ON RECORD 1991 G. BROWN

CONTENTS

ON RECORD ENTRIES ARE NOT ORDERED ALPHABETICALLY, BUT ORGANIZED INTUITIVELY— A MIXTURE OF SEGUES BY MUSICAL GENRE OR STYLE.

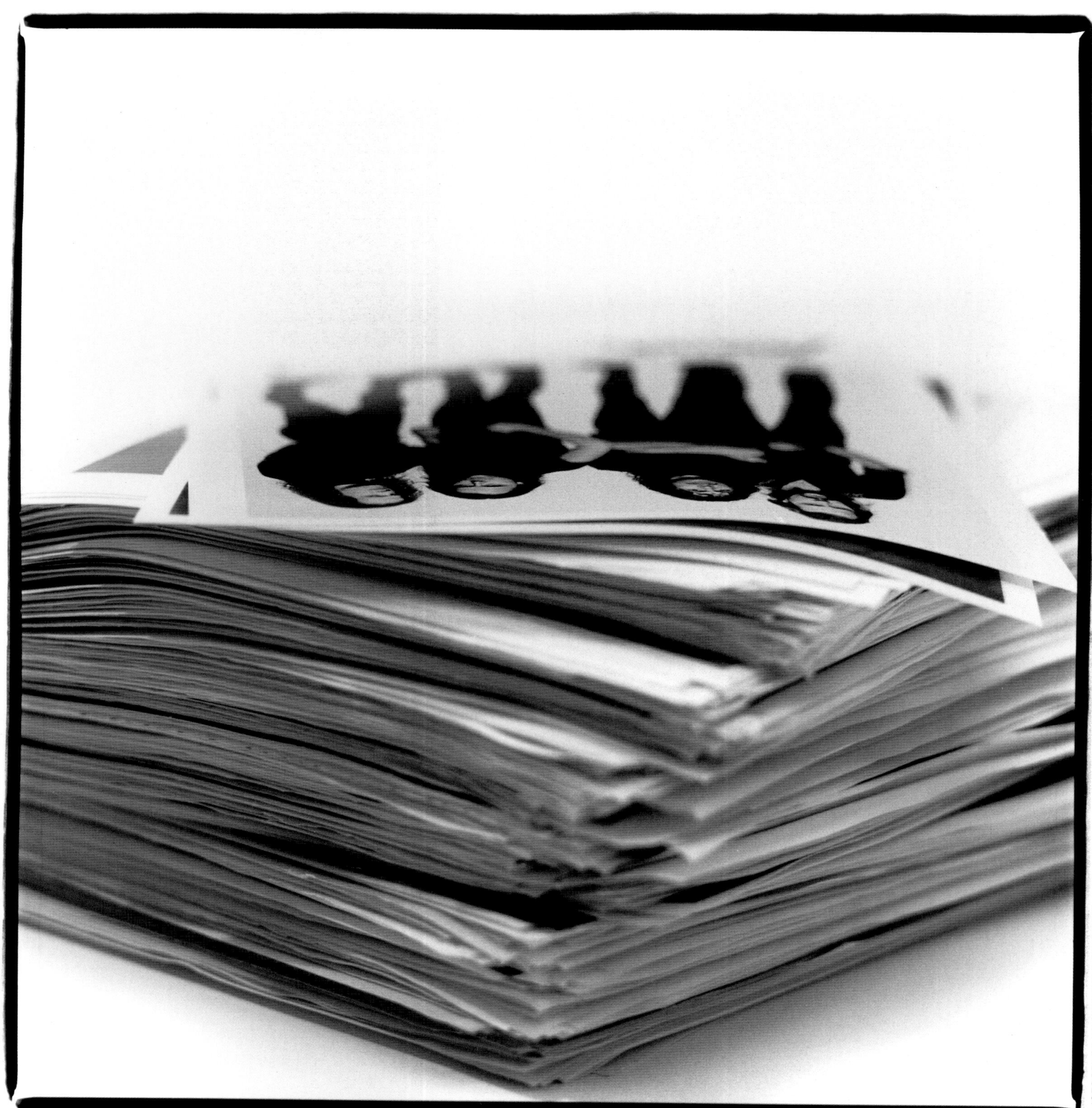

PHOTOGRAPH BY STEPHEN COLLECTOR

ON RECORD VOL.3 1991

BY 1991, a man defined in New York media outlets for his brash personality and giant ego had transitioned from a figure of note in the Big Apple to a household name. The ubiquitous Donald Trump took stock in rock by playing the title role of "Mr. Big Stuff" in a video by Precious Metal, an all-female hard-rock band. "Mr. Big Stuff," a remake of Jean Knight's 1971 soul hit, was featured on the group's self-titled album, and the promo shot from the taping received heavy trade and consumer press exposure.

"The Donald" didn't get to be a video star after all, however—the vainglorious real-estate developer seemingly pulled a power play on Precious Metal.

"He agreed to do the video for $10,000, which would go to charity," guitarist Mara Fox told me. "It was supposed to be contingent on whether he liked the way he looked, on his being able to edit out shots of himself that he didn't think were flattering. We said fine, no problem—it was all done on a handshake. We went to New York and filmed the whole thing.

"After it was done, he said, 'I really love it, I'm into it, I look 10 years younger—but I changed my mind, I want $250,000.' No record company would give that kind of money to that creep."

Precious Metal had final say-so over the edit, and Trump was snipped out of the video.

"We wanted to release it with black tape over his eyes, or put a money bag instead of his head," Fox said. "But our management and record label were so nervous about it, they made us cut out the Trump appearance entirely—all that's left is band footage, totally a performance clip. It's been a pain in the butt for us—he really strung us out."

When I called Trump, he declined to comment, but his advisers opined that the video would have been bad for his image at a time when he was trying to look as squeaky-clean as possible for his divorce battle.

Far more serious things happened that year. With sadness, I wrote tributes to Freddie Mercury, lead singer of Queen, who died from AIDS-related complications at age 45, one day after making his diagnosis public, and to the three people crushed to death when audience members rushed the stage during an AC/DC concert in Salt Lake City.

When it came to music, 1991 was a very good year. Grunge made its popular breakthrough with bands such as Nirvana, Pearl Jam, Soundgarden and Alice in Chains. The reign of the glam-metal groups was in its decline, but no one told Guns N' Roses. Garth Brooks and Amy Grant achieved massive pop success, crossing over from country and contemporary Christian music, respectively. U2, Metallica, the Red Hot Chili Peppers, R.E.M. and Primus released successful mainstream albums.

As a popular music reporter, I received all of their records for review, waded through their press kits and went to their concerts. I was and am a very lucky boy. Please allow me to share. **—G. Brown**

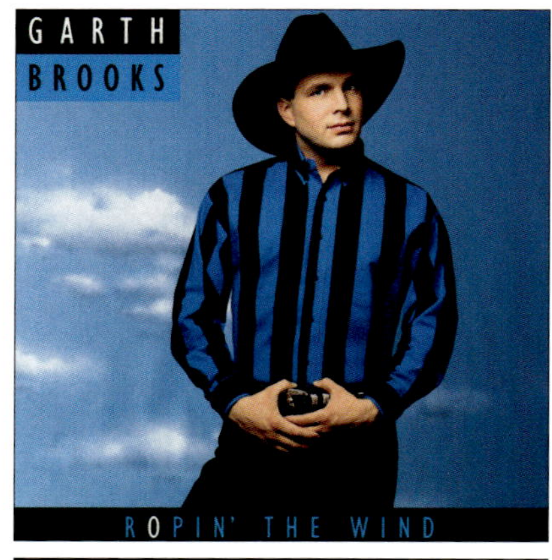

Billboard 200: *Ropin' the Wind* (No. 1)

Garth Brooks' *Ropin' the Wind* entered the *Billboard* 200 at No. 1, a remarkable first for a country artist.

FOR DECADES, rock 'n' roll fans viewed country music as the entertainment choice of hayseeds, cowboys and truckers. But over time, it had gained a new respectability and shown rock audiences a thing or two, thanks to Garth Brooks' gigantic breakthrough.

Brooks sold more records in 1991 than any other performer, and his *Ropin' the Wind* album beat out releases by Michael Jackson, U2, Guns N' Roses and Hammer to claim the No. 1 spot on *Billboard*'s chart.

Obviously, the mainstream was ready for someone like Brooks. Rap and heavy metal had driven baby boomer radio listeners away in droves, dispatching them to the contemporary country side of the dial, where Brooks' sentimental songs blurred the lines between straight-ahead country and pop. The second single released from *Ropin' the Wind* was his honest cover of Billy Joel's "Shameless."

Brooks was 29, raised on Seventies singer-songwriters like James Taylor. But he also drew inspiration from some unconventional sources.

"My music is country—definitely George Jones, Chris LeDoux and George Strait are in there," Brooks said. "But I would have to say that Boston and Journey are in there as well. I was a big fan of Kiss when I was growing up. I was really into their music—the early stuff is great. I'm a sum of my influences."

Brooks told of seeing kids in Megadeth T-shirts at his concerts, where he tore up audiences with animated theatrics like climbing up into the lighting rigs and throwing water on his band. In 1977, it probably would have made the humble jock a certifiable rock star. ■

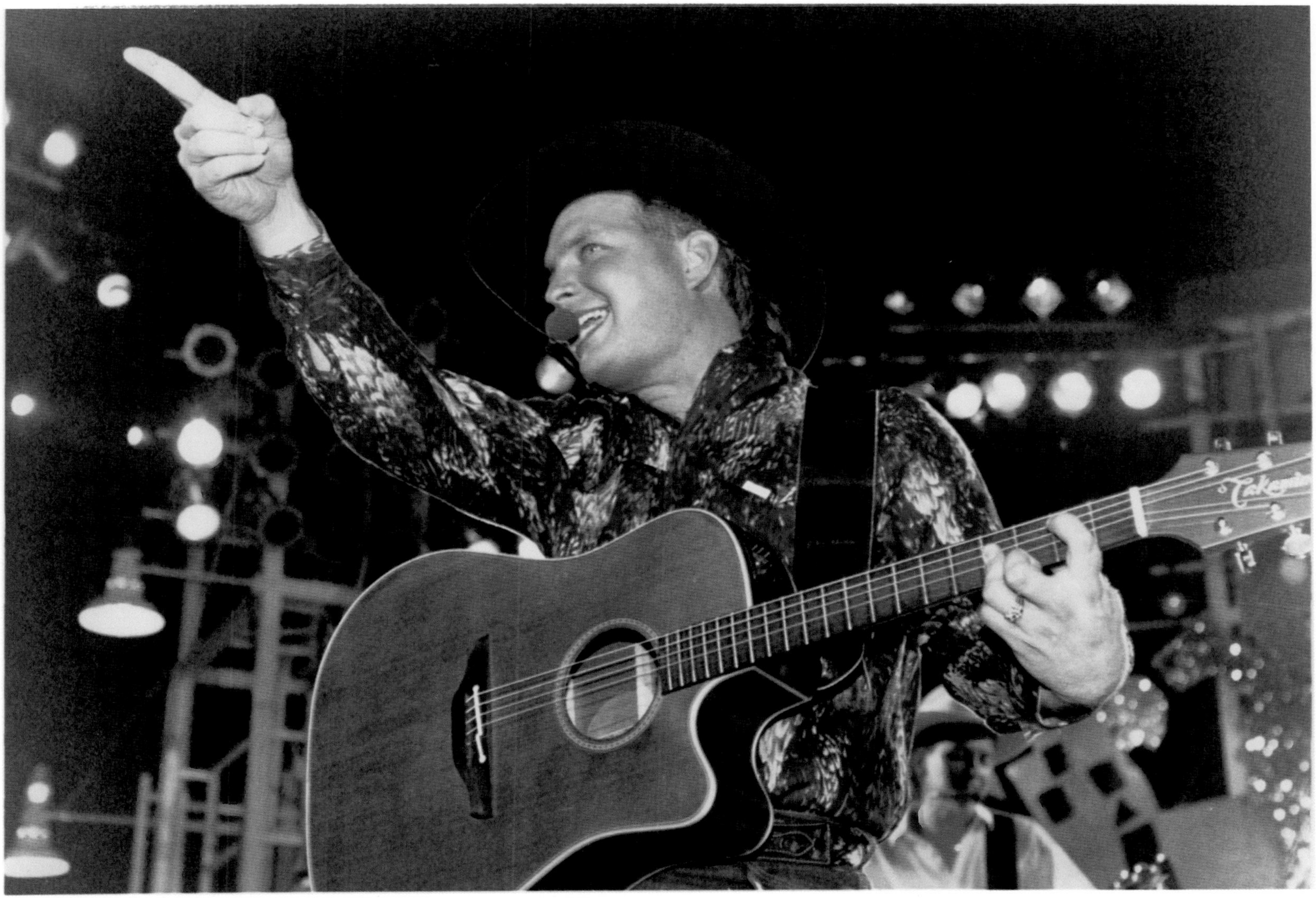

GARTH BROOKS

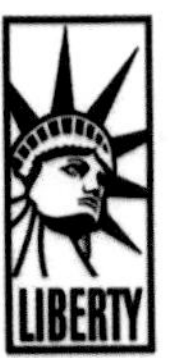

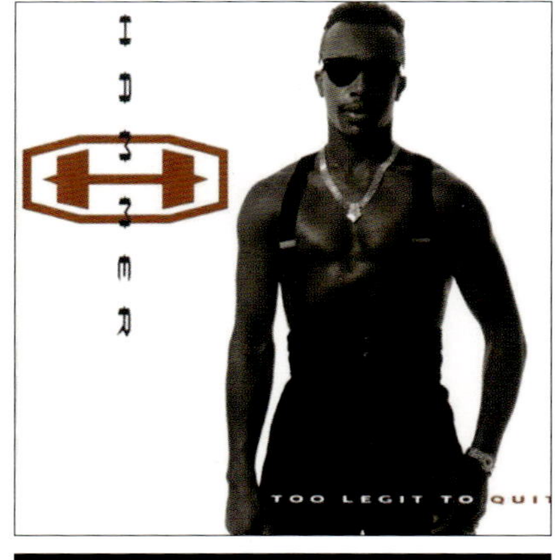

Billboard 200: *Too Legit to Quit* (#2)
Billboard Hot 100: "Too Legit to Quit" (#5);
"Addams Groove" (#7); "Do Not Pass Me By" (#62);
"This Is the Way We Roll" (#86)

After officiallly dropping the "MC" from his stage name, hip-hop's Hammer released *Too Legit to Quit.*

IN THE Eighties, it was rebel art. In the Nineties, it was commerce. Rap music had totally crossed over, appealing to whites and blacks, country folks as well as urbanites. And Hammer was the charismatic artist who'd advanced the genre to a mass-appeal level.

He'd done it with catchy, high-energy music, but there was a thoughtful, moral side to his lyrical swagger—he refuted the notion that rap was simply an expression of misogyny, explicit language or racial hatred. He showed that it could compete as family entertainment. Part of his appeal lay in his enthralling dance steps, which were an integral part of his dazzling videos. His breakthrough second release, 1990's *Please Hammer Don't Hurt 'Em*, was the first rap album of the decade to reach No. 1 on the pop charts.

But in the wake of his rapid rise to fame, Hammer had drawn flak. His biggest hits, "U Can't Touch This" and "Pray," relied extensively on sampling—sounds electronically borrowed from Rick James' "Super Freak" and Prince's "When Doves Cry," respectively. Some critics regarded his records as mere piracy.

Yet no sampling appeared on his *Too Legit to Quit* album. Hammer composed the majority of songs with his co-producer and used live instrumentation. "I want this to be the album that ends the narrow thinking that rap is one-dimensional," he said. "When people think of Hammer, I want them to think of music."

His growing business empire bore him out. A virtual cottage industry, the entertainer employed 200 people at his corporation. He even starred in a Saturday morning cartoon called *Hammerman*. Still, other rap artists accused Hammer of paying more attention to his loose-limbed dance skills than to his lyrics, the cornerstone of hip-hop. Others said his show-biz instincts didn't compensate for his less-than-skillful rap delivery.

"My peers want me to apologize for being successful, and I'm not going to," he stated. "I don't make a record saying, 'I hope this is a hit in the black community.' I make a record saying, 'I hope everybody likes this.' I grew up in an integrated inner city. There was a Chinese family across the street, the Gonzaleses lived three houses down, and my next-door neighbors were white Americans. Consequently, I didn't grow up worrying about the color of a person's skin. Now I'm at the point where my music is appealing to more than just people of my own color, and I'm elated. If their music appeals to 200,000 people and mine appeals to 5 million of any color, I think I've got a slightly better idea of what the people like." ■

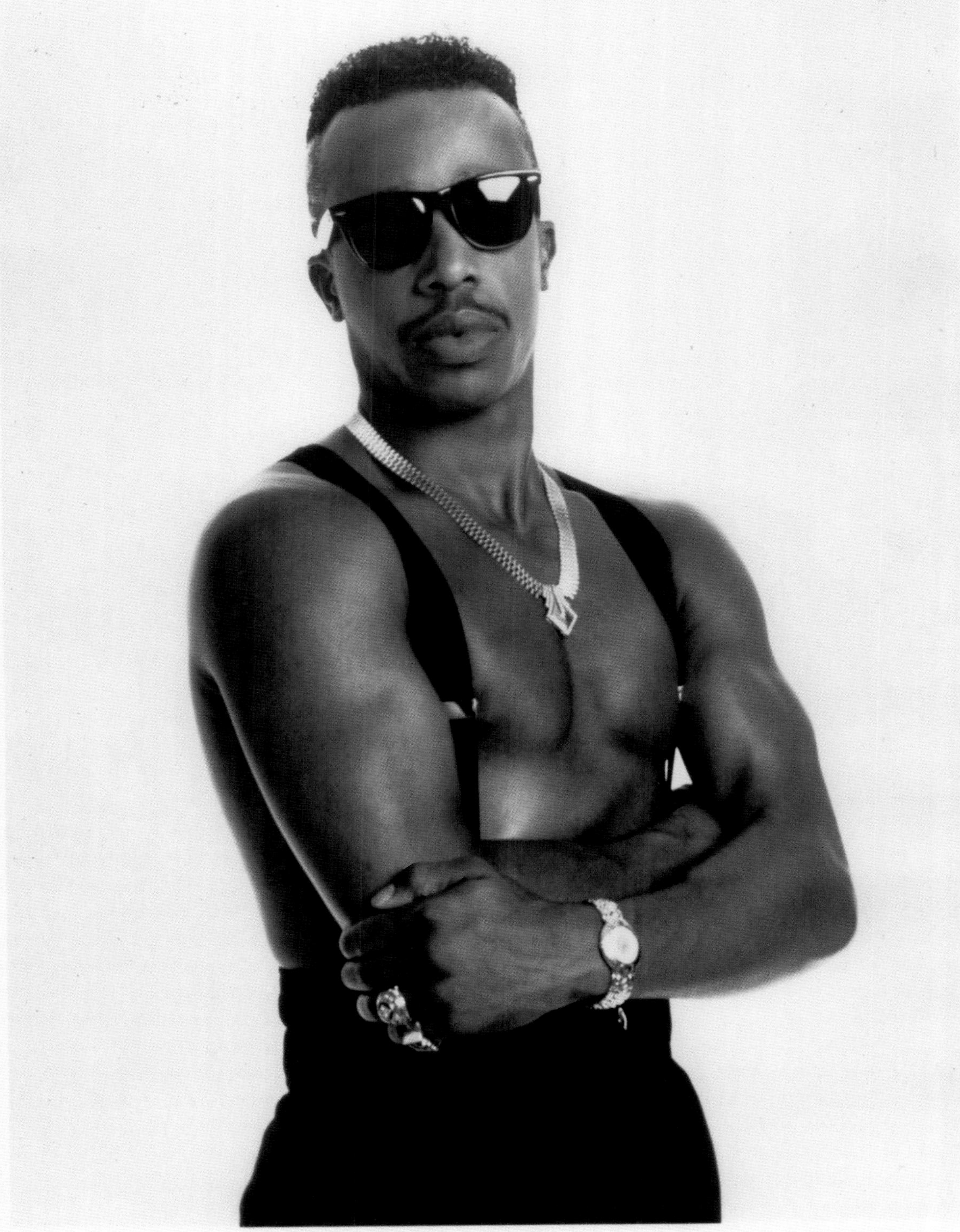

HAMMER

Photo: Annie Leibowitz / 1991

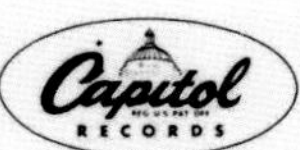

MARKY MARK AND THE FUNKY BUNCH
MUSIC FOR THE PEOPLE

Led by Mark Wahlberg, Marky Mark & the Funky Bunch reached No. 1 with the song, "Good Vibrations."

Billboard 200: *Music for the People* (#21)
Billboard Hot 100: "Good Vibrations" (No. 1); "Wildside" (#10); "I Need Money" (#61)

"MARKY MARK" Wahlberg was only 20 years old, but he was enough of a businessman to hedge his bets. He'd become one of the most popular acts in contemporary music, so he didn't complain that his fans were generally squealing adolescent girls—in videos and the poses he adopted for photos, he had his t-shirt off revealing his sculpted pecs. And he expressed himself by pulling down his pants and exposing his skivvies.

"They're Calvin Kleins—they're hooking me up, sending free underwear to me," the hip-hop hunk said.

But Wahlberg wanted people to respond to his respect for the B-boy art form. His debut album, the platinum *Music for the People*, was a hard-hitting synthesis of hip-hop and funk. What did a baby-faced Irish-Catholic boy have to say to the hip-hop community? That all white rappers weren't like Vanilla Ice.

"I'm just being myself," he insisted. "I don't think it matters that I'm a white dude doing black music. Some people grew up on R&B or rock 'n' roll. I listened to hip-hop—it's been around since before my teenage years, and I feel for the pioneers who have worked so hard. If you make a real dope record, it doesn't matter what color you are. I know white rappers, Hispanic rappers, even an Oriental rapper."

The little brother of New Kids on the Block's Donnie Wahlberg deviated from the New Kids' clean-teen image. He touted himself as an example of triumphing over circumstances. The siblings grew up the youngest in a family of nine in the lower-middle-class Boston neighborhood of Dorchester. He got his start as a break-dancer, and was initially enlisted as a New Kid himself. But he quit after six months—"I couldn't sing," he admitted.

A few million dollars poorer than his big brother, he dropped out of the 10th grade and got into bouts of juvenile delinquency—fighting, truancy, drinking, vagrancy, shoplifting. But he was also into rapping to better himself. Donnie funded and produced the *Music for the People* project, and Marky Mark credited him for much of the musical strength. The album spawned two contagious Top 10 hits. The feel-good dance rap "Good Vibrations" featured house piano and a splice of Loleatta Holloway's 1980 disco hit, "Love Sensation." The thoughtful "Wildside" borrowed Lou Reed's 1973 classic "Walk on the Wild Side" groove to deal with real-life tales of urban death.

"It was a good way of fitting in all the issues I wanted to talk about," Marky Mark recalled. "I have a positive message." He walked the talk. Amid all his other commitments, he was taking the tests required for a high school equivalency diploma, and he was confirmed in the Catholic Church. ■

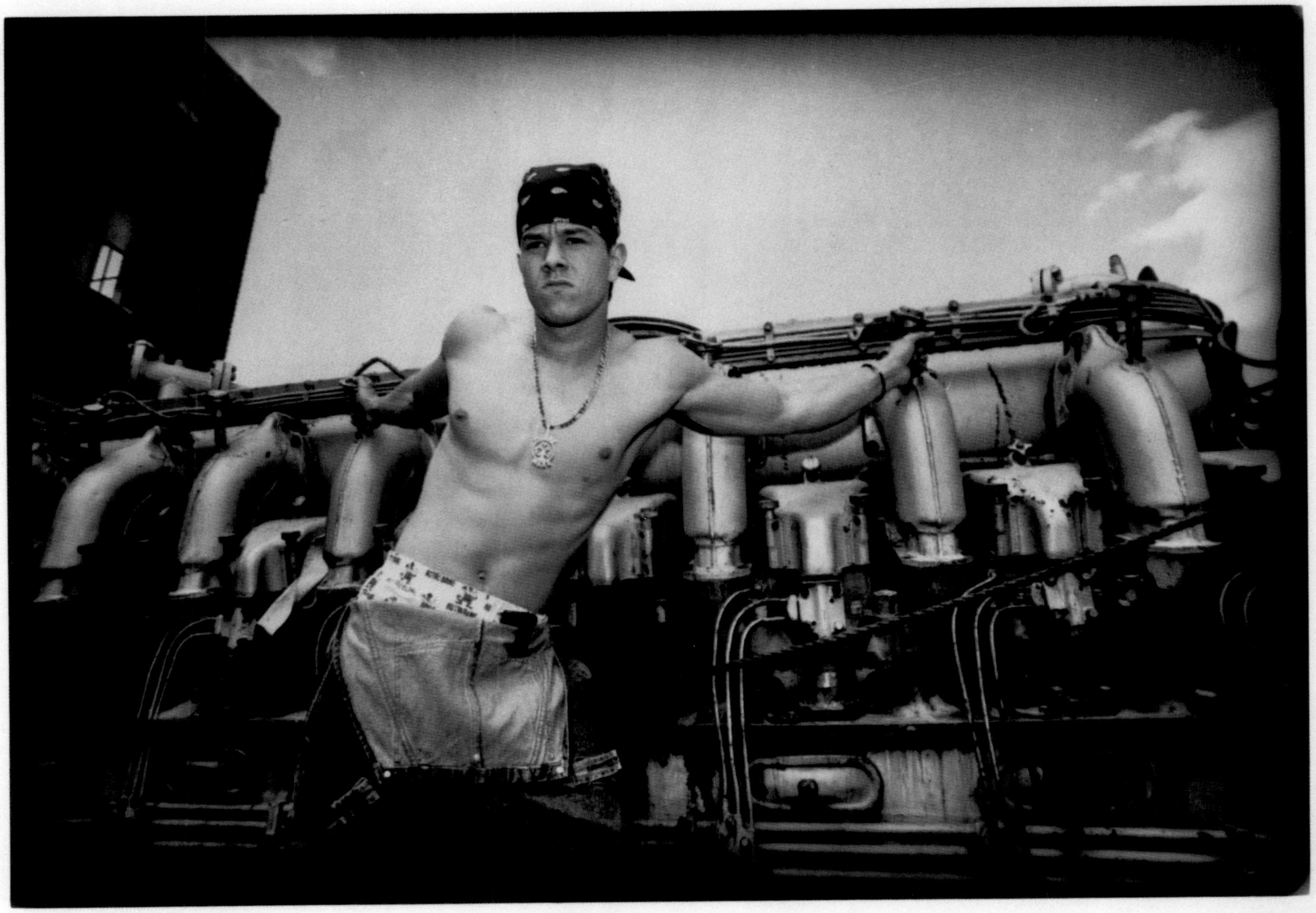

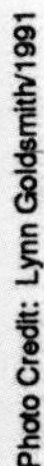

MARKY MARK

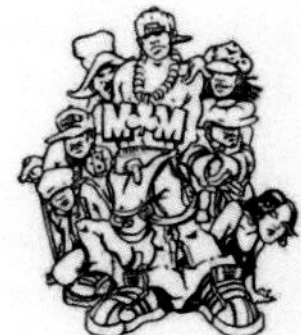

©1990 Interscope Records, Inc./ Permission to reproduce limited to editorial uses in newspapers and other regularly published periodicals and television news programming. All other rights are reserved.

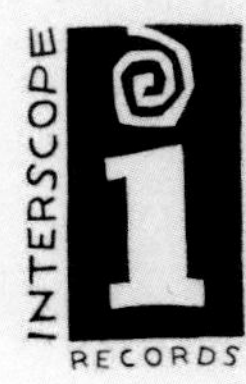

Paula Abdul's *Spellbound* bore two more No. 1 singles, "Rush Rush" and "The Promise of a New Day."

Billboard 200: *Spellbound* (No. 1)
Billboard Hot 100: "Rush Rush" (No. 1); "The Promise of a New Day" (No. 1); "Blowing Kisses in the Wind" (#6); "Vibeology" (#16); "Will You Marry Me?" (#19)

PAULA ABDUL took a quick ride to the heights of pop stardom. The pop-dance singer achieved massive commercial success with her 1988 debut album, *Forever Your Girl*, making news for statistical feats—it yielded worldwide sales of more than 10 million copies, she scored four No. 1 singles (the most ever from a debut album) and won a Grammy Award.

But the credibility of Abdul's dance-pop product was suspect. Prior to *Forever Your Girl*, she had never made a record. Her renown was as a former Los Angeles Lakers cheerleader and a choreographer (her credits ranged from TV's *The Tracey Ullman Show* to videos by Janet Jackson).

Attention focused on her voice. Her name came up constantly in discussions about lip-synching (she was part of the ill-fated "Club MTV" tour featuring the Milli Vanilli fraud), and a backup singer filed a suit claiming she sang lead on many of the *Forever Your Girl* songs.

Abdul angrily denied the brief flourishes of controversy. "I knew there would be a lot of skepticism since I was coming from the field of choreography—'How is this girl going to be a pop singer?'" she mused. "But I knew it would be a long, hard struggle to be accepted as an all-around entertainer. When I was growing up, I idolized Gene Kelly, Judy Garland—they could do it all. To be a star in their era, you had to excel in every area. I think now, after a few years, people are understanding what I'm all about."

Abdul started working with a vocal coach, and the training transformed her voice. She abandoned her kittenish image in favor of a more elegant look. But the biggest change was musical. She toyed with the *Forever Your Girl* formula, and her *Spellbound* album was more ambitious and mature. For eight songs, she turned to a fine team of collaborators—Paul Lord, V. Jeffrey Smith and Sandra St. Victor of a promising Brooklyn-based funk-rock trio, the Family Stand.

Spellbound peaked at No. 1 on the *Billboard* album chart, and the singles—the anthemic "The Promise of a New Day" and the playful dance number "Vibeology"—were warmly received. The ballad "Rush Rush" featured a music video that starred Keanu Reeves re-enacting the 1955 Natalie Wood/James Dean film *Rebel Without a Cause*. Her bravura performance of "Blowing Kisses in the Wind" laid to rest the disputes regarding her singing. On "Will You Marry Me?" Abdul's charming vocal tumbled headlong into a marriage proposal. She became not only a profitable commodity but a self-assured adult contemporary artist.

"I'm a pure example of conviction of the heart, going for what I believe in," she said. "And I believe in my talent." ■

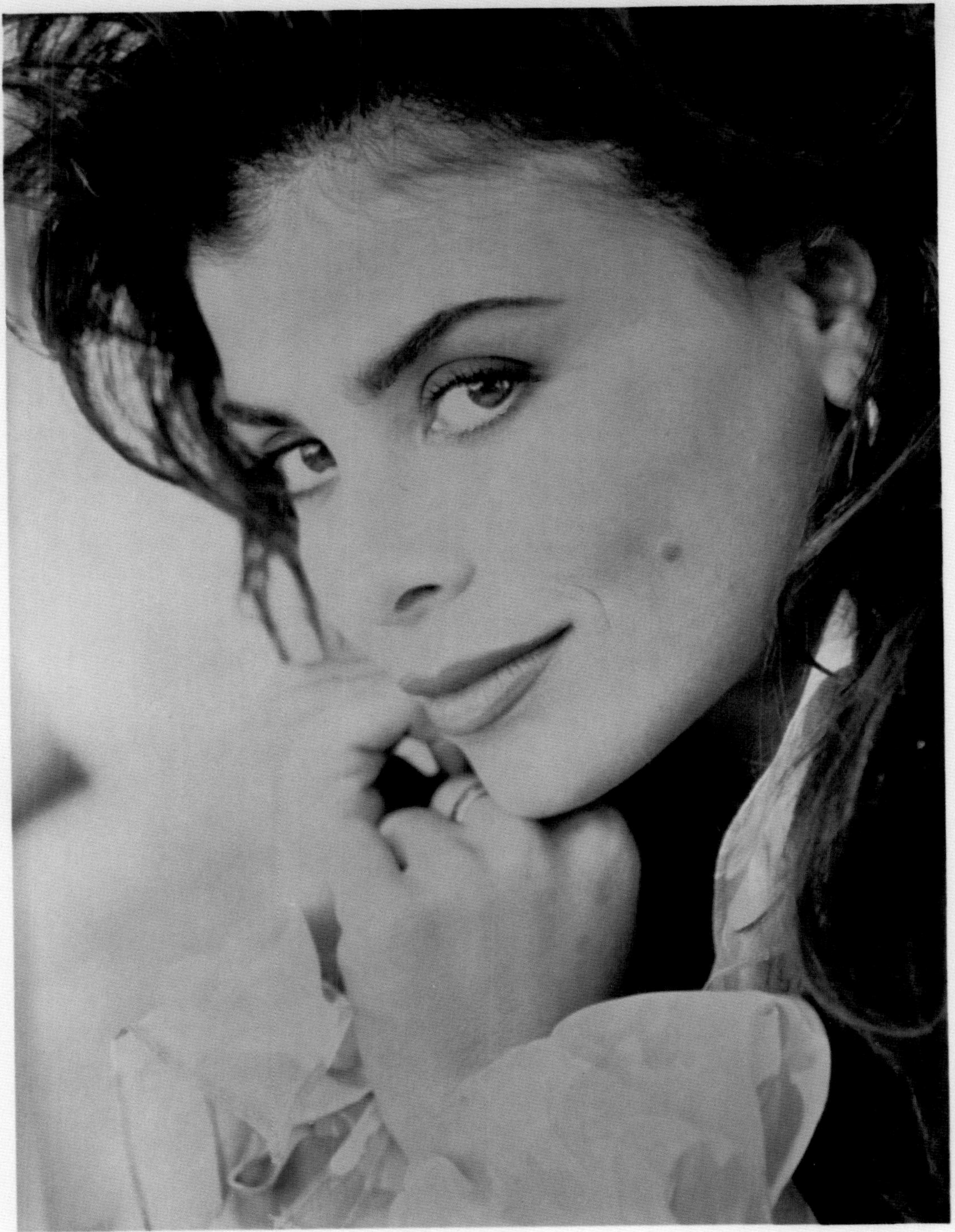

PHOTO: ALBERTO TOLOT 0591

captive

Paula Abdul

Virgin

The challenging *Achtung Baby* represented a dramatic shift in thematic and musical direction for U2.

Billboard 200: *Achtung Baby* (No. 1)
Billboard Hot 100: "The Fly" (#61); "Mysterious Ways" (#9); "One" (#10); "Even Better Than the Real Thing" (#32); "Who's Gonna Ride Your Wild Horses" (#35)

U2 HAD wrestled with the notion of rock stardom from the start. The band had such difficulty reconciling its Christian beliefs with the rock 'n' roll lifestyle that it nearly broke up after releasing two albums. For most of the Eighties, U2 was regarded as rock music's last cornerstone of authenticity, an icon carrying the torch for unabashed idealism with evangelical seriousness.

By the end of the decade, the group members found themselves caught between their dreams and the hard, suffocating truth of superfame. After being mocked and caricatured for their mighty anthems and righteous pouts, they went into the making of *Achtung Baby* determined to start fresh and broaden their musical palette. Songs like the corrosive "The Fly" and the dark "One" attempted to plumb for the unexpected, bold sounds of U2 reflected off a fun house mirror. *Achtung Baby* met with unanimous critical acclaim and debuted at No. 1 throughout the world. What had U2 hoped to accomplish with the album? Lead singer Bono quoted Sam Shephard.

"Right in the middle of a contradiction, that's the place to be," he said. "And rock 'n' roll has a lot of contradictions."

U2 had gone camp, and the Zoo TV tour to support *Achtung Baby* was the frontline offensive—a massive audio-visual jungle that both milked and mocked rock-star self-indulgence with colorful totems of the band's brave new postmodern world. Banks of video monitors and TV screens flashed a dizzying array of words and images. Boxy East German Trabant cars hung from the scaffolding, their headlights converted into spotlights as aircraft warning lights blinked atop eleven-story towers. The staggering enormity of the set matched the thrust of the tough-sounding *Achtung Baby* material perfectly.

A costumed ringmaster orchestrated this whirlwind of gadgetry. With guitarist The Edge, bassist Adam Clayton and drummer Larry Mullen more engrossed in the music than the theater of live performing, Bono devised an alter ego called the Fly, swaddled in hip-hugging black leather, Cuban heels and wraparound bug-eye sunglasses. There were onstage phone calls, relentlessly dialing the White House switchboard to get through to President George H. W. Bush.

"I've started feeling like I know some of these ladies," Bono said. "I can tell as soon as they answer 'White House' whether it's going to be one of the friendly chatty ones or one of the very formal types."

When the giant video screens suddenly flickered to life, they showed Bush calling the congregation to order with cleverly doctored news footage, chanting Queen's "We will, we will rock you!" "Bush has given us so much fodder," Bono laughed. "We don't know what we'll do after the next election." ■

U2

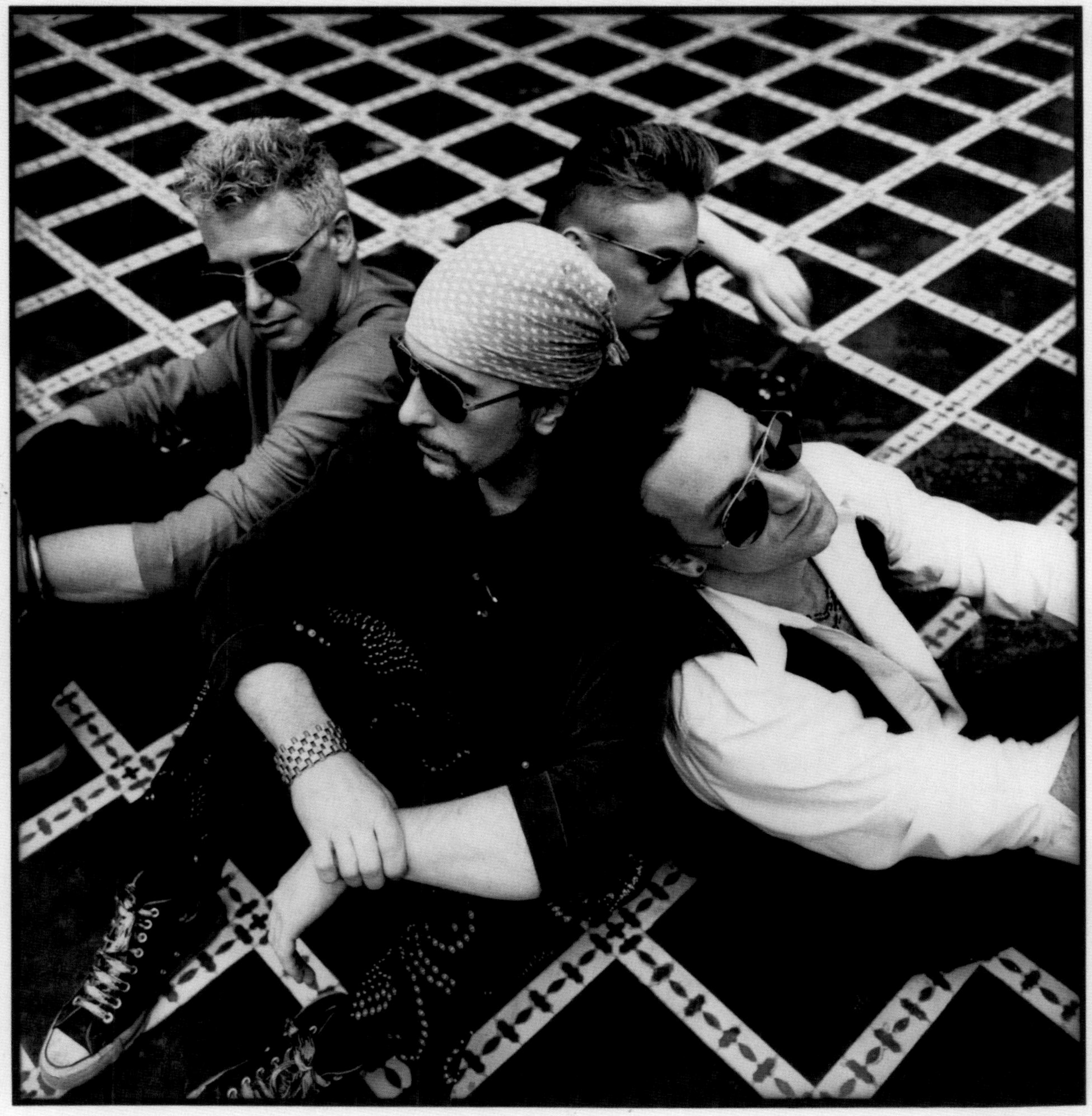

FOR EDITORIAL USE IN PERIODICALS ONLY. NO SINGLE SUBJECT USE. ALL OTHER RIGHTS RESERVED.

PHOTO CREDIT: ANTON CORBIJN

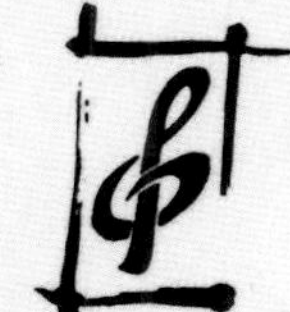

PolyGram Label Group

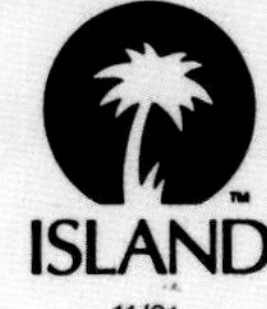

11/91

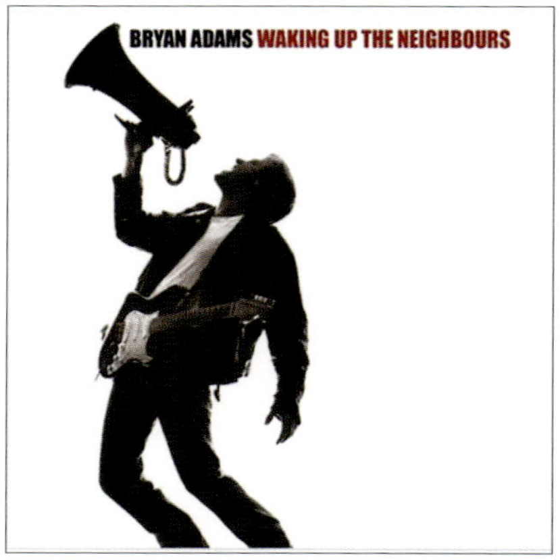

Bryan Adams' "(Everything I Do) I Do It for You" emerged as one of the most successful songs of all time.

Billboard 200: *Waking Up the Neighbours* (#6)
Billboard Hot 100: "(Everything I Do) I Do It for You" (No. 1); "Can't Stop This Thing We Started" (#2); "There Will Never Be Another Tonight" (#31); "Thought I'd Died and Gone to Heaven" (#13); "Do I Have to Say the Words?" (#11)

BRYAN ADAMS had few equals when it came to canny commercial instincts. He affirmed his hit-making credentials in the Eighties, balancing love songs ("Heaven," "Straight from the Heart") and hard-edged rockers ("Run to You," "Summer of '69") on precisely produced albums. After his 1987 album, *Into the Fire*, he holed up in writing dens and recording studios for a year and a half with an array of producers before he finally found producer-songwriter Robert "Mutt" Lange, a notorious studio perfectionist known for his high-impact guitar and vocal sounds (his credits included Def Leppard records).

They had a dozen songs before composer Michael Kamen approached Adams with "(Everything I Do) I Do It for You." He first heard the song as a snippet of Kamen's instrumental score for the film *Robin Hood: Prince of Thieves*. Played on lutes, harpsichord and mandolins with Kamen humming a melody, the aural sketch sounded nothing like a pop hit. "But I recognized it had great potential," Adams recalled. "It had this gorgeous melody running through it—an 'international' melody, the kind your mom would like. I thought, 'That's half of a beautiful song right there.'"

Originally, Adams and Lange were expected only to write lyrics for the song for another artist to record. But as they worked on the track, they decided for Adams to cut it for inclusion in the movie soundtrack as well as his own album. To express Robin Hood's undying devotion to Maid Marian, Adams made a list of "a lot of commitment-oriented lines like 'I'd walk the wire for you' and 'I'd fly with you,'" he said.

"The *Robin Hood* executives were second-guessing it. They wanted to change the tempo, make it a duet (with Kate Bush, but the idea was nixed). During the final mix, they wanted to call the song 'I'd Die for You.' But there's no guy who'd say that—he might think it, but he wouldn't say it!"

"(Everything I Do) I Do It for You" hit No. 1 in 21 countries and earned Adams his first Grammy award and an Oscar nomination, propelling sales of his *Waking Up the Neighbours* album, a scrupulously crafted yet resoundingly tuneful piece of work. Adams called the surprise success "mind-boggling," but he maintained he didn't really care what he'd accomplished with a ballad labeled "the wedding song of the Nineties."

"It's eclipsed everything I've ever done—heck, it's eclipsed most people's entire careers," he mused. "I don't think about it, to be honest. I think about sustaining that interest and enthusiasm in my work. Writing songs is easy, but writing another good one is really hard." ■

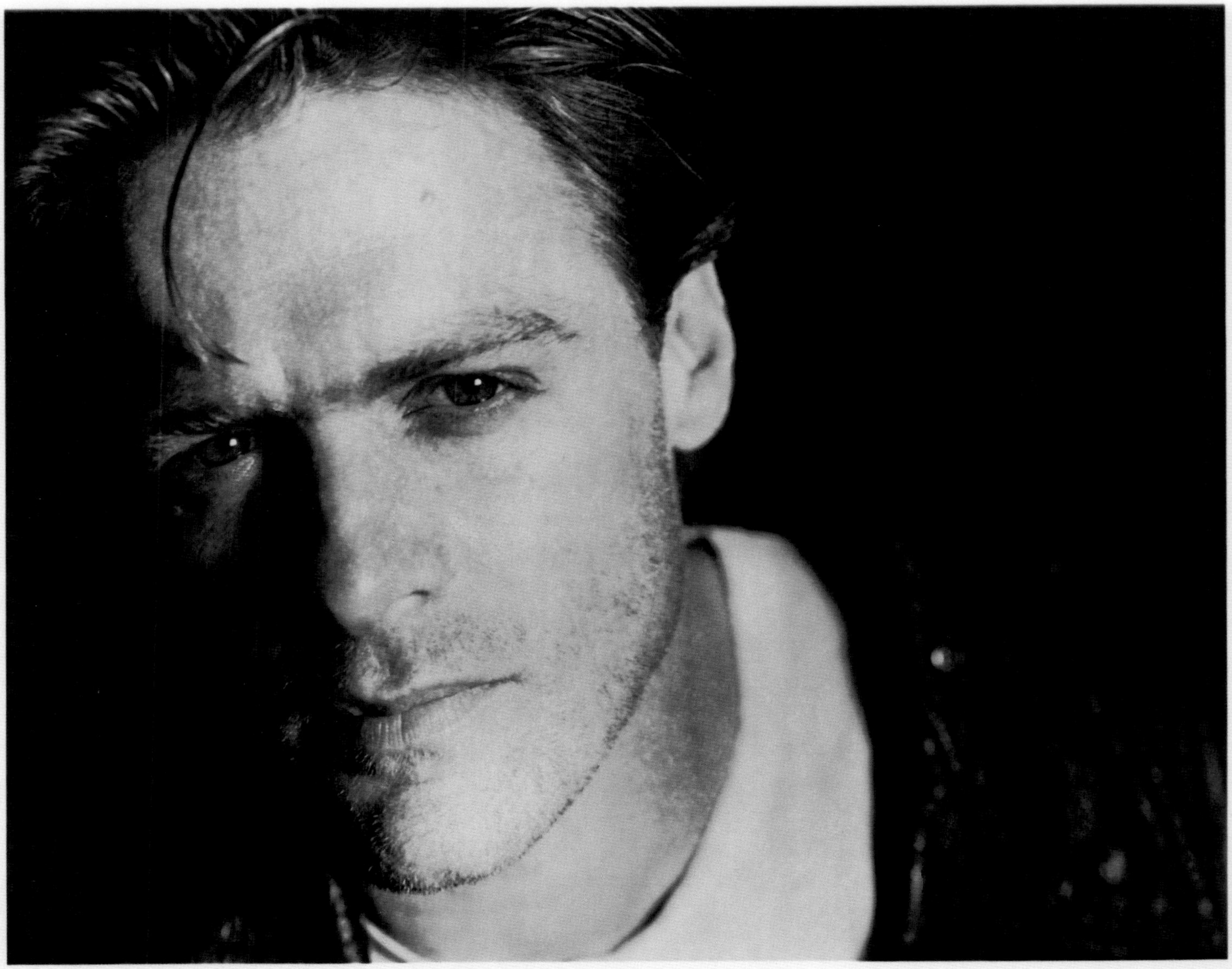

Photo: Catlin

BRYAN ADAMS

bruce allen
talent
604-688-7274

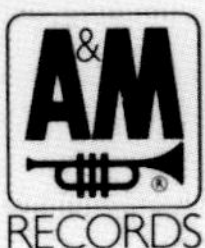

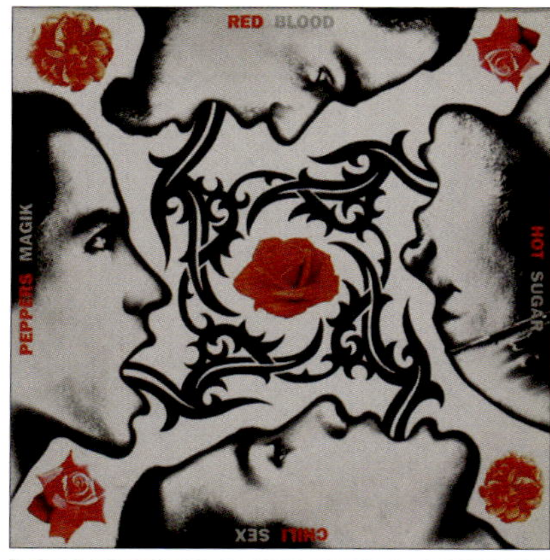

Red Hot Chili Peppers catapulted to alt-rock fame with the juggernaut album, *Blood Sugar Sex Magik*.

Billboard 200: *Blood Sugar Sex Magik* (#3)
Billboard Hot 100: "Give It Away" (#73); "Under the Bridge" (#2)

INFAMOUS FOR their anarchic live shows and goofy flexed-pecs-and-strained-necks photo opps, the Red Hot Chili Peppers never gave their wild image a second thought. The Peppers broke out of cult status and celebrated their first gold album for 1989's *Mother's Milk*, with a warp-speed cover of Stevie Wonder's "Higher Ground" landing them on radio and MTV. Then the untamed party band entered a major-label bidding war, ultimately signing with Warner Brothers Records.

The Red Hot Chili Peppers—singer Anthony Kiedis, bassist Flea, drummer Chad Smith and guitarist John Frusciante—remained hormonally pumped-up funk/punk celebrators on *Blood Sugar Sex Magik*. The band and producer Rick Rubin (known for his work with the Beastie Boys, the Cult, Slayer and the Black Crowes) secluded themselves in a legendary "haunted" house in the Hollywood hills, where they lived and recorded the album over a two-month period.

"It was a four-story, 13-bedroom dilapidated stone mansion. Allegedly, it's where the Beatles first took acid and where everyone from Valentino to Hendrix lived," Kiedis said. "We found the mansion had a wandering 'presence.' Our full-time cook held a séance and confirmed there's been a male ghost there for years. And a photographer who took publicity shots of us found a 'ghostly image' in four of them."

"Give It Away" reached No. 1 on the *Billboard* Modern Rock Tracks chart. In the wake of that success, the Los Angeles foursome was steered toward worldwide popularity with a cool, soulful ballad—the #2 hit, "Under the Bridge," was uncommonly pensive, but it demonstrated the loony band's versatility.

"We're still known as 'that hyperkinetic California quartet that's been known to perform wearing nothing but strategically placed sweat socks,'" Kiedis said. "So when a band as underground as we are can get through to that many people, it's nice."

The success led in part to the departure of Frusciante, who grew uncomfortable with the band's popularity and left abruptly in the middle of the supporting tour. ■

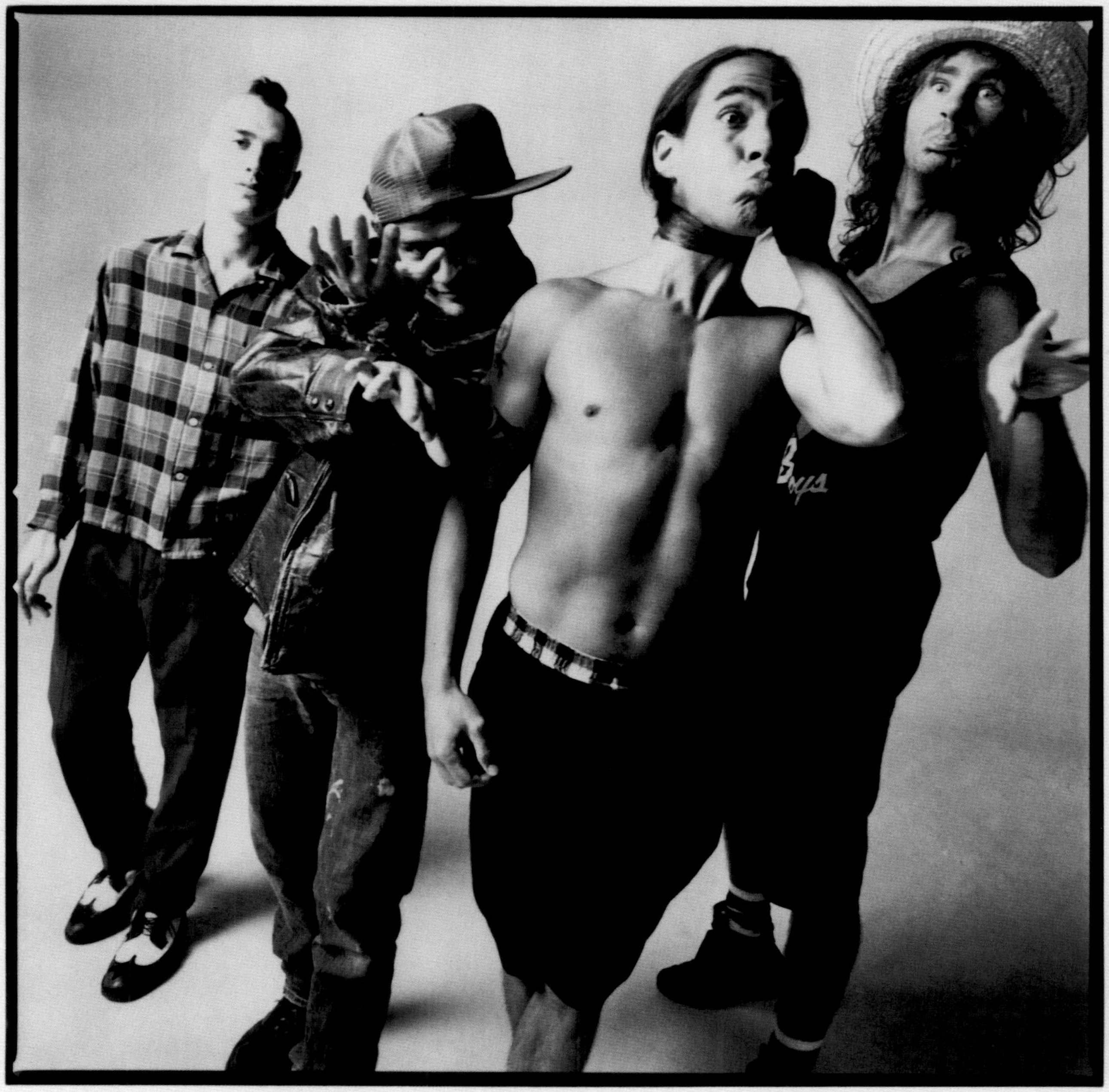

Photo Credit: Chris Cuffaro/Visages

John Frusciante Flea Anthony Kiedis Chad Smith

RED HOT CHILI PEPPERS

© 1991 Warner Bros. Records/Permission to reproduce limited to editorial uses in newspapers and other regularly published periodicals and television news programming.

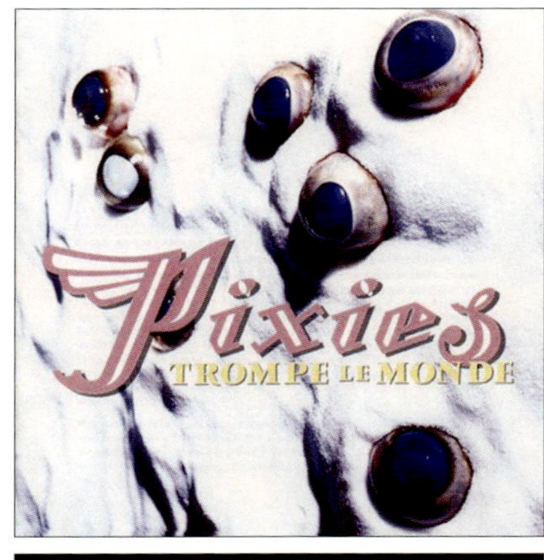

Pixies' version of the Jesus and Mary Chain tune "Head On" made *Billboard*'s Modern Rock Tracks chart.

Billboard 200: *Trompe le Monde* (#92)

PIXIES CALLED their 1991 album *Trompe le Monde*—"trick the world" in French. Did the title refer to the Boston band's own bewilderment at success?

"Yeah, I can't figure out why everyone is so interested in my life," vocalist and guitarist Black Francis said. "There are bands that are so much bigger. I still consider Pixies to be fringe entertainers no matter how you cut it up."

But Pixies were the darlings of America's college-rock underground, claiming the noisy margins of alternative guitar music. And they were one of Europe's most important bands.

"We work a lot over there, tour all the time. The kids don't listen to radio as much, so there's nothing else for them to do but go to a lot of gigs," Francis mused. "That's it for our international marketing plan."

Francis led Pixies' throbbing, grating sound, writing lyrics about his obsessions ("Eyeballs, astronauts, Cuban culture") and pushing his insistent shrieking out of the mix. He had reputation for being somewhat reclusive, usually shunning interviews. A University of Massachusetts Amherst dropout, Francis (a.k.a. Charles Thompson IV) formed Pixies in 1986 with Joey Santiago (guitar), Kim Deal (bass) and David Lovering (drums). The enigmatic band's first EP garnered international recognition, and 1989's *Doolittle* and 1990's *Bossanova* were major-label shriek-alongs.

For *Trompe le Monde*, Francis said Pixies "wanted to keep the guitars plenty loud, go for the throat." The harsh, grungy "Planet of Sound," the delicately melodic "Letter to Memphis" and an explosive cover of the Jesus and Mary Chain classic "Head On" justified Francis' declaration that pop music was comprised of the hard and soft. Critics said Pixies were approaching mainstream acceptance.

"Certainly I make career decisions that aren't always out of love for music, but I have to deny catering to the pop end of things," Francis said. "I make pop music, but it's a different thing than Top 40. I don't have anything in common with the charts. Hopefully I'm increasing an audience strictly through work, just putting out records on a regular basis." ■

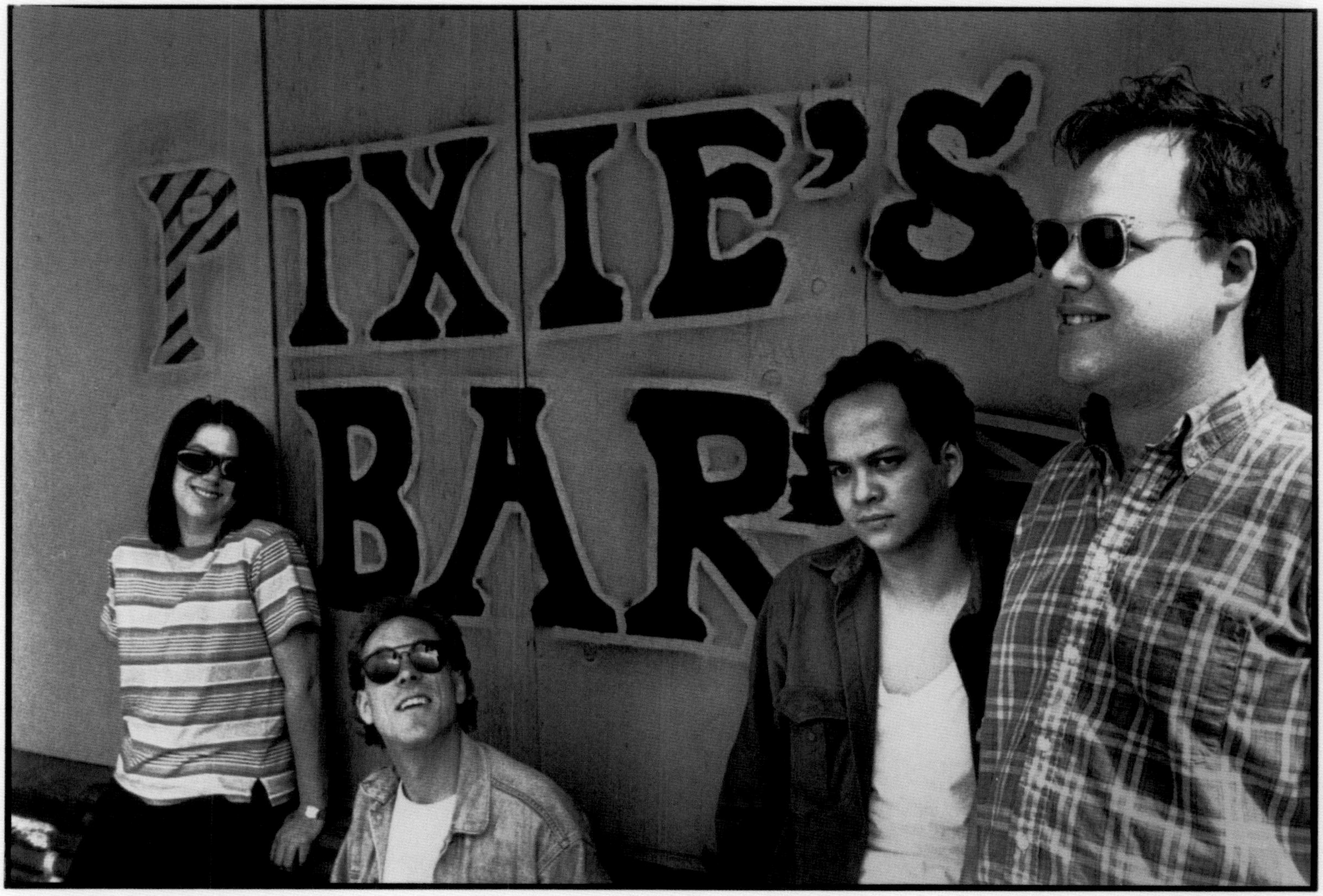

KIM DEAL DAVID LOVERING JOEY SANTIAGO BLACK FRANCIS

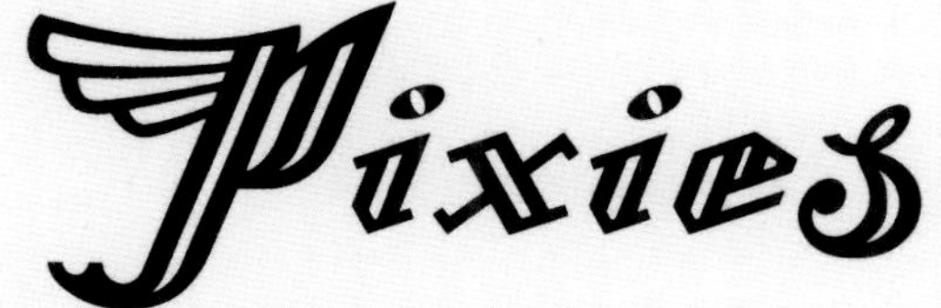

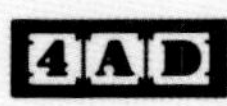

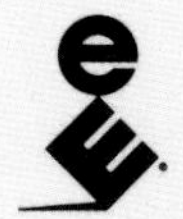

Elektra Entertainment

With *Badmotorfinger*, the members of Soundgarden set the tone for the proliferant Seattle rock scene.

Billboard 200: *Badmotorfinger* (#39)

ONE OF the earliest practitioners of the psychedelic-punk-metal "Seattle sound," Soundgarden—singer Chris Cornell, Kim Thayil (guitar), Ben Shepherd (bass) and Matt Cameron (drums)—built a fan base with independent releases and 1989's *Louder Than Love*, a major label debut. The loyal following grew through frequent tours—devotees were fascinated with the quartet's primal attitude (the chorus of "Big Dumb Sex" and a cover of Spinal Tap's "Big Bottom"). In early 1991, Cornell and Cameron added to their Seattle bona fides with Temple of the Dog, a band composed of hometown brethren (including Pearl Jam's Eddie Vedder) whose lone-self-titled album was a blues-influenced tribute to Mother Love Bone singer Andrew Wood (who had died of a drug overdose).

"All of us bands have an association, and it's not that it rains a lot here," Cornell said. "For years, there was no possibility of a record company coming to the Northwest and signing an act, but we filled tiny clubs and halls. Now we're putting out some important records internationally, and a lot of outside people are moving to Seattle to say they're part of the scene. It's a lot more convoluted."

The *Badmotorfinger* album paved the way to alternative music and mainstream success. There was a brainy part to the band's loud and aggressive style, but there was also a skull-crushing low end. Thayil revved up riffs influenced by Black Sabbath, and Cornell, a long-haired shirtless beast, roared through flamboyant vocals. His trademark passionate wail defined "Jesus Christ Pose," a thundering seven-minute single steeped in religious symbolism that Cornell claimed was a criticism of fashion magazines using images of persecution.

"Models laying in the shape of the cross, rock stars posing as if they're crucified—it's just irritating," he said. "For recognition, they're taking what they know is a sacred symbol to a lot of people."

Badmotorfinger went platinum and received a Grammy nomination, yet a big hit song eluded the band.

"So far, we've successfully avoided the pop Top 40 aspect of ourselves, and we're content with that," Thayil said. "Every subsequent record, we think it's going to be louder, heavier and weirder." ■

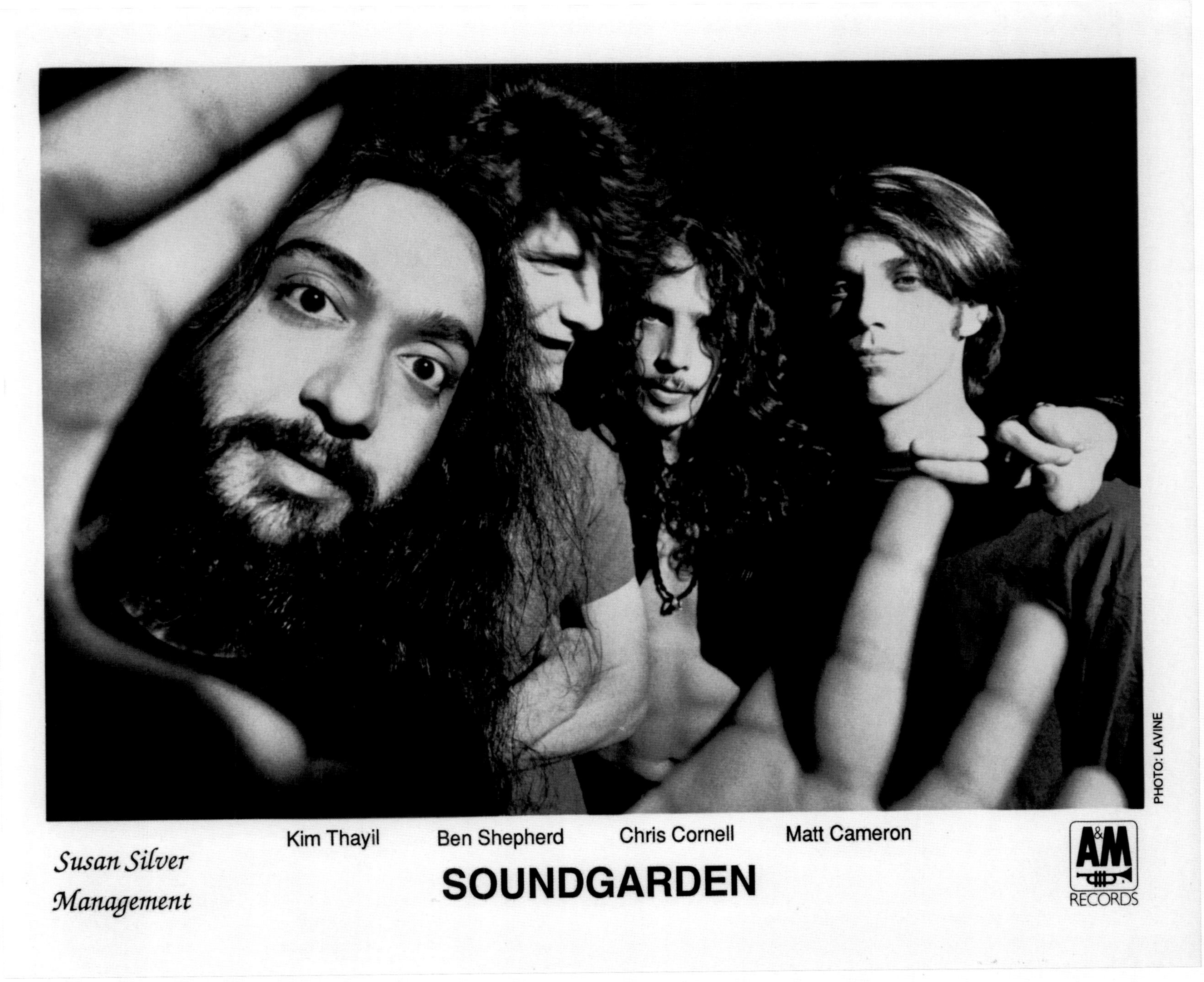

PHOTO: LAVINE

Kim Thayil Ben Shepherd Chris Cornell Matt Cameron

Susan Silver
Management

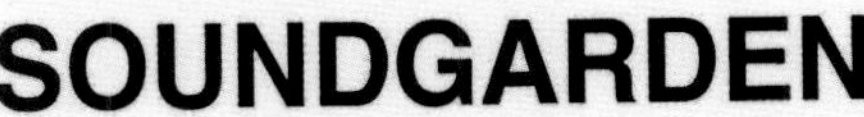

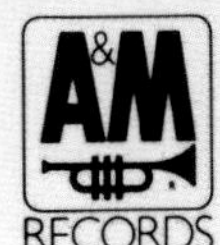

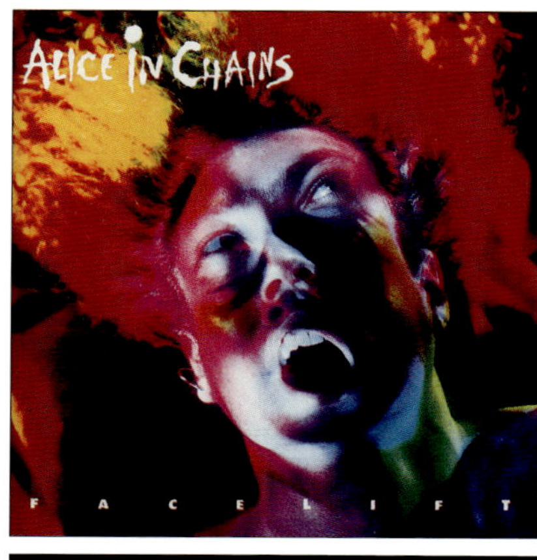

Billboard 200: *Facelift* (#42)

"Man in the Box" helped Alice in Chains' *Facelift* emerge as the first grunge release to crack the Top 50.

FORMED DURING the late Eighties, Alice in Chains emerged from the same bulging Seattle grunge swell that brought locals like Soundgarden, Mother Love Bone and the Posies to major labels.

"We were living at a rehearsal hall, working shifts all night and practicing during the day," guitarist and songwriter Jerry Cantrell said. "It was incredibly hectic, and kind of a sad scene because we had this tyrannical, psychotic boss. It was hell. But a lot of the roots of our frustration came from that particular time.

"After a while—when we had a few songs together—we would find people standing outside our practice room listening and saying, 'You guys are really good.' We didn't think we were that great, but it was slowly coming together. We got on a few bills with our friends, Mother Love Bone, and played in front of their crowd and got a good response."

Alice in Chains became one of the Northwest's most popular bands with the throbbing, gloomy *Facelift*. The sheer power of the debut album and the single "Man in the Box" had alternative and metal freaks quivering in their Chuck Taylors.

"Yes, this is a mind game," Cantrell said. "We like to pull the strings at the right time. I think we're very focused and heavy, but still jagged around the edges."

Second-billing factored into the band's success. During 1990 and 1991, AIC opened for everyone from Extreme to Iggy Pop to Van Halen, as well as appearing on the infamous "Clash of the Titans" speed-metal package with Slayer, Megadeth and Anthrax.

"Slayer told us that no opening act had ever been successful," singer Layne Staley recalled. "We were the first band to please their audience." ■

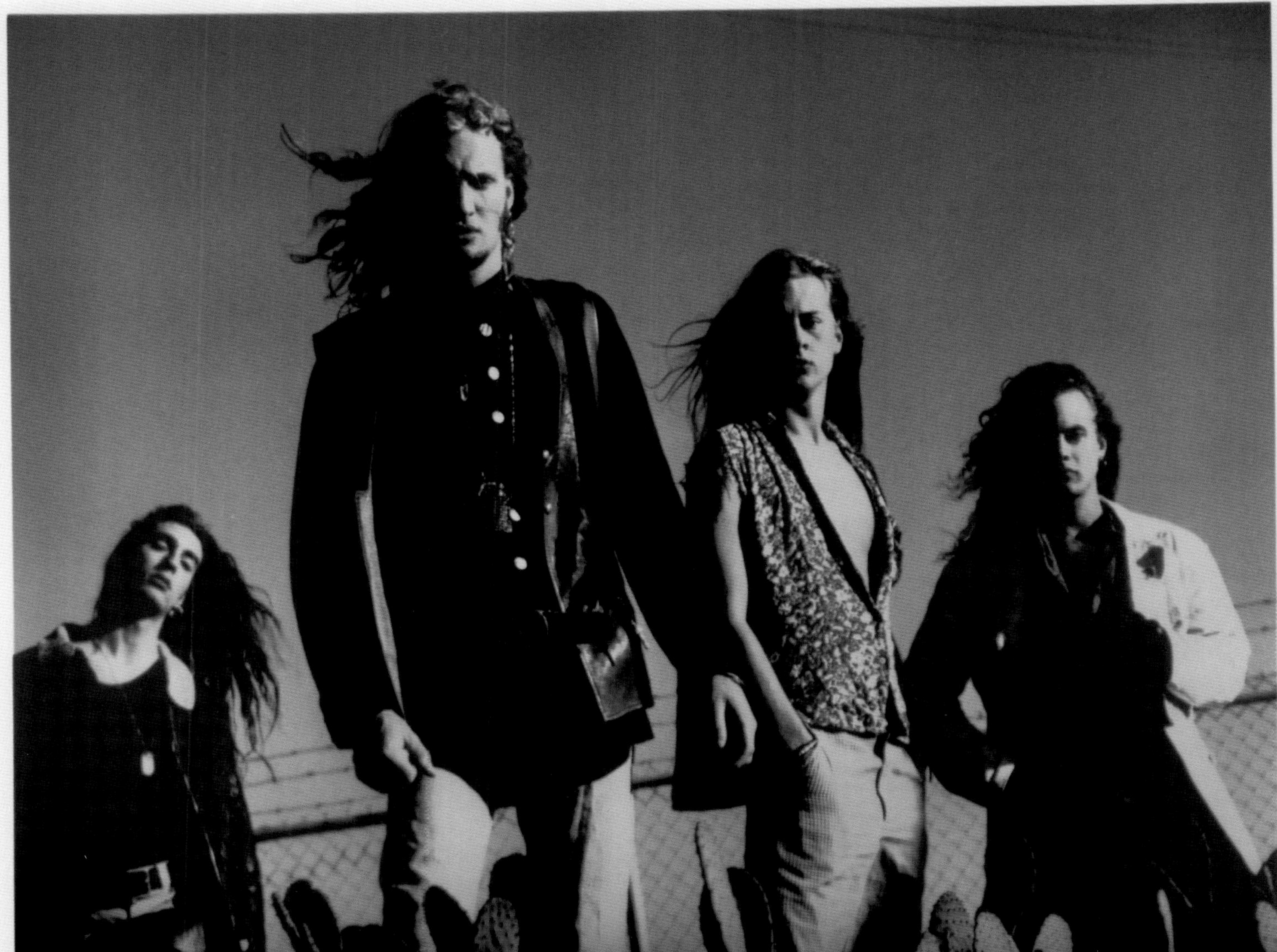

Sean Kinney | Layne Staley | Jerry Cantrell | Mike Starr

Management
Susan Silver 206/623-9268
Kelly Curtis 206/725-8927

ALICE IN CHAINS

Columbia
9103

© 1991 Sony Music. Permission to reproduce this photography is limited to editorial uses in regular issues of newspapers and other regularly published periodicals and television news programming.

Photo Credit: Rocky Schenck

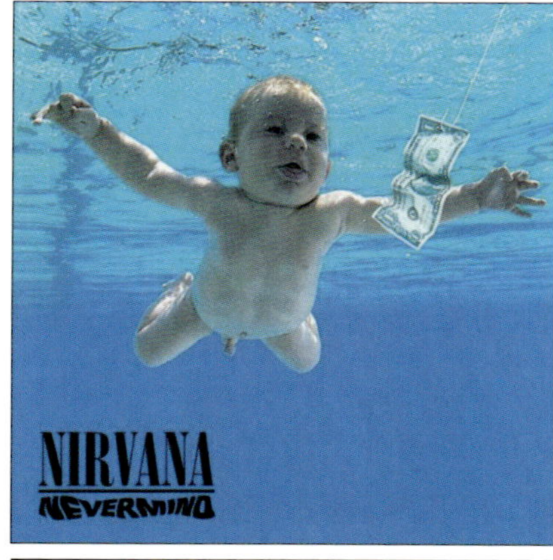

Despite low expectations, Nirvana's *Nevermind* turned into the grunge movement's first No. 1 album.

Billboard 200: *Nevermind* (No. 1)
Billboard Hot 100: "Smells Like Teen Spirit" (#6); "Come as You Are" (#32); "Lithium" (#64)

SINGER-SONGWRITER-GUITARIST KURT Cobain and bassist Chris Novoselic came from the rural logging town of Aberdeen, 100 miles south of Seattle. They met soon after leaving high school, sharing an affection for early-Eighties punk. They started a cover band to make a few bucks.

"We were broke, but we couldn't bear to play country music," the amiable Novoselic laughed. "So we thought we'd play Creedence Clearwater Revival songs. I don't remember if we actually got a gig."

In 1987, they formed Nirvana and were signed by Sub Pop Records, an independent label that released *Bleach*. Recorded for a reported $600, the album eventually sold 35,000 copies and elevated the band's status among alternative rockers. After a procession of drummers, Cobain and Novoselic recruited Dave Grohl and hit the road.

"We toured in a Ford van—you couldn't sleep," Novoselic said. "We were pretty burned out on it, you can't imagine. We did it for 24 months, easy."

The punky, metallic threesome signed with Geffen Records and put out *Nevermind*. The album stormed to the top of the charts and sold millions of copies worldwide. MTV ran the sensational "Smells Like Teen Spirit" single night and day, with the song's screaming, sardonic hook line, "Here we are now, entertain us," construed as a youthful call to arms, the Nineties equivalent of "I can't get no satisfaction." In months, Cobain went from being an absolute nobody to a new savior with microphones crammed in his face. The burden of popularity fell hard on him.

"We hoped *Nevermind* would put us on the level of (indie kingpins) Sonic Youth," he said. "Instead, we made it to No. 1."

Nirvana's career explosion resulted in a "feeding frenzy." Major labels scurried to sign any band that identified itself as "alternative" or "grunge," words that suddenly became valuable marketing tools.

"I don't have much use for the mainstream," Novoselic noted. "Before we came along, the people in power wanted to play it safe, didn't want to push—or maybe they had plain bad taste. Poison and Winger were making money, and it was like a chemical waste dump. They wanted to keep it going. Quality bands are out there, but they're suppressed somehow. But that's the music industry. It chews 'em up and spits 'em out." ■

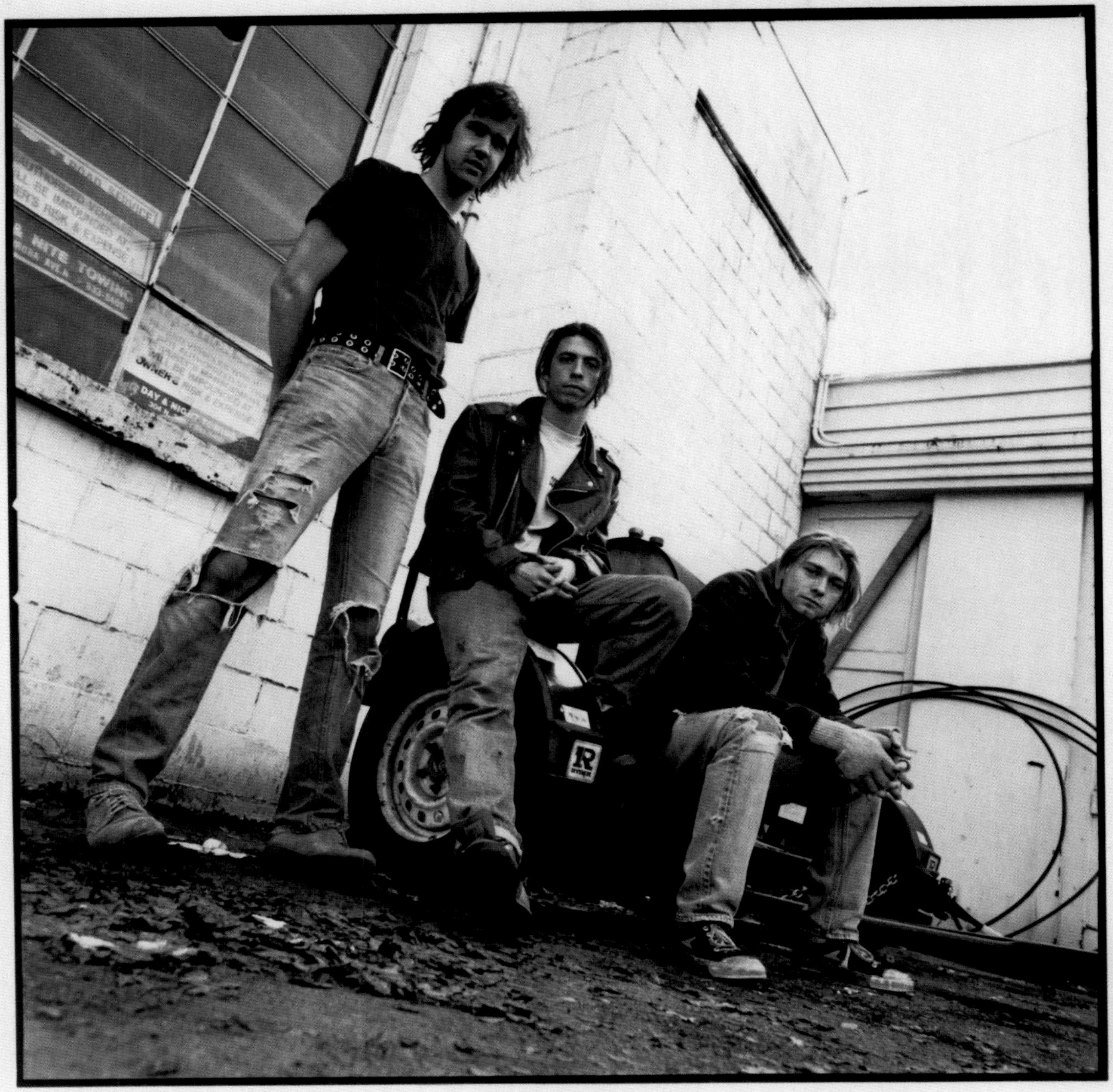

Photo Credit: Chris Cuffaro

Chris Novoselic David Grohl Kurt Cobain

NIRVANA

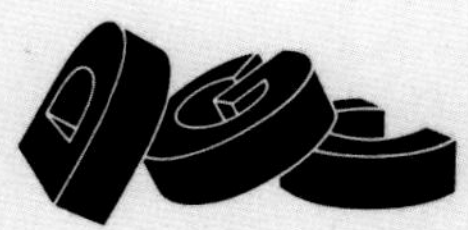

DAVID GEFFEN COMPANY

© 1991 The David Geffen Company/Permission to reproduce limited to editorial uses in newspapers and other regularly published periodicals and television news programming.

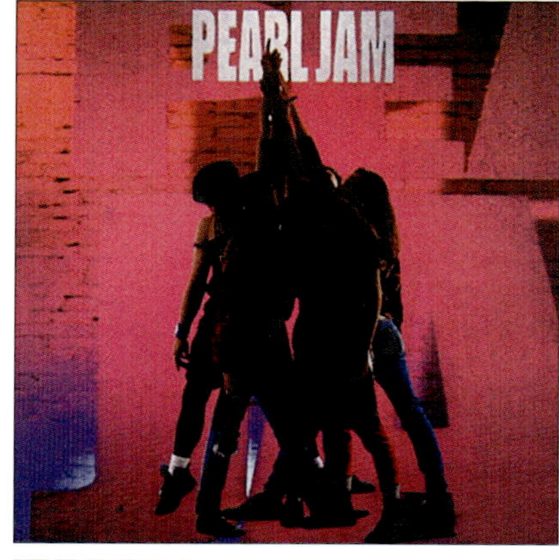

The frenzy for *Ten*, Pearl Jam's debut album, came with a distressing outlook for vocalist Eddie Vedder.

Billboard 200: *Ten* (#2)
Billboard Hot 100: "Jeremy" (#79)

AFTER NIRVANA'S *Nevermind* broke grunge and alternative rock into the mainstream, it was Pearl Jam's turn as rock's hottest new band. Popularized by the songs "Alive," "Even Flow" and "Jeremy," *Ten* clicked with a mass audience. Pearl Jam's magic was a group effort—members Stone Gossard and Mike McCready (guitars), Jeff Ament (bass) and Dave Abbruzzese (drums) rocked hard—but singer Eddie Vedder shouldered the onus of the band's popularity.

Historically, rock's young men of the moment became angry, bitter realists. Vedder fought that injustice inside himself. Part Native American, he was a kid who felt disconnected from his family, school and town, then found an intimate connection in music. Now a body of infatuated, disenfranchised kids looked to his songs for catharsis. Vedder's lyrics tackled weighty topics—depression, homelessness and abuse.

"I'm really surprised how all this happened," the reluctant messiah said. "You just become this huge band."

Pearl Jam refused to succumb to the accepted conventions of the music industry. When the Seattle quintet made the covers of the publications *Time*, *Rolling Stone* and *Spin*, Vedder said he was unhappy.

"So many things are fucked up, the way people manipulate us," he muttered, his mood darkening. "Betrayal is the worst. And I'm bad—I don't forget. I carry that stuff around down here." He clutched his stomach. "And I'm afraid it's going to come out in twisted ways. It's saturation in a bad way. It'd be a shame if we did all this and couldn't change anything."

His mood brightened momentarily. "But there's this little movement that's taking hold. It's not about girls' bustiers and slick guitars. It's a feeling that anyone can do anything." ■

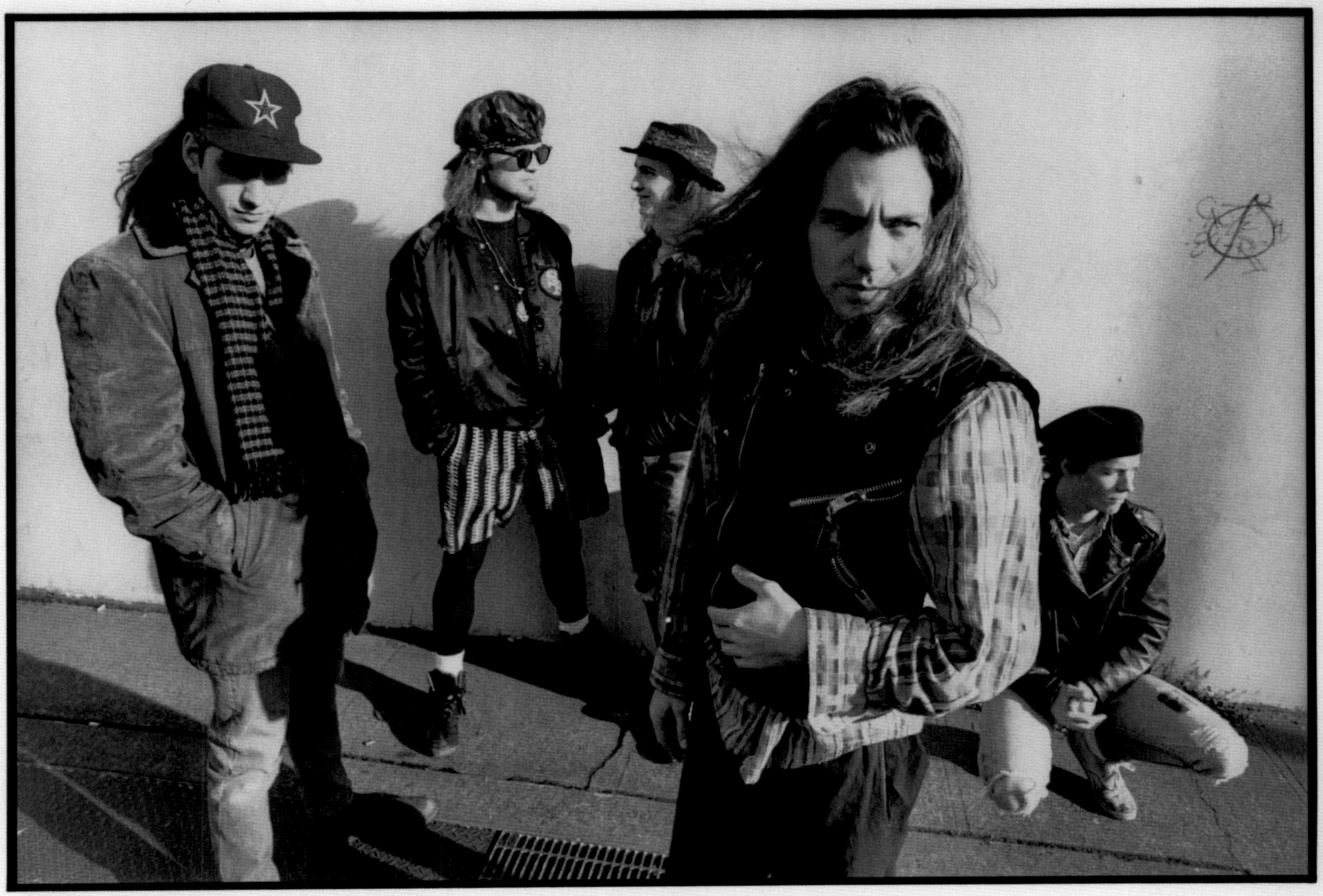

Photo Credit: Lance Mercer

L-R: Stone Gossard, Jeff Ament, Mike McCready, Eddie Vedder, Dave Krusen

PEARL JAM

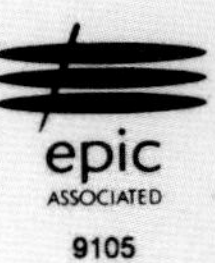

9105

© 1991 Sony Music. Permission to reproduce this photography is limited to editorial uses in regular issues of newspapers and other regularly published periodicals and television news programming.

Metallica unconditionally crossed over to mainstream awareness with *Metallica*, a.k.a. *The Black Album*.

Billboard 200: *Metallica* (No. 1)
Billboard Hot 100: "Enter Sandman" (#16)
"The Unforgiven" (#35); "Nothing Else Matters" (#34);
"Wherever I May Roam" (#82); "Sad but True" (#98)

THE FOUR members of Metallica had spent the better part of a decade on the outside of the music business looking in. They were the scourge of mainstream rock, rebelling against heavy-metal stereotypes and the standard marketing machinery. Their music too brutal and thrashing for commercial rock airplay, they also refused to make a promotional video for their first three albums. They built their reputation through relentless touring, fanzines and word of mouth. Sales were through the roof, but industry folks thought they were crazy.

But 1991 was a different story. *Metallica* entered the *Billboard* album chart at No. 1 and stayed there an entire month, conquering radio and MTV and attracting a whole new base of fans.

The product of eight months of banging around in a North Hollywood studio, *Metallica* featured a commercial producer, Bob Rock, known for his work on Mötley Crüe's *Dr. Feelgood* album. Rock tinkered with the recording mechanics, making Metallica's brand of metal deeper, clearer and somewhat more conventional but without dulling the band's loud but very musical edge. The wallop came from more focused songs—four- to six-minute models of punch and clarity featuring only one or two key streamlined riffs.

"It was hard at first to let someone like Bob have an opinion in the studio—we're pretty stubborn when it comes to that," singer-guitarist James Hetfield noted. "But we like to freak people out, too. Everybody thought we were going to sound like Bon Jovi. The challenge was to write the shorter song and put a little more emphasis on individual playing—we simplified, concentrated, let the guitars breathe."

Rock jacked up the aural bluster in the rhythm section on the roaring hit single, "Enter Sandman," a scary bedtime story delivered with Hetfield's usual attack-dog-from-hell posture. Rock also expanded the group's instrumental palette, like the subtle bed of cellos lurking deep in the mix of "The Unforgiven." Hetfield sang the confessional ballad "Nothing Else Matters" in an unexpectedly deep tenor, accompanied by a romantic acoustic guitar passage (with one flashy electric solo), harmonies and orchestra.

With the slowed-down tempos and super-spiffy engineering job, *Metallica* made it safe to like Metallica. The band's hardcore following quickly branded the members as "sellouts," claiming the album was crap and not "heavy" enough.

"I've heard that word since our second album," Hetfield said in response. "I don't know what it means to people—to me, 'sellout' means you've done something you didn't want to do just for the sake of money or a trade-off, give so you can take. We're too stubborn to do any of that shit. We write only for ourselves. Success is being able to do what you want to do. This is my music, and I'm proud of it right now." ■

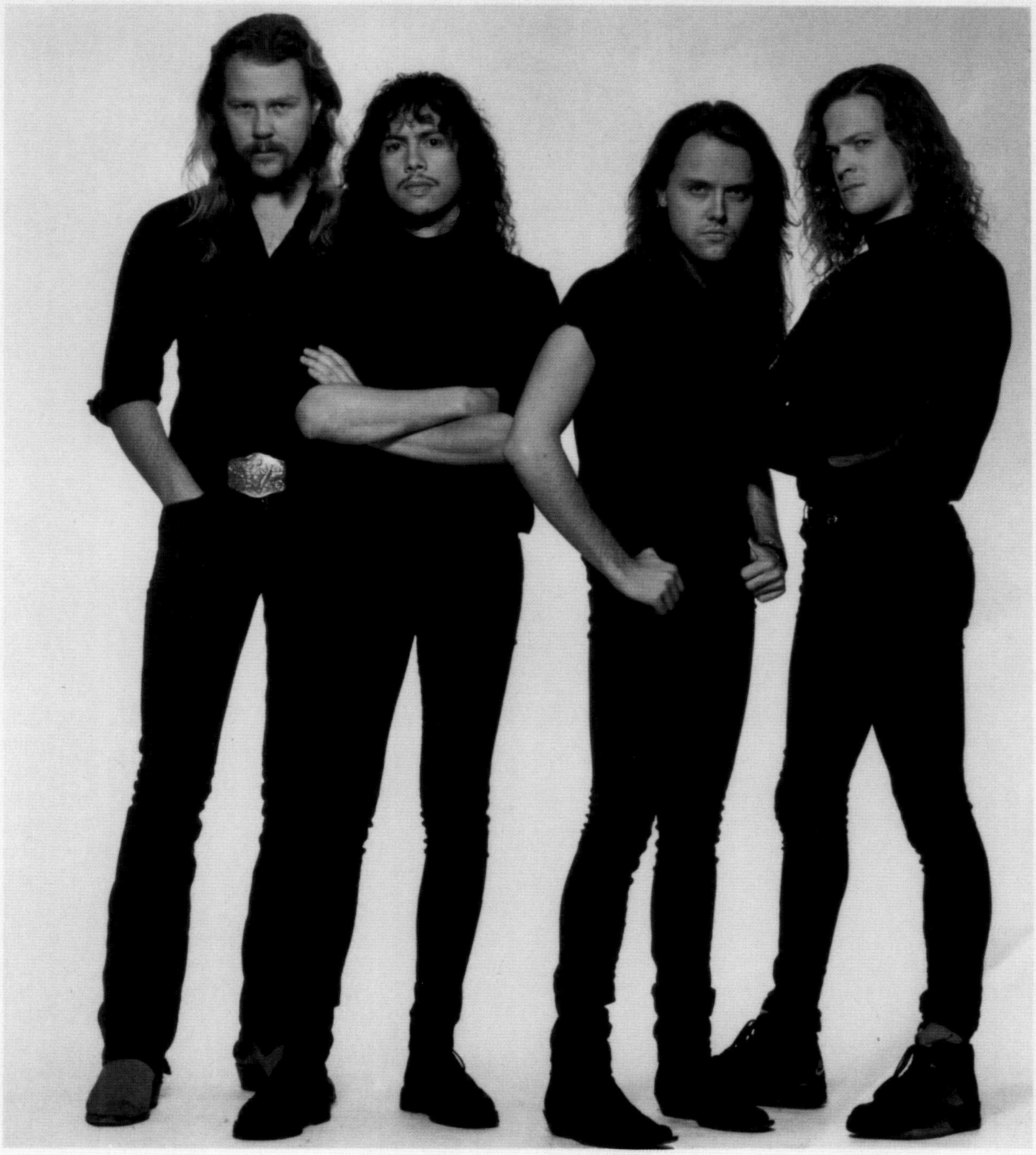

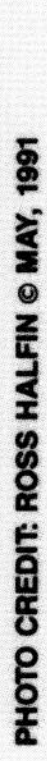

JAMES HETFIELD KIRK HAMMETT LARS ULRICH JASON NEWSTED

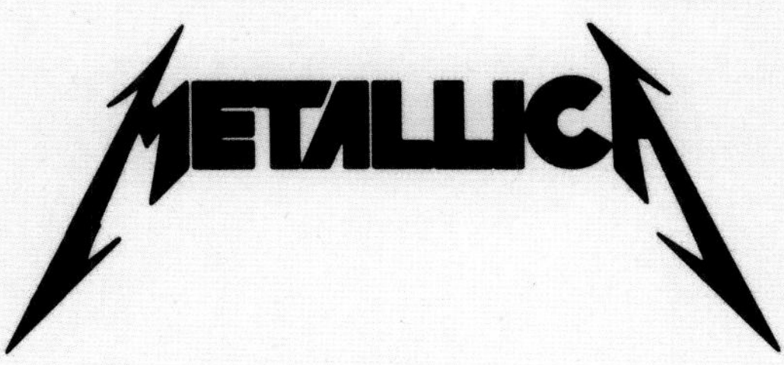

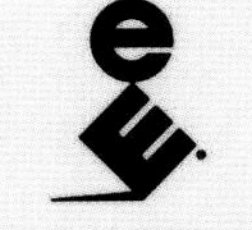

Elektra Entertainment

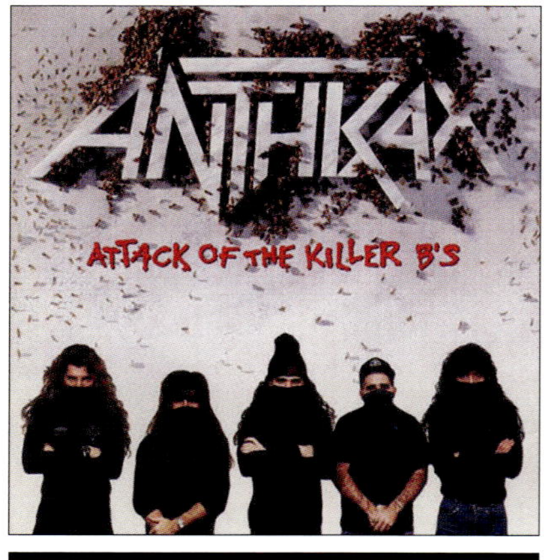

Anthrax's *Attack of the Killer B's* featured the thrash-metal band's cover of Public Enemy's "Bring the Noise."

Billboard 200: *Attack of the Killer B's* (#27)

FORMED IN New York in the early Eighties, Anthrax sparked the emergence of speed metal, focusing on tight, furious ensemble playing, catchy choruses and reference humor. 1990's *Persistence of Time* was decidedly more contemplative and mature, the cartoonish side of the band reduced in favor of philosophical views of war and racism. Drummer Charlie Benante expected people to be surprised that the band's music was a vehicle for compassion.

"A Detroit kid earned an Eagle Scout badge from 'Who Cares Wins,' a song about the homeless," Benante recounted. "It inspired him to raise food and money for a homeless shelter. We spent a day with him, and he's just a normal kid who went out of his way to do something. Stuff like that doesn't get reported. If the kid had gone out and killed somebody and blamed a heavy-metal song, it'd be all over the place."

The rockers were still unapologetically fast and loud, but Anthrax also earned respect for being receptive to uncompromising rap music. The band released *Attack of the Killer B's*, a compilation of B-sides, covers and rarities including a collaboration with Public Enemy on a slamming version of PE's classic "Bring the Noise" featuring Chuck D. rhyming over Anthrax's whining, chugging guitars.

"Bring the Noise" became one of Anthrax's biggest singles, the heaviest rock-rap alliance since Run-D.M.C. covered Aerosmith's "Walk This Way" in 1986. As an audience of young white metal fans found common ground with black youth in their love of rap, Anthrax and Public Enemy cemented the connection with a successful tour that integrated Anthrax's brand of aggressive, intense thrash with Public Enemy's hip-hop attack.

"I give our audience a little credit, even if it's not something they're really aware of," guitarist Scott Ian said. "I think they're less racist than some other metal bands' followings." ■

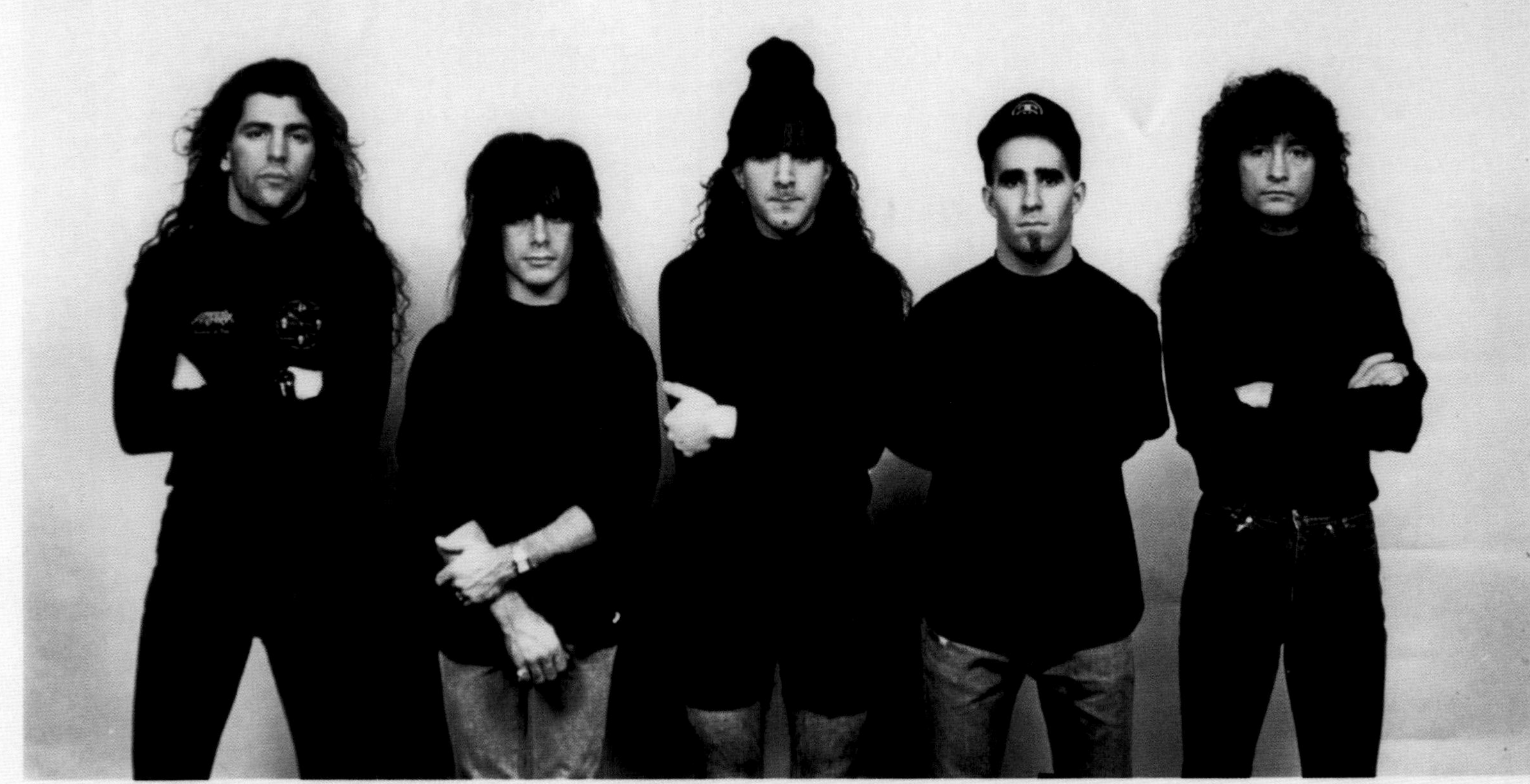

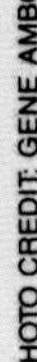

L TO R: FRANK BELLO, DAN SPITZ, CHARLIE BENANTE, SCOTT IAN, JOEY BELLADONNA

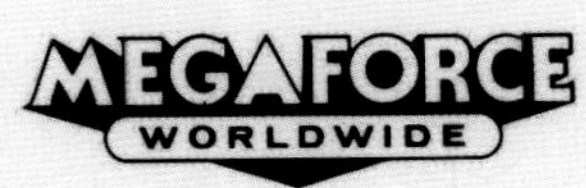

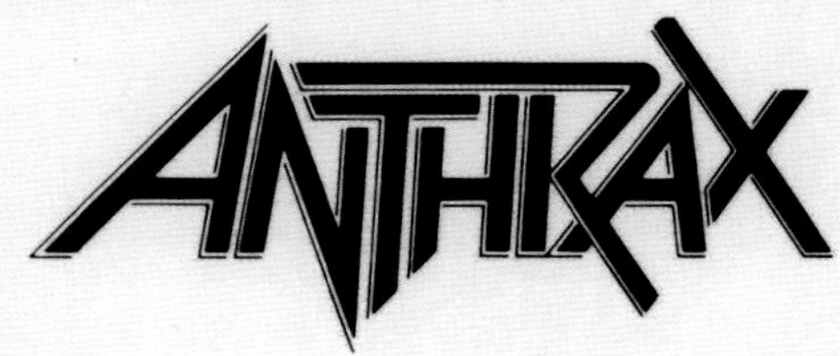

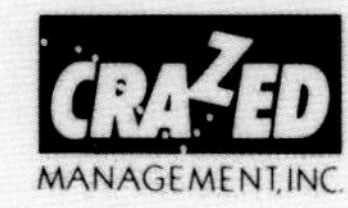

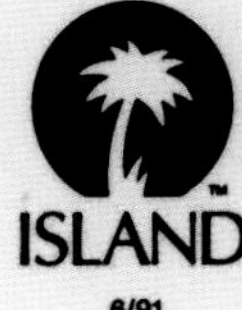

6/91

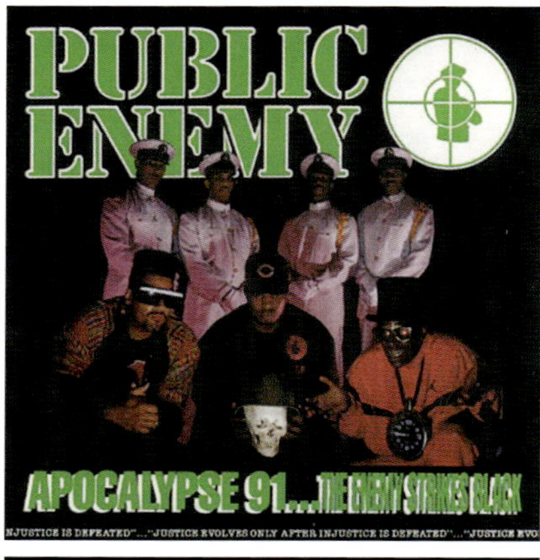

Bidding to consolidate its white audience, Public Enemy rerecorded "Bring tha Noise" beside Anthrax.

Billboard 200: *Apocalypse 91...The Enemy Strikes Black* (#4)
Billboard Hot 100: "Can't Truss It" (#50)

SINCE PUBLIC Enemy's inception, the members of the rap group had made it clear they stood for African-American pride and might. Through three controversial albums—*Yo! Bum Rush the Show*, *It Takes a Nation of Millions to Hold Us Back* and *Fear of a Black Planet*—lead rapper Chuck D had built a reputation as a confrontational, high-profile spokesman for a modern-day black power movement. And that made "Ol' Whitey" uncomfortable, leading to assaults on Public Enemy's credibility and charges of racism.

"When people are uneasy, it's usually because someone is challenging their way of thinking," Chuck D countered. "What we say may not be popular in certain quarters, but that doesn't make us stupid or our music invalid. I like to call rap 'black America's CNN.'"

The platinum-selling act returned with *Apocalypse 91...The Enemy Strikes Black*. The album's content was scrutinized because of Public Enemy's militant pro-black stance and subscription to the Nation of Islam's whites-devolved-from-blacks theory. But instead of inciting contempt, consternation and intimidation, *Apocalypse 91...* met with unanimous critical praise and climbed to #4 on the *Billboard* 200—the highest position in the band's history.

Chuck D put the album in context. "On our first album we said, 'Hey, we got a black nationalist point of view—even if they can't accept it, we're gonna let everybody know about it.' The next album revolved around the corruption of the white system. And the third, *Fear of a Black Planet*, was about the theories of the white mainstream, the effects of racism on blacks. This new album is just hard-punching, focusing on *our* problems, us versus us—black accountability."

Produced by the Bomb Squad, Public Enemy's studio phalanx, *Apocalypse 91...* burst with futuristic, thickly layered soundscapes and assertive, buzzing beats. The uncompromising lyrics catalogued failures within the black community, such as crime and the lack of economic self-sufficiency. "1 Million Bottlebags" was an anti-malt liquor song, extending rap's rhetoric against drugs into alcohol.

"Behind every empty bottle is an argument or a murder," Chuck D articulated. "My thing isn't toward the brothers, it's toward the corporations that irresponsibly target black society. I'm going after the companies' throats."

Public Enemy also demonstrated a commitment to reaching a larger rock audience, ending the album with "Bring tha Noize," a collaboration with the rebel headbangers Anthrax. Even though they shared an outlaw vanity and anger, black rap fans and white metal audiences often were divided by prejudice. But "Bring tha Noize," one of rap's great call-to-arms anthems, brought the two camps closer together—a video became the first ever to appear on both *Yo! MTV Raps* and *Headbanger's Ball*.

"People resist being exposed to different things," Chuck D explained. "Part of it is fear, and part of it is that they grow up receiving certain information that's pumped through radio and TV. That becomes their reality. But it isn't our reality." ■

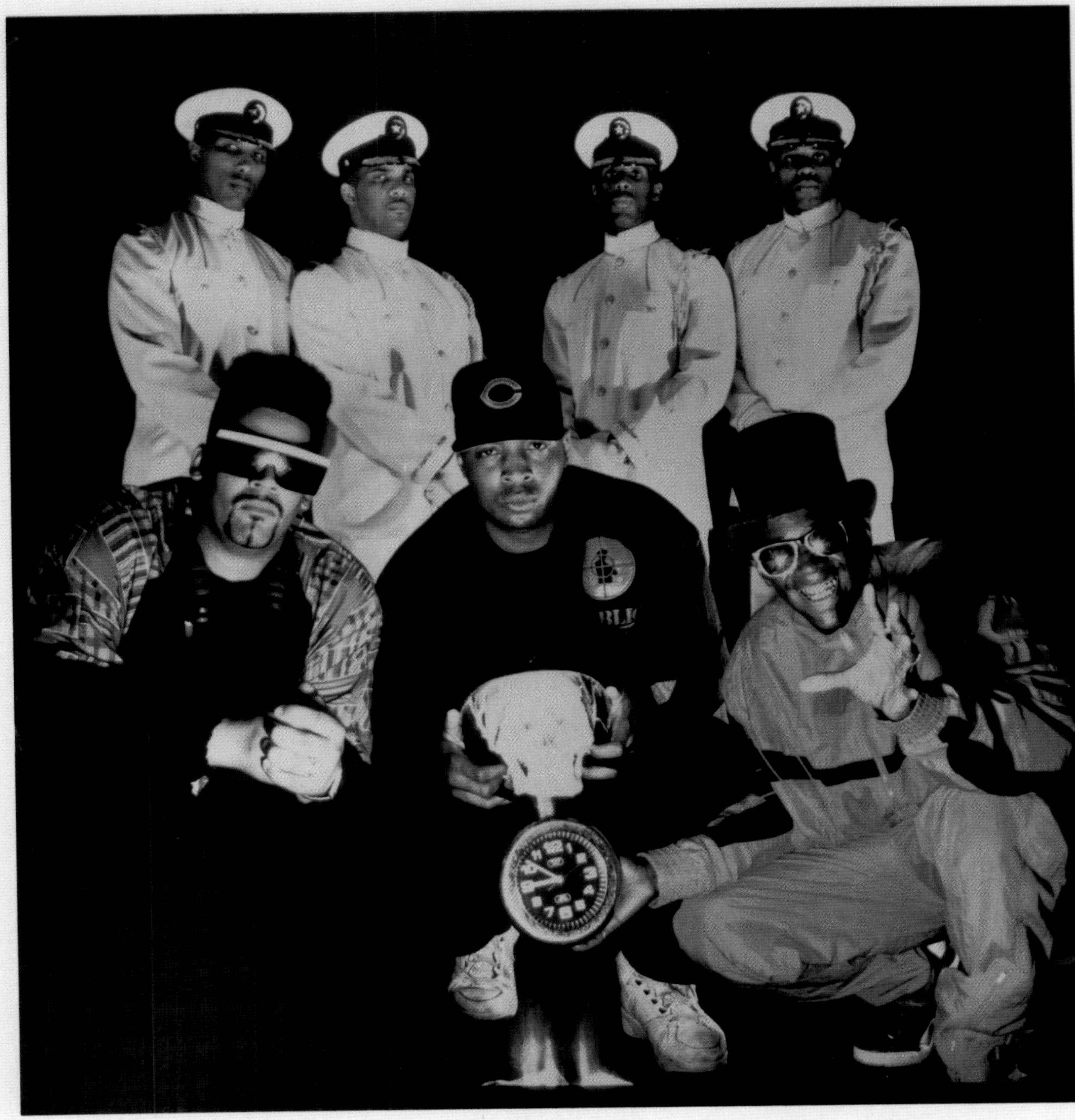

From left: (front) TERMINATOR X, CHUCK D, and FLAVOR FLAV; (back row) THE S1Ws.

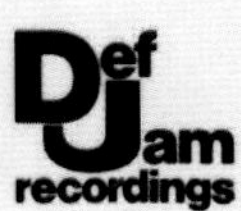

PUBLIC ENEMY

Columbia
9107

PHOTOGRAPH: ERNIE PANICIOLI

© 1991 Sony Music. Permission to reproduce this photography is limited to editorial uses in regular issues of newspapers and other regularly published periodicals and television news programming.

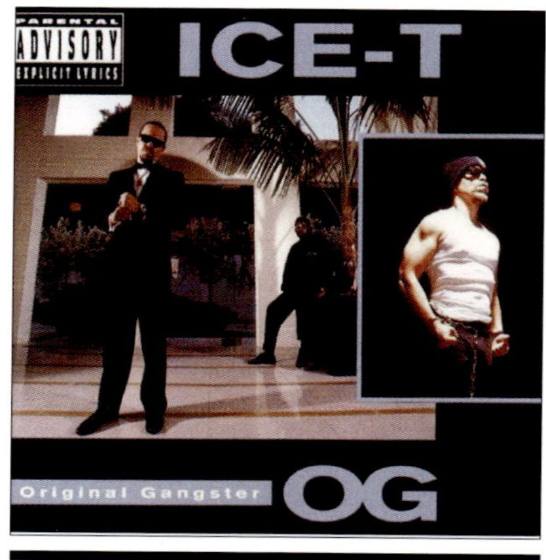

L.A.-raised rapper **Ice-T** released *O.G. Original Gangster*, one of gangsta rap's genre-defining albums.

Billboard 200: *O.G. Original Gangster* (#15)

ICE-T HAD been dubbed the godfather of hard-hitting, reality-based "gangsta" rap. There were no happy endings to his tales of gang violence and despair from the streets of South Central L.A. The beats and samples made it hard to sit down, but there was deeply felt rage and contempt behind his profanity.

With his *O.G. Original Gangster* album, Ice-T was bringing his rap to a whole new audience. He introduced Body Count, a heavy-metal band, on the track titled "Body Count." Did rap have more in common with metal than just volume and energy?

"White kids are getting hipper to black culture—'Yo, this is kind of different' is the attitude," he said. "With R&B, the kids didn't want to meet us, but rap is rock 'n' roll all over again, everybody chillin' together."

The outspoken rapper was a prolific performer. He co-starred as a streetwise cop in the feature film *New Jack City*. Ice-T fronted Body Count on the first annual Lollapalooza tour in 1991 and introduced a metal song called "Cop Killer" without much notice. Representing the street-side view of police corruption, harassment and racism, it had white suburban kids singing along.

"I identify with musical anarchy—I like a lot of intense punk bands," he said. "We're happy to connect with anyone who wants to listen. The black rap kids are radical, and so are the white rock kids." ■

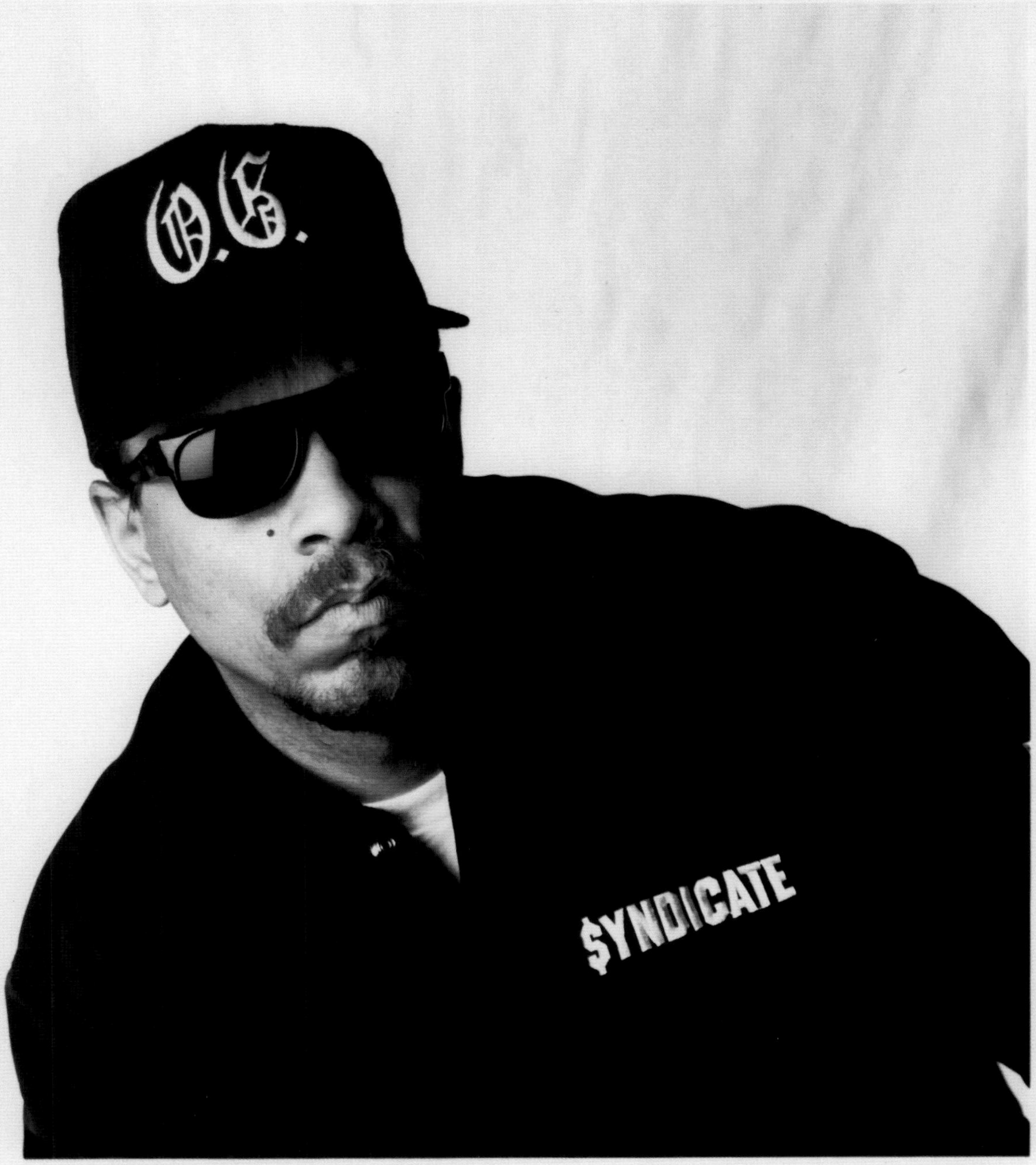

ICE-T

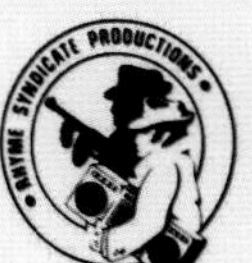

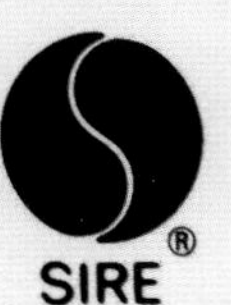

Photo Credit: Harrison Funk

© 1991 Sire Records Company/Permission to reproduce limited to editorial uses in newspapers and other regularly published periodicals and television news programming.

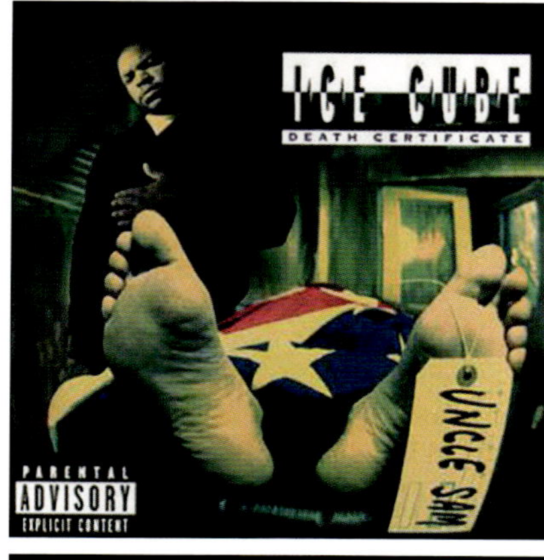

Billboard 200: *Death Certificate* (#2)

Ice Cube was equally praised and reviled for his racially and politically charged *Death Certificate* album.

FOR SOME liberal rap enthusiasts, there were reasons to like Ice Cube. He depicted real-life situations with a sharp eye for detail and a slick rhyming style.

But since his early days with hardcore rappers N.W.A., Cube had perfected a role as the self-proclaimed "nigga you love to hate," supporting Minister Louis Farrakhan of the Nation of Islam and lobbing pathetically ignorant and savage verbal grenades at Jews, gays, police and "bitches."

Ice Cube's *Death Certificate* album reflected on a world where life was nothing but violence and money. "No Vaseline" was a malicious dis to N.W.A., and "Black Korea" was taken as a racist petition to burn down all Korean-owned grocery stores. The ugly, angry lyrics were denounced by anti-defamation activists, Korean citizen groups, syndicated columnists and even the editors of *Billboard*. But the popular West Coast rapper disavowed literal interpretations of his records.

"The worst thing for someone to do is to tell you the truth about yourself and you know it's true," he said. "That's what I try to do. I try to hit people where it hurts, so I can take them to another level."

None of Ice Cube's inflammatory pronouncements damaged his standing in the hip-hop community or his sales. *Death Certificate* debuted at #2 on *Billboard*'s albums chart. His popularity was further increased by his role in the film *Boyz n the Hood*, where his performance as one of the titular characters earned critical praise. ■

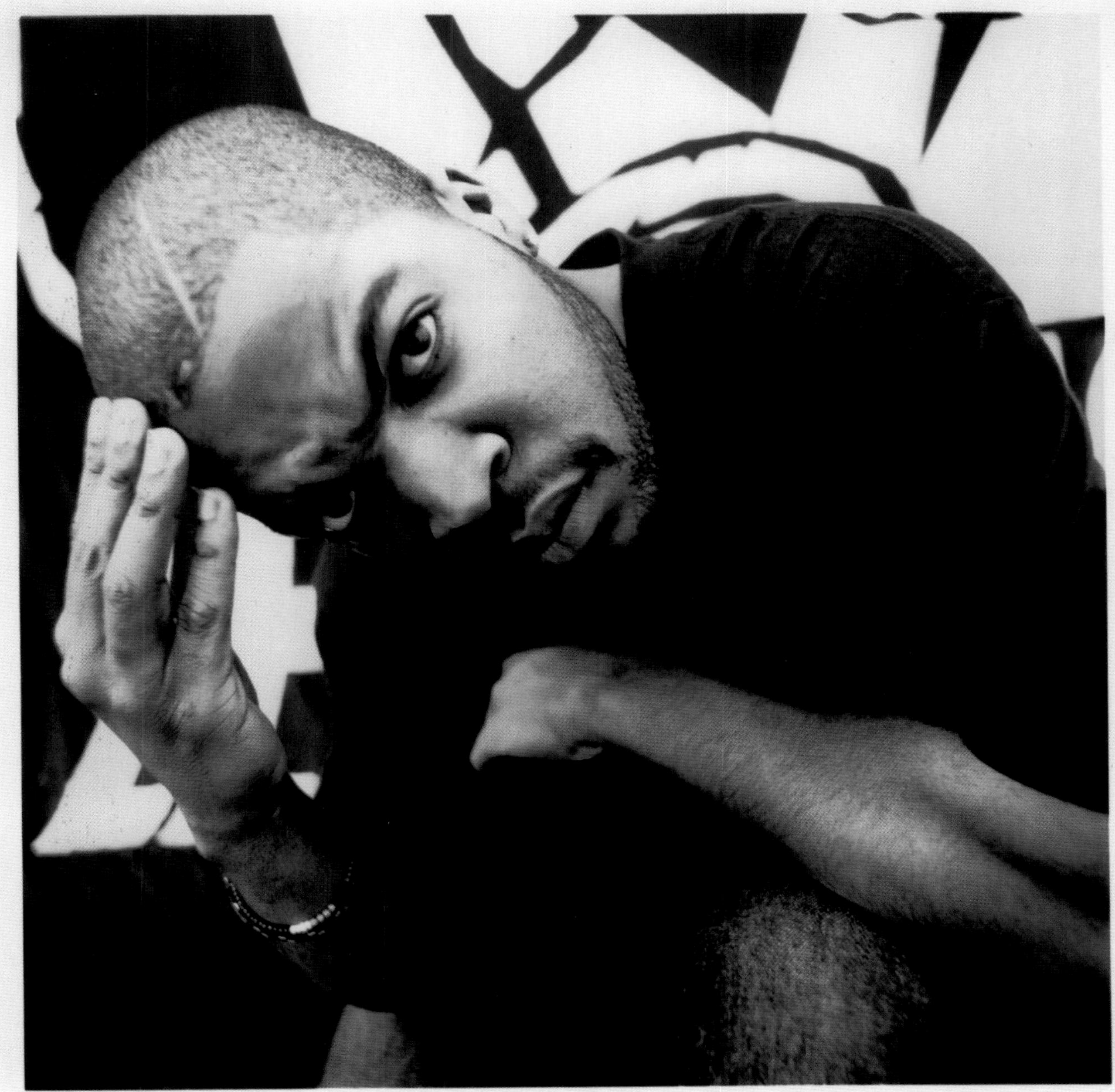

I·C·E C·U·B·E

DEATH CERTIFICATE

213.467.0151 PRIORITY RECORDS 800.235.2300

Billboard 200: *Quik is the Name* (#29)
Billboard Hot 100: "Tonite" (#49)

With *Quik Is the Name*, Compton native DJ Quik emerged as a revered West Coast producer and rapper.

AFTER GENERATING buzz in the streets of Compton from his self-made mixtapes, DJ Quik signed to Profile Records and released his debut album, *Quik Is the Name*. Led by the success of "Tonite" and "Born and Raised in Compton," *Quik Is the Name* blasted rough humor-laced rhymes about sex, alcohol and drugs and provided a soundtrack to the Los Angeles gangsta scene, making him a household name in hip-hop circles.

But on tour, exposed to life outside of South Central L.A., Quik (a.k.a. David Blake) experienced gangsta 'hood resistance. There were outbreaks of violence in Oakland and San Antonio, and serious scenarios in Houston, Memphis and Phoenix. In St. Louis, it was a Blood/Crips gunfight. In Denver, Quik was arrested for allegedly throwing a bottle into the crowd.

"A long time ago I made an underground tape and it contained some Blood shit in it. I wasn't gangbanging, I made it for some friends—I knew they would buy it. I didn't know motherfuckers everywhere were liking the raps—it went everywhere. It's a word-of-mouth thing, it all is. And one thing led to another."

Denver concertgoers saw Quik flashing gang signs and inciting fans in the crowd.

"So I was the aggressor then? I got more to lose—I'm out here trying to do something for myself. I go through this shit everywhere. I'm not singled out as a Blood, I'm singled out as a successful little motherfucker." ■

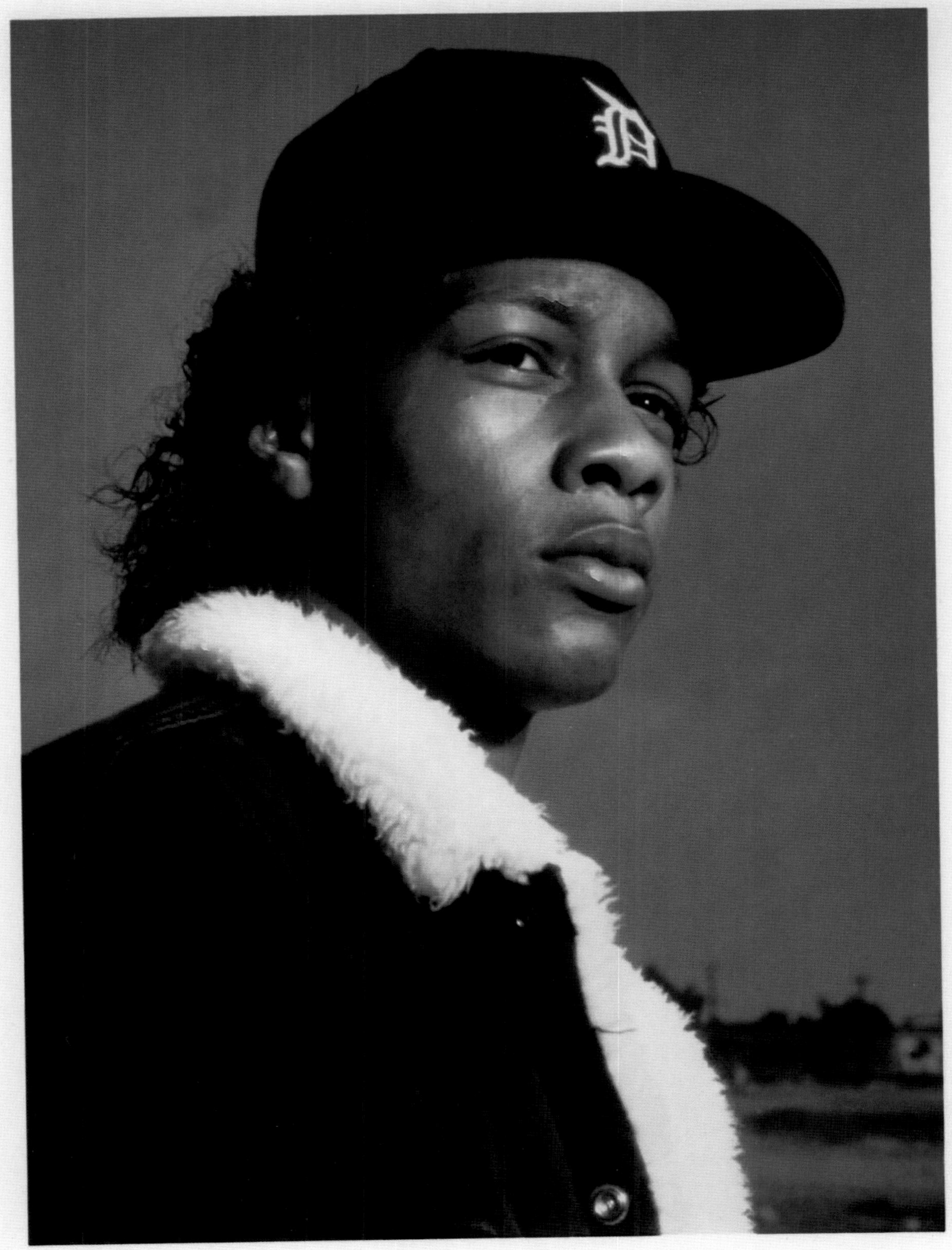

D J Q U I K

PROFILE®
RECORDS, INC

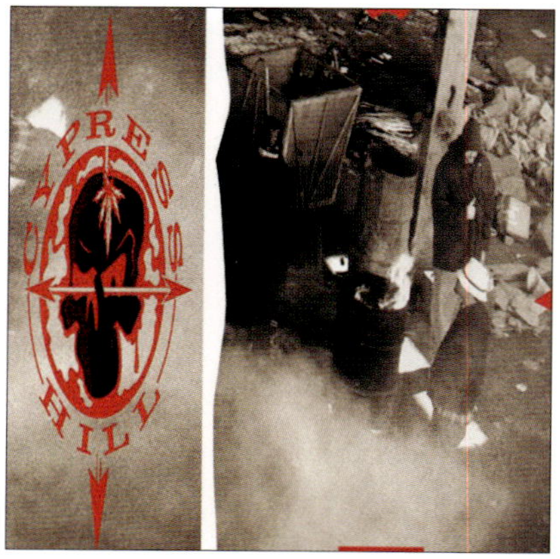

Billboard 200: *Cypress Hill* (#31)
Billboard Hot 100: "How I Could Just Kill a Man"/"The Phuncky Feel One" (#77)

Cypress Hill recast hip-hop with stoned bass-and-drums loops, cartoony violence and B-Real's nasal raps.

LIVING IN South Central L.A., Cypress Hill broke out dramatically to become one of the biggest-selling rap acts. The mostly Latin crew's *Cypress Hill* laid a vehement pro-marijuana stance and dark, gun-toting gangsta tales on top of stark hip-hop grooves. Mixmaster Muggs raked the songs with braying screeches and eerie tones, while Sen Dog demonstrated his booming braggadocio and B-Real related via his altered cartoonish crazed-convict weed-fiend persona.

"When we did our earlier demos, I didn't sound that great rapping in my normal voice," B-Real (a.k.a. Louis Freese) said. "One day, we were messing around and came up with something—if I rap loud, it's in a higher tone. It sounded better."

The ominous style of "How I Could Just Kill a Man"/"The Phuncky Feel One," a double A-side single, received heavy airplay on urban and college radio.

"It's looking at it from the point of an individual, not a gang," B-Real drawled. "When your gang ain't there and you're by yourself, whatcha gonna do? You're gonna protect yourself. But people don't realize that shit."

Other songs depicted the hip-hoppers' obsession with smoking weed—the members of Cypress Hill were the first rappers to openly support cannabis legislation.

"This ain't for everybody," B-Real exhaled. "I wouldn't want to force this on anybody. But we stick to what we know. When we were underground, we didn't care if the government liked it or not." ■

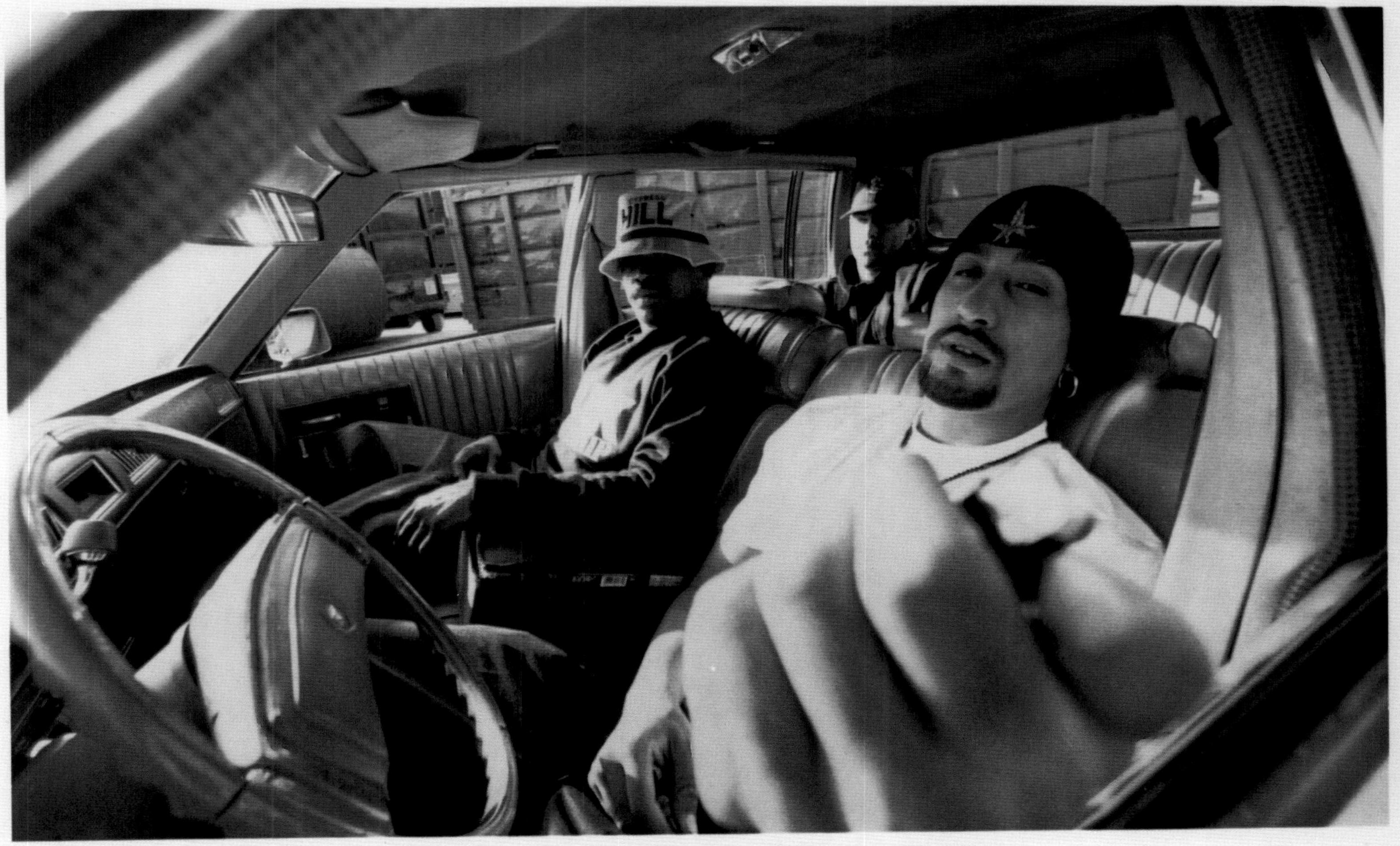

© 1991 Sony Music. Permission to reproduce this photography is limited to editorial uses in regular issues of newspapers and other regularly published periodicals and television news programming.

PHOTOGRAPH: MICHAEL MILLER

From left: SEN DOG, MIXMASTER MUGGS, and B-REAL.

Management:
Buzz Tone
1502 Gardner
Hollywood, CA 90046
Phone: 213.878.1900

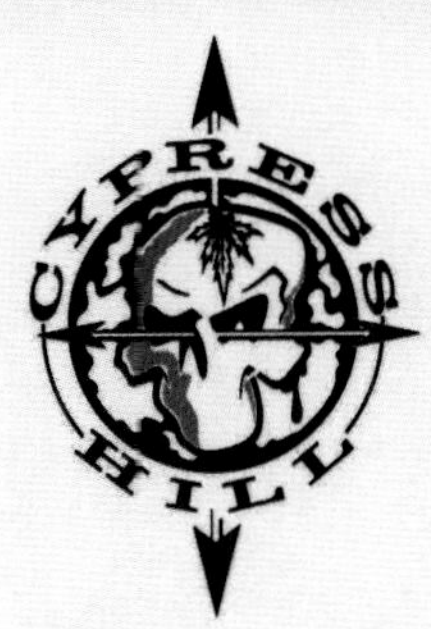

CYPRESS HILL

Columbia
9107

Billboard 200: *The Reality of My Surroundings* (#49)

Fishbone built on its underground following, wrangling respect with *The Reality of My Surroundings.*

IN 1979, five African-American teens from South Central L.A. found themselves being bused to the predominantly white Hale Junior High School in the San Fernando Valley. They coped by forming a band with one of their few black classmates, Angelo Hall. Within a few years, the members of Fishbone were being hailed in West Coast circles as the crown princes of modern funk—a feat accomplished without the benefit of radio airplay. They'd converted their fans through the spasmodic mayhem of live shows with the credo: "If someone pays ten bucks to see us, they ought to see a heart attack or something."

"In the beginning, we knew a lot more what we didn't want to do than what we wanted to do," guitarist Kendall Jones reflected. "Our inspiration came from seeing bands that were really shitty live. We'd see shows by these pompous Euro groups who went more for mood than activity. They'd doll up before the show and then they wouldn't perform—they acted like it was the audience's privilege to see them. We decided early on that we wanted to do the most exciting, energetic shows that we could."

Fishbone jumped musical genres, a mad, dense rush of musical styles—from funk to soul to hard rock to Jamaican ska by way of urban Los Angeles. But the band's party spirit and social conscience (angry political lyrics about inner-city decay) had yet to attract a significant black audience.

"We're not just entertainers—we say what's on our minds," Jones said. "Fishbone's got to address the problems that are happening now in L.A., and we're making a concerted effort to reach out to a wider audience, to some of the brothers. But we're not going to sound like Bobby Brown to do it."

Adding second guitarist John Bigham, a former Miles Davis sideman, Fishbone released *The Reality of My Surroundings*. The group performed "Sunless Saturday" and "Everyday Sunshine" on *Saturday Night Live*, and both tracks made the modern rock charts. ■

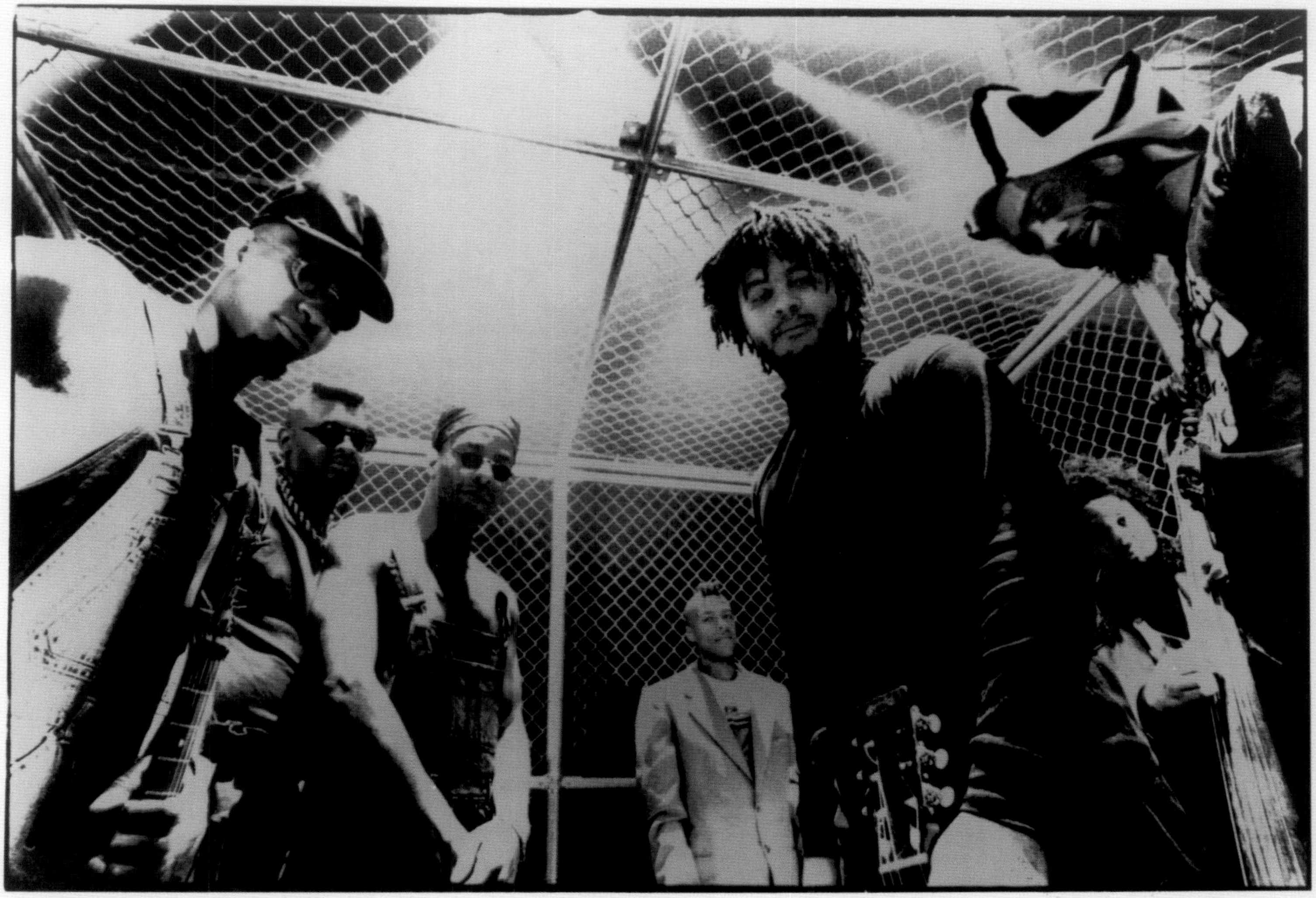

L to R: Phillip "Fish" Fisher, Walter A. Kibby II, John Bigham, Angelo C. Moore, Kendall Rey Jones, Christopher Dowd, John Norwood Fisher

© 1991 Sony Music. Permission to reproduce this photography is limited to editorial uses in regular issues of newspapers and other regularly published periodicals and television news programming.

Photo Credit: Sikay Tang

Management:
Elliot Roberts
Frank Gironda Lookout Management
506 Santa Monica Boulevard
Penthouse
Santa Monica, California 90401

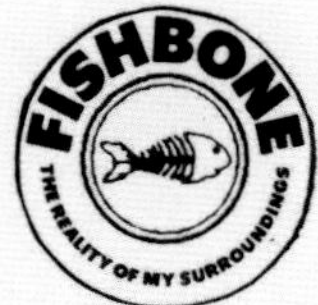

Columbia
9104

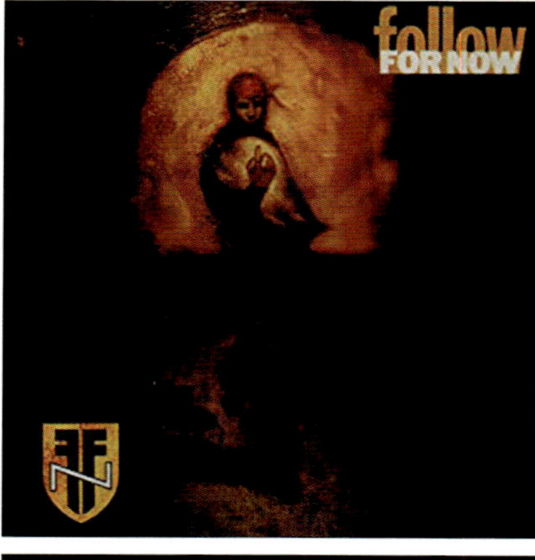

Follow for Now, a newly formed band from Atlanta, was bent on expanding its dedicated live following.

THE MARKET seemed flooded with like-minded acts attempting to reclaim rock music as a black birthright. Follow for Now played music steeped in black consciousness and influences, and the group's manic live shows garnered rave reviews. After headlining Atlanta's Center Stage Theater on New Year's Eve without a record contract, the band signed to Chrysalis Records and released *Follow for Now*. The music was described as everything from Sly Stone meets Black Sabbath to Jimi Hendrix meets Metallica.

But Follow for Now faced the inevitable—its urban rock sound endured comparisons with Living Colour, and its audience was white.

"People are waiting for a bridge between rock and rap, plus there's the retro Seventies vibe going around," singer David Ryan-Harris mused. "Black radio makes it seem if you're black and play guitar, you're freaky. If it's not drum-machine stuff, then it doesn't get played."

Though Chrysalis Records initiated a major promotional campaign for the album—the videos for "Holy Moses" and "Evil Wheel" aired on MTV—Follow for Now never achieved mainstream success. ■

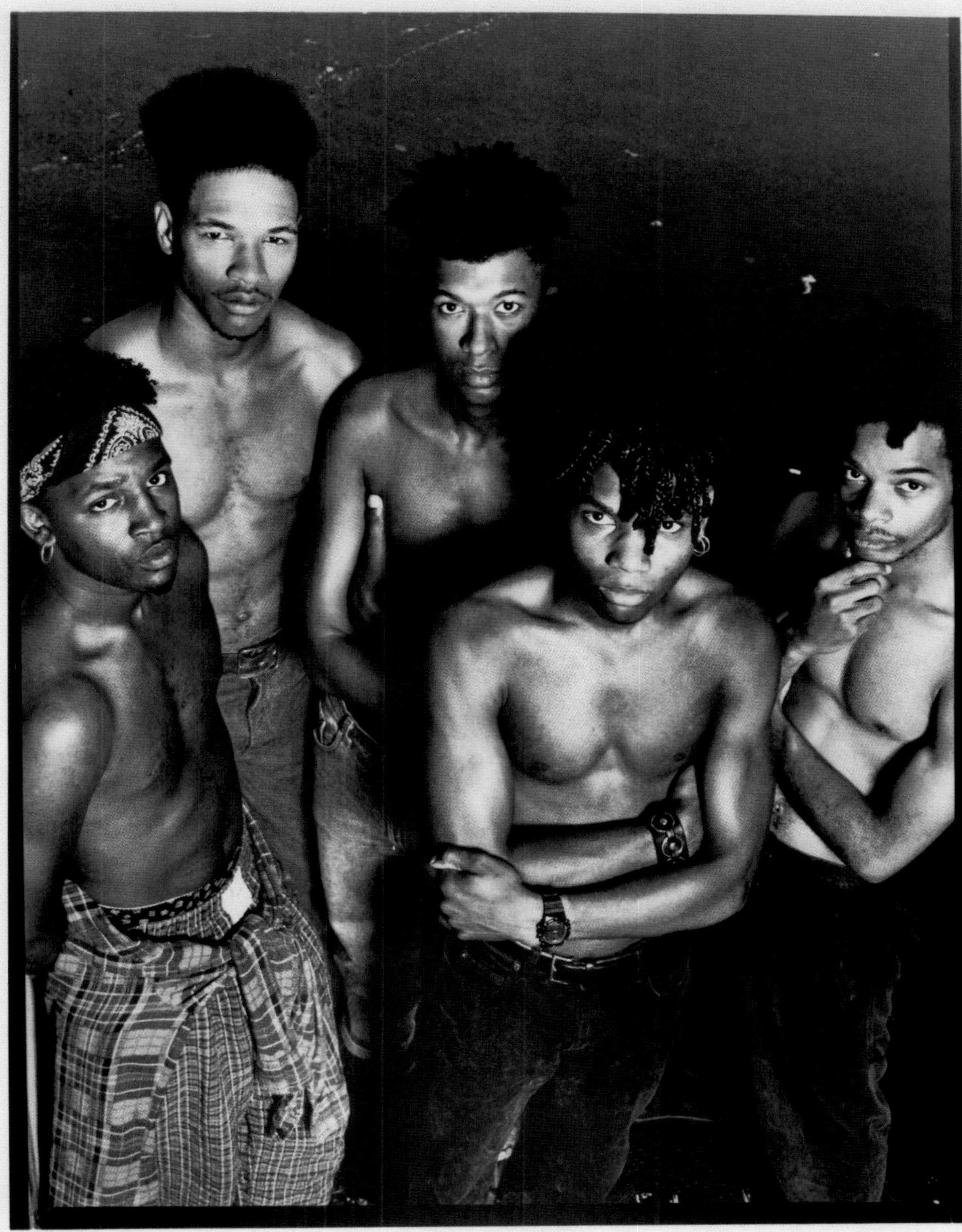

PHOTO: RUTH LEITMAN

follow FOR NOW

Chrysalis®

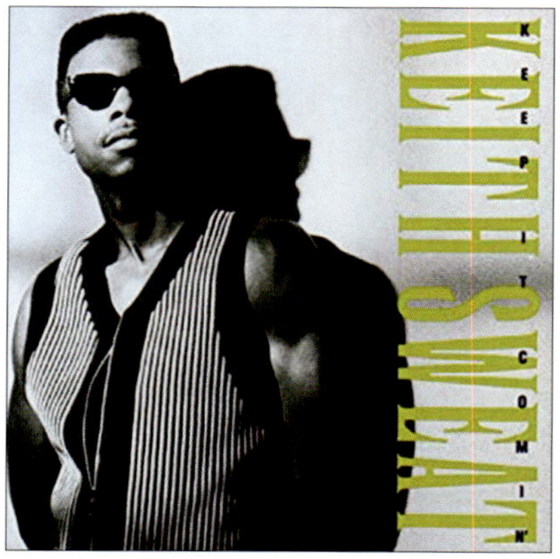

Billboard 200: *Keep It Comin'* (#19)
Billboard Hot 100: "Keep It Comin'" (#17);
"Why Me Baby?" (#44)

Keep It Comin' by Keith Sweat briefly unseated Michael Jackson from the top spot on the R&B charts.

KEITH SWEAT was an early proponent of new jack swing, a hardcore mix of hip-hop and soulful sounds. Known for a pleading, whining vocal style, he released "I Want Her," a seductive 1987 single that topped the R&B chart and reached #3 on *Billboard*'s pop chart. The Harlem born-and-raised entertainer sold 3 million albums and was up for stardom.

"I grew up two blocks from the Apollo Theater, and Marvin Gaye was my idol," Sweat said. "I watched entertainment shows on television, I saw concerts, I hung around studios—and I picked up things about performing and recording."

On *I'll Give All My Love to You*, his second album, Sweat wrote or co-wrote and produced every song.

"How did I get control of my work?" Sweat asked rherotically. "If my record company won't let me do it my way, they get nothin'."

Sweat released his third album, *Keep It Comin'*. The title track, his fourth No. 1 R&B hit, sampled Kool & the Gang's 1973 smash, "Jungle Boogie."

"If you write songs, nobody else knows better how they should sound," Sweat said. "I try to imagine what people like to hear on the radio. Sometimes you get tired of hearing boom-boom-boom, you just want to lay back and relax. And sometimes you're in the mood for a good dancing-party groove." ■

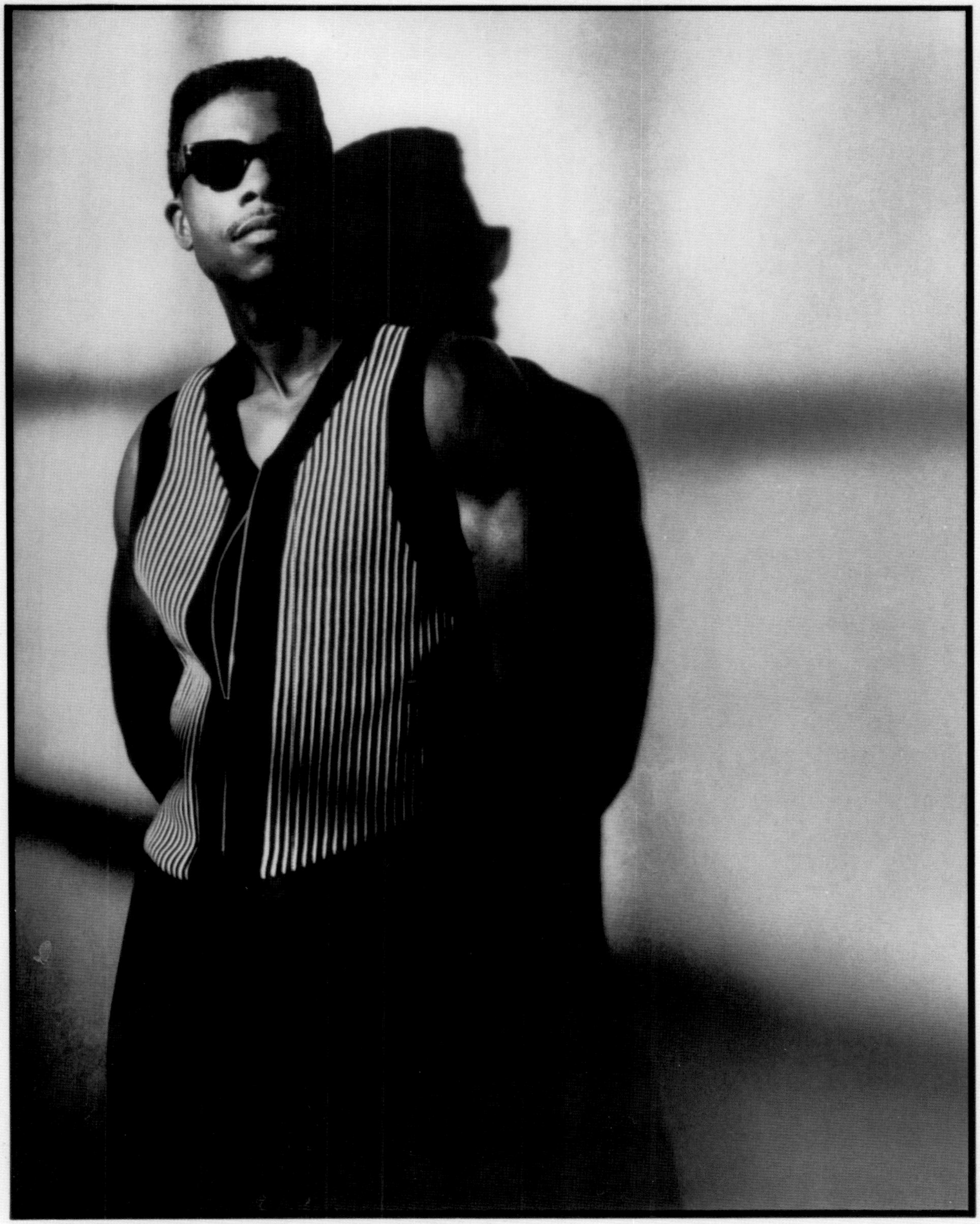

PHOTO CREDIT: RANDEE ST. NICHOLAS/1991

KEITH SWEAT

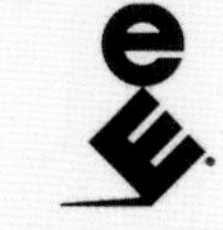

Elektra Entertainment

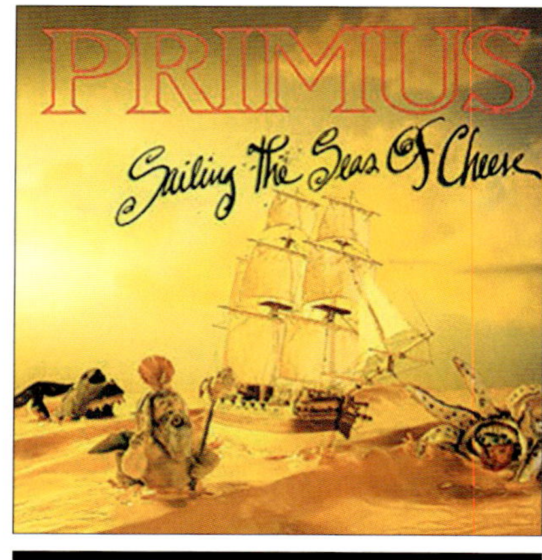

Billboard 200: *Sailing the Seas of Cheese* (#116)

A commercial breakthrough, *Sailing the Seas of Cheese* brought **Primus**' alt-rock sound to the masses.

ALTERNATIVE-MUSIC fans could generally agree on one thing: Primus was aggressively weird. The triumvirate—lanky frontman Les Claypool, guitarist Larry Lalonde and drummer Tim "Herb" Alexander—succeeded largely on its own terms despite its eccentric and devoutly anti-commercial body of work. Critics described their compositions as post-punk avant-rock with Rush's exactness and Frank Zappa's humor, a goofy, heavy, unique evocation of insanity and a neuromuscular disorder.

Sailing the Seas of Cheese was Primus' major-label debut, supported by the singles "Jerry Was a Race Car Driver" (#23 on *Billboard*'s Modern Rock Tracks chart), "Tommy the Cat" (Tom Waits provided the voice of the titular feline) and "Those Damned Blue Collar Tweekers." Anchored by Claypool's vigorous bass playing and comical vocals, the album parlayed the oddball trio's idiosyncratic funhouse funk into popularity and recognition.

Onstage, the thrash-rock pioneers had fans standing, dancing and pumping fists in the air—and expressing their collective adoration with the chant "Primus sucks!"

"People used to come up to us and go, 'You're cool,'" Claypool said. "We'd answer, 'Nah, we suck.' Well, it just caught on." ■

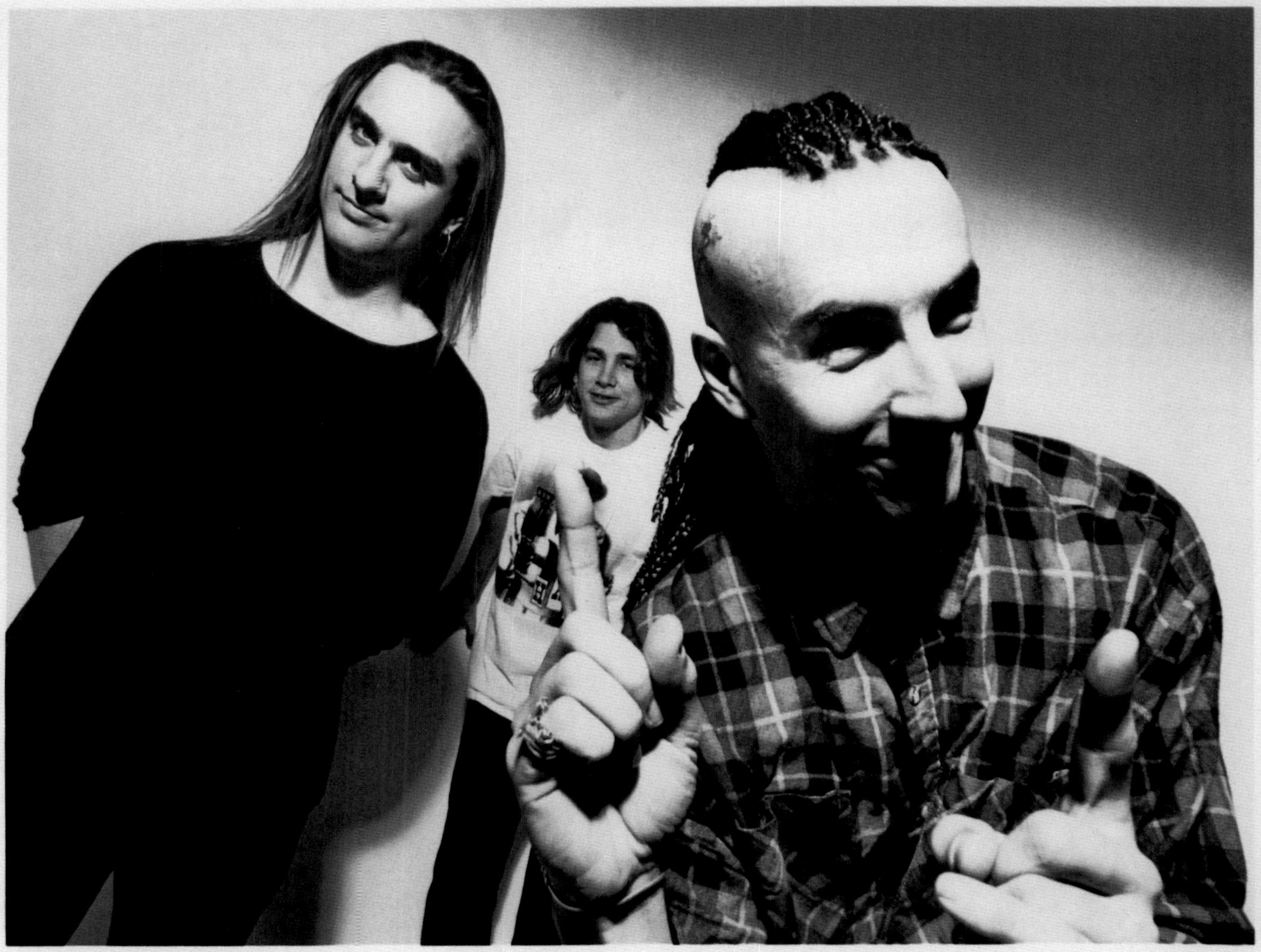

Photo Credit: Michael Lavine/1991

Tim Alexander Larry Lalonde Les Claypool

PRIMUS

©1990 Interscope Records, Inc./ Permission to reproduce limited to editorial uses in newspapers and other regularly published periodicals and television news programming. All other rights are reserved.

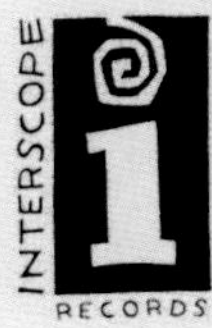

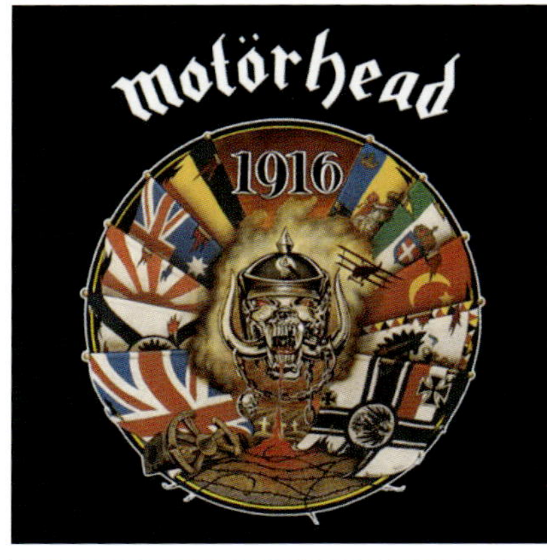

1916 by **Motörhead** was its first nomination in the Best Metal Performance category at the Grammys.

Billboard 200: *1916* (#142)

BACK IN 1977, when heavy metal and punk rock were estranged, Britain's Motörhead united them in an overwhelmingly loud and fast style and pioneered thrash-metal. With vocalist and bassist Lemmy (real name Ian Kilmister) at the helm, the band delivered classics like "Ace of Spades" and "Overkill." But international popularity stayed on an underground level, thanks to shifts in personnel—Lemmy was the only remaining original—and bad management.

"Rather than it skyrocketing one day and then you've fallen flat on your ass the next day, it's been pretty steady with us—we've been able to have a long career out of it," Lemmy said. "We could get a show somewhere on the planet just about every night of the year. We're lucky—we've got some hardcore fans."

Lemmy had moved from England to the US, settling in West Hollywood. *1916*, Motörhead's first record in four years, clarified the band's grimy attack but didn't compromise its commitment to power and speed. Some sharp departures were pulled off—a ballad ("Love Me Forever") and a 1:25 tribute to a classic band ("R.A.M.O.N.E.S."). *1916* concluded with the title track, a surreal, lump-in-the-throat account of World War I's Battle of the Somme.

"We don't play it live—we love it, but it's too intense," drummer Phil "Philthy Animal" Taylor said. "A heavy-metal audience wants bam-bam-bam-bam." ■

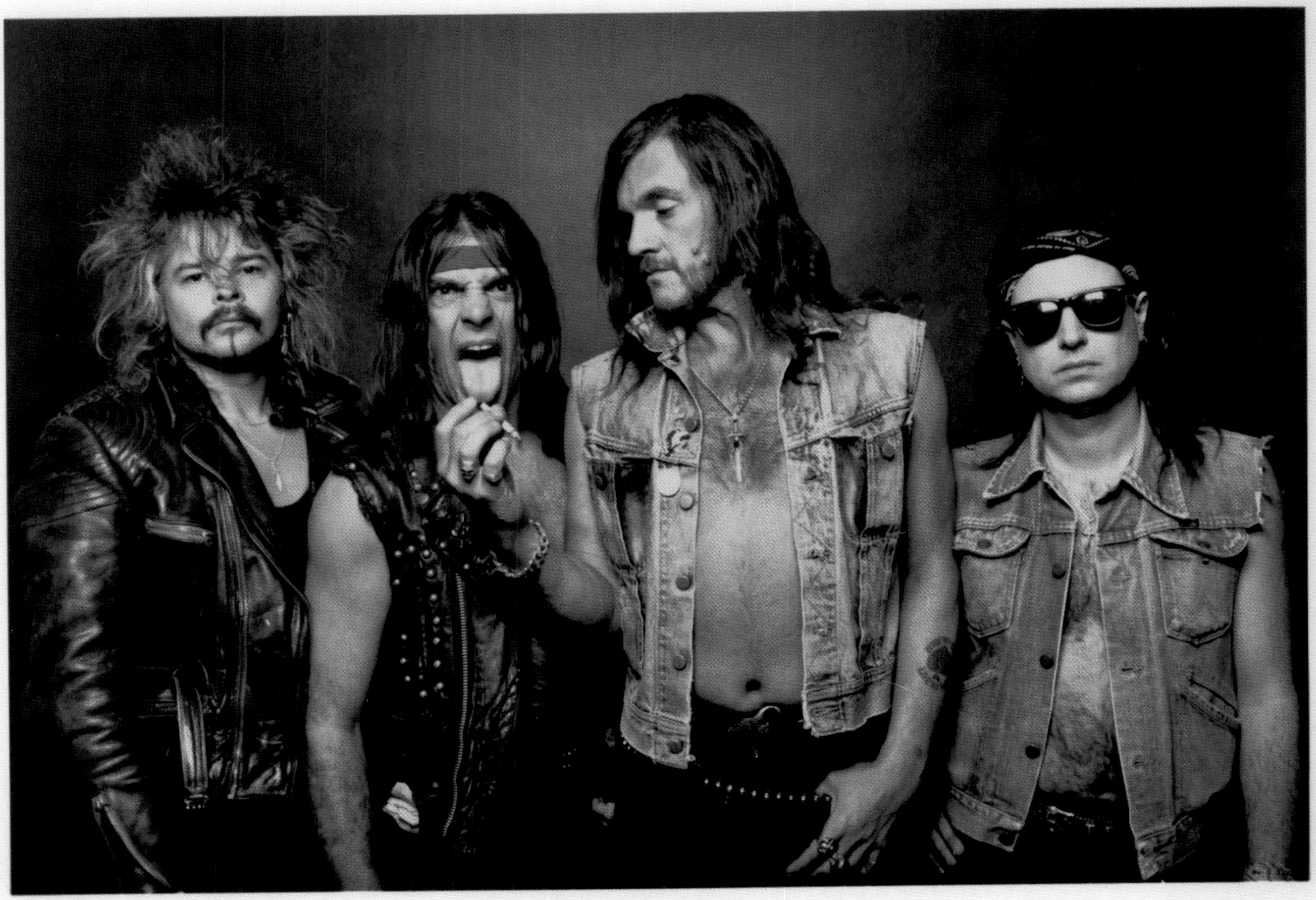

L to R: Philthy Animal Taylor Wurzel, Lemmy, Phil Campbell

motörhead

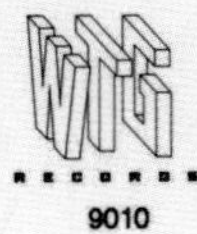

9010

© 1991 Sony Music. Permission to reproduce this photography is limited to editorial uses in regular issues of newspapers and other regularly published periodicals and television news programming.

Photo Credit: Robert John

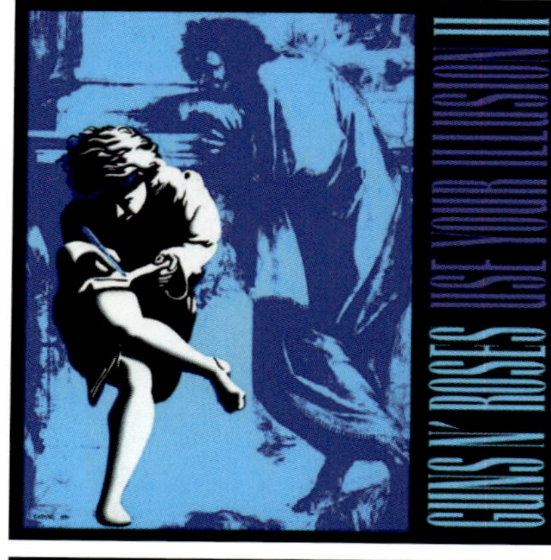

Billboard 200: *Use Your Illusion I* (#2); *Use Your Illusion II* (No. 1)
Billboard Hot 100: "Don't Cry" (#10); "Live and Let Die" (#33); "November Rain" (#3); "Yesterdays" (#72)

Guns N' Roses released two different albums the same day, *Use Your Illusion I* and *Use Your Illusion II*.

IN THE mid-Eighties, five Los Angeles youths set out to blow away all the other Sunset Boulevard club bands. The members of Guns N' Roses were special—the complementary personalities of volatile singer Axl Rose and charismatic guitarist Slash brought an element of danger and energy to the scene. They fought it out with the endless wave of hard-rock hopefuls to become the genre's last authentic bad boys. 1987's *Appetite for Destruction*, Guns N' Roses' debut album, sold 12 million copies worldwide. Troubled street kids related to the group's mystique more than that of the average MTV hair band.

But in the years following *Appetite for Destruction*, Guns N' Roses had offered little in the way of creativity and much in the way of debilitating controversy. The highly publicized scandals had ranged from detox programs, divorces and charges of racism and sexism to the use of vulgar language on the televised American Music Awards.

"Guns N' Roses is a street band—we come from a 'nonexistent existence,'" Slash laughed. "Just guys out there with nothing. Suddenly we're a stadium band. I haven't changed at all. Axl is really into this whole star-status thing. We obviously don't see eye to eye there."

A 1991 world tour marked the debut of a revamped lineup. Founding members Rose, Slash, guitarist Izzy Stadlin and bassist Duff McKagan had added former Cult drummer Matt Sorum to replace Steven Adler, whose drug dependency had caused him to play poorly.

With Sorum, Guns N' Roses recorded the tunes for *Use Your Illusion I* and *Use Your Illusion II*, taking the unprecedented step of simultaneously releasing the two separate full-length studio albums. The idea drew mixed reactions from the music industry. Some record-store chains praised the idea as an attention-getting device, while others claimed competition between two albums would confuse fans and split sales. The tactic paid off when *Use Your Illusion I* debuted in the charts at #2 and *Use Your Illusion II* at No. 1, but critics charged that the band members were starting to believe their own hype, thinking that they had 36 great songs to release.

"More songs just kept coming out," Sorum said. "Some of the better ones were actually written in the studio. Some were done on the first or second take, real spur-of-the-moment stuff. We went, 'God, how are we gonna put all this on an album?'"

Dizzy Reed joined as a full-time member; the keyboardist provided support on the two *Use Your Illusion* albums. "In any band, there's one or two principal people, and in Guns N' Roses, it's Axl and Slash. Obviously, a lot of what happens goes through them," Reed said. "We do share, um, certain elements. We like to have fun, we party. We've all been through a lot of shit." ■

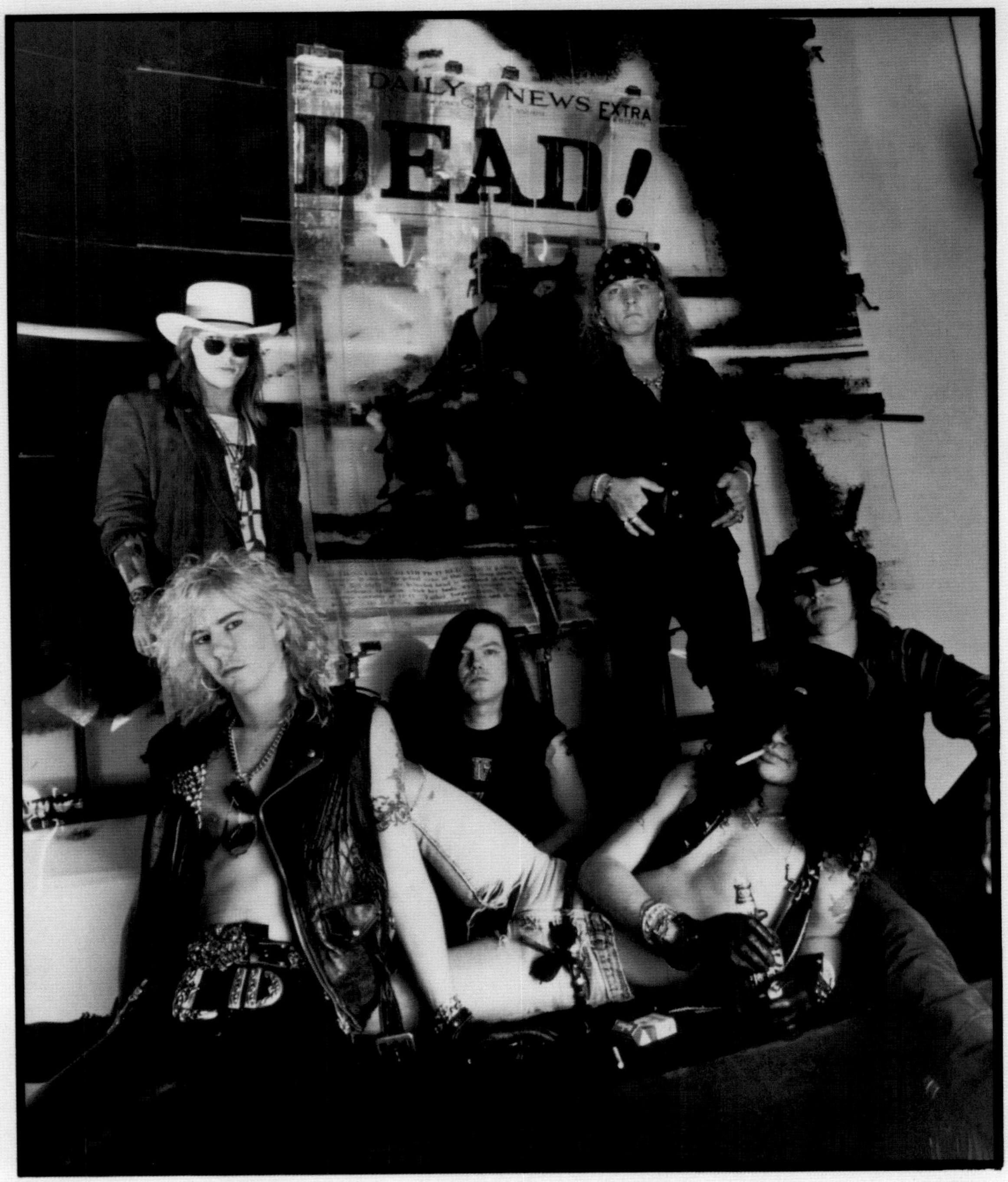

Photo Credit: Robert John

W. Axl Rose | Duff McKagan | Dizzy Reed | Matt Sorum | Slash | Izzy Stradlin

GUNS N' ROSES

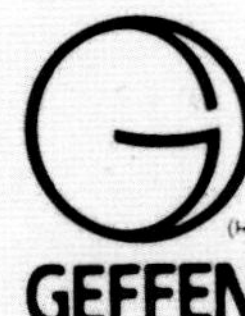

GEFFEN

© 1991 The David Geffen Company/Permission to reproduce limited to editorial uses in newspapers and other regularly published periodicals and television news programming.

FOR UNLAWFUL CARNAL KNOWLEDGE

With the thorny mood of *For Unlawful Carnal Knowledge*, Van Halen reclaimed the heavy-metal crown.

Billboard 200: *For Unlawful Carnal Knowledge* (No. 1)
Billboard Hot 100: "Top of the World" (#27); "Right Now" (#55)

SEVENTEEN YEARS had passed since brothers Eddie and Alex Van Halen hooked up with Michael Anthony, forming the foundation of what was arguably the most popular hard-rock band in America. Van Halen's nine albums had never failed to achieve platinum status, and *For Unlawful Carnal Knowledge* was the latest of three consecutive No. 1 releases since Sammy Hagar replaced original vocalist David Lee Roth in 1985. The album with the ribald acronym also broke the spell that had seemingly kept rock music from the top of the charts for the past two years.

"A lot of bands get so much money and success and power, they start getting lazy and taking it for granted," Hagar said. "And we're good enough to just blow and have it be pretty darn great. But we want to work even harder now, to lift ourselves up a little higher. All you dream for in this business is for something to inspire you, and Van Halen has that between us—Eddie will play a riff, I'll tell him a song title I have, Alex will kick off a beat, and whoa! It takes off."

For Unlawful Carnal Knowledge was characterized by a much denser, multilayered sound than the previous two albums. Produced at the band's Los Angeles studio, the album paired veteran Van Halen producer Ted Templeman with former Led Zeppelin engineer and Rolling Stones producer Andy Johns. Featuring salacious numbers with plenty of macho lyrics about sex and girls, the music was intelligent and intricate, stuffed with Eddie Van Halen's new set of guitar tricks. A very upfront rhythm section pounded heavy beats throughout, capturing Alex Van Halen's drums-from-hell sound.

Hagar was a blustery, forceful vocal presence."Singing is real personal. You can't blame your guitar or your amplifier," he mused. "I wanted to refine lyrics and work things out—'Does that word sing better than that word?' I wrote seven different lyrics for 'Poundcake.'"

Van Halen's strategy was not to release commercial singles from the album, but four songs hit No. 1 on the album-rock charts. "Poundcake," the rip-roaring opening track, wasn't talking about Sara Lee. "Runaround" was a romp with a singalong chorus. "Right Now," the album's only keyboard song, stood out for its incessant chorus and hit MTV video. And "Top of the World," the catchy closer, was the only melody that even remotely resembled obvious Top 40 fodder.

"We didn't want to be strapped to having to write hits," Hagar said. "This band is burnt on pop radio today—it's a formula. So we just took the songs that would make good videos. They seem to be the vehicles nowadays." ■

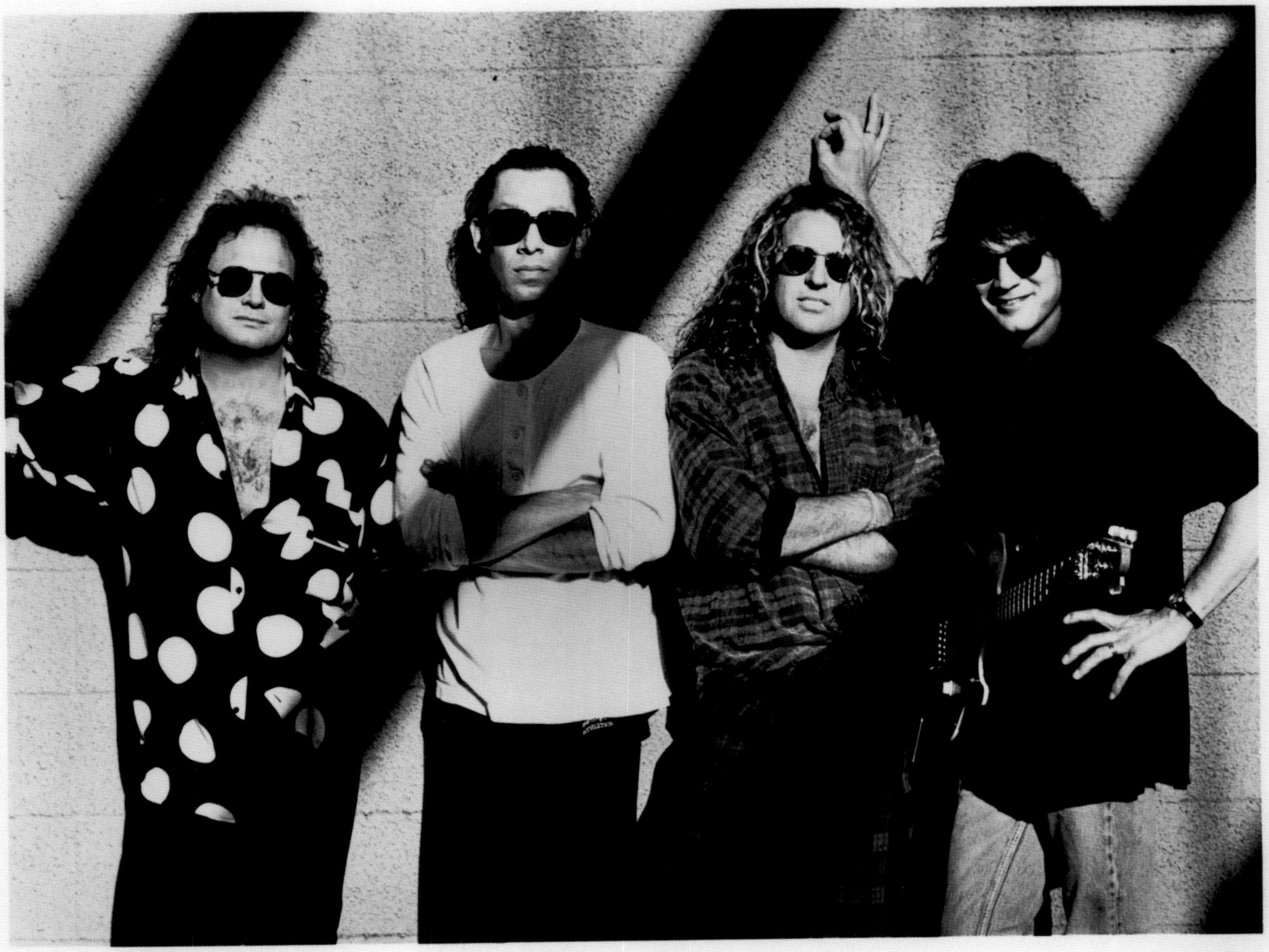

Photo Credit: Bob Sebree

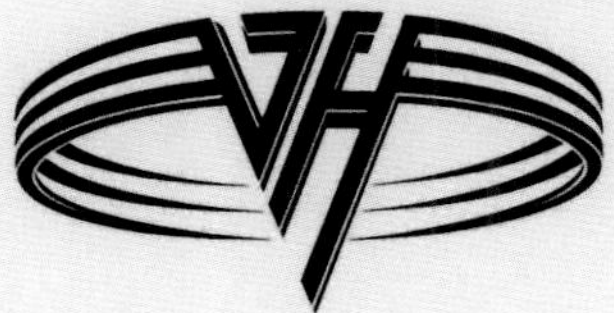

VAN HALEN

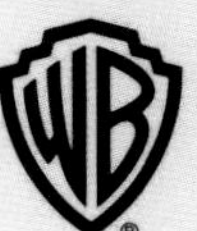

© 1991 Warner Bros. Records/Permission to reproduce limited to editorial uses in newspapers and other regularly published periodicals and television news programming.

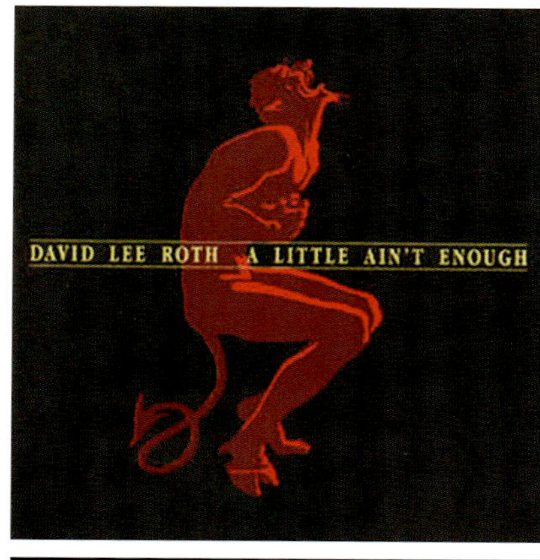

Billboard 200: *A Little Ain't Enough* (#18)

Grunge made his brand of hard rock seem obsolete, yet David Lee Roth's spirit hadn't been dampened.

DAVID LEE Roth, the notorious hard-rock frontman, was a big part of the party-hearty appeal of the first six Van Halen albums, and his three solo efforts were platinum-sellers in the US. The hyperactive singer reinvigorated his muse on *A Little Ain't Enough*, featuring the twin guitar attack of veteran Steve Hunter and 20-year-old Jason Becker to replace Steve Vai. To work with producer extraordinaire Bob Rock, Roth and his band had to make the trek to Rock's studio in Vancouver. Checking into a $15-a-night dive, they found themselves in the middle of a tough neighborhood for nearly half a year, with hookers out front and a nightclub in the basement.

"We removed ourselves geographically and immersed ourselves," Roth said. "I told the band, 'There's going to be strippers fist-fighting outside your room at 4:30 in the morning, and if you're a little testy from lack of sleep, fine—put that in your amplifier and we'll play the fast song. And if you get lonesome up here because you're away from a loved one or your dog or whatever, that's the day for the blues.'"

Although songs like "Hammerhead Shark" and the strutting "Sensible Shoes" told the story—big, high-octane music with sleazy but funny lyrics—*A Little Ain't Enough* resulted in a disappointing drop-off in sales from Roth's prior albums. Hard rock's clown prince hit the road with his most over-the-top production, romping around a fantastic set—while he rode a huge microphone, his drummer was set squarely between two fishnet-clad legs, and two demon statues sprayed Jack Daniels on the crowd every night. But low attendance doomed the tour, and nearly half of the shows were cancelled due to poor ticket sales.

"When you've been around as long as I have, you're up and down, you're going to be all over the place," Roth said. "That is part and parcel of the part you play as a public figure. We're like living characters for people who don't read books. One day you're a hero, the pick to win, and the next, you're a pillar of salt. That's half the fun of reading the Bible! So your own confidence had better not come from what side of the *Billboard* chart you're on. Here today, gone later today. Hey, if you love what I do, tell a friend. If you hate what I do, tell an enemy, because I'm still going to be here tomorrow—and the day after that. Now to some people, that sounds like a vile threat. Well, that's kinda rock 'n' roll, ain't it?" ■

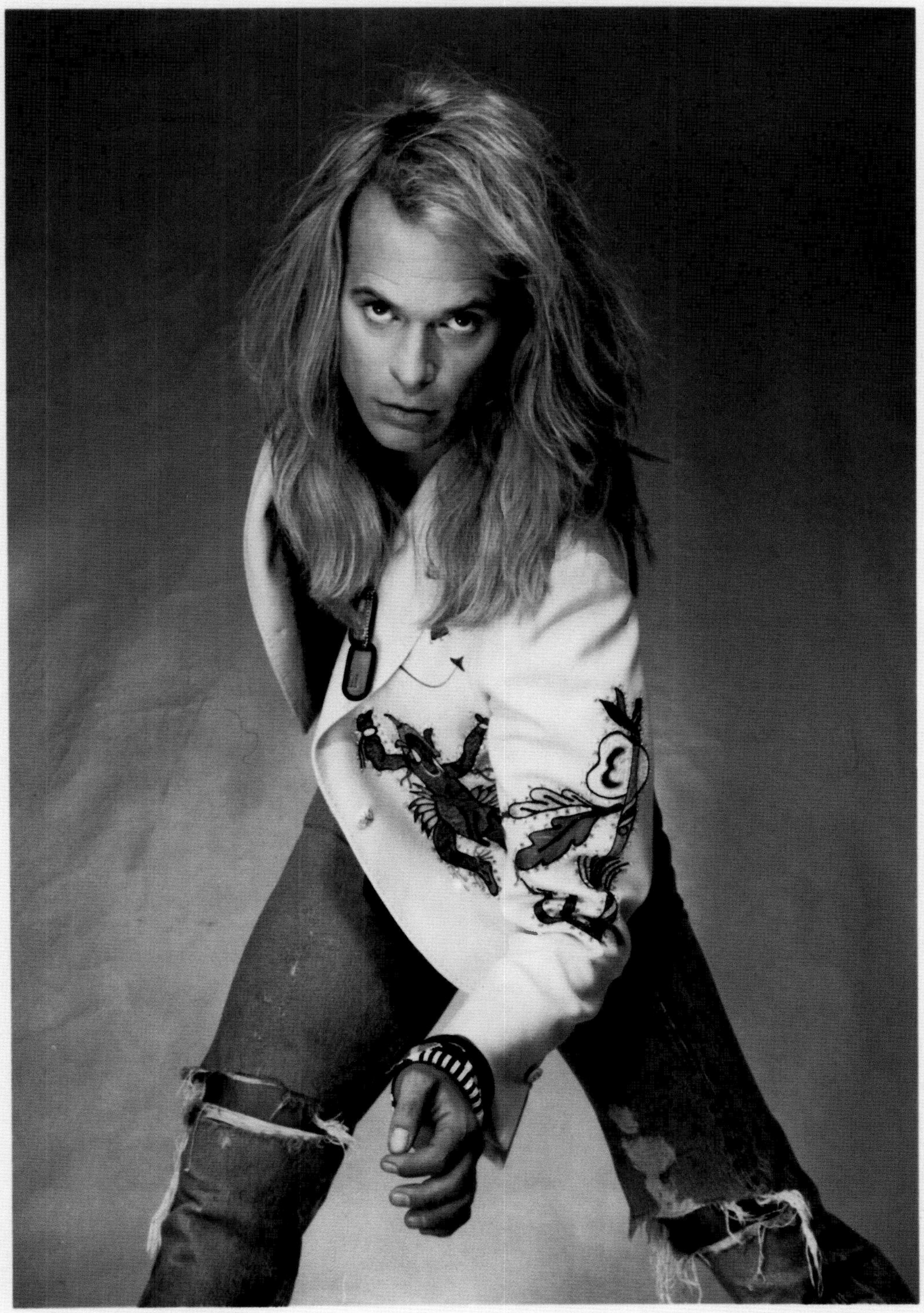

Photo Credit: Jim Hagopian

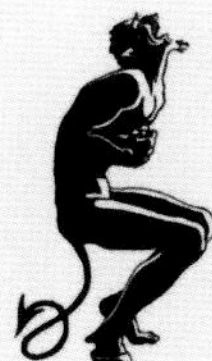

DAVID LEE ROTH

© 1990 Warner Bros. Records Permission to reproduce limited to editorial uses in newspapers and other regularly published periodicals and television news programming.

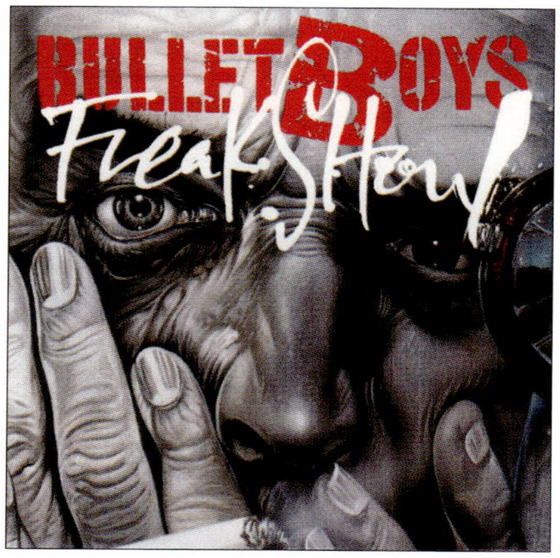

BulletBoys caught the last wave of the glam-metal scene covering Tom Waits' "Hang On St. Christopher."

Billboard 200: *Freakshow* (#69)

BULLETBOYS' SELF-TITLED debut album was a million-selling success, but it also drew unwelcome comparisons—that howling Marq Torien learned everything from David Lee Roth, that producer Ted Templeman molded the Los Angeles-based outfit into a clone of early Van Halen.

"We had that strike against us, but we talked about it on the road," guitarist Mick Sweda said. "We knew the second record would be heavier, darker."

The band's second album, *Freakshow*, went off on that tangent, showcased on the first single, "THC Groove."

"The record company screamed for something more accessible—they were flat-out afraid of the track, thinking it was too heavy, thrash stuff," Sweda said. "But we thought it would shock people—it upset the complacency that's going on in radio. It was a statement that we're not going to play this game of lightening up to get played."

A rendition of Tom Waits' "Hang On St. Christopher" interpreted the acoustic original with moody results; the single reached #22 on *Billboard*'s Album Rock Tracks chart.

"Ted played us the Waits song—the horns are barely in tune, everything dumps along on this steam-train track—and we looked at each other and said, 'What is this?' But it was cool—we gave it a shot and came out with something that's our own." ■

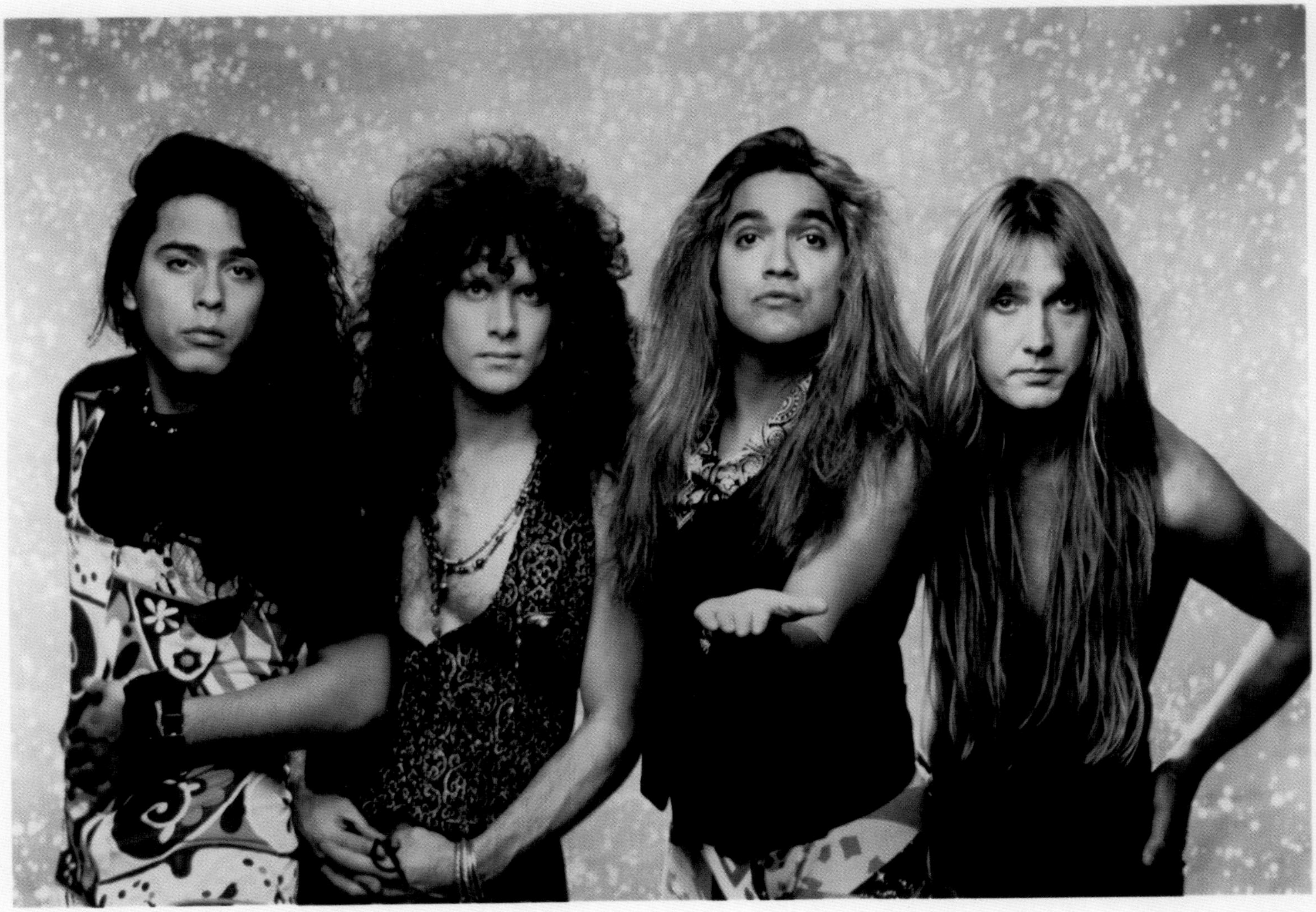

BULLETBOYS

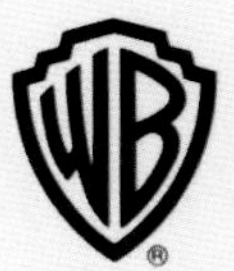

© 1991 Warner Bros. Records Permission to reproduce limited to editorial uses in newspapers and other regularly published periodicals and television news programming

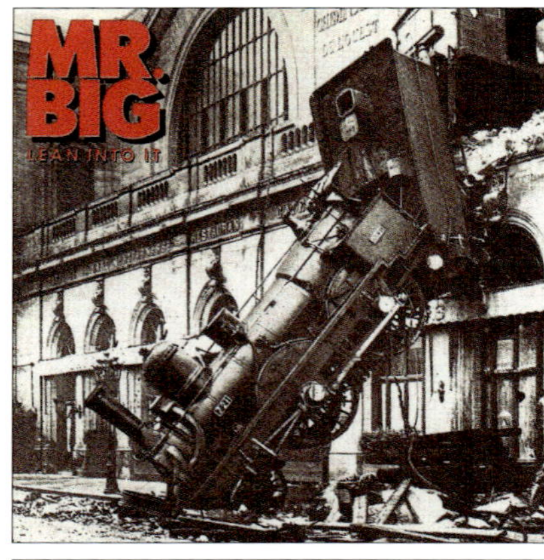

Mr. Big's pop-metal career was propelled into a higher gear with the acoustic ballad "To Be with You."

Billboard 200: *Lean into It* (#15)
Billboard Hot 100: "To Be with You" (No. 1);
"Just Take My Heart" (#16)

MR. BIG was organized in 1988 by singer Eric Martin, drummer Pat Torpey and the virtuoso guitar and bass of Paul Gilbert and Billy Sheehan.

"We started out as a heavy-metal band," Martin said. "We were just playing in front of guys, and that was no fun for me."

"To Be with You," an acoustic love song, was never intended to be a single from Mr. Big's *Lean into It* album, but a radio station in Lincoln, Nebraska, began having amazing success playing it regularly—much to the chagrin of the staff of Mr. Big's record company, which was diligently trying to break another single at the time. Finally released as a single, "To Be with You" climbed to No. 1 on the *Billboard* chart and pushed the album close to the one million sales mark.

Rather than following the beaten path and turning the song into a power ballad, Mr. Big kept it soft and simple.

"The song was almost an afterthought," Martin revealed. "It's a nice melody expressing something all guys have been through, saying to a girl, 'If you come with me, I'll treat you right.'"

The Los Angeles band found the suddenness of their popularity strange. "We have a hit song, and now the guys bring their girlfriends—I love it," Martin said. "For the one thing that works out right, there are a thousand things that don't quite happen the way you expected. So it's hard for most experienced musicians to get really excited, because you always figure it's not gonna last. I'm just glad this is happening while it is."

Corporate sponsorship of rock tours had attracted the attention and financing of Makita. Since Mr. Big's inception, Gilbert and Sheehan had played their instruments in concert running cordless electric drills over their guitar strings. Mr. Big prominently incorporated images of the tool-making company in the stage design and drum riser—adding a whole new dimension to the term "garage band."

Gilbert and Sheehan's drill-as-guitar-pick practice was usually in harmony, but Gilbert did get his drill caught in his hair at an Atlanta show. As he noted in the aftermath, "I'll bet even Makita doesn't know all the uses its products have." ■

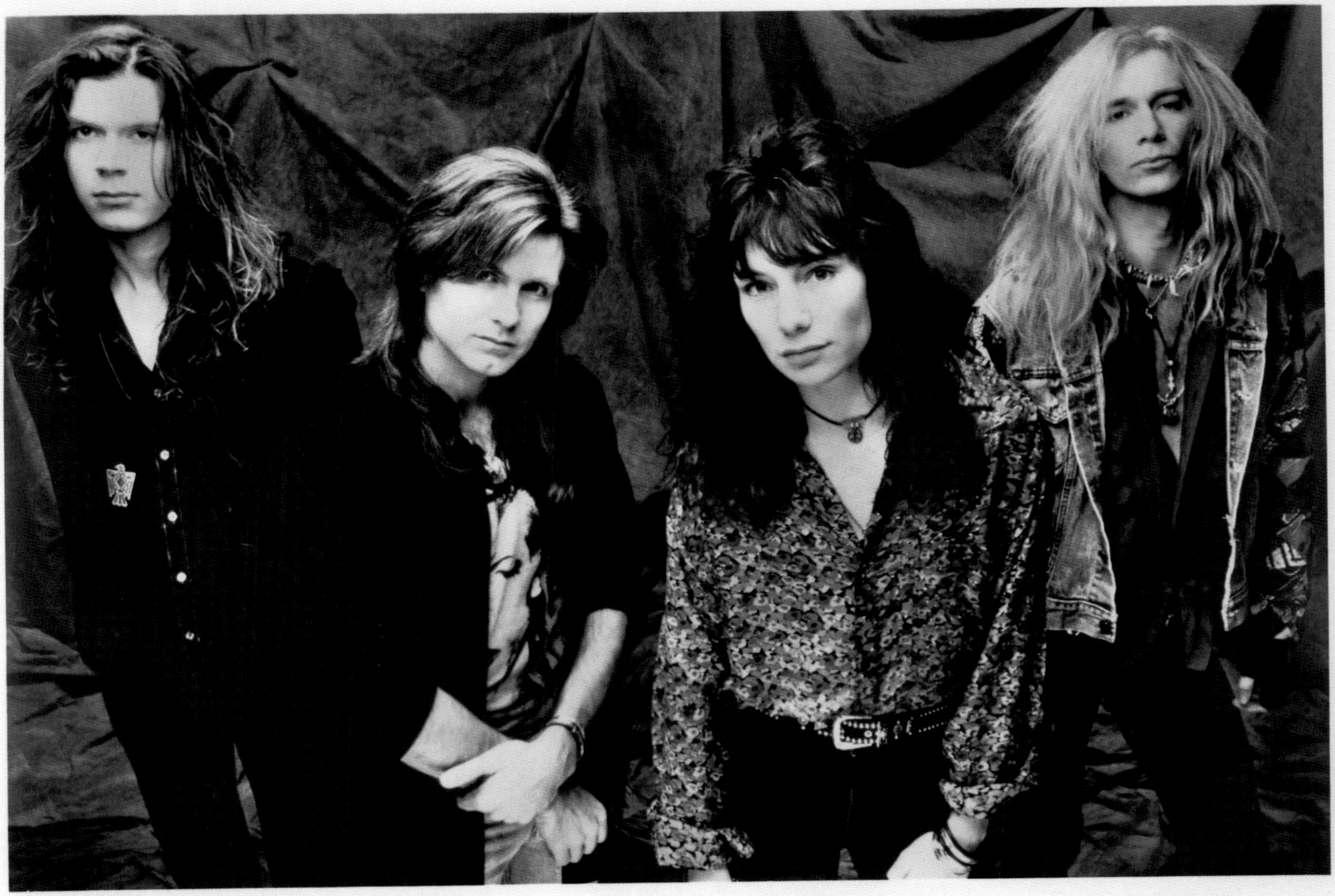

PAUL GILBERT PAT TORPEY ERIC MARTIN BILLY SHEEHAN

Photo credit: William Hames

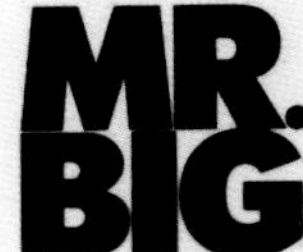

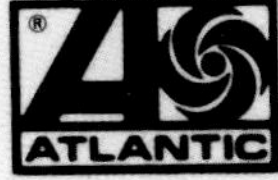

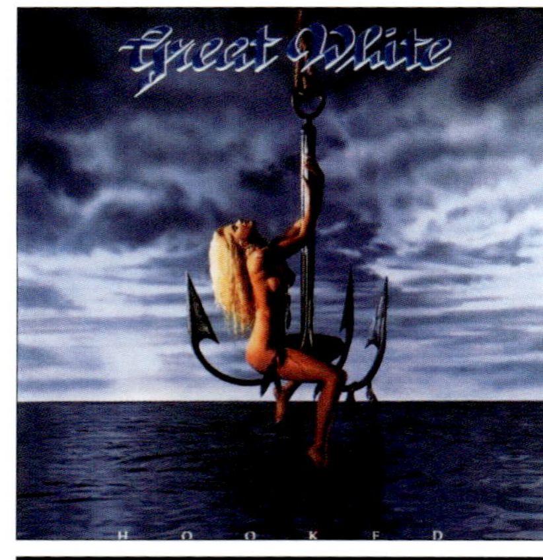

Relying on bluesy, mid-tempo songs, Great White served up polished hard rock on the *Hooked* album.

Billboard 200: *Hooked* (#18)
Billboard Hot 100: "Call It Rock N' Roll" (#53)

IN THE late Eighties, a blues-derived sound set Great White apart from Los Angeles' pack of pedestrian glam-rock acts. The band earned multiplatinum success when radio embraced the hits "Rock Me," "Save Your Love," "House of Broken Love" and a breakthrough cover of Ian Hunter's "Once Bitten, Twice Shy."

"We're getting to play stuff in that 2/4 groove, that bluesy vibe," guitarist and keyboardist Michael Lardie said. "What helps our execution is that we understand the concept behind real blues. Obviously, we grew up chronologically with bands like Led Zeppelin and Aerosmith, but it's simple to see where they borrowed their music. In the last few years, our manager has made us aware of Muddy Waters, Willie Dixon and Robert Johnson, and now blues is very much a part of our listening experience. You gain true affection for it, because it was really the forerunner of rock 'n' roll."

Hooked included the singles "Call It Rock N' Roll" and "Desert Moon."

"The lyrics are pretty simple, straight to the point," vocalist Jack Russell, the rambunctious leader of the gang, said. "We try to get the tunes where we want them in terms of writing and arranging. That way we don't have to spend a lot of time messing around in the studio. 'Call It Rock N' Roll' was written at soundcheck—we were smarting around, I went back in a trailer and wrote the lyrics. Other songs took a little work. The trick is to write for yourself, not anybody else."

But it wasn't always easy being in a hard-rock band—the California outfit had hit it big, then had to battle being labeled as "another hair band" and struggled with the "wimp" factor. And then *Hooked* sold less than its predecessor.

"I've been doing this for a dozen years. About six of those years, I can actually say I made some money, so I'm batting a little above 50 percent—not bad for rock 'n' roll," Russell said. "But let's not forget the years before that—we did it for nothing. Music is still the thing that gives you all the pleasure in the world." ■

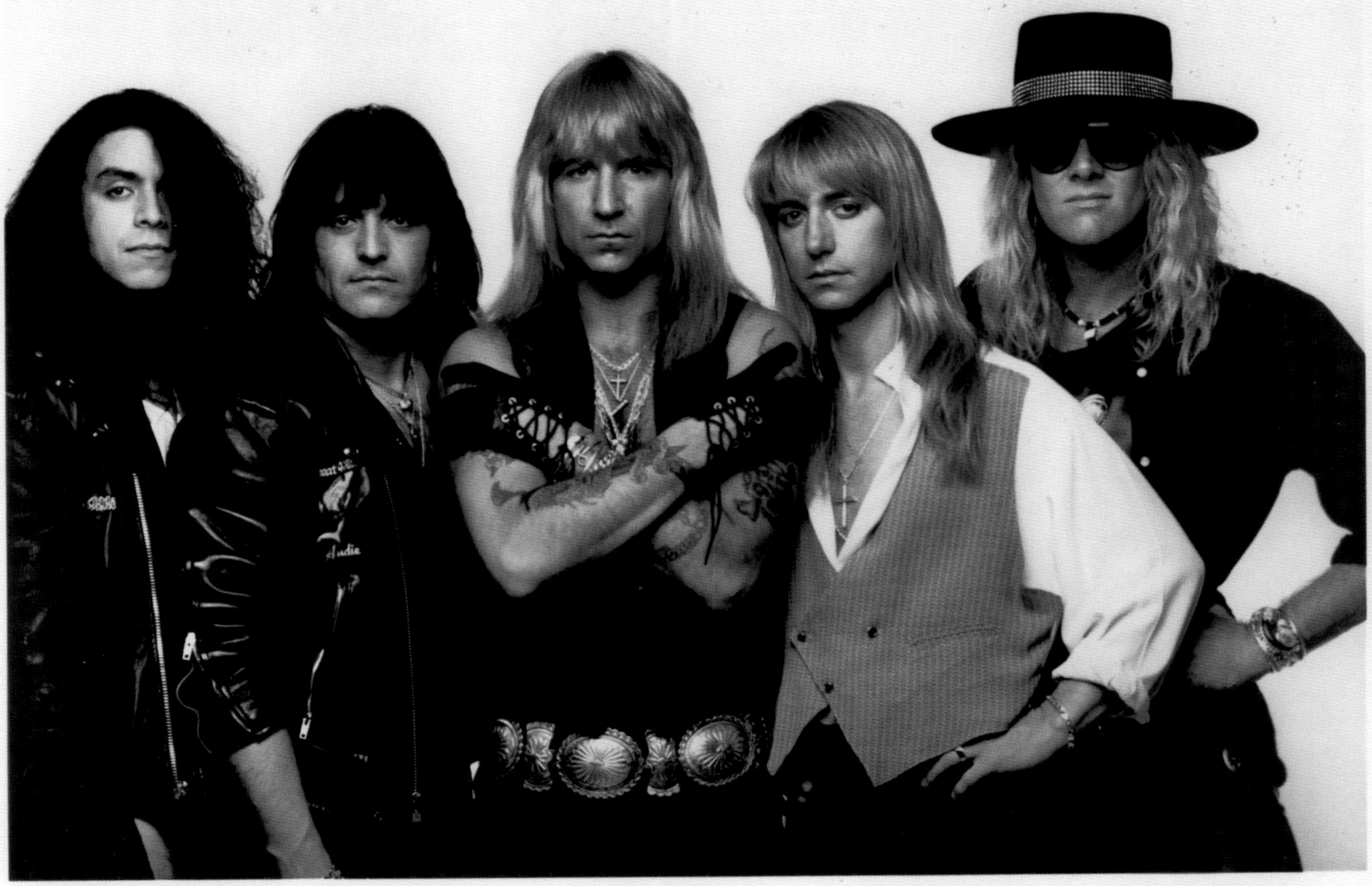

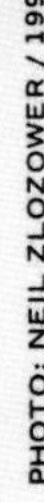

TONY MONTANA AUDIE DESBROW JACK RUSSELL MICHAEL LARDIE MARK KENDALL

Great White

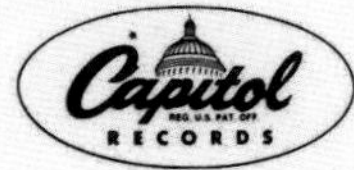

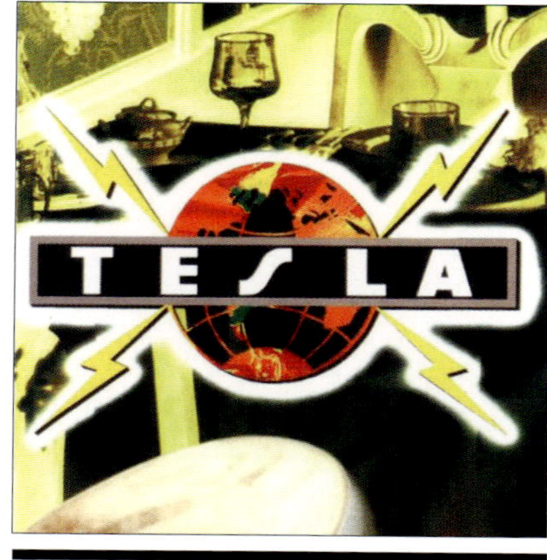

Tesla put its faith in guitar-heavy, melodic hard rock on the mainstream radio smash "What You Give."

Billboard 200: *Psychotic Supper* (#13)
Billboard Hot 100: "What You Give" (#86)

SUBSCRIBERS TO the *Encyclopædia Britannica* could use its Instant Research Service to ask about historical luminaries. The Top 10 inquiries? John F. Kennedy, Martin Luther King, Jr., Albert Einstein, Adolf Hitler, Edgar Allan Poe, Abraham Lincoln, Jesus, Pablo Picasso, Al Capone and—last but not least—Nikola Tesla. "I don't know what has caused the interest in Tesla," the service's director said.

She should have paid more attention to MTV. It stemmed from the hard-rock group of the same name with three consecutive platinum albums. Tesla the band had always championed Tesla the maverick scientist—at concerts, petition drives were held to persuade the Smithsonian Institute to recognize his contributions. Supporters insisted he invented radio and was responsible for AC power.

"It's gratifying to see the guy get the due he deserves," bassist Brian Wheat said. "There's already an exhibit on (Guglielmo) Marconi and (Thomas) Edison. They got all the credit. We were taught about them in school, but Tesla did so much and no one talks about it. He's been maligned."

The titles of the Sacramento quintet's albums of gritty, blues-based rock made a connection to the Tesla namesake. *Psychotic Supper* referred to the mad genius' germaphobia—before eating, he would ritually clean every dish, glass and piece of silverware.

"And we were all going psychotic when we started the record," Wheat said. "We'd had success pretty quick, and we'd gotten to the point where people outside the band had pretty high expectations for our fourth album. We got a bit freaked out before we settled down. We're happy being ourselves. The continuing inclusion of Tesla the dude isn't a gimmick because it has nothing to do with our music. This band has always been concerned with the songs. It wasn't a gimmick when we did *Five Man Acoustical Jam*."

That 1990 live all-acoustic album boasted a Top 10 single—a reworking of "Signs," a 1971 hit by the Five Man Electrical Band.

"We didn't want people to think Tesla had turned into an acoustic band, and it made *Psychotic Supper* a heavier album," Wheat explained. "And we moved away from rural upstate New York where we made our first two albums and into the city. We drew off the energy—just walking from your hotel to the studio was cool." ■

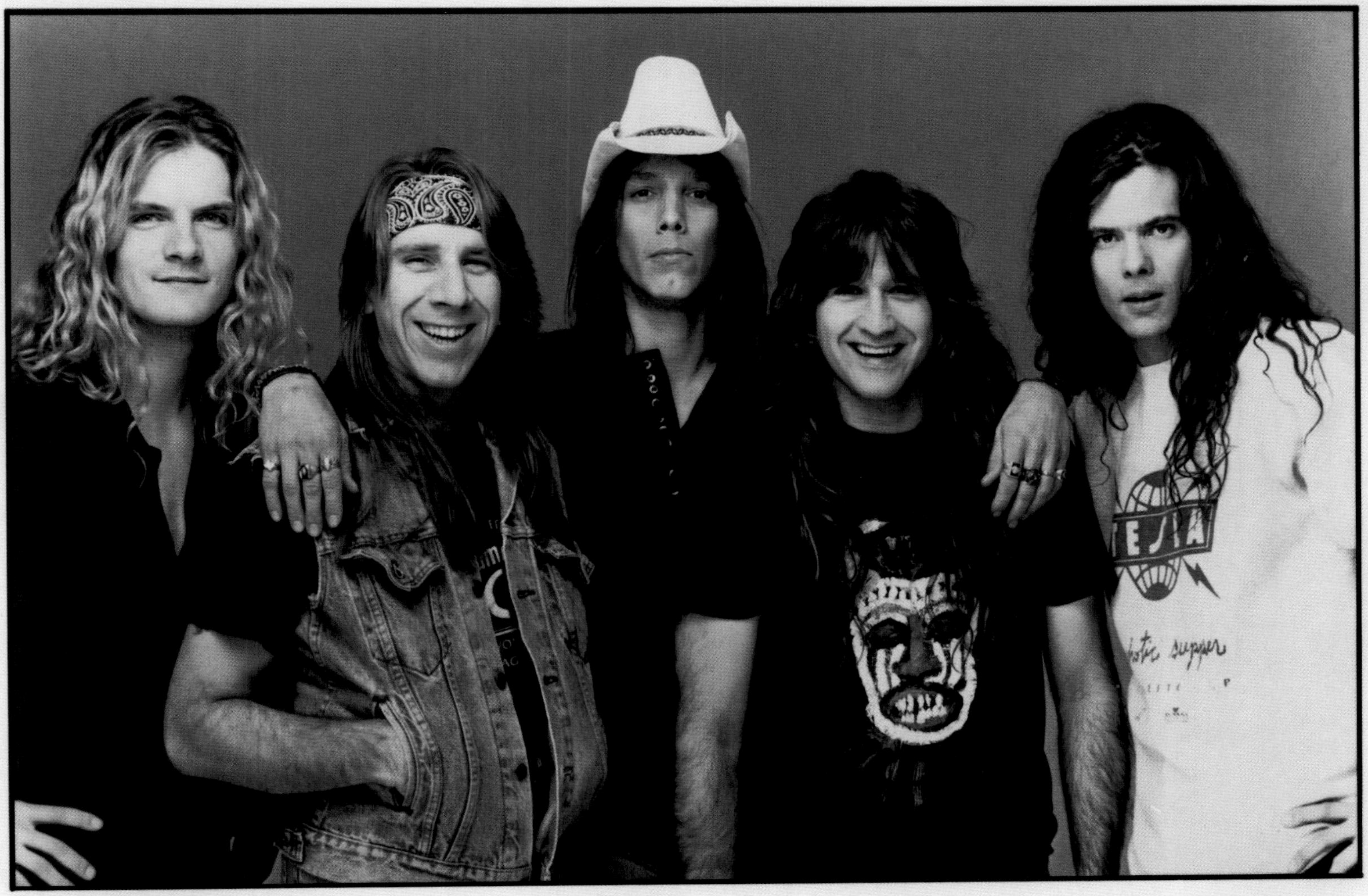

Frank Hannon Troy Luccketta Jeff Keith Brian Wheat Tommy Skeoch

Photo Credit: Ross Halfin

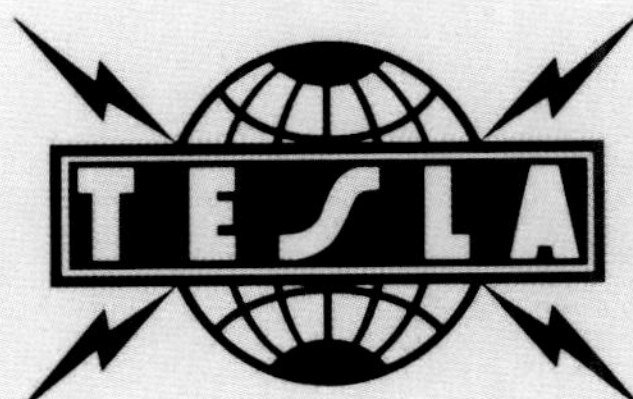

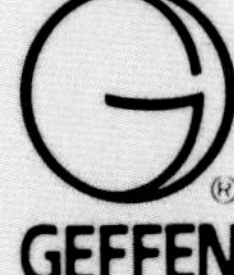

© 1991 The David Geffen Company/Permission to reproduce limited to editorial uses in newspapers and other regularly published periodicals and television news programming

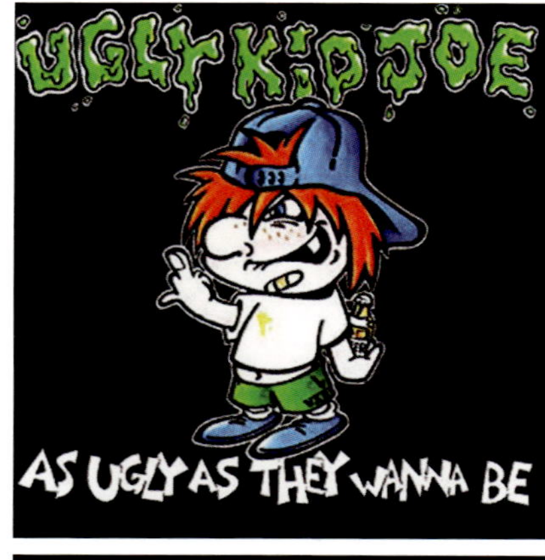

Billboard 200: *As Ugly as They Wanna Be* (#4)
Billboard Hot 100: "Everything About You" (#9)

Ugly Kid Joe's *As Ugly as They Wanna Be* became the first EP to sell more than a million copies in the US.

UGLY KID Joe, a five-piece band of diehard Ozzy Osbourne fans celebrating simple party-time urges, hailed from Isla Vista, California.

"The town is the most densely populated square mile west of the Mississippi," vocalist Whitfield Crane said. "Suburbia, dude! It's just a bunch of college kids smoking dope—the big sticky green buds—and grooving to our music."

Ugly Kid Joe (no one was named Joe—the name was taken in response to the L.A. glam band Pretty Boy Floyd) unleashed a wild brand of bratty humor and garage-band funk-metal. The EP *As Ugly as They Wanna Be* served as an introduction. The title of the short-form album parodied 2 Live Crew's 1989 album *As Nasty as They Wanna Be*; the logo was a cartoon embodiment of an "ugly kid" wearing a backwards baseball cap and giving the finger. The single "Everything About You," which listed things Crane hated or didn't care about, made it into the *Billboard* Top 10.

"We're a breath of fresh air," Crane said. ■

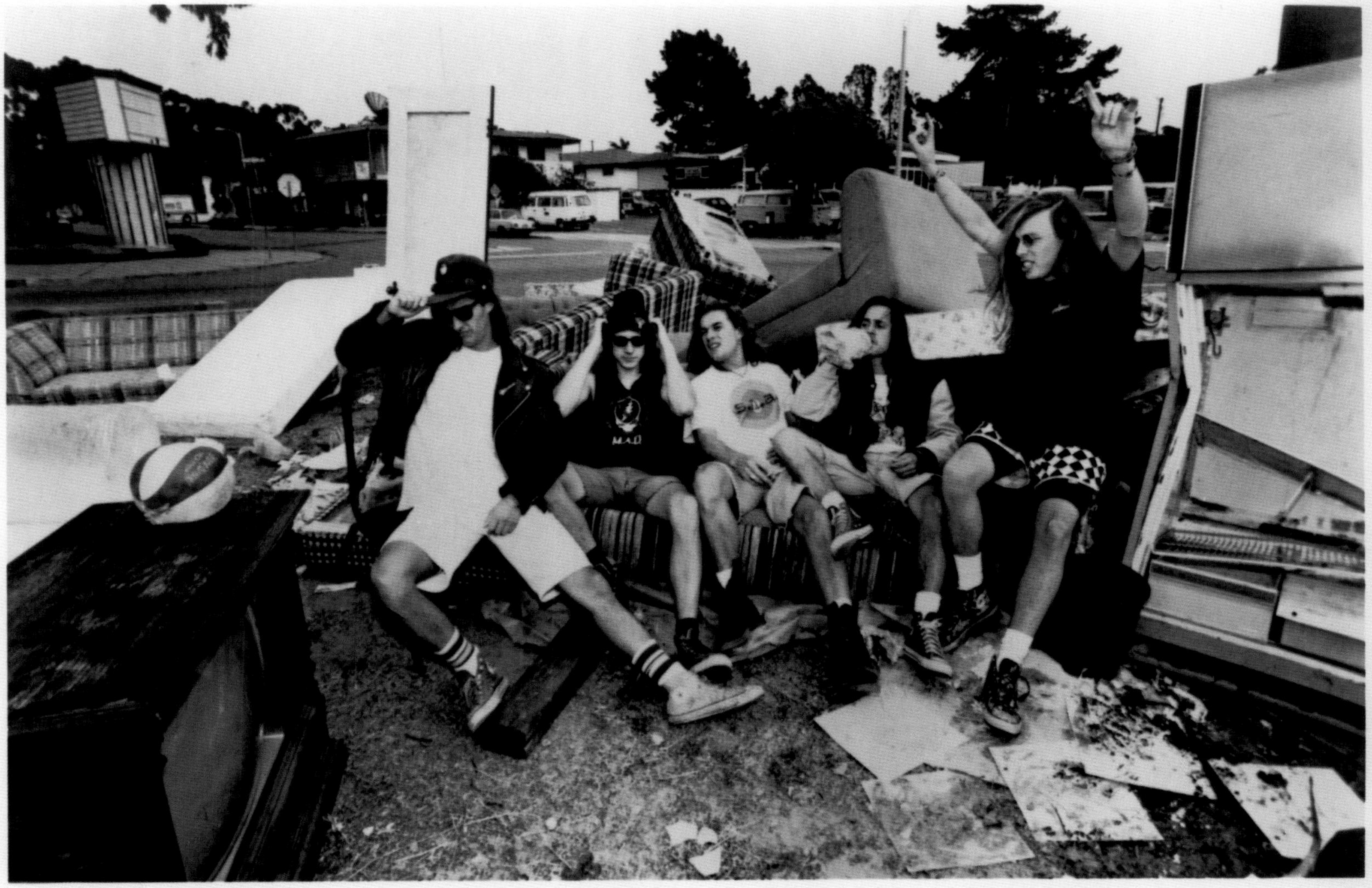

Roger Lahr **Klaus Eichstadt** **Whitfield** **Mark Davis** **Cordell Crockett**

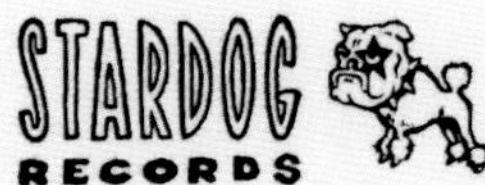

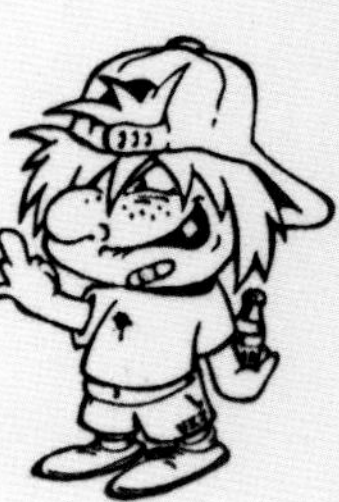

Distributed By Important Records Distributor

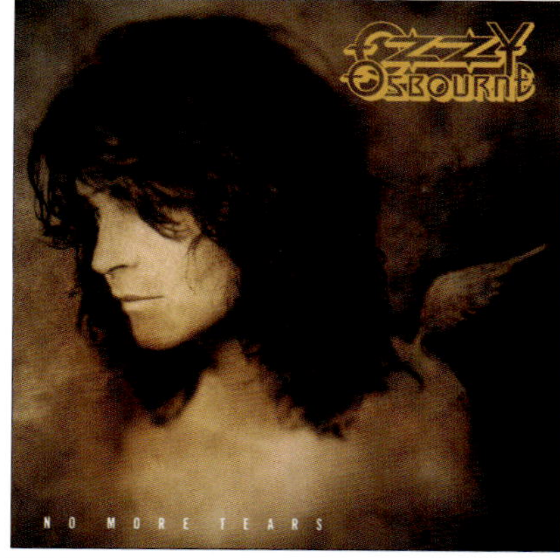

Billboard 200: *No More Tears* (#7)
Billboard Hot 100: "No More Tears" (#71); "Mama, I'm Coming Home" (#28)

With the restrained ballad, "Mama, I'm Coming Home," Ozzy Osbourne kept up his commercial success.

EARLY IN 1991, Ozzy Osbourne was cleared in another lawsuit alleging that he promoted suicide in his songs. Not cowed by his court case, he recorded a new album, *No More Tears*.

"All I can do is go into a studio and make a record. None of us ever say, 'Okay, I've had a good run, let's make a pile of shit for a change,'" Osbourne said. "There are so many bloody pigeonholes, brand names they keep giving it—punk, metal, rap, soul, blues. The bottom line is, it's all music. You've got a choice—you either like it or you don't. I don't know what key I'm singing in. I don't know a guitar from a trumpet. I look at my arms, and if my hairs stand on end, it's a good song."

The triple-platinum *No More Tears* became known for "Mama, I'm Coming Home," Osborne's first solo Top 40 hit in the US, but he found himself without the usual enthusiasm to perform. He claimed his body could no longer handle the physical demands of a rigorous touring schedule, and his mind couldn't handle the burden of being Ozzy Osbourne, heavy metal's most famous radical—that former drunken drug addict who peed on the Alamo and tried to strangle his wife and gobble the heads off bats.

When his publicist confirmed that the "No More Tours" dates would be his last before retirement, the announcement surprised many. But you had to be nuts to think his retirement could last very long.

"For years, I felt like a mouse on a wheel going round and round—it became routine," Osbourne explained. "I shouldn't complain, because my popularity kept going. But from the first album I ever made, from Black Sabbath on, every album was a winner—I got instant success. I was traveling around aimlessly buying houses that I was never living in, buying animals that never knew me, having children that thought I was a voice on the phone—basically living out of a suitcase for 25 years." ■

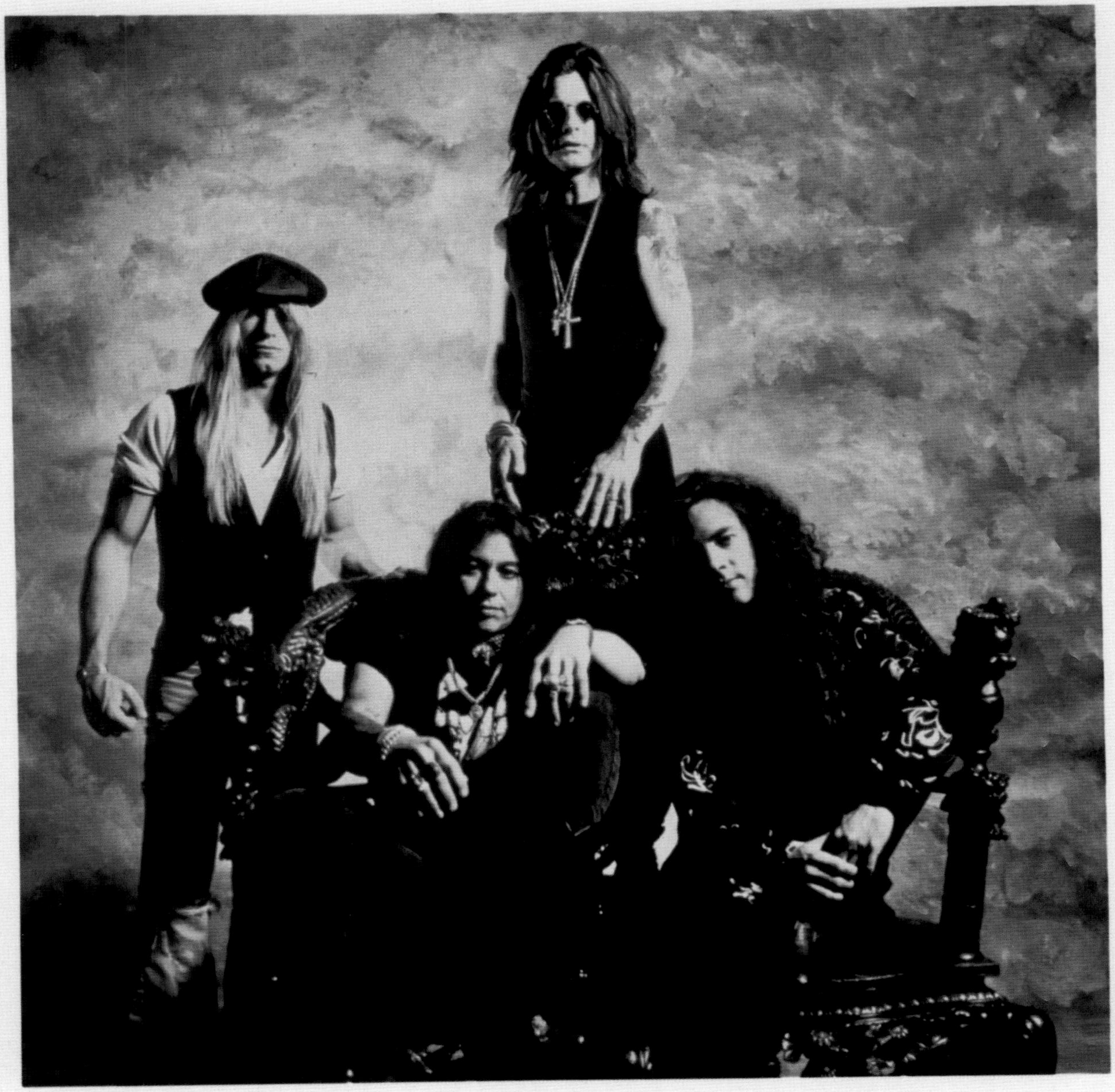

Photo Credit: Jeff Katz

L to R: Zakk Wylde (standing), Randy Castillo (sitting), Ozzy Osbourne (standing) and Michael Inez (sitting)

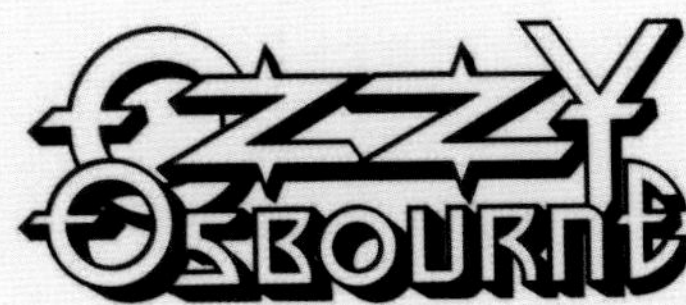

9109

© 1991 Sony Music. Permission to reproduce this photography is limited to editorial uses in regular issues of newspapers and other regularly published periodicals and television news programming.

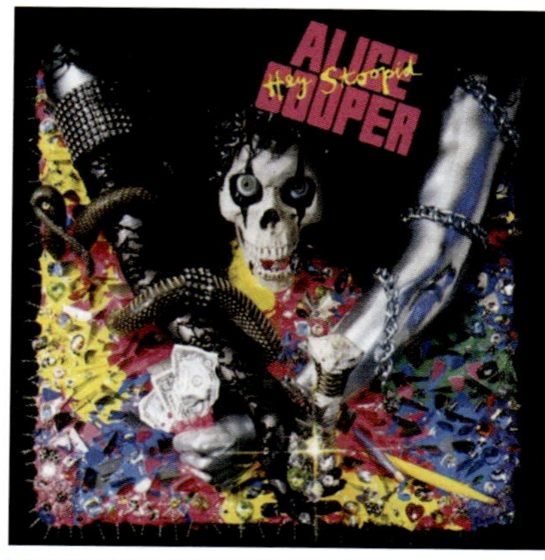

Billboard 200: *Hey Stoopid* (#47)
Billboard Hot 100: "Hey Stoopid" (#76)

Following his success with *Trash*, Alice Cooper attempted to maintain the good times with *Hey Stoopid*.

WITH STAGE shows featuring huge boa constrictors, chopped-up baby dolls, guillotines, electric chairs and fake blood during his early Seventies heyday, Alice Cooper was the first to take shock rock to theatrical extremes. In 1989, rock's maestro of the macabre returned to the spotlight with his clean-living comeback album, the multi-platinum *Trash*.

The followup, *Hey Stoopid*, featured several notable guest performances from Nikki Sixx and Mick Mars (both of Mötley Crüe), Slash, Ozzy Osbourne, Joe Satriani and Steve Vai. The title track advised Cooper's cohorts in the business not to self-destruct. He wanted real rattlesnakes to shake their tails on the track "Snakebite," so three live rattlers were brought to the studio. "I paid them *scale*," Cooper joked.

Cooper had exorcised his well-known alcohol problem.

"When you have a character as defined as Alice, you have to battle so that it's not such a cartoon, a parody of itself. I've gone out of my way to turn Alice into a character that, years from now, anybody could play. He's as much a fictitious American literature character as Batman. I can get up in the morning and shoot 70 on any golf course, and then that night play this horrific character for two hours. And when I walk off the stage I don't have to be him. That's the fun of having played Alice for 20 years. Now I have control of him.

"What kind of music survives through all of rock 'n' roll's changes? It's always the hard-rock garage band—guitar bass, drums and a lead singer. The cockroach of rock 'n' roll."

But glam metal's popularity had begun to wane just before the grunge explosion, and *Hey Stoopid* didn't make as much of a commercial impact as its predecessor. The tour was "less bloody and splatter-oriented, but it's full-scale Alice-style," Cooper said. "I haven't lost the hardcore audience—they're still there. But now I'm getting an entirely new audience that's 15-17 years old, and they walk in like lambs to the slaughter. They've only heard about the legend, now they want to see the guillotine." ■

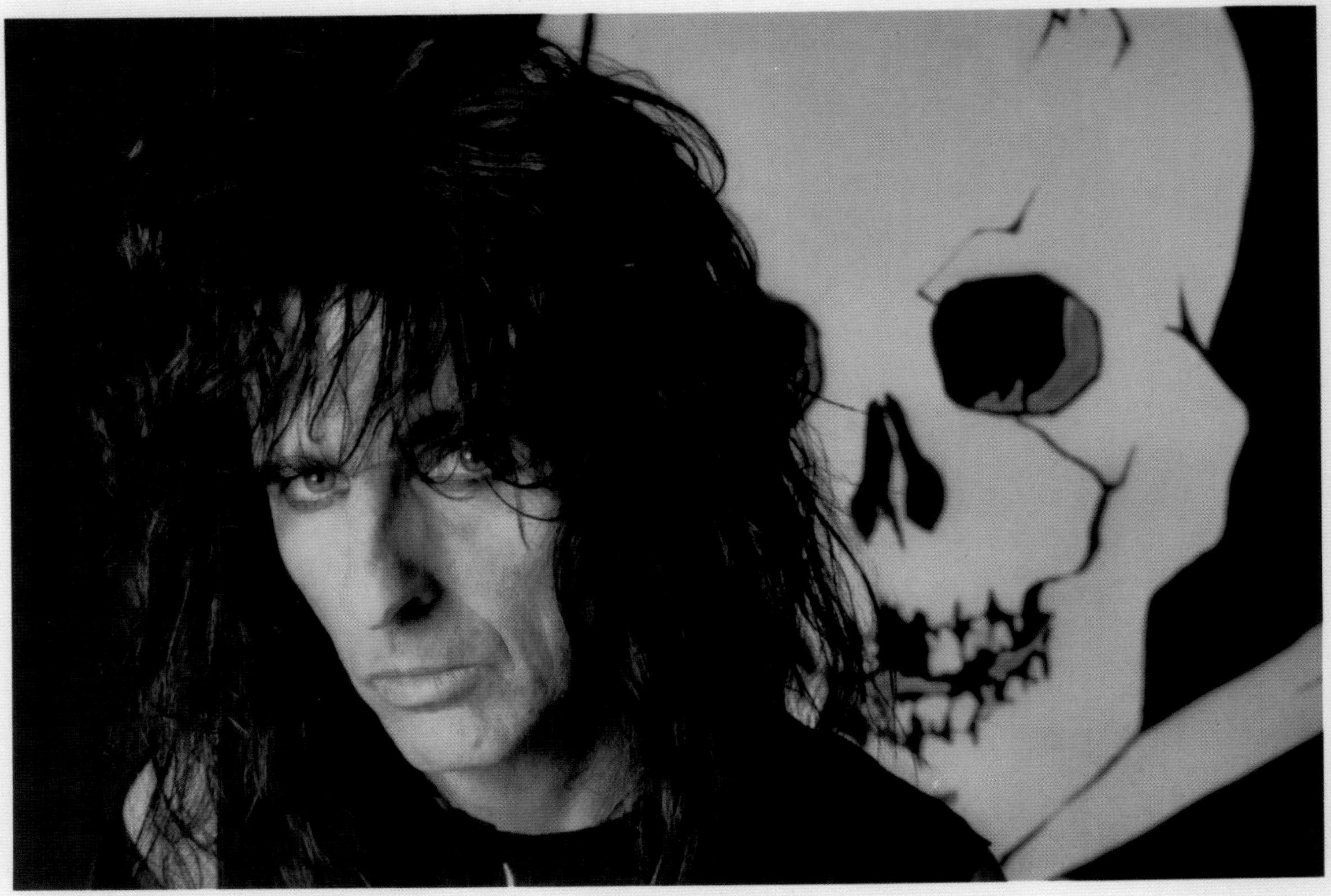

Alive

ALICE COOPER

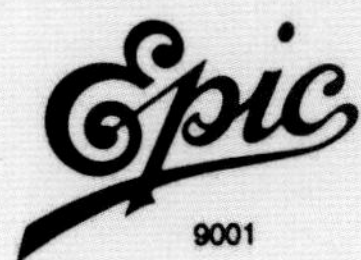

© 1990 CBS Records Inc. Permission to reproduce this photography is limited to editorial uses in regular issues of newspapers and other regularly published periodicals and television news programming.

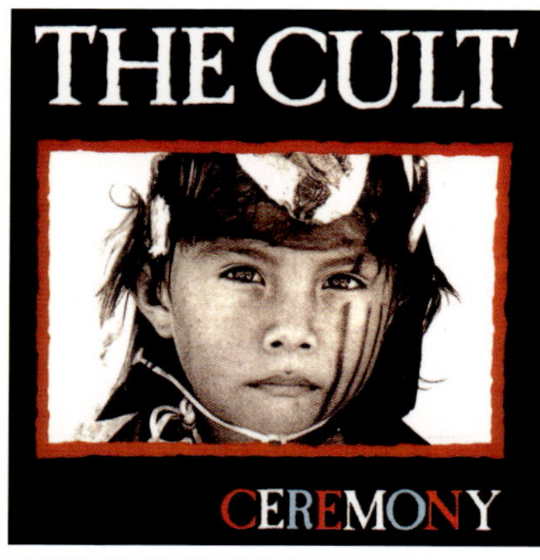

Billboard 200: *Ceremony* (#25)

The Cult's *Ceremony* represented a season of upheaval within the ranks of the British hard-rock band.

IN THE Eighties, before alternative rock became a marketing category, the Cult emerged from the UK and flirted with great commercial success. The band's heavy sound was built out of Billy Duffy's penchant for monster guitar riffs, Ian Astbury's unmistakable voice and love of a neo-hippie mysticism. For those not about to rock, it might have seemed pompous and silly, but for a generation of heavy-metal kids, the Cult albums *Electric* and *Sonic Temple* defined the genre.

"On one level, it's just good, kickin' rock 'n' roll music," Duffy said. "On another level, there's a spiritual, sensitive side nature to it, but when you start analyzing that stuff…"

Astbury's interest in the plight of Native Americans inspired the *Ceremony* album. "Wild Hearted Son," the first single, began with the beat of an American Indian dance. (The band was sued by the parents of the Native American boy pictured on the cover, delaying the release of the album in many countries.) Duffy pulled out a lot of guitar aggression, and Astbury inveighed the lyrics like a latter-day Jim Morrison.

But behind the scenes, substance abuse and infighting had thrown the Cult into turmoil. Duffy and Astbury had reportedly opted to record their parts separately at different times. The pair had squandered their edge.

"But people want rock stars, they always have—a little glamour, a little escapism, something to get out of the daily grind," Duffy said. "Led Zeppelin got slaughtered in the press when they started. They just got on with what they did and people loved it. That's what the Cult's all about." ■

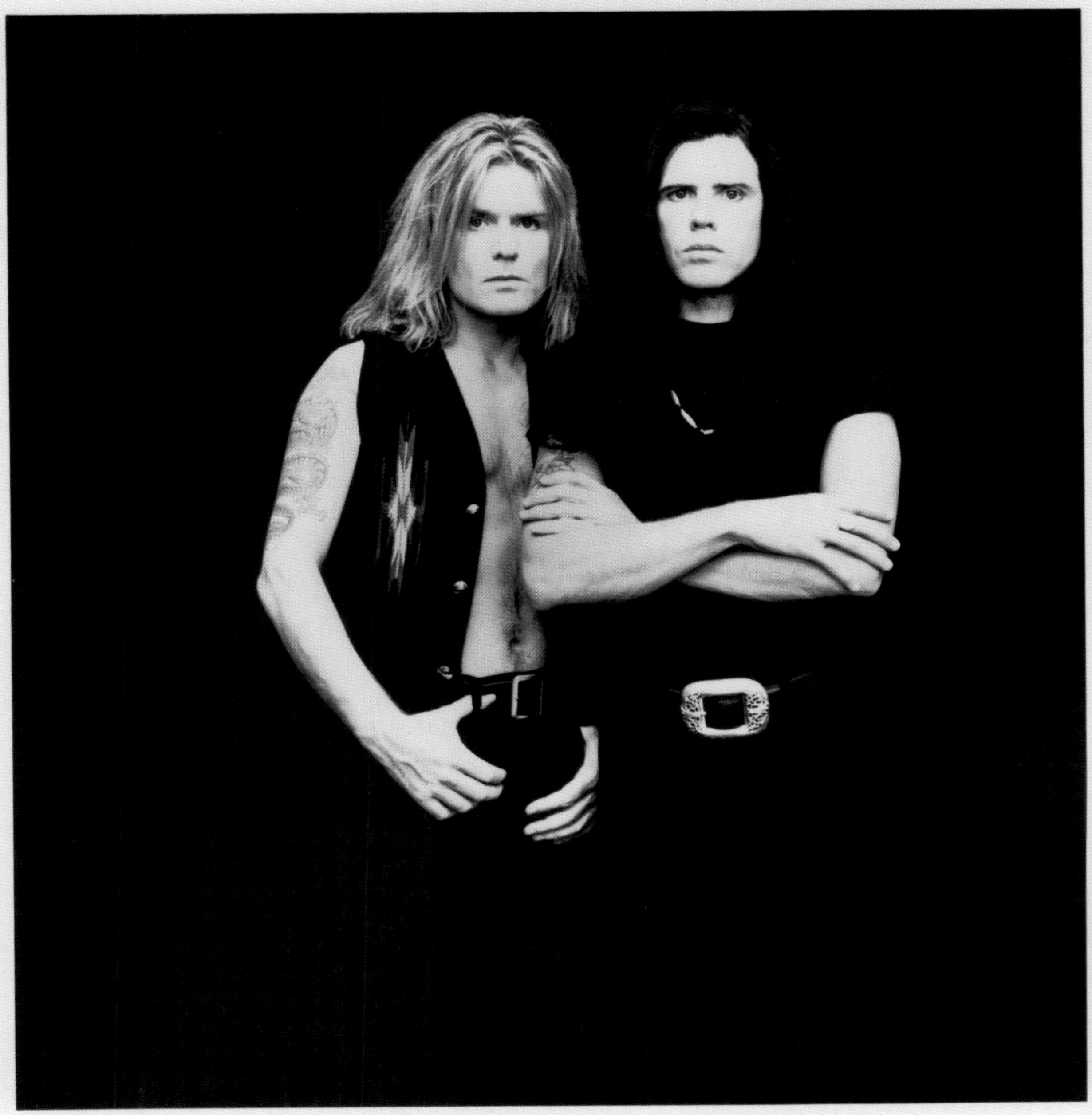

Billy Duffy

Ian Astbury

Photo Credit: Peter Dokus/NG1

THE CULT

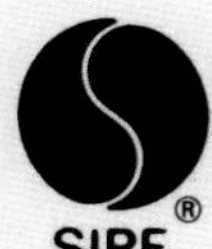

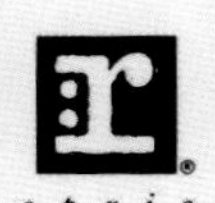

© 1990 Reprise Records/Permission to reproduce limited to editorial uses in newspapers and other regularly published periodicals and television news programming.

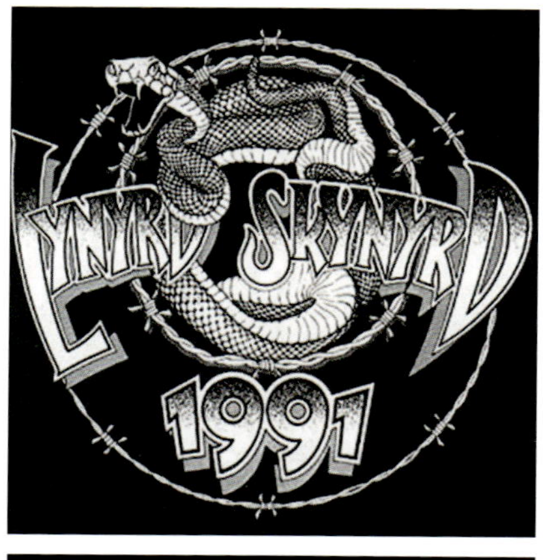

Billboard 200: *Lynyrd Skynyrd 1991* (#64)

The retooled Lynyrd Skynyrd returned to recording with the barroom boogie of *Lynyrd Skynyrd 1991*.

THE SOUTH was rising again. The great Southern rock bands of the Seventies—Lynyrd Skynyrd, the Allman Brothers Band, 38 Special—had released new recordings, and their skills were intact. They all had Top 10 songs on *Billboard*'s Album Rock Tracks chart.

"Music happens in circles—Southern rock was gone for a decade, and now it's back," Lynryd Skynyrd guitarist Gary Rossington noted. "We always said we weren't Southern music, we were a band from the South that was British-influenced. But I'm happy to see Southern rock return. Too often today, music is secondary to dancing and Broadway-type performances. It's fun for us to walk out, plug in an amp and play with no effects or synthesizers or tapes—it's the real deal. That's why our fans relate to us—we say simple things in simple songs. Working-class people like to hear that."

In the mid-Seventies, Lynyrd Skynyrd, spearheaded by an unprecedented triple-guitar attack and the rabble-rousing charisma of frontman Ronnie Van Zant, was poised on the edge of superstardom when tragedy struck in October 1977—a plane accident in the backwoods of Mississippi killed four members of the entourage including Van Zant. The survivors suffered crippling injuries, emotionally as well as physically, and Skynyrd was laid to rest. But as the 10th anniversary of the crash approached, the guys (Rossington, Billy Powell, Leon Wilkerson, Artimus Pyle and Ed King) realized how much they missed playing together.

"We're just real tight—we grew up together, went to school together, went through so many life tragedies like the plane crash," Rossington explained. "We were always a family and best of friends."

They reunited for the successful "Tribute" tour in celebration of the original band, and then they started writing. *Lynyrd Skynyrd 1991* picked up where Skynyrd left off, turning out rhythm-oriented hard rock with the signature three-guitar assault on "Smokestack Lightning." Ronnie Van Zant's younger brother, Johnny, performed vocals.

"We made a vow that we wouldn't come back with a record if we didn't think it was up to Skynyrd standards," Rossington mused. "But we found out we have something here, and we're proud of it. Like George Foreman says, just because you're old doesn't mean you're over the hill." ■

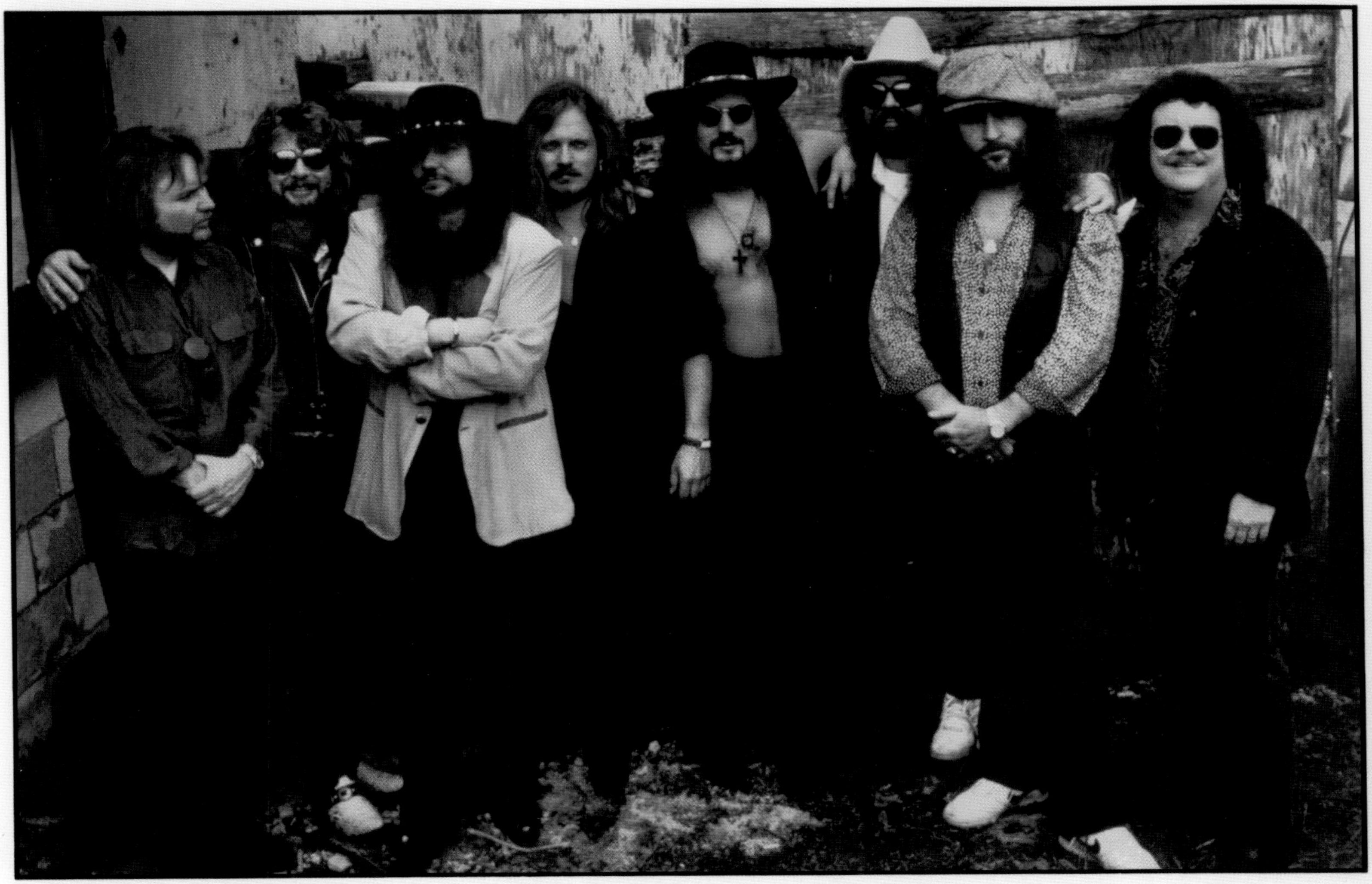

LEON WILKESON JOHNNY VAN ZANT ARTIMUS PYLE

ED KING GARY ROSSINGTON CUSTER RANDALL HALL BILLY POWELL

Photo credit: CAROL FRIEDMAN

LYNYRD SKYNYRD 1991

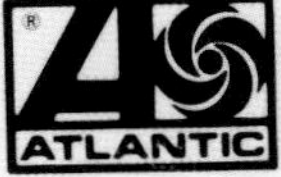

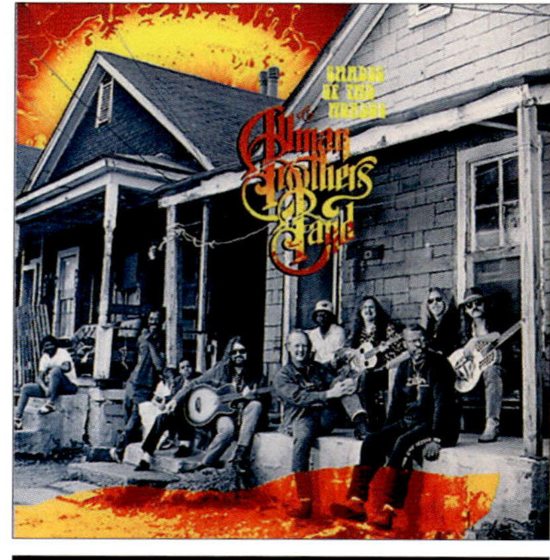

The Allman Brothers Band rose above past obstacles and came near peak form on *Shades of Two Worlds.*

Billboard 200: *Shades of Two Worlds* (#85)

DURING THE late Sixties and early Seventies, the Allman Brothers Band conjured a mix of virtually every American musical form—blues, country, R&B, jazz and rock. Bound by unsurpassed musicianship and improvisational skills, the group defined the Southern rock genre.

"I was always, from the beginning, the doubting Thomas," frontman Gregg Allman noted. "In 1963, I said, 'Look, the Beatles just came out. Everybody on the block and their brother has a damn band. Man, the competition...' And there were some pickers out there who just came out of the woodwork, because they saw it—'Hell, I can grow my hair, play a few Beatles tunes and get me a job, no problem.' We did the same thing, and playing other people's songs got real old with me real fast. In 1966, I sat down and started to write—I was 17 years old. The first 200 went in the garbage, and then I wrote one called 'Melissa.' I didn't show that one to anybody until the Brothers formed in '69. Hell, by then I couldn't tell if it was worth a damn or not."

The Allmans' benchmark early albums were noted for the graceful interplay between Duane Allman and Dickey Betts, one of rock's most gifted guitar duos. The classic *At Fillmore East* established the band's reputation for awesome skills, but the live album was Duane Allman's last testament. In October 1971, he died in a motorcycle accident at age 24. One year later, original bassist Berry Oakley, also 24, met the same fate. Though the band regrouped and continued to tour and enjoy success—Betts' role became more prominent, and the breezy "Ramblin' Man" and the instrumental "Jessica" became the band's biggest hits—things were never quite the same. Over the years, the vagaries of substance abuse, legal wrangling and internal discontent led to several breakups and reunions with different rosters.

The four surviving original members—Allman, Betts, Butch Trucks (drums and timpani) and Jaimoe (drums)—regrouped again in 1990 and re-earned a place in the rock pantheon. *Shades of Two Worlds* recalled their greatest albums of the past—the group's forceful jamming, Gregg Allman's gripping vocals and Betts' classic twin-guitar harmony lines and expansive duels with Warren Haynes.

"Dickey and I played together for three years before we put the Allman Brothers back together," Haynes said. "So by the time I joined the band, I didn't have that kind of immediate pressure to 'replace' Duane Allman. As a fan of the band, I want to stay true to Duane's spirit, but they've always left it totally up to me how much of his influence to show. I was a Duane Allman freak, but he was only my very favorite out of a dozen other guitarists."

Gregg Allman, who played a drug dealer in the movie *Rush*, had reawakened from his Eighties nightmare, which he attributed to alcohol. "There have been difficult times," he mused. "But now I think of a lot of good times when I look back." ■

© 1991 Sony Music. Permission to reproduce this photography is limited to editorial uses in regular issues of newspapers and other regularly published periodicals and television news programming.

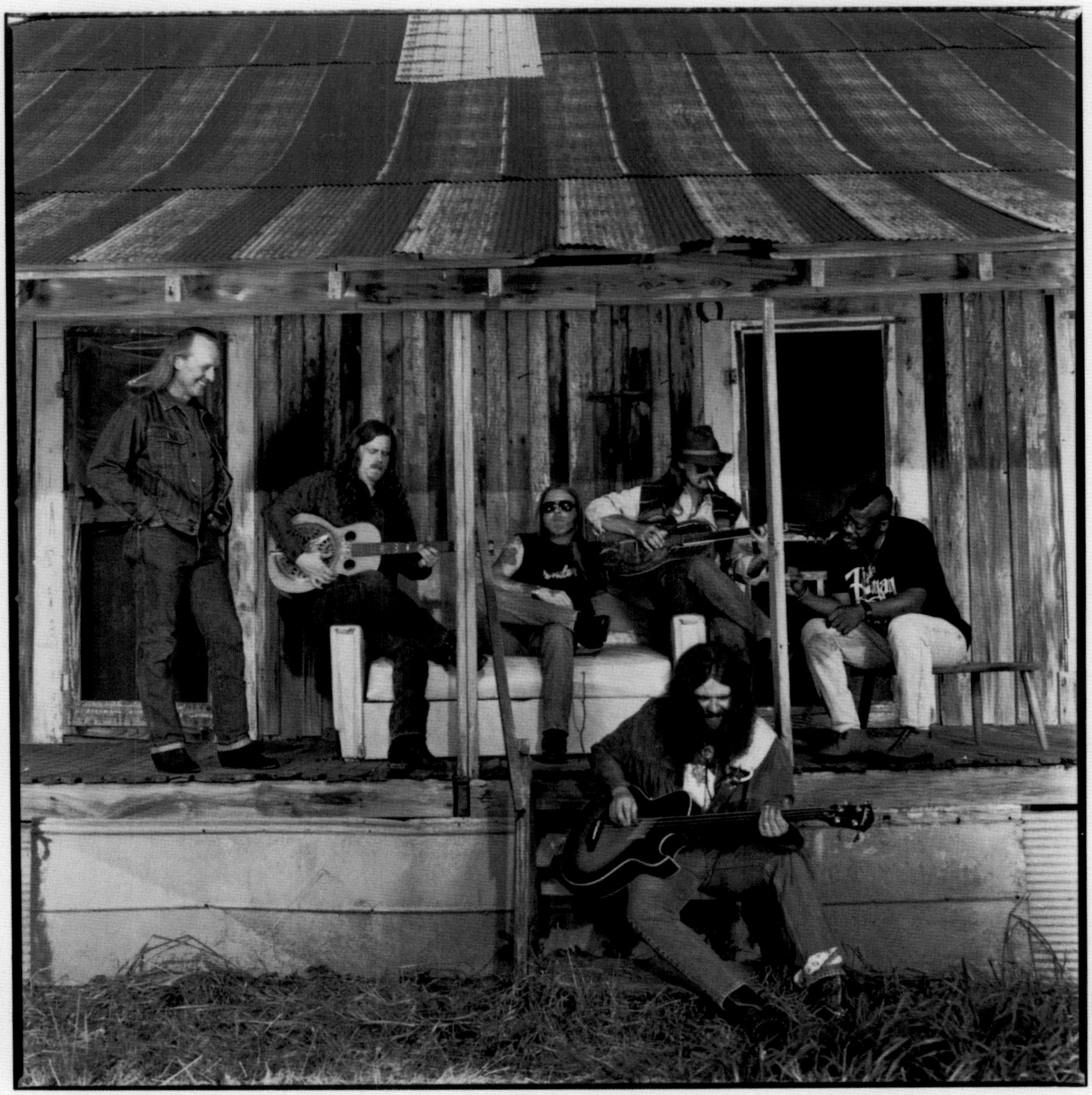

PHOTO CREDIT: KIRK WEST

BUTCH TRUCKS WARREN HAYNES GREGG ALLMAN DICKEY BETTS ALLEN WOODY JAIMOE

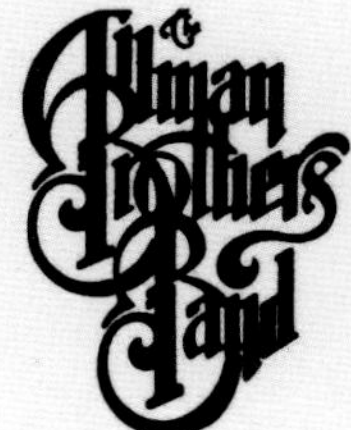

9105

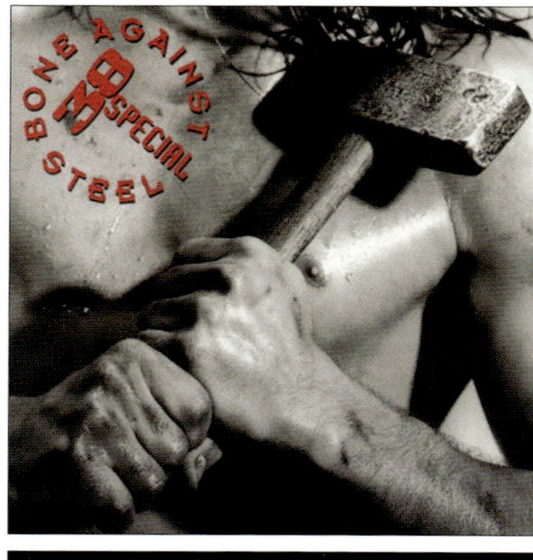

38 Special released one more great single, "The Sound of Your Voice," from the *Bone Against Steel* album.

Billboard 200: *Bone Against Steel* (#170)
Billboard Hot 100: "The Sound of Your Voice" (#33)

A PROGENITOR of Southern rock, 38 Special came into its own in the early Eighties with such crunching guitar-driven pop hits as "Hold on Loosely," "Fantasy Girl" and "Caught Up in You." But in 1988, the band underwent its first personnel change in a decade when singer Don Barnes departed for a solo career.

So whom did 38 Special recruit? Singer and keyboardist Max Carl, a guy from Nebraska who'd lived in Los Angeles for 12 years and had a long run as vocalist with Jack Mack & the Heart Attack, a ten-piece R&B group. Carl's songs put a spark back into 38 Special, yielding the most versatile albums in the Atlanta-based band's history.

"I'm tired of being pointed out for not being a 'wild-eyed Southern boy'—I don't care about that anymore. All I know is that what I'm doing is working," Carl said. "Georgia's been a great place for me. In L.A., you're surrounded by so many creative environments and people, it tends to be a negative effect personally—you're influenced by what somebody else is doing, or somebody who you respect says, 'Gee, that's not as good as what you were doing.'"

1988's *Rock and Roll Strategy* album made a lot of new 38 Special fans. Some people thought "Second Chance," a ballad, would ruin the band's career, but it became a No. 1 adult contemporary hit and three-format smash. Three years later, 38 Special's signature sound was reinvented on the *Bone Against Steel* album. "The Sound of Your Voice" reached #2 on *Billboard*'s Album Rock Tracks chart, with Carl carrying the tune's irresistible hook. On the anthemic "Rebel to Rebel," Donnie Van Zant paid homage to the legacy of his brother, Ronnie Van Zant of Lynyrd Skynyrd.

"All I've ever seen Donnie do is run around the stage and sing rock 'n' roll, being light-hearted, funny and a little crazy," Carl said. "And suddenly, here he is center stage with his eyes closed and the lights down low, singing a song that really means a lot to him. It goes over great live. I feel like we're up there with guys like Robert Bly—a rock concert is a bit of a ritual for people, the only place you can go and jump up and down and holler without anyone telling you to sit down and turn that stuff down. Everybody needs that outlet. And in the throes of that, we have a handful of moments that can raise the hair on your arm, make you stop for a second and think." ■

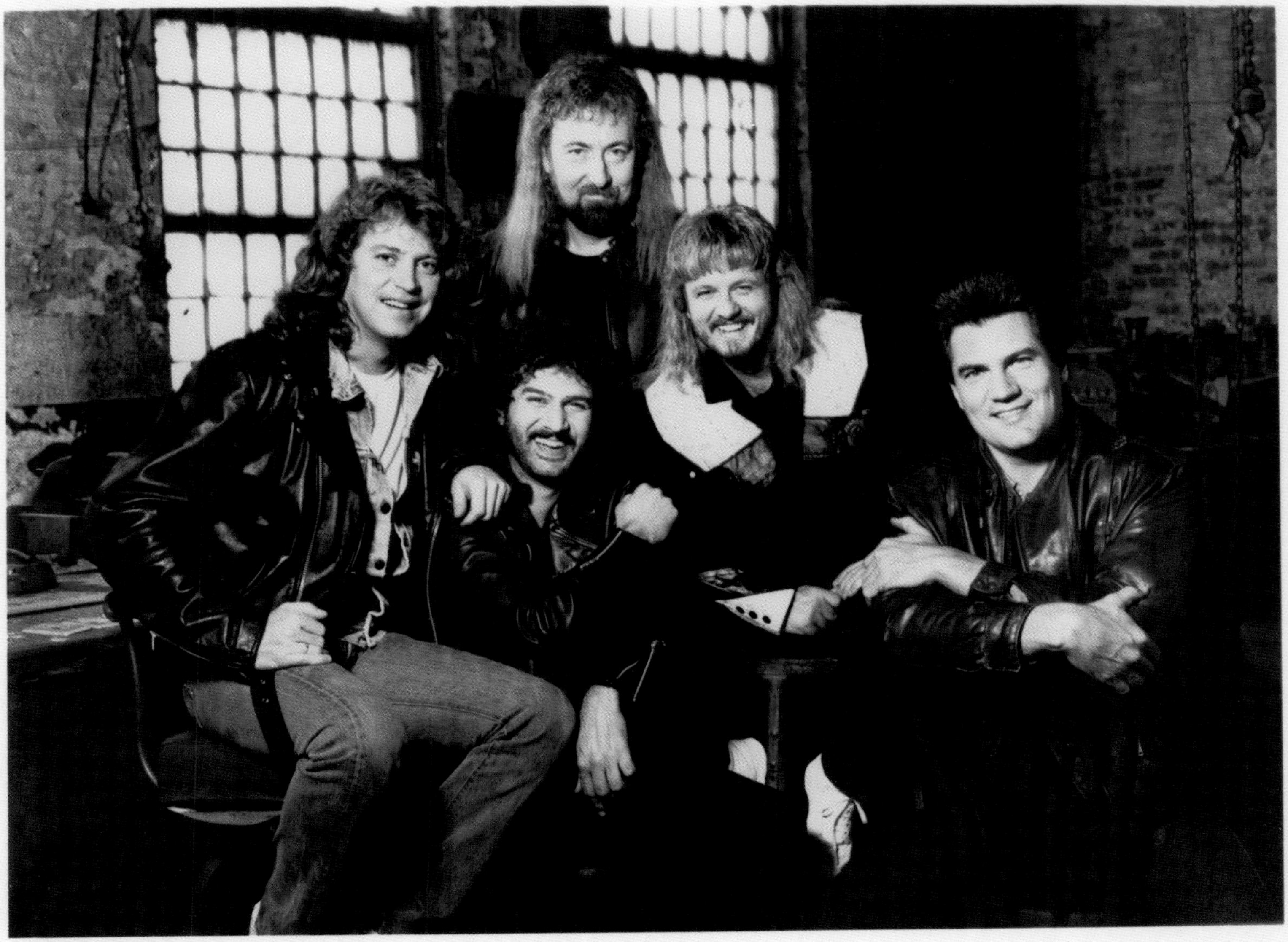

Photo Credit: John Halpern

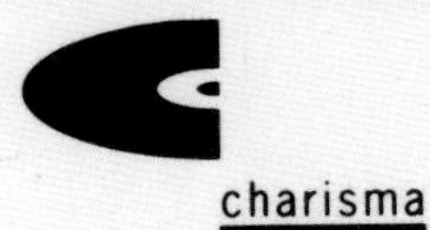

38 SPECIAL

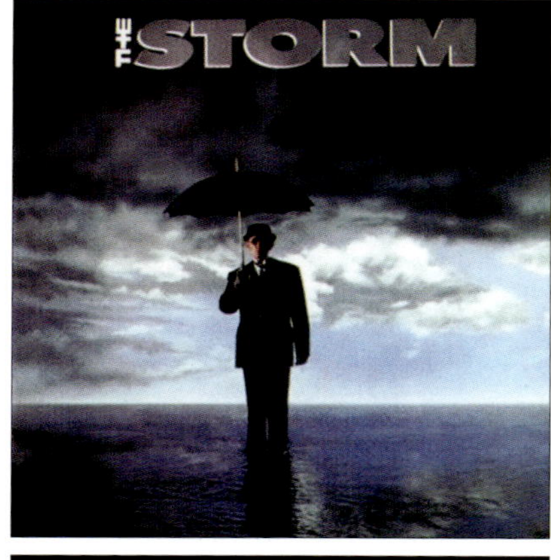

The Storm, featuring three ex-Journey members, scored a hit with "I've Got a Lot to Learn About Love."

Billboard 200: *The Storm* (#133)
Billboard Hot 100: "I've Got a Lot to Learn About Love" (#26)

PEOPLE KEPT saying how much the Storm's polished, radio-friendly rock sounded like Journey. "I've Got a Lot to Learn About Love" was obviously Journey-esque, given the hook-filled melody and Kevin Chalfant's strong vocals. Keyboardist Gregg Rolie realized the comparisons would continue.

"Do we try to sound like Journey?" Rolie asked and answered. "Well, you've got three ex-members of the band (Rolie, bassist Ross Valory and drummer Steve Smith). I'm not gonna change my style of hearing or presenting music."

Rolie had stopped being defensive about Chalfant's voice. As lead vocalist for the band 707, Chalfant sang the 1982 hit, "Mega Force."

"It's a matter of who got to the box office first, and that was Steve (Perry, Journey's singer)," Rolie said. "Kevin's been working his ass off for ten years to get somewhere. He can't help the way he sounds—you can't fake that kind of quality timbre. In black music, a lot of guys sound like Stevie Wonder, but nobody beats them up about it."

Rolie, who co-founded both Santana (he was lead singer on the Top 10 hits, "Evil Ways" and "Black Magic Woman") and Journey, exited the latter band after the 1981 live album, *Captured*.

"The last year of Journey was torment—I wanted to see the other side of life," he explained. "Touring and being in the back of buses wasn't enough for me after 14 years. You can't write good music for people if you know nothing about them, and it got to the point where I didn't know anything, just stages and other people's stories. Now I'm a family guy, and I like being a dad—but the music side of me hasn't quit. And the Storm fell into my lap."

The Storm's self-titled debut album was produced by Beau Hill, who had helmed multi-platinum albums for hard-rock bands Winger and Ratt.

"I've done this three times now, and it's easier than it's ever been—we take care of business, do a good job and enjoy it," Rolie said. "A lot of the audience that used to listen to Journey has gone to country and western. It's because the music went away, not the audience. They switched to a guy like Garth Brooks because song value was there. And song value is the key thing with us." ■

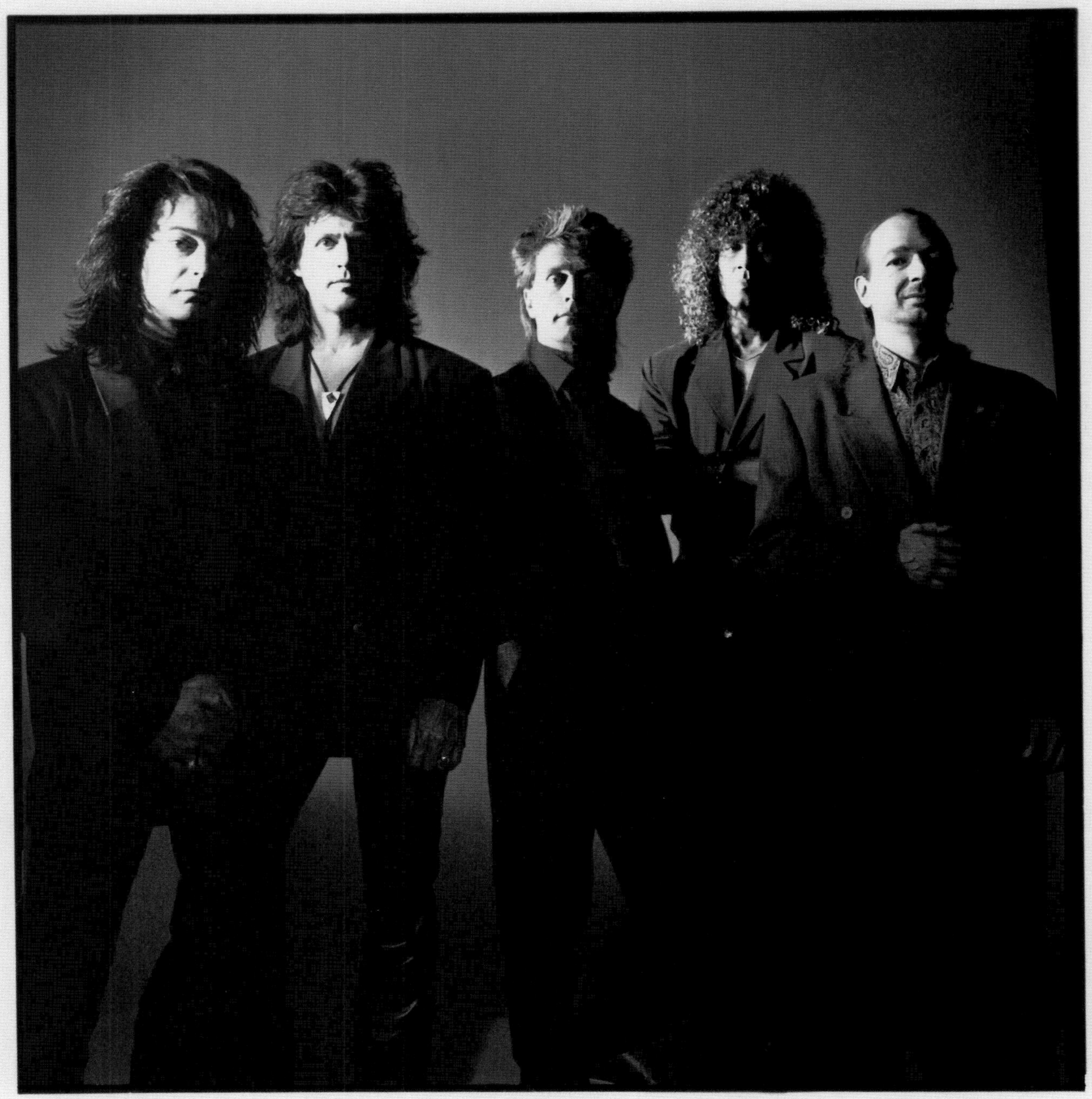

Photo Credit: Jeff Katz / 1991

Kevin Chalfant Gregg Rolie Ross Valory Josh Ramos Steve Smith

THE STORM

© 1991 Interscope Records, Inc./Permission to reproduce limited to editorial uses in newspapers and other regularly published periodicals and television news programming. All other rights reserved.

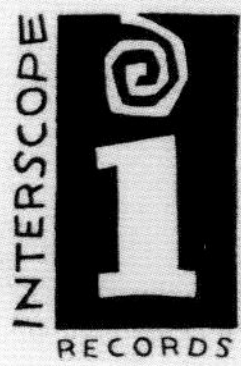

With his *Whenever We Wanted* album, John Mellencamp officially shed "Cougar" from his moniker.

Billboard 200: *Whenever We Wanted* (#17)
Billboard Hot 100: "Get a Leg Up" (#14); "Again Tonight" (#36)

JOHN MELLENCAMP began his career in the Seventies billed by his manager as Johnny Cougar. "I was 22 and had absolutely no vision," he said. "I thought making records was something fun and cool to do." Following the success of his 1982 *American Fool* album, he added his given surname, becoming John Cougar Mellencamp. He also cemented his reputation as a brat with an attitude.

The Indiana native had since matured, a fact well documented through the poignant social commentary of his best-selling albums in the Eighties. Often writing about the shattered dreams of America's common folk, he explored and defined his heartland rock 'n' roll, with violins, accordions, pedal steel guitars and dulcimers surfacing in his guitar-based style.

"Someone said I had my finger on what America wanted to hear," he said. "I just don't see it that way—I think I got real lucky with the songs."

Mellencamp returned to straight-ahead rock 'n' roll with *Whenever We Wanted*, the first album to drop the "Cougar" from his name. It yielded the Top 40 hits, "Get a Leg Up" and "Again Tonight," and "Last Chance," "Love and Happiness" and "Now More Than Ever" all garnered airplay on rock radio.

As a teenager, Mellencamp was influenced by the movie *Hud*, based on a novel by author Larry McMurtry (*The Last Picture Show, Lonesome Dove*, *Tears of Endearment*).

"I saw it several times," Mellencamp said. "It's about this young guy, Paul Newman's character, who hates work, loves to drink and rides around in a big ol' Cadillac raising hell. At one point he has a fight with his father, who says, 'You've got all the charm it takes to make youngsters like you, but you don't give a damn about people.'

"When I first saw *Hud*, I wanted to be just like him. I was the first one to start a fight, the first one to get thrown out of a high school basketball game for drinking, the first one to go cruising for girls. Now it's the opposite of what I want to be. I began to identify with the old man's idea that 'slowly the face of the nation is changing because of the people we admire.'" ■

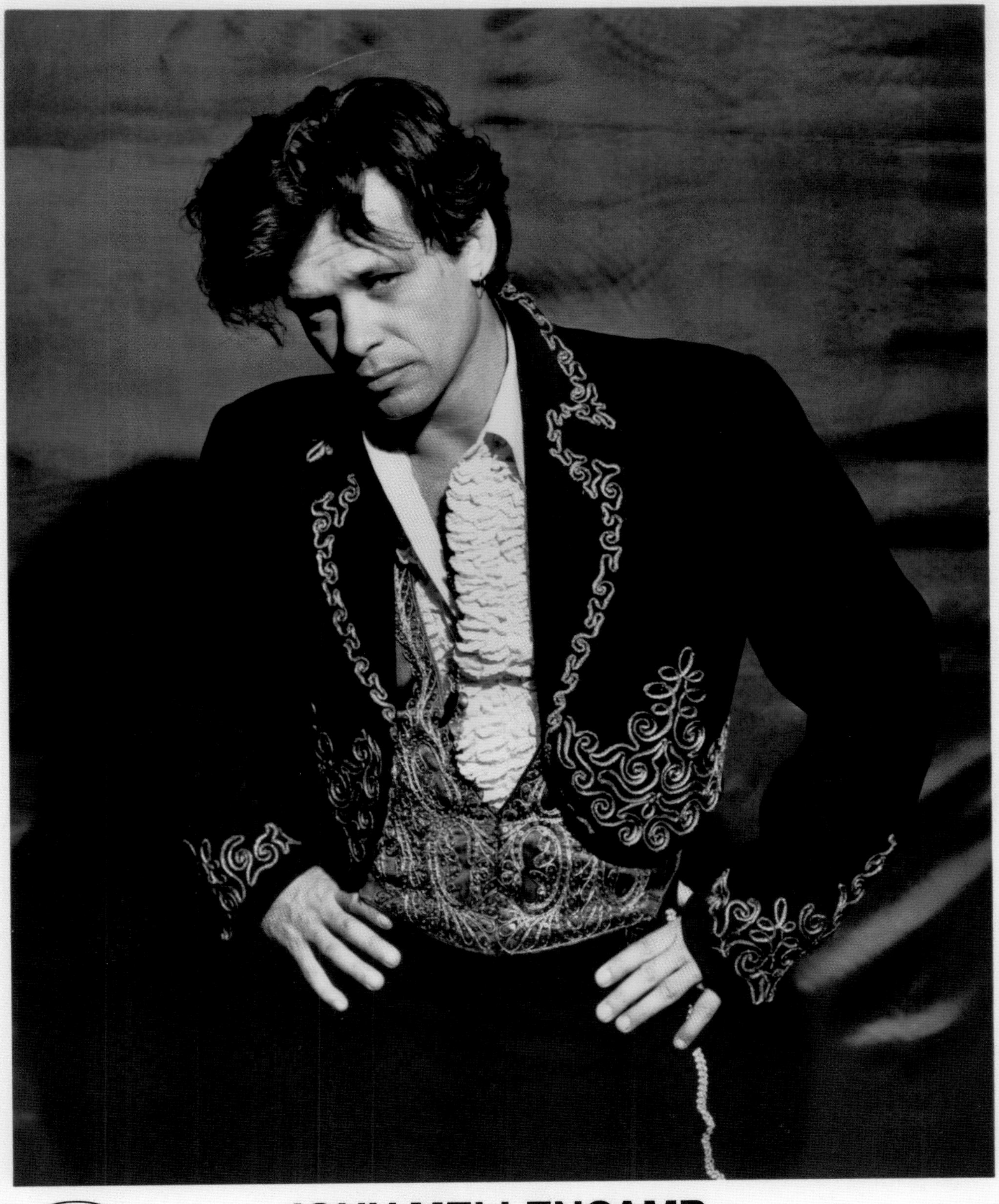

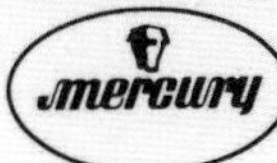

JOHN MELLENCAMP

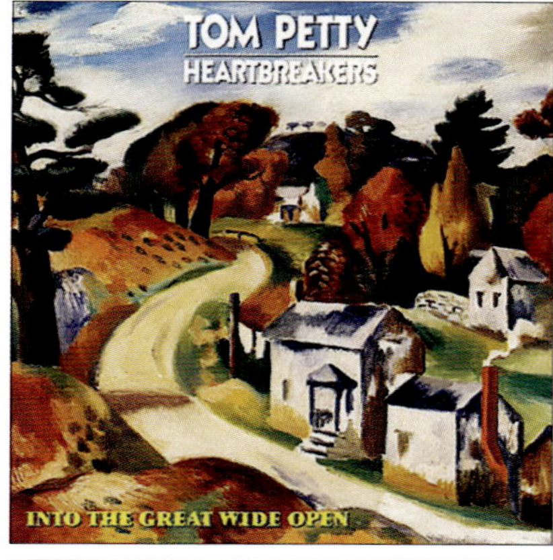

Billboard 200: *Into the Great Wide Open* (#13)
Billboard Hot 100: "Learning to Fly" (#28);
"Into the Great Wide Open" (#92)

Sustaining their leader's commercial pinnacle, "Learning to Fly" soared for Tom Petty & the Heartbreakers.

TOM PETTY should have been a satisfied man, given his reemergence as one of rock music's most vital artists. *Full Moon Fever*, his 1989 album, marked the biggest-seller of his career, and he had tenure as the youngest member of the Traveling Wilburys supergroup. But on *Into the Great Wide Open*, the songwriter avoided complacency. He'd turned 40 the night before he started making the album and sang reflectively about the state of the American dream, the tough choices facing the middle class.

"At first I thought I was going to write a nice happy album," Petty said. "But it was almost impossible. The country is incredibly fucked up at the moment. We have to trace that to our leaders. I think they're very corrupt people with no regard for human life or dignity, and I intend to give them a very hard time."

Petty described the late Eighties as "a personally dark period," but he'd regained his belief in the power rock 'n' roll could have in changing lives.

"In the last five years, you've seen the industry become fragmented, a lot of specific labels put on it. I don't want to get in a position where I can only be allowed to release what's expected of me. That's all wrong—artists are supposed to open people up to things. I'm a little annoyed at how much business has crept into music. It's getting awfully professional; the radio is completely out of whack. But I don't know that I can do any good preaching on the state of rock 'n' roll. So I've just ignored the musical climate. I'm not above anybody else. I'm just trying to present my music as honestly as I can."

As the result of his *Full Moon Fever* success, many people seriously thought Petty would continue as a solo artist. That album started as a busman's holiday with fellow Wilbury and former Electric Light Orchestra leader Jeff Lynne and ended up bringing him a degree of recognition never accorded with the Heartbreakers, his longtime backup band. When it came time to go back in the studio, Petty decided that he, Lynne and the Heartbreakers—guitarist Mike Campbell, keyboardist Benmont Tench, drummer Stan Lynch and bassist Howie Epstein—should all collaborate.

Into the Great Wide Open blended the Heartbreakers' gritty verve with Lynne's striking electric and acoustic rock textures burnished to a pleasantly crisp sheen. Petty rendered his spare but powerful lyrics with nuance and subtlety, saying "They're not the kind of songs I wanted to scream." "Learning to Fly," which reached the top of the *Billboard* Album Rock Tracks chart, concerned overcoming obstacles.

"I saw a pilot interviewed on TV," Petty revealed. "They asked him what the most difficult part of flying was, and he said, 'Coming down.' I thought that was a good metaphor for a lot of things in life. Rock 'n' roll was only a teenage music in the Fifties. The audience has obviously grown up quite a bit since then. It's a challenge to see if the music can grow, too." ■

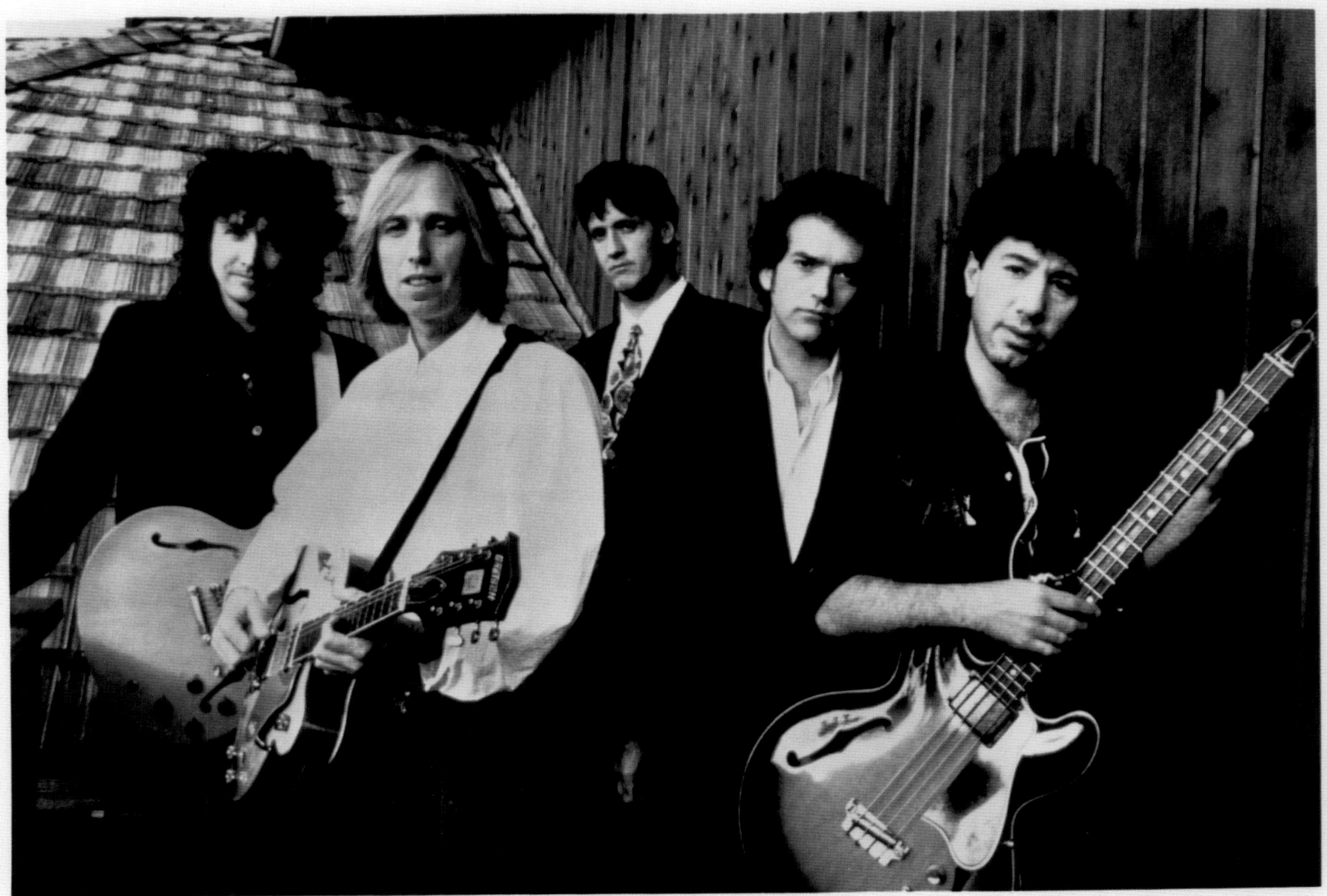

Photo credit: Caroline Greyshock

MIKE CAMPBELL TOM PETTY STAN LYNCH BENMONT TENCH HOWIE EPSTEIN

TOM PETTY AND THE HEARTBREAKERS

7/91

MCA

McGUINN
BACK FROM RIO

"King of the Hill," featuring Tom Petty, sparked *Back from Rio*, Roger McGuinn's lauded comeback album.

Billboard 200: *Back from Rio* (#44)

ONE OF the most innovative American bands of all time, the Byrds were enjoying renewed appreciation, as a four-CD boxed set marked their 25th anniversary and the Rock and Roll Hall of Fame inducted the legendary Sixties outfit in January 1991.

The timing was perfect for Roger McGuinn, the co-founder and guiding force behind the Byrds, to release *Back from Rio*, his first solo recording in more than a decade.

"'To everything there is a season, turn, turn, turn'—it was just time for something like this to happen naturally," the soft-spoken artist said of his career resurgence. "The Byrds wrote a song about the subject back in the Sixties—'So You Want to Be a Rock 'n' Roll Star.' The highs and lows are something that I've never taken too seriously."

McGuinn had certainly had his share of lows. He struggled to keep the Byrds intact before a final 1973 breakup, and various reunion efforts proved short-lived. His series of solo albums met with limited commercial success. He soon found himself in a downward spiral—without a record contract, divorced and doing a lot of drugs. Close to bankruptcy, McGuinn withdrew from the music business and went through a period of Christian reawakening. In the Eighties, he returned to his folk roots and barnstormed the country with his trusty acoustic 12-string, playing small clubs or opening for other acts.

"It's logical to assume there's been a dark cloud over me, because I haven't been making records," McGuinn said. "But dwelling on that isn't in my character. Going on the road isn't the public's idea of what makes you happy in the business, but I was having a good time."

McGuinn and his wife and manager, Camilla, resisted offers they felt wouldn't make business sense, but a demo deal with the producers of the John Candy movie *Uncle Buck* allowed him to record songs. He re-emerged via *Back from Rio* with his unmistakable voice and chiming guitar riffs. The project featured plenty of big-name contributions and collaborations. McGuinn had renewed his friendship with David Crosby and Chris Hillman, two of his former partners in the Byrds, and the trio performed three songs together on McGuinn's album. Songwriting contributions came from Elvis Costello and Eurythmics' Dave Stewart. And Tom Petty co-wrote and sang on "King of the Hill," which peaked at #2 on the *Billboard* Mainstream Rock Tracks chart.

"I never met Tom until he recorded 'American Girl' (a song with an enormous debt to the Byrds' music) in 1976," McGuinn enthused. "My manager played it for me, I liked it and put in on *Thunderbyrd*, my last solo album." ■

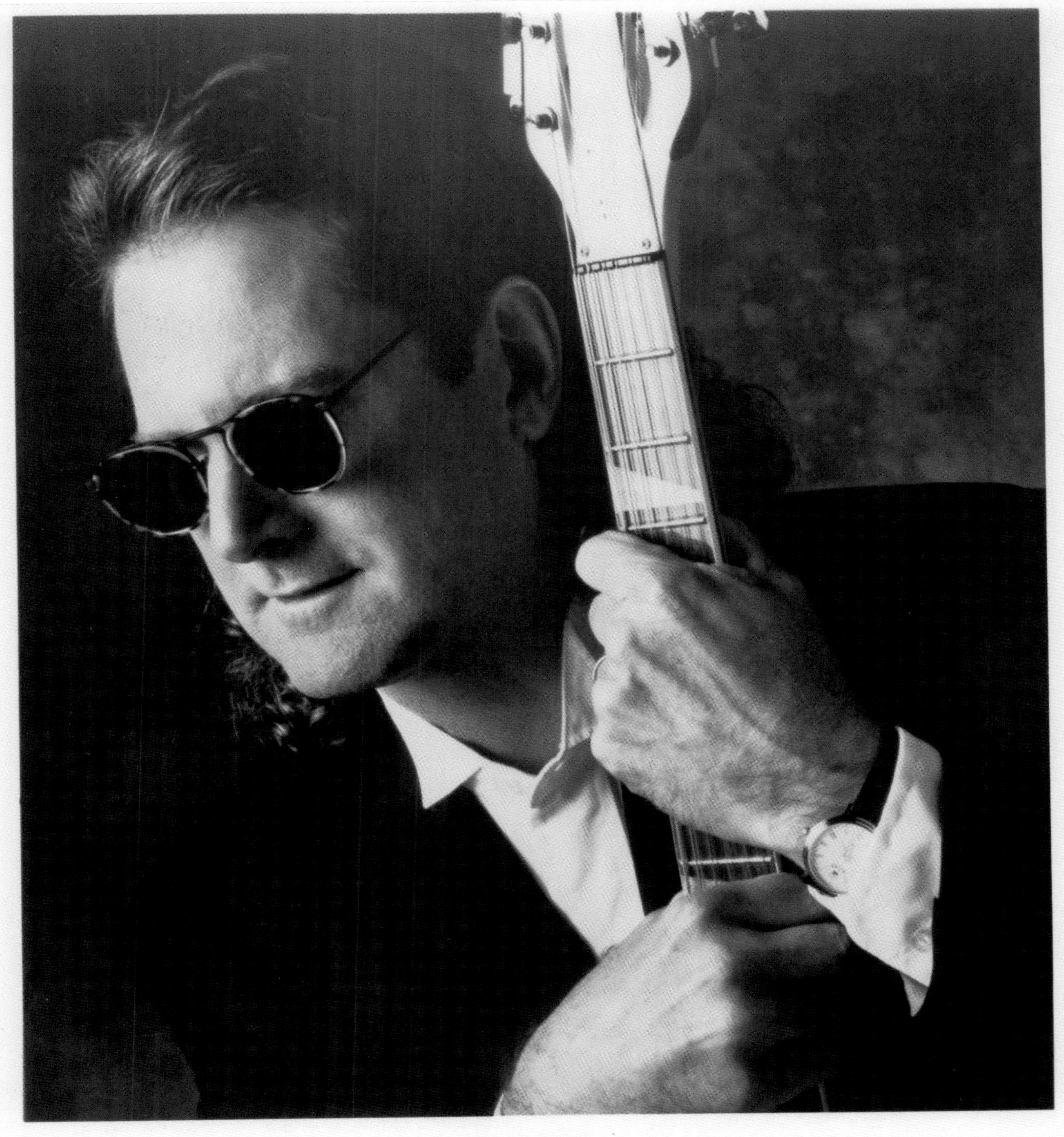

ROGER McGUINN

ARISTA

Nestled on the charts for almost a year, James Taylor's *New Moon Shine* was finally certified platinum.

Billboard 200: *New Moon Shine* (#37)

MORE THAN two decades had passed since James Taylor left North Carolina with guitar in hand and songs in his head. No longer anchored at home, he had to create his future—and that future began in 1969 hanging out with the Beatles in England. He recorded *James Taylor*, his auspicious debut, at 21. The album, the first for Apple Records, included "Carolina in My Mind" and featured Paul McCartney on bass. The appealing warmth of his material proved him to be one of the most talented, genuine and durable figures of the early Seventies, when *Sweet Baby James*, his landmark second release, heralded the arrival of pop music's "sensitive singer-songwriter" era.

"My best stuff was early on, I think," Taylor admitted. "But I'm not ready to quit. I try to keep things in the present."

Fast forward—through hits like "Fire and Rain" and "You've Got a Friend," a long bout with drugs and depression, a failed marriage to fellow superstar Carly Simon—to 1991. With his personal battles in the past, he remained a top concert attraction no matter how his records did. *New Moon Shine*, his 13th studio release and biggest album in years, showcased his patented thoughtful material and the startling purity of his voice and delivery. The doleful, folkish "Copperline," an adult contemporary radio hit co-written with Southern author Reynolds Price, spun the tale of a man's return to his hometown.

But several songs reflected Taylor's political approach. "Shed a Little Light" was inspired by a biography of the late Martin Luther King, Jr. "Slap Leather" expressed his cynicism over the Persian Gulf War and former president Reagan's legacy. "Native Son" was an anti-war tune written in support of Vietnam veterans. Taylor promoted *New Moon Shine* by touring, and the concerts supported of the Natural Resources Defense Council (NDRC), a leading environmental organization with which Taylor had long been affiliated.

"It bugs me to see somebody run as 'the environmental president' and see nothing done about the environment," he said, referring to George H.W. Bush. "Conservation is the route we need to take. There are other things that can be done through technology or tapping new resources. But, basically, the frame of mind that needs to be engaged is one of using less energy, of making less noise, less waste, less pollution. There should be an aggressive push—tax incentives, legislation. This country should also have a forward-looking and aggressive commitment to global population control. Overpopulation is driving the destruction of the environment more than anything else. I know it's not a popular political point—ever since the Reagan administration, our leadership has dropped all commitment. But it needs to be back in the forefront of our foreign aid picture." ■

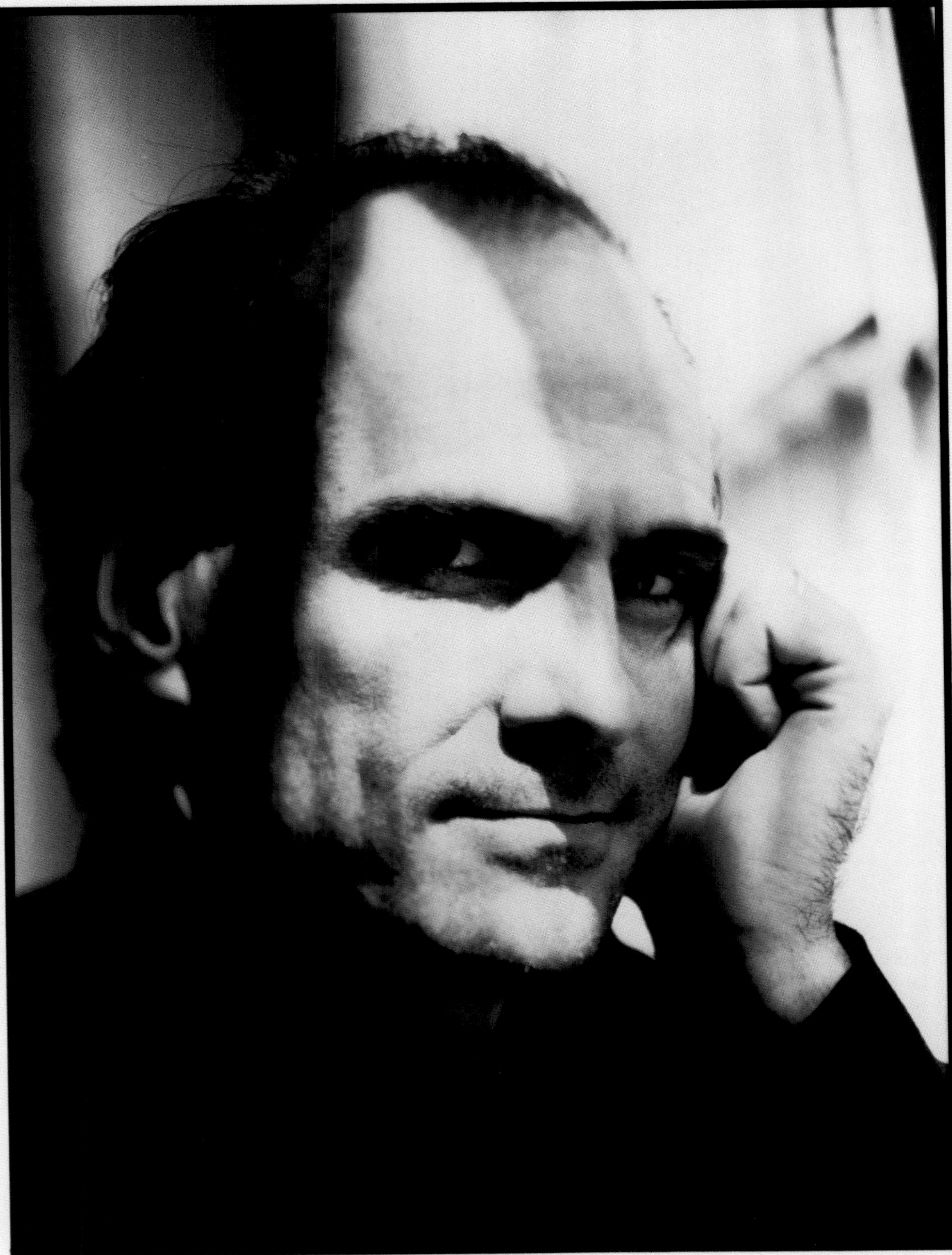

© 1991 Sony Music. Permission to reproduce this photography is limited to editorial uses in regular issues of newspapers and other regularly published periodicals and television news programming.

Photo Credit: Lee Crum

PETER ASHER MANAGEMENT INC.

JAMES TAYLOR

Columbia

9109

Billboard 200: *The Fire Inside* (#7)
Billboard Hot 100: "The Real Love" (#24)

The nostalgic appeal of "The Real Love," a prototypically restless Bob Seger song, retained his following.

***THE FIRE** Inside* was Bob Seger's first album in more than five years—the longest layoff of his 25-year recording career, and an eternity considering the pop audience's short attention span and capricious tastes. Did people still remember the man who sang "Rock and Roll Never Forgets"?

"All I can do is go by the numbers," the senior statesman of heartland rock said. "And based on the sales charts, it looks like my fans are still out there—they were willing to wait."

Seger spent a decade gigging in journeymen bars and clubs before finally ensuring his legacy as one of America's premier songwriters with 17 Top 30 singles (such rock radio staples as "Night Moves," "Against the Wind" and "Hollywood Nights") and six consecutive Top 10 albums. After Seger toured behind 1986's *Like a Rock*, no one questioned his right to semi-retirement.

In 1987, "Shakedown" became his first-ever No. 1 single, a smash from the *Beverly Hills Cop II* motion picture ("It was fast," he said, "done as a favor"). But that year Seger made an admittedly "bad move" from his hometown Detroit to Los Angeles.

"I got married, we tried to settle down in L.A. because my wife wanted to work there, and then my mother got ill," he recalled. "She was in and out of hospitals, and I had to be in Michigan all the time. I missed my career, but it didn't matter—taking care of her took precedence. The marriage ended up going down—we were long parted by the time my mother passed away. Then I got serious about my music again."

The Fire Inside, a collection of reflective ballads and passionate rockers, took more than two years to make. Seger was joined by his Silver Bullet Band and performers including Joe Walsh, Bruce Hornsby, Don Was, Little Feat's Bill Payne and Bruce Springsteen sideman Roy Bittan.

"I probably wrote too many songs and worked on too much at once, but I wanted a high-quality product—I wanted to come back strong," he admitted. "I'm glad to be back—I'm a long-term worker in this business. Videos and radio formats have changed everything, but you have to be true to what you do, and hopefully it's a little bit better than last time. That's all you can really do." ■

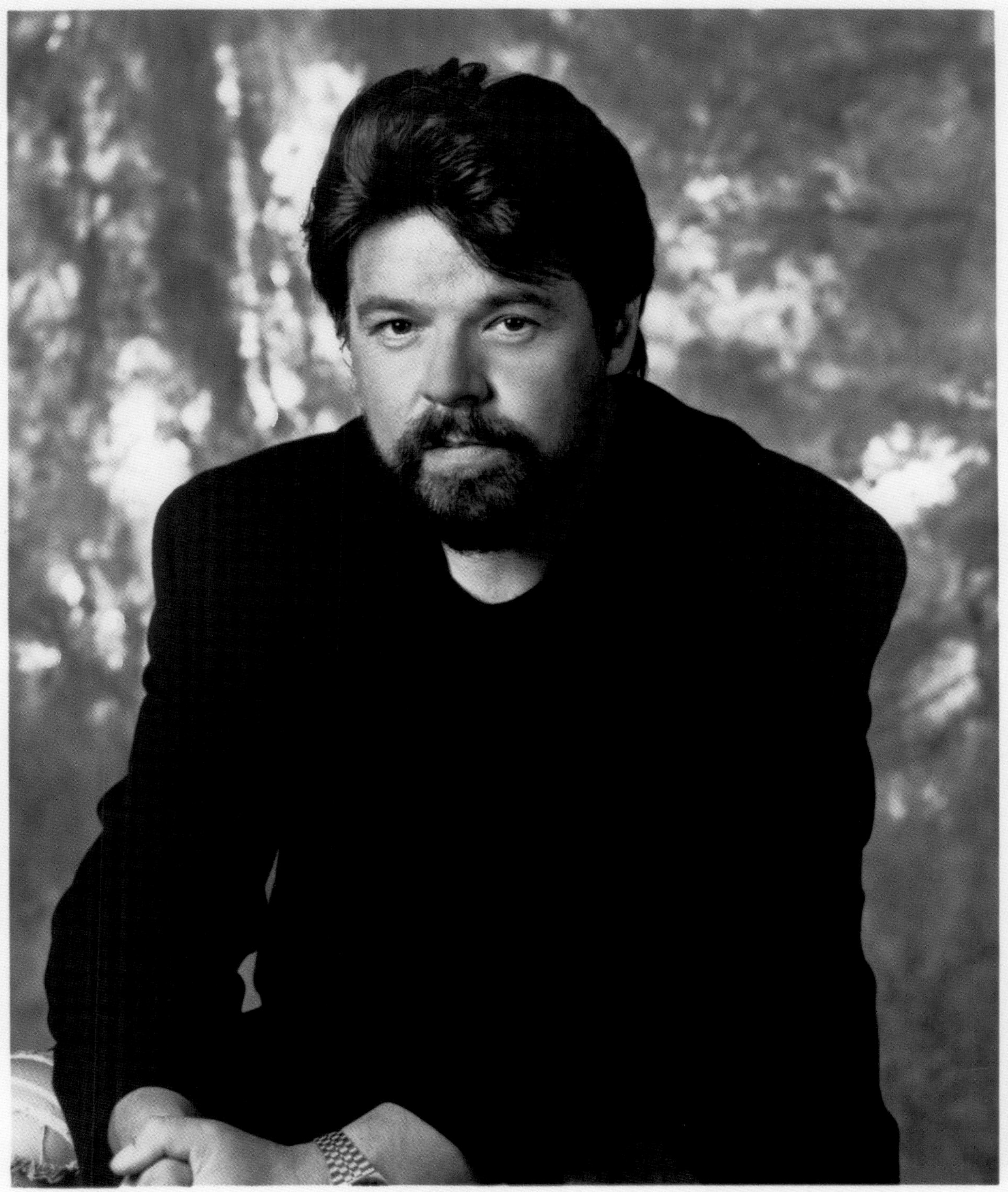

PHOTO: LESTER COHEN / 1991

BOB SEGER

Dubbing himself an *Ordinary Average Guy*, guitar great **Joe Walsh** announced his run for vice president.

Billboard 200: *Ordinary Average Guy* (#112)

THREE YEARS removed from his last recording, Joe Walsh was again rocking in the style of his Seventies heyday on *Ordinary Average Guy*. Yet he also showed why the album was aptly named.

"It's no big deal to put a record out," Walsh said. "Everybody's excited but me. I stopped writing for a while because I didn't want to have to deliver just 'product.' What is this, my 20th or something? If it does good, it does good. I can't get my hopes up."

But the former James Gang (1968-71) and Eagles (1975-82) guitarist did care about something. He planned to run as a vice presidential candidate in the 1992 election.

In 1979, Walsh endeared himself to fans with a semi-serious campaign for the presidency. His qualification? "Has never lied to the American public." His promise regarding the then-in-progress Iranian hostage standoff? "Give me a Learjet and a chainsaw and I'll take care of *that*!" He lost as a write-in candidate to Ronald Reagan, but he said he managed to register 100,000 voters.

Eleven years after that bid, Walsh was "throwing his hat in the ring" for VP, running in the New Hampshire primary under the official campaign slogan "Enough is Enough!" Normally, vice presidents were picked as running mates by a presidential candidate, and voters cast their ballots for a combined ticket. But there was an interesting quirk in US constitutional law, according to a spokesman in Walsh's camp. Walsh felt he had a much better chance of running against Dan Quayle than George Bush—"What's Quayle done for you lately besides being in charge of taking up space?" Walsh eventually ran for vice president on a ticket with "Blues Party" candidate and political activist Rev. Goat Carson.

Ordinary Average Guy's title track reached #3 on *Billboard*'s album rock chart, but Walsh hadn't announced his candidacy to make a statement on rock stardom. Among the planks in his campaign platform were "Register and Vote" and "Save the Earth."

"That's the reason I chose vice president," he mused. "I know I can't become VP, but I want to raise consciousness. Vote for anything, anytime, anywhere you can—just vote. I've spent the last four months traveling across America, and all I've seen is good people needing jobs, food and homes. We were driving through a town in the tour bus, and at a stop light I saw a guy, his wife and their three kids in a shopping cart. I got out and talked to him. He told me he had lost his employment, his savings and his house because the bank had closed. Maybe he was bullshitting me, but something's wrong. These atrocities have to be addressed. We need to take care of our people before we take care of other countries." ■

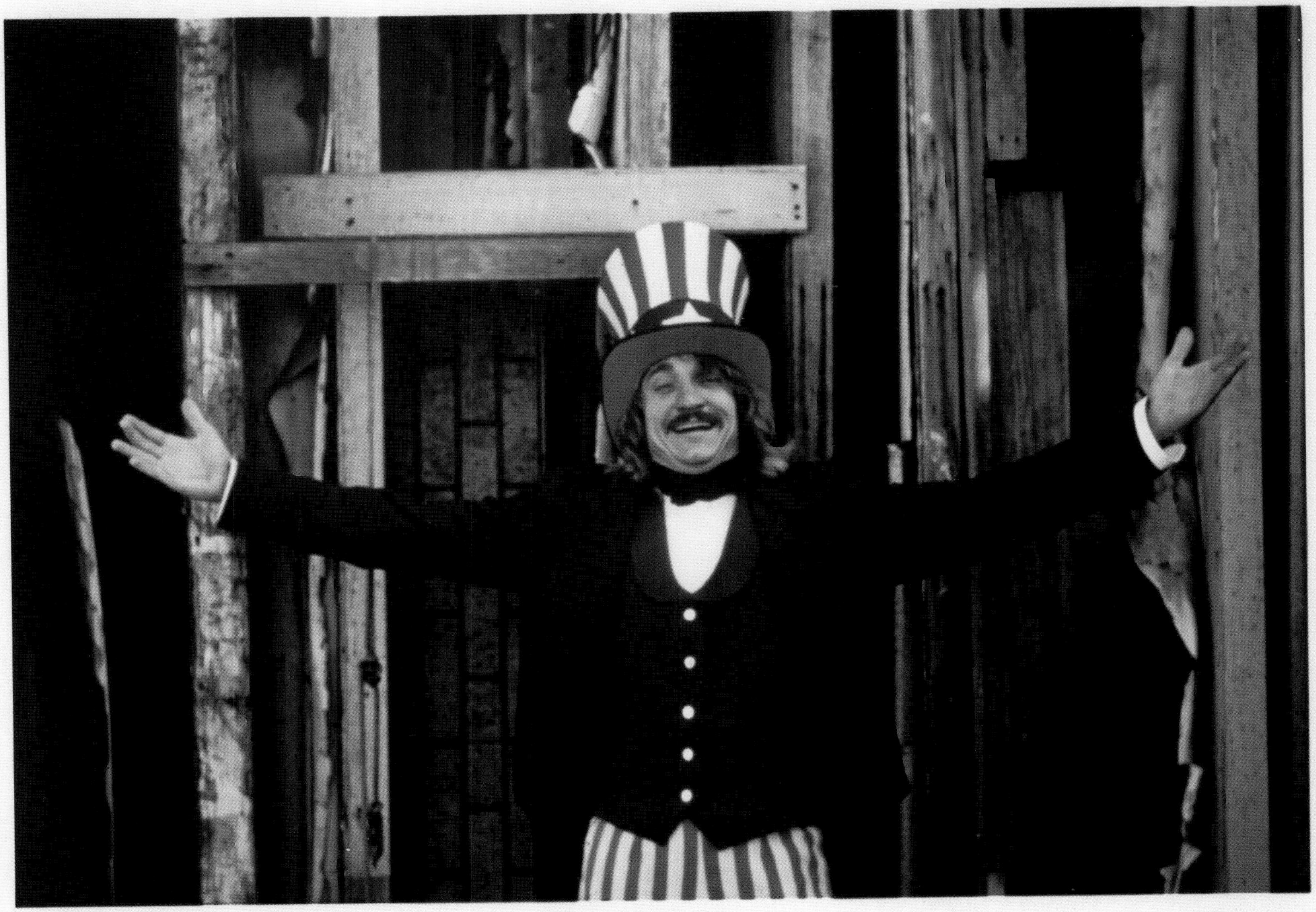

JOE WALSH

© 1991 Sony Music. Permission to reproduce this photography is limited to editorial uses in regular issues of newspapers and other regularly published periodicals and television news programming.

The New York Rock and Soul Revue's all-star lineup saw its concerts documented with *Live at the Beacon.*

DONALD FAGEN made his name for his role in Steely Dan, the legendary duo that defined a cerebral brand of rock music in the Seventies. But he was known nearly as much for his reclusive nature. After his acclaimed first solo record, 1982's *The Nightfly*, the singer-keyboardist dropped from sight.

Fagen resurfaced with a new project—and a mellower outlook on life, relaxing with some classic soul-era tunes. The New York Rock and Soul Revue grew out of informal jam sessions in New York City clubs and restaurants, eventually expanding to two performances at the Beacon Theater with an all-star group of singers and players. *The New York Rock and Soul Revue: Live at the Beacon*, a warm, generous compilation of material, was recorded with Michael McDonald, Boz Scaggs, Phoebe Snow, Charles Brown, Eddie and David Brigati of the Rascals and others. The group burned through such soul masterpieces as Eddie Floyd's "Knock on Wood" and Jackie Wilson's "Lonely Teardrops."

"These great soul songs have a nostalgic component, but for me, that's not the main thing," Fagen said. "A lot of them are beautifully constructed standards, the same way the Gershwin or Cole Porter songs are—they can be interpreted in many ways. The original versions are great. You'll never match them for authenticity, but you can use them as a basis to do all kinds of interesting things, to experiment with arrangements."

Fagen added a few more contemporary tunes to the Revue, including McDonald's monster Doobie Brothers-era hit, "Minute by Minute," as well as robust renditions of Steely Dan's "Pretzel Logic" (which peaked at #17 on *Billboard*'s Mainstream Rock Tracks chart) as well as "Chain Lightning," and "Green Flower Street" from *The Nightfly*. But making the record was like a vacation from his more exacting work during Steely Dan's heyday, when he and partner Walter Becker famously used hundreds of studio hours and dozens of the country's top session musicians to finish a track.

"It's a whole different thing," Fagen reflected. "All I really care about is that the band is tight and that everyone listens to each other when they're playing. The rest is in the hands of the gods. Everyone's tired of sitting at the sequencer, planning out every bar. It's fun just coming in with other musicians and finding the groove with bass, drums and piano." ■

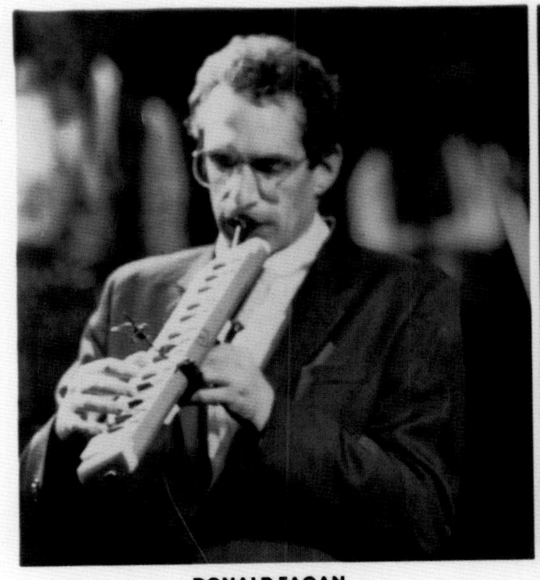

DONALD FAGAN

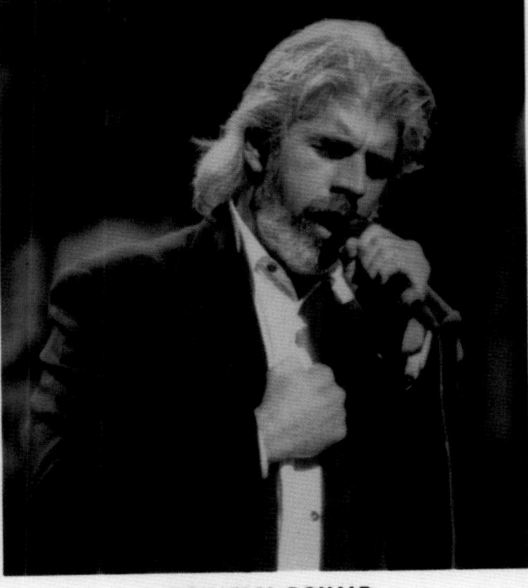

MICHAEL McDONALD

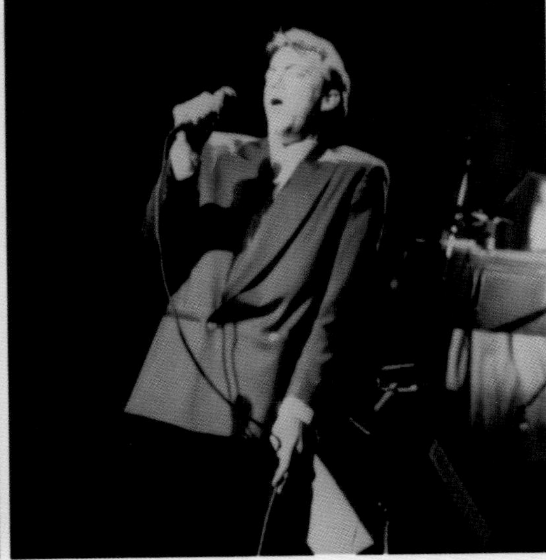

BOZ SCAGGS

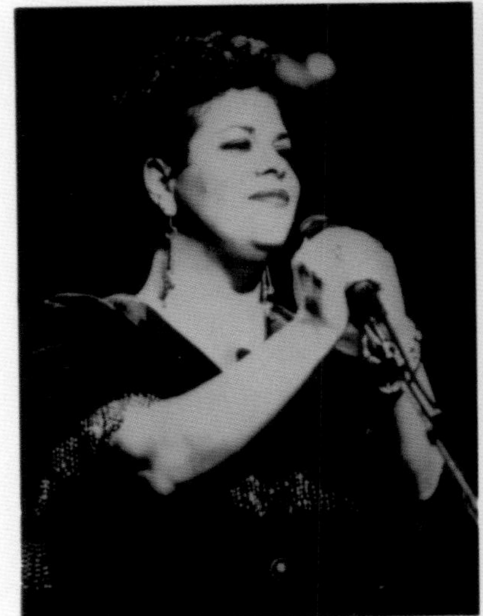

PHOEBE SNOW

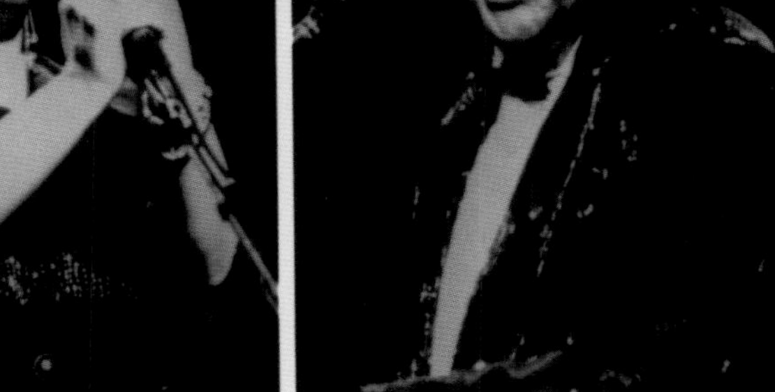

CHARLES BROWN

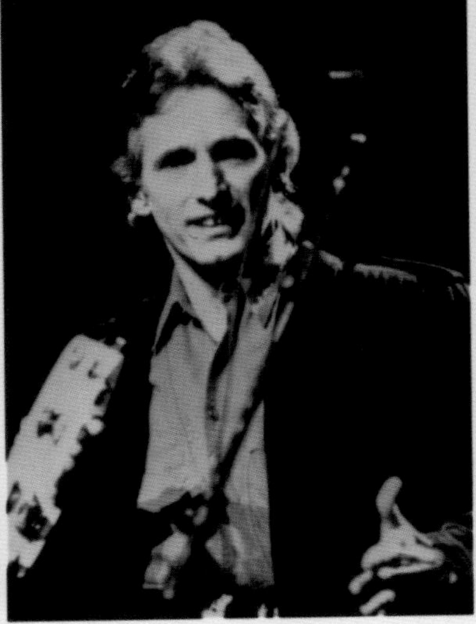

DAVID BRIGATI

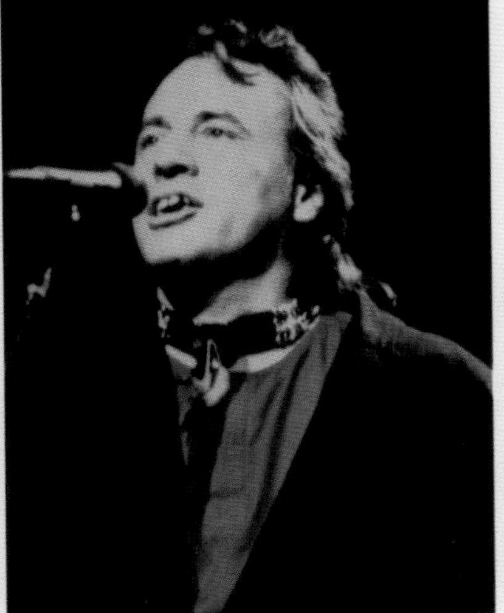

EDDIE BRIGATI

PHOTO CREDIT: CESAR VERA

THE NEW YORK ROCK AND SOUL REVUE

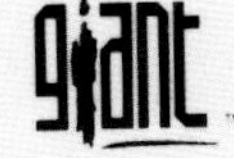

1991 Warner Bros. Records/Permission to reproduce limited to editorial uses in newspapers and other regularly published periodicals and television news programming.

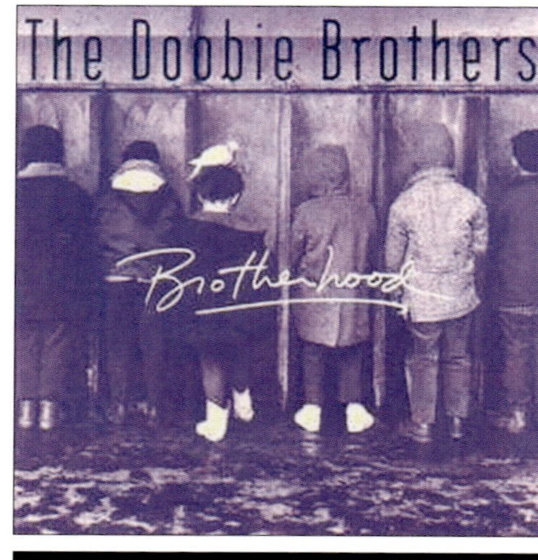

Billboard 200: *Brotherhood* (#82)

The Doobie Brothers' "Dangerous," a loving appreciation of motorcycles, typified the roots of the band.

WHEN THE Doobie Brothers started out in San Jose during the late Sixties, they had a reputation as a hard-rocking biker band.

"It's not like everybody had Harleys," guitarist Tom Johnston laughed. "Pat (Simmons, guitarist) and I were the only nuts for bikes, and we played to whoever and whatever showed up, and that included hippies, mountain mamas and crazy suckers as well as bikers. But we used to play a lot of Hell's Angels bars. I was a lot nuttier in those days, so the bikers used to come over to our house. We even looked like a bunch of young bikers on the cover of our first album."

That was essentially the same lineup that recorded the classics *Toulouse Street* in 1972 and *The Captain and Me* in 1973. Johnston was responsible for such early hit singles as "China Grove" and "Long Train Running," and in 1975 Simmons contributed "Black Water," which became the group's first No. 1 song.

Then the Michael McDonald era changed the band's style from Johnston's hard-rocking tunes to McDonald's slicker R&B syncopations and high, impassioned voice ("What a Fool Believes"). When Johnston officially left the band in 1977, observers assumed he resented McDonald's role in the spotlight.

"Michael and I get along famously," Johnston insisted. "He even bought a bike, which really surprised the hell out of me."

All of the band's members, from every one of its incarnations, joined together for a reunion tour in 1987. *Brotherhood*, the Doobies' 14th album release, featured all five of the original group members and attempted to recreate their biker image.

"Well, you can never get enough of those highway blues," Simmons sang on the single "Dangerous," a familiar groove that rocked with the kind of peril one might experience taking a Harley for a joyride. The track peaked at #2 on *Billboard*'s Album Rock Tracks chart.

"It's a rebel tune, about motorbikes, street bikes," Simmons admitted. "I wrote it from my own experiences as a biker, and I have the scars to prove it." ■

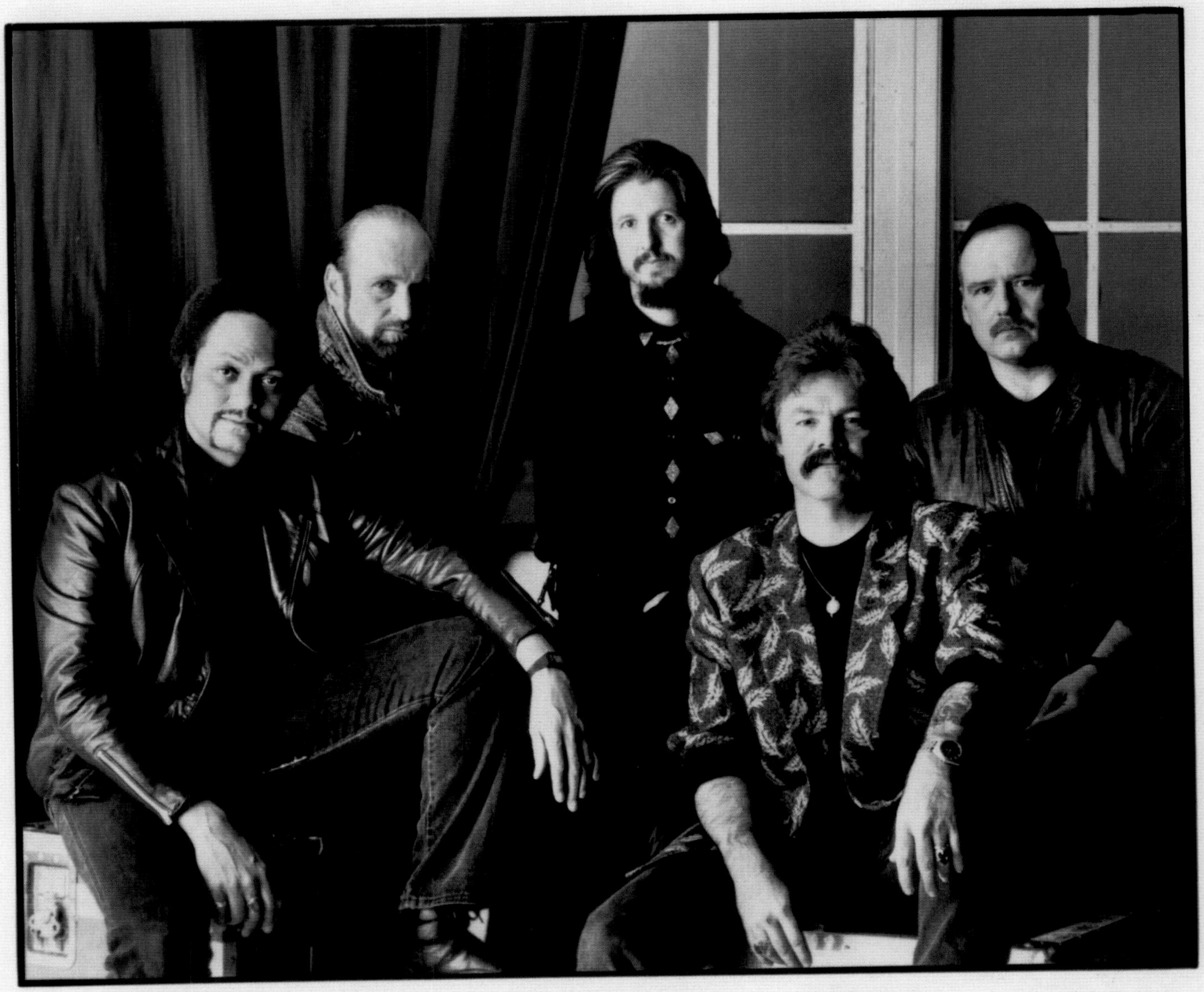

Tiran Porter Michael Hossack Patrick Simmons Tom Johnston John Hartman

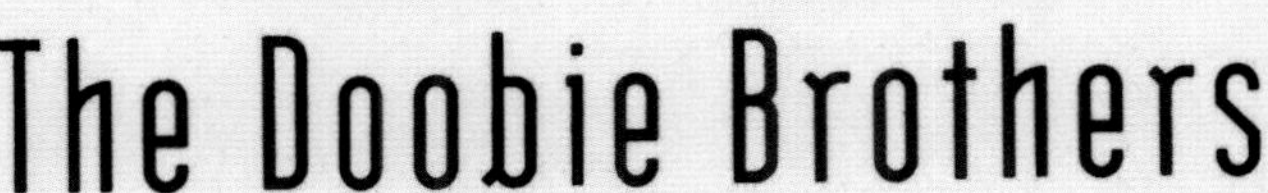

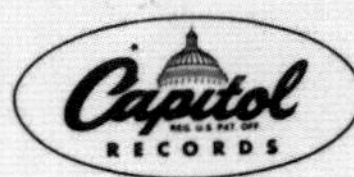

PHOTO: PETER DARLEY MILLER / 1991

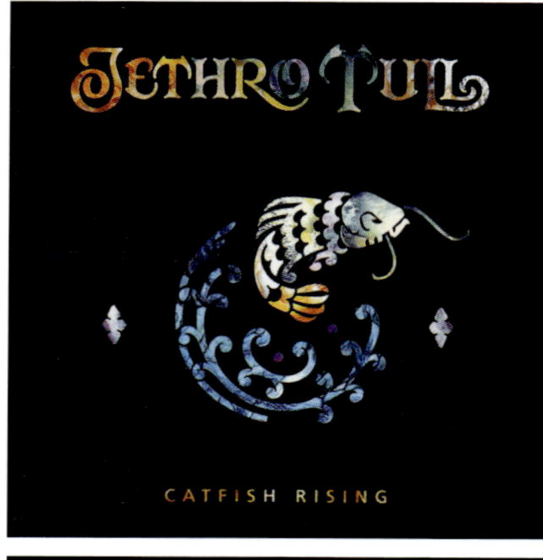

Billboard 200: *Catfish Rising* (#88)

Jethro Tull continued to carve its own place in rock with *Catfish Rising*, the British group's 18th album.

IAN ANDERSON had been at Jethro Tull's helm since 1967. Despite declining album sales, the British group's catalog performed extremely well.

"By 1971 I had created a good balance between my Chicago blues roots and my modern folk roots," Tull's flautist and vocalist said. "But it's the lyrical subject that still stands up over the test of time. I write songs with a picture in my head, maybe because I trained briefly as an artist. With 'Aqualung,' I had an image of a derelict, down-and-out hobo character. And that's the picture I have in my head when I'm singing it onstage every night. When a radio station plays Tull, it's going to be that classic. Young fans coming through the ranks are more likely to buy that album than the new one. We lose a lot of people who say, 'I'm gonna buy the CD of *Aqualung* instead.'"

Catfish Rising, Jethro Tull's 18th album of new material, featured noticeably less keyboards than any Tull release of the past decade.

"In the early Eighties, we tried to use a more modern approach, but I'm fed up with all of the synthesizer noises," Anderson explained. "Now I quite like things that are made of wood. I love doing acoustic music that's got a pushy, aggressive attack to it, and that's what I've tried to do on this album. I wrote three quarters of the songs on open-tuning mandolins, so they have a kind of bluesy feeling about them. The way the other guys react determines the sound—there's nothing in anybody's mind except a general feel. You can't calculate that any more than you can calculate the results of conception."

Tull continued performing to good-sized houses when the band toured. "People have strong feelings about us, like us or not—I've met a lot who think of Tull with utter loathing and contempt," Anderson said. "You don't find too many people just going down the middle. And I'm happy to be in that category. We're blessed with a fervent and loyal following, sort of like the Grateful Dead."

Anderson had no use for the conventions of the music industry. "I've always hated showbiz people who kiss you on both cheeks," he mused. "When they ask me if I choreograph my movements onstage, I'm horrified. To me, it means some mincing guy saying, 'Let's try it again, one-two-three-four.' I've been on the periphery of that world for two decades, and I still don't like the ambience." ■

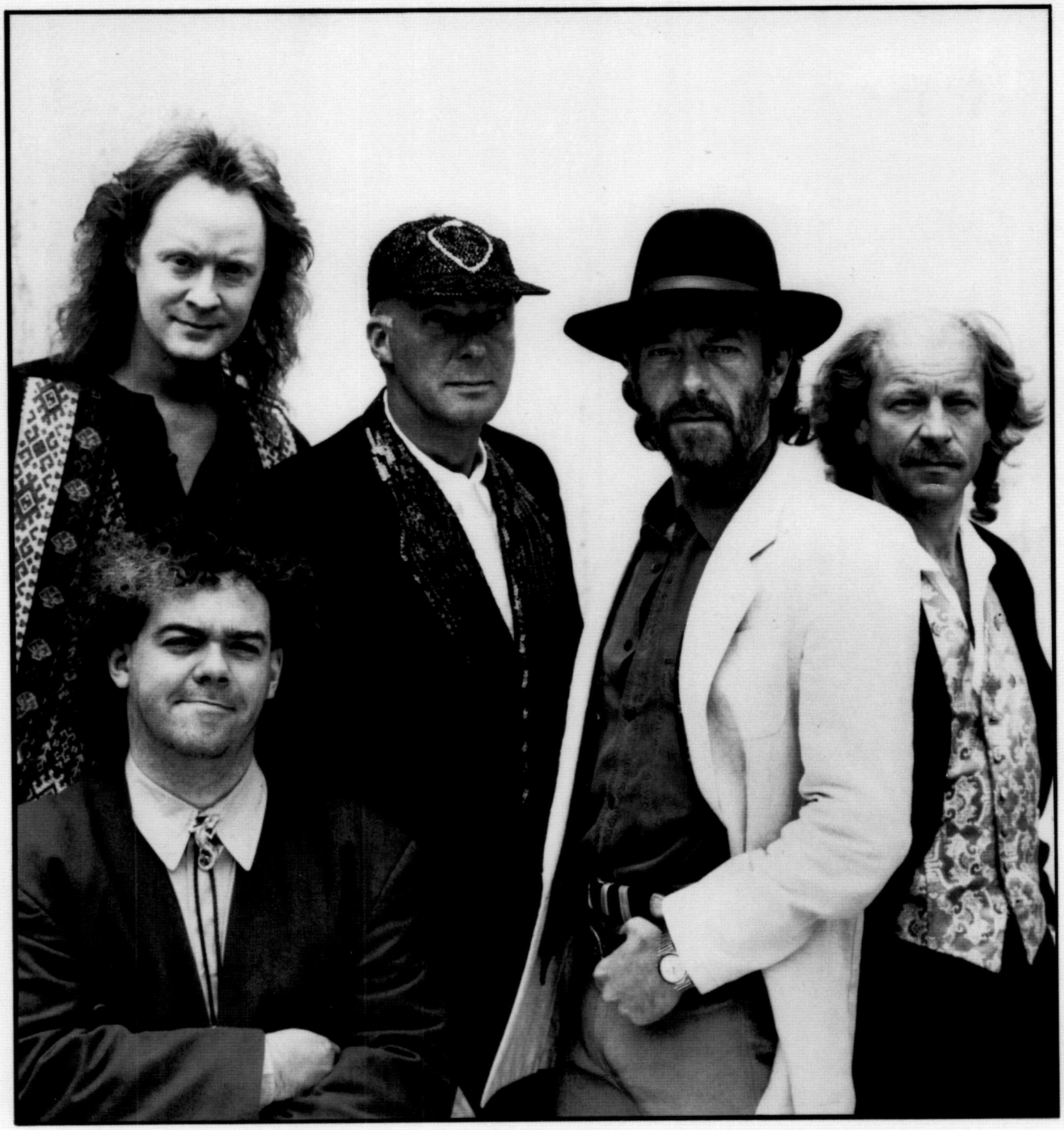

August 1991

Clockwise from bottom left: Martin Allcock, Doane Perry, Dave Pegg, Ian Anderson, Martin Barre

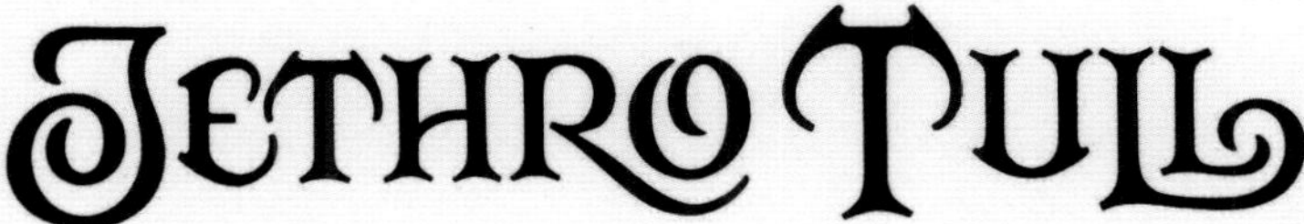

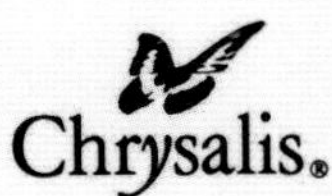

The smash "Rhythm of my Heart" from *Vagabond Heart* evinced Rod Stewart's permanance and panache.

Billboard 200: *Vagabond Heart* (#10)
Billboard Hot 100: "Rhythm of My Heart" (#3); "The Motown Song" (#10); "Broken Arrow" (#54)

DECADES INTO a hit-filled career, Rod Stewart was growing old not at all unbecomingly.

"Everybody wants to know—'How long can you keep doing it?' Because we're the pioneers, really, of baby-boomer rockers," Stewart said. "As long as I've got my hair and I'm nice and thin and I've got a voice and the energy and I keep loving it, I'm thinking what a lucky bastard I am."

On *Vagabond Heart*, a platoon of producers and songwriters gave Stewart a surge. The two biggest hits from the album were "Rhythm of My Heart" (a Great Highland bagpipe could be heard adapting the "The Bonnie Banks o' Loch Lomond," a nod to Stewart's Scottish heritage) and "The Motown Song," featuring the Temptations. He also released a cover of Robbie Robertson's song "Broken Arrow" as a single.

"My vocals were done in Los Angeles," Stewart said. "I live in the States, and I'm not allowed to record in the UK because of tax reasons. I left there in 1975, when the taxation was 89 pence on the pound. And if you were really silly, you could actually pay more tax than you earned! Everybody left in those days—Clapton, the Stones…" ■

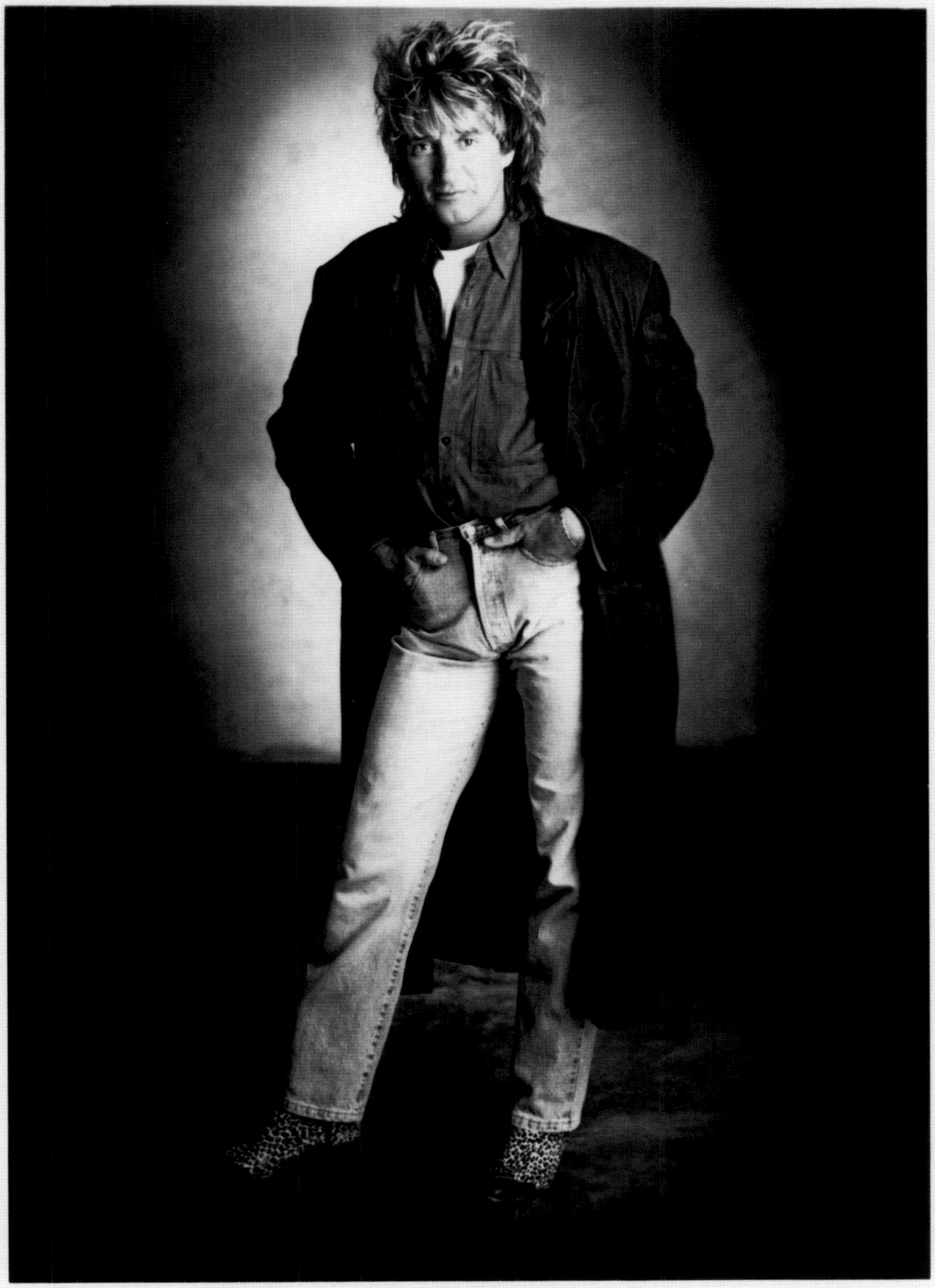

Photo Credit: Diego Uchitel

ROD STEWART

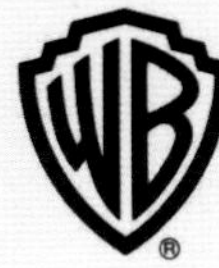

© 1991 Warner Bros. Records/Permission to reproduce limited to editorial uses in newspapers and other regularly published periodicals and television news programming.

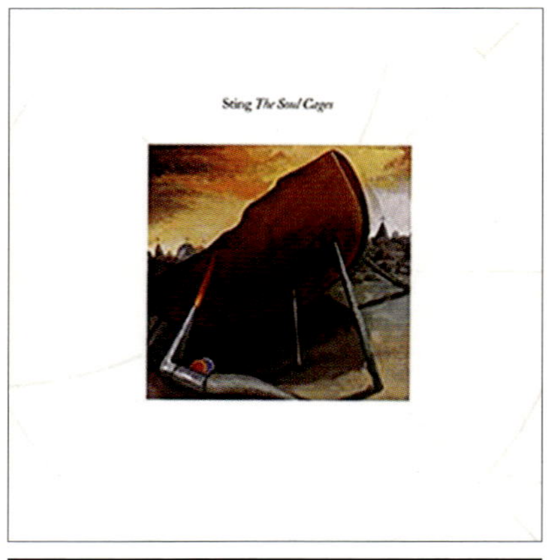

The Soul Cages, a rite-of-passage concept album, found Sting ruminating about the death of his father.

Billboard 200: *The Soul Cages* (#2)
Billboard Hot 100: "All This Time" (#5)

***THE SOUL** Cages* was Sting's first album since 1987's *Nothing Like the Sun*—a situation he blamed on writer's block.

"I had a critical case," the singer and bassist admitted. "I had a lot of problems trying to figure out what I was going to write about."

The death of his father, a dockyard worker, inspired Sting to compose the songs on *The Soul Cages*. Most of the ambitious album was somber and moody, a meditation on his confused and painful feelings, an examination of his value system using recurring images of rivers, the sea and spectral ships. Only "All This Time" had a catchy pop melody and bouncy rhythm, but the hit song's lyrics concerned a boy's first glimpse of death.

"The record is a musical way of making the journey to understanding my father. I was getting around to being able to tell him what I felt about him, and then he died. And a few other people I cared about, kind of father figures, were abruptly taken off the planet—John Dexter (a Broadway director), Gil Evans (the jazz arranger), Ethyl Eichelberger (a transvestite performance artist). People kept dying on me. Modern people almost pretend death doesn't happen—I couldn't write because I hadn't gone through the right process when my father died. But I have the tool of music to process my emotions, and it helped me reconcile. Now I feel like he's been mourned in some way. I get the feeling something has fallen into place."

Sting was often typecast as a cerebral rock star who went for big statements and rarely cracked a smile—an image further heightened by *The Soul Cages*.

"The album has been personal and confessional—and therapeutic in terms of facing death and loss. I hadn't dealt with it successfully, personally as well as publicly. I feel a whole lot better. Once you've realized how mortal we are, you can live life to the fullest. Because you're next. Life is short." ■

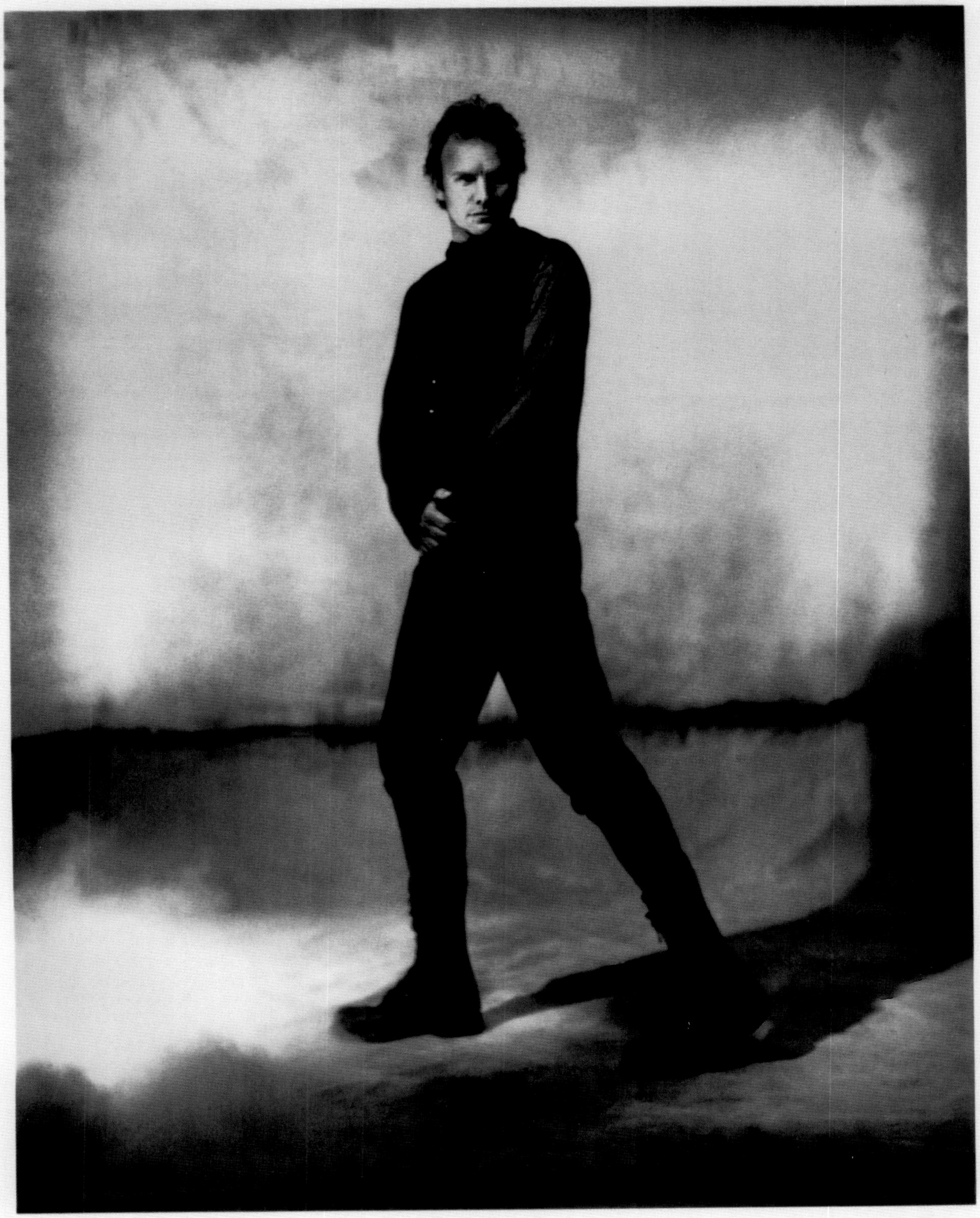

Photo Credit Guzman

STING

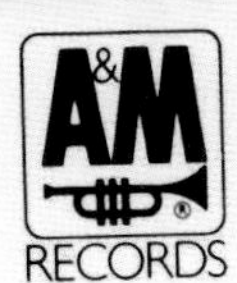

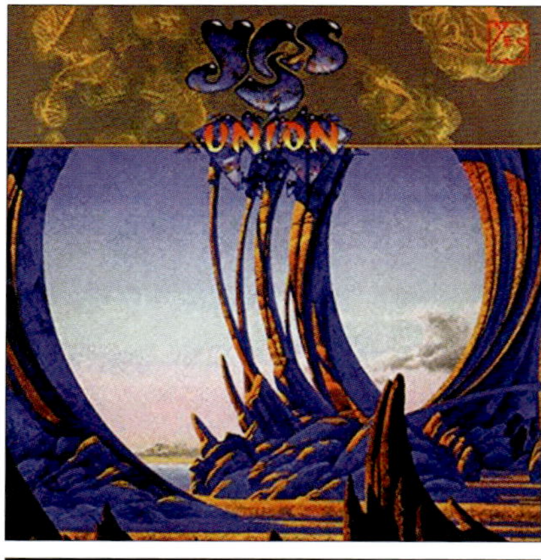

The British progressive-rock band Yes' key contributors over the years collaborated on the making of *Union*.

Billboard 200: *Union* (#15)
Billboard Hot 100: "Lift Me Up" (#86)

"IF CHRIS Squire and I can iron out our disagreements, then certainly George Bush and Saddam Hussein can iron out theirs."

That was Jon Anderson's way of describing how the most prominent members of Yes, past and present—Anderson (vocals), Squire (bass), guitarists Steve Howe and Trevor Rabin, keyboardists Rick Wakeman and Tony Kaye, and drummers Bill Buford and Alan White—had put aside their differences long enough to record an album, *Union*, and hit the road for a worldwide concert tour. According to Anderson, it took lots of lawyers, three managers, two record labels and four months of negotiations to clear the way.

"We have kind of a gentleman's agreement to make it work," Anderson said. "That means there needs to be a lot of give and take."

The success of "Roundabout," the single from the 1972 tour de force, *Fragile*, established Yes as the definitive purveyor of British progressive-rock, seeking to merge the symphonic craft of classical music with the spirit of rock.

"At the time, many rock bands were looking to the musical horizon," White said. "In Yes, we liked to think we were looking beyond the horizon."

But Yes also set the precedent for the excessive musical inclinations that plagued art-rock—cynics savaged such albums as 1974's *Tales of Topographic Oceans* as overindulgent and pretentious shows of instrumental finesse. Yes became a contrivance, and many members pursued solo records.

When Rabin became part of Yes in 1984, the band became more pop-oriented, capturing new devotees with the chart-topping "Owner of a Lonely Heart." By 1989, two versions of Yes wrangled over rights to the name, and Anderson was the only player in both camps. Yet eight of the 12 musicians who had been Yes members at one time or another had merged, and *Union* was the first album from a band called Yes in more than three years. There was no mistaking the signature sound on the single, "Lift Me Up," which hit No. 1 on *Billboard*'s Album Rock Tracks chart.

"It's commercial, heavy rock 'n' roll, some very cosmic and earthy music," Anderson said. "It feels good to bring in the Nineties as a full unit again—everybody is flexing their musical muscles."

"Everyone is trying to find musical parts for the others. The extra musicians have added strength to the sound," White added. "It's all been better than I anticipated—I thought we'd have a lot of problems for sure." ■

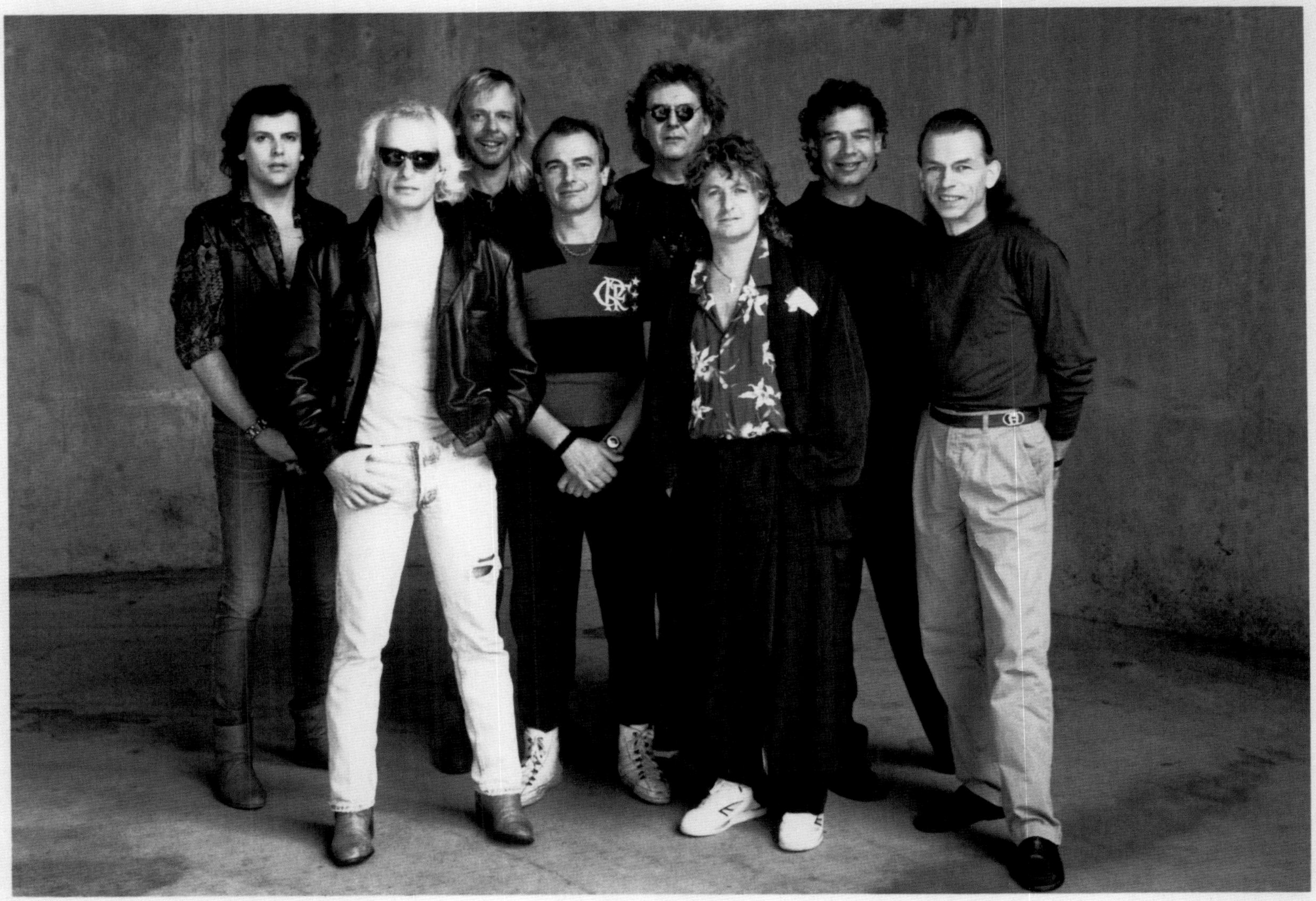

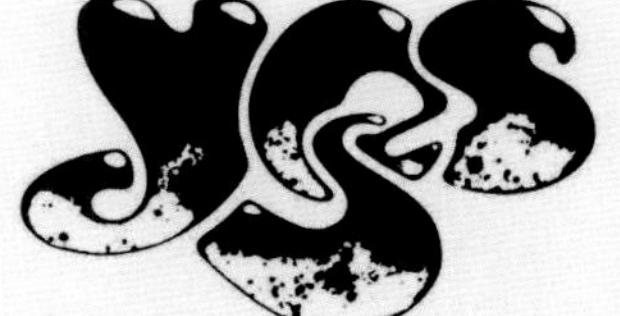

ARISTA™

KEYS OF THE KINGDOM THE MOODY BLUES

The Moody Blues, pared down to a quartet, persisted with their appreciation for pleasing, upbeat songs.

Billboard 200: *Keys of the Kingdom* (#94)

THE LATE Eighties hits, "Your Wildest Dreams" and "I Know You're Out There Somewhere," introduced the Moody Blues' music to a new generation of fans, many of whom weren't familiar with the British band's history of progressive concept albums characterized by orchestral overtones.

"Making our music accessible to a wider audience has brought more personal satisfaction to ourselves," singer-guitarist Justin Hayward said. "It's only been in the last decade that I've been able to let the early hits be in my past and look toward other kinds of satisfaction—apart from the occasional flashback."

The "veteran cosmic rockers" released their 17th album, *Keys of the Kingdom*, and had modest commercial success. It failed to produce any major hit singles, but "Say It with Love" charted at #22 on *Billboard*'s Mainstream Rock Tracks chart.

"A carpenter was working in my home studio at Christmastime," Hayward recalled. "He said he had an old keyboard sitting in his living room that his wife really hated because it wasn't exactly a nice piece of furniture. It was a Juno 60 (a Roland synthesizer). You had a few basic sounds, and then you had to use little sliders to make up your own. I borrowed it and made up this one great sound and wrote 'Say It with Love' that night. It really inspired me. Then he wanted it back, and all of a sudden this old keyboard became really important."

The group fired keyboardist Patrick Moraz after completing only a few tracks for the album. "His touring contributions were great," Hayward said. "He always had much greater plans outside the band, and I respect him for that." ■

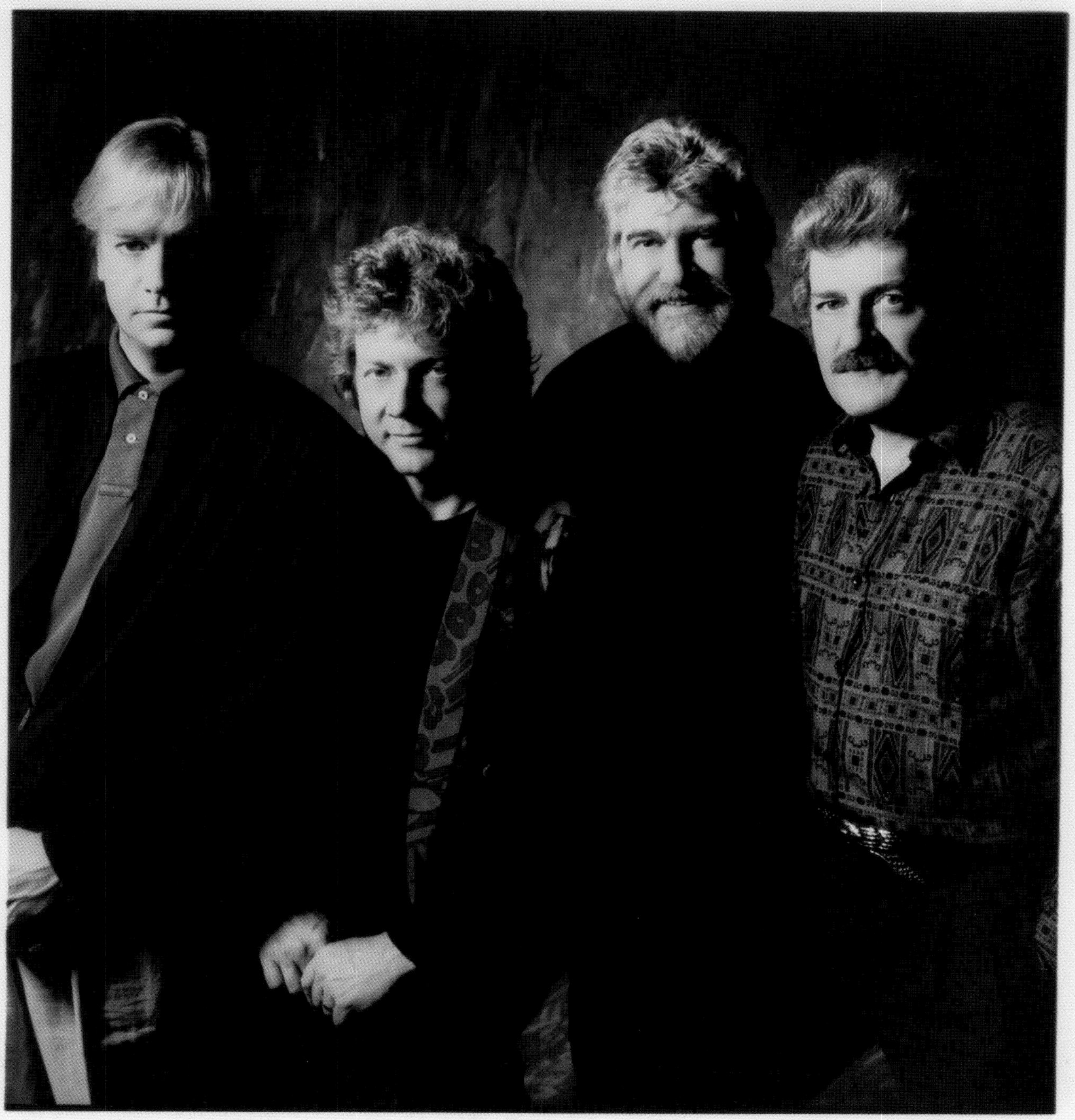

MNGT: TOM HUELETT AND ASSOC.

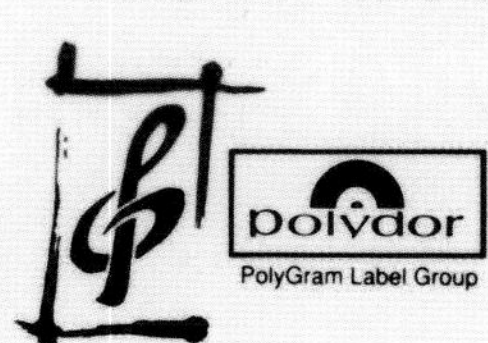

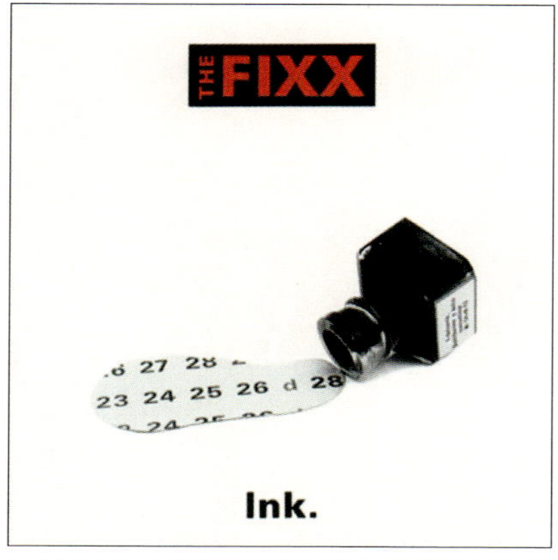

Billboard 200: *Ink* (#111)
Billboard Hot 100: "How Much Is Enough?" (#35)

The Fixx, no longer topping the charts, reemerged with *Ink* following a three-year recording interlude.

OVER A decade-long career, the Fixx's hit singles had confronted the issues of peace ("Stand or Fall"), materialism ("Saved by Zero") and ecology ("Driven On"). "How Much Is Enough?" took a stand against personal greed. Vocalist Cy Curnin overheard the line "Good enough's not good enough" amid cocktail-party chatter.

"I thought, 'Geez, perfectionism is poisoning this guy if he can never be satisfied,'" Curnin explained. "In one sense, always wanting more is good, but you can miss the moment by planning the future."

Curnin spoke from recent personal experience. The cut "Driven Out," from the Fixx's 1988 *Calm Animals* album, had produced the British quartet's first No. 1 song on *Billboard*'s Album Rock Tracks chart, but the album sold disappointingly. Curnin compared the showing to "a cold slap 'round the face—it showed us we can't assume there's always going to be a big audience for us to rely on."

The Fixx learned to enjoy life more by surviving on very little, including cutting back touring expenses.

"*Calm Animals* was an all-time low for the band commercially, but it was an all-time high for realizing we still wanted to do it," Curnin said. "It seems to match the way we should be doing things anyway today. You can waste so much just by getting used to things."

The Fixx resumed recording with *Ink*, an album that marked the first time the band had collaborated with outside songwriter Scott Cutler, who wrote and co-produced "How Much Is Enough?," a Top 10 single on the modern rock charts.

"He's a young guy with a lot of energy," Curnin noted. "It was interesting to work with someone who has known about the band for so long without actually being a part of it. To sit down with a third party and justify the way I work gave me a new way of looking at things."

A more personal approach to the words transpired. "In the early days, there was this naïve feeling of being on some sort of a crusade. But it all becomes rather impersonal after that. We're all surrounded with kids now—I've got two—and I think we're turning into softies." ■

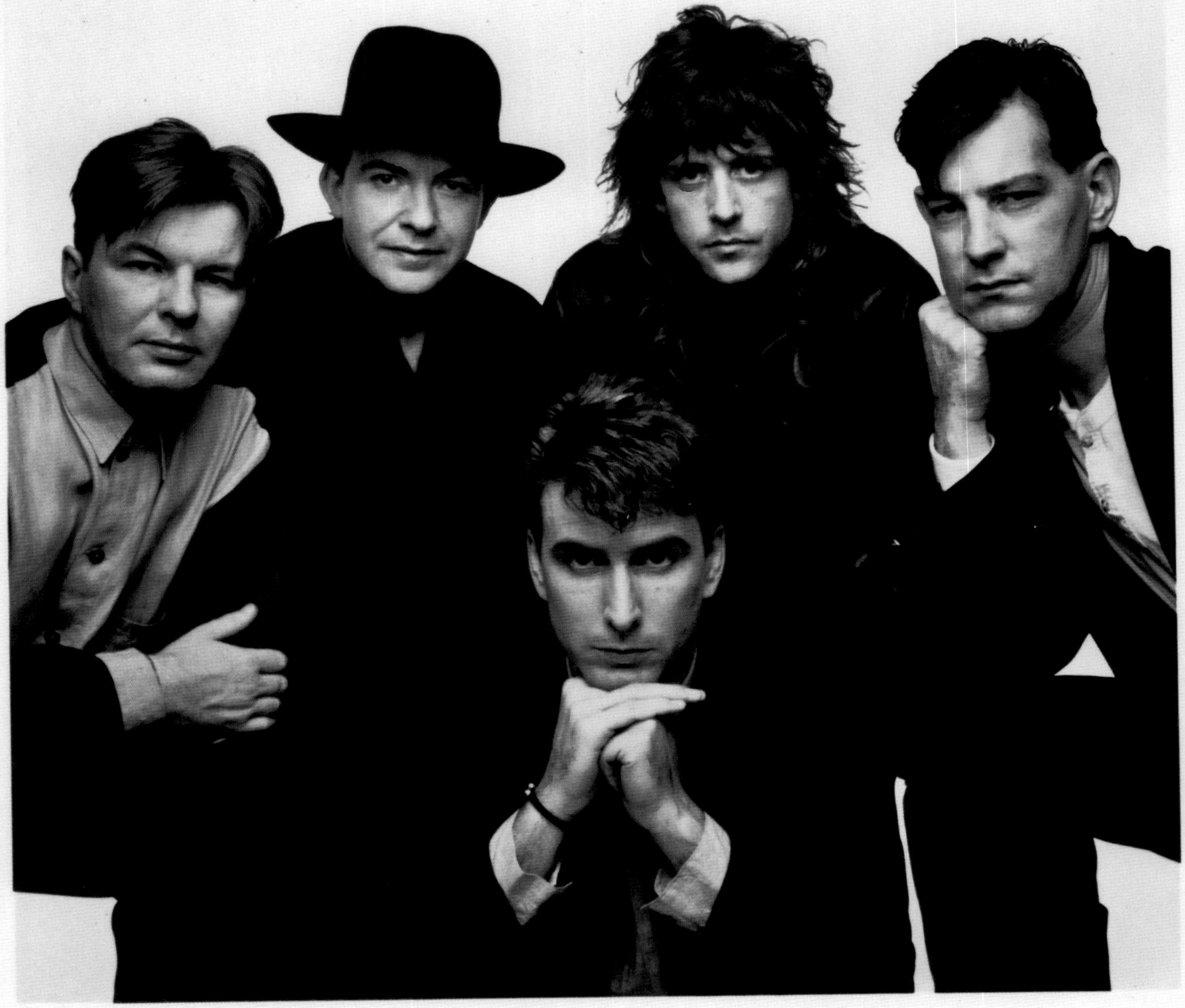

Photo credit Steve Rapport

ADAM WOODS DAN K. BROWN CY CURNIN JAMIE WEST-ORAM RUPERT GREENALL

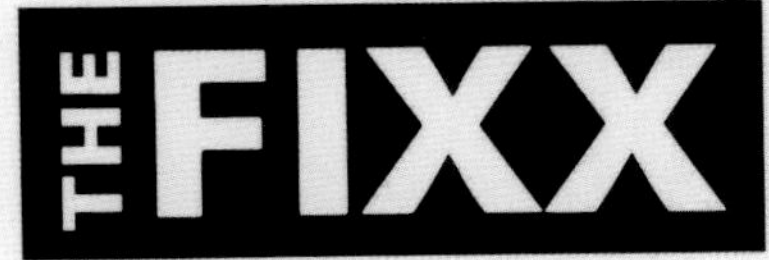

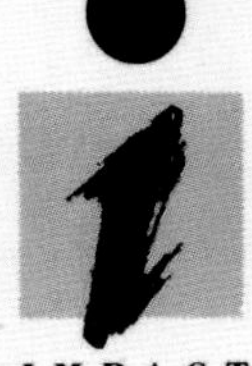

IMPACT

2/91

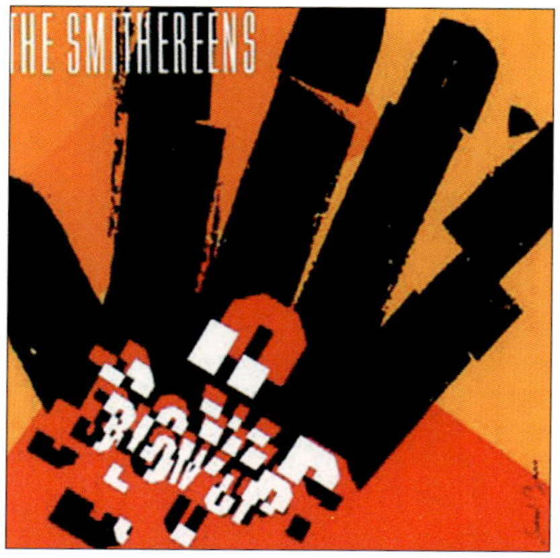

The Smithereens added striking strings to the pop-rock ballad "Too Much Passion" for a Top 40 single.

Billboard 200: *Blow Up* (#120)
Billboard Hot 100: "Too Much Passion" (#37)

IN THE back half of the Eighties, the Smithereens drew media attention and scored radio hits with catchy Sixties-influenced power-pop.

"But I used to be a metalhead, even before the music was known as metal," singer, songwriter and rhythm guitarist Pat DiNizio said. "In the early Seventies, I was playing guitar in power trios doing songs by Uriah Heep and Budgie—that was the easiest stuff to play as a teenager. Then I went through a jazz fusion period—at one point I was taking drum lessons from Tony Williams. But one night I took a bus into New York City and got stuck at a record store in the Brill Building, where the legendary songwriters from the Fifties and Sixties were based. I found the first Buddy Holly album—it was expensive, but something told me I had to buy it. I took it home, and it was magical for me. It brought everything back into focus, things like melody and simplicity of song structure. It choked me up, and I realized that was the direction I wanted to pursue as a writer. It led me to start listening to my old Beatles, Stones and Beach Boys records again. I left the family business at age 24—everybody thought I was insane to join a rock 'n' roll band."

DiNizio met guitarist Jim Babjak, Dennis Diken (drums) and Mike Mesaros (bass) through a classified ad in a local music paper. The other three had been elementary-school friends and Kinks freaks, and the band members became known as pop culture historians and record collectors. DiNizio had a knack for crafting tight three-minute guitar-driven songs, a meeting of Sixties British Invasion tunefulness and garage-rock crunch. The Smithereens gained publicity with a string of hits, including the brooding "Blood and Roses," "Only a Memory" and the classic "A Girl Like You"—intelligent, passionate work that DiNizio described as the crisp in-your-face sound of AC/DC guitars meets the melodic sense of the Beatles.

The exuberant, edgy sound on *Blow Up*, the group's fourth album, was aggressive and focused. "Too Much Passion" became the New Jersey rockers' second Top 40 smash.

"My strength is songs that are comprised of three chords and a melody," DiNizio said. "I'm fortunate that I have my own unique voice. When people hear it on the radio, they do know that it's me. That's a blessing, something that you're born with." ■

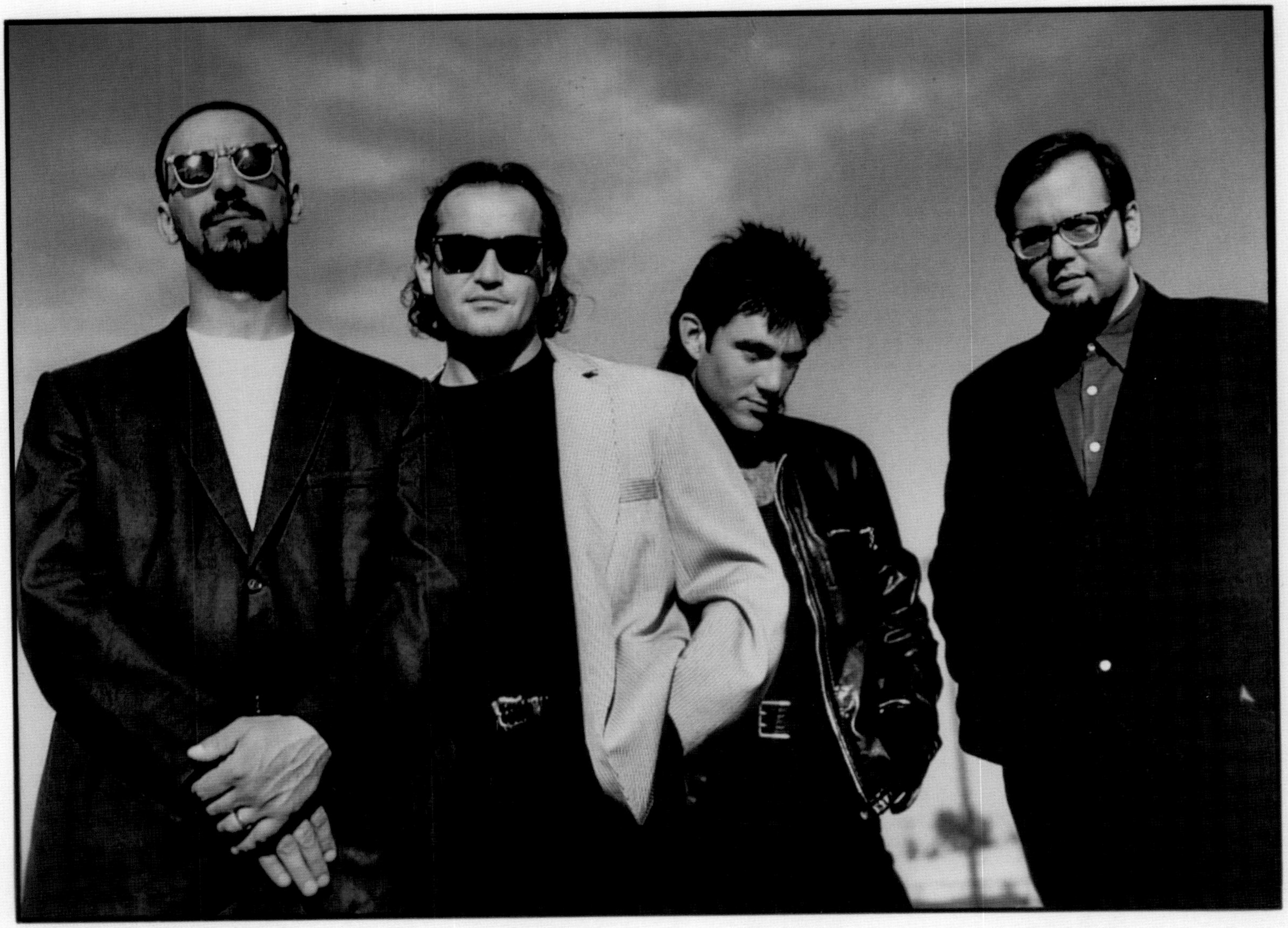

PHOTO: DEWEY NICKS / 1991

Pat DiNizio Jim Babjak Mike Mesaros Dennis Diken

THE SMITHEREENS

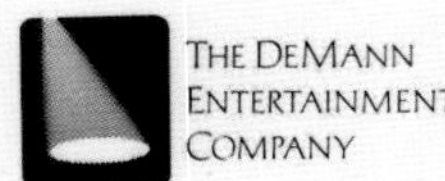

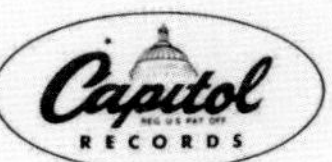

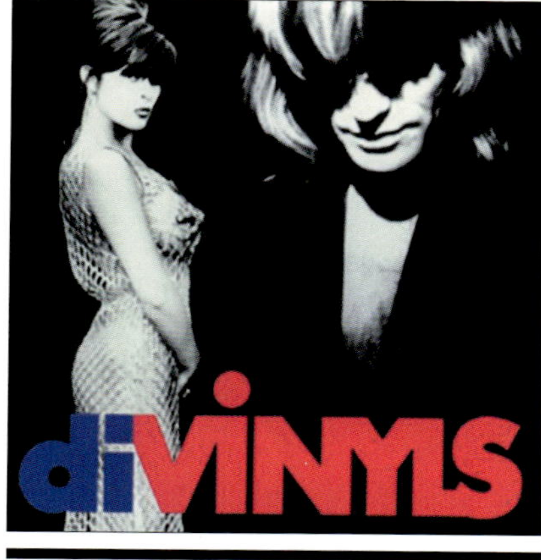

"I Touch Myself," a melodic paean to self-gratification, thrust Divinyls from obscurity to pop stardom.

Billboard 200: *Divinyls* (#15)
Billboard Hot 100: "I Touch Myself" (#4)

DIVINYLS FORMED in Australia in 1981 when guitarist Mark McEntee was captivated by singer Christina Amphlett's choir singing at a religious concert. *Desperate*, the debut album released in 1983, exotically coupled Amphlett's unusual vocal mannerisms with a rowdy pop sound. The chanteuse added a naughty, teasing touch by shoehorning herself into short schoolgirl's plaid dresses and torn stockings. "I am just a red brassiere/To all the boys in town," she sang with a possessed demeanor.

Her affinity for coquettish uniforms became something of a trademark on 1985's *What a Life!*, which spawned the pop hit, "Pleasure and Pain," written by producer Mike Chapman and preeminent rock songstress Holly Knight. Reduced to the songwriting team of Amphlett and McEntee, Divinyls followed with the *Temperamental* album in 1988.

But the duo had garnered only a small cult of fans. A year later, Divinyls were without a record contract.

"However, instead of being depressed, we decided to have fun," Amphlett explained.

She and McEntee went to Paris and, inspired by the city's red-light district, wrote at least half of the *Divinyls* album, including "I Touch Myself" (a collaboration with songwriters Tom Kelly and Billy Steinberg). The in-your-face wild child had become a glamourous adult temptress. On *Divinyls*, Amphlett appeared all in black, from her fishnet hose to her brassiere. Critics lauded her distinctive, seductive, carnal growl.

It helped make "I Touch Myself" a Top 10 hit in America. But Divinyls' new success was mostly due to the sexual implications of the song, bolstered by a steamy video that sparked controversy. The clip was banned in Australia (which only served to draw more attention to the group—the song was the first No. 1 hit they'd had in their homeland) and was heavily edited before being aired on Britain's popular TV chart show *Top of the Pops*.

"We have a hit, and all of a sudden the Divinyls are about sex. But the Divinyls have always been about that," Amphlett said. "It's a fun song, a love song. I can't remember being calculated about writing it. It's really strange in Australia. It would be played all day on the radio, but not on the TV. And when we did *Top of the Pops* in person, the announcer wouldn't even say the name of the song." ■

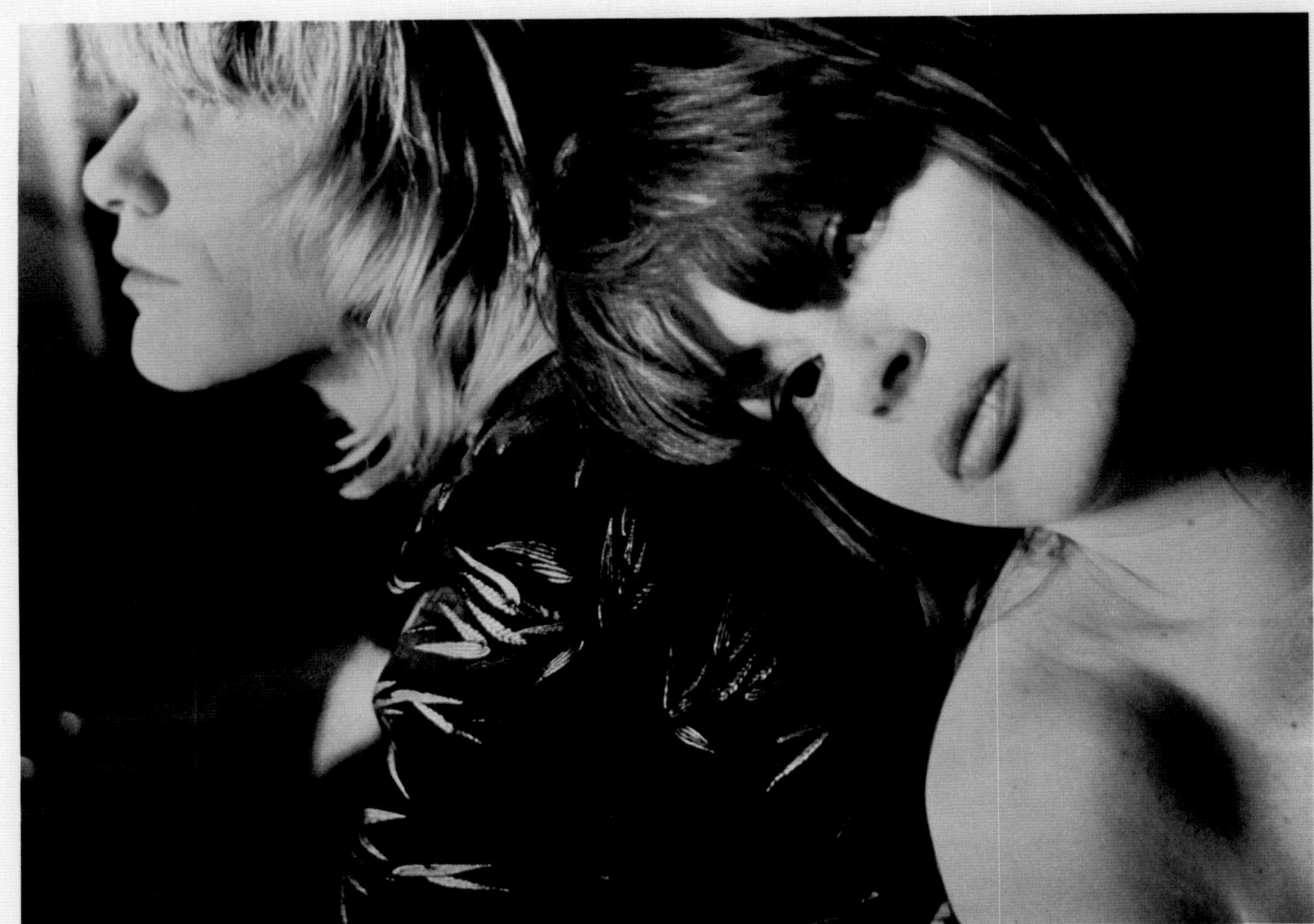

PHOTO: MELANIE NISSEN 0491

divinyls

Virgin

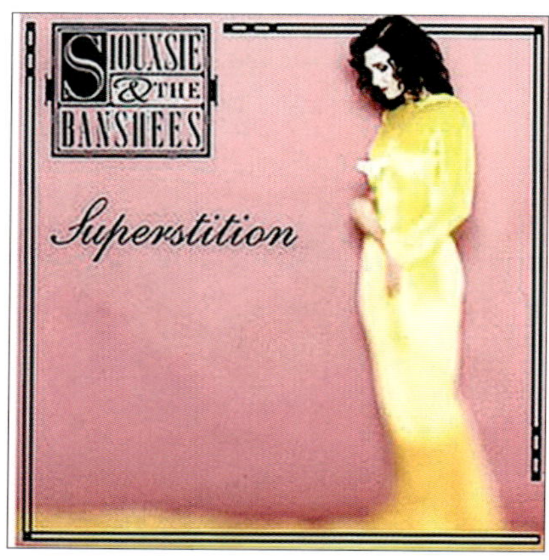

Siouxsie & the Banshees' *Superstition* album spawned the band's first US Top 40 hit, "Kiss Them for Me."

Billboard 200: *Superstition* (#65)
Billboard Hot 100: "Kiss Them for Me" (#23)

SIOUXSIE & THE Banshees made an uncertain debut at the height of the British punk era. Fifteen years later, they were among the scene's few survivors, and their musical mysticism reaped mainstream success in the US. Siouxsie Sioux (née Susan Dallion) and her crew toured in the second-to-the-top slot in the inaugural Lollapalooza festival, the summer's most successful concert bill. From the *Superstition* album, the single, "Kiss Them for Me," topped *Billboard*'s Modern Rock Tracks chart and gave the band a left-field Top 40 hit.

"Now we spend more time in Los Angeles than in England—for Christmas we decorated a rubber tree with garlands," drummer Budgie said. "But when you've been together as long as we have, you have to sort yourself out. It's like having a well-worn woolly jumper—lots of snags you've got to get rid of, you have to pull the belt and make it fit properly. The downside is the preconception of what we are. When we started, naturally we didn't think we'd have been around this long."

In 1976, Siouxsie & the Banshees were the embodiment of the punk rock ethos—their public beginning was a London punk festival, stumbling through a 20-minute-plus free-form version of "The Lord's Prayer" (with the then unknown Sid Vicious on drums) and stopping only after they'd gotten bored. They admittedly intended to annoy the crowd and be thrown offstage.

"But now we're not carrying any flags or banners for that period," Budgie said. "People ask, 'Was it really exciting?' and whatever you say won't change the picture in their minds. It was a whole different way of life, fending for yourself and what you wanted to do."

For most of the Eighties, Siouxsie & the Banshees influenced the gothic rock scene with a succession of albums. With her deathly white makeup, teased jet-black hair and Cleopatra-meets-the-Addams-Family demeanor, Sioux was a distant, mysterious performer who never seemed interested in her audience. However, after the band's success with 1988's "Peek-a-Boo"—an off-kilter cabaret techno-dance single from the *Peepshow* album that charted in America—Sioux thawed her icy veneer, shed her punk priestess garb and become more extroverted.

"It's a confidence thing, being able to reveal sides of yourself," Sioux said. "There's an undercurrent of black humor going on in the writing that people miss—a line like 'Are you still dying, darling?' treats a serious subject that way."

"And we sidestepped the album-tour treadmill by joining up with Lollapalooza," Budgie noted. "When you get seven bands hanging out, you realize that it's not just you that's against the world on tour. We're having fun doing it because we're still doing it." ■

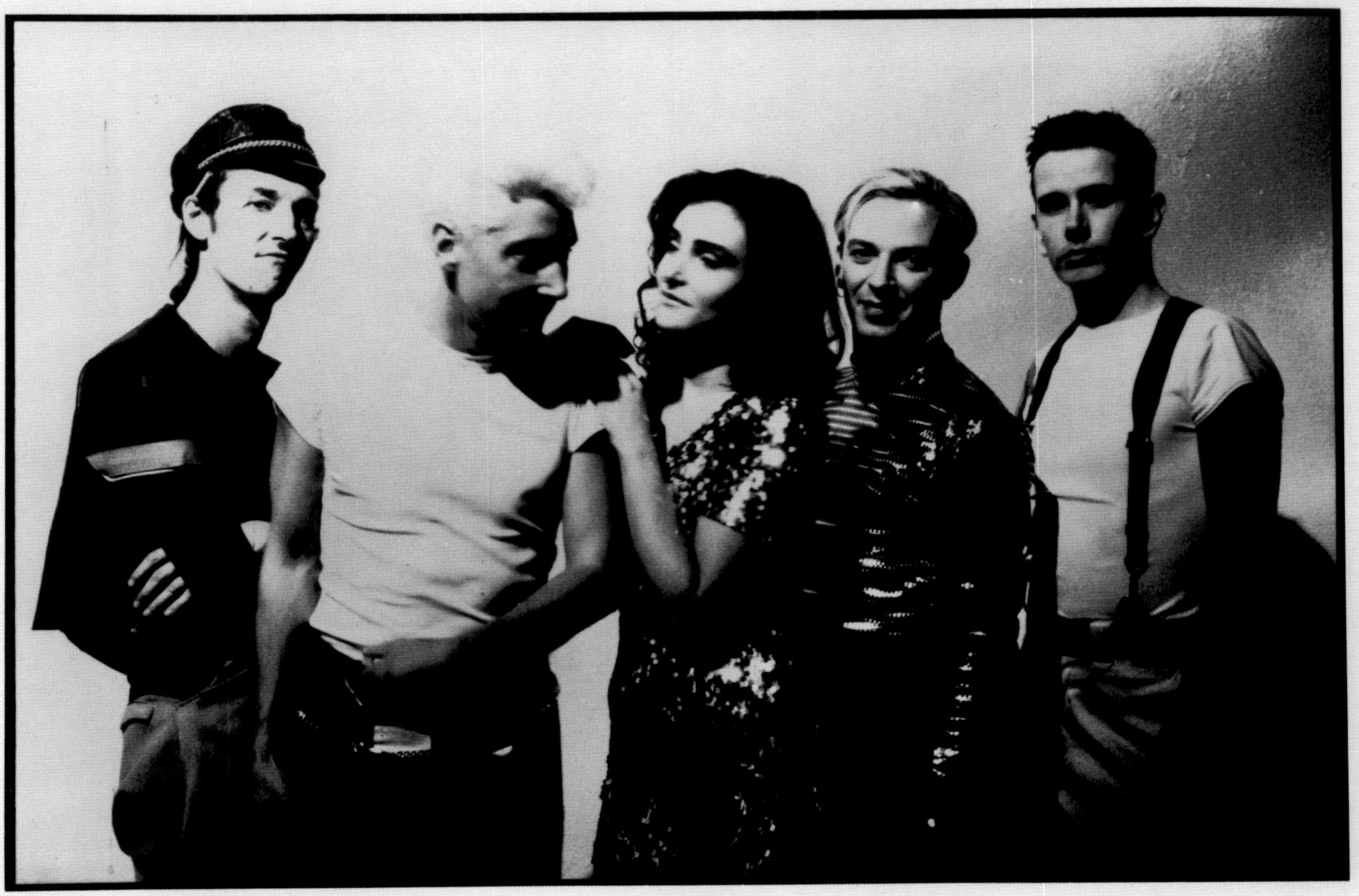

Jon Klein Budgie Siouxsie Sioux Steven Severin Martin McCarrick

Photo Credit: Donna Francesca

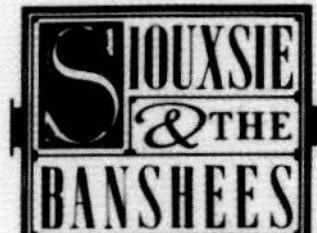

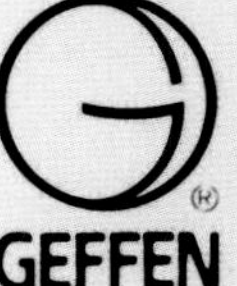

© 1991 The David Geffen Company/Permission to reproduce limited to editorial uses in newspapers and other regularly published periodicals and television news programming.

Toad the Wet Sprocket achieved fame on the strength of the hits, "All I Want" and "Walk on the Ocean."

Billboard 200: *Fear* (#49)
Billboard Hot 100: "All I Want" (#15);
"Walk on the Ocean" (#18)

FETTERED BY comparisons to R.E.M., Toad the Wet Sprocket still had a leg up on its peers. The childhood friends from Santa Monica, California—singer Glen Phillips, guitarist Todd Nichols, bassist Dean Dinning and drummer Randy Guss—had taken their band's name from an old Monty Python skit and recorded two albums on their own. They self-produced their debut, 1989's *Bread & Circus*, in a living room for $650, and it turned heads at major labels. The members since had become better players, and *Fear*, Toad's third album, was the first not to rely on parental loans.

"Dealing with so little money on the first two records, we just played live takes like it was a club," Dinning said. "This time we could do overdubbing, different tracking on some things. It proved we could make a polished record."

Toad moved up to the big league with the melodic songs on *Fear*. The multilayered instrumentation that blended folk and rock, combined with the mid-tempo, understated hooks and Phillips' warm, compelling voice, made the album a smash. Radio and MTV constantly played the breakthrough single "All I Want" and the plaintive ballad "Walk on the Ocean," and the band logged many miles on the road. Toad's appeal was potentially universal—the absorbing, thoughtful lyrics appealed to a new college-aged generation—but the commercial breakthrough came as a surprise.

"That's been a fluky thing," Guss said. "Glen's platinum record is in his bedroom under a pile of dirty sheets. Our intent is to be independent of radio and MTV and the press. So we tour, and that's a different story." ■

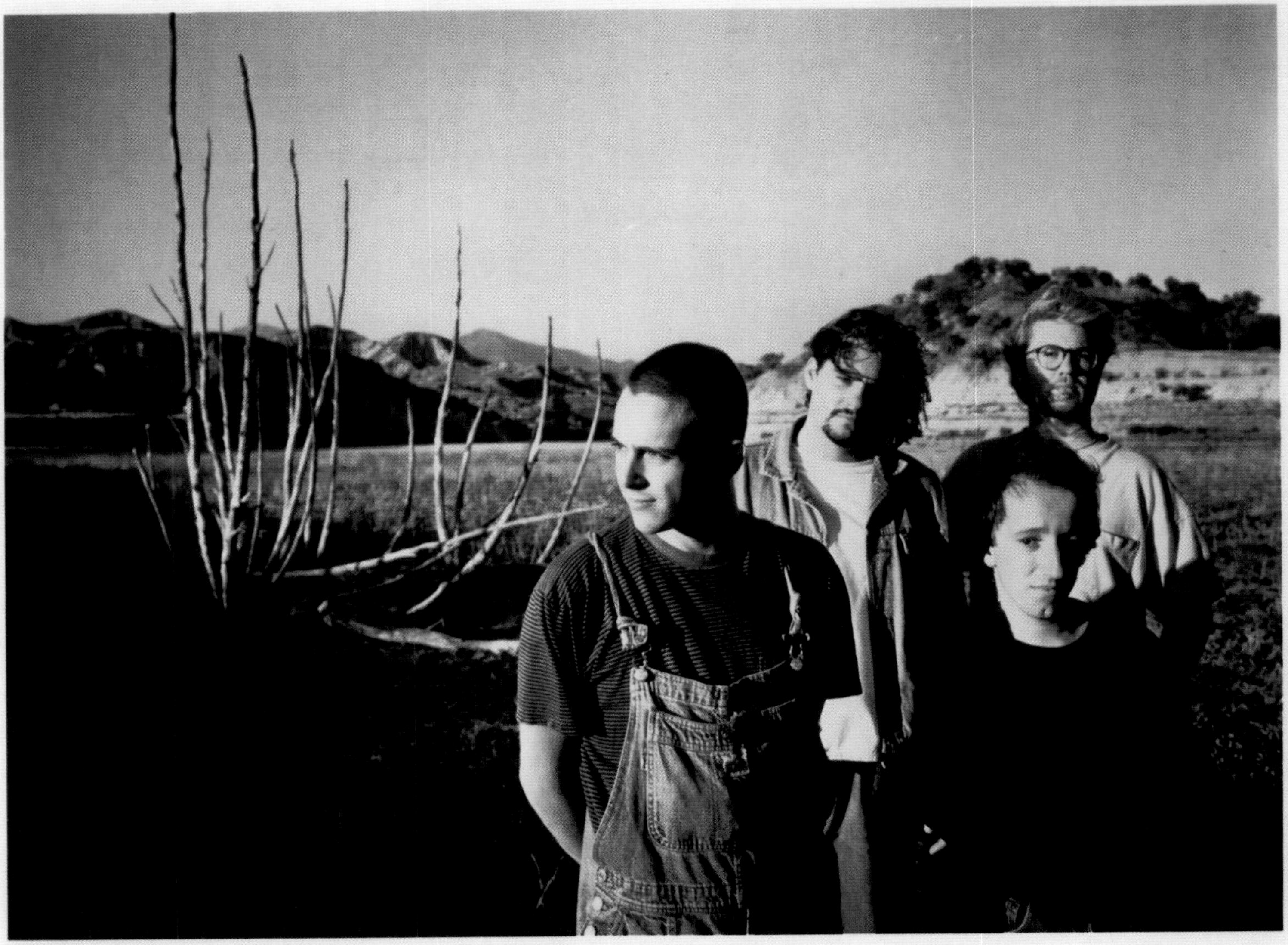

Left to Right: Glen Phillips, Todd Nichols, Randy Guss, Dean Dinning

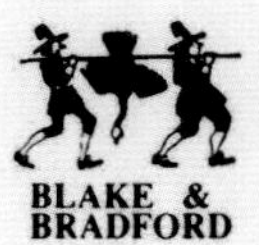

toad the wet sprocket

Columbia
9108

Photo Credit: Dana Tynan

© 1991 Sony Music. Permission to reproduce this photography is limited to editorial uses in regular issues of newspapers and other regularly published periodicals and television news programming.

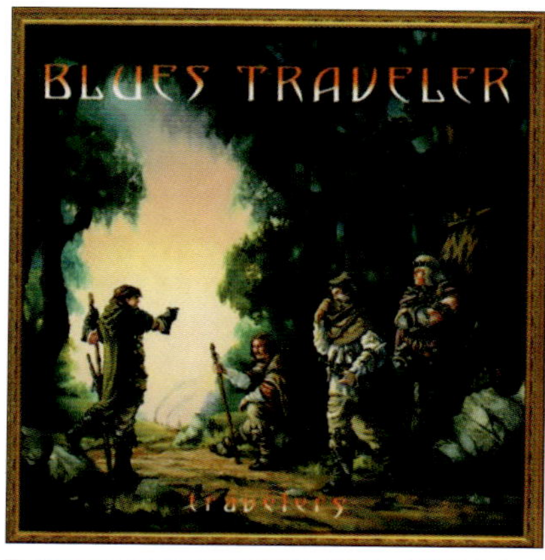

Harp player John Popper's bursts of piercingly high notes sustained Blues Traveler's *Travelers and Thieves.*

Billboard 200: *Travelers and Thieves* (#125)

FOR A generation weaned on MTV, Blues Traveler represented the rebirth of live music as communion rather than commodity.

"It's such a pain in the ass to make records, or even videos. We're musicians, not actors," frontman John Popper explained. "The live show is our thing—we really believe in improvising and jamming. Our fans have come to expect us to compose on stage. In a way, it's like we're going to sleep. We shut off what we're thinking about and go on autopilot."

Blues Traveler was a "blues band" of sorts, but all kinds of extended Sixties rock styles—psychedelia, jazz-rock, hard-rock—found their way into the hard-blowing young group's physical, hypnotic sets. Friends since high school in New Jersey, Popper and drummer Brendan Hill met guitarist Chan Kinchla in 1986 and bassist Bobby Sheehan a year later. The group got started playing at keg parties and took the name Blues Traveler (after Gozer the Traveler, the demon in the movie *Ghostbusters*). Relocating in New York, Blues Traveler became one of the city's most popular club bands by packing NYC's Wetlands every week for a year.

Impresario Bill Graham's high-powered management company "discovered" the group at a benefit concert. Popper had fit his harmonica prowess into the modern framework of rock and blues; one major label executive described Blues Traveler as "Charlie Parker on harmonica fronting the Meters." Blues Traveler released a self-titled debut album in 1990, and the tireless band followed it a year later with *Travelers and Thieves*. Produced by Jim Gaines (noted for his work with Stevie Ray Vaughan and Huey Lewis & the News), the band's sophomore effort was tighter and more controlled than its live jams. "All in the Groove" and "Mountain Cry," featuring a guest appearance by Gregg Allman on keyboards and backing vocals, got airplay on college radio stations.

But no studio recording could fully convey Blues Traveler's concert presence. Followers of the Grateful Dead had taken Blues Traveler to heart. The band members didn't agree with the comparisons musically, but similarities existed—the segues between songs, the extended jams and three-hour shows.

"Deadheads like the kind of music that we play—free-form pelvic rock 'n' roll that makes you groove," Sheehan explained.

"The main thing we learned from the Dead is to be original," the portly Popper added. "We don't want to lose fans because of the stereotype. We're not the next Grateful Dead, we're the first Blues Traveler. Who knows what we'll do? We may all end up dead in a hotel room from a gunfight." ■

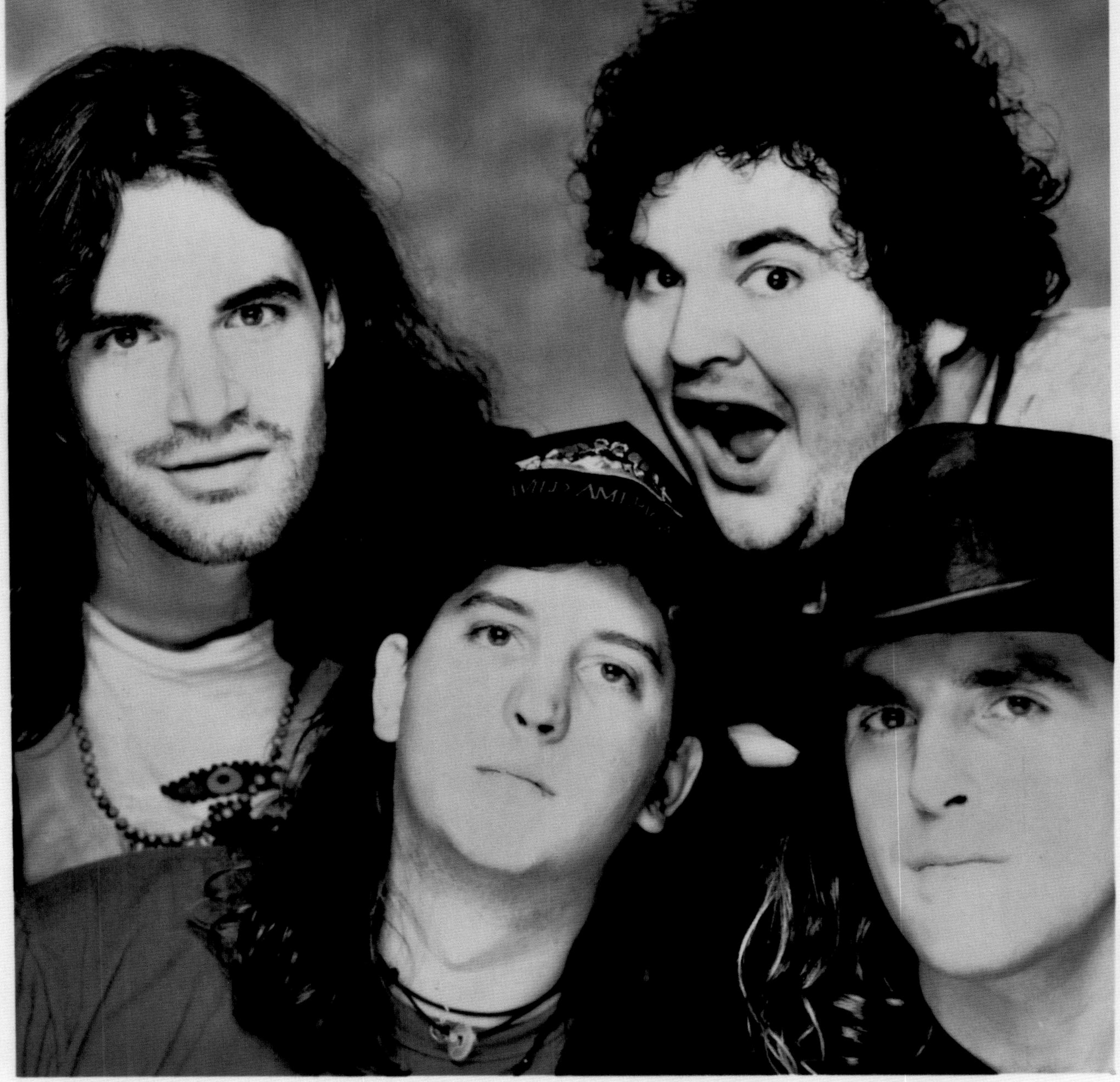

PHOTO: CHRIS CASTLE

CHAN KINCHLA BOBBY SHEEHAN JOHN POPPER BRENDAN HILL

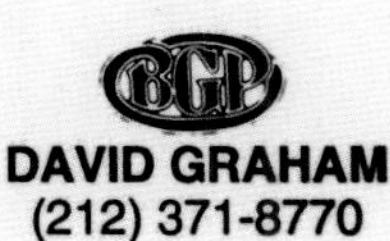

DAVID GRAHAM
(212) 371-8770

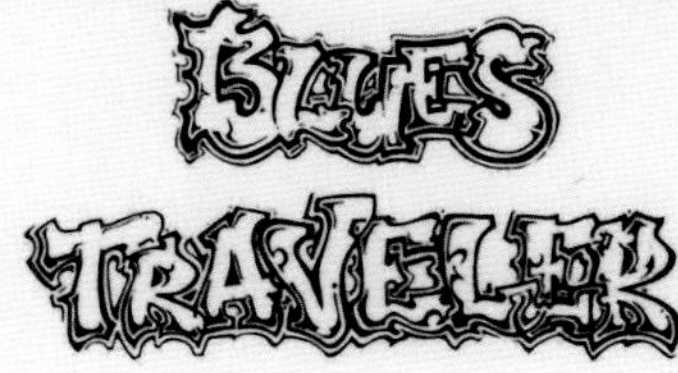

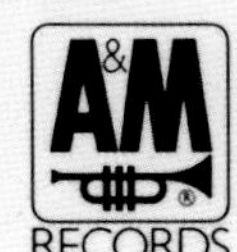

Spin Doctors grew up on the road and produced *Pocket Full of Kryptonite*, the album that refused to die.

Billboard 200: Pocket Full of Kryptonite (#3)
Billboard Hot 100: "Little Miss Can't Be Wrong" (#17); "Two Princes" (#7); "Jimmy Olsen's Blues" (#78)

SPIN DOCTORS played their first gig at a frat party in the basement of the Delta Phi house at Columbia University in 1988. The New York quartet then jammed four to six nights every week, gaining a crazed following in the Northeast. Singer Chris Barron's loony, neo-hippie charm and guitarist Eric Schenkman's solos powered the band's brand of bluesy rock, while bassist Mark White and drummer Aaron Comess comprised a funk-busting rhythm section.

"That campus and bar scene made the clay, and maybe we're just shaping it," Barron surmised.

Spin Doctors made their recording debut with *Up for Grabs...Live*, a six-track EP recorded at a Lower Manhattan spawning ground called Wetlands Preserve (aka "the Wetlands"). Both Spin Doctors and their "soul brothers," Blues Traveler, incubated at the club.

In August 1991, Spin Doctors issued *Pocket Full of Kryptonite*, a full-length album.

As radio exposure and rotation on MTV had become the paths to the top of the charts, Spin Doctors managed to do it the old-fashioned way—by tirelessly touring. The band's record company initially overlooked the *Kryptonite* release, considering the group road dogs like Blues Traveler (whose harmonica man, John Popper, appeared on three tracks).

But Spin Doctors just kept doing their job. Live, the band always gave the crowd its money's worth.

"Just by going through that, we've cemented our interpersonal relationships," Schenkman said. "For us, the brotherhood of the band and the crew is reactive to the music. We've learned a lot about how to live together and not be adversely affected by the traveling conditions. You get through all the basic problems that usually break people up, and then you grow into the next level."

It took over a year for Spin Doctors' infectious, concise singles—the kiss-off "Little Miss Can't Be Wrong" and "Two Princes"—to get going. Belatedly impressed by the band's fan base of young "Spinheads," the label went the distance, courting a network fronted by college and commercial DJs hip to the group's charm. "Little Miss Can't Be Wrong" and "Two Princes" eventually became Top 20 smashes, and *Pocket Full of Kryptonite* blossomed into a massive hit.

"I was taught at a pretty early age that music is a funny business," Schenkman said. "You can never be so self-centered. You don't know—you could be making all the money you'll ever make this year. As soon as I get some time, man, I'm just going to get me some land and a dog to put on it." ■

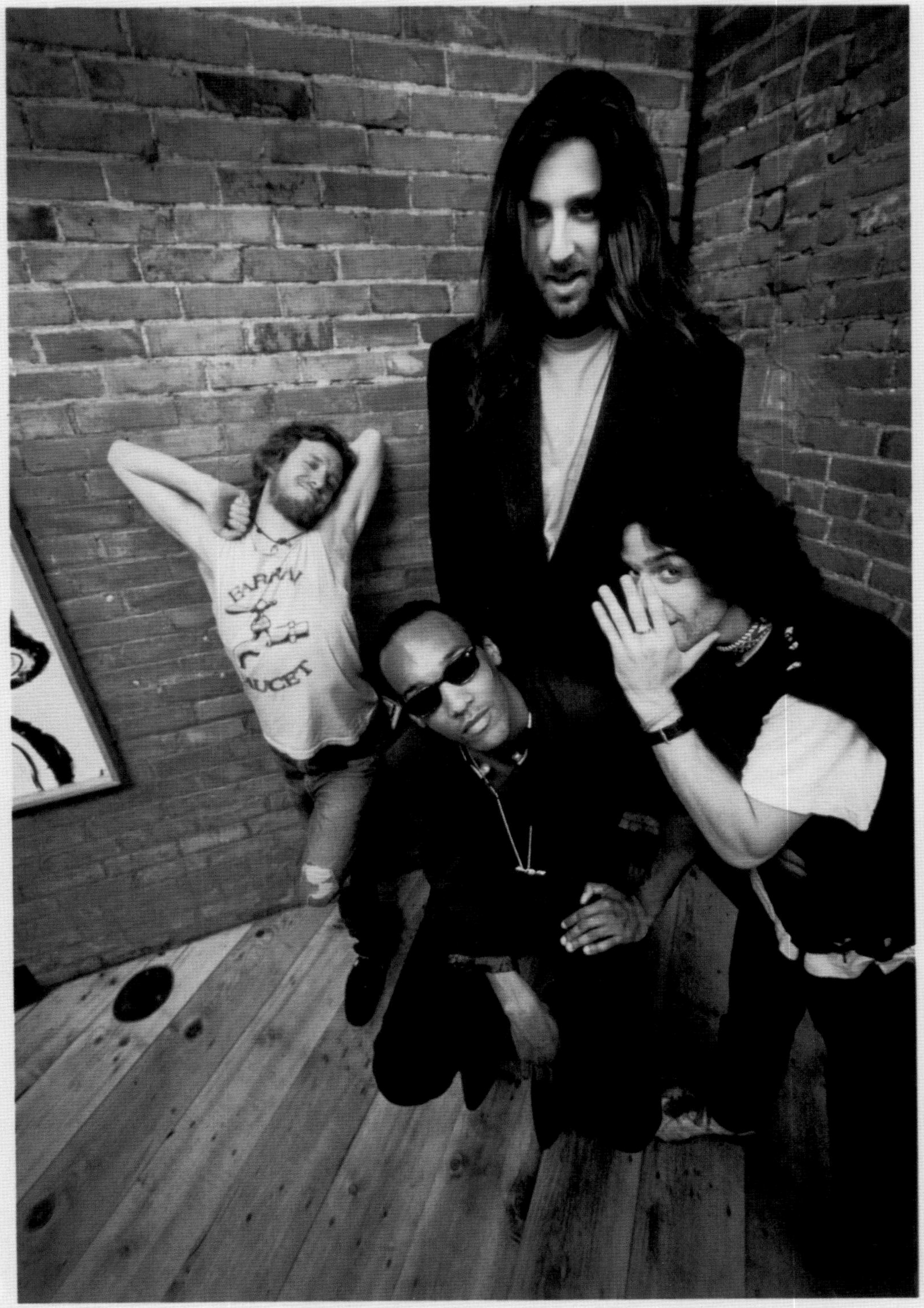

©1991 Sony Music Entertainment Inc.

PHOTO CREDIT: PAUL LaRAIA

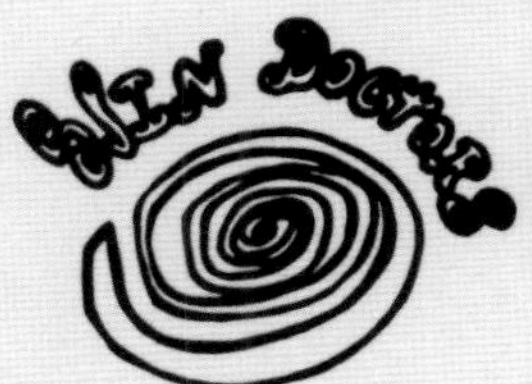

CLOCKWISE FROM LEFT: CHRISTOPHER BARRON (VOCALS), AARON COMESS (DRUMS), ERIC SCHENKMAN (GUITAR, BACKING VOCALS), MARK WHITE (BASS)

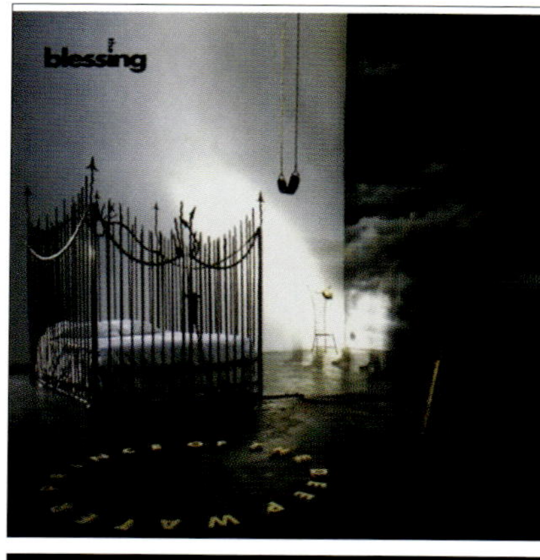

The Blessing arrived from England with a confident, fully realized collection of soulfully crafted songs.

LIKE, SAY, Dire Straits' debut, the Blessing's *Prince of the Deep Water* was intelligent, wide-ranging and forceful. The quartet mixed delta blues, reggae and a touch of gospel to express a dark, mysterious, languid look at tropical and Southern life. It seemed the equivalent of an F. Scott Fitzgerald novel put to music. William Topley, the Blessing's lead singer and primary writer, permeated his songs with wonder and emotion.

The highlight was "Delta Rain," a stirring duet with background vocalist Rebecca Price. Unleashing a rich, deep voice that rose directly from his soul, Topley was hailed as a modern-day Van Morrison, but his singing was lusher and more powerful—one of those hefty, R&B-influenced vocal styles that made a listener believe every word:

And through the gutters there will be water running wilder than the sea

And as the rain comes down a thousand circles fade like you and me.

A boarding school kid from England, Topley listened to the BBC and immersed himself in the values of American blues, Southern rock 'n' roll and soul. He'd turned his early infatuation into a career.

"I go back to the time I started listening to rock music, in the late Seventies—almost everything in Britain was in decline," Topley explained. "The one thing that wasn't was classic rock. Groups like the Who, the Rolling Stones and Led Zeppelin were on top of the world, the only successful things coming out of the country. And the more I looked at them, the more I realized that their music was paying tribute to the rock 'n' roll and black music of the Fifties and early Sixties. That goes back to the cultural exchange that happened during World War II, when close to a million US service personnel came over to Britain prior to the liberation of Europe, and they brought with them their music. The Sixties generation of classic rockers were brought up in an environment when all things American were held in great esteem."

The imposing Londoner with the deep, charismatic voice had called many parts of the globe home.

"I had a job singing in a bar in Spain when I was about 19," Topley recalled. "I did that for nearly a year, and it certainly lowered the tone of my voice. It was an intimate café where people were right in your face. There was a lot of smoke in the atmosphere (cough). But I always wanted to play low-down and dirty music."

According to Topley, 100,000 copies of the Blessing's *Prince of the Deep Water* were sold worldwide. But in America, the vital and engrossing record fared unremarkably. Topley's soulful baritone didn't quite fit in at a major record label, or on rock or alternative radio, or at MTV or VH1.

"Every Englishman who is into music wants to do tours of America," he said, "but very few people in America actually understand what the Blessing is trying to do." ■

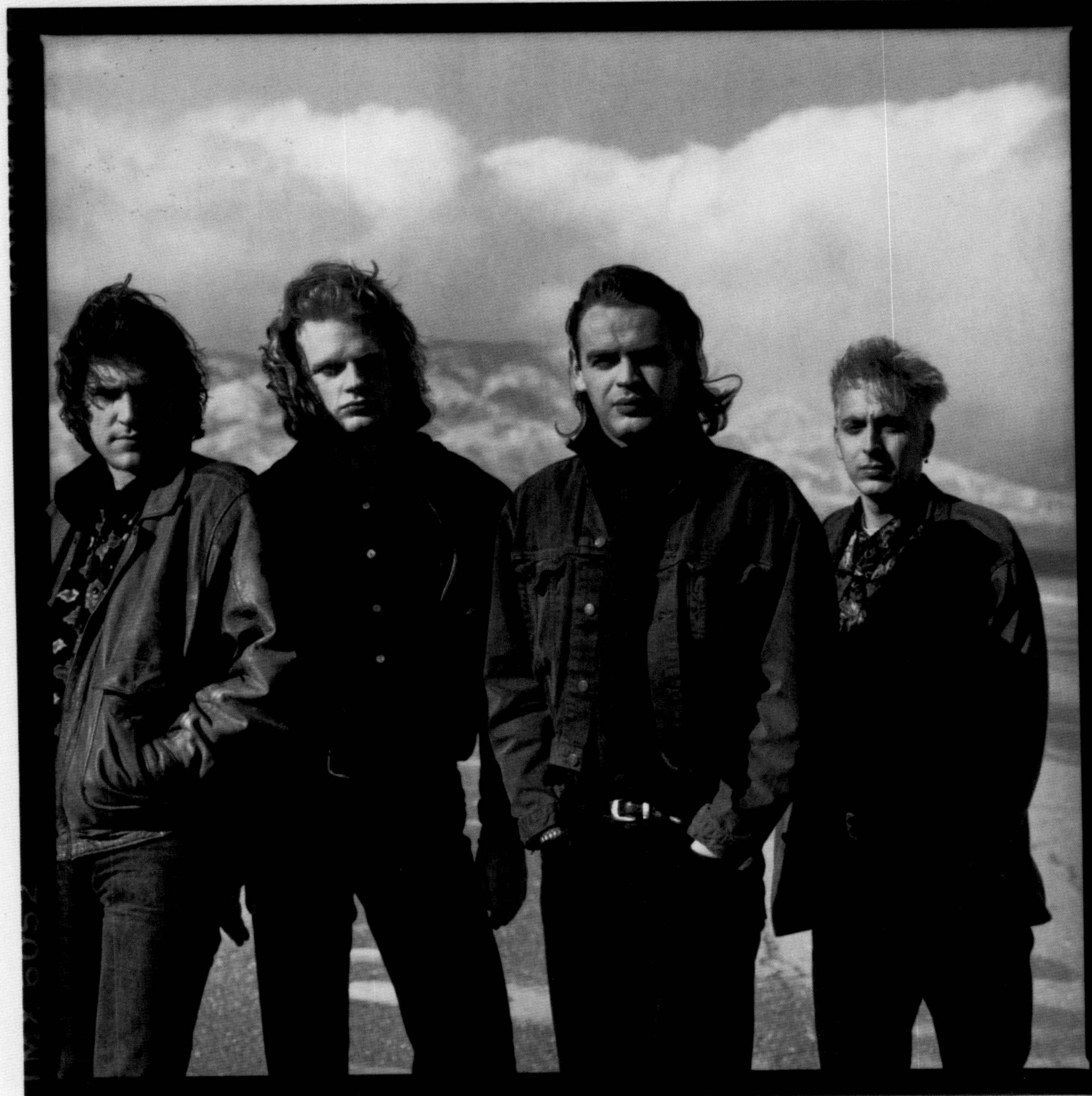

Photo credit: Peter Darley Miller

KEVIN HIME-KNOWLES LUKE BRIGHTY WILLIAM TOPLEY MIKE WESTERGAARD

the blessing

2/91

MCA

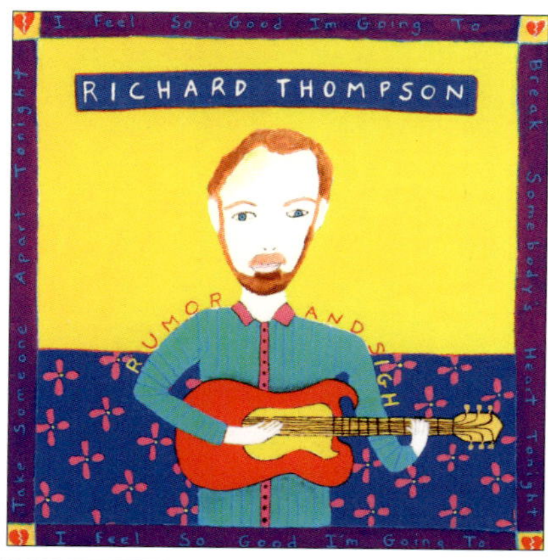

The estimable **Richard Thompson** grew his following with the folk ballad, "1952 Vincent Black Lightning."

AS A teen, Richard Thompson was a member of Fairport Convention, the seminal London-based group that used electric instruments to play traditional British folk music. He then became half of the husband-and-wife team of Richard & Linda Thompson—a pairing that produced six albums, two of which *Rolling Stone* ranked in 1987 among the best 100 of the last 20 years. Since 1984, he'd been a solo artist lauded for intelligent lyrics, loony wit and exceptional guitar playing, pursuing a career just out of range of the mainstream.

"But live performances are the best yardstick for me, and over the last decade they've improved," he said. "I don't aim my records at a broad market. I enjoy myself and try to be true to whatever ideals I have left."

Rumor and Sigh didn't change Thompson's status as a beloved cult figure, but it satisfied his old fans and beguiled some new ones. He worked once again with L.A. producer Mitchell Froom (Los Lobos, Crowded House). *Rumor and Sigh* didn't chart in the US, but the album greatly advanced Thompson's reputation—it was nominated for a Grammy, and "I Feel So Good" peaked at #15 on the *Billboard* Modern Rock Tracks chart. The album featured "1952 Vincent Black Lightning," which became one of his most acclaimed compositions.

Thompson remained humble. "'Career' is a funny word," he mused. "It's more of a 'careen,' I think, than 'career'—a downhill, out-of-control careen, not something actually calculated. There's life in the old dog. 'My monkey ain't dead, show ain't over,' as they say." ■

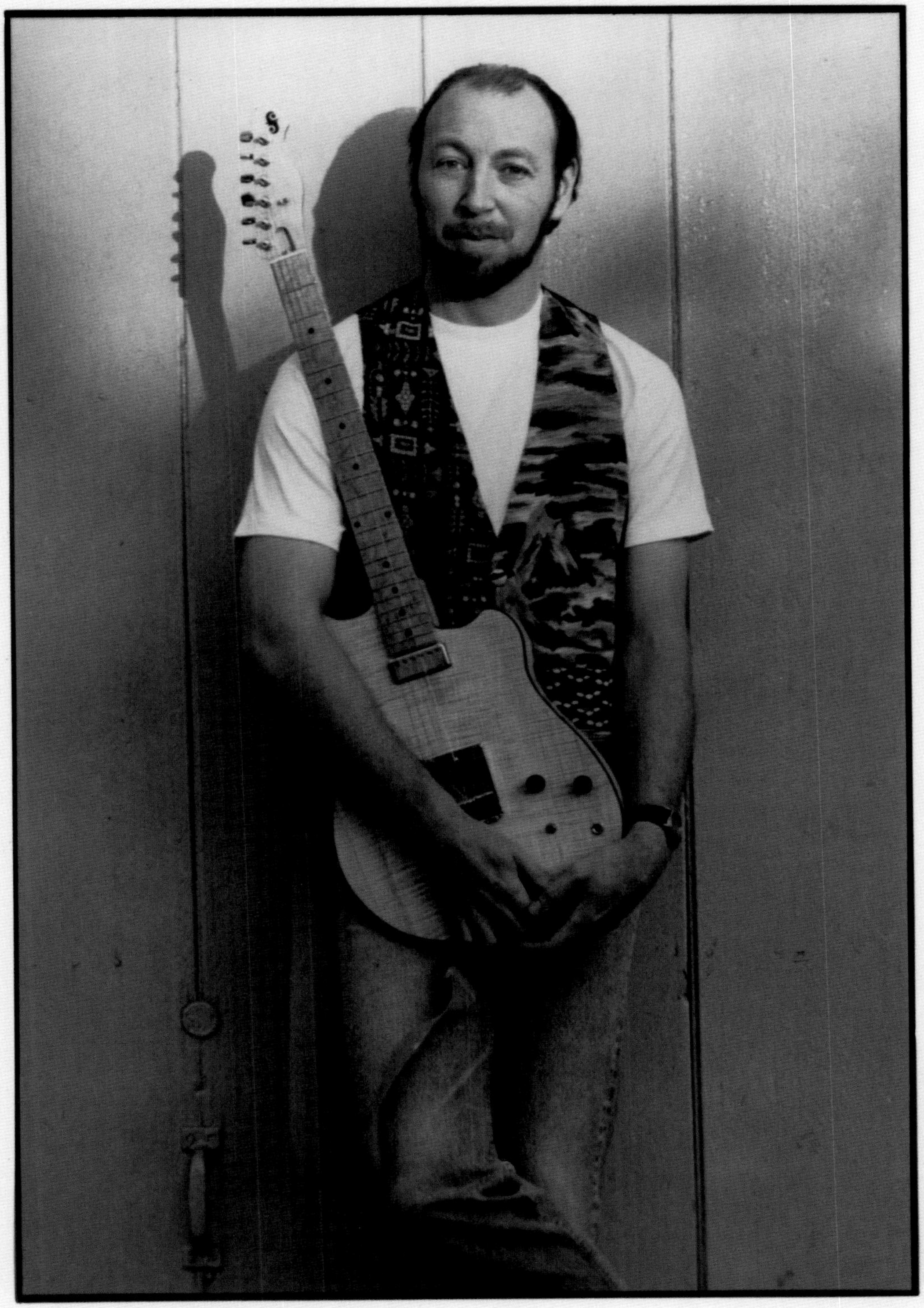

PHOTO: LAURA LEVINE / 1991

RICHARD THOMPSON

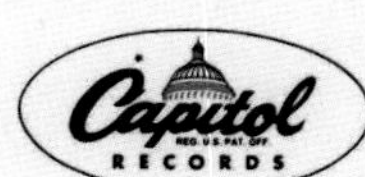

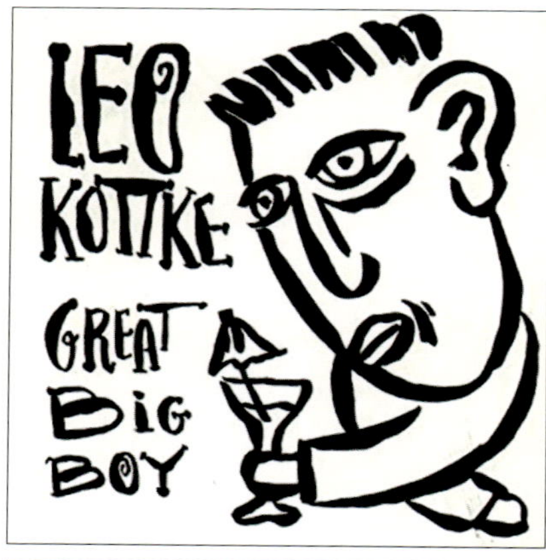

One of the world's most skilled acoustic guitar players, Leo Kottke released his first all-vocal offering.

OVER THE course of 20-plus albums, acoustic guitarist Leo Kottke had lived down his own putdown. With his first release, 1971's *6- and 12-String Guitar* (on John Fahey's Takoma label), the self-taught virtuoso from Minneapolis became a favorite among progressive radio jocks. But in his liner notes, Kottke wrote there were no vocals because his baritone sounded "like geese farts on a muggy day." He was trying to explain why the album was all instrumental, yet the quote had plagued him for most of his recording career.

"I'm the only guy I know who buried half his lifework at the beginning because I labeled myself," Kottke said. "More than any piece of music I've ever done, that really did stick."

Kottke had never had a platinum record or a hit single, but he'd crafted a reasonably successful string of albums by cultivating a loyal audience with his unified, distinctive playing style—an innovative, sonorous fingerpicking technique integrating classical, folk, jazz, country, ragtime and bottleneck forms.

He'd also learned to love his deep, resonant voice. *Great Big Boy* was his first release to feature vocals throughout, built around the slightly warped humor he communicated onstage.

During concerts, Kottke had always juxtaposed amazing musicianship with stream-of-consciousness patter involving long, often surreal narratives. "I've heard me going on and on like I do," he allowed, "which can hold together live. Yet it doesn't hold together on tape. It had been in the back of my mind for many years to do an entire vocal album, but I couldn't find the right way to get that dimension of what I do in performance onto a record, an overall character that rang true. I could write enough vocal tunes, but it sounded like a pile of tunes."

On 1990's *My Father's Face*, Kottke got his first clue with a different, personal, marvelously original track called "Jack Gets Up." His oblique, freeform lyric, grounded in esoteric wordplay and overlapping images, was incredible. From there he metamorphosed into an eccentric off-kilter singer-songwriter, displaying a repertoire of verbal storytelling in his endearing bemused baritone. *Great Big Boy*, produced by Steve Berlin of Los Lobos, got more radio airplay and media coverage than anything Kottke had done in 15 years.

"Something fell into place," Kottke said. "I found my voice." ■

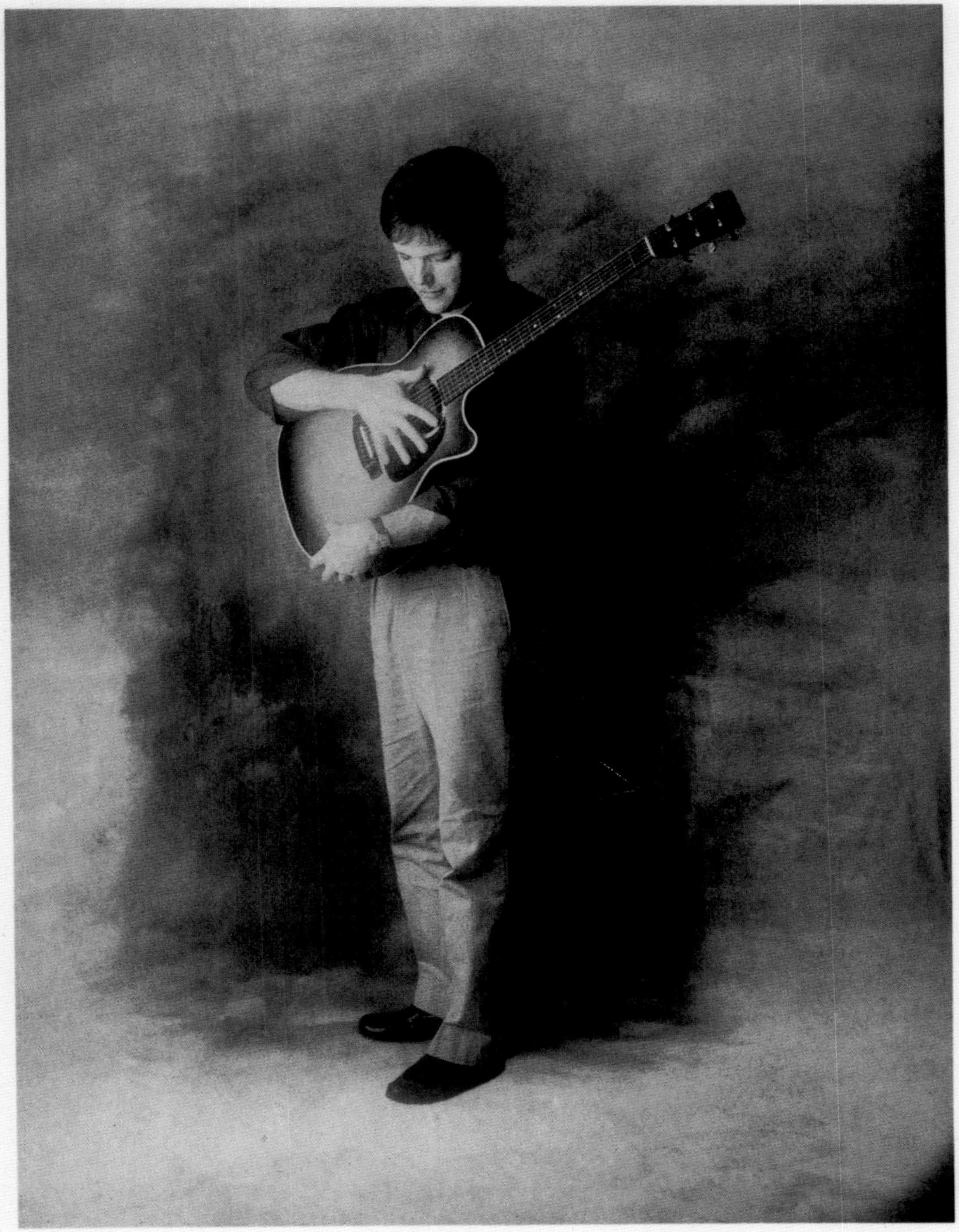

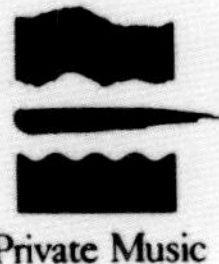

LEO KOTTKE

Morris, Bliesener
& ASSOCIATES
Phone: (303) 782-9292 Fax: (303) 758-3750
4155 East Jewell Ave. #412 Denver, CO 80222

Photo Credit: Kip Lott

Moving away from the sound of their earlier recordings, **BoDeans** took a pop sheen to *Black and White*.

Billboard 200: *Black and White* (#105)

BODEANS' THREE albums had generated critical success and a sizable Midwestern following. Characterized by a refreshing lack of pretention and the plaintive harmonies of Kurt Neumann and Sammy Llanas, the Wisconsin-based band achieved critical acclaim as harbingers of a roots-rock trend. In 1987, *Rolling Stone* readers voted BoDeans the Best New American Band

But the five-man group had yet to score a hit single. Prompted to try a new direction, the band recruited David Z., a more mainstream producer best known for his work with Prince. *Black and White* took a more pop approach than the previous releases, placing greater emphasis on synthesizers, drum machines and processed guitar tones.

But *Black and White* didn't perform any better than the first albums. "Black, White and Blood Red," the single, did not sell, but "Good Things" received noteworthy radio airplay and became a staple in the band's live set.

"The record company wanted us to work with someone, so we picked David. It was his project from start to finish," Llanas said. "We thought it'd be interesting, and he made a record that had a great big arena sound. It just wasn't what we would have done if we were at the helm." ■

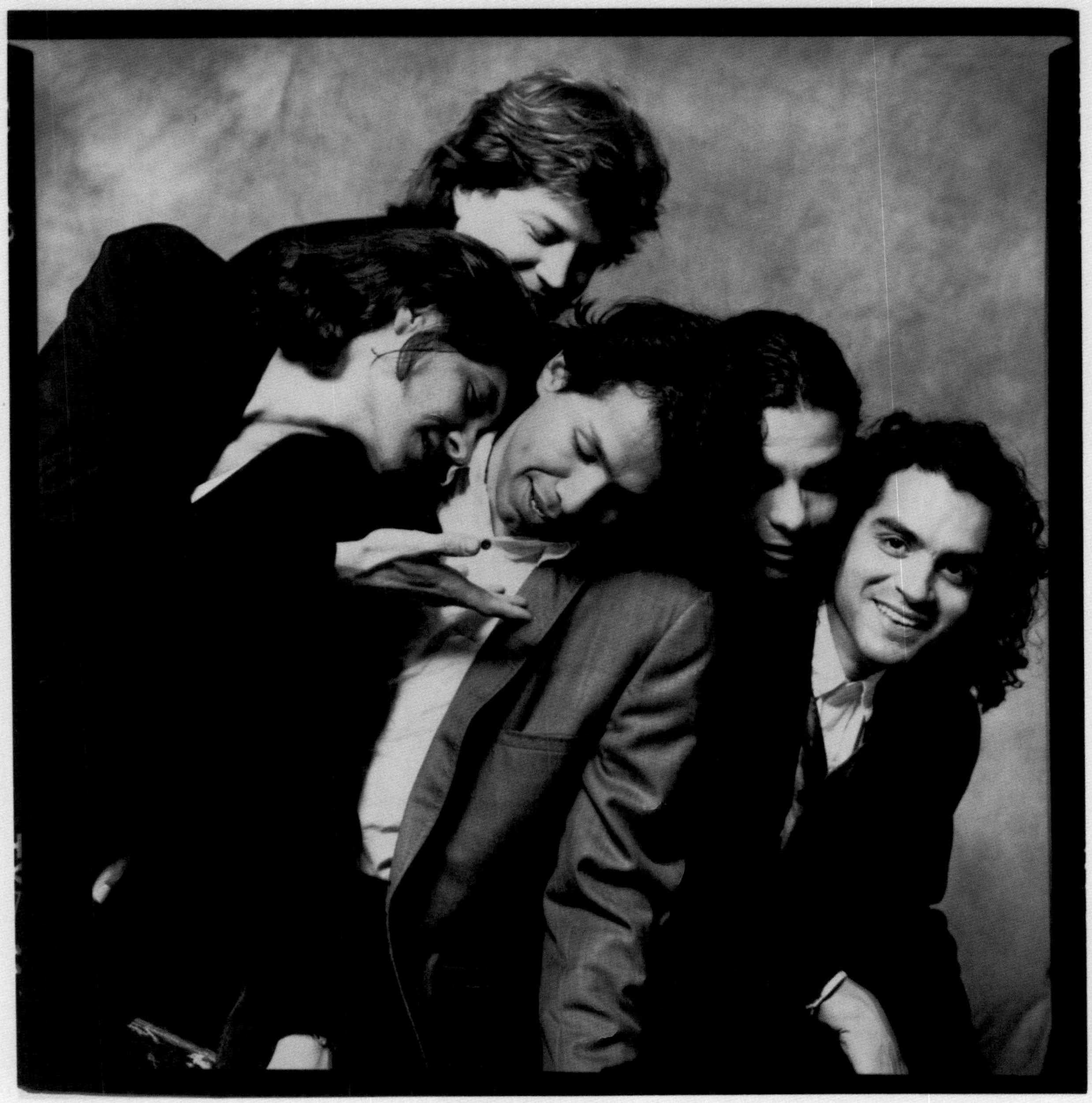

FROM LEFT TO RIGHT· KURT NEUMANN, BOB GRIFFIN, SAM LLANAS, DANNY GAYOL, MICHAEL RAMOS

Photo Credit: Michael Wilson

BoDeans

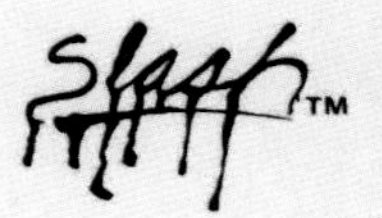

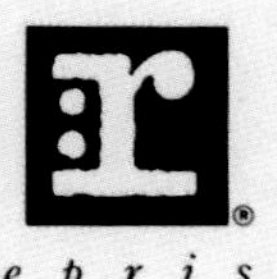

reprise

© 1991 Reprise Records/Permission to reproduce limited to editorial uses in news papers and other regularly published periodicals and television news programming

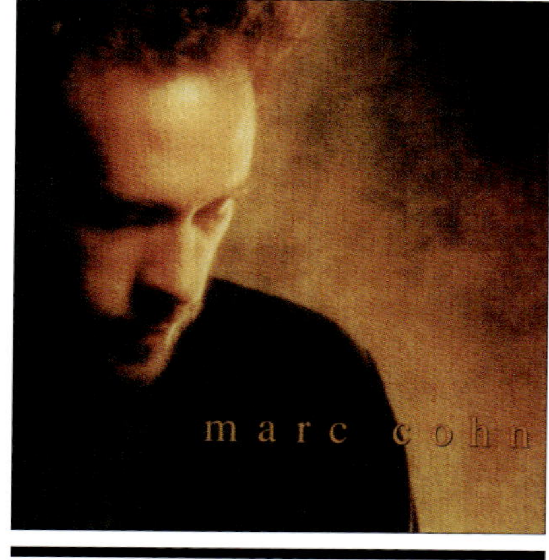

"Walking in Memphis" made its mark, and Marc Cohn walked off with a Grammy for Best New Artist.

Billboard 200: *Marc Cohn* (#38)
Billboard Hot 100: "Walking in Memphis" (#13);
"Silver Thunderbird" (#63); "True Companion" (#80)

WITH VIRTUALLY no fanfare, Marc Cohn released a modestly produced debut album and his life changed forever. "Walking in Memphis," a romantic and soulful vision of a musical mecca, shot him to the forefront of the contemporary music scene.

"It's a pretty literal transcription of a visit I made there in 1985," the Cleveland native said. "I went to Graceland, I heard Al Green preach the gospel, I saw W.C. Handy's statue. But the song is about more than just a place—it's about a kind of spiritual awakening, one of those trips where you're different when you leave. The main part of the trip is the last verse—a lady named Muriel."

Cohn met Muriel Witkins, a little-known club singer and pianist, at a restaurant an hour outside town.

"I didn't go searching for anyone like her. She was the entertainment on weekends. I was immediately overwhelmed by her presence and her voice, which was a beautiful, lovely instrument. I walked up to her at a break just to tell her, 'You're background music, nobody seems to be listening, but I am.' I talked to her for an hour and then she invited me up to sing. She ended up having an incredible effect on me, not only as a musician, but as a person. She saw things in me and shared things with me that I don't normally talk about, mostly revolving around my parents, who died when I was pretty young."

Witkins inspired Cohn to write "Walking in Memphis" and the other songs that appeared on *Marc Cohn*, his debut album. She got to hear it before she died in 1990 at age 68.

Cohn almost regretted mentioning Elvis Presley in "Walking in Memphis." "To me, the song is so minimally about him, but I worry that it gets cast off as another Elvis tribute. It's a testament to the power of his name—even if you just mention it in one verse, the song becomes about him because people focus on it."

The album also produced the outstanding "True Companion" and "Silver Thunderbird," which was seemingly about an unsophisticated father driving a hip automobile. "It's also about an element of being a kid—that sort of wonder about your dad, where he works, what he thinks," explained Cohn, who'd just become a father for the first time.

In the early Seventies, Cohn heard Van Morrison's *Astral Weeks* album on a progressive FM radio outlet in Cleveland. He became a devotee of Joni Mitchell and Jackson Browne, but he considered James Taylor his "most pervasive and least audible" influence.

When Cohn moved to New York to be with his fiancée during the Eighties, he put together a 14-piece band called the Supreme Court. After Carly Simon recommended the group to Jackie Onassis, the Supreme Court played Caroline Kennedy's wedding.

"It was fun once it became clear that they didn't want us to play 'We've Only Just Begun,'" Cohn laughed. ■

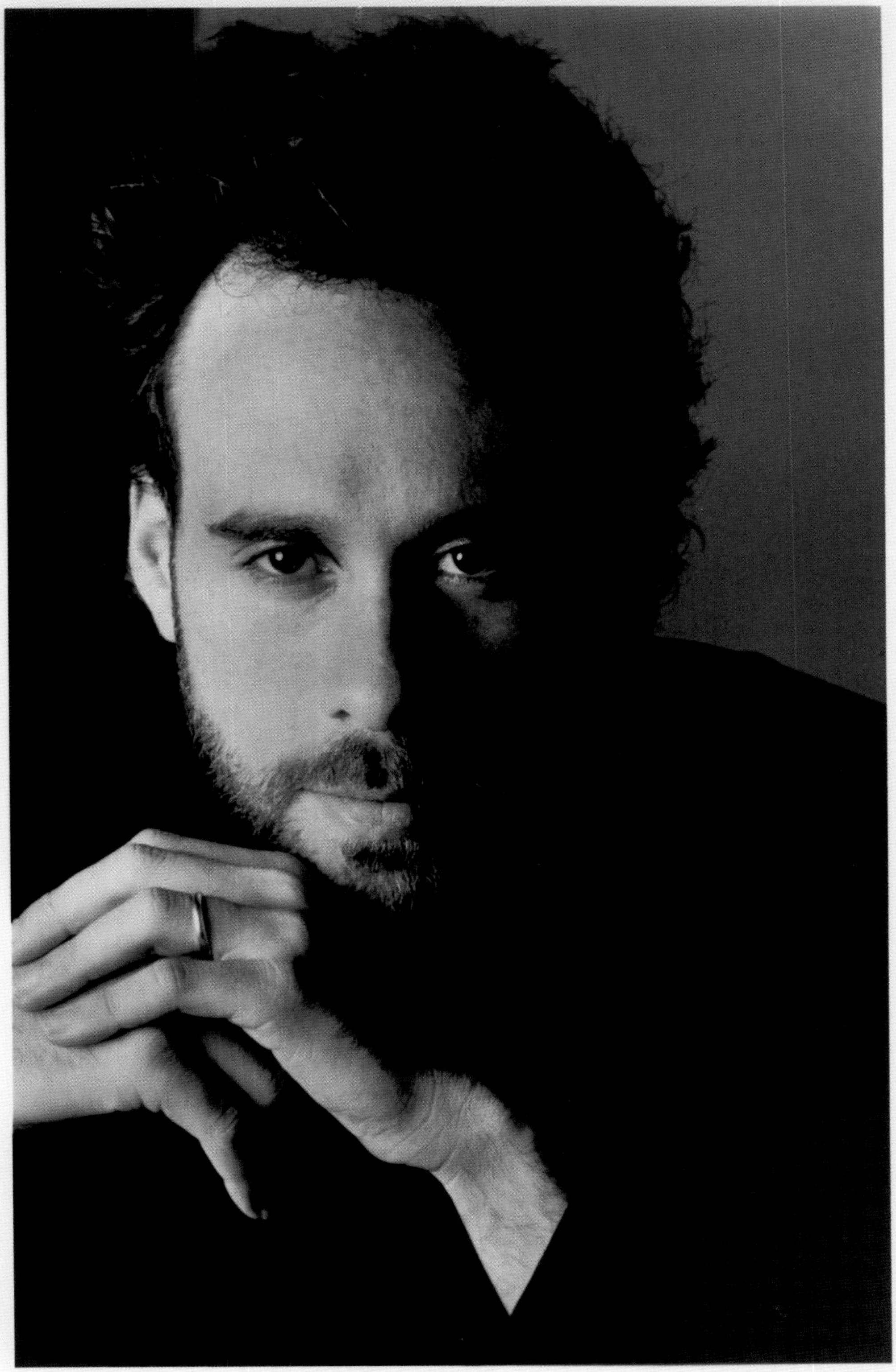

marc cohn

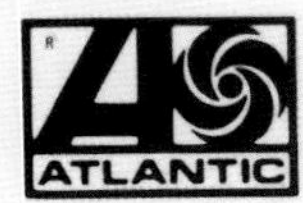

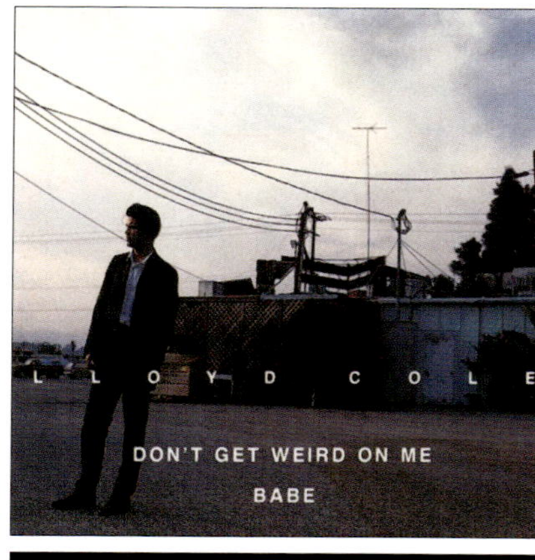

Don't Get Weird on Me Babe marked a significant shift artistically for UK singer-songwriter Lloyd Cole.

DURING HIS tenure as leader of Lloyd Cole & the Commotions, Cole's dark, cynical songs were frequently praised as some of the most literate rock compositions to come along since the works of Ray Davies, Lou Reed and Bob Dylan.

"I don't know where we fit in," Cole said. "All I would say is there were probably only five or six good bands of the Eighties, and we were one of them."

But despite his poised confidence and chart-topping success in Europe, Cole had remained relatively unknown in the US, save for a series of amaretto print ads he did in a financial pinch. So, after three albums (the best was 1984's *Rattlesnakes*), Cole was sans Commotions.

"I was tired of band democracy, not the music," he explained. "You can't make decisions that aren't dependent on four other people's livelihoods. I did that for six years, and I didn't want to be in an organization anymore. I wanted to have more control over my life."

Cole followed his first solo effort, 1990's *Lloyd Cole*, with *Don't Get Weird on Me Babe*, a concept album recorded in two parts. One side continued the jangling guitar pop of *Lloyd Cole*, while the other side featured a session orchestra conducted by Paul Buckmaster (known for his arrangements for Elton John, David Bowie and the Rolling Stones). Cole described it as his "farewell to rock." "She's a Girl and I'm a Man" and "Tell Your Sister" flirted with becoming American hit singles, both appearing on the modern rock charts.

Joining Cole was guitar whiz Robert Quine, who had raised some hell with Lou Reed and Richard Hell & the Voidoids.

"Now it's even worse," Cole said. "Instead of being a band member, I'm suddenly a band member and also an employer." ■

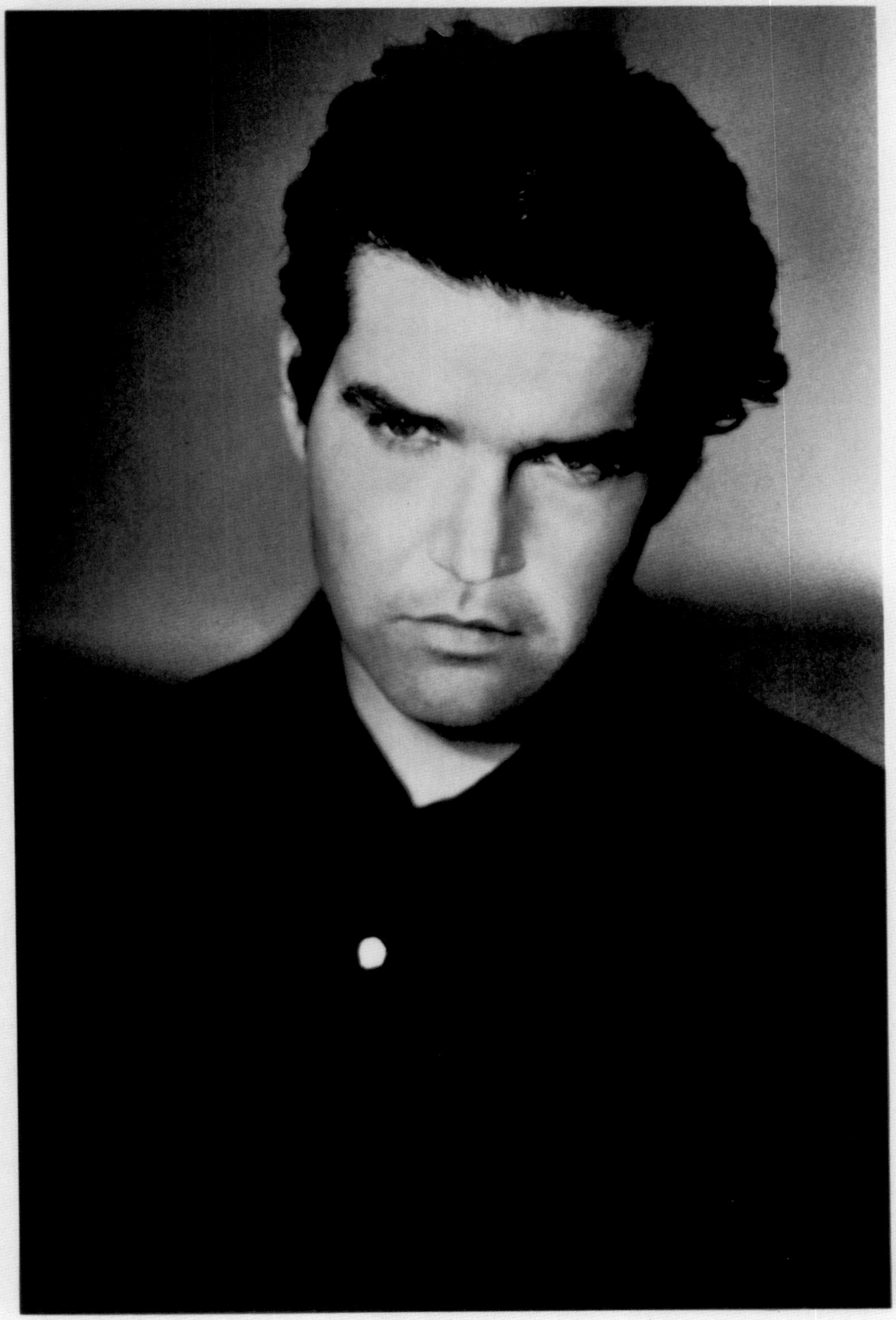

1991

LLOYD COLE

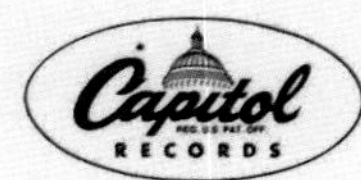

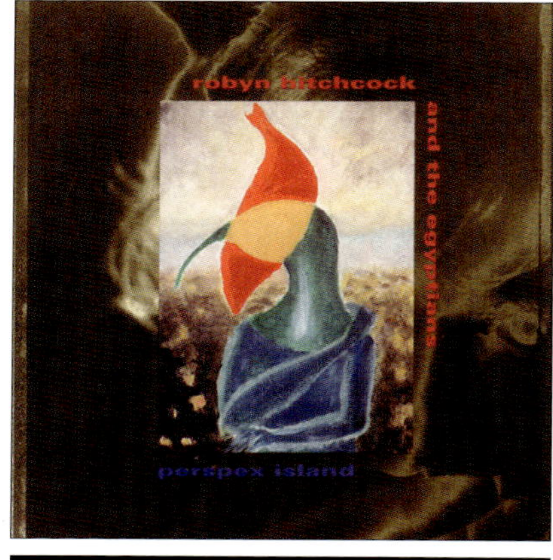

Lovable oddball Robyn Hitchcock topped the alternative charts via the simple "So You Think You're in Love."

LITERATURE AND any number of musical gurus had informed Robyn Hitchcock's forays into jangly and melodic Sixties folk-rock and shades of psychedelia. His best ballad was "Raymond Chandler Evening," and he was clearly influenced by John Lennon's plain but appealing voice and Pink Floyd founder Syd Barrett's obsession with slightly ominous but strangely beautiful stream-of-consciousness lyrics.

But the British singer-songwriter's entire body of work, both as a leader of the Soft Boys and as a solo performer, had gone undiscovered because of his avid pursuit of weirdness. His typically deranged concerns had included insects, dwarfs, lobsters, dead wives and man-eating vegetation.

"I'd rather people listen to the music, but people are more interested in checking you out on the attitude meter," Hitchcock said. "People who like me come along to cop that attitude. People who don't like me are just like me, wise guys—'I can do that wacky stuff, too.'"

Feeling trapped by and disenchanted with the madcap persona he'd created, Hitchcock seemed to break free with *Perspex Island*, an album recorded with his longtime backup band, the Egyptians, that knocked on the door of record-buying middle America. The apparently sincere "So You Think You're in Love" peaked at No. 1 on *Billboard*'s Modern Rock Tracks chart.

"I was burned out on a certain way of being perceived," he admitted. "I was hoping I'd get something more coherent in writing these songs, but you never know. I don't write out of conscious intent. It has to come to me. You hope you're a magnet."

Perspex Island struck a balance between eccentric wordplay and heartfelt emotion. Produced by Paul Fox, who'd worked with XTC, the album reflected a new tenderness and introspection for Hitchcock.

"We could carry on making the same record indefinitely if we didn't add something to the mix," he mused. "It's easy to dig your own grave and climb out of it when people are shoveling dirt in—it's common in show biz. 'I only dug the grave to make a hole.' Escape my eccentric persona? The truth is subtler, more boring—you have to have an angle pinned on you, and you can only hope it's one you pinned on yourself. No one ever accused me of being a major-league footballer or a gangster." ■

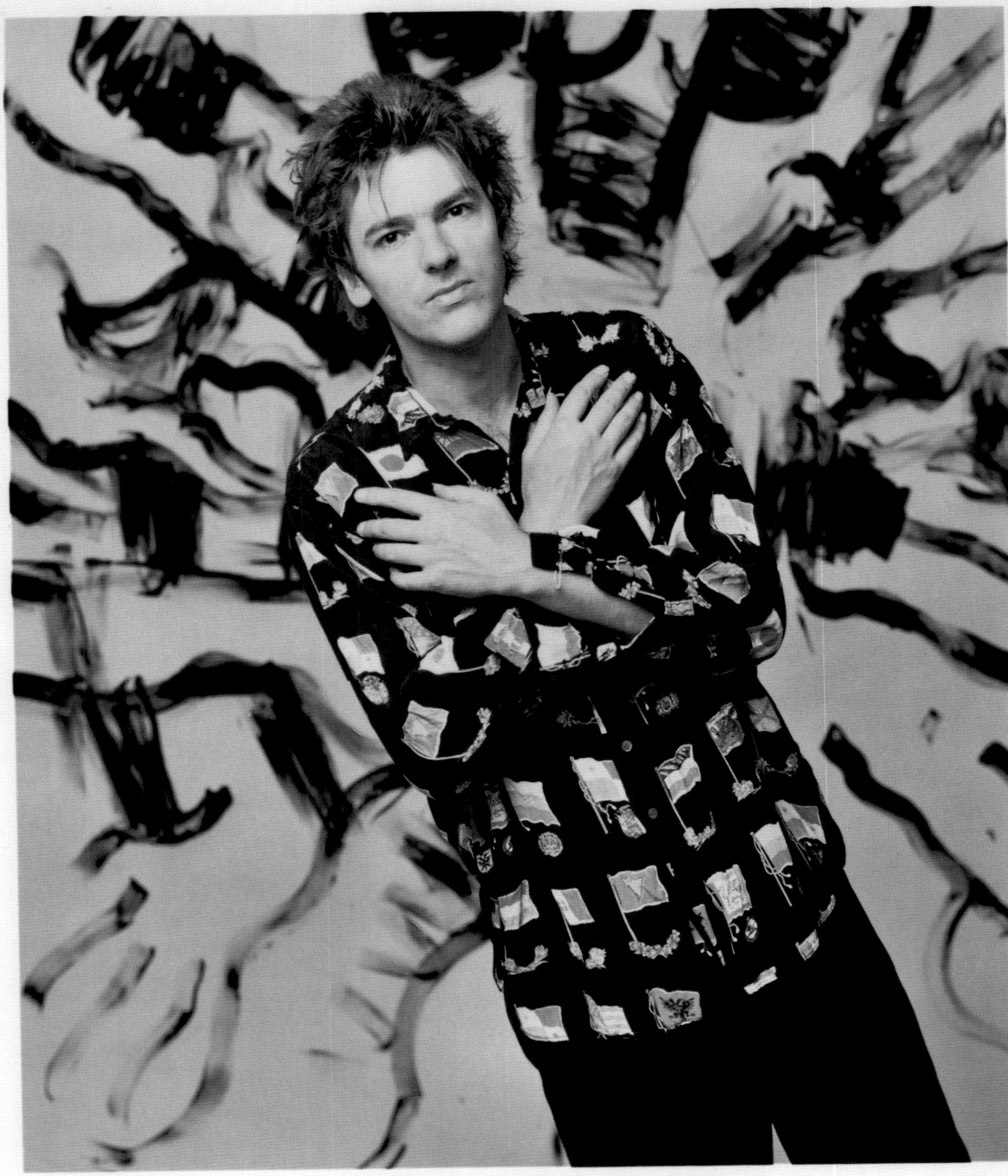

PHOTO: CHRIS CARROLL

ROBYN HITCHCOCK

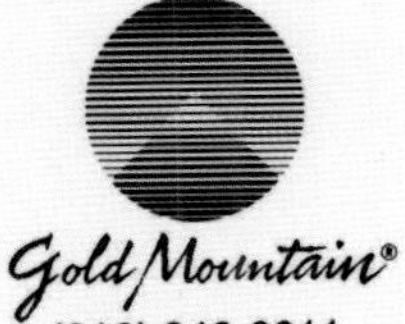

(212) 840-6011

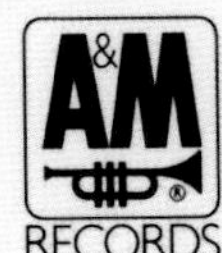

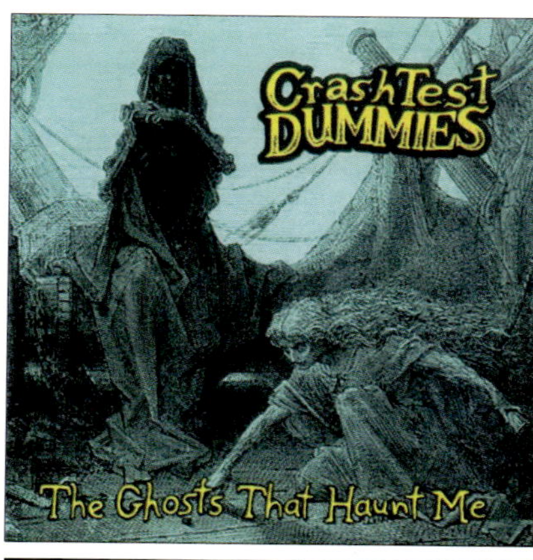

Billboard Hot 100: "Superman's Song" (#56)

From the album *The Ghosts That Haunt Me*, "Superman's Song" surfaced as Crash Test Dummies' first hit.

FORMED CIRCA 1987 as the house band at a Winnipeg after-hours club, the members of Crash Test Dummies had found innovative uses for accordion, mandolin, pennywhistle and harmonica in a sparse country-folk setting. At home, the Canadian band's twist on acoustic roots music was a smash—the debut album *The Ghosts That Haunt Me* was a No. 1 record. In the American market, the elegiac "Superman's Song" garnered radio airplay.

"Superman's Song" was the first song that singer and guitarist Brad Roberts ever wrote. He cited as his pivotal influence Lyle Lovett, whom he'd seen perform at the Winnipeg Folk Festival in 1988.

"For the longest time I couldn't imagine myself actually writing anything, because I just didn't see a way to make my voice and the influences I'd had add up to anything," Roberts said. "Then I saw Lyle's workshop at the festival, and he sang these gorgeous songs in a completely stripped-down setting, with nothing more than an acoustic guitar and a cello. I thought, 'Wow, I'd like to write like that.' So I went home and wrote 'Superman's Song' the next weekend."

Roberts, who had university degrees in both English and philosophy, fused dry wit with literary allusions in his lyrics. "Superman's Song" was typical of his sardonic style, an entertaining face-off between two larger-than-life comic book heroes—the Man of Steel and Tarzan—sung in his distinctive bass-baritone voice.

"I wanted to write a political song," he explained. "But a great deal of the time, I find politically motivated popular music sounds very preachy, didactic, heavy-handed, moralistic and earnest. I wanted to avoid that, so using comic book characters gave me a way to delineate a theme yet add an amount of levity and humor. It's a semi-philosophical look at two antithetical approaches to the good life. I thought it would be interesting to juxtapose Superman, the altruistic hero who's vitally active in community life, against Tarzan, who lives in the solitary world. He basically swings through the jungle, scoops up Jane and looks out for himself."

However, Roberts wasn't a comic book fan. Although he mentioned Solomon Grundy in the song, he couldn't recall who Grundy was, not having read about him since he was eight years old. (Solomon Grundy was a gigantic humanoid with vast strength whose greatest passion had been fighting Green Lantern over the years.)

"I imagine comic-book-collector freaks would know," he laughed. "I had to come up with an antihero to pit against Superman, and Grundy rhymed with money." ■

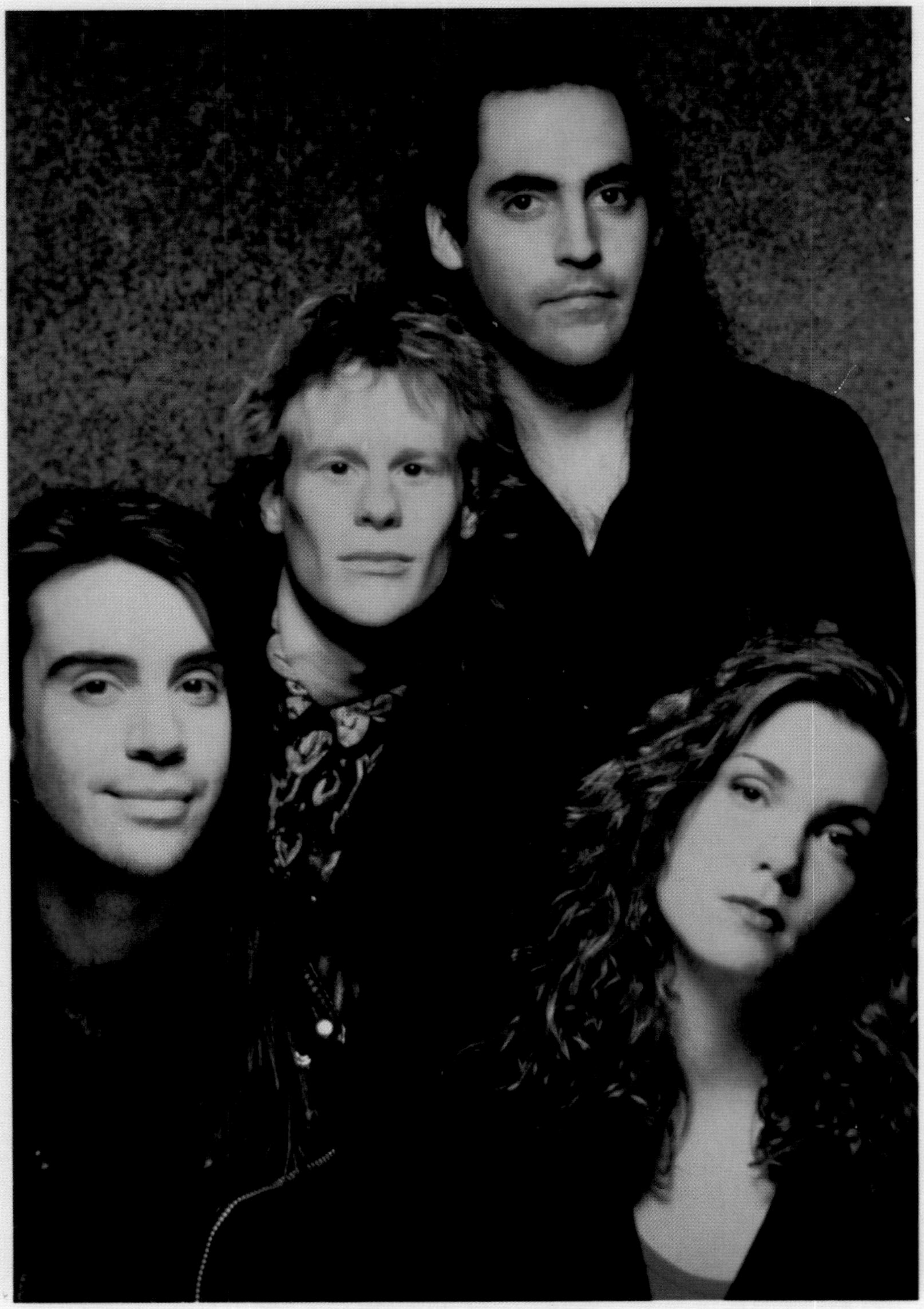

ARISTA

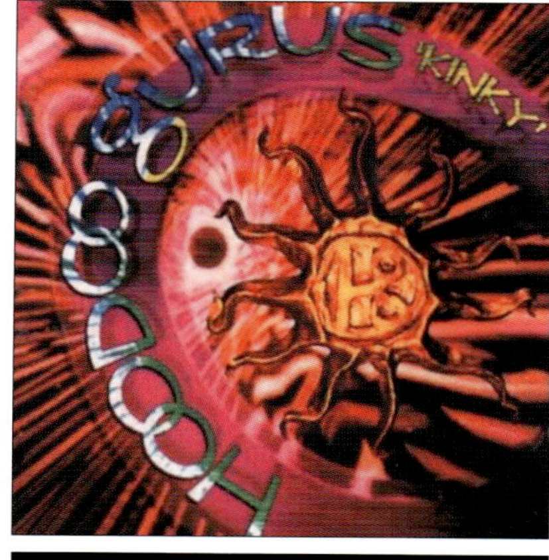

Billboard 200: *Kinky* (#172)

Australia's Hoodoo Gurus returned with "Miss Freelove '69," the latest in a lengthy line of near-hits.

AUSTRALIA HAD borne few bands as crassly entertaining as the Hoodoo Gurus. The maverick Sydney quartet would have made a wonderful Sixties British Invasion group. They tooled crazy, loud fun with guitars, drums, swell hooks and an addiction to trashy pop culture.

The hardy Hoodoos were veterans of five albums, three record labels and seven years of intensive touring, and they had garnered considerable airplay on college radio with some top-notch singles—"I Want You Back," "Bittersweet," "What's My Scene," "Come Anytime." But the general public still hadn't caught on to their energetic synthesis of gonzo garage-rock and demi-psychedelia.

"Our type of melodic, guitar-oriented pop-rock seems to be a purist form these days," lead guitarist Brad Shepherd said. "But it's all we do. A strong song, an interesting arrangement and a four-on-the-floor backbeat still moves me. We just don't play the game well enough, and it's probably to our detriment. We're embarrassed to do promotions or suck up to the record company. But because we haven't subjected ourselves to that sort of indignity, we're not jaded. We're in our own universe. We have fun, and anyone who wants to buy into it has a good time."

The Hoodoo Gurus were still eager to conquer the American airwaves. Their album *Kinky* was mixed by Ed Stasium (of Living Colour, Smithereens, Jeff Healey and Ramones fame), and he added simple but terrific sonic details like feedback and phasing. "Miss Freelove '69" reached #3 on *Billboard*'s Modern Rock Tracks chart. The single captured the retro feel of *Kinky*, opening with a tinny riff suggestive of some hip television show circa 1969. The story matched the tune's wild mood—it chronicled a hedonistic homecoming party at frontman Dave Faulkner's place.

"The song just came out of Dave the next day," Shepherd explained. "We'd started this party at his flat on the beach at three in the afternoon. We'd just come back from a tour of Japan and we had some sake to celebrate, and a few people came around and started playing some groovy disco tunes—Spinners, Gloria Gaynor, Village People. It wasn't even meant to be a party. It accidently exploded, getting louder and louder until we had this swinging shindig happening. The police came around three in the morning, and that's the last verse—'Check their badges at the door, join the action on the floor.'

"But they didn't really join in as they do in the lyrics. They gave us a noise abatement order and went away. They were sure debauchery was occurring, and they might have had to arrest us if they saw it. Dave was standing there in his boxer shorts at that point. He thinks it's just cooler to dance in underwear." ■

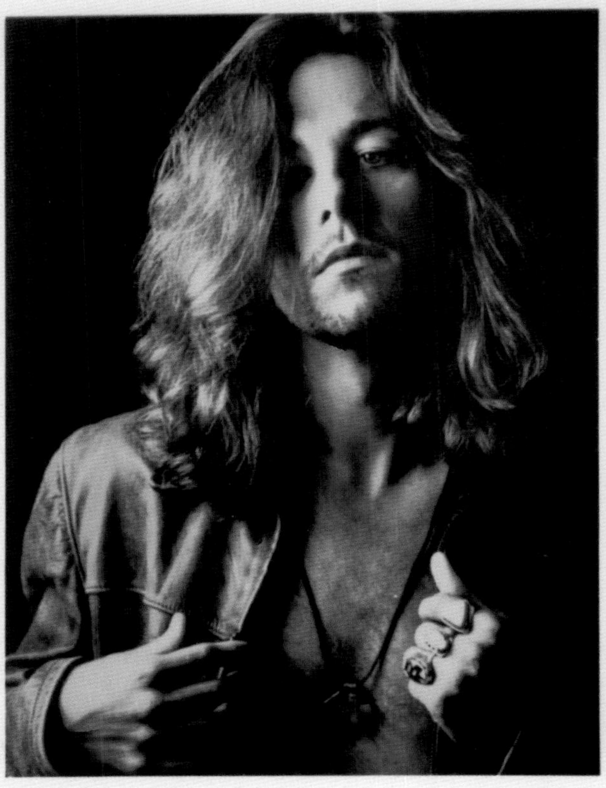

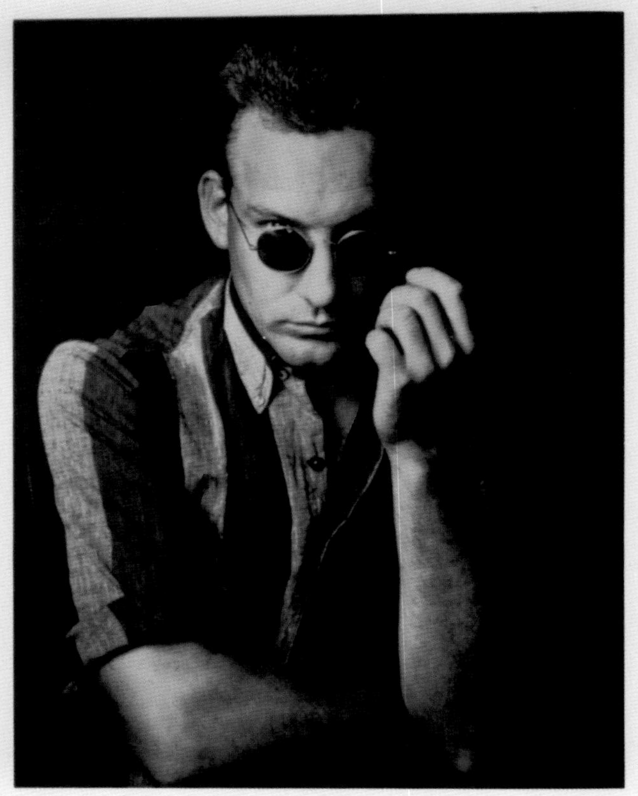

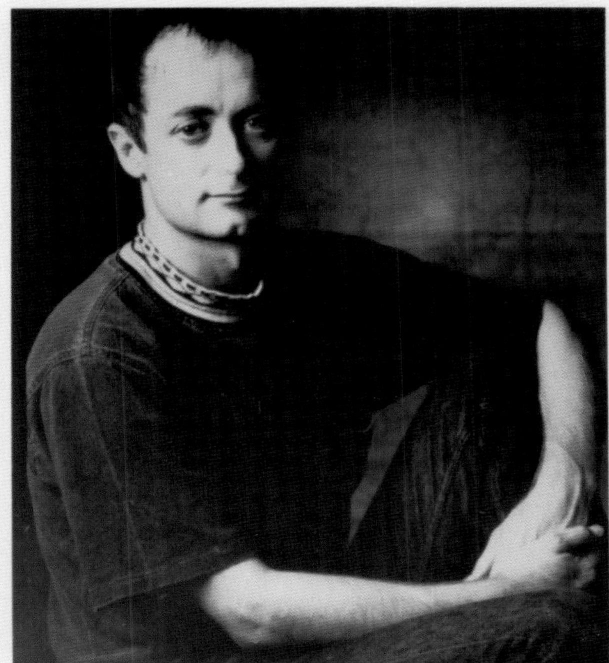

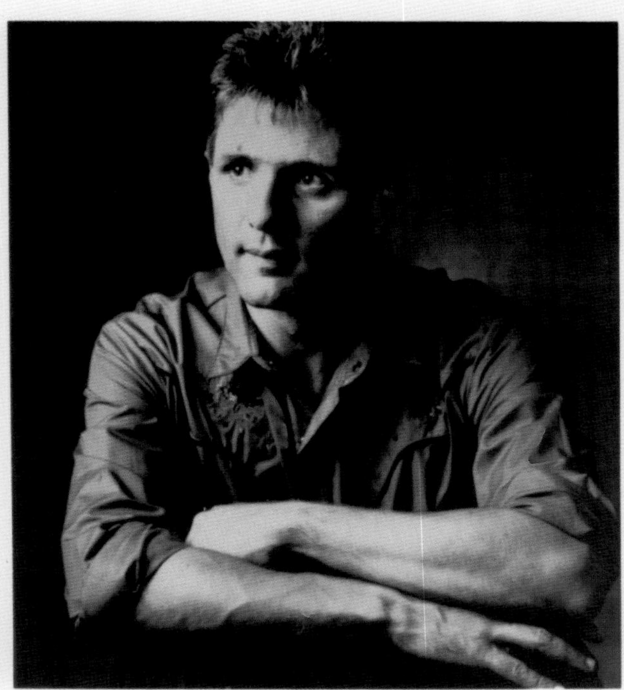

Photographer : Adrienne Overall

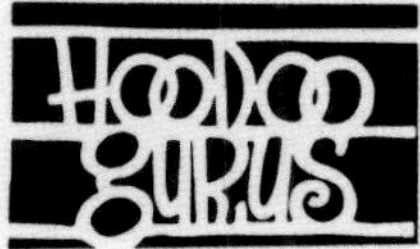

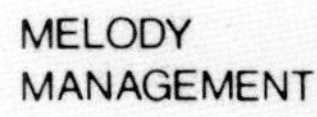

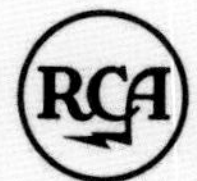

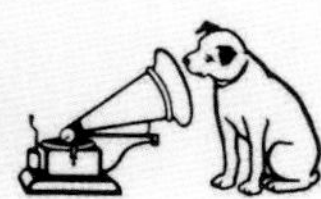

Crowded House's *Woodface* featured tracks co-written by frontman Neil Finn and his older brother Tim.

Billboard 200: *Woodface* (#83)
Billboard Hot 100: "Fall at Your Feet" (#75)

CROWDED HOUSE had gotten a little more crowded. Chief singer-songwriter Neil Finn had renewed his musical partnership with his brother Tim, best known as a founder of Split Enz, New Zealand's most famous pop export.

Growing up, Neil was strongly influenced by Tim, who put together Split Enz's quirky sound and vision in the early Seventies. The band was visually flamboyant (sculpted hair, day-glo suits, layers of make-up) and musically jarring (cockeyed art-rock instincts).

"It started off as a mission for all the guys involved," Neil said of Split Enz. "It was in many ways quite naïve and extreme. They thought the world would embrace their eccentric vision. A lot of those songs had an album's worth of ideas crammed in."

Ironically, it wasn't until Neil joined the band at age 18 that Split Enz became stars Down Under. He penned most of the band's successes, notably 1980's international smash "I Got You." Tim left Split Enz in 1983. Neil found good fortune with Crowded House—the threesome (Finn, drummer Paul Hester and bassist Nick Seymour) homered on their first at-bat, a platinum-selling self-titled debut album that delivered the entrancing singles "Don't Dream It's Over" and "Something So Strong."

The second Crowded House album, the less outgoing *Temple of Low Men*, came out in 1988. The band's trademark was an intelligent, passionate approach to commercial pop music, creating canny, handsome melodies on record and jokey onstage interplay.

The Finns finally got around to making their first record as a duo. They worked on material for a separate album of their own, to precede a new Crowded House record. But the two projects were merged for *Woodface*, and the eight songs Neil and Tim wrote marked a rare collaboration—most Split Enz material was written separately.

"It's weird, really—sometimes these things take a long time to reveal themselves," Neil mused. "We never had the motivation before, or maybe the roles of big brother and little brother were a little strict."

Tim deferred to his younger sibling in Crowded House, but the group's chemistry remained intact on *Woodface*. The bold, romantic tunes displayed soothing, standout Beatles-esque harmonies.

"That's one of the things that knocked us out when we got back together, the sound of our voices," Neil said.

Beneath Mitchell Froom's finely executed production details, introspective meditations on life and love gave a pleasing tension to the tracks. "Chocolate Cake," a sardonic jab at American-style materialism, and the rapturous "Fall at Your Feet" were released as singles.

"This band has always had a fragile relationship—we're all quite different from each other, although we're close," Neil concluded. "But people can see the chemistry."

Crowded House's live shows were full of "in" jokes, singalongs and even the occasional food fight or striptease. Tim Finn proved extraneous to the notoriously loose and lively affairs. He left the band in November 1991, in the middle of its UK tour. ■

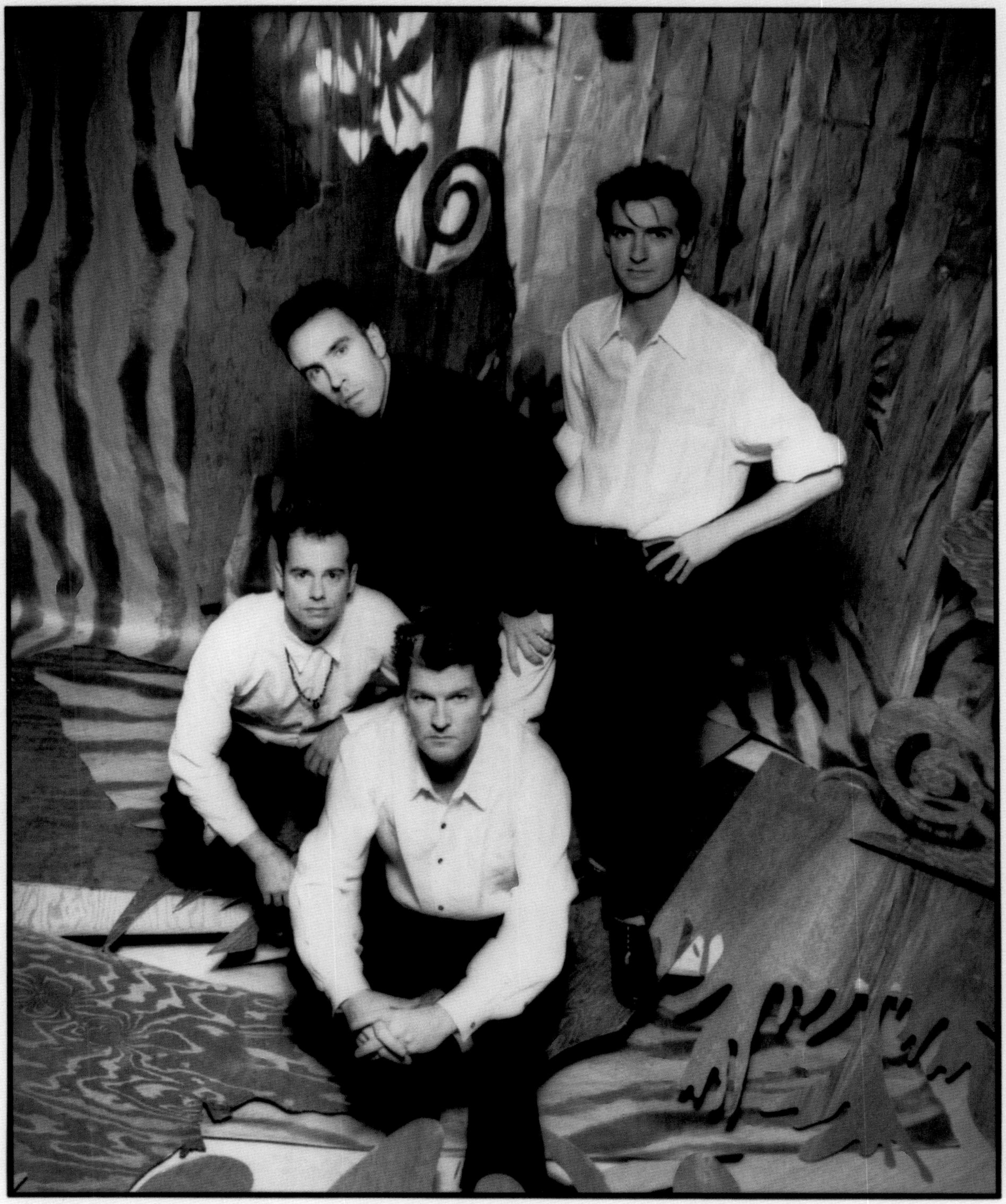

PHOTO: DENNIS KEELEY / 1991

Clockwise from top: Neil Finn, Tim Finn, Paul Hester, Nick Seymour

CROWDED HOUSE

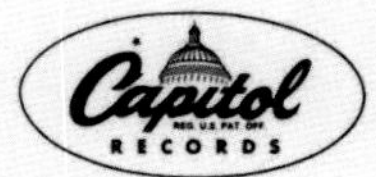

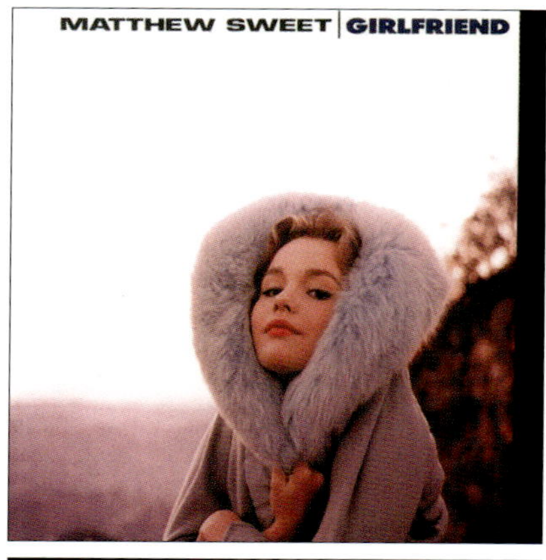

Billboard 200: *Girlfriend* (#100)

With the classic guitar pop of *Girlfriend*, Matthew Sweet enjoyed an artistic and critical breakthrough.

ONE OF America's most talented champions of smart power-pop, Matthew Sweet was part of the Athens, Georgia, scene for two years in the early Eighties before migrating to New York and solo travails. The struggling rocker apparently wrote *Girlfriend*, his third album, while in the middle of both divorce proceedings and his first romance since the marital breakup, and then a home-heating accident ruined all of his records and guitars.

"It gives the impression that my life has been shattered, when really I've been pretty lucky," the Nebraska native said. "The thing that really impacted me was when I decided to throw away my drum machine—it led me to a basic organic sound, to make an exciting, immediate kind of record."

Girlfriend overflowed with melodic hooks, solid guitar-and-drums punch and winsome, impassioned vocals with just enough emotional angst. But Sweet watched the impeccable rock-pop record hang in limbo before being released. Prior to finishing it, his label dropped him, and he shopped the album around without success. Then a label president happened to hear Sweet's music playing in a fellow executive's office and signed him immediately.

"Girlfriend" went on to make inroads at alternative radio, climbing to #2 on *Billboard*'s Modern Rock Tracks chart. Critics gave it loads of praise and MTV constantly aired the inventive Japanese animation video.

"It's a pretty dumb song. It's like an advertisement—'I'm free, you're free, let's do it,'" Sweet said.

A coquettish picture of Fifties starlet Tuesday Weld graced the cover of *Girlfriend*.

"I'm a collector of movie memorabilia. When I saw the photo, it reminded me of an old Bill Evans jazz album—the look in her eyes, she's young but knows everything." ■

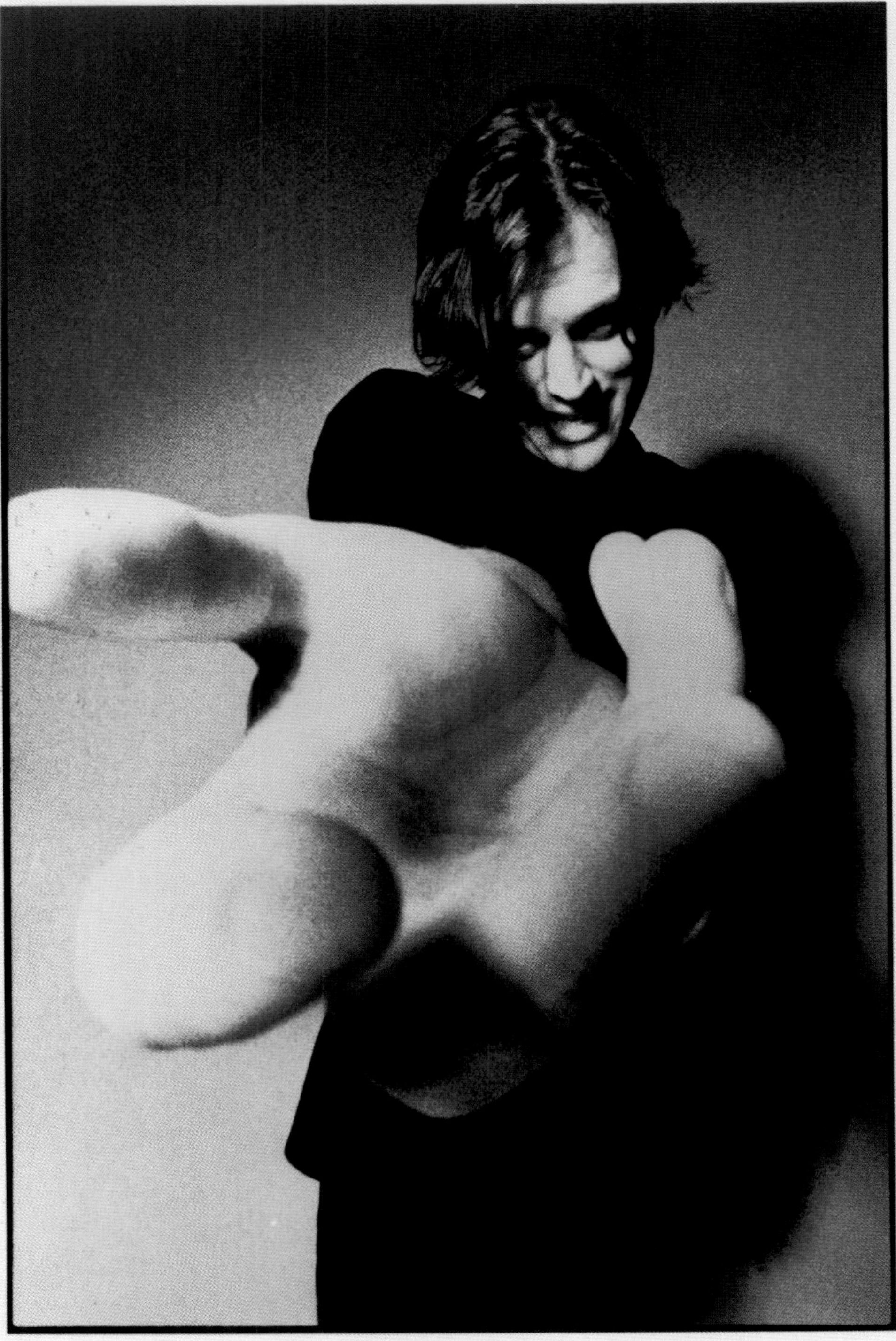

Photo Credit: Michael Lavine

MATTHEW SWEET

management: RUSSELL CARTER ARTIST MANAGEMENT

ZOO ENTERTAINMENT 6363 Sunset Boulevard, Hollywood, California 90028 TEL 213 468 4200 FAX 213 468 4207

9111

© 1991 Zoo Entertainment. Permission to reproduce this photography is limited to editorial uses in regular issues of newspapers and other regularly published periodicals and television news programming.

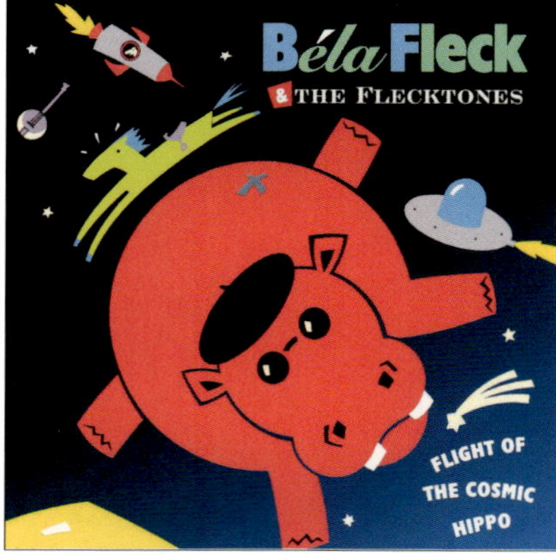

Béla Fleck & the Flecktones thrilled with exciting musical virtuosity and a fondness for playing together.

NO OTHER genre loved strict tradition quite like bluegrass, but Béla Fleck managed to reach beyond the constraints of Kentucky's "high lonesome" mountain music by enlarging the vocabulary of his instrument for a new generation. The pioneering banjo player quoted everyone from Earl Scruggs to the Rev. Gary Davis in his playing, and he and his band, the Flecktones, were known in jazz as well as bluegrass circles. It came as little surprise that Fleck's hometown was New York, hardly a bastion of traditional bluegrass.

"In the Sixties, it was a musical revolution—I grew up on the Beatles and Joni Mitchell, and even more direct folk music by Pete Seeger and Joan Baez," Fleck said. "I didn't know what bluegrass was. By the time I was 15 in the early Seventies, when I finally got my first banjo and fell in love with it, we were into Yes and Return to Forever and Mahavishnu Orchestra—that was the cutting edge.

"My mother said, 'I think I have a banjo record in the closet that we've never listened to.' It was Flatt & Scruggs. I'd heard them on television, on *The Beverly Hillbillies*. In New York City, there were kids trying to play the Grateful Dead and Led Zeppelin who thought I was pretty weird. In the beginning there was a lot of arm-flapping—*Hee-Haw* was the thing that came to mind when anybody saw a banjo. But by the end of high school, they were used to me and we were all friends. Ever since, I've been playing pretty much full time. It's almost like being an athlete in training. My hands and brain get quicker, in shape. It's a good feeling when it becomes like talking or breathing to me."

A nine-year run with New Grass Revival in the Eighties defined Fleck's creative charm. In 1990, he formed Béla Fleck & the Flecktones, which made extremely intricate music approachable and fun for their fans. Howard Levy played piano, harmonica and ocarina, among other instruments. Victor Wooten pushed his bass beyond its conventional rhythmic supporting role. And percussionist Future Man had created a new instrument altogether—the Synth-Axe Drumitar was a guitar-shaped portable electronic drum trigger of his own invention that accessed tonal and percussive sounds.

The band's second album, *Flight of the Cosmic Hippo*, reached No. 1 on *Billboard*'s Contemporary Jazz Albums chart, and the song "Blu-Bop" (the group's style owed more to bebop than bluegrass) received a Grammy nomination for Best Instrumental Composition.

"I haven't had the backlash that some people had before me," Fleck said. "My banjo teacher, Tony Trischka, and my bandmate from New Grass Revival, Sam Bush, both went through more angriness from people about distorting bluegrass. By the time I came along, a lot of those battles had already been fought and people were grudgingly putting up with it." ■

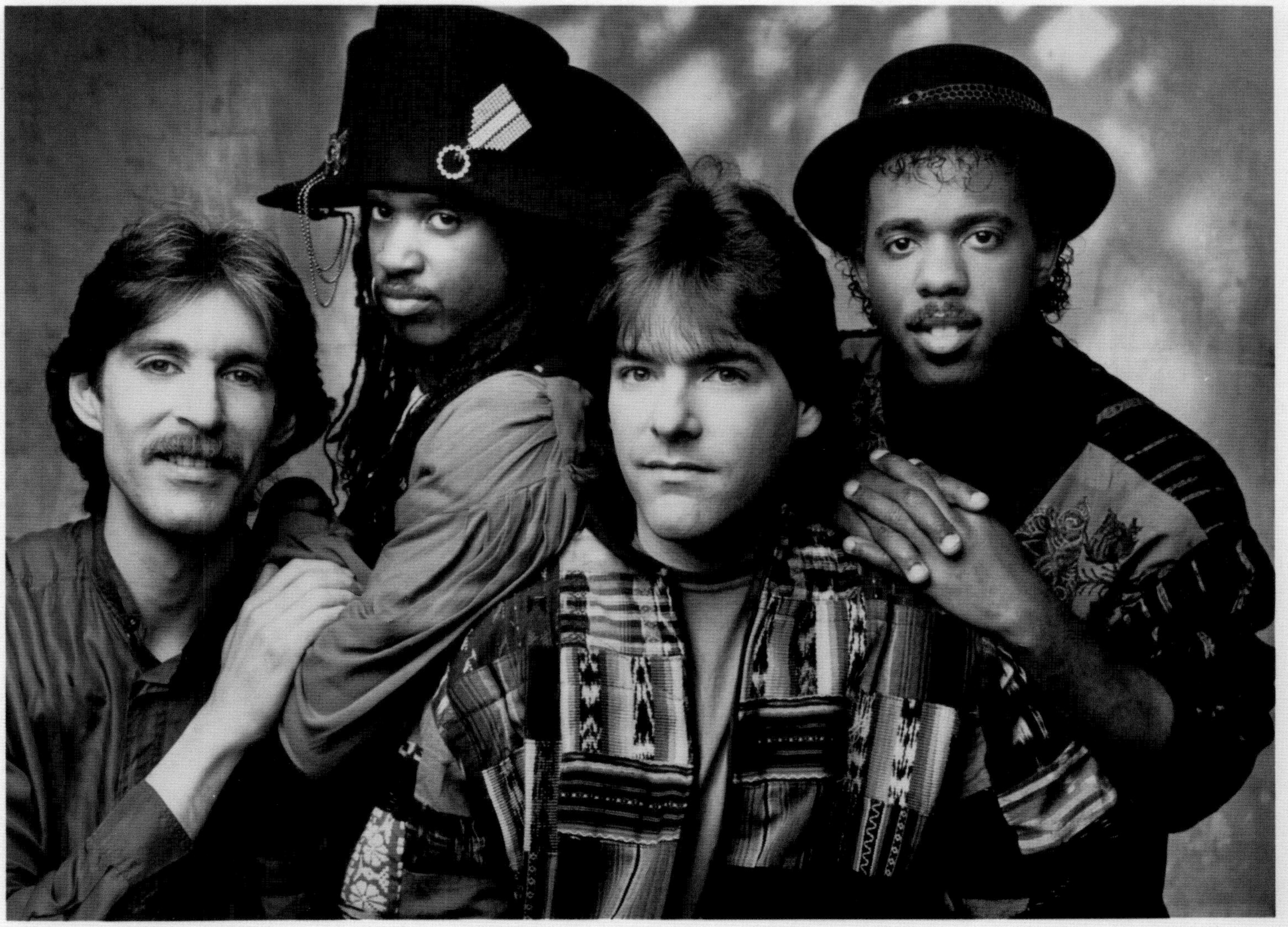

Howard Levy Future Man Bela Fleck Victor Wooten

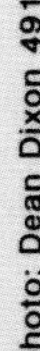

BELA FLECK & THE FLECKTONES

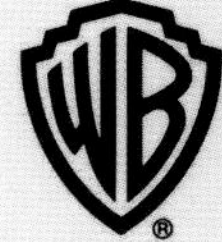

© 1991 Warner Bros. Records/Permission to reproduce limited to editorial uses in newspapers and other regularly published periodicals and television news programming.

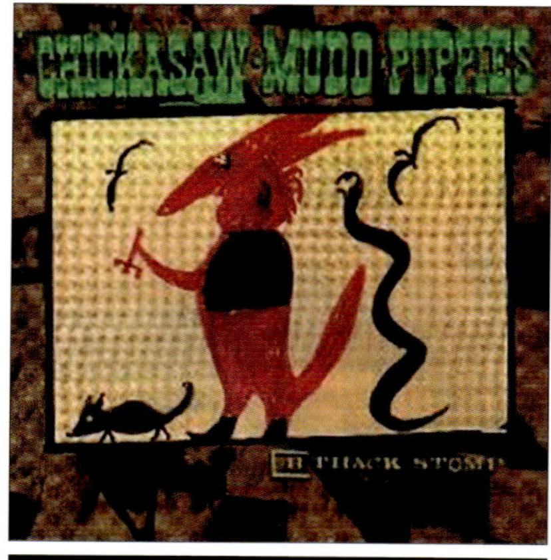

Chickasaw Mudd Puppies, an uninhibited swamp-rock duo, were protégés of R.E.M. singer Michael Stipe.

WHEN THEY met at art school, Ben Reynolds and Brant Slay discovered a shared interest in classic Delta blues records by Muddy Waters and Howlin' Wolf and obscure recordings of field hollers. The Georgia natives soon started a buzz going as the Chickasaw Mudd Puppies, with a series of showcase dates featuring low-tech yet engaging recreations of a front-porch jamboree—the two-man band decorated the stage like an old Southern lot and dressed in floppy hats, overalls and work boots.

Chickasaw Mudd Puppies didn't pretend to be authentic hillbillies or a true blues group, but they made up in enthusiasm and chemistry what they lacked in expertise on guitar, harp and quirky traditional and homemade percussion (stomp board, washboard, cowbell and even cans).

"I give us credit for putting our souls behind our music—I'm proud when that comes across—but we have absolutely no talent," Reynolds laughed.

The *8 Track Stomp* album was alternately produced by R.E.M.'s Michael Stipe and one of their heroes. Willie Dixon, who was pushing 75, was arguably the greatest living blues songwriter, responsible for "Hoochie Coochie Man," "Spoonful," "Wang Dang Doodle" and "I Just Want to Make Love to You," among others.

"We don't want to be seen as the two white boys trying to do this typically black style of music," Reynolds insisted. "Willie Dixon accepted us fine—he custom-wrote a song for us—and I don't need any more approval than that. It's not about color, it's about where your heart is." ■

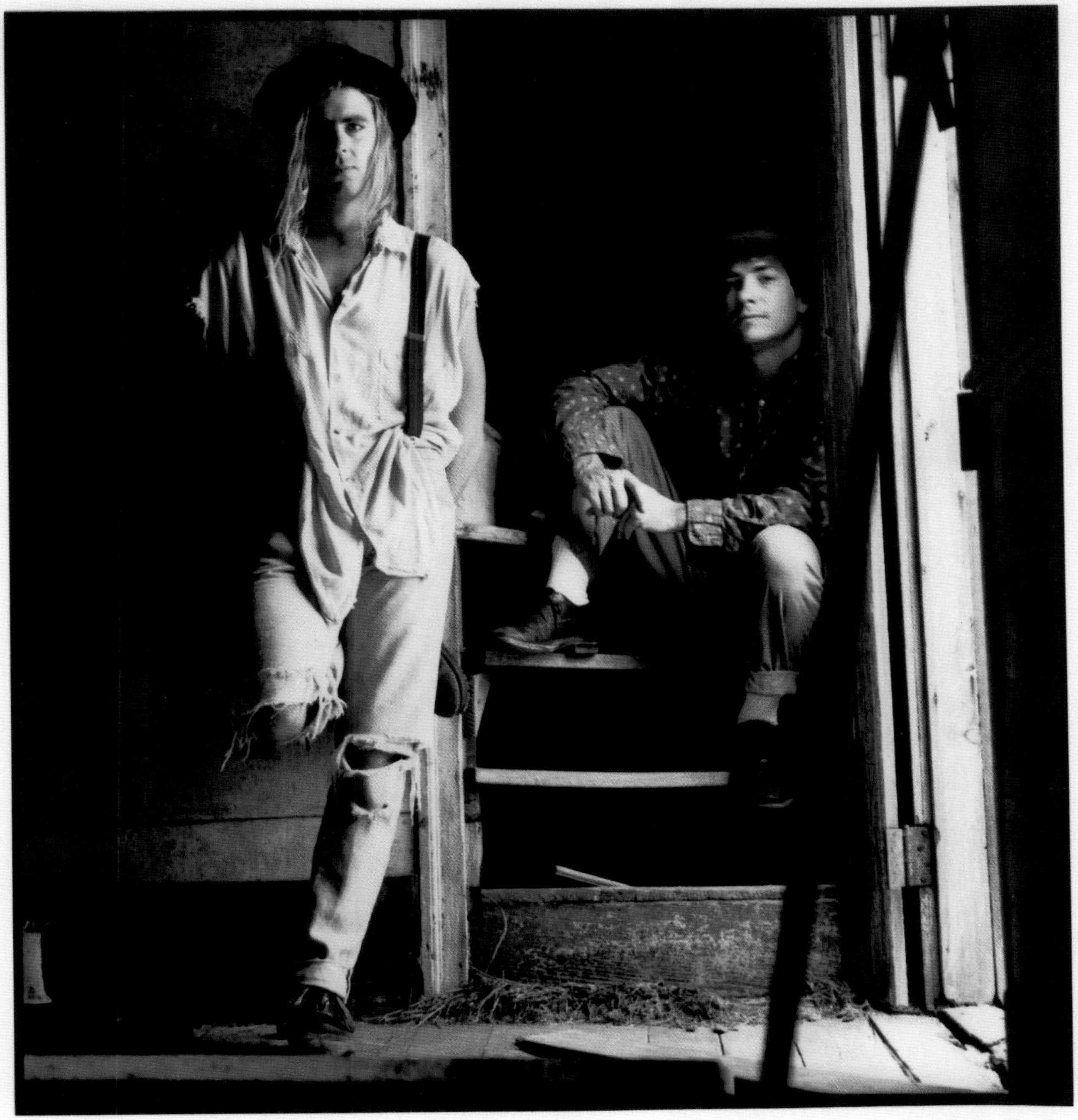

© PolyGram 1991

BRANT SLAY

BEN REYNOLDS

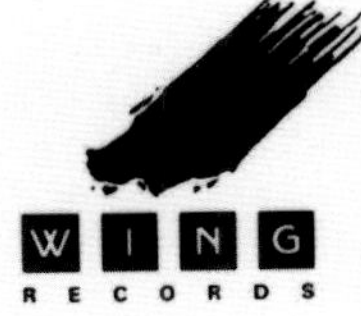

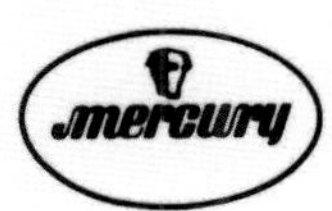

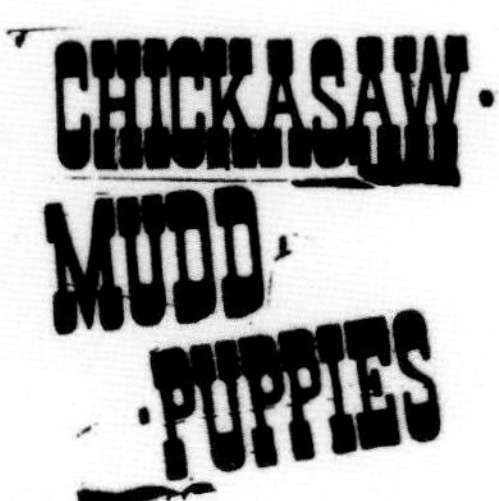

PolyGram™

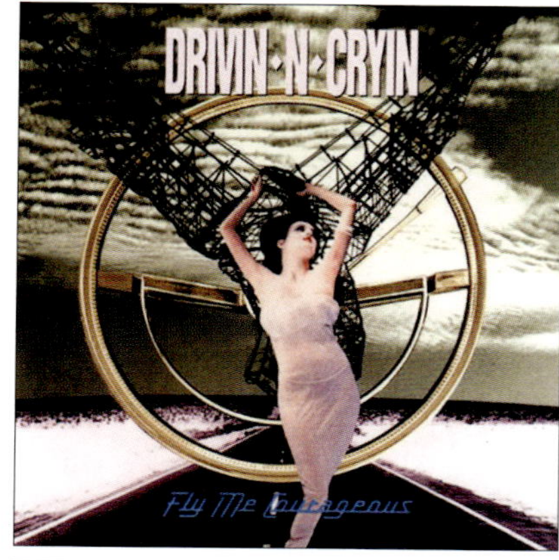

Billboard 200: *Fly Me Courageous* (#90)

Fly Me Courageous earned the Southern hard-rock band Drivin N Cryin its first gold-record certification.

DRIVIN N Cryin's rocking but roots-conscious sound had helped the Atlanta band land many tour dates and college radio success, but lead singer Kevn Kinney admitted the first three albums were "too eclectic." For *Fly Me Courageous*, the group's most cohesive and listenable effort, veteran producer/engineer Geoff Workman streamlined the punchy rock accents, and the title track reached *Billboard*'s Modern Rock Tracks and Album Rock Tracks charts.

"I love to play that riff," Kinney said. "It's a rip of 'What'd I Say' by Ray Charles. You might as well steal from the best—steal from Georgians!"

The song's emphasis was on cranked-up guitars, but Kinney's evocative lyrics drew Drivin N Cryin into the fray of the Middle East conflict: "Mother America is brandishing her weapons/To keep you safe and warm by threats and misconceptions." Kinney wrote the words as the US began sending troops to the Persian Gulf.

"We got banned from a couple of stations—people think that line is un-American," Kinney said. "The thing is, I'm the biggest, proudest American you'll ever meet. But my patriotism doesn't stop at the current faddish definition. It's time to start calling it as we see it. I was taught by my father that you can say what you want to say, but follow the Golden Rule." ■

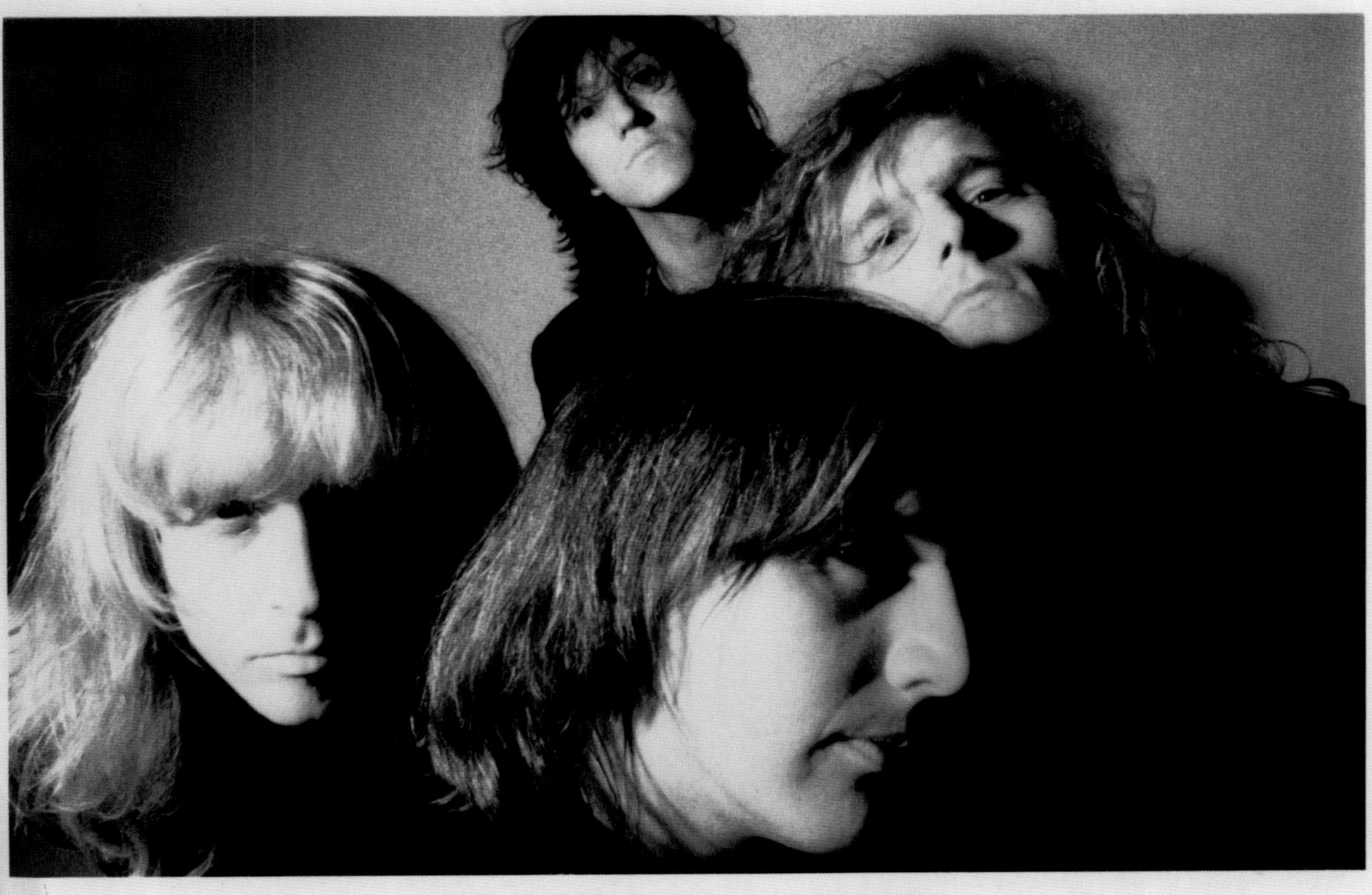

L TO R: BUREN FOWLER, KEVN KINNEY, JEFF SULLIVAN, TIM NIELSEN

DRIVIN◆N◆CRYIN

PHOTO CREDIT: MICHAEL LAVINE

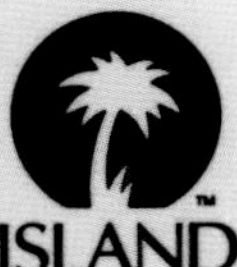

Billboard 200: *International Pop Overthrow* (#86)

Material Issue found a place on modern rock radio with the smart, hooky *International Pop Overthrow.*

SONGWRITER JIM Ellison acquired his talent for crafting shameless power pop from the record collection he inherited from his father. He formed Material Issue and scored with *International Pop Overthrow*, the Chicago-based trio's big-label debut after three years' worth of independent releases. The album's cleverest moments harkened back to mid-Sixties innocence in its songcraft and marketing (a fondness for mod fashion and a red-white-and-blue stars-and-stripes logo).

"We got an affliction for Herman's Hermits while everybody else was listening to Billy Squier," Ellison said. "Live, we're somewhat on the punk side, but in the writing we always go for melody."

Ellison's bouncy songs revolved around the girls in his life. The tuneful single "Valerie Loves Me," a tale of unrequited love, peaked at #3 on *Billboard*'s Modern Rock Tracks chart. Other three-minute jingles were titled "Diane" and "Renee Remains the Same."

"All the women I sing about are real, but they're not aware of that," Ellison declared. "I could just tell them my feelings if I wanted to, but it's much sneakier to write a song. And I'll never run out of girls' names before I run out of riffs." ■

© PolyGram 1991

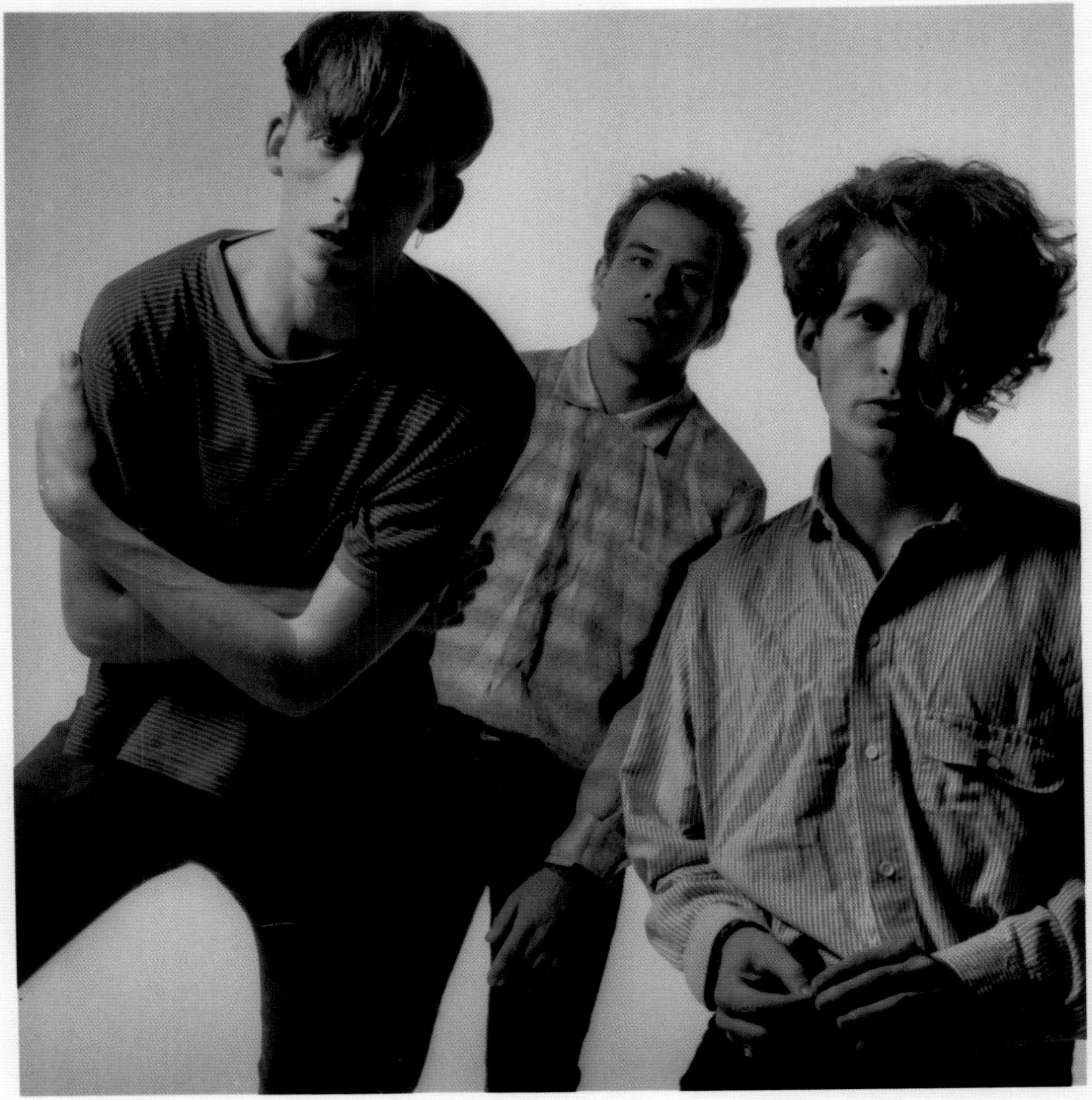

JIM ELLISON MIKE ZELENKO TED ANSANI

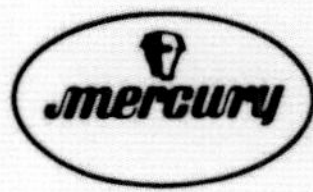

MATERIALISSUE

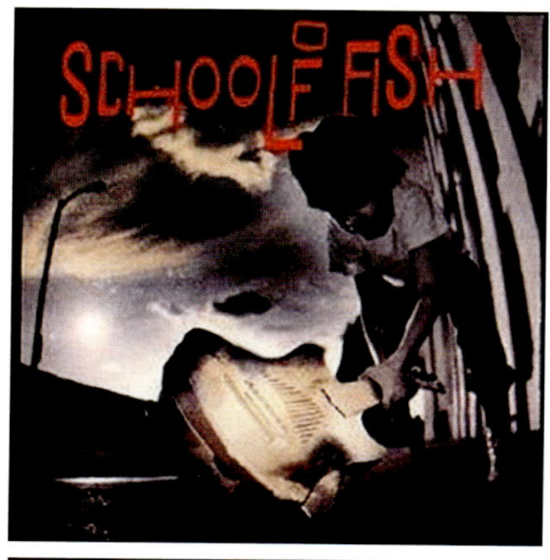

Billboard 200: *School of Fish* (#142)

Rock radio stations took School of Fish's bait, playing the enchanting, hook-laden single, "3 Strange Days."

THE YOUNG members of School of Fish converged on the Los Angeles music scene. Their demo version of "3 Strange Days" was so impressive that it was heard in the film *Reversal of Fortune*.

"Our manager worked at a company that did soundtracks for movies," guitarist Michael Ward explained. "It was a serious blink-and-you-miss-it thing. It was playing out of a jukebox for 10 seconds. Great movie, though."

"3 Strange Days" was a song worth checking out in its entirety, representing the band's sound with a swirling, trippy guitar riff and Josh Clayton-Felt's meandering vocal.

"Everybody thinks the lyrics are about drugs and tripping. They're not," Ward said. "The title is about 'being outside' of yourself for a while, where you feel weird, déjà vu. Josh wanted to write a song with these three chords, and he said, 'Play one of those Arabic scales that Prince would use.' I did it as a joke, and he thought it was perfect. We've since found out firsthand that it's the perfect 4½-minute cure for a hangover."

The band's self-titled debut album was produced by John Porter, best known as Roxy Music's bass player during the Eno days. The intriguing, diverse record blended guitar-driven grunge with melodic instincts that were…"I don't like the word 'psychedelic' because it's applied to everything," Ward said. "I don't think we sound retro or Sixties at all, although I can see why people say 'Beatles' to some of the melodies. But it's 1991—what can we do but rock 'n' roll?" ■

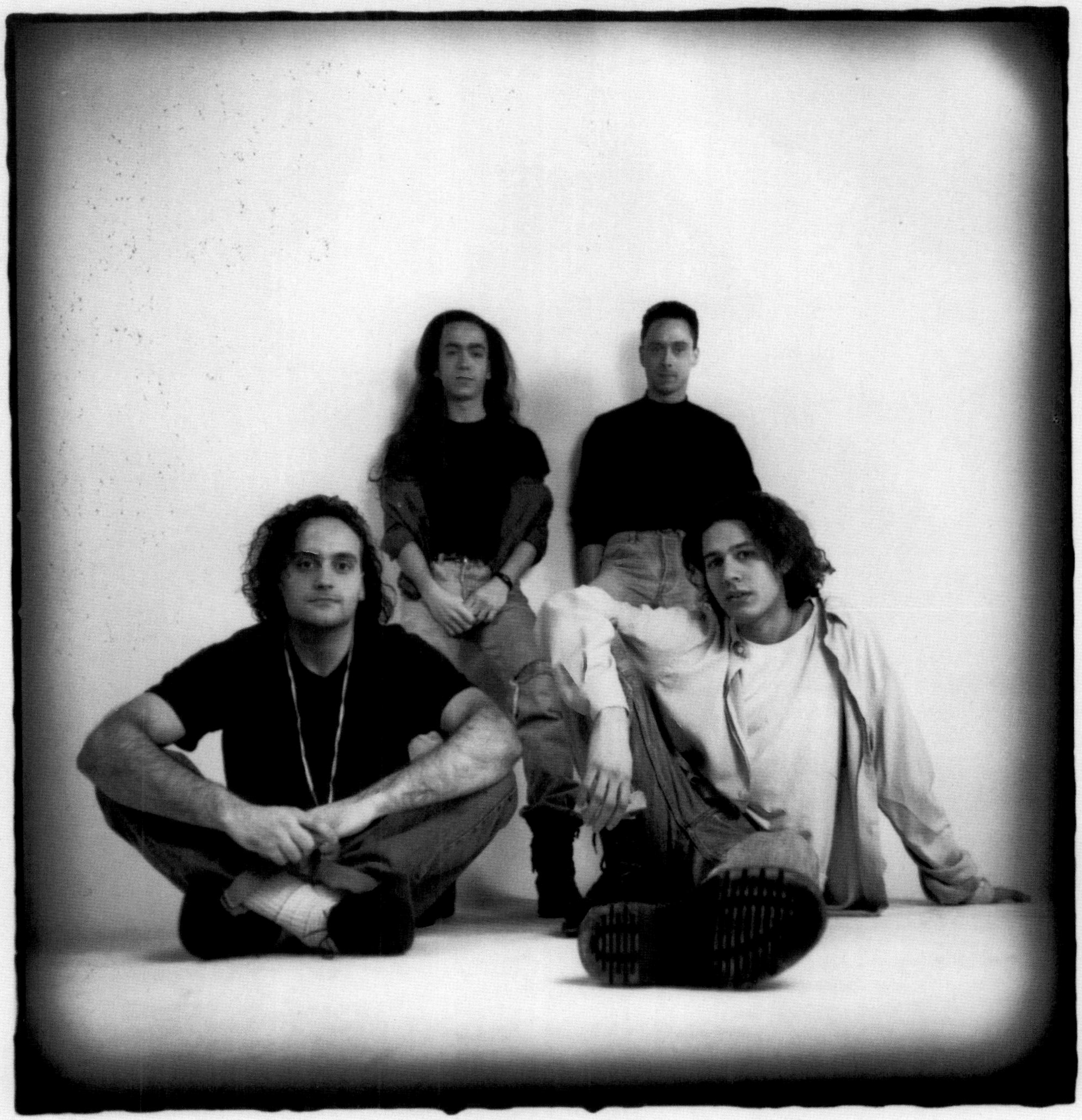

PHOTO: CHRIS CUFFARO/VISAGES, 1991

Michael Ward Dominic Nardini M.P Josh Clayton-Felt (seated)

SCHOOL OF FISH

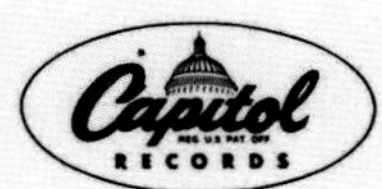

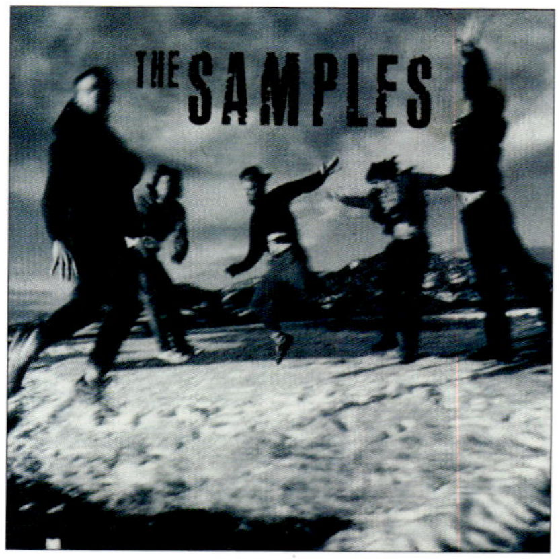

The Samples knew, after achieving regional success, that other bands didn't have to "feed the machine."

THE SAMPLES' emergence out of the burgeoning Colorado music scene had been no fluke. In 1986, vocalist and lead guitarist Sean Kelly and bassist Andy Sheldon moved from Vermont to the University of Colorado in Boulder. They put a drummer-wanted ad on a campus bulletin board, and fellow student Jeep MacNichol answered it. They then met keyboardist Al Laughlin (a Boston transplant) at a party. Mixing rock melodies and reggae rhythms, the Samples—naming themselves for their survival technique of making meals from free food samples at local supermarkets—toured incessantly.

"Most bands set out for a recording contract, but we didn't set out to do anything but play in Colorado," Kelly explained. "We just kinda happened by ourselves. Our fans were supportive students. They would buy our tapes, and during summer vacation they'd spread out across the country to go home. We created a big base. We knew there was an audience that liked the music, that we were onto something fresh."

In four years, the Samples rose from a free-thinking Boulder band to a group with national impact, opening for UB40, the Wailers and Johnny Clegg & Savuka. The quintet was close to a major label deal with Arista Records, but negotiations foundered over creative control. The band chose to release 5,000 copies of *The Samples* on their own label. When the initial shipment all but sold out, the Samples signed with Arista under their own terms.

The Samples cut down on the band's lengthy live jamming for well-constructed songs like "Waited Up." Instrumental strengths included MacNichol's inventive drumming and Kelly's sharp guitar leads. Kelly expected a nationwide barrage of comparisons to Sting (there was an undeniable vocal similarity).

The situation should have meant wide distribution, promotion and possible financial stability. The label told the Samples they would be placed under the wing of a new alternative music department. It never developed. *The Samples* sold more than 50,000 copies nationally, but the band soon found the A&R executives too preoccupied with trying to change the lyrics and style of what was to have become the second album. When asked specifically to write "hits" to push to radio and MTV, the Samples opted to be dropped from the label.

"I came up with a metaphor as to what major labels are—they're like driftnets," Kelly said. "They go out to sea and cast their big nets to get tunas like Mariah Carey and Whitney Houston, but they kill everything else that gets tangled in the nets, the beautiful dolphins. We were lucky enough to slip through the netting and survive." ■

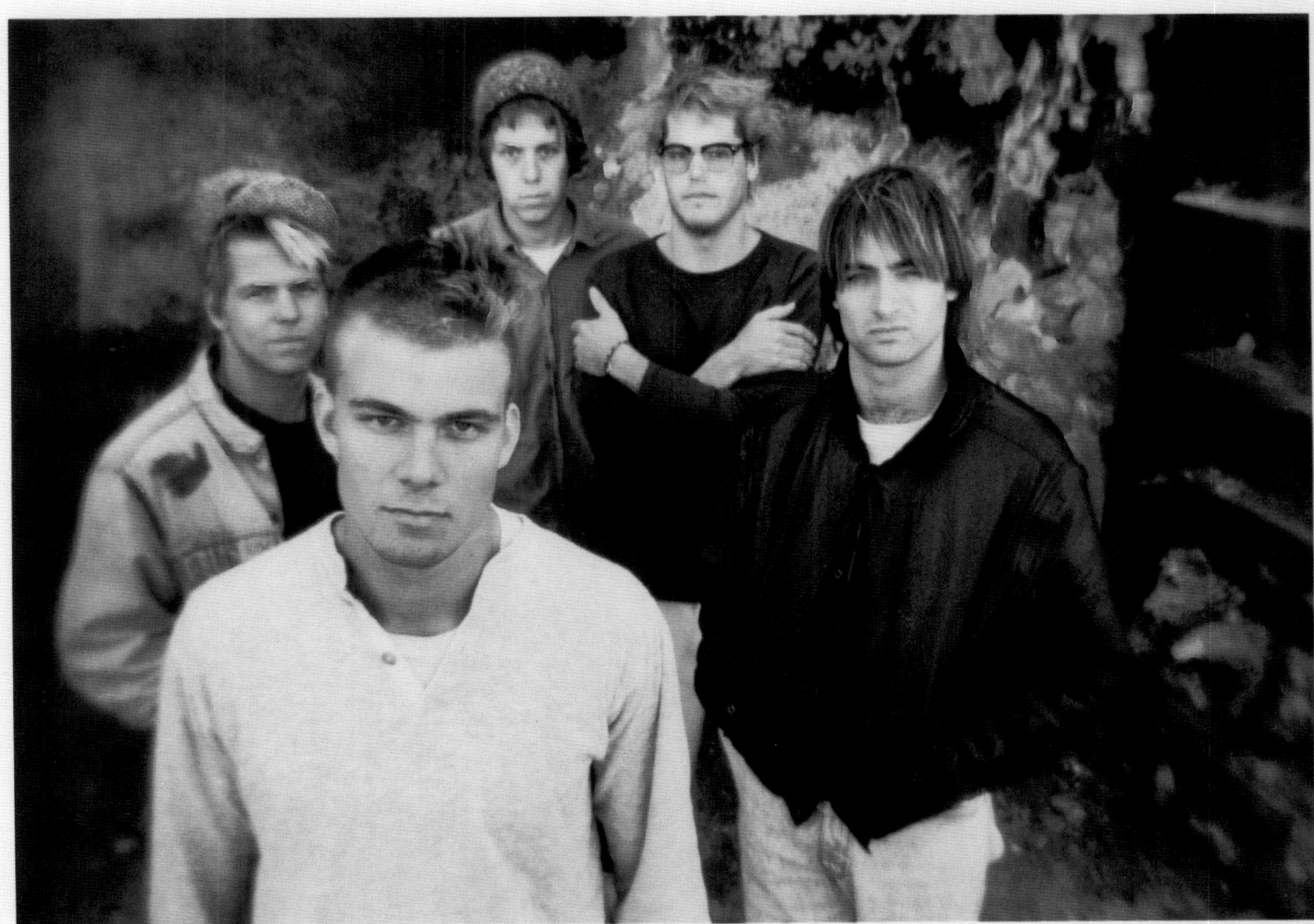

KRT Management Inc.
1776 Broadway
Suite 1710
NY NY 10019
(212) 265-9590

THE SAMPLES

ARISTA™

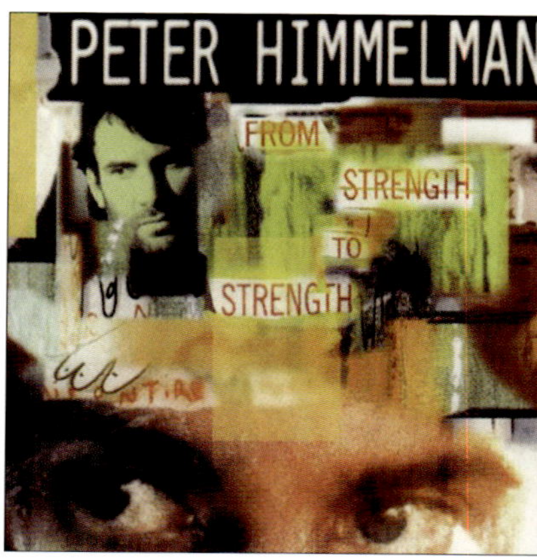

Peter Himmelman achieved significant radio airplay with his "Woman with the Strength of 10,000 Men."

PETER HIMMELMAN'S special gift was his uncommon emotional candor—the teeming passion on his albums put him among the most underrated talents in America. At the same time, the songs revealed his orthodox religious beliefs. Himmelman, a student of Jewish mysticism and law, integrated an overall "spirituality," but that was just another word for common sense.

"Anyone who's thinking straight understands that if you don't provide for your family and have peace in your home, there will never be peace in the world," Himmelman explained. "People are in control—you have to do moral deeds within your own sphere. There's merit to broad issues, but you don't find yourself in the Arctic Ocean to save the whales every day. Yet you do have the ability to listen to your wife and provide for her happiness, these things that sound so prosaic."

As an Orthodox Jew, Himmelman observed Shabbat, which meant he refused to perform on Friday nights—prime time in the music biz—and he ate only kosher foods, which wasn't easy on tour (he took up intense religious studies after a less strict upbringing). He also refused to trade on his relationship with his father-in-law—he married Bob Dylan's daughter, Maria, in 1988. For the singer-songwriter from Minnesota, searching out higher truths amid the wreckage of modern-age real-life situations was the true sound of rock 'n' roll rebellion. His album *From Strength to Strength* featured "Woman with the Strength of 10,000 Men," a moving song about the determination of a paralyzed woman.

"That's what mysticism is—transforming a person into a wiser, more compassionate, more moral character. It's very mysterious and awesome, much more so to me than Madonna grabbing her crotch on TV. Not that I have any problem with that, it doesn't offend me at all. She's great 'cause she's smart—I'm sure she doesn't think she's a visionary. But I have a problem with people ascribing a great value to what she presents—it disturbs me because people find it rebellious. It's not rebellious at all. We know it taunts a puritanical mindset, but so what? What's the next Madonna gonna do, go completely naked and writhe around with an alligator? It's all one and the same—completely boring."

Despite the introspective, personal, sharply observant nature of his music, Himmelman's live shows were riotous, free-form affairs. He did whatever struck him—between songs, he was a consistently challenging, insightful and weird storyteller. Audiences had come to expect the unexpected from his performances.

"I try to find something new every night," Himmelman admitted. "I set myself up for either great success or abysmal failure." ■

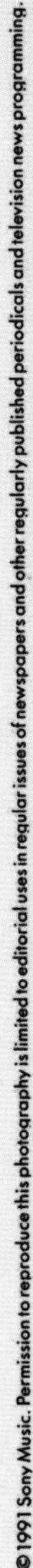
© 1991 Sony Music. Permission to reproduce this photography is limited to editorial uses in regular issues of newspapers and other regularly published periodicals and television news programming.

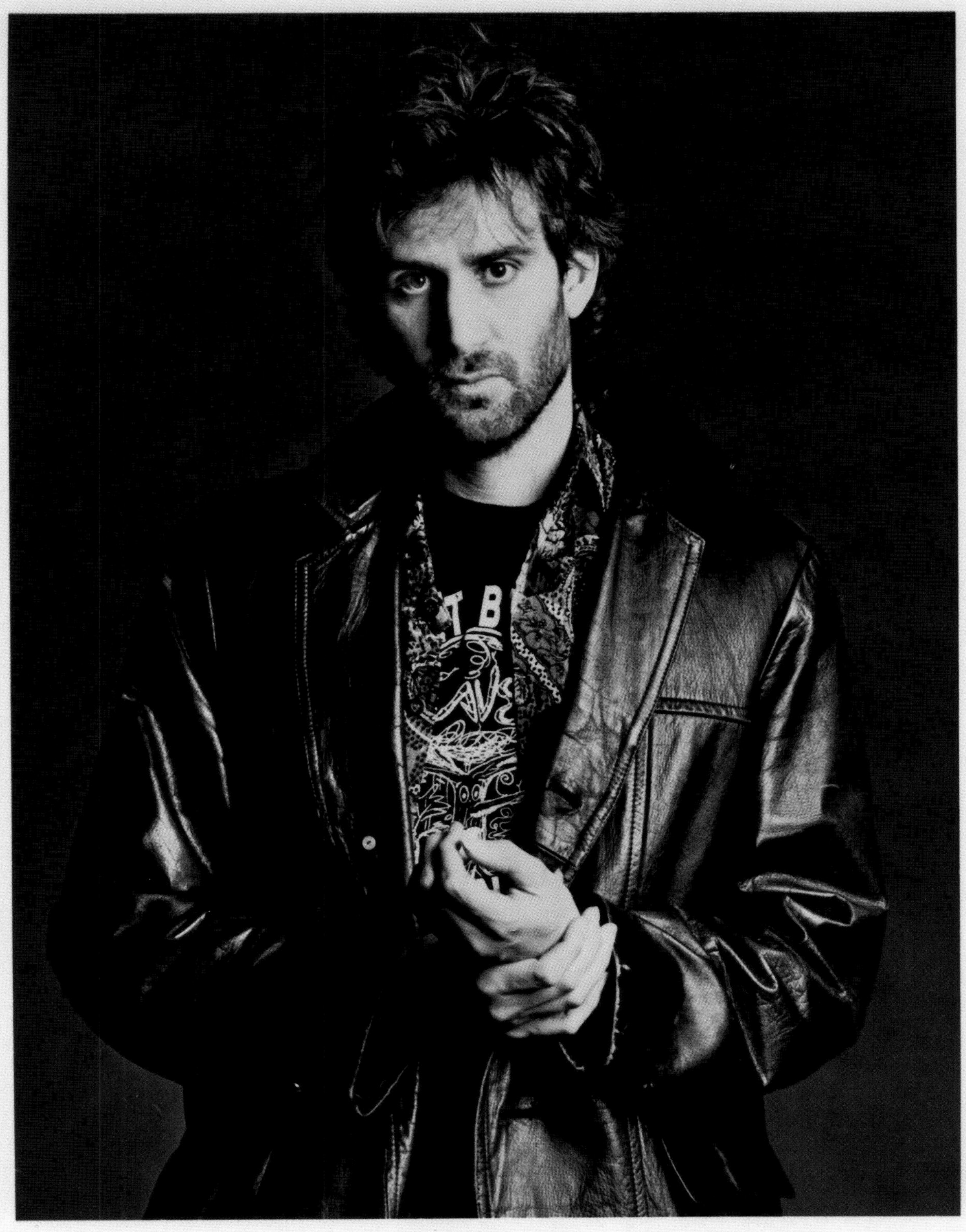

PHOTO: LYNN GOLDSMITH

PETER HIMMELMAN

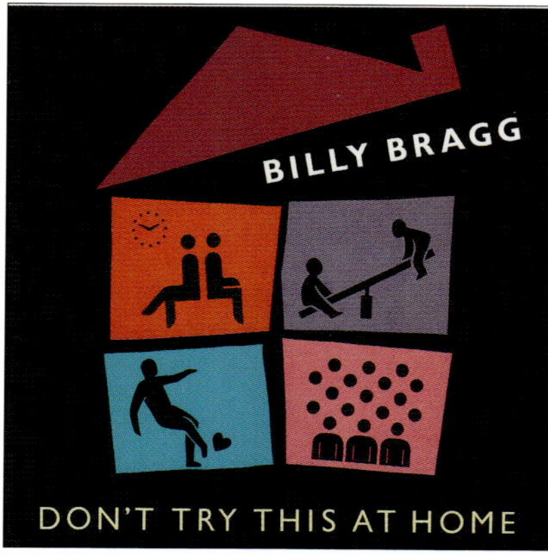

Transitioning from angry, edgy issues, *Don't Try This at Home* was Billy Bragg's warmest set of songs.

BILLY BRAGG grew up in a suburb of London, where he established an eye for the nuances of working-class principles and customs. Inspired by the Clash, the Jam and the songwriting of Elvis Costello, Bragg gained public attention with his strident political wake-up calls. He'd been recognized as the "Swingin' Socialist" for singing radical socialist dogma, the "Cuddly Commie" for playing in communist countries, and the "Lovable Laborite" for doing countless benefits for labor organizations and trade unions and campaigning for his native country's Labour Party.

But he had also been capable of touching, warm love songs—1986's "Levi Stubbs' Tears" was a chilling tale of a tragic couple.

"I'm disappointed that any number of soul divas haven't had a go at those songs," Bragg admitted. "I can't sing them like they could."

So the rough-hewn troubadour had branched out musically from singing pithy compositions playing a solitary electric guitar. *Don't Try This at Home* had less left-wing propaganda and more human emotion, cloaking his biting commentary in catchy arrangements.

"I'm very proud of finally making a record that makes more sense to the American audience," Bragg said. "From a career standpoint, I was getting annoyed that people who didn't know my material thought of me as a political solo singer. But most important, the ideological language of the mid-Eighties has changed now that we're in the post-Marxist period. It isn't relevant at the moment. It will be again, but if I wrote those songs, it'd be, 'Bill, the game's up, you can't keep plowing that rut.'"

Don't Try This at Home was his first album to feature a full-band sound. The pop direction of "Sexuality" was a collaboration with Johnny Marr of the Smiths. The infectious single poked fun at Bragg's image: "I've had relations/With girls from many nations/I've made passes/At women of all classes/And just because you're gay/I won't turn you away/If you stick around/I'm sure that we can find some common ground." "Sexuality" reached #2 on *Billboard*'s modern rock chart in the US.

"The moment of inspiration came from watching those macho sexist videos you see on channels in hotel rooms around the world, talking about the sexual prowess of the singer," Bragg explained. "I thought it was so ripe for twisting around, to be an expression of sexual identity instead of sexual prowess. The most important thing was getting Johnny involved with the whole project. He lifted it from a good idea to a great song." ■

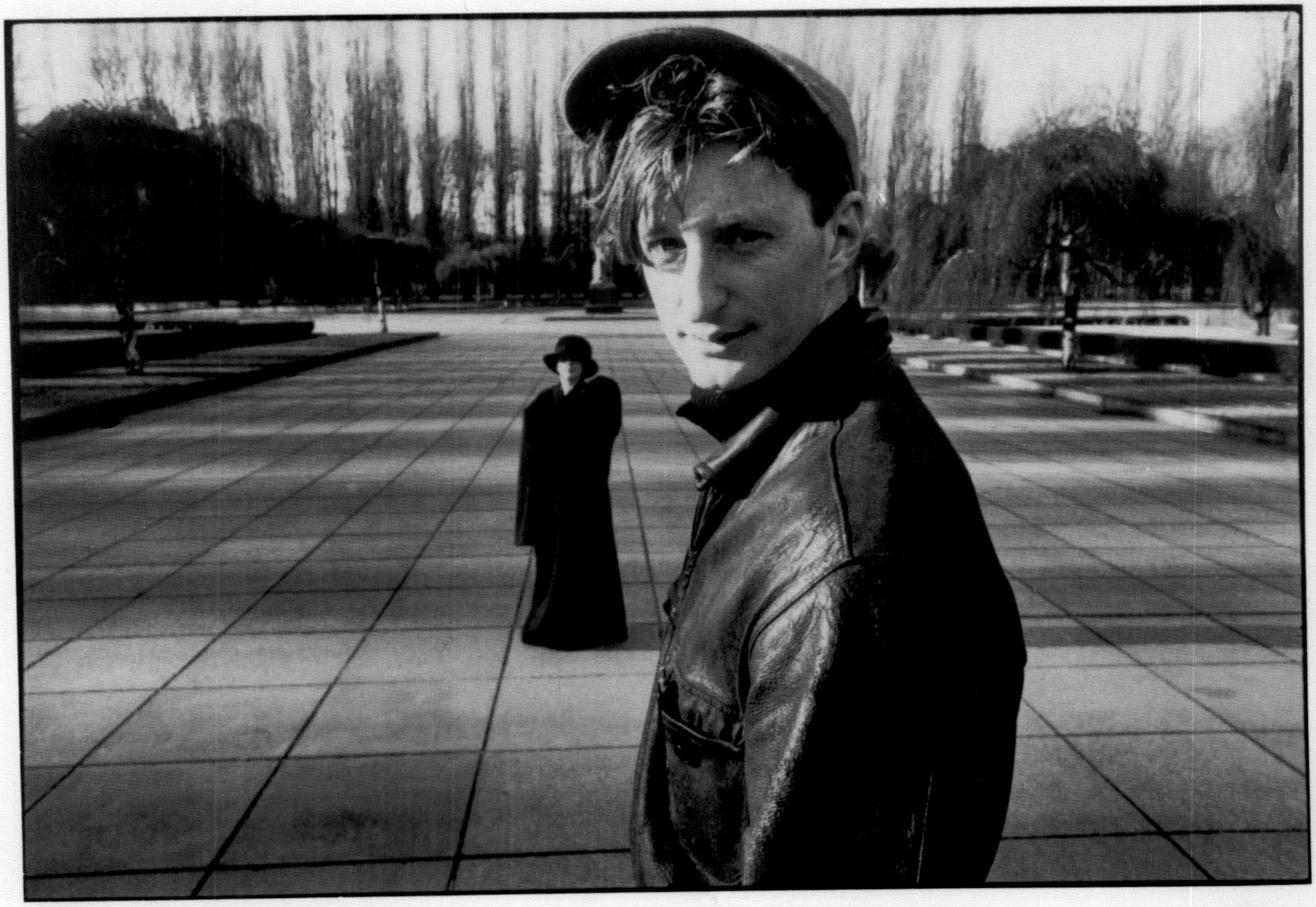

BILLY BRAGG

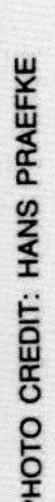

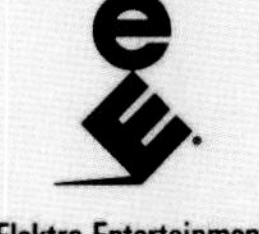

Elektra Entertainment

Patty Larkin delivered *Tango*, a highly praised release of romantic reflections and contemplative ballads.

AMONG THE growing chorus of new singer-songwriters, Patty Larkin was becoming a familiar voice. She was excited about being part of the resurgence, hearing people speak of an "urban folk," "new acoustic," "neo-folk" or "fringe-folk" movement.

"But once you use the word 'folk,' people have an image of a woman with a guitar and a muumuu, ironing her hair," Larkin laughed. "It's unfortunate that we're dragging that behind us. It's been a grassroots thing. When it first started bubbling up five years ago, we used to say, 'Where is this folk revival? I'll move there!' But then Suzanne Vega and Tracy Chapman and even Edie Brickell drew from those rootsier sounds. Now you see songwriters like Nanci Griffith or Shawn Colvin on *The Tonight Show*, and you know something's happening."

A powerful presence with her emotive vocals and intelligent songwriting, Larkin had been tearing up stages in New England and at festivals around the country for many years. Backed by a spare ensemble on *Tango*, the Boston-based musician documented heartfelt love songs and assertive expressions of social conscience ("Metal Drums," about toxic waste). Her clean, accomplished acoustic guitar technique was a recording strength as well.

"After my college days, I played electric guitar in a jazz context and a rock 'n' roll band. I loved the Pretenders and the Police. I didn't play punk, but I liked it because it was anti-Bee Gees. But I found myself doing some acoustic gigs and really getting into the idea that people were listening. There was an attention being paid to words and music coming from the heart. That's what drew me back in as a writer."

In concert, Larkin was a jokester, weaving ironic stories and comic sendups into her tapestry of songs. On *Tango*, her satirical side was represented by the gleeful "Dave's Barbeque," about a strange vacationer who sets up "a bug-zapper barbeque."

"It's funny to mix regular singer-songwriter staples with humor in performance—it helps make a connection with the audience," she said. "That's entertainment, it livens things up. But when I get to recording, it doesn't always transfer. Unless it's something you're known for, there's a problem of hearing a joke too many times. I think we got something with 'Dave's Holiday,' and if people disagree, I figure they can just skip ahead on the CD." ■

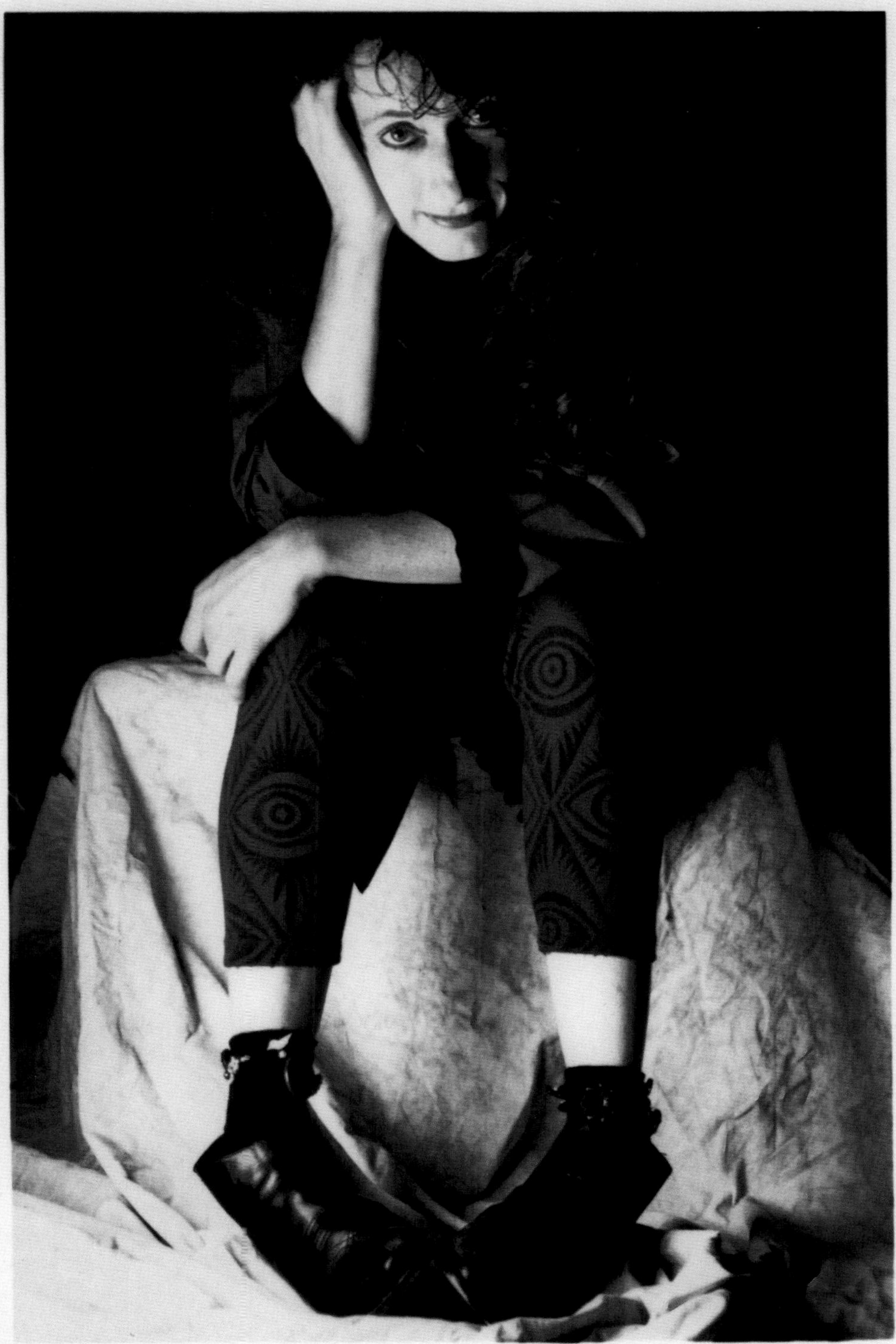

High Street Records™ Recording Artist

Patty Larkin

High Street Records™ Publicity Office,

3500 West Olive Avenue, Suite 1430, Burbank, CA

91505 (818) 972-4242

FLEMING TAMULEVICH & Associates INC.

Artist Representatives (313) 995-9066

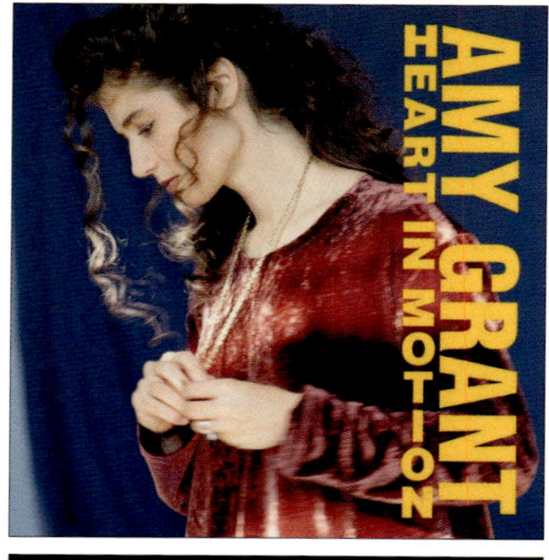

In pursuit of secular fame, Amy Grant's *Heart in Motion* bore five Top 20 pop hits, including "Baby Baby."

Billboard 200: *Heart in Motion* (#10)
Billboard Hot 100: "Baby Baby" (No. 1); "Every Heartbeat" (#2); "That's What Love Is For" (#7); "Good for Me" (#8); "I Will Remember You" (#20)

WITH HER earliest albums, Amy Grant earned five Grammys and sold more than 10 million records as a superstar in the so-called "gospel ghetto" of contemporary Christian music. She then stretched beyond her traditional boundaries and presented music with more temporal themes. The foray struck a positive chord with her fans—"Baby Baby" and "Every Heartbeat," from her *Heart in Motion* album, had no obvious spiritual overtones, but they hit the top of the pop and adult contemporary charts as well as the Christian charts.

"There was a time when it was important for me not to cross over. Ten years ago, I said, 'I want to write songs for Christian kids, I want to make an impact on them,'" Grant noted. "But today it's important to go into the prevailing trends of music. I'm not going to cling to what I was doing back in 1981 just because it's safe. If somebody says, 'You're trying to go secular,' I say, 'Of course I am—that's the whole point.' I'll always want to make my old crowd proud, but this album has to do with me as a Christian stepping out on the platform and being a voice in our culture. I want to be a great songwriter and write about what we're all going through. And that naturally draws me into the mainstream pop world."

Grant hadn't lost her inspiring vocal edge, but she'd acquired a sleeker image—she said she wrote the No. 1 "Baby Baby" about her infant daughter Millie, yet the song's video found her cuddling with a cute guy, gently singing in his ear and looking stylish. That departure from her straight-and-narrow character had some of her religious fans wondering if she'd "bitten the apple" and forsaken her spiritual roots for mainstream fame. A few Christian radio stations excluded "Baby Baby" from their playlists, and a small number of Christian bookstores pulled the album. But Grant had raised the ire of fundamentalist Christians ever since she began flirting with secular success five years earlier.

"I don't see what could be 'controversial' about a simple, innocent love song," she mused. "Some people feel that if music doesn't have any evangelical content, then it doesn't have any value. I have a different thought process—I feel like what I'm trying to do is very important and necessary. There's a part of me saying, 'I want to be able to turn on the radio and hear some good, fun songs where I'm not being pressured materially, sexually or violence-wise.' I just wanted to challenge misconceptions of gospel musicians by showing they're not bloodless Barbie & Ken dolls. Because of music, my view through the window is a lot broader than it ever would have been before. But as a person, I feel like I'm right in stride with my sisters—I'm (the youngest) of four girls. I don't think I took a hard left at any point along the way and turned into somebody else. And I'm sure if I had, they'd have taken me out behind the house and killed me." ■

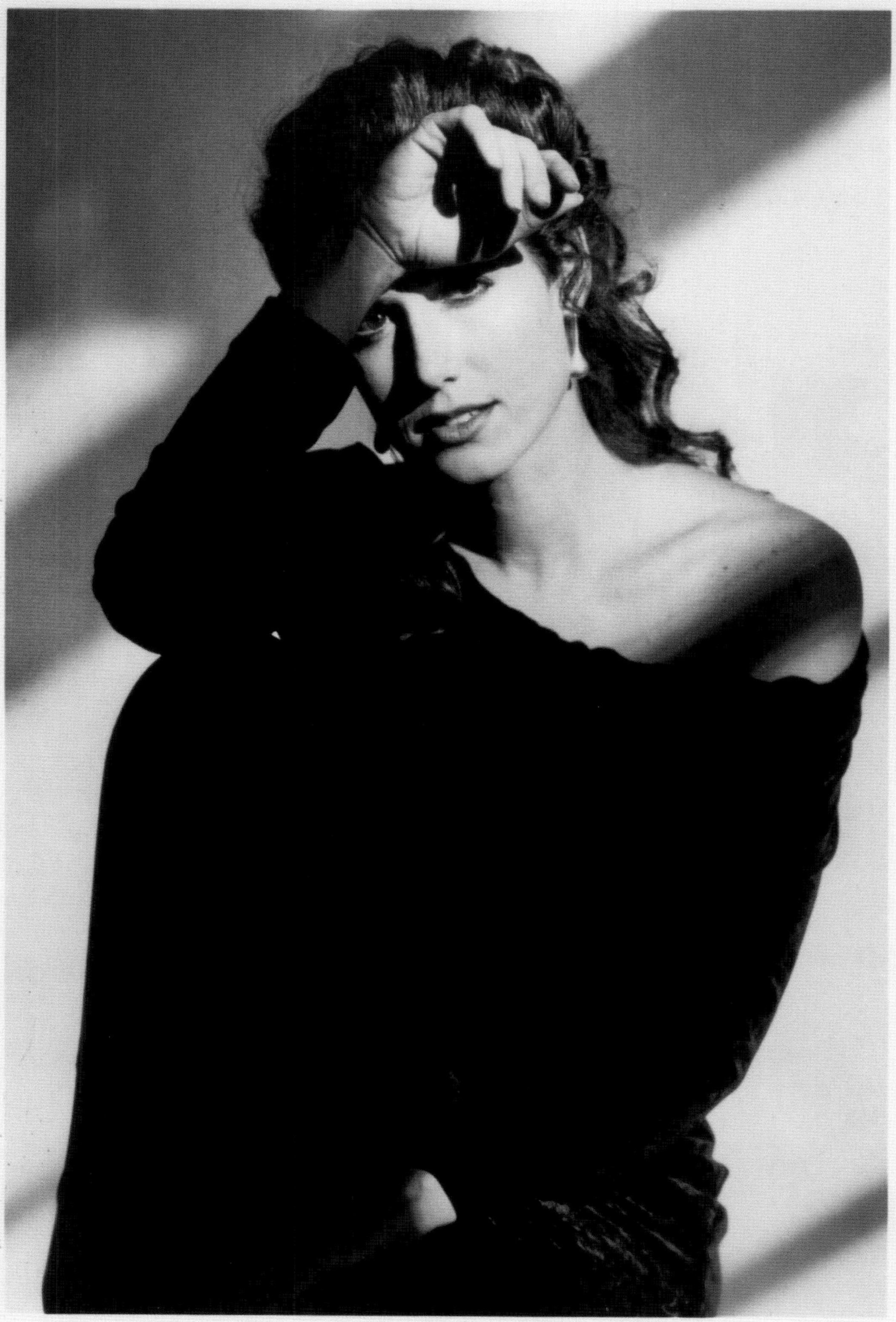

Photo Credit: Victoria Pearson-Cameron

AMY GRANT

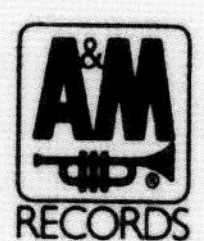

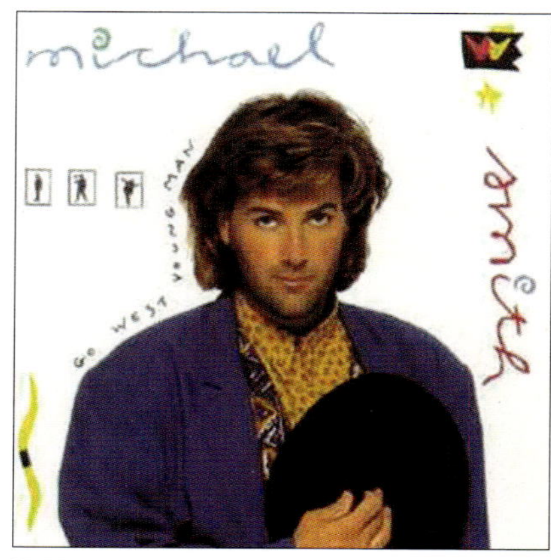

Michael W. Smith bridged his mainstream aspirations and Christian roots with "Place in This World."

Billboard 200: *Go West Young Man* (#74)
Billboard Hot 100: "Place in This World" (#6)

POPULAR CONTEMPORARY Christian artist Michael W. Smith had scored seven No. 1 hits on Christian radio, releasing six previous albums. His label, Reunion Records, allowed Geffen Records to distribute his *Go West Young Man* album in 1991, providing the singer-songwriter with a chance to tap into the mainstream market. The single, "Place in the World," crossed over and hit #6 on the *Billboard* Hot 100.

"I think it's interesting because I'm hardly an overnight sensation—a lot of people have been with me for so long," the Nashville-based musician explained. "But it's great that I'm gaining a new audience. It's just that it's too early to think that you've got tons of new fans."

In 1982, Smith signed on as a keyboard player in Amy Grant's touring band and was opening her shows before the year was out. As contemporary Christian music became a full-fledged industry, Smith and Grant had broken through to mainstream pop success as clean-living rock stars.

"Some of my favorite musicians are Elton John, Bryan Adams and Janet Jackson," Smith said. "But my faith is the most important thing in my life. I think pop-rock music could use some more positive role models."

Smith's music had an esteem-building message, but his "Christian sex symbol" image was unusual. He wasn't flirtatious, but he was good-looking and very charming. *People* magazine chose him as one of the world's "50 Most Beautiful People."

"I'm sure there's a lot of stuff said that I wouldn't appreciate," he concluded. "I don't pay too much attention to the external. The marketing people are just doing their jobs—'Hey, he's got pretty blue eyes!' It all has to do with who you hang with, who your friends are. It can go to your head and you can get into the schmooze thing, but I don't play that game. I'm really a normal guy—a family guy, a husband and father of five. That's my priority." ■

michael W smith

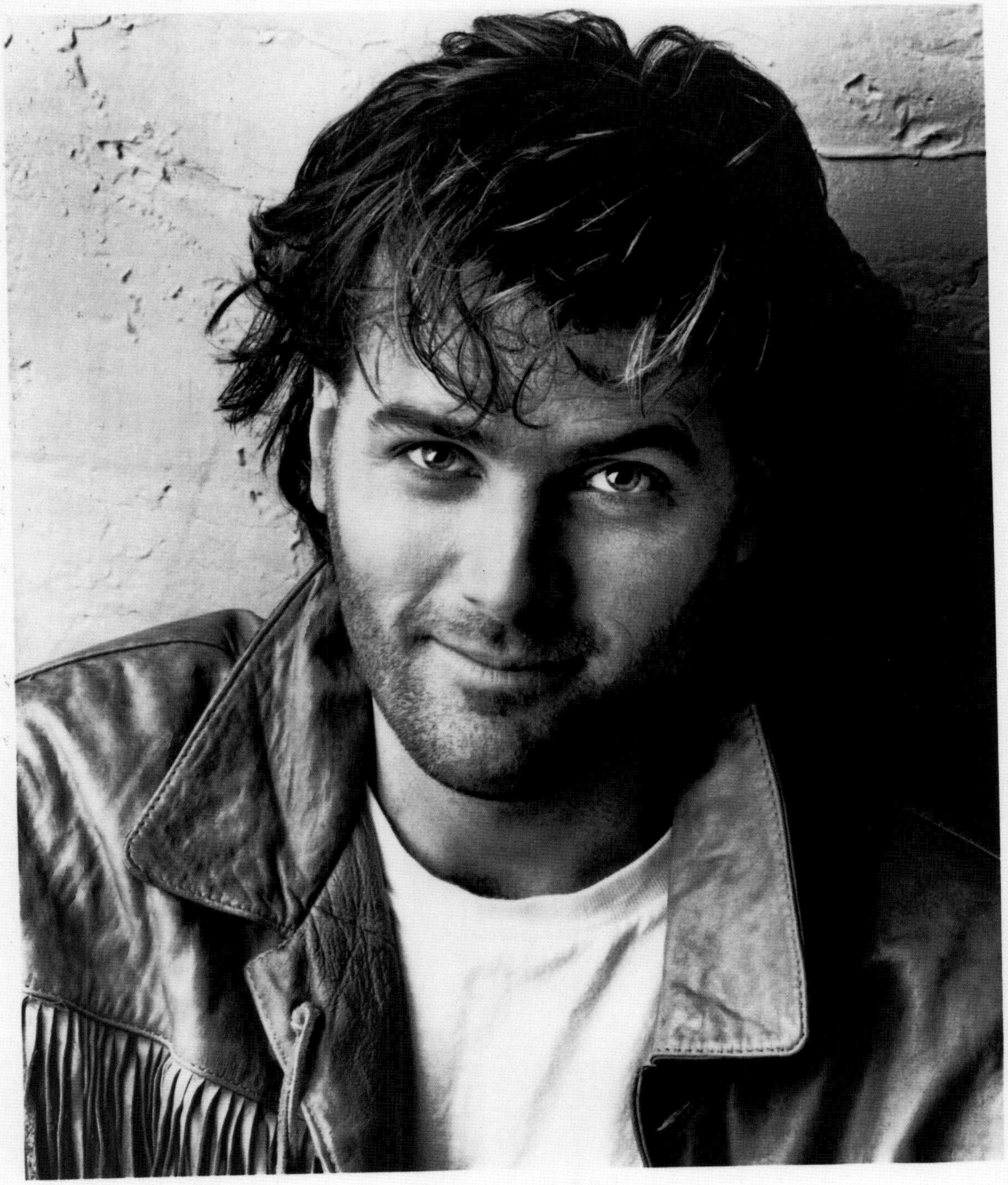

Photo credit: Mark Tucker

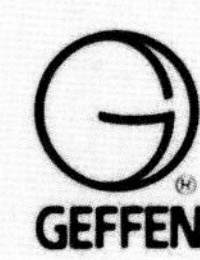

NEIL DIAMOND
Lovescape

Dominant pop force **Neil Diamond** continued to enchant his fans and challenge his critics with *Lovescape*.

Billboard 200: *Lovescape* (#44)

CONSIDERING THE ephemeral nature of pop culture, the response of Neil Diamond's fans remained astounding. For years, his massive following had never wavered, turning out in droves and setting attendance records at major venues across the country.

How had Diamond endured and continued the love affair between him and his fans, packing arenas at will? Why did his public respond to him so extraordinarily?

"They're the ones who make the show great for me—they've been loyal," Diamond said. "I made a promise I would do this as best I could for as long as I could, if they would keep their minds open to the music. That's the unspoken deal. It's the greatest job in the world, and I'm dedicated to it. But the little things make it hard. I don't like being in a hotel room eating a peanut butter and jelly sandwich while my kid is off school today, home alone. He's 14, he takes it like a man, he understands. I've been gone 140 days this year, my wife is a champ about it. But that's part of the price a person has to pay."

Diamond's remarkable course as a songwriter started at the Brill Building, the early-Fifties tune factory, where he wrote such songs-to-order as "I'm a Believer" for the Monkees. He eventually started performing and scored a breakthrough in the mid-Sixties with "Solitary Man" and "Cherry, Cherry."

"It was an amazing time, exciting, frightening, and there was always hope, because we were young and dumb and the whole world was open for us. But it was a long time coming. I spent eight years in Tin Pan Alley trying to figure out what the hell I was doing and where I was going. In those days, you were living from single to single, from advance to advance. If you picked up $50 for a song, that meant that you could feed yourself for another week."

Since 1975, Diamond had evolved into an easy-listening crooner, establishing himself with ballads. *Lovescape* marked his 19th studio album. "Hooked on the Memory of You," a duet with Kim Carnes, made #23 on *Billboard*'s Adult Contemporary chart; a version of "Don't Turn Around," co-written by Albert Hammond and Diane Warren, reached #19.

Diamond was sometimes dismissed by rockers who said he was unhip, that a tendency for ponderous middle-of-the-road schlock had overwhelmed his talent—in some cases, deservedly so. But Diamond was amiable about it.

"We all live and die in the hope that what we do is of enough quality and artistic merit to have validity," he mused. "But I know I don't fit in." ■

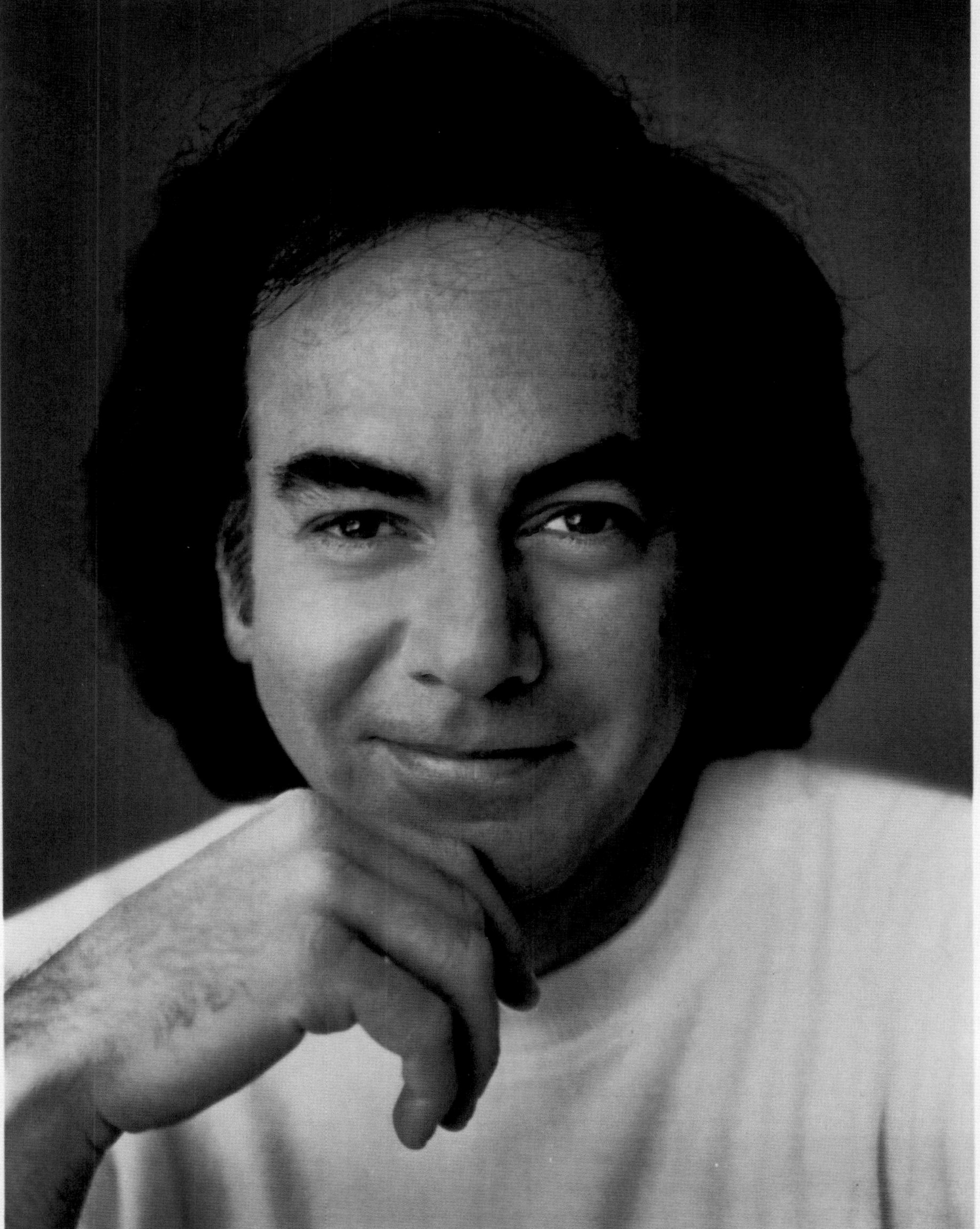

© 1991 Sony Music. Permission to reproduce this photography is limited to editorial uses in regular issues of newspapers and other regularly published periodicals and television news programming.

Photo Credit: Matthew Rolston

GALLIN·MOREY·ASSOCIATES
8730 SUNSET BOULEVARD PENTHOUSE WEST LOS ANGELES, CALIFORNIA 90069

NEIL DIAMOND

Columbia
9108

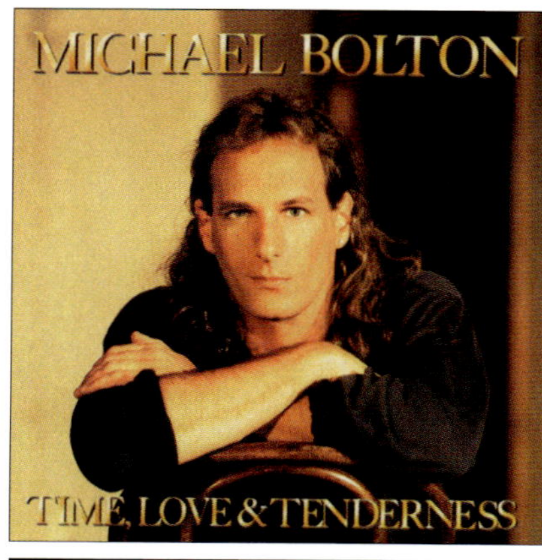

Billboard 200: *Time, Love & Tenderness* (No. 1)
Billboard Hot 100: "When a Man Loves a Woman" (No. 1); "Love Is a Wonderful Thing" (#4); "Time, Love and Tenderness" (#7); "Missing You Now" (#12)

Michael Bolton's *Time, Love & Tenderness* included a cover of Percy Sledge's "When a Man Loves a Woman."

MICHAEL BOLTON'S full-throated adult-pop ballads were guaranteed to make his mostly female, mostly white disciples swoon. He was the dream lover who knew how they felt—the kind of guy who would never forget an anniversary or go out partying with the boys.

"It's too bad that their boyfriends get jealous sometimes," Bolton said with a laugh. Bolton had originally performed pop-tinged hard rock. He became better known as a soft-rock balladeer after a stylistic change in the late Eighties. The massive commercial success of *Time, Love & Tenderness* was hardly a joke, but rock critics everywhere loved to pick on him anyway. He had a few excesses—his voice lacked subtlety, and his hernia-patient singing style was chronically overdone.

Bolton's version of Percy Sledge's "When a Man Loves a Woman" soared to No. 1 and scored him a Grammy. For those old enough to remember the original version, that rendition was cause to mourn. His idea of blue-eyed soul was to turn up the screech quotient, robustly bellowing out the familiar R&B classic.

Bolton didn't put up with the abuse.

"The most compelling factor in music, for me, has always been the vocal performance," he said. "That's what makes my spine tingle, the way the human spirit comes through in a great vocal."

Another hit, "Love Is a Wonderful Thing," later became the subject of a successful plagiarism suit brought against Bolton by the Isley Brothers. ■

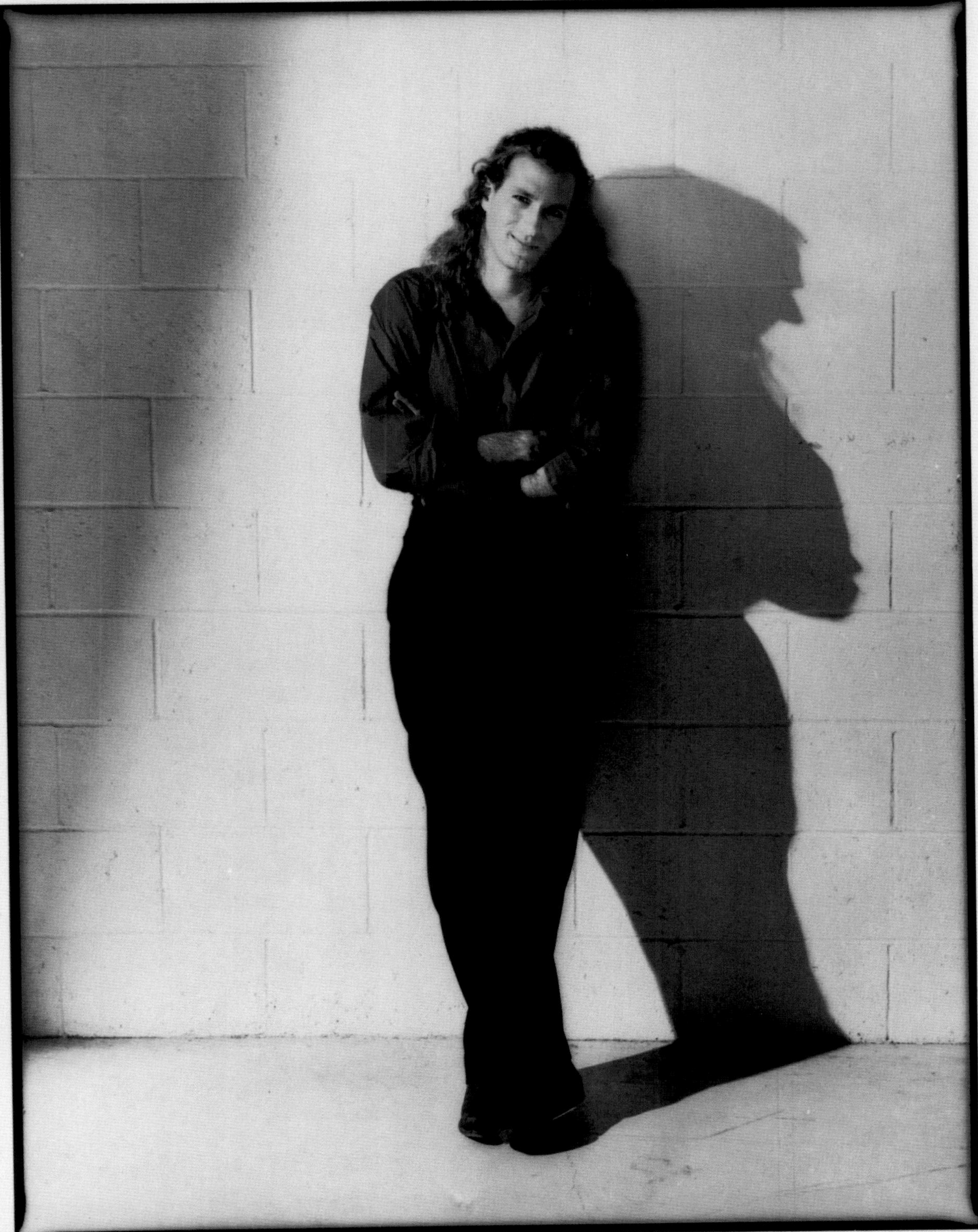

PHOTOGRAPH: TIMOTHY WHITE

© 1991 Sony Music. Permission to reproduce this photography is limited to editorial uses in regular issues of newspapers and other regularly published periodicals and television news programming.

Direction:
Louis Levin Management
130 West 57th St. #10-B
New York, NY 10019
Phone: 212.489.5738
FAX: 212.489.6319

MICHAEL BOLTON

Columbia
9105

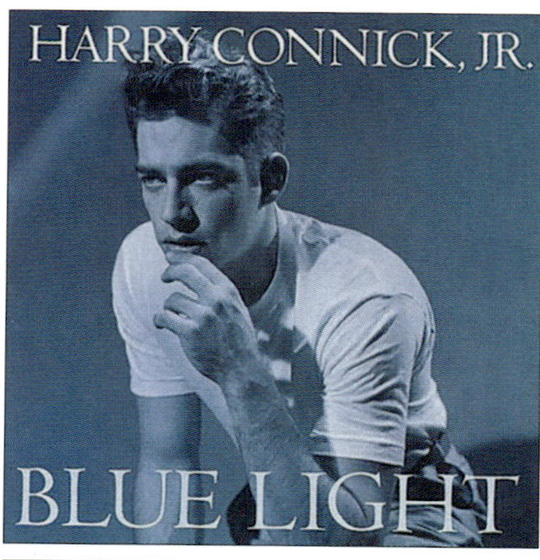

Billboard 200: *Blue Light, Red Light* (#17)

Harry Connick Jr.'s Grammy-nominated album *Blue Light, Red Light* debuted at No.1 on the jazz charts.

CELEBRATED AS one of modern music's top emerging young singers and performers, Harry Connick Jr. was an improbable superstar. In the era of rap and rock, he was an accomplished pianist reestablishing a classic American idiom—the jazz and swing of the Forties and Fifties.

With his slicked-back hair, Armani suits and youthful good looks, the ingratiating Connick personified style, quality and excitement to his millions of adoring fans. Yet with all the attention had come an adjustment to his sudden wunderkind status. He'd taken savage knocks from critics for his "vanilla" sound and phrasing, a pallid derivative of the vintage black artists of the past. He could sound arrogant, brashly speaking of his distaste for contemporary pop ("kiddie music," he called it). And he worked under the weight of endless comparisons with a young Frank Sinatra that suggested his inferiority.

But Connick was a born entertainer who aimed to please and succeed. Disarmingly honest and self-deprecating, he knew he had a whole life of music ahead of him.

"I'm not burdened by criticism, the people making it are burdened," Connick said in his honeyed Louisiana accent. "It's not a big deal. Anyone who knows anything about music knows I'm not a masterful singer yet. I have a lot to work on. I'm just doing it my way, at my pace, writing and performing—and enjoying it. Everybody has his own place in the world. That's the only attitude I've ever had."

Connick first came to prominence with covers of standards—by the time he was 20, he already had two well-received albums of solo piano and trio. The soundtrack for the 1989 movie *When Harry Met Sally* marked the first time Connick recorded with a big band and orchestra, and it turbocharged his career. He won a Grammy for the album, which sold more than a million copies in the United States, a phenomenal amount by jazz criteria. It catapulted him from clubs to concert halls overnight.

Blue Light, Red Light was a dazzling exercise, a big band recording featuring 12 songs all written or co-written, arranged and orchestrated by Connick."There wasn't a lot of mystery to it," he said of commanding horns and woodwinds. "I taught myself how to orchestrate by sitting down and doing it. When you have to score something for 18 people, it's not that spontaneous."

Connick launched an ambitious big band tour that took him around the world. He also seemed poised to become a movie star. In 1990, he portrayed a tail gunner in the motion picture *Memphis Belle*.

"I take life day to day. It's boring from the media's point of view, but there's too much philosophizing going on about me. What's the big deal? I haven't done anything that spectacular. There are other musicians far greater than I'll ever be. I'm just real fortunate to have a big band. It's expensive on the road, but it's important that people have the opportunity to hear it." ■

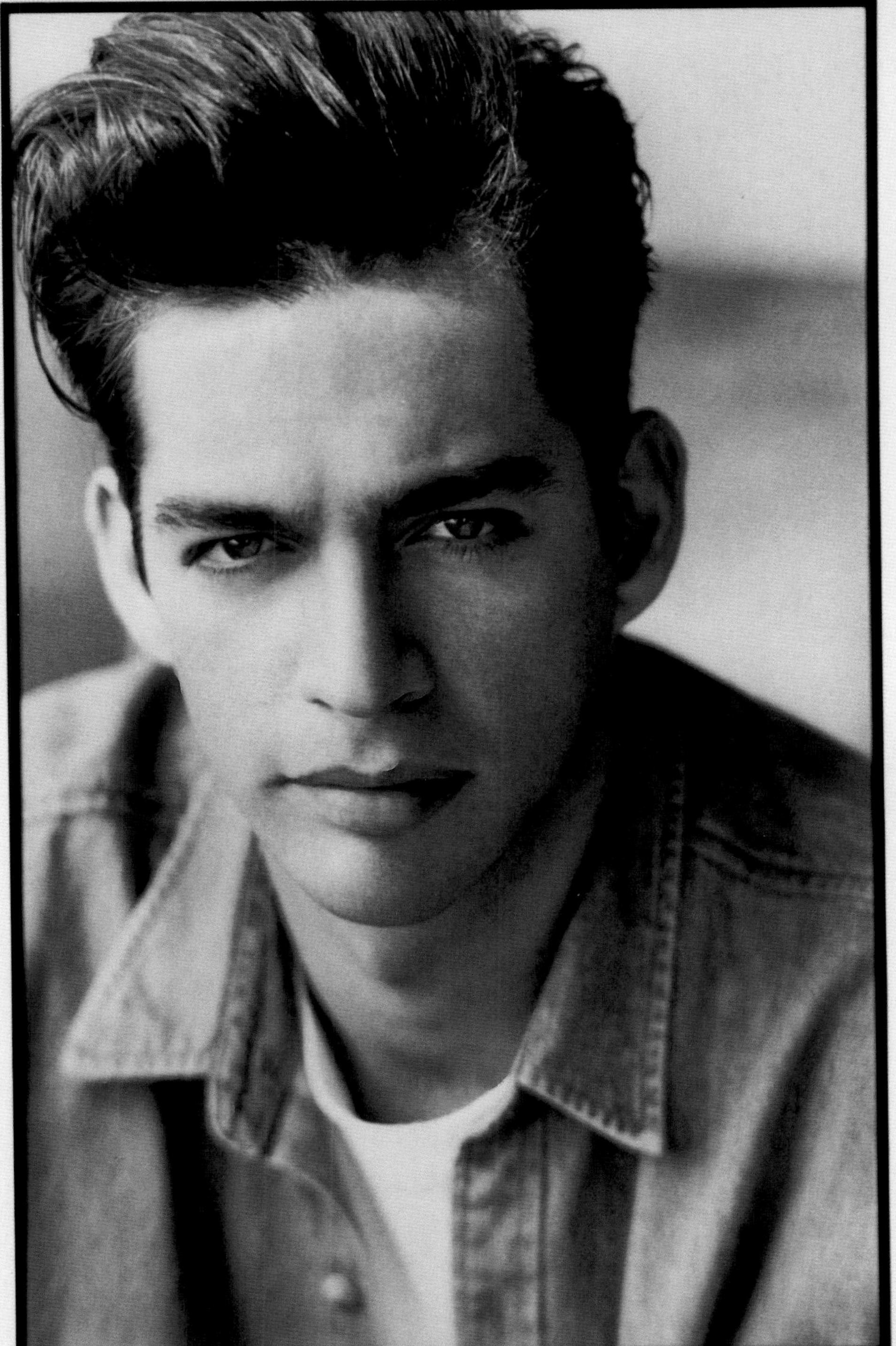

© 1991 Sony Music. Permission to reproduce this photography is limited to editorial uses in regular issues of newspapers and other regularly published periodicals and television news programming.

Photo Credit: Palma Kolansky

HARRY CONNICK, JR.

Columbia
9108

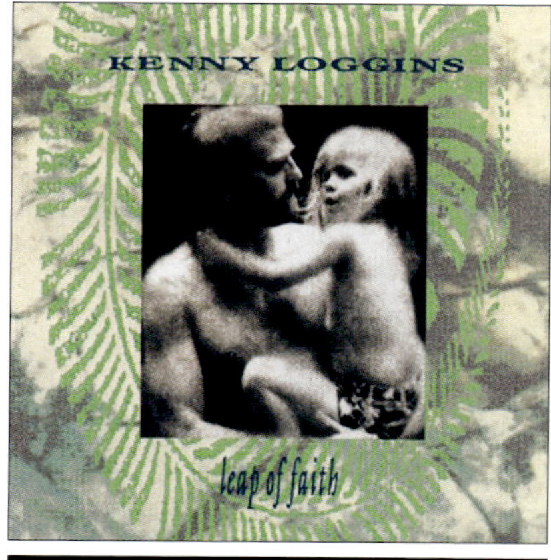

The self-revealing, cathartic *Leap of Faith* was a far cry from some of Kenny Loggins' lighter albums.

Billboard 200: *Leap of Faith* (#71)
Billboard Hot 100: "Conviction of the Heart" (#65)

HE'D BEEN one of pop music's top singer-songwriters for the past two decades, from his early days as one-half of Loggins & Messina through his years as a premier hitmaker—"Whenever I Call You 'Friend'," "This Is It," "I'm Alright," "Footloose," "Danger Zone."

But that was the old Kenny Loggins. The new one was more concerned with spreading a reverent message on his *Leap of Faith* album. He appeared on virtually every television and radio program in America, explaining that *Leap of Faith* chronicled "a painful period of decision and separation."

In 1990, Loggins owned a multimillion-dollar Santa Barbara house, 20 acres of land and three cars. But he gave it all up, separating from his wife of 13 years (they had three children). His rebirth since that time informed the unabashedly emotional statement behind *Leap of Faith*.

"We still cared for and respected each other. We liked the same movies, we shared the same sense of humor. That's valid, and a lot of people settle for that. I might have, too, if the cards had been dealt differently," he said softly. "But at a certain point I realized that I wanted something more. We did everything to save the relationship, but no technique can fill in for love.

"We mutually split, which is important. *Leap of Faith* isn't about leaving your wife for another woman. *Leap of Faith* is about leaving a situation, believing that love exists and trusting that somehow you're going to have it. Saying, 'I'm not where I belong and I will push myself out in the void and see where I land and trust that it's where I belong.' That's the driving force of the album—love exists, courage is rewarded."

With Loggins' positive spiritual attitude and supple falsetto to lead the way, *Leap of Faith* addressed the upheaval of his divorce, the mystery of his new love, his struggle to make peace with his late father and the strains and joys of parenthood. "Conviction of the Heart," a Top 5 adult contemporary single, was a plea for the suffering planet.

The earnest, revelatory nature of the album set up Loggins as an easy target for cynics.

"When they say that I'm naïve or a romantic fool, I have to know that I'm painting colors they haven't seen, they haven't experienced what I'm talking about," Loggins reflected. "I didn't fabricate this. I didn't say, 'Oh, now's a good time to come out with my sensitive music—I'll catch the Robert Bly wave.' This is just what's happened to me, and the music came through. But there must be something in the air. There's an authenticity that's touching people. They crave the truth, content in music. They want to feel, and my album assists people in feeling." ■

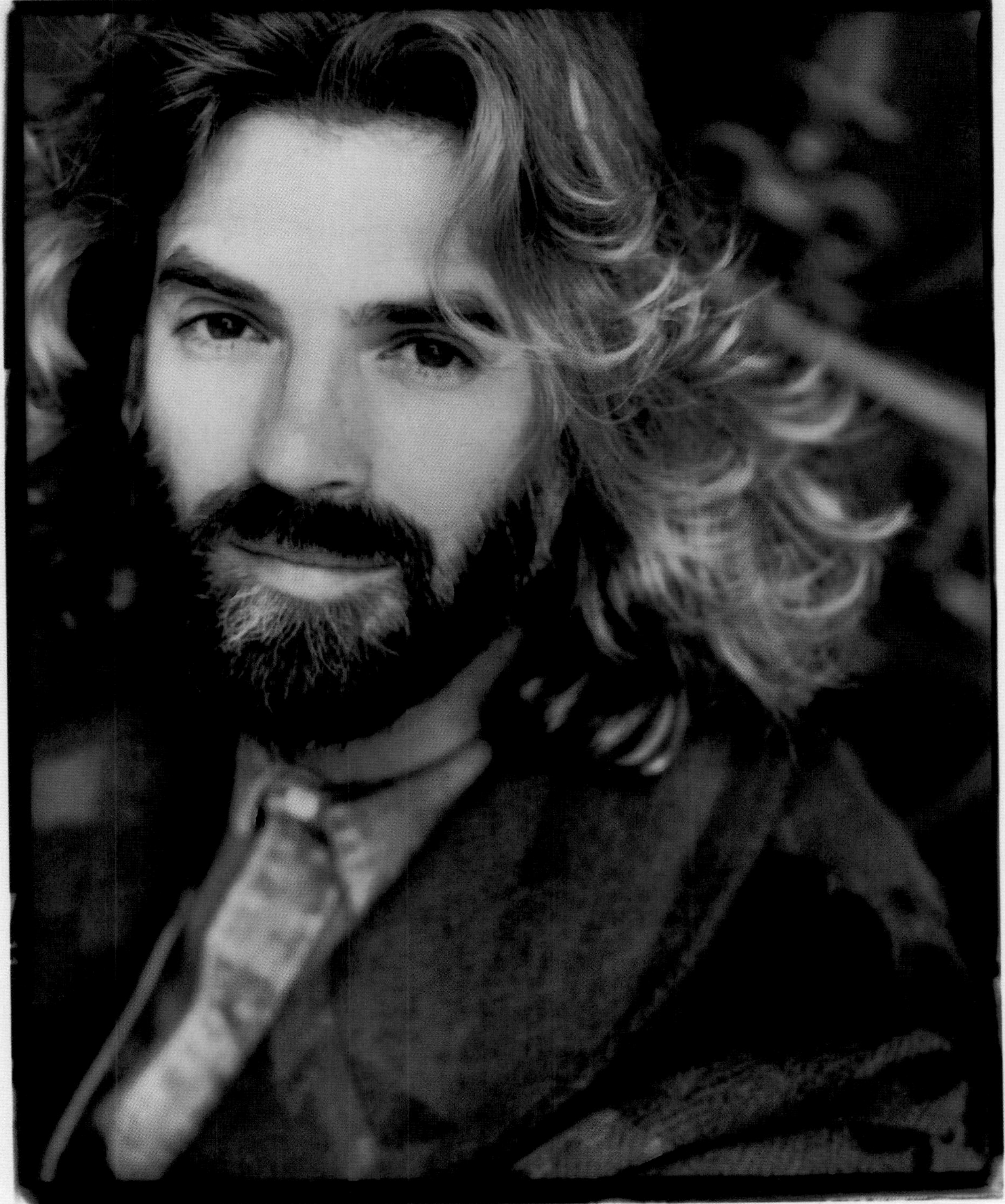

© 1991 Sony Music. Permission to reproduce this photography is limited to editorial uses in regular issues of newspapers and other regularly published periodicals and television news programming.

Photo Credit: Ann Cutting

KENNY LOGGINS

Columbia
9109

Alive

ALIVE ENTERPRISES, INC.
213-247-7800

Aaron Neville Warm Your Heart

Aaron Neville's cover version of "Everybody Plays the Fool" hit No. 1 on the adult contemporary charts.

Billboard 200: *Warm Your Heart* (#44)
Billboard Hot 100: "Everybody Plays the Fool" (#8)

AARON NEVILLE personified one of music's most intriguing dichotomies. He was a forbidding-looking man who dressed in black leather and blue denim. Jailhouse tattoos adorned his massive body, which appeared suited for middle-linebacking duties. But when he sang, he cut the air with his fluid, melismatic trill. His unique style was so exquisite and delicate that it conjured images of angels floating into the heavens.

How did Neville develop his heart-breaking tenor and that fluttering falsetto?

"When I was younger, I was into yodeling, the singing cowboys in the movies—Roy Rogers, Gene Autry," he recalled. "My father had Nat King Cole's records. He was my favorite. And I was mesmerized by the doo-wop groups. Clyde McPhatter, the Clovers, the Flamingos—they'd just sit on a park bench and sing. In school, they'd always find me in the bathroom singing with my doo-wop group. There was better sound in there."

Although he'd been the voice of the Neville Brothers since 1977, Neville's pop profile rose significantly when he received a 1990 Grammy Award as Linda Ronstadt's vocal partner for "Don't Know Much." His market-friendly solo album *Warm Your Heart* introduced him to a larger audience, and he enjoyed a Top 10 hit with "Everybody Plays the Fool," a remake of the 1972 Main Ingredient song.

"I've been pinpointed as an R&B singer—I've been hearing it all my life," he mused. "But as far as I'm concerned, music is music. I can sing 'Ave Maria' and the 'Mickey Mouse' theme. You tell me what R&B is."

As a member of the Neville Brothers, Aaron had been the divinely voiced spirit of New Orleans, almost single-handedly pushing the band beyond cult status. But Art, Charles, Cyril and Aaron were all New Orleans R&B institutions. Together they represented more than a century of the city's musical heritage.

"Doing solo stuff actually helps, it brings up the Neville name," Aaron said. "I'll always be a Neville Brother, and I don't feel like I've made it until we all have. Art (the oldest brother) does things with the Meters, Charles has a jazz band called Diversity, Cyril has a reggae band. I'm the only one without a band." ■

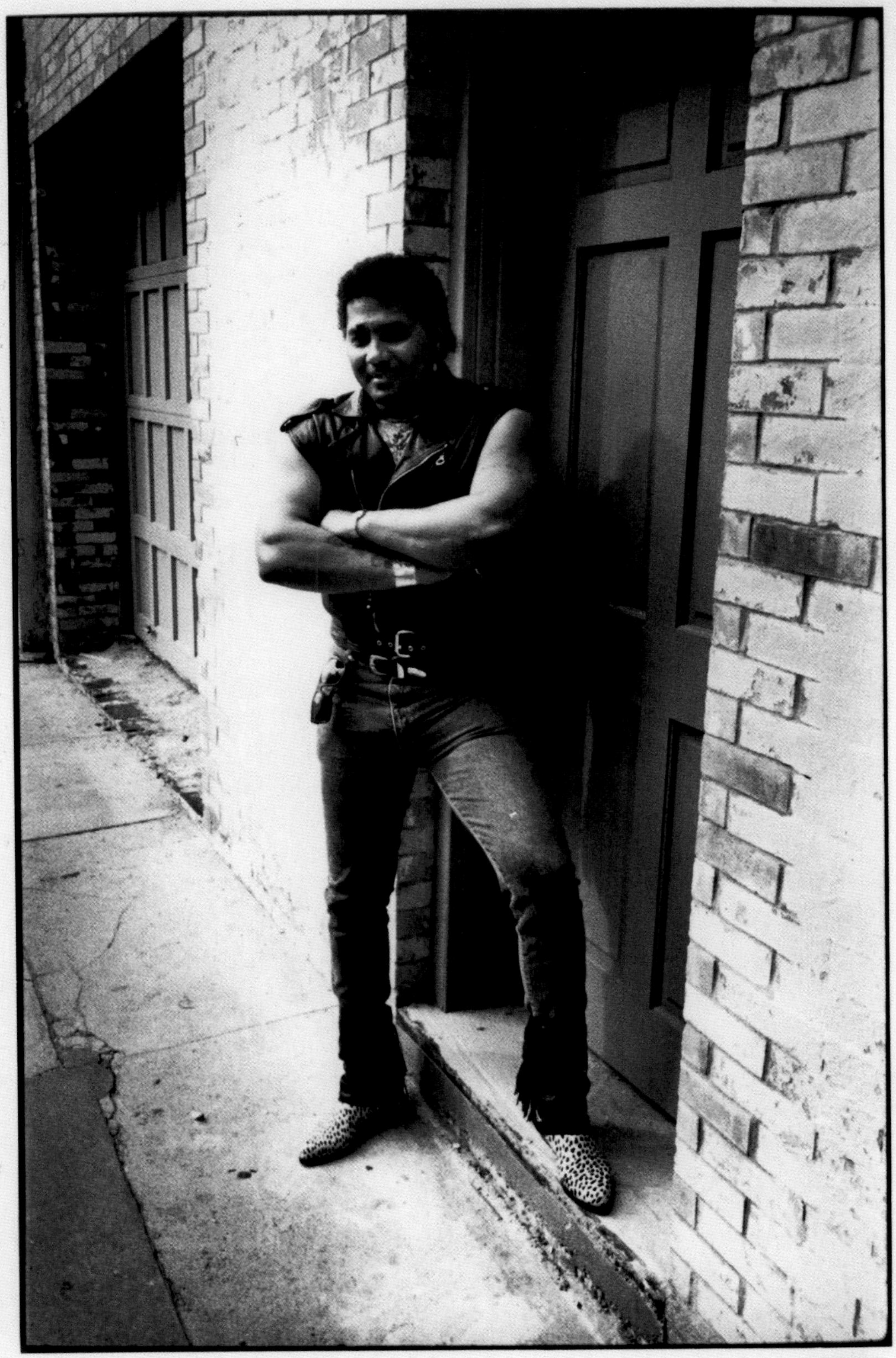

Photo Credit: Larry Williams

AARON NEVILLE

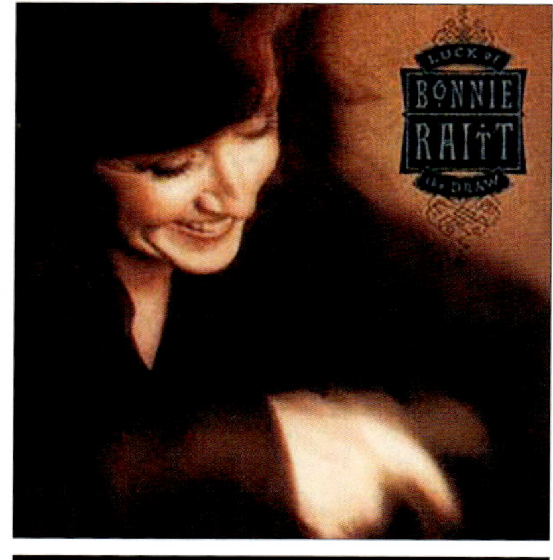

Bonnie Raitt's *Luck of the Draw* netted hits with "Something to Talk About" and "I Can't Make You Love Me."

Billboard 200: *Luck of the Draw* (#2)
Billboard Hot 100: "Something to Talk About" (#5);
"I Can't Make You Love Me" (#18);
"Not the Only One" (#34)

IN THE early Seventies, there weren't many women performing Bonnie Raitt's blend of blues, folk and R&B. Nor were there many who could keep up with her partying for days at a time—a lifestyle choice that led to alcoholism and a temporary career stoppage.

Clearheaded, Raitt made 1989's *Nick of Time*, a musical rumination about growing up and being an adult that brought her plaintive brassy vocals and stellar slide guitar work to center stage. Hailed as her best album ever, it resuscitated her career, selling more than 3 million copies, hitting No. 1 on the *Billboard* chart and snatching three Grammy awards.

"It's so convenient, with the buzzwords that are being attached—like 'comeback,' 'clean and sober' and 'harbinger of middle age,'" she said, laughing.

The follow-up, *Luck of the Draw*, was also a multimillion seller, generating several hit singles, including "Something to Talk About" and a ballad, "I Can't Make You Love Me," with Bruce Hornsby's instantly recognizable piano tones.

"Bruce is the one who raises the bar on an artistic level—he is just pure music," Raitt said with admiration.

"In the summer of 1988, I was sitting in a hotel coffee shop in Tulsa, when all of a sudden the receptionist comes over and says, 'Excuse me, you have a call from Bonnie Raitt,'" Hornsby recalled. "So sure enough, Bonnie was calling me out of the blue—she had tracked me down just to say she was a fan, which was an amazing thing. We became friends after that."

In the liner notes, Raitt dedicated the album to the blues guitarist Stevie Ray Vaughan, who had died in a plane crash the previous year. "He was one of the greatest embodiments of the blues, and there'll never be anyone like him," she wrote.

The past few years had been the best of Raitt's two decades-plus as a performer. She'd sown fewer wild oats and married for the first time.

"Now I'm able to play to 15,000 people who are fans," she said. "I'm playing a lot of markets that were closed to me before, so it's exciting and thrilling. But the great bluesmen are singing into their 90s. I think I've built up enough of a following that I could be around that long." ■

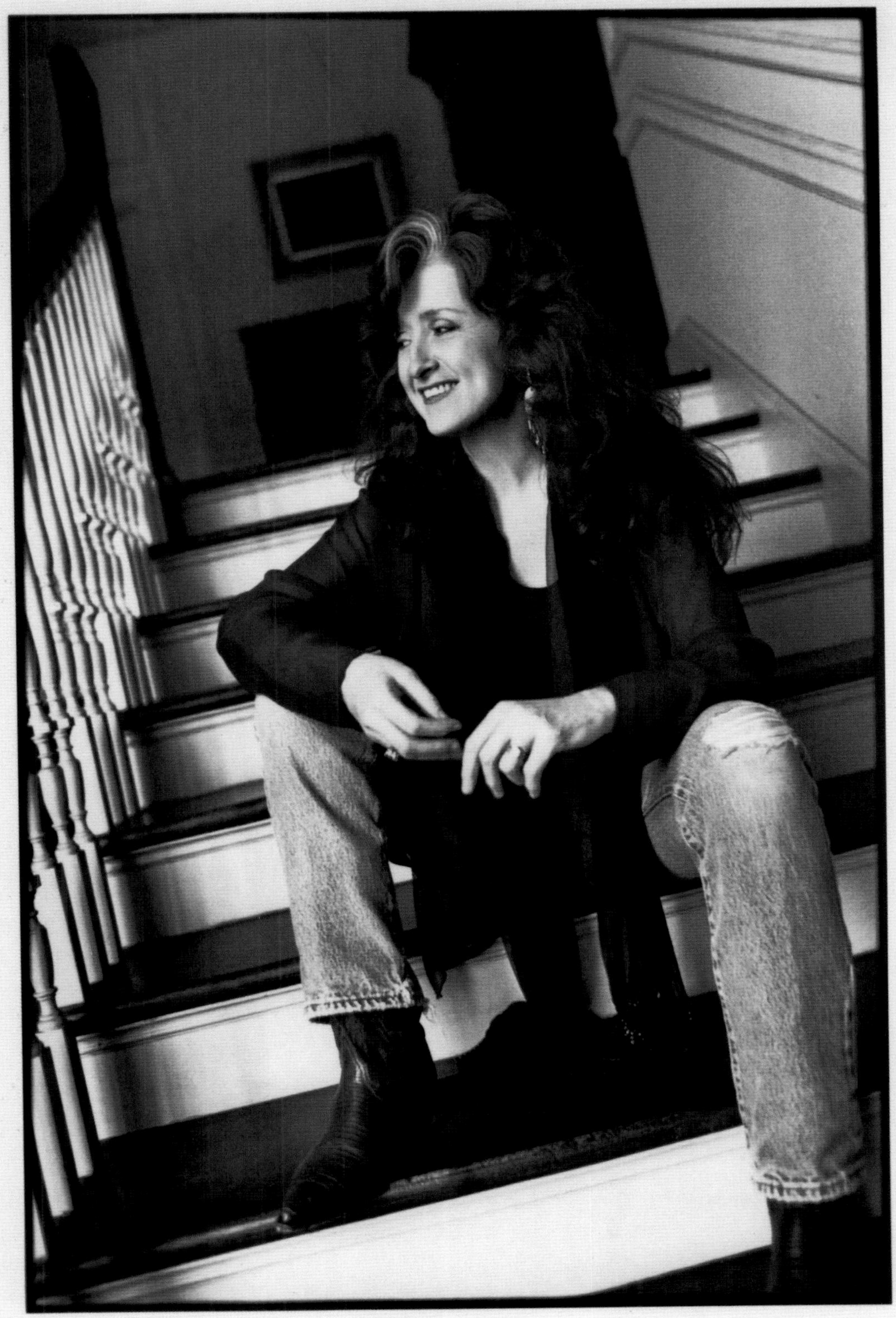

BONNIE RAITT

PHOTO: MERLYN ROSENBERG / 1991

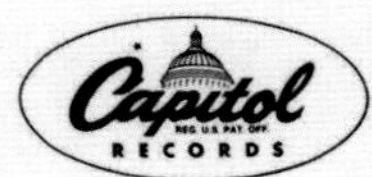

A consistently popular female rock artist of the Eighties, Stevie Nicks enlisted songs by Nineties rockers.

Billboard 200: *Timespace: The Best of Stevie Nicks* (#30);
Billboard Hot 100: "Sometimes It's a Bitch" (#56)

STEVIE NICKS earned fame for her chart-topping work with Fleetwood Mac and as a solo artist. So when it came time to release *Timespace: The Best of Stevie Nicks*, the singer-songwriter naturally culled tracks from her solo albums—but also recorded new songs composed and produced by Jon Bon Jovi and Poison's Bret Michaels.

"Everybody feels I should have a relationship with a whole other generation of rock 'n' rollers," Nicks said. "At first I was very hostile about it—and I'm not a very fun person when I'm hostile. 'Is my career finished if I don't? Can I not write songs anymore?' They explained that it might open up an audience of people who are a whole lot younger than me. And I can dig that, but I happen to have my own baby fans that I love a lot—people send me videos of 6-year-olds who know my entire set, little girls who know every word and move. So I said, 'Let me meet the people, hear the songs—I'll see if I can relate to them."

Thus arrived Bon Jovi's "Sometimes It's a Bitch" and Michaels' "Love's a Hard Game to Play." The former was the only single released from *Timespace*.

"Jon played me his song, and I said, 'I'm going to have to interpret this to sing this.' I wasn't nuts about saying, 'Sometimes it's a bitch, sometimes it's a breeze,' because I've never sort of swore in a song before. And his generation cannot possibly understand what my life has been like since 1974 with Fleetwood Mac, and I could never explain it to anybody. How in the world could he figure out how to write a song for Stevie Nicks?

"Well, he did, like he was on my shoulder or something, took a time machine back and fast-forwarded through the real bad parts and the real great parts of rock 'n' roll—'I've run through castles of candy and darkness,' 'I've laid down with love and I've broke up with life,' 'It's not what's in the mirror, but what's left inside.'"

But Bon Jovi had a specific way that he wanted Nicks to sing the custom-made tune.

"I'm not real good at being told how to sing," Nicks admitted. "I did exactly what he told me, and after we worked on it for 10 days, I stood up and said, 'I've been very sweet, I have sung it your way, it's done.' Jon said, 'I'm bailing to a beach—later.' I went in the next night, lit my incense and candles, drank my strong coffee and re-sang the song myself. I got it on the first take—now it sounds like I wrote it. Jon came back two weeks later, and I don't think he was really pleased with what I did—but after what we'd been through, I don't think he was gonna come up and tell me that." ■

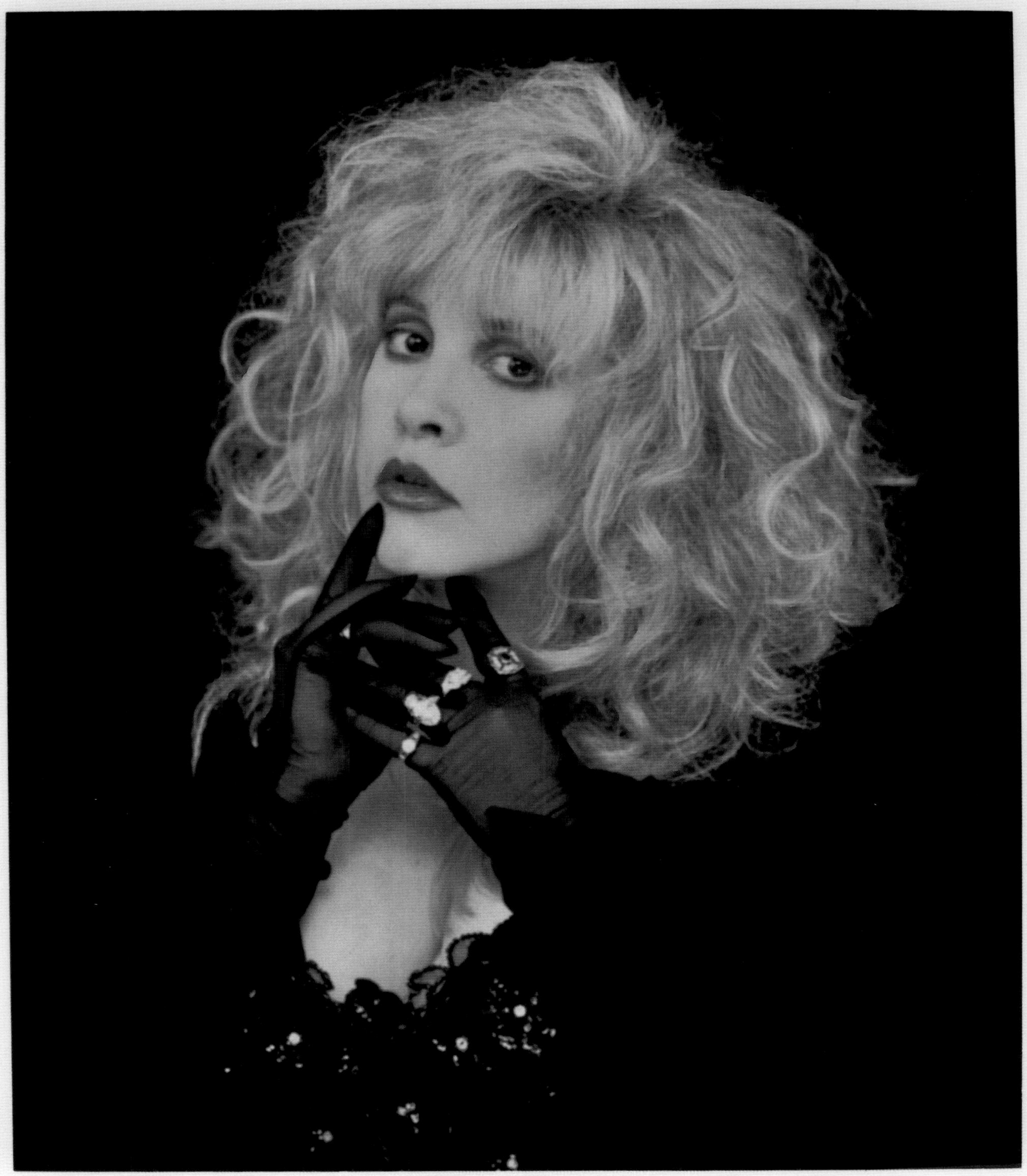

1991 / 27627

©MODERN RECORDS – PHOTOGRAPHER: NEAL PRESTON

STEVIE NICKS

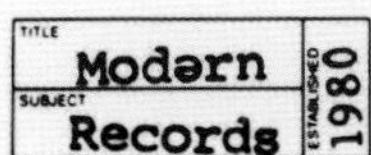

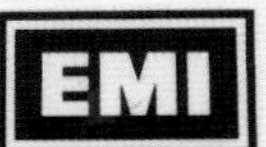

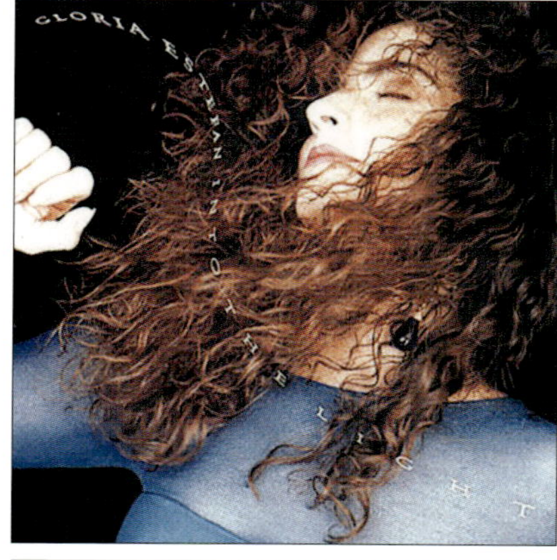

Stirred by a near-fatal accident, Gloria Estefan resurfaced with the hit ballad, "Coming Out of the Dark."

Billboard 200: *Into the Light* (#5)
Billboard Hot 100: "Coming Out of the Dark" (No. 1); "Seal Our Fate" (#53); "Can't Forget You" (#43); "Live for Loving You" (#22)

GLORIA ESTEFAN didn't know if she would ever walk again, much less romp around and dance the conga onstage. En route to a concert date in March 1990, the queen of Latin pop was seriously injured when a tractor-trailer rammed her tour bus on a snowy Pennsylvania interstate. The impact threw Estefan off her bunk and she fractured and dislocated vertebrae in her spine. Doctors performed a spinal fusion and implanted a pair of eight-inch steel rods to buttress her back.

But by the summer, the singer-songwriter, still devoting most of her day to exercise and physical therapy, had returned to making music. In March 1991, she launched her comeback with a year-long world tour and concept album called *Into the Light*.

"I didn't think about performing for a long time," Estefan said. "I've been doing it for 15 years, and if I wasn't the same, I wouldn't have gotten back onstage again. My main concern was to do things on my own, to put on my own shoes, to walk to the front gate. But when I saw my body responding after six or seven months, I had to get back out there fast. I wanted people to know beyond a shadow of a doubt that I was okay."

Before her accident, Estefan and Miami Sound Machine fashioned nine Top 10 singles with a catchy blend of pop, rock, dance and Latin strains. *Into the Light* was the highest-charting album of her career, a collection of dramatic pop infused with personal testimony.

"I had a year to write—it's been an introspective time of my life," she mused. "I got a letter from my voice doctor telling me that a spinal injury affects your singing in the majority of cases. Your diaphragm, the main muscle you use for control and tone, is right by the middle of the spine. I couldn't even laugh because it hurt. The first song I tried to sing was 'Coming Out of the Dark.' And a lot of emotion was there for me. It was from the heart."

The No. 1 single (Estefan's third, joining 1988's "Anything for You" and 1989's "Don't Wanna Lose You") reflected upon her extraordinary recovery.

"When we were flying in a helicopter over to the hospital for my operation, it was really dark and cloudy. Some sun came over my husband Emilio's face. He was so depressed and traumatized, and the line 'Coming out of the dark' came to him. A few months after the accident, we hadn't written anything. I was taken over to our office and we had the song in 15 minutes. Everything came flooding out. I'd seen so much loving support from my family and fans, and I wanted it to be a message, how much they helped me through this ordeal. We definitely heard a big chorus, and we chose a black gospel choir because the sound is so uplifting and positive, even spiritual." ■

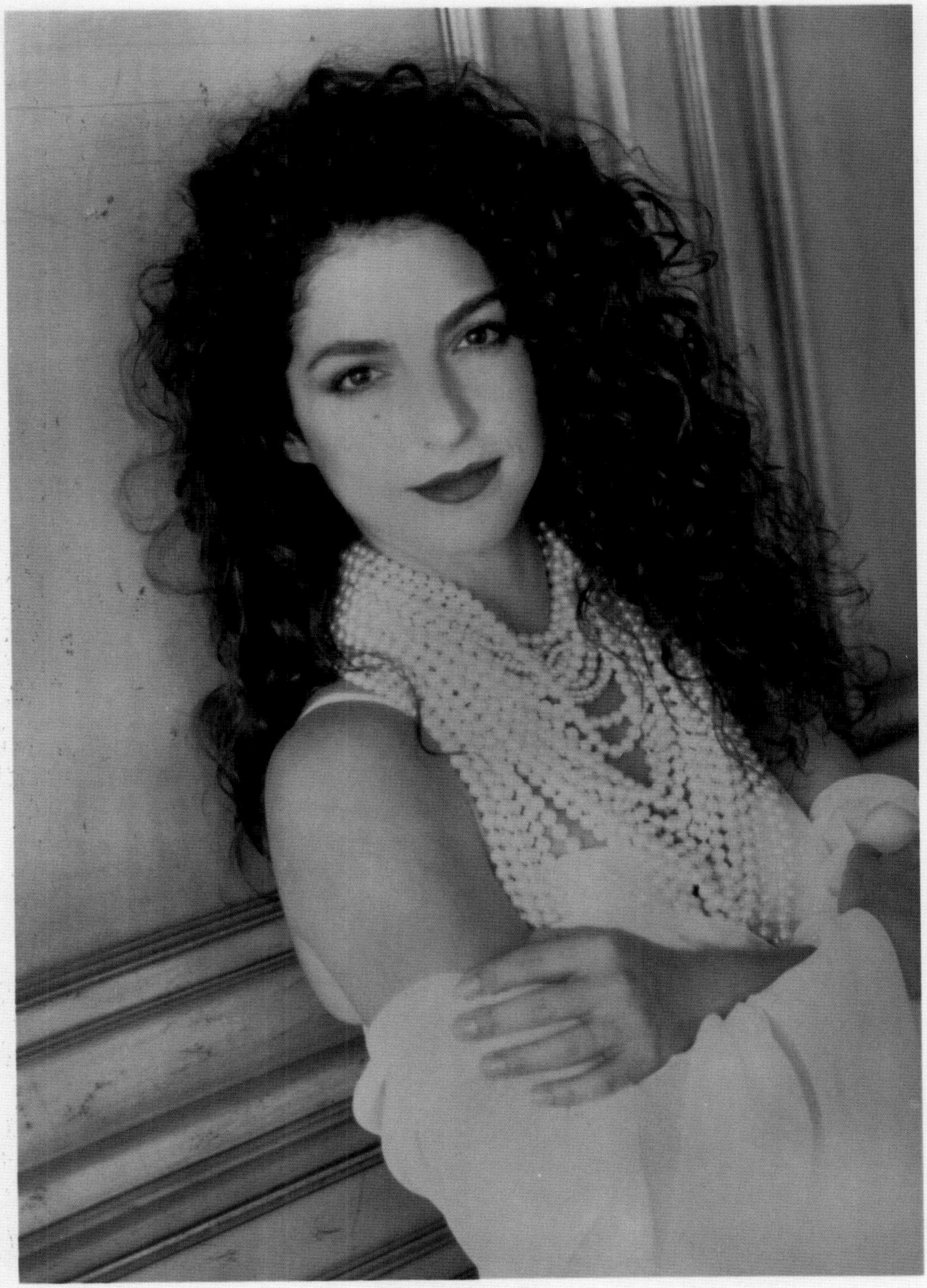

Photo Credit: Alberto Tolot

GLORIA ESTEFAN

9101

© 1990 CBS Records Inc. Permission to reproduce this photography is limited to editorial uses in regular issues of newspapers and other regularly published periodicals and television news programming.

Billboard 200: *Eagle When She Flies* (#24)

"Rockin' Years," Dolly Parton's duet with Ricky Van Shelton, was her 23rd single to top the country charts.

DOLLY PARTON'S image—her trademark big wigs and bigger bust—was confusing to some folks and comic to others. She'd been exposed to every possible "dumb blonde" barb. But the real-life Dolly Parton was soft-spoken and attractive in a dignified way. Exuding perspicacity and self-confidence, she'd developed from a country music superstar to a reigning pop star to a film star (*9 to 5*, *The Best Little Whorehouse in Texas*, *Rhinestone*, *Steel Magnolias*).

Eagle When She Flies marked Parton's full returned to her country sound. The record reached No. 1 on *Billboard*'s Top Country Albums chart, and a duet with Ricky Van Shelton, "Rockin' Years," reached No. 1 on the singles chart. "Silver and Gold," co-written by Carl Perkins, was a #15 country single, and the title song, an ode to female strength, spent 20 weeks on the chart, reaching #33.

A *National Enquirer* article reported that silicone implants would rupture and kill Parton. She reassured her fans the story wasn't true.

"I expect it, so I don't mind," she reasoned. "You become public property once you get in show business. I take some sort of pride in being the 'tabloid queen.' They keep me hot between flop movies and flop records."

She giggled. "I say, 'It could be worse—they could tell the truth.'" ■

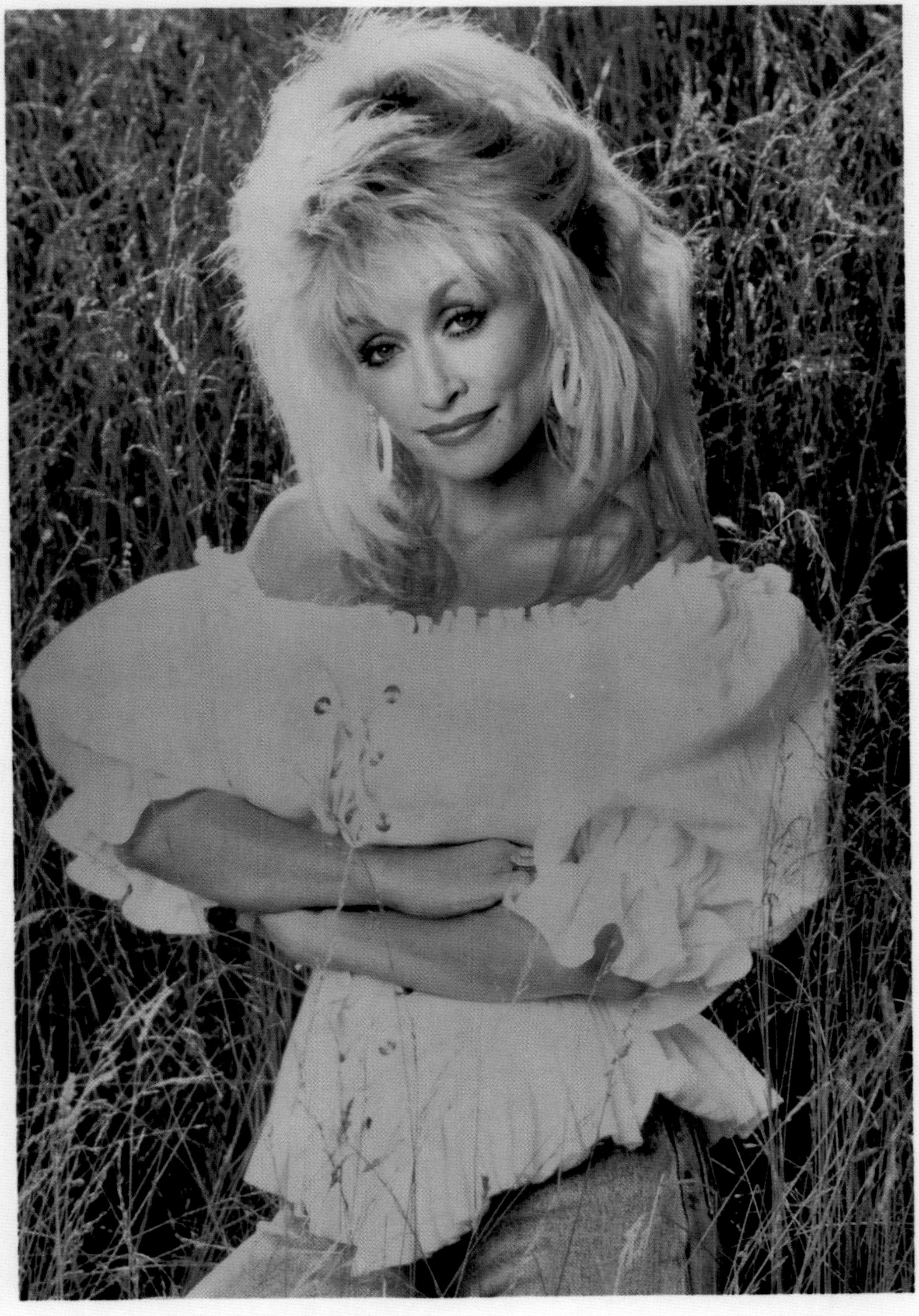

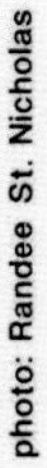

DOLLY PARTON

Columbia

9101

©1991 Sony Music Entertainment Inc. Permission to reproduce this photography is limited to editorial uses in regular issues of newspapers and other regularly published periodicals and television news programming.

Billboard 200: *The Force Behind the Power* (#102)

The Force Behind the Power touched off an international comeback for legendary entertainer **Diana Ross**.

DIANA ROSS was a legend, a global superstar applauded by fans for her glitzy effervescence and her multifaceted career as a recording artist, actress and producer. Yet she had trouble selling records in the second half of the Eighties. 1989's *Workin' Overtime* saw her return to Motown Records, but it missed the mark, jolting her fans with a new image (leather jacket, torn jeans) and a new sound (hip-hop).

"I wanted to understand what my teenagers were hearing in the clubs," she said. "I hope I'm never limited to one type of music. You do the things you enjoy and hope other people enjoy them, too. I wanted to do an album of African sounds, but Paul Simon beat me to that. So I looked for other material."

For *The Force Behind the Power*, Ross chose three producers—Peter Asher, James Carmichael and Stevie Wonder. Carmichael had achieved success with Lionel Richie. Wonder, another early Motown artist, wrote the title song, a hymn with a background choir extolling love. Asher, the 1989 Grammy Award winner for his work with Linda Ronstadt and Aaron Neville, produced the first single, "When You Tell Me That You Love Me."

Led by that hit—Ross considered the sentimental ballad one of her signature songs—the album achieved more global than domestic success, going double platinum in the UK and performing well in Japan and various European countries. Seven singles appeared across international territories, and Ross' world tour lasted nearly two years.

"People love to hear ballads with beautiful lyrics from me," Ross said. "And there are quite a few on my record." ■

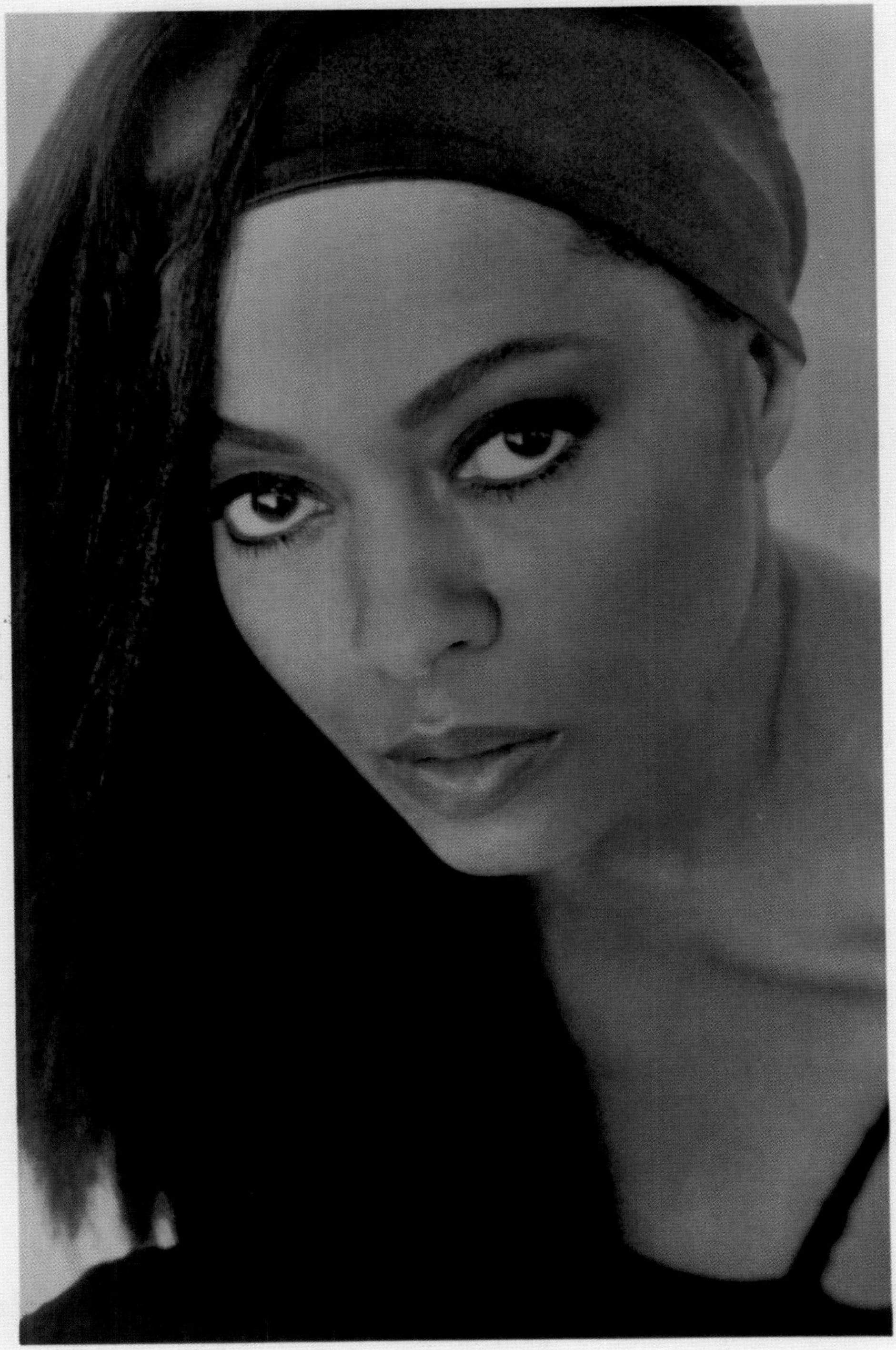

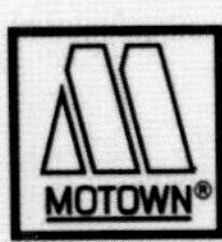

diana

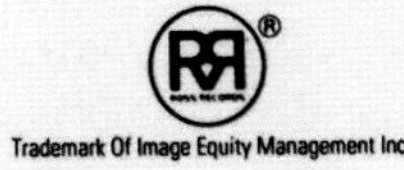

Trademark Of Image Equity Management Inc.

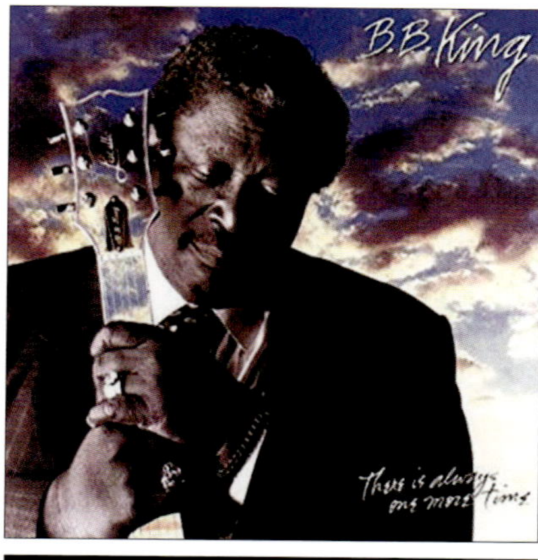

There is Always One More Time marked the 32nd studio release of blues dignitary **B.B. King**'s career.

B.B. KING had had an extraordinary career. There was a period when he was a big favorite with the blues crowd but unknown to the general public. Then the electric guitarist played the Fillmore West in the Sixties and got a surprise—his black audience had become "90 percent white."

"It was hippies, young kids with long hair all over the place," the Mississippi-born King said. "I got a standing ovation before I even played a note, and I cried—that had never happened to me before."

Over the years, the man universally hailed as "the King of the Blues" had become an international icon through his consistently excellent performances and sophisticated recordings. Pianist Joe Sample and Will Jennings co-composed most of the tracks on *There is Always One More Time*.

"But the younger blacks aren't tuned in to what I do," King mused. "Some of them tell me that when they were growing up and they'd hear their parents playing B.B. King on Saturday morning, they knew they were gonna get it. A lot of older blacks are still blues fans, but they buy my records and stay at home." ■

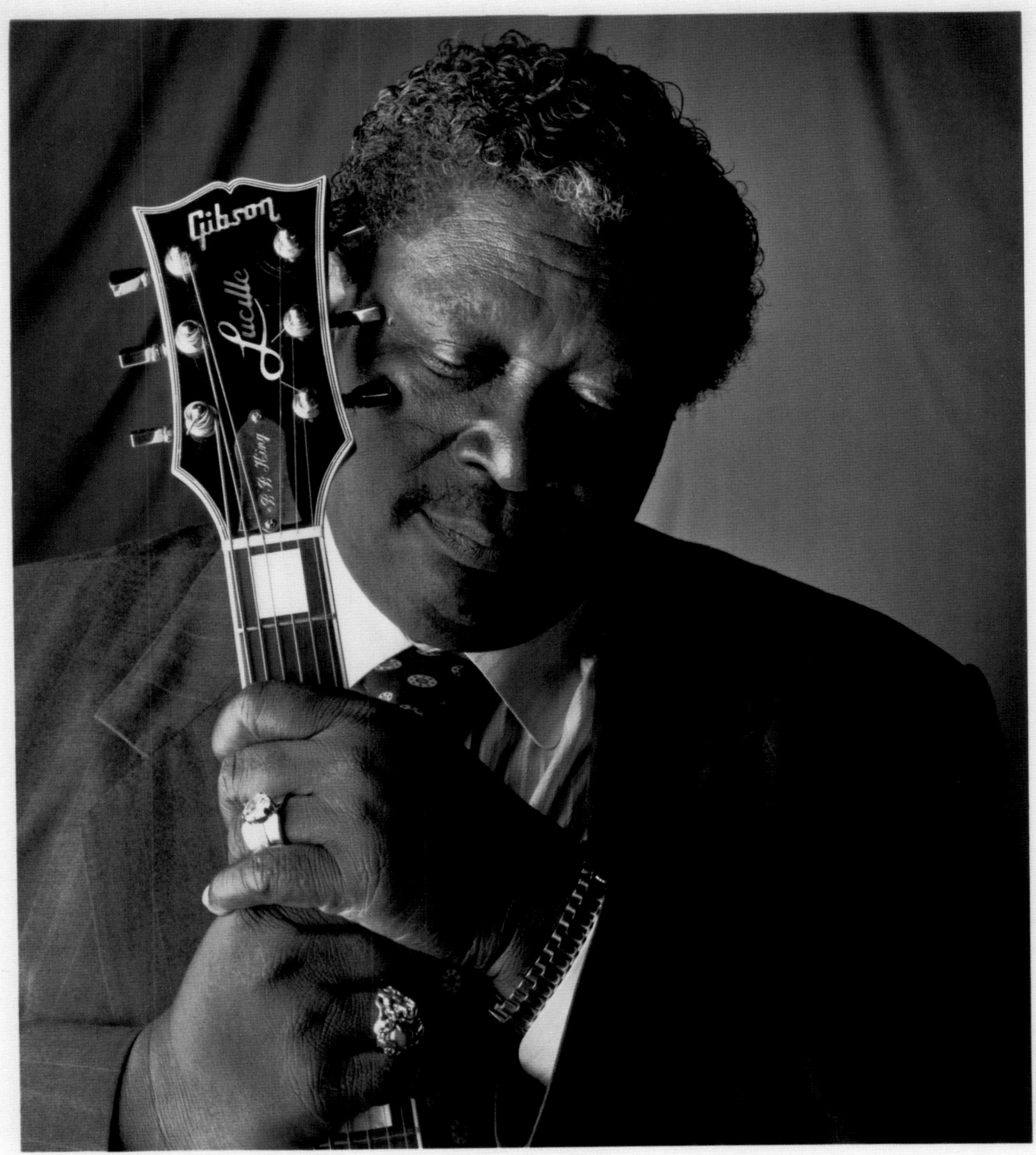

B.B. King

10/91

MCA

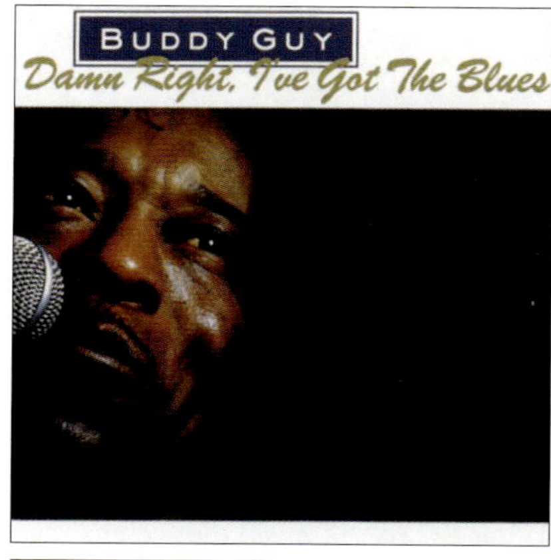

Damn Right, I've Got the Blues, Buddy Guy's first album in years, returned the guitarist to blues celebrity.

Billboard 200: *Damn Right, I've Got the Blues* (#136)

BUDDY GUY'S good health and hard work had made him a survivor in a tough field. Born in Louisiana, he moved in 1957 to Chicago, where blues masters Muddy Waters and Howlin' Wolf dominated the scene. The guitarist proved himself to the older, established fraternity—first as a session player at the legendary Chess Records studio, and then as a sideman in various bands. Finally, as a headliner, he brought the raw, gritty Chicago sound into the blues-rock of the Sixties. He opened gigs for the Rolling Stones, and guitar heroes Eric Clapton and Jeff Beck acknowledged his influence.

Guy's recordings had rarely captured the intensity of his live shows—his reputation as Chicago's hottest bluesman was based on jaw-dropping showmanship and go-for-broke dynamics—a wild virtuoso wading into crowds, wailing on his guitar, flashing a huge grin. But he was still undiscovered outside Chicago and the national blues community. He suffered most of the Eighties without a record deal.

"I didn't say, 'Whoa, this isn't for me—I'd better go learn how to fly a plane or something.' I kept my guitar," Guy said. "I went three days hungry in Chicago trying to get back to Louisiana. A guy said, 'I'm not going to give you money to get a hamburger and a cup of coffee—you've got a guitar, pawn it.' I looked at him and said, 'Well, I'd better take a walk, because my wife doesn't come between me and my guitar.' I found the thing I could have an affair with that she won't pitch a fit about!

"I'm religious—I believe God put us all here for a reason, not a season. When I didn't have a record contract, I kept saying, 'If I keep playing, somebody somewhere is going to hear me. I'll give it my best shot.'"

Guy's resurgence began when he joined Eric Clapton onstage at London's Royal Albert Hall at the beginning of the Nineties. That prompted refocused attention on the bluesman and landed him on Silvertone Records. On his comeback album, *Damn Right, I've Got the Blues*, he went the superstar-collaboration route, teaming up with Clapton, Jeff Beck and Mark Knopfler in cameo roles. It clicked with record buyers and won the Grammy Award for Best Contemporary Blues Album.

Without many of the original greats remaining to carry on the blues tradition and celebrate its roots, Guy acknowledged he'd become an old hand. "I make mistakes, but sometimes I make them sound good—it's called experience," he said. "It's like a horse race. If I can come all the way from the back and win, I get the big payoff." ■

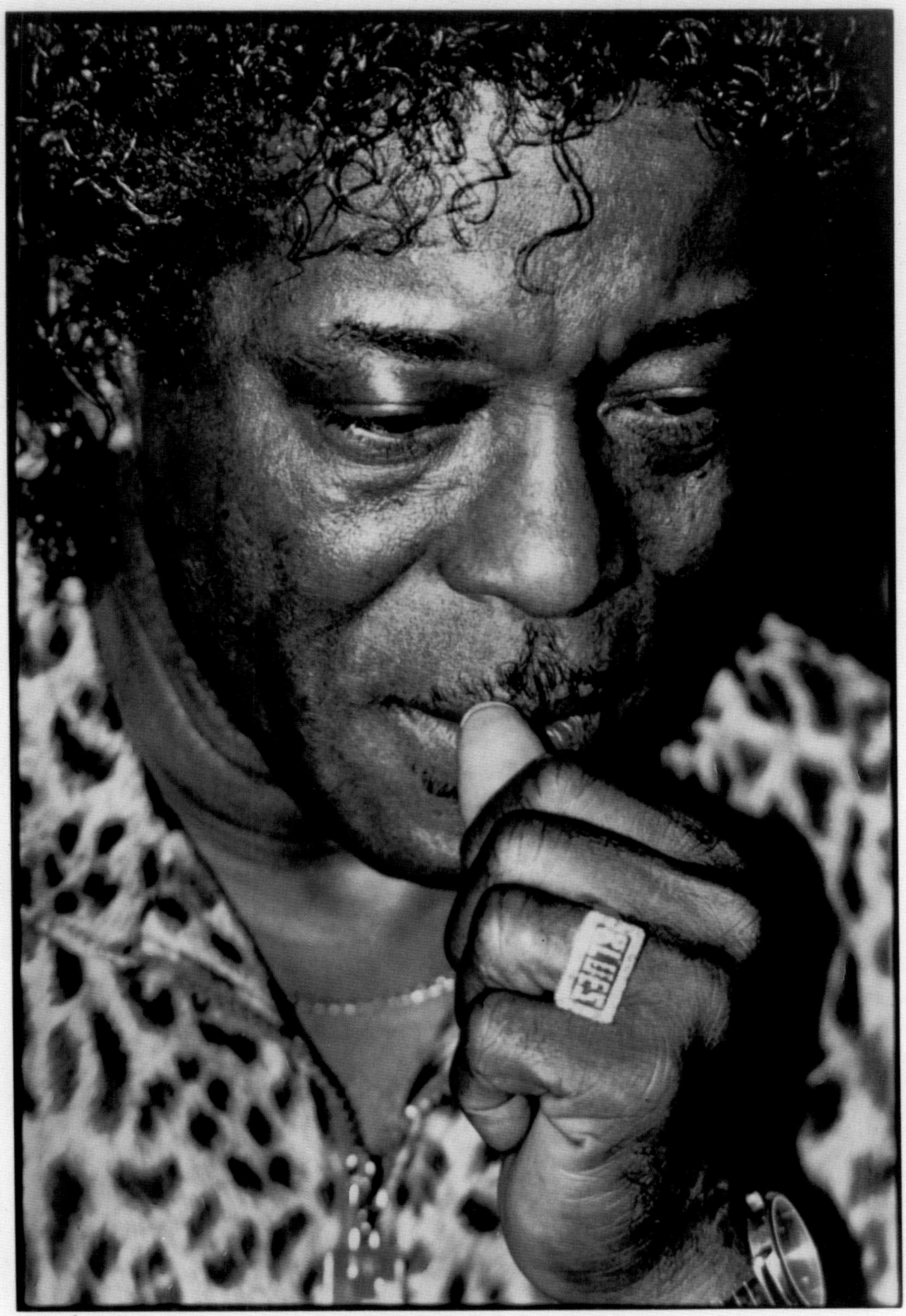

BUDDY GUY

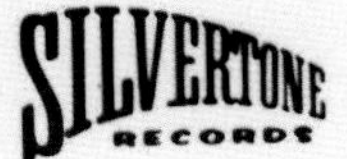

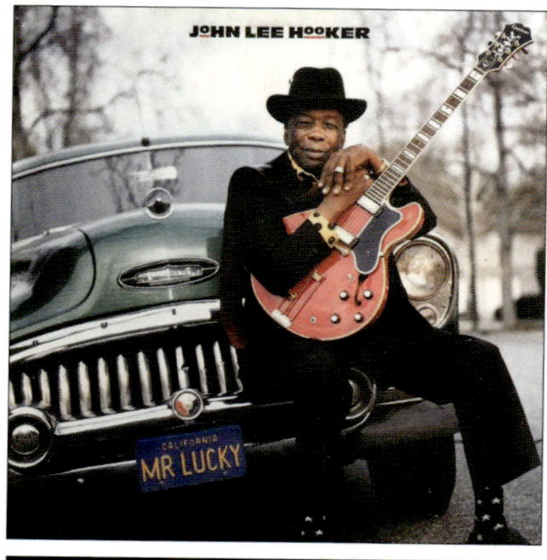

Billboard 200: *Mr. Lucky* (#101)

Elder blues statesman John Lee Hooker delivered *Mr. Lucky*, another of his guest star-loaded albums.

JUST WHEN he'd seemed on the verge of being relegated to the history books, John Lee Hooker had come back into fashion. In 1991, the 74-year-old bluesman was more popular than he had ever been during his lengthy career. In January, he was inducted into the Rock and Roll Hall of Fame.

"I want my flowers while I'm living," he said. "I can't smell no flowers when I'm gone."

So often, the blues performers who were rock's progenitors never enjoyed the financial rewards reaped by their young imitators. But Hooker socked away enough to allow him to live comfortably in Vallejo, California, where he enjoyed more trappings of success than perhaps any of his peers.

Hooker had recorded more than 100 albums for a profusion of labels, and he cut for others under pseudonyms like Texas Slim, Birmingham Sam, the Boogie Man, even John Lee Booker. Whereas blues artists frequently sold their song rights, Hooker held on to his. In the late Eighties, he decided to collect what was owed him. His lawyer asked him whether he had contracts, and Hooker had some 40 years' worth.

"I had given them all to a man in Detroit for safekeeping, and I wrote and got them all," Hooker said, "We took the companies to court, and they were in a panic when they found out I had the papers. And I've been getting my royalties ever since then. Now I'm set for life. I got a pretty nice split-level house, and I'm into real estate. I got three properties in Oakland that I lease. But I learned it the hard way. I could have lived the fast life and I wouldn't have nothing."

In 1989, Hooker's booking agent came up with the idea of recording him with some of the musicians he'd influenced. *The Healer* was an all-star extravaganza including performances by friends and disciples. It sold more than a million copies, a phenomenal feat for a blues album. It was no problem getting a major label to handle his follow-up album. *Mr. Lucky* featured guest artists Keith Richards, Albert Collins, Johnny Winter, Booker T. Jones, John Hammond and Johnnie Johnson. The most stirring cut, his duet with Van Morrison on the moving anthem "I Cover the Waterfront," smoldered with masterful spiritual fervor.

"They didn't do it for money—they got more than I do," he laughed. "They did it for love and friendship and music."

With his legacy secure, Hooker insisted he was semi-retired.

"I have no more special goals. I wanted to be remembered by my music, and now John Lee Hooker will be remembered as long as there's a world." ■

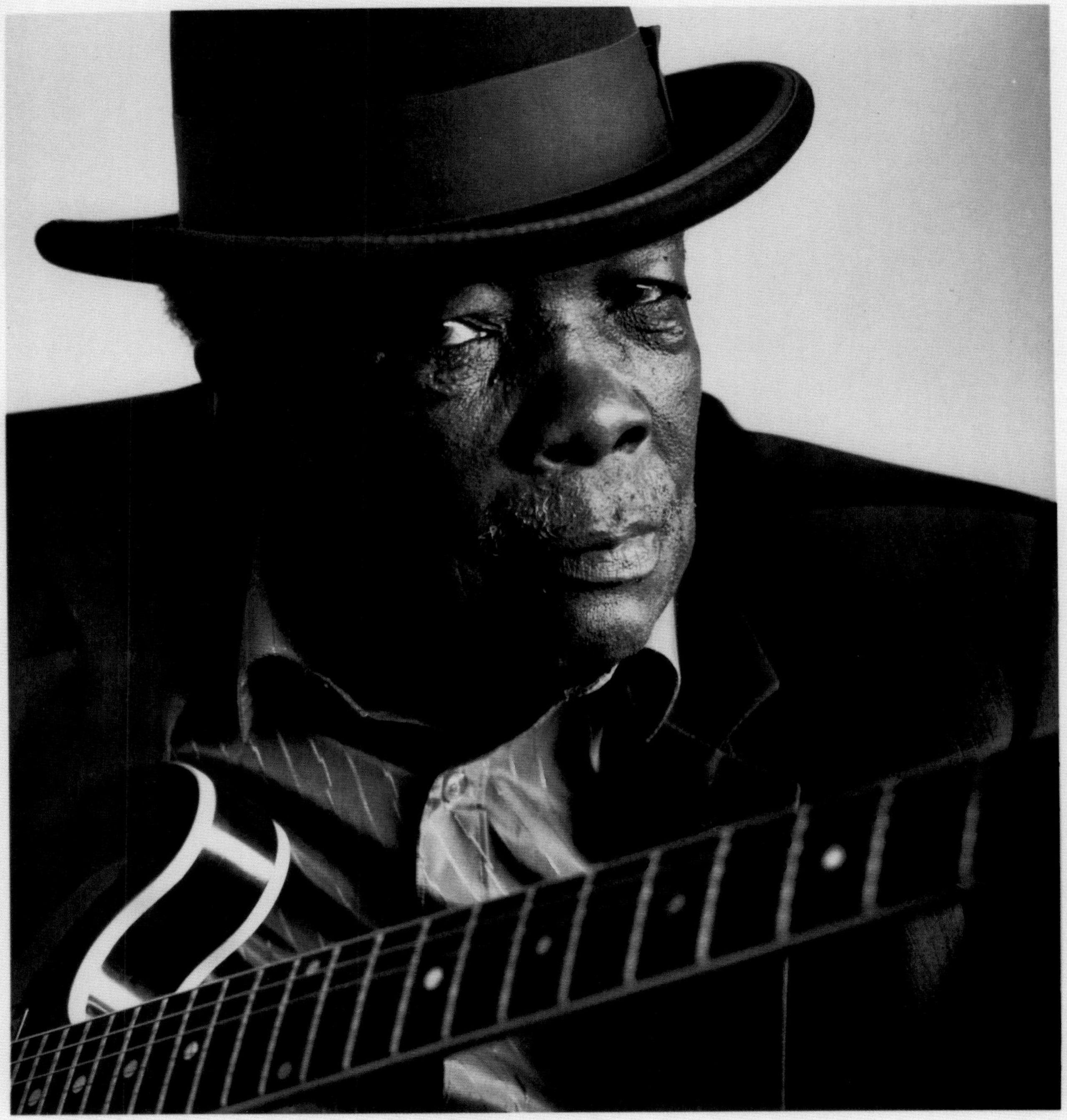

PEOPLE WEEKLY (c) 1991 Kim Komenich 8/91

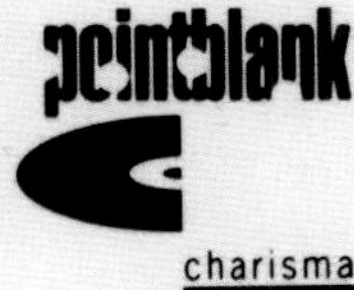

JOHN LEE HOOKER

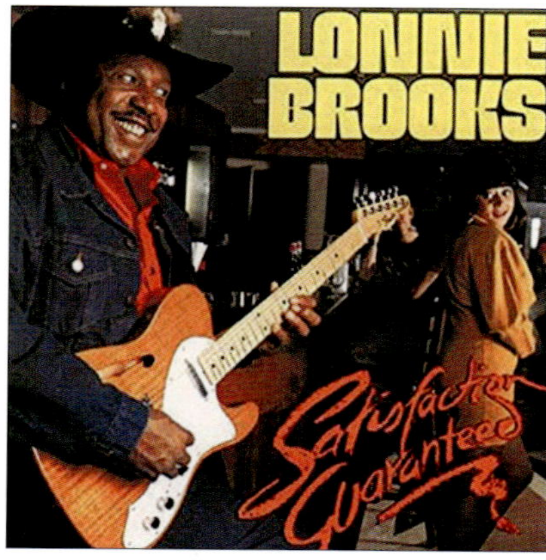

Lonnie Brooks released *Satisfaction Guaranteed*, duetting with his adult offspring on "Like Father Like Son."

SINCE THE mid-Fifties, Lonnie Brooks had recorded under his own name and as Guitar Junior, building a party-time reputation with his high-energy amalgamation of New Orleans R&B and Chicago blues.

"I'm a native of Louisiana, deep in the bayou," Brooks said. "I took up the guitar in my early 20s. My first job was with Clifton Chenier. I traveled to Chicago with Sam Cooke in 1959. I was playing rock 'n' roll then, but I then I started listening to a lot of the guys around Chicago and got hung up in the blues."

Brooks forged a career as a bluesman, but with the economic pressures of supporting a family, he performed less and less. A contract with Alligator Records gave him another chance, leading to 1979's electrifying *Bayou Lightning* album. For the next decade, Brooks worked hard, averaging more than 250 shows a year and winning enthusiastic reaction at clubs and festivals. In 1989, his son Ronnie Baker Brooks, who had been touring with his father for two years, took over the full-time rhythm guitar job in his old man's band.

Brooks' *Satisfaction Guaranteed* recording featured "Like Father Like Son," which focused on vocal and guitar trade-offs between the family members. As Lonnie sang about the mischief his son had gotten into over the years, Ronnie reminded him, "Daddy, I'm just doing what you've done."

"I'd played songs like that, built around a phrase, but they were about women," Brooks said. "Ronnie kinda took that idea and applied it to us. He took off after a rehearsal and came back the next day with the song. It's so much fun for me. Blues music is passed on from generation to generation, and having my son on the bandstand with me is an indescribable feeling."

One of the highlights of Brooks' shows came when dad and son played lead guitar at the same time—both on the same instrument, with Lonnie on the bottom three strings and Ronnie on the top. ■

GEORGE THOROGOOD

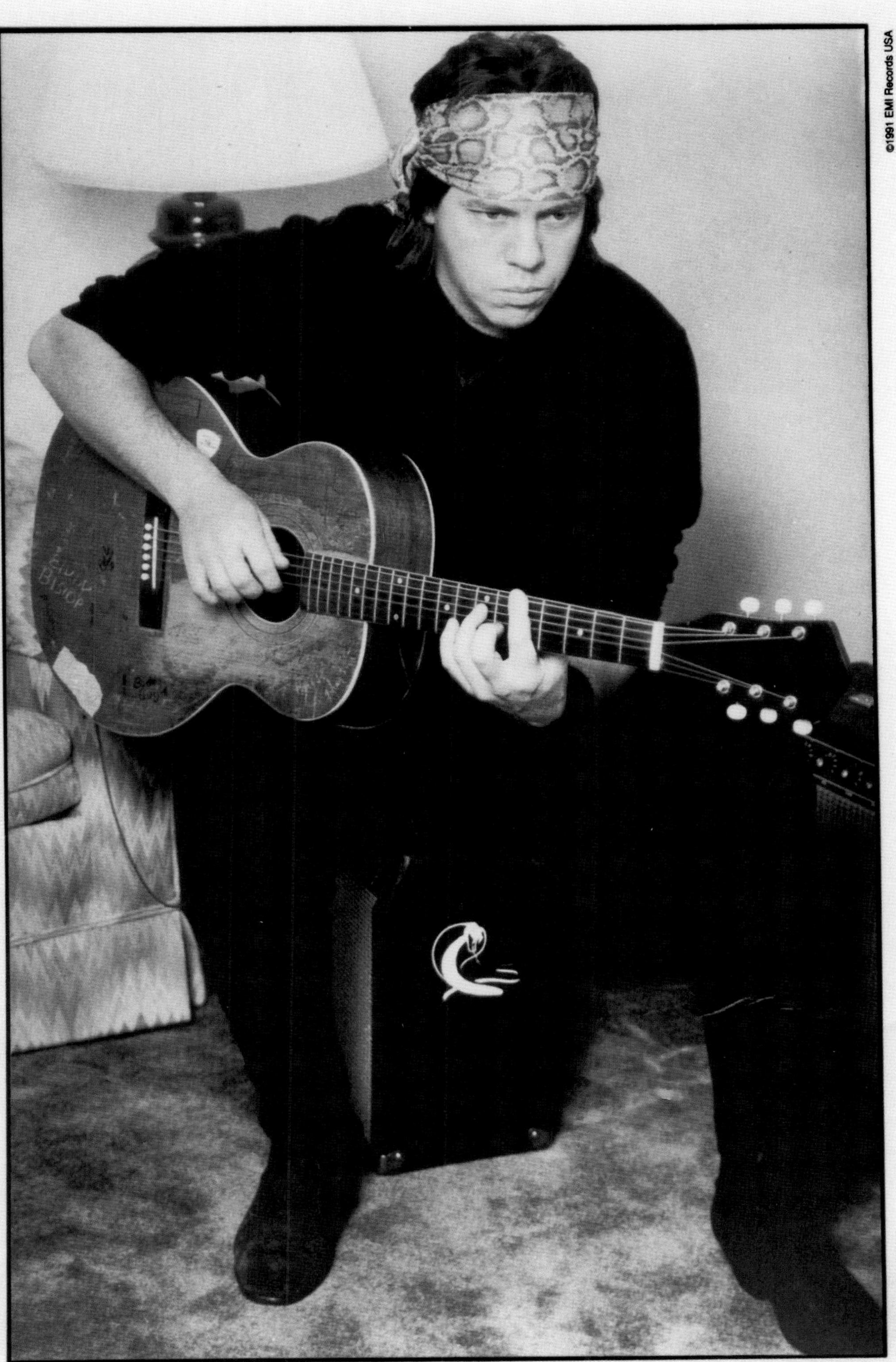

©1991 EMI Records USA

Photography: Allen Messer

EMI

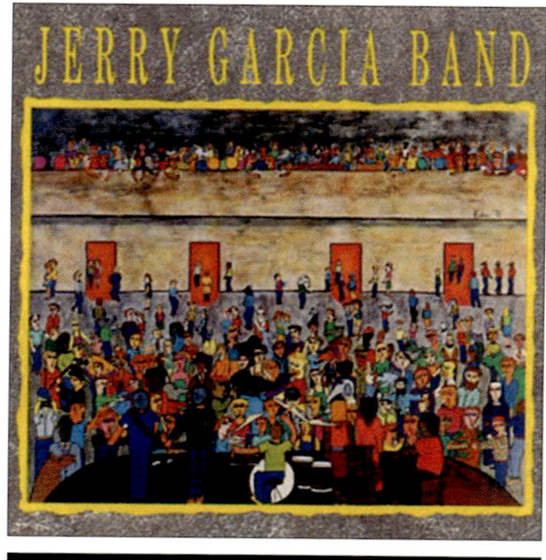

Billboard 200: *Jerry Garcia Band* (#97)

The Bay Area's Jerry Garcia Band was led by the seminal guitarist, singer and heart of the Grateful Dead.

1991 WAS an intriguing time for the Grateful Dead and Deadheads, the migrating tribe of campers who shadowed the durable San Francisco band around the country. After years of cultdom, the Dead had drifted into mainstream acceptance during the late Seventies and exploded to megastar status in the Eighties, more as a result of legendary gigs than of record sales or radio exposure. The band became America's most consistent concert draw.

At the same time, however, the band's fan base had expanded from a core of knowledgeable loyalists in psychedelic regalia and bus caravans to those apparently less concerned with the music than the scene, acquiring a reputation for trashing communities in the wake of concerts. This subculture created problems on the environmental front and on the police lines—arrests came after ticketless fans tried to crash concerts and some cities banned the group.

The Dead pleaded for decorum, and guitarist Jerry Garcia said they were getting through. "In the typical situation, we would play two or three nights at a venue. That was enough time for a whole cottage economy to set up, the 'Deadhead mall' with vendors selling stuff. That became an attraction on its own. Many people started camping outside, and it just got too visible—it scared people in the towns. It became, 'Something's gotta change or you guys can't play her anymore.' So it's something we have to keep monitoring and addressing—'Hey, Deadheads, behave yourselves.' A Grateful Dead concert isn't free turf."

Garcia was a musician, not a diplomat. His most widely-known non-Dead project was the Jerry Garcia Band. In the Seventies, Garcia began to spend his "off" Monday nights jamming at the Keystone, a small club in San Francisco. His cohorts varied, except for his bass-playing buddy John Kahn, once of the Butterfield Blues Band. Eventually the loose aggregation became the Jerry Garcia Band, a regular item in Bay Area clubs, developing an eclectic repertoire ranging from gospel to rock to Garcia's solo tunes. In 1981, they added local gospel musician and producer Melvin Seals on keyboards.

The group had released one studio album, 1978's *Cats Under the Stars*. A 2-disc live album, *Jerry Garcia Band*, documented a series of 1990 shows at San Francisco's Warfield Theater. Garcia was in the best shape of his career—"Captain Trips" had become "Captain Dips"—he was into scuba diving and went to Hawaii every chance he got. But the Jerry Garcia Band's tour had been postponed, sparking rumors among Deadheads that the guitarist's substance abuse days were no longer in the past.

"Nah, the timing's not working out right, that's all," Garcia demurred. "The Garcia Band is an 'opportunistic theater'—we have to work into the cracks." ■

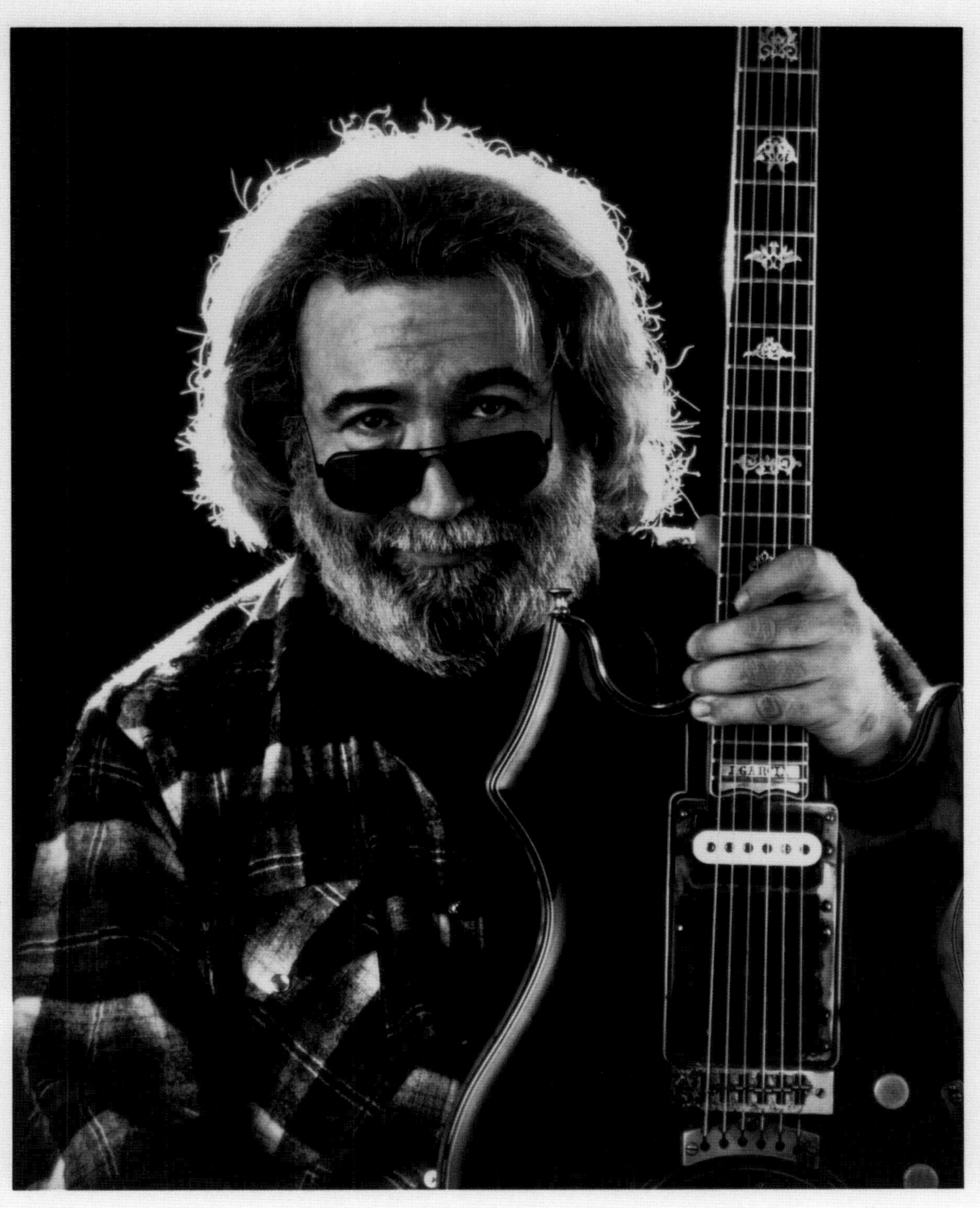

JERRY GARCIA

ARISTA

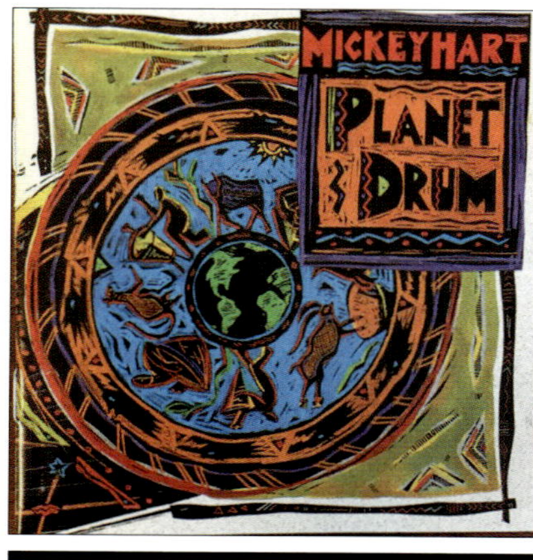

Mickey Hart produced *Planet Drum*, which won the first Grammy awarded for Best World Music Album.

ROCK STARS such as Paul Simon to David Byrne had become famously preoccupied with the "World Beat," but Mickey Hart's obsession was more erudite.

Hart had spent most of his adult life as a "Rhythm Devil," one of two drummers in the Grateful Dead. But he began to recognize that he knew very little about percussion. A muscular bundle of energy, he launched into a self-imposed project to research everything he could about the primal power of drums. On globe-spanning tours with the Dead, he'd collected music, rhythms and songs. He recorded drummers from Africa to the Arctic, from the Golden Gate Gypsy Orchestra to the Gyuto Monks chanting the holy scriptures in Sanskrit. He studied the folklore of percussion instruments, especially in regard to their religious and ceremonial uses.

"I love to hit a drum, and that makes me a practitioner of the oldest form of music-making on the planet," Hart explained. "It's always had a spiritual and physical effect on me, including various degrees of trance and ecstasy. I'm trying to fill in the puzzle, the roadmap. It's for me and other drummers who intuitively knew this stuff and couldn't articulate it."

A lifelong dream reached fruition with Planet Drum. Hart brought together many of the world's foremost percussionists, distilling new rhythms from their different musical cultures and disciplines. The *Planet Drum* album was recorded at his home studio in Northern California, employing percussion instruments ranging from the human body ("Jewe" featured hands slapping on the chest, using the thorax cavity as a resonator) to Hart's high-tech "beam," an electronic monochord played with a steel pipe (familiar to fans of Grateful Dead shows).

The global sound was popular with an eclectic audience. There were ethnomusicologists, anthropologists and the Dead's ever-faithful fans, who took interest in anything the band members did. And members of numerous men's movements often used drumming as part of the group process.

"They're using it as a focusing technique to establish community and ritual," Hart said. "It's not music, it's about making noise—musicians need not apply. And it's not just for men—my girlfriend drums with a feminist drum circle of hundreds every week."

Planet Drum remained at No. 1 on the *Billboard* World Music chart for 26 weeks, and audiences rejoiced when the fusion masters were brought on tour. ■

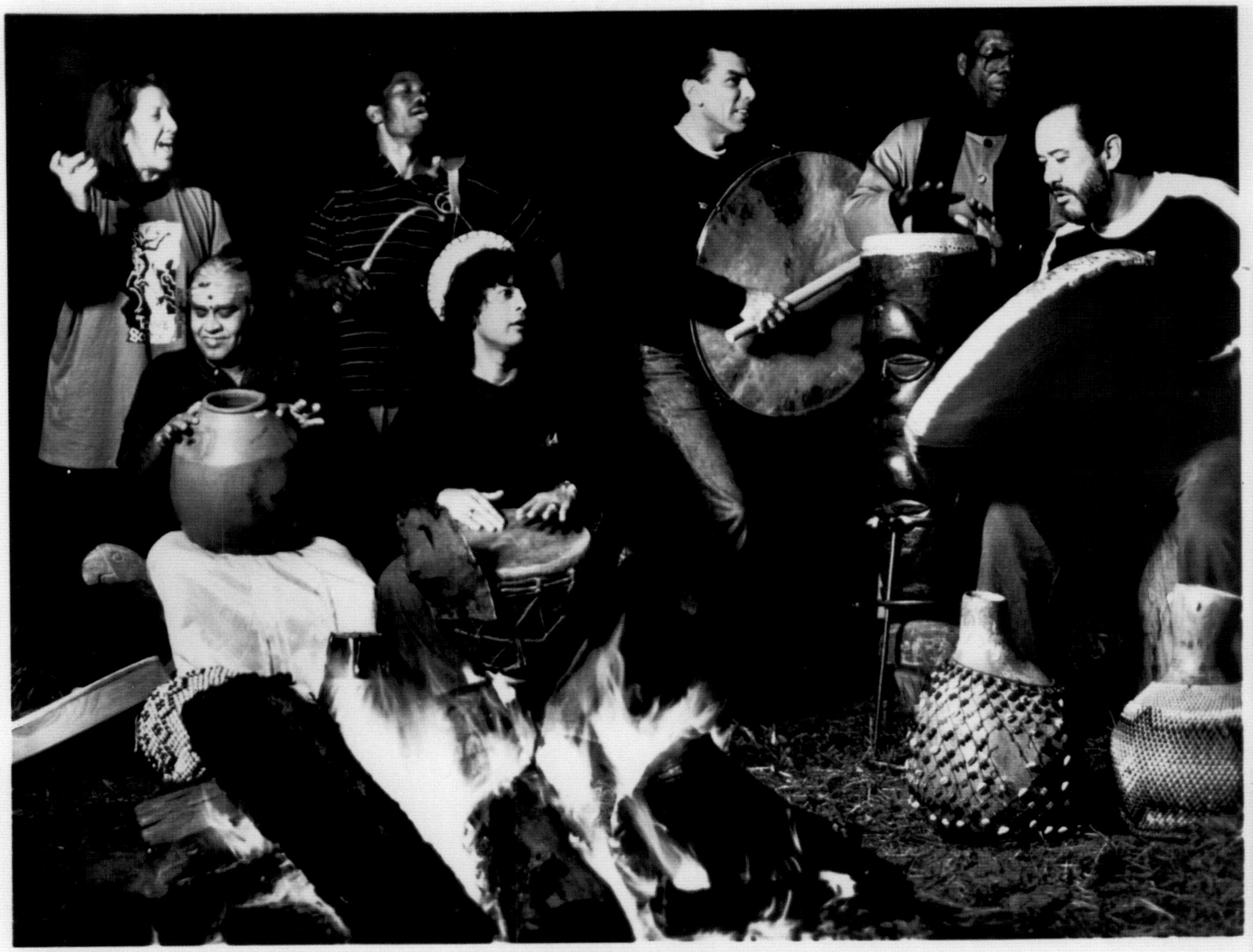

PLANET DRUM

(L-R: Flora Purim; T.H. ("Vikku") Vinayakram; Sikiru Adepoju; Zakir Hussain; Mickey Hart; Babatunde Olatunji; Airto Moreira)

PHOTO CREDIT: JOHN WERNER

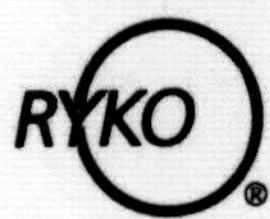

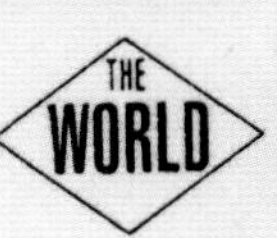

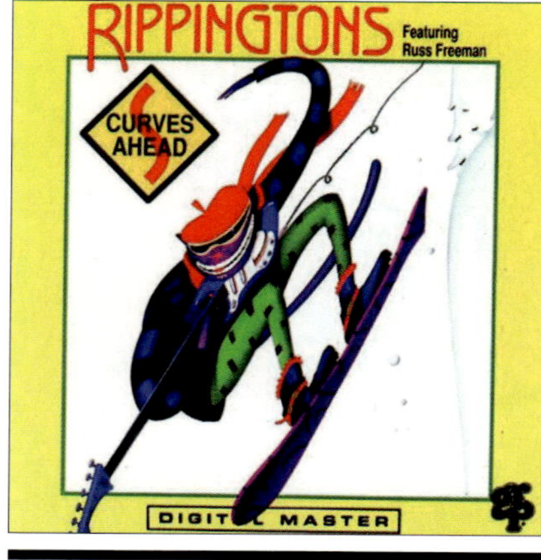

Rippingtons' *Curves Ahead* featured songs influenced by a move to Colorado and the ski atmosphere.

BY BRIDGING pop and jazz music, the Rippingtons had become a fixture on the contemporary jazz charts. 1990's *Welcome to the St. James' Club* album made No. 1 in *Billboard*, and *Curves Ahead*, the instrumental act's fifth release, followed suit.

"We haven't touted ourselves as a jazz act. The instrumental aspect is the only thing we've borrowed," leader Russ Freeman said. "My goal has been to reach the audience that doesn't know about—or doesn't like—jazz. I want to take the rock and pop vocabulary that we've grown up with and apply touches of pure jazz to that."

Freeman was the Rippingtons' creative force. In the early days, he wrote, produced, arranged and played virtually all of the instruments on albums. For concert performances, he depended on other young musicians, and in the studio and on tour the Rippingtons project evolved into a six-member unit—none of them a singer. The Rippingtons used wordless vocalizing techniques, but Freeman resisted recording a straight vocal tune, even though he had seen how, say, Kenny G had benefited from his duet with Michael Bolton.

"We're feeling pressure from the record company to do that," he admitted. "I'm not opposed; I just realize how precious it is to have success in the instrumental field, to do this accessible type of jazz. As soon as we do a vocal tune, we'll be known for that and the unique status we've established goes away forever."

After several performances in Colorado, Freeman fell in love with the area and relocated, building a home and the Cheyenne Mountain Ranch recording studio. The Rippingtons' electric bassist Kim Stone also resided in the state. "On *Curves Ahead*, the title song, 'Snowbound' and 'Aspen' were inspired by the beauty of the place," Freeman noted. ■

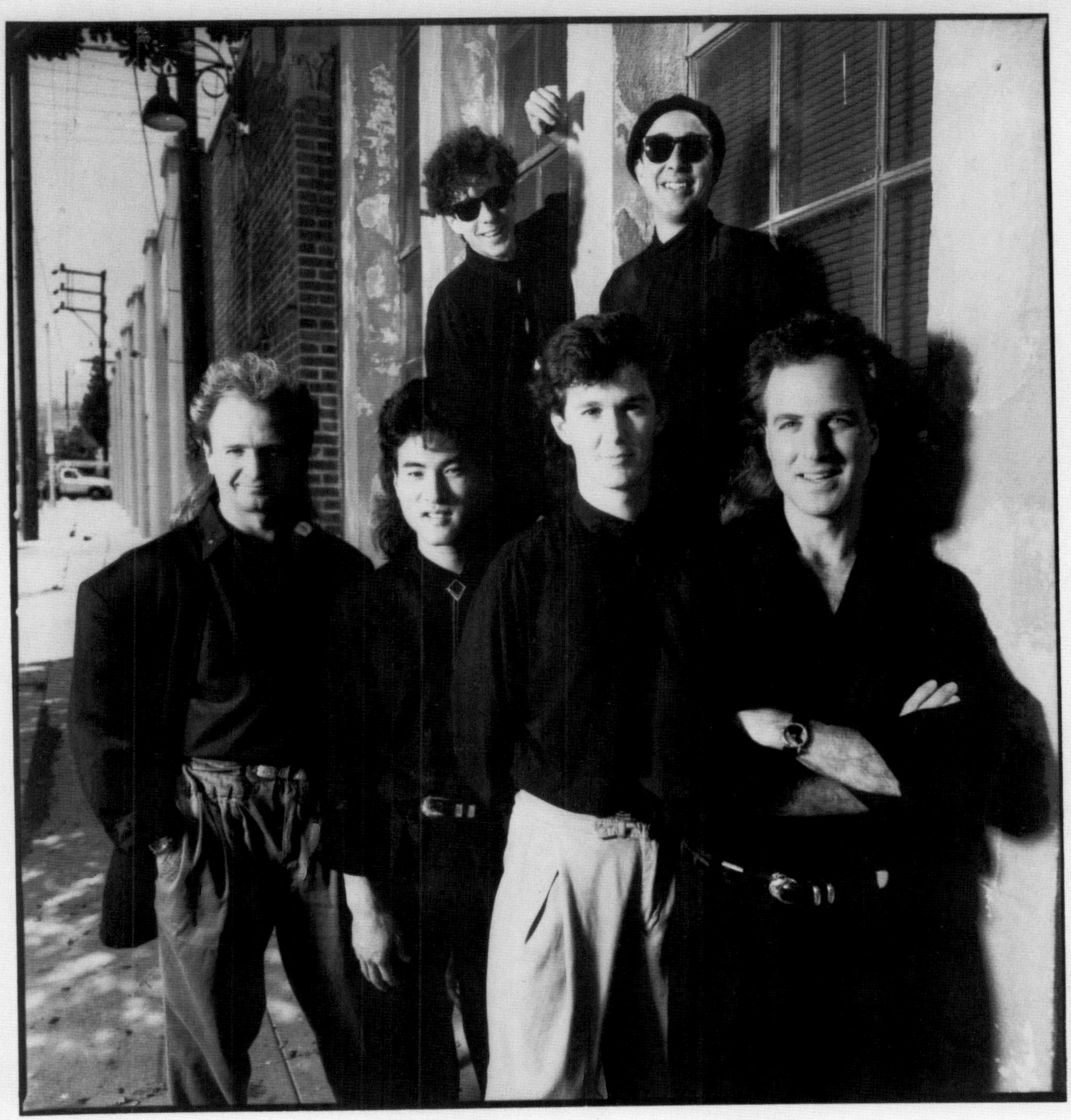

photography: Jeff Katz

STEVE REID JEFF KASHIWA TONY MORALES MARK PORTMAN KIM STONE RUSS FREEMAN

RIPPINGTONS

Featuring Russ Freeman

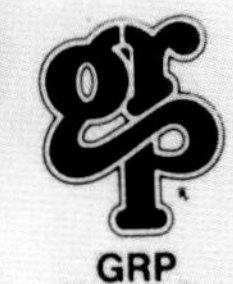

GRP Records

Jesus Jones' *Doubt* sold a million copies in America and spun off the kinetic hit, "Right Here, Right Now."

Billboard 200: *Doubt* (#25)
Billboard Hot 100: "Right Here, Right Now" (#2); "Real, Real, Real" (#4)

THE BRIGHTEST light on the alternative scene was Jesus Jones, the British quintet whose "Right Here, Right Now" spent five weeks at No. 1 on *Billboard*'s Modern Rock Tracks chart. On the pulsating single, lead singer Mike Edwards avowed, "Right here, right now/ There is no other place I want to be/Right here, right now/Watching the world wake up from history."

"It was written at the beginning of 1990, a new year and a new decade," Edwards declared. "It was inspired by the incredible events around us—the revolutions in Czechoslovakia and Romania, the coming down of the Berlin wall, things that our parents never thought they'd see in their lifetimes. I wanted to write a song that wasn't so factual or anecdotal—'70 years of communism has ended'—but personal, what I'm sure it felt like to a lot of people. Six months later, the song was completely out of date, but now I think optimism is back in vogue. Part of the song's success in America has been the public's emotions in the aftermath of the Gulf War."

The genre-bending *Doubt*, Jesus Jones' sophomore effort, was an exceptionally tuneful hybrid of rock and dance music. The band belonged to the faction of groups that emerged in the late Eighties out of London's "acid house" scene, in which the contemporary grooves of rap and house music were augmented with noisy guitar-dominated psychedelic textures.

"In attitude, we're very much a part of that scene," Edwards noted. "It was massively influential, like punk. It had all the elements of youth culture, its own clothing, drugs and sounds. It was one of those exhilarating times that only occur every decade or so. It hasn't had a chance to happen in America yet, but I think it's in the process. The vast size of the country means any new idea takes a while to get across to the general public. The arrival of our band signals the re-exporting of American music by British groups. We want to be the missing link that fills the parts between the best music."

Rap's sampling technique—reusing key melodies and beats from other records—was an element to the sound, but Jesus Jones transformed what it appropriated. "We've grasped the idea that technology is the important part of society today—it makes music affordable to everyone, but I see sampling as taking influences to an extreme," Edwards insisted.

"If you use an arrangement of samples in an unaccustomed way, then you don't end up sounding like everybody else. That's our function in rock music." ■

© 1991 SBK Records. Permission to reproduce this photography is limited to editorial use in regular issues of newspapers and other regularly published periodicals and television news programming.

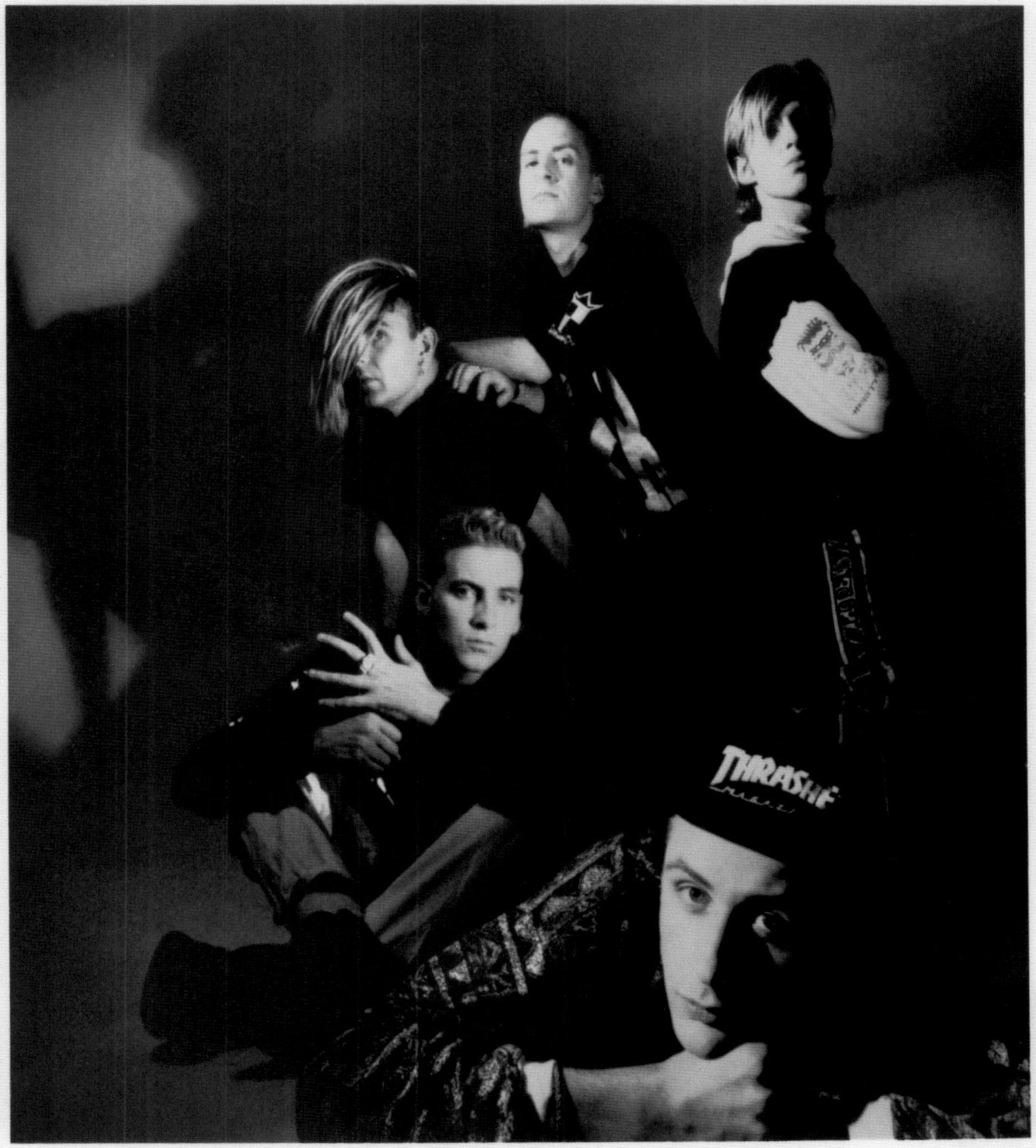

Photo Credit: Simon Fowler

Front to back Mike Edwards Barry D. Al Jaworski Jerry De Borg Gen

JESUS JONES

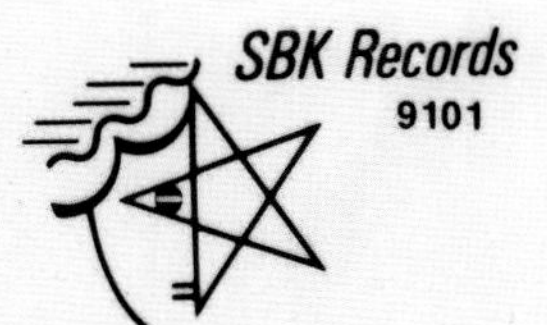

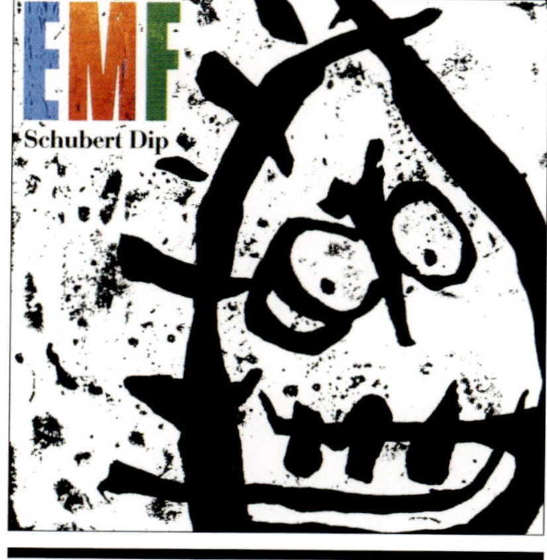

The dance-rock quintet EMF occupied the international charts with the utterly British "Unbelievable."

Billboard 200: *Schubert Dip* (#12)
Billboard Hot 100: "Unbelievable" (No. 1); "Lies" (#18)

IT HAD become trendy in England to make records meshing dance music with guitars—and export the most popular results to America. EMF, a rock-dance quintet in existence for less than two years, sprang from nowhere to international success by concocting an insanely catchy debut single, "Unbelievable," which hit No. 1 in the U.S. aided by a tidal wave of hype.

The five working-class funkateers hailed from the Forest of Dean, a rural district west of London. They played in local bands before meeting at keyboardist Derry Brownson's clothes shop. Excited by the burgeoning acid-house movement but too far from London to participate, they used Brownson's funds to launch EMF.

"All we had was attitude and a big drinking problem," Brownson, 20, said. "But we played in the back of a local pub for our fourth gig and got signed to a recording contract. 'Unbelievable' was the first song we recorded. The way we worked together seemed special, but it was a bit like throwing a bottle with a message in it into the sea. We released it thinking it wouldn't get anywhere."

Yet five months later, "Unbelievable" went Top 5 in the UK, followed by a debut album, *Schubert Dip*. EMF's fresh-faced appeal catapulted them into the British tabloids, which typecast the group as risqué alter egos to New Kids on the Block (there were five of them, and they wore baseball caps) or the Sex Pistols of the independent dance scene (they behaved in a mildly delinquent manner and favored naughty language).

"They've tried to put their foot on our heads because we're young and energetic, but those are purely cosmetic comparisons," Brownson noted. "We like America—our fans here climb onto the stage and dive into their friends' arms, slam-dancing with each other."

Controversy arose over the band's follow-up single. "Lies" contained a sample from the taped confession of John Lennon's assassin, Mark David Chapman, reciting a lyric from Lennon's "Watching the Wheels" after his arrest. Under legal threats from Yoko Ono, EMF had to remove Chapman's voice on future pressings of *Schubert Dip*.

"We taped it off the telly, from a Lennon documentary," Brownson explained. "We weren't sensationalizing his death, but Yoko kicked up a fuss and wanted royalties, which sort of belittles the whole thing. We're not really bad boys. There's an intelligence in what we do, but we are spontaneous. Success hasn't hit us yet." ■

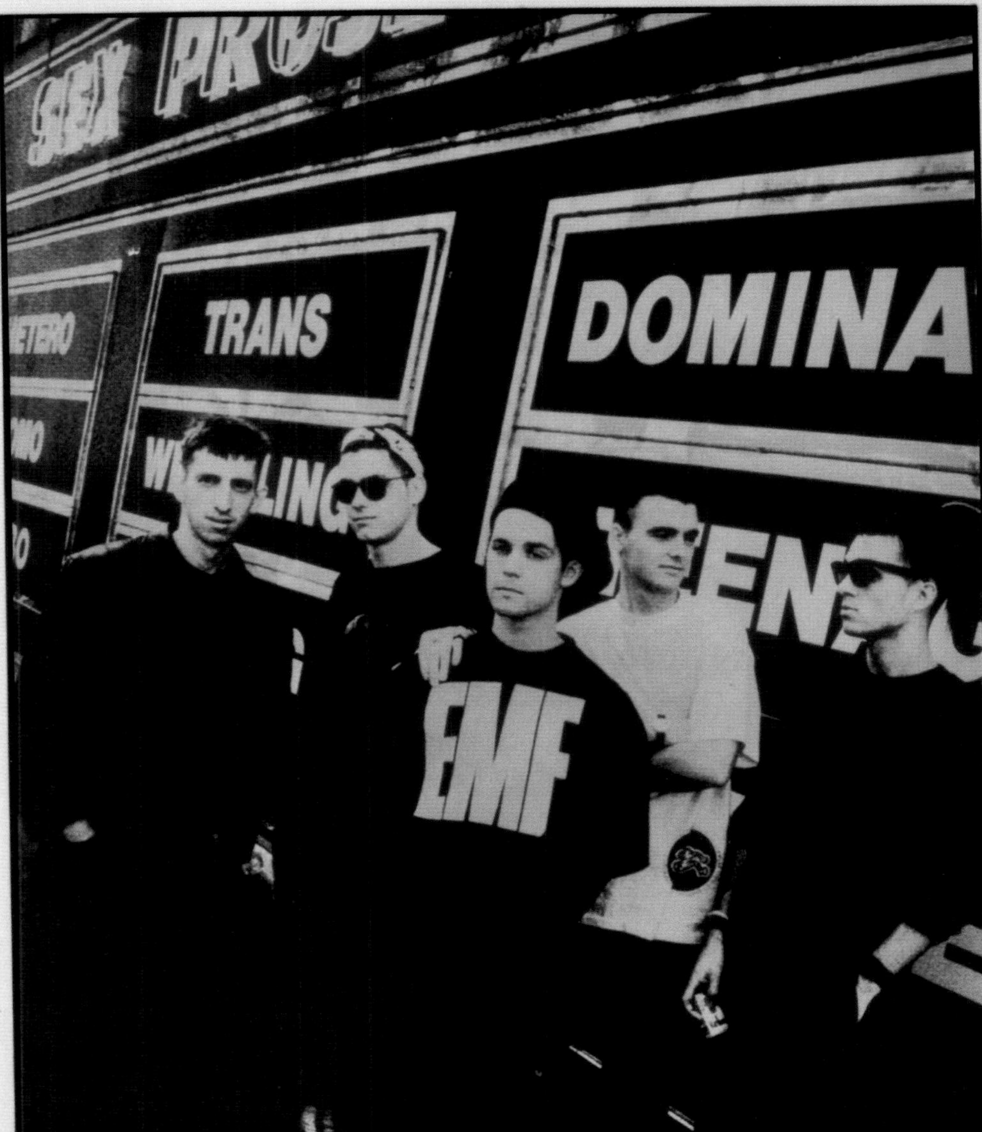

PHOTOGRAPHER: KEVIN WESTENBERG

©1991 EMI Records USA

EMF

FROM EMI

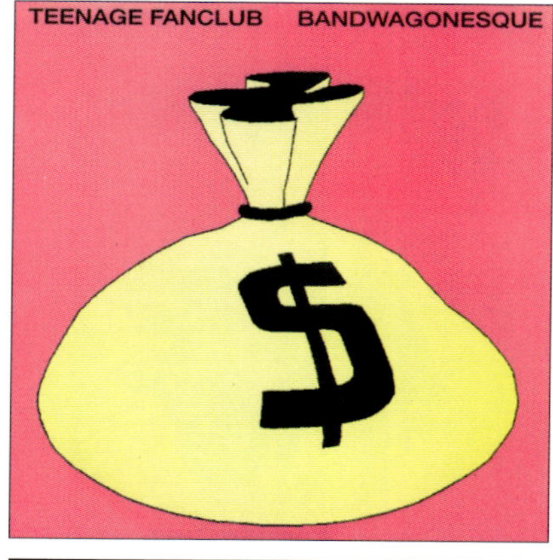

Emerging from the Glasgow scene, Teenage Fanclub was declared the modern-rock band of the moment.

Billboard 200: *Bandwagonesque* (#137)

THE ENGLISH press had dubbed Teenage Fanclub rock's bright new hope. *Bandwagonesque* topped *Rolling Stone* magazine's college albums chart, and *Spin* magazine identified it as the No. 1 record of the year. But the accolades all made lead singer and guitarist Norman Blake just a wee bit uncomfortable. He apologized for the band from Scotland not being smarter or more ambitious.

"In the UK, there's a big house-music dance scene going on. Everyone's in a trance, jumping on the bandwagon," Blake said. "Maybe that's one reason we've been sort of popular—we don't have any image at all. We're totally into playing music, we love playing records and we're fans. That's it."

Teenage Fanclub's 1990 independent release, *A Catholic Education*, landed on every British best-of tally. *Bandwagonesque*, the band's first major-label release, wasn't innovative, but it was compelling and effective. The members of the group, aged between 25 and 28, used the basic guitar-and-drums tools of rock to pull off a noisy reconstruction of pop and punk. "Star Sign" reached #4 on *Billboard*'s Modern Rock Tracks chart.

"We try to get a good performance and record it live, get the one good take, even if it's slightly flawed," Blake said. "Technology is too complicated. We've got amps that sound warm, 'valve-y.' We're interested in getting purity of sound, putting guitars directly onto tape instead of through three or four different processes."

With their loose-limbed grooves and sharply developed melodies, a couple of the songs on *Bandwagonesque* displayed the decided influence of the Great American Pop Band of the Seventies, Big Star.

"I got into music when the Sex Pistols and the Clash came out," Blake explained. "But as a young punk, I swallowed this line of bullshit—you were taught not to like old records. So I missed early Seventies pop music, power-pop like Big Star. Only in the last five years have I gotten into that. We all like melody. I'm into the Beach Boys, the music of the Beatles. I know from the mid-Sixties onwards."

Beneath the guitar-saturated din, many of the lyrics were laced with a touch of irreverence.

"Compared to London, Glasgow is provincial," Blake said. "We Glaswegians have a self-deprecating sense of humor. We can't take anything that seriously. The massive shipbuilding industry is gone, so it's grin and bear it. We have that attitude in a rock band." ■

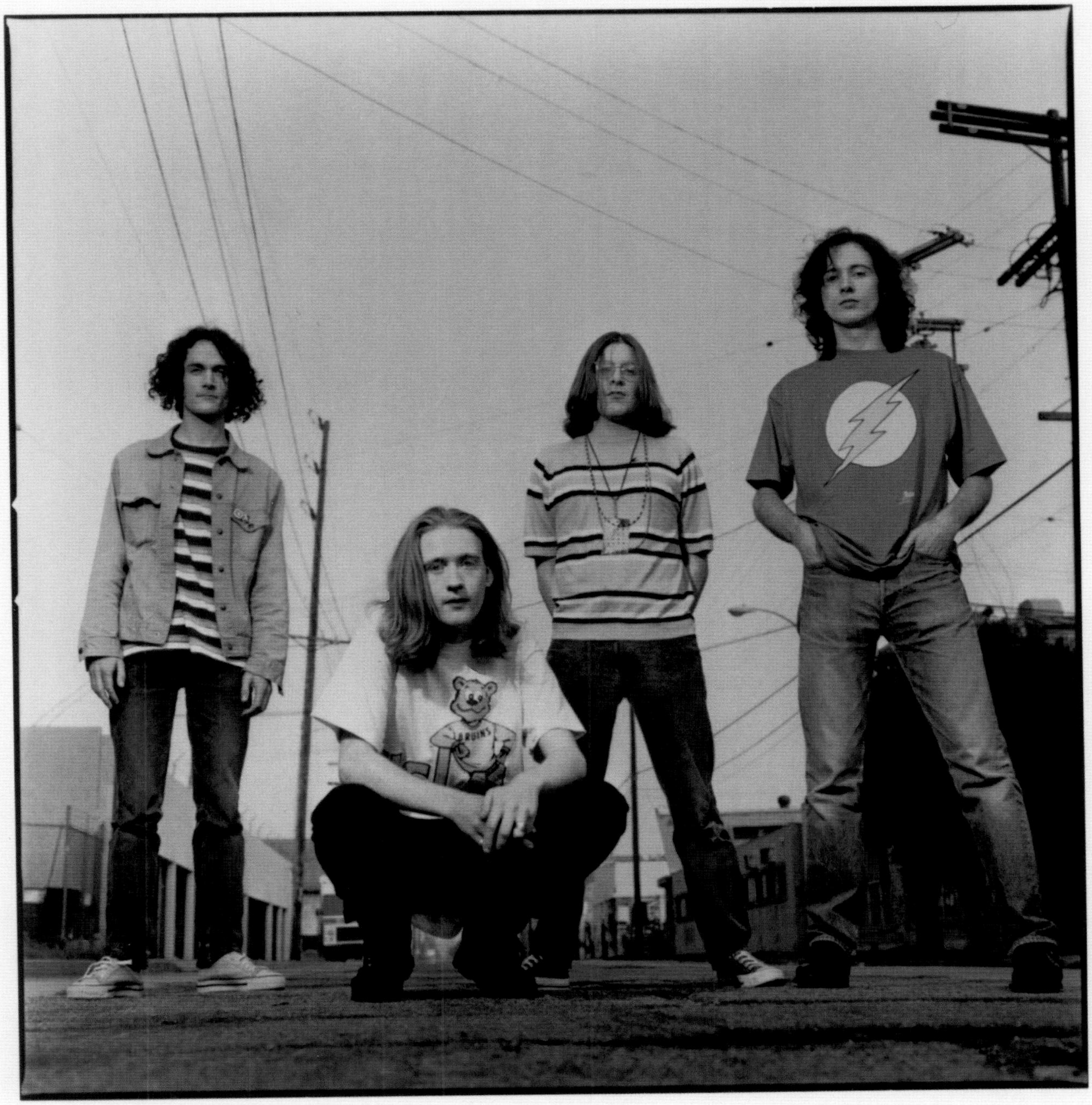

Photo Credit: Michael Lavine

Gerry Love Brendan O'hare Norman Blake Raymond McGinnley

Teenage Fanclub

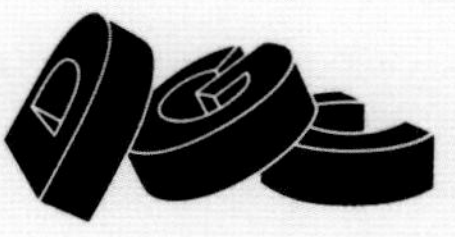

DAVID GEFFEN COMPANY

© 1991 The David Geffen Company/Permission to reproduce limited to editorial uses in newspapers and other regularly published periodicals and television news programming.

Big Audio Dynamite II, formed by former Clash guitarist Mick Jones, experienced the surprise hit, "Rush."

Billboard 200: *The Globe* (#76)
Billboard Hot 100: "Rush" (#32); "The Globe" (#72)

MICK JONES was a driving force behind the Clash, perhaps the most politically and musically inspiring band to emerge from the British punk scene. After the group unceremoniously ousted him in 1983, the scruffy-voiced rocker recouped from the acrimonious split by forming Big Audio Dynamite two years later. B.A.D. released four innovative albums that mixed rock with an urban dance beat and electronic effects, but Jones disbanded the original lineup at the end of 1989.

"Everything has been written and then rewritten over," Jones said. "It must have been great being in, say, the Ink Spots. Back then you could have the idea to write about lips and not worry that someone had written that before. I would like to get back to writing something simple that everybody can understand. That's what I'm really aiming for, not to be too clever."

When the Nineties dawned, Jones had surrounded himself with young talent to form his newest career incarnation, Big Audio Dynamite II. Bassist Gary Stonadge was an old soccer-watching buddy.

"I've known Mick since the Clash—this was luck," Stonadge said. "We were going to a football match and he asked if I wanted to try something musically. I thought he was joking, but he lined up some gigs. The first couple were terrible. We thought it wasn't going to work."

The Globe featured "Rush," the top hit on the Modern Rock Tracks chart of 1991 in *Billboard*. The song manipulated the synthesizer riff from the Who's "Baba O'Riley" to add snap to a dance rhythm. Jones confessed that he was driven by a need for constant change.

"It's like Mick's version of 'My Way,' I suppose," Stonadge said, referring to the Sex Pistols' rendition of the Frank Sinatra standard. "When he wrote that song, it was a new start, a new band in a new decade. If he had the chance, he wouldn't change a thing."

The single, "The Globe," borrowed the martial beat and pealing guitar chords of Jones' Clash days, but whereas his songs used to call for political action, the message was now "It's party time—do what you like." Live, fans got the traditional two guitars, bass and drums lineup, but Big Audio Dynamite got a little help from some nifty high-tech racks.

"And we play records before our set," Stonadge enthused. "People in America are starting to get into that English rave thing, the psychedelic dance parties." ■

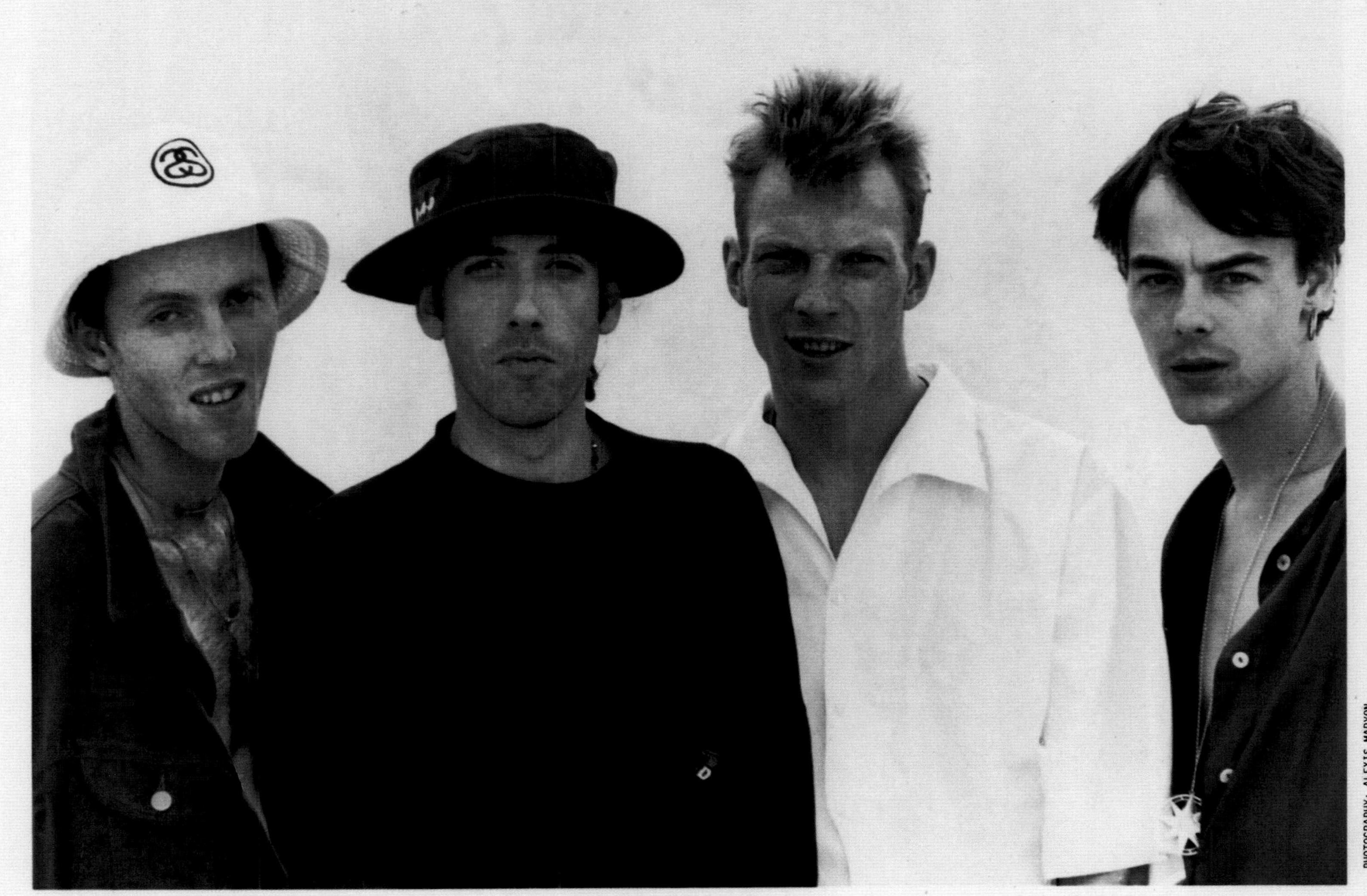

From left: NICK HAWKINS, MICK JONES, GARY STONADGE, and CHRIS KAVANAGH.

© 1991 Sony Music. Permission to reproduce this photography is limited to editorial uses in regular issues of newspapers and other regularly published periodicals and television news programming.

BIG AUDIO DYNAMITE II

Columbia

9105

Primal Scream's *Screamadelica* picked up the first-ever Mercury Music Prize for the UK's best album.

TO BRITISH youth, Primal Scream's sound—hip dashes of Sixties psychedelia and the Rolling Stones mixed with modernized dance beats—was brilliant. But it didn't make as much sense to American kids.

"The scene can't happen here—it's unique to English culture, to a small country," founder Bobby Gillespie said while on tour in the US. "Even in the punk days, you had British punk and American punk. But our music is exotic because we're not from here. Maybe Americans can find that appealing."

Primal Scream was spawned in 1984 in Glasgow when Gillespie took time from another Scottish group, the Jesus and Mary Chain. With his own band, he emerged as a marginal leather-trousered rock outlaw, only to redefine himself in 1989 as a party guy on the acid-house scene. He immersed himself in Britain's thriving "rave" culture, where "strangers got rid of their inhibitions and opened up." It was a hedonistic lifestyle of sex ("Screaming 15-year-old girls wearing hot pants would fly by you") and drugs (Ecstasy) and rock 'n' roll.

"Rock gigs had ceased to excite me—they were sad, sterile," Gillespie explained. "Hundreds of kindred spirits crammed together in a room, but too cool to talk to each other. I was through being cool."

Having discovered the joy of dance-floor communion, Primal Scream fused late-Sixties retro-pop melodies with contemporary rhythms—and had a seismic effect on the UK music scene. The *Screamadelica* album was diverse to the point of paradox. It was a rock record—"Movin' On Up" reworked a Stones-y guitar groove with a percolating Soul II Soul edge (the song was produced by Jimmy Miller, who worked on the Stones' "Let It Bleed"). But it also reflected Gillespie's many musical influences and the mind-bending substances he'd absorbed. There were astonishingly trippy trance/dance anthems ("Higher Than the Sun") and creamy, uplifting techno-gospel tunes ("Don't Fight It, Feel It"). Lyrically, "Loaded" (as in "let's get...") repeatedly sampled Peter Fonda's lines in Roger Corman's Sixties biker movie, *The Wild Bunch*.

On tour in America, Gillespie saw himself as a solitary sage in a musical wasteland.

"It's an eight-piece band live—heavy drum licks, pianos, lead guitars, two singers," he said. "We create an atmosphere. But it's always frustrating if you ain't getting anything back. I'm getting pretty cynical. People go see Band A that's putting out, and then they enjoy Band B that walks through the motions. I don't think they can tell the difference." ■

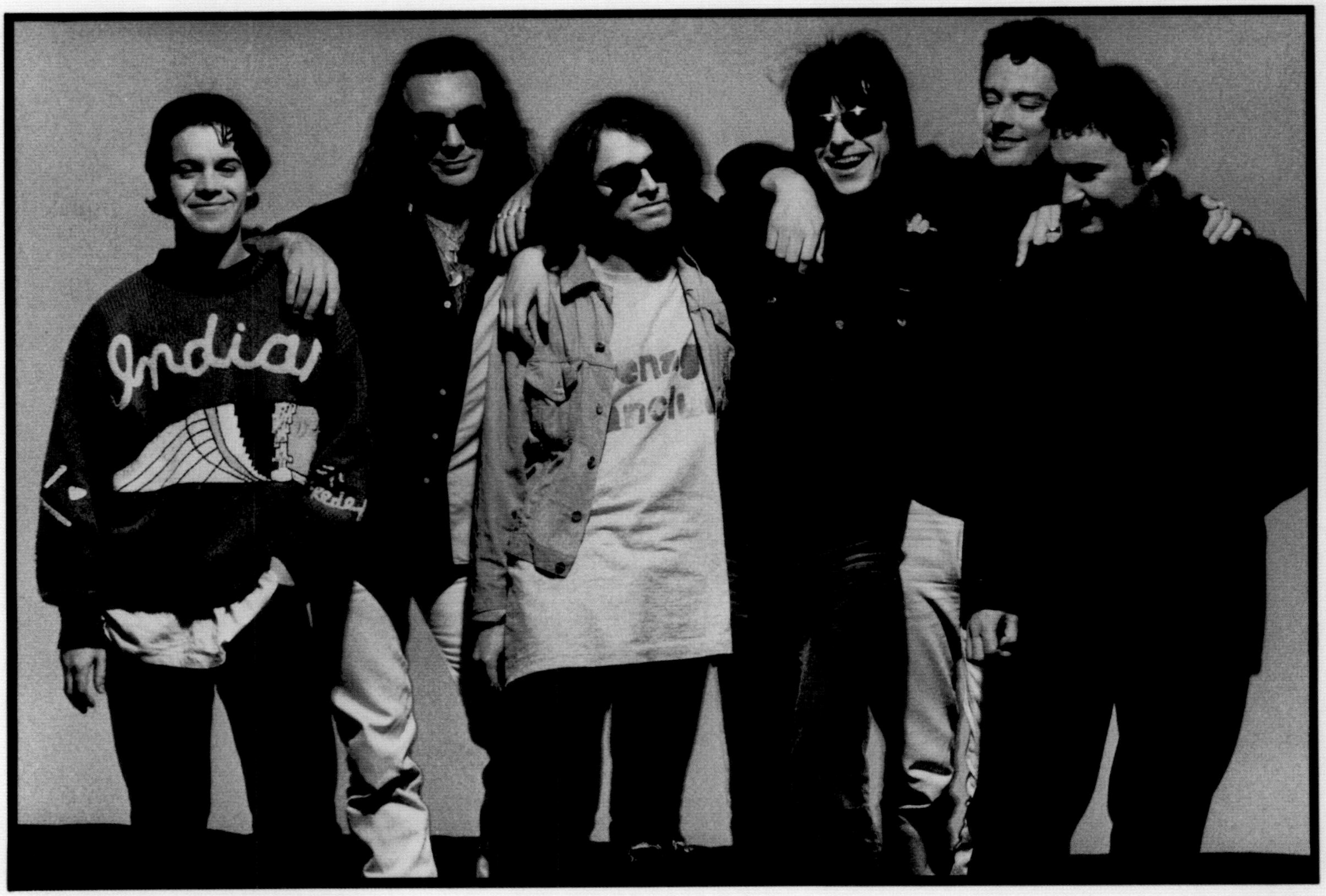

Photo Credit: Kevin Westenberg

primal scream

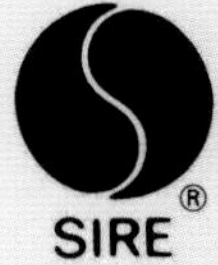

© 1991 Sire Records Company/Permission to reproduce limited to editorial uses in newspapers and other regularly published periodicals and television news programming.

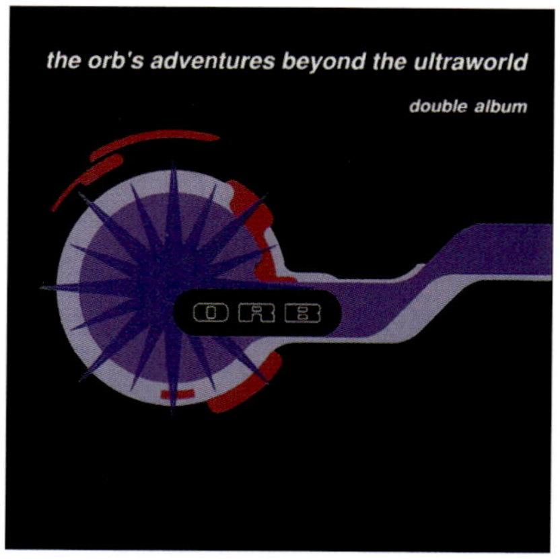

The Orb, a British ambient house group, provided "Fluffy Little Clouds" with a laid-back dancefloor vibe.

THE ORB was the name for the electronic music ventures of Britain's Alex Paterson and his pals. Instead of drum machines, the Orb used ambient elements in the aural graffiti of house music, creating compelling rhythms from esoteric pulses. The trippiness provided a soundtrack for ravers coming down from drugs once the clubs had closed their doors—the vibe of "tune in, turn on and chill out" rooms—and England was hailing Paterson as the successor to Pink Floyd.

"That's a bit over the top, to be compared to a band that's accomplished so much," Paterson said. "The Orb is a three-pronged effort. I'm a DJ in the dance clubs. I also remix numerous records in the studio—I've done Primal Scream and Front 242, to name a few. And then I record as the Orb. It started off as a hobby, something to do on weekends. The musical backing is for the dance floor, but I bury the beats far enough to make the music suitable for the living room."

Or the flotation tank. Manhattan's Center for Creative Well-Being was the site of an Orb listening party—individuals lay in 10 inches of water saturated with Dead Sea salt as underwater speakers pumped *The Orb's Adventures Beyond the Ultraworld.* On the album, Paterson subtly mixed in samples of choral ensembles, jet airplanes, astronaut broadcasts and even an Oxy 10 commercial.

Most of the album's grooves were instrumental, but "Little Fluffy Clouds" featured Rickie Lee Jones wondering about the sky over a galactic bed of throbbing techno house (the unauthorized use of her work led to a dispute settled out of court for an undisclosed sum). The original UK release, a 110-minute double CD featuring the 18:47 epic "A Huge Ever Growing Pulsating Brain That Rules from the Centre of the Underworld," was condensed into a 70-minute single disc in America, where Paterson did some club dates.

"We've remixed the backing tapes so they are unlike the album, and we layer sequencers, keyboards and samplers on top so it's spontaneous," Paterson explained. "Sometimes a crowd dances, and other times people just stand and listen. It's funny—I slipped in Led Zeppelin's 'When the Levee Breaks' during a British show, and people came up afterwards to ask me where it came from. Kids under 20 don't know that music existed back then, and now that drum sound is sampled on every hip-hop record." ■

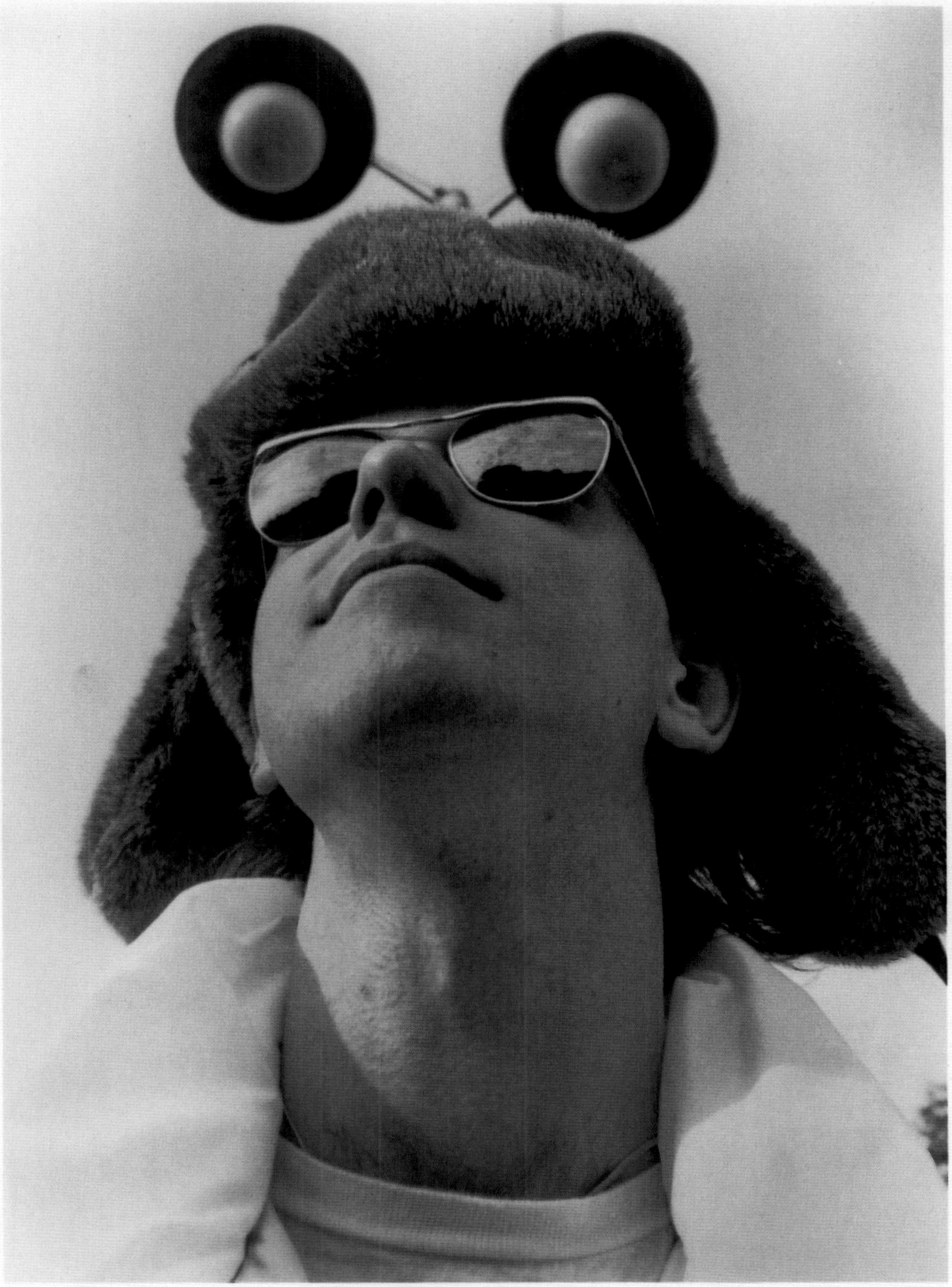

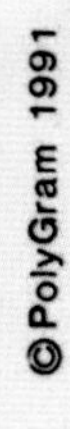

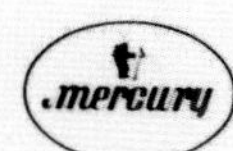

THE ORB

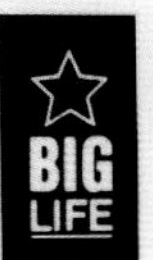

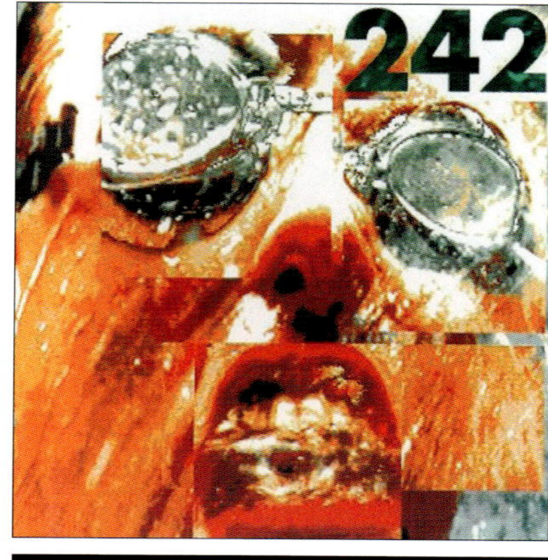

Front 242 consolidated the sounds of the electronic and industrial music genres with *Tyranny (For You)*.

Billboard 200: *Tyranny (For You)* (#95)

WHEN FRONT 242 formed in Belgium in 1981, its members didn't plan on mainstream acceptance. Disowning such designations as "industrial disco" and "dancecore," they invented an "electronic body music" concept—an aura of relentless beats, bombastic sequencer flourishes and overbearing chanted vocals. The band's cold, domineering music left many disco denizens reaching for the Advil, but the bleak, impersonal racket became a dance-club phenomenon, as a cult audience praised the group's collage of extreme sound as being more in tune with tumultuous times than escapist fare.

"In America, if you need a drummer or bass player, you look in the paper. In Belgium, there is not a musicians' market—everybody is pushed to work with machines," synthesizer player Rodney Codneys explained. "Being in the middle of Europe, we were also influenced by the German 'anti-rock' of the Seventies, bands like Can and Kraftwerk. They made music without being musicians, with noises and sound mixes rather than melodies.

"We're horrible musicians. We're good cheaters with machines. We approach music differently. It's a landscape of sounds from anywhere. We just take an idea, we talk, and we put noise and harmony samples together to express something. So there's no writing in the musical sense. We have no choice—we cannot play."

Front 242's music verged on going overground—*Tyranny (For You)*, the band's first release for a major label, rose on the album charts despite a lack of commercial airplay. The song "Rhythm of Time" proved an alternative club hit.

"It's a miracle," Codneys admitted. "We've always been convinced that electronic music was a complete concept, but the big move to more sophisticated, less commercial sounds has come from the public. There are a thousand reasons—Prince did some weird productions with those tougher sounds, motion pictures started using synthesized soundtracks, rap came from the streets by applying low-tech machines. That's all brought an audience to Front 242." ■

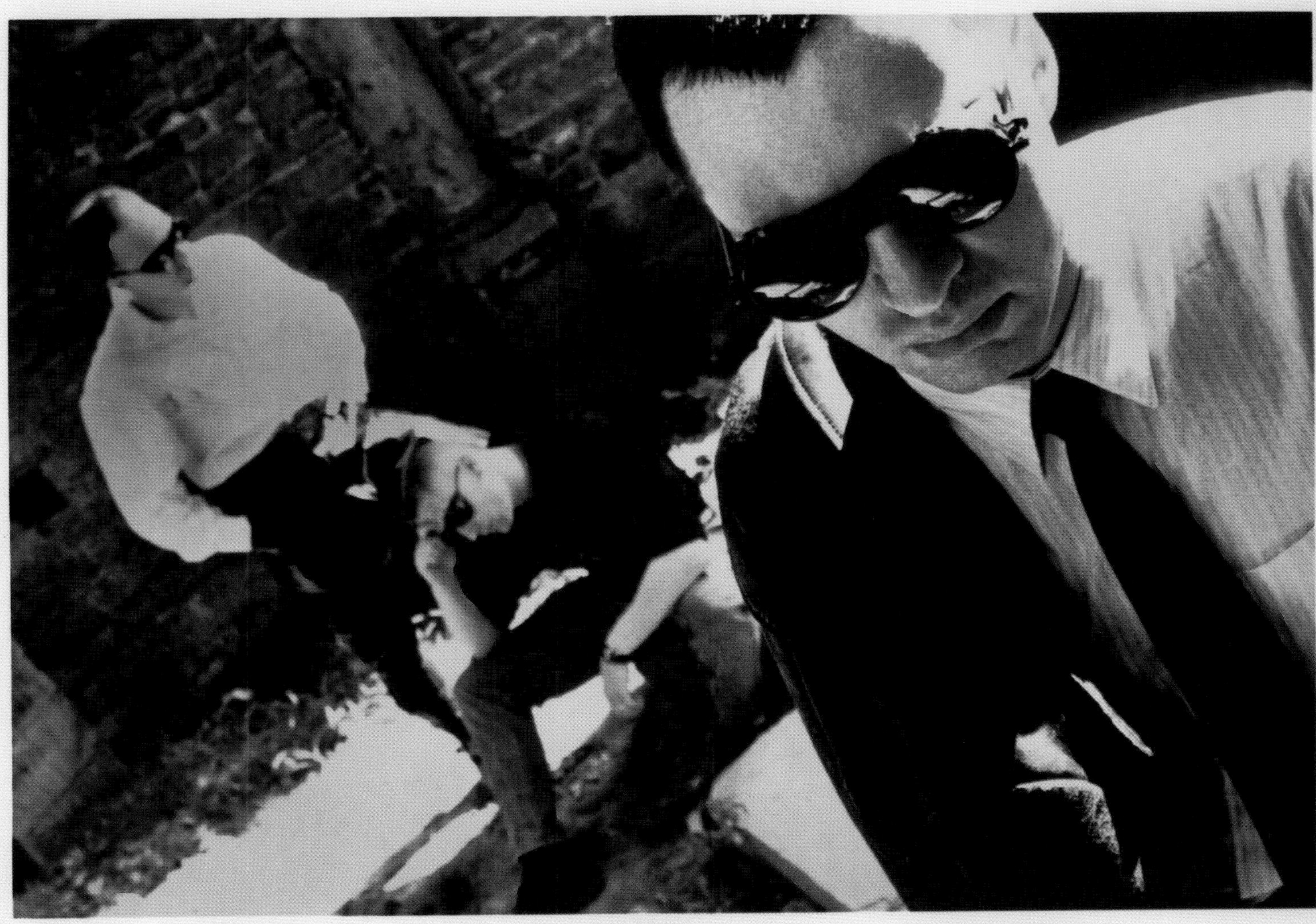

PATRICK CODENYS RICHARD 23 JEAN-LUC DeMEYER

FRONT 242

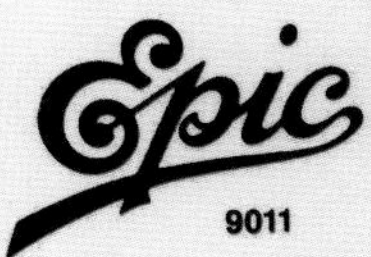

PHOTO CREDIT: A. VERBAERT

© 1990 CBS Records Inc. Permission to reproduce this photography is limited to editorial uses in regular issues of newspapers and other regularly published periodicals and television news programming.

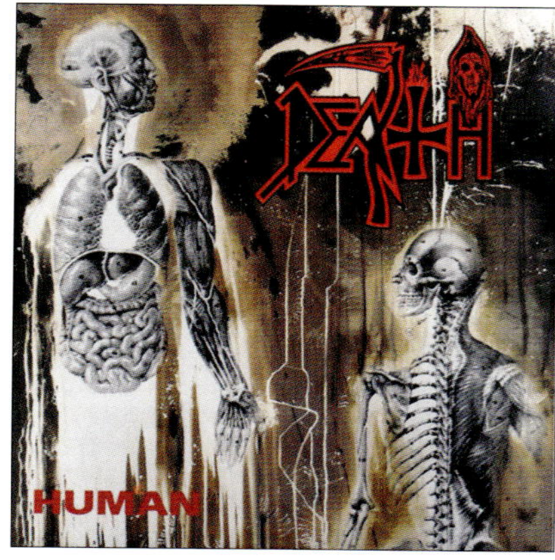

Death's breakthrough album, *Human*, opened the doors for other extreme acts in the death-metal genre.

CHUCK SCHULDINER got credit for kick-starting the death-metal scene—primarily because nobody had ever been so blunt as to call a band Death, and the guitar virtuoso took the doomy sound one step further with ominous, lower-key dynamics and growling about all manner of destruction. Schuldiner had had problems finding Death members—he was the only one who had appeared on all four of the group's brutal, albeit increasingly accomplished, albums.

"When I started, this was considered the most unacceptable music ever," he explained.

But there would always be teenagers who wanted to annoy their parents and neighbors. They had caught up to the land's most vile, extreme bands—death-metal movements were burgeoning in the US and the UK. Death released *Human*, the Florida metal band's most technical and progressive album. Why didn't the lyrics on *Human* have the blood-and-guts propensity of early Death?

"What goes on in relationships between human beings can be just as brutal as any satanic schlock," Schuldiner mused. "Some people only see the chaos connected with the music, and they expect me to act out the band name and be wild. But I like puppies and flowers when I'm not onstage." He said that with a straight face. ■

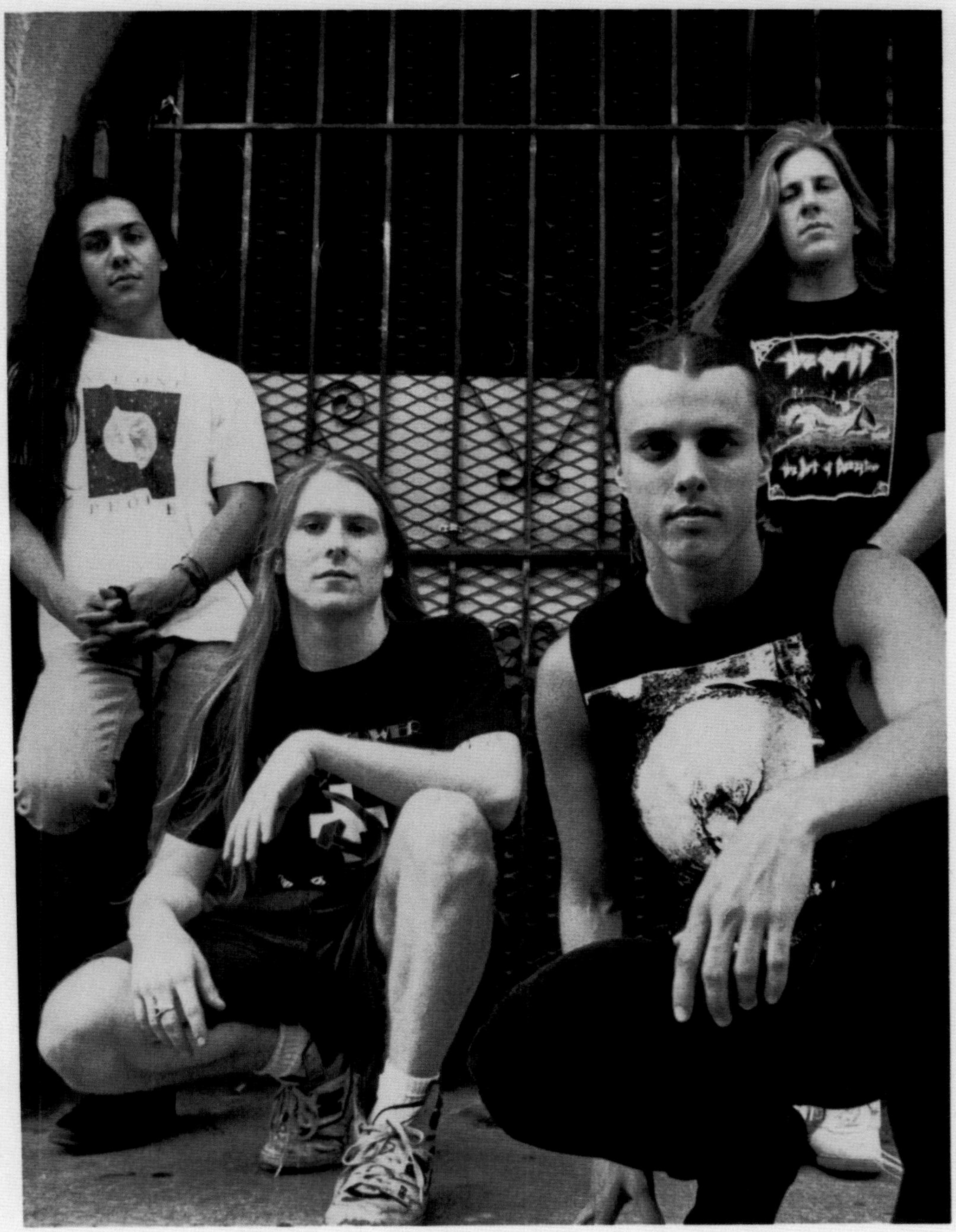

PHOTO BY MICHAEL HAYNES

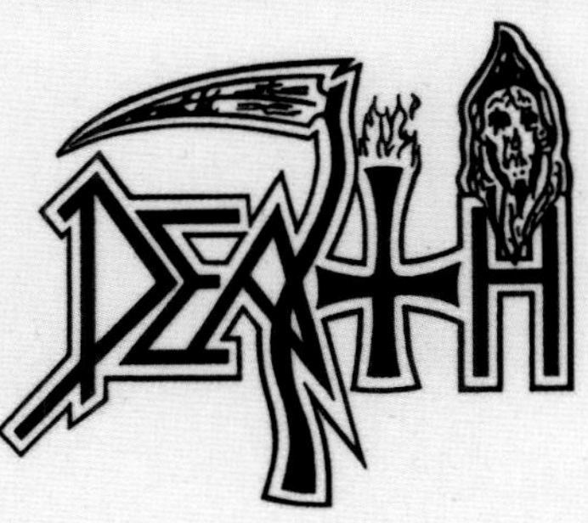

HUMAN

RELATIVITY

Billboard 200: *The Doors: Original Soundtrack Recording* (#8)

The Doors, Oliver Stone's somewhat divisive film, offered a cross-section of the band's classic rock hits.

IN THE 20 years since his death in a Paris bathtub, Jim Morrison's legend had remained the subject of public fascination—and blossomed into the realm of myth. His complex psyche had been obscured by a barrage of misinformation and hype. Was he an erotic politician or an abusive alcoholic? A hippie shaman or a doped-up rebel? The Lizard King or a Dionysian debaucher?

Director Oliver Stone made *The Doors*, a provocative feature film starring Val Kilmer as Morrison. The surviving members of the Doors didn't review Stone's biopic when it was released. Keyboardist Ray Manzarek said they had a "monetary, contractual agreement" not to criticize the project for a while. But then he excoriated *The Doors*.

"Oliver Stone with the strange 'white powder' take on Jim Morrison…it's a speed-freak meth-head movie," Manzarek said.

In response, Stone claimed that Manzarek objected to the film's portrayal of the band because Manzarek wanted to make his own movie. Morrison and Manzarek were UCLA film students when they formed the Doors in Los Angeles circa 1965 with drummer John Densmore and guitarist Robbie Krieger. Together, they created a classic rock sound dominated by Manzarek's electric organ work and the charismatic Morrison's deep, sonorous voice.

"I went to UCLA film school, so of course I want to make my own movie—but it's not about the Doors! That's Stone's stupidity," Manzarek countered. "The Doors have gone through ups and down ever since 'Light My Fire' hit No. 1 in 1967. This time it's a two-pronged attack—it's a great worshipping of Jim, plus a reduction of his myth by nitpicking about his negative qualities, a *National Enquirer* phase. We have to show that Jim Morrison was weak, that he did this and that with a girl, that he drank booze. My God, show me a writer who doesn't drink! Jim Morrison isn't the guy who died in a bathtub in Paris. Where are the words, the poetry that he wrote? That's what he was all about. That's the next cycle that will come three or four years from now."

The Doors hadn't made an album in two decades, but the release of the film generated a revival of interest in the band. *Best of the Doors* re-entered *Billboard*'s album chart. *In Concert*, a live double album, was compiled from a variety of different releases and concerts. And the movie soundtrack, containing over two dozen of the Doors' songs, reached the Top 10.

The well-read Manzarek assessed his best friend's life. "The man was a human being just like you and me—but incredibly intelligent, funny, artistic, poetic and driven," he said. "That was the dichotomy of Jim Morrison." ■

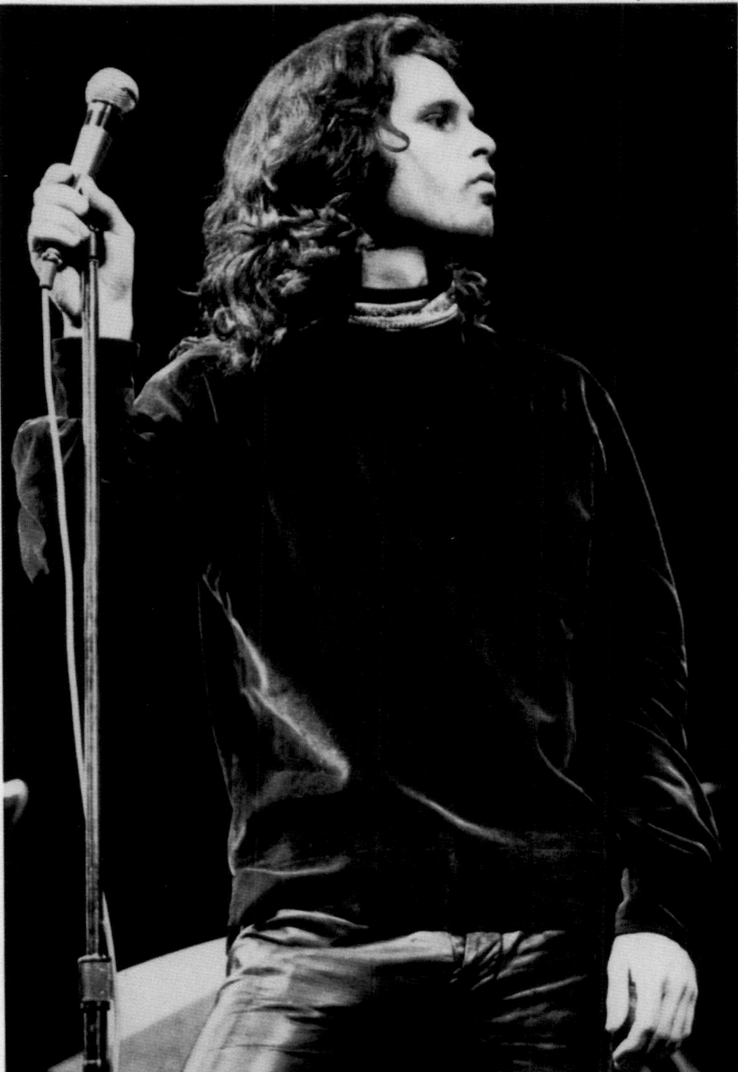

JIM MORRISON

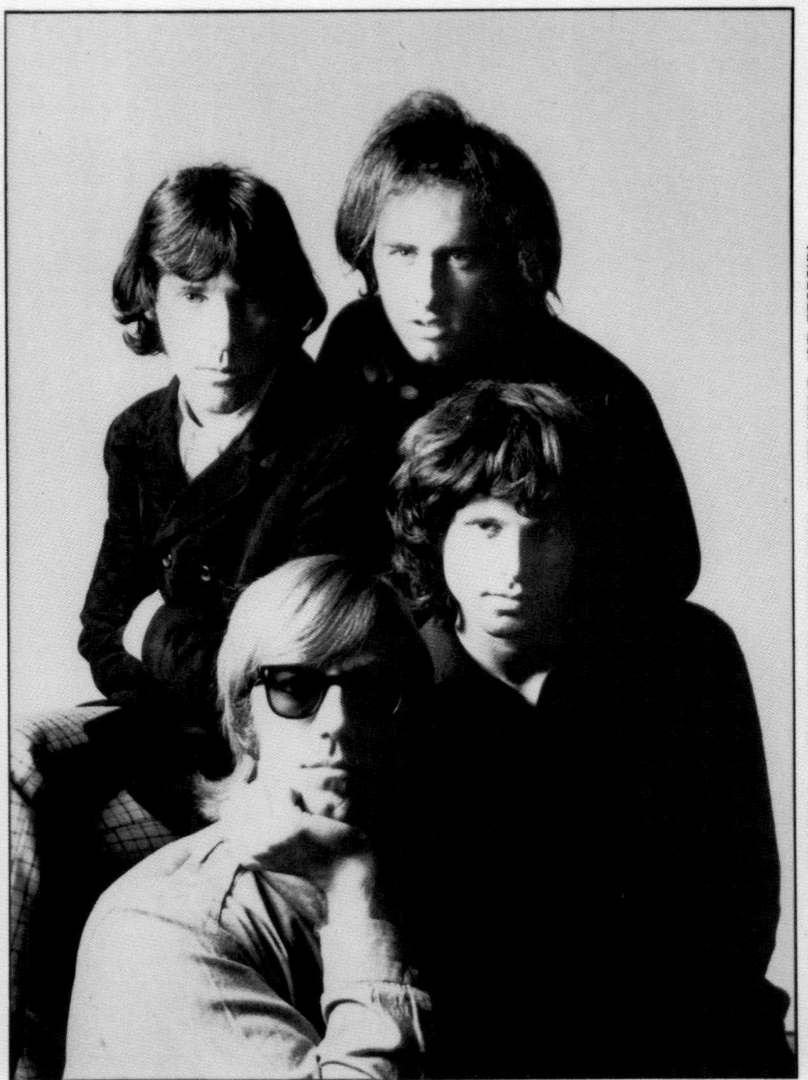

PHOTO COURTESY OF: THE DOORS – THE ILLUSTRATED HISTORY (1983) PHOTO CREDIT : JOEL BRODSKY

JOHN DENSMORE
RAY MANZAREK
ROBBIE KRIEGER
JIM MORRISON

THE DOORS

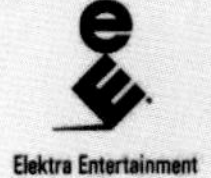

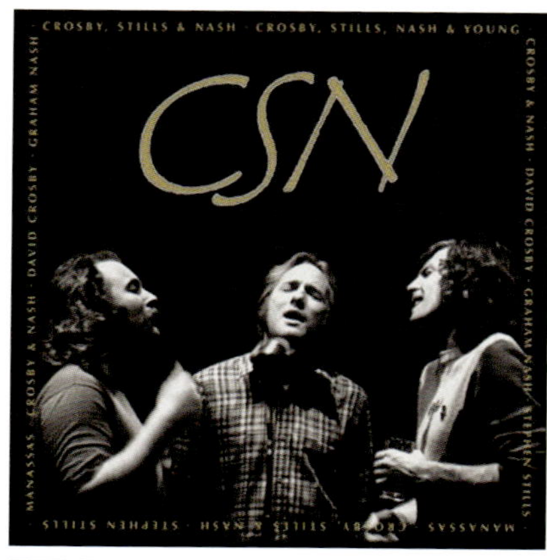

Billboard Hot 100: *CSN* (#109)

Crosby, Stills & Nash issued *CSN*, a box set of collective highlights amid tracks from various solo projects.

DAVID CROSBY, Stephen Stills and Graham Nash had spent nearly half their lives making music together, withstanding innumerable distractions as well as personal and musical differences to become a cornerstone of vocal harmony and social relevance.

"The noise we make together is like an act of God," Stills said. "The marriage—and that's what it's been—has been a bitch."

The most recent example of Crosby, Stills & Nash's durability was *CSN*, a box set on four discs featuring material spanning 1969 through 1990—from their catalog of recordings as a group in addition to selections from Crosby & Nash, Manassas and their individual solo efforts. Crosby's "Laughing" was a philosophical "revelation" of sorts that questioned spiritual gurus: "And I thought I'd seen someone/Who seemed at last/I was mistaken/It was only a child—laughing—in the sun/Ah! In the sun."

"It was on my first solo album, my response to George Harrison and the Maharishi," Crosby explained. "Harrison was thinking he had found somebody who had the answers, but my general response to that was, 'I don't know if there is one answer.' I'm suspicious of anyone who says they have the answer."

Prior to the compilation's release, complications arose when manager Elliot Roberts—no longer representing the trio but Neil Young, the group's occasional fourth member—yanked most of Young's material designated for *CSN*.

"It's for the aficionados," Crosby noted. "What do they want? Something special—they're deep into it or they wouldn't have worn out the vinyl records." ■

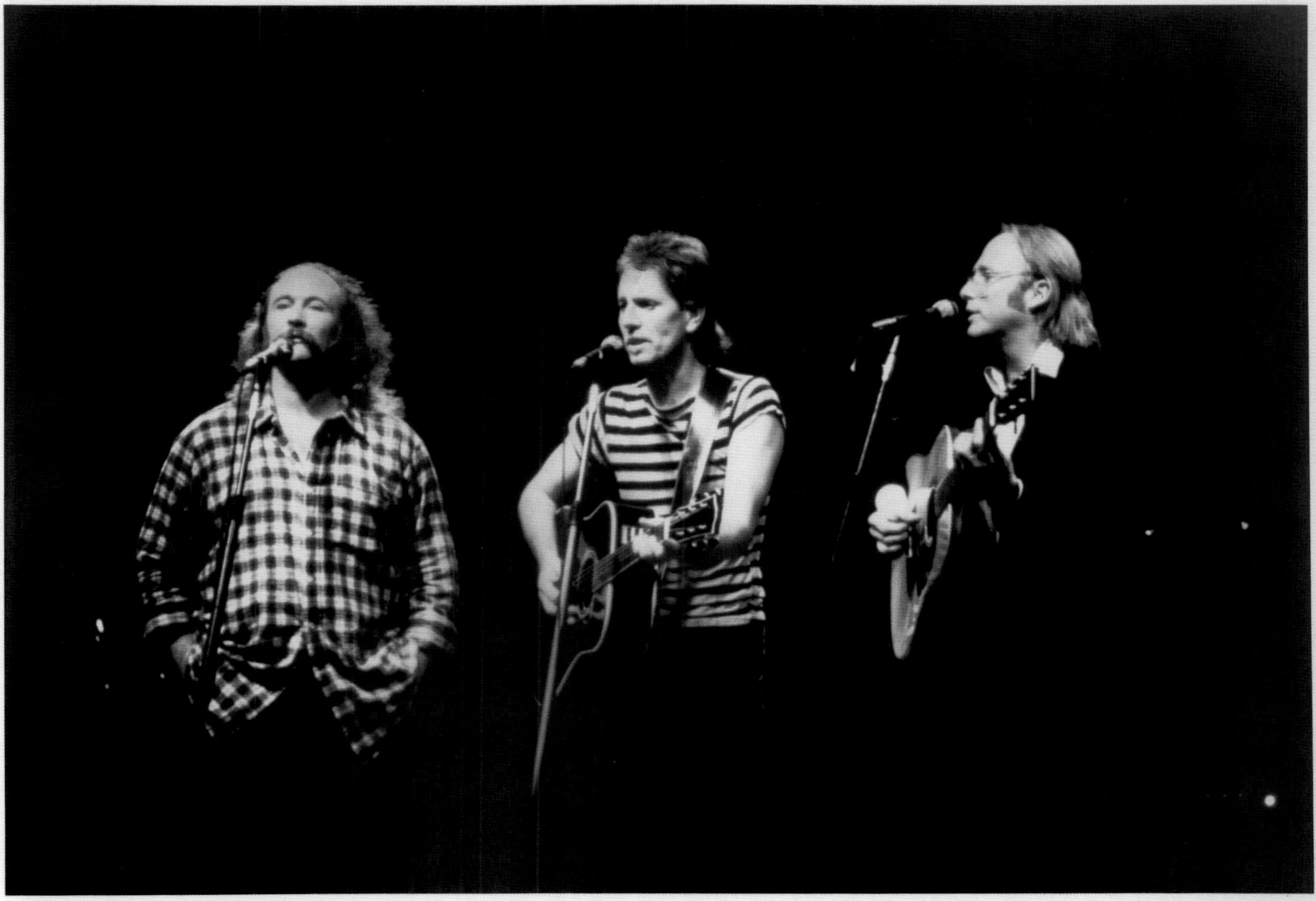

CROSBY, STILLS & NASH

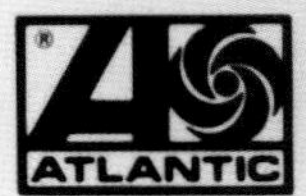

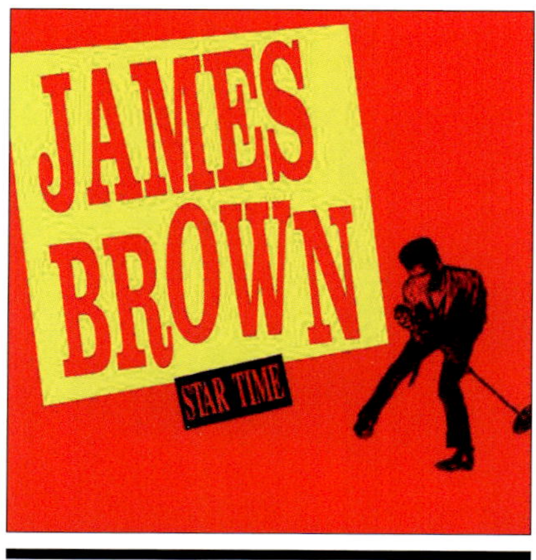

James Brown's *Star Time* assured his standing as one of America's most influential living entertainers.

SOUL LEGEND James Brown's early life was a thicket of extreme poverty, prejudice, the temptations of crime and drugs and the severity of prison. He overcame it all to become the first and most potent symbol of successful black America. Brown had recorded his fair share of banal, repetitive music, but during his prime, which stretched over 15 years, he pioneered new directions.

Yet because his recorded catalog had been in poor condition, most people were more familiar with Brown's legend than with his art. The disappearance of his first label, King Records, had made it a challenge to find many of his albums released before 1970, and he'd never been the subject of a well-referenced greatest-hits collection.

To celebrate 35 years of his professional career, PolyGram released a comprehensive look at the Godfather of Soul's work. *Star Time*, a 72-song, four-CD box set, included all of Brown's big hits arranged chronologically, from his 1956 debut, "Please Please Please," to a succession of seminal classics, such as "Papa's Got a Brand New Bag," "I Got You (I Feel Good)" and the impassioned "It's a Man's Man's Man's World."

Convicted of aggravated assault in October 1988, Brown served two-and-a-half years of a six-year sentence. The parole board granted him an early release in January 1991. During his incarceration, Brown was sustained by the public's appreciation for his pivotal role in developing modern black music. As the Hardest Working Man in Show Business, his whirling dervish style created a whole new set of criteria for thrilling live shows, and he led some of the most well-rehearsed bands ever.

"I'm a good man to work for, but a hard man to work for," he said. "I'm very demanding—you got to be on your Ps and Qs all of the time. You're working with the Godfather of Soul, you can't expect to get away with any less. And if you do, then you're not good enough to be on my stage."

Brown's powerful recordings virtually invented funk singlehandedly. He directly influenced Sly & the Family Stone's link between R&B and rock. His use of Afro-rhythms and jazz helped pave the way for George Clinton's extraterrestrial soul of the Seventies. And rappers ascribed to him the brusque, jerky, minimally accompanied speechifying that distinguished their genre.

Brown said current music was harmful to young people "by creating a false hope and telling them things that don't exist. I try to sing about life, things that uplift and motivate. Over the last seven or eight years, I have been disgusted—I always say, 'Don't play any music you wouldn't play for your mother.'"

With his South Carolina jail sentence behind him, Brown had faced another struggle and come back.

"A lot of silly things been put on me that I got nothing to do with," he said. "God will get me through it. God bless you, you hear?" ■

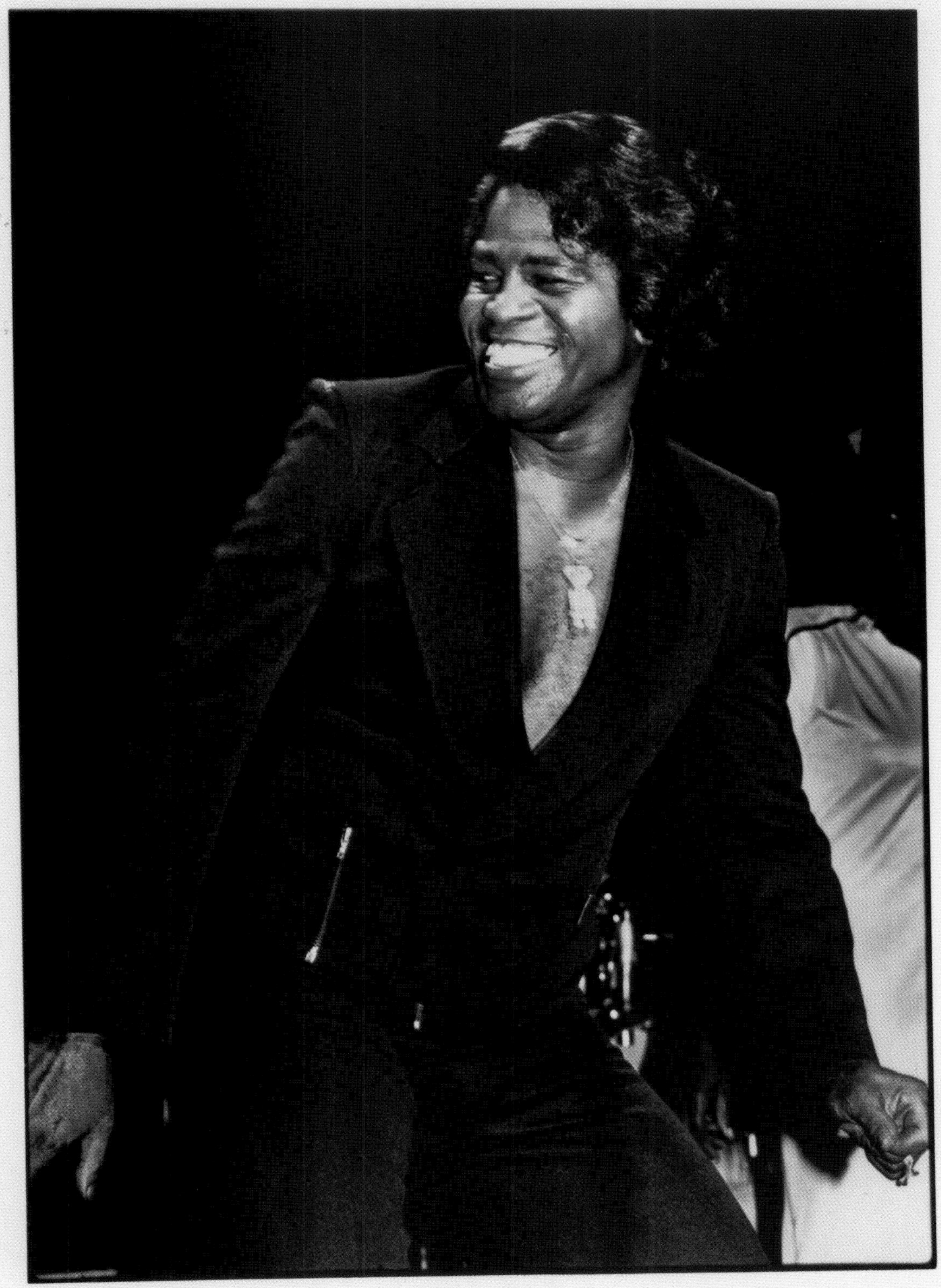

JAMES BROWN ★ STAR TIME

PolyGram Label Group

From the forthcoming career retrospective box set

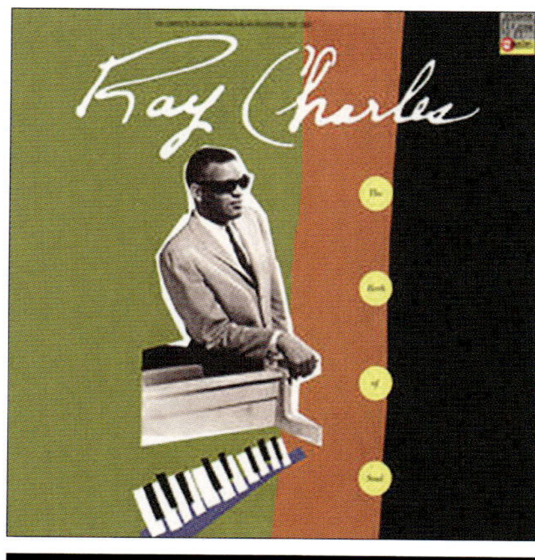

The Birth of Soul, an essential three-disc box set, gleaned the brilliance of **Ray Charles'** early recordings.

AT AGE 60, Ray Charles remained one of America's most important and influential musical personalities, singing and playing on nearly constant tours around the world. But while honors and adulation kept coming his way, the soul music giant still resisted personal categorization.

"Long after I'm gone, I would be perfectly happy if people would just say that Ray was sincere, true to his music," Charles mused. "That's it. I'd be thrilled to death, because that's what I'm about. I enjoy being me! That may sound weird, but I get a kick out of myself. And whenever I don't do a good job—that happens, I miss a note—I get pissed at myself, too."

Musical trends came and went, but Charles never seemed to bow to fashion, remaining as free-spirited as he was in the Fifties. Whether it was pop, rock 'n' roll, country or jazz, Charles made it his own without the slightest sense of strain, dissolving the barriers that divided music and people. *The Birth of Soul: The Complete Atlantic Rhythm and Blues Recordings*, a 3-CD box set, covered his groundbreaking work from the Fifties and Sixties. For good or ill, he also ensured his imprint upon the American mass consciousness by validating a Diet Pepsi commercial, wailing "You got the right one baby, uh-huh."

"They wanted a saying that would stand out, trying to sell that 'hook.' And I liked the jingle. If I don't like the music or the company doesn't have integrity, I don't feel I need the money that bad, to be honest with you. I don't know why they chose me to do it, but it turned out pretty good for them."

Despite his long uphill fight to overcome the hindrances of blindness and racial prejudice, Charles had managed to remain funny and witty, singularly free from the bitterness and self-pity that might have accrued under the circumstances. But he was outspoken about his experience as a heroin addict for nearly two decades.

"'Just say no,' that's a sick bunch of BS, frankly," he fumed. "That's sweet and nice, but in the real world, baby, it ain't that way. In my situation, I made a decision one day in the Sixties to stop—boom. Damn near killed me to do it, but it's a commitment you make to yourself. Whatever pain they say you have to go through, you're just gonna go through it. That ain't 'Just say no.' It just looks good in print and makes the president feel like he's doing something. But you've got to educate, and they don't want to educate. They just want to tell people what to do. You could teach things that will wise them up as to what will happen in their lives. But they keep learning in the streets, and we just keep going around in circles." ■

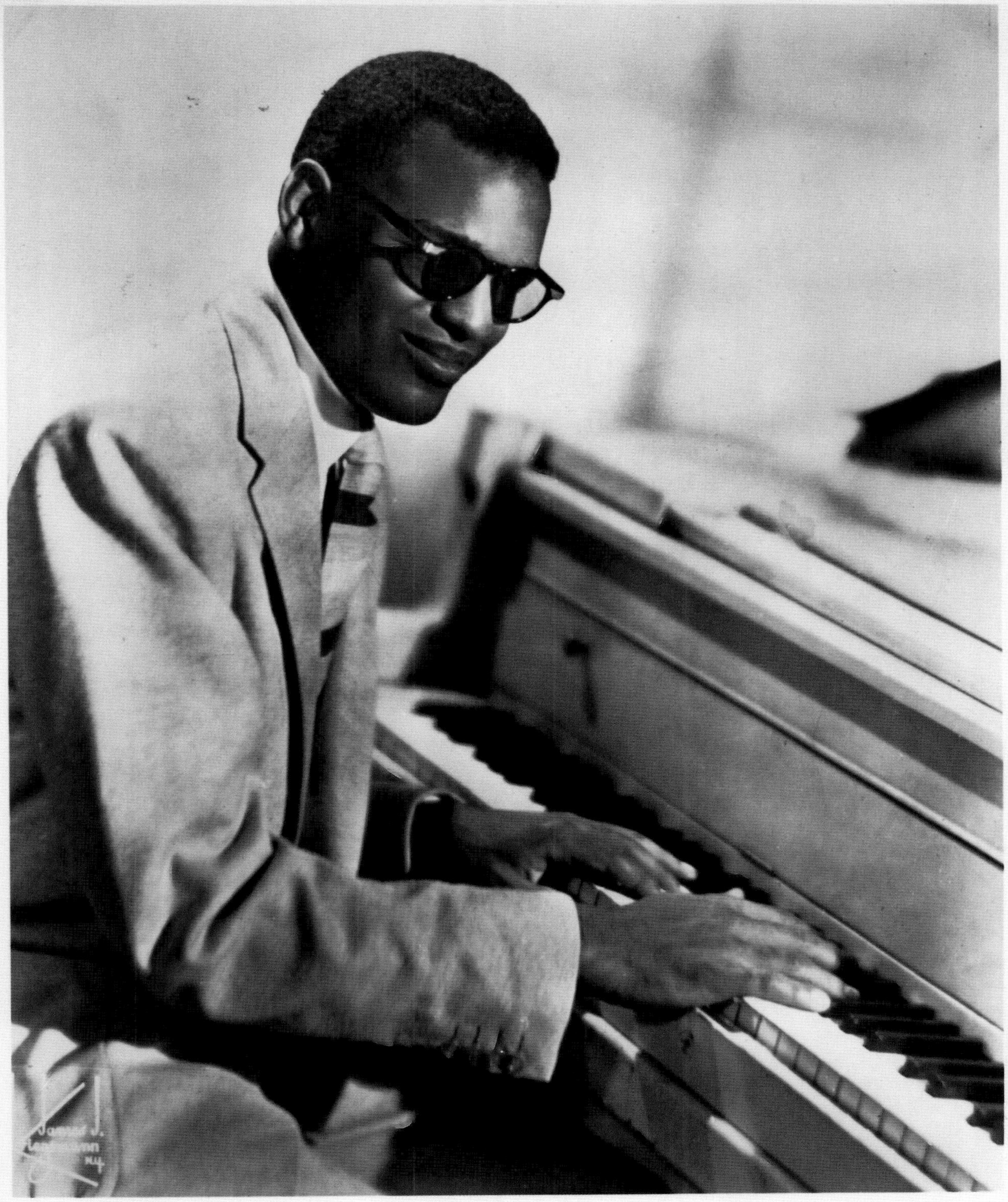

RAY CHARLES

Exclusively on

MOSS PHOTO SERVICE, INC., 350 W. 50TH ST., NEW YORK 19, N.Y.

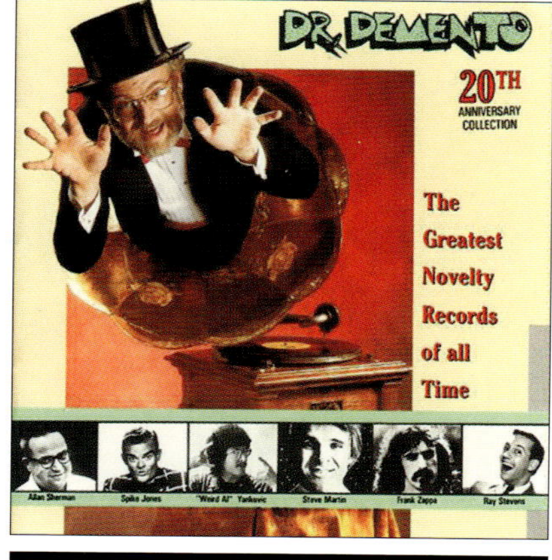

Dr. Demento's *20th Anniversary Collection* celebrated the disc jockey's radio career and novelty-song show.

OVER THE course of two decades, Dr. Demento had become a radio icon. He was the host of *The Dr. Demento Show*, a weekly two-hour clearinghouse for disturbed and deranged recordings. Enormously popular with listeners nationwide and throughout the world (it was broadcast on Armed Forces Radio), his show always finished with "The Funny Five," the five most "demented" discs and tapes as determined by listeners. The Doctor's No. 1 discovery had been "Weird Al" Yankovic, the pop satirist best known for his parodies like "Eat It" and "Another One Rides the Bus."

"In the early years, I played mostly older stuff from my private collection," the Doctor reminisced. "But the late Seventies were great. That's when 'Weird Al' started doing his thing on my show. 'Fish Heads' (by Barnes & Barnes) and 'Dead Puppies' (Ogden Edsl), my two most-requested songs, both arrived at the same time. People have access to better recording equipment now, but the number of submissions has remained remarkably constant, around 20 a week. I get a whole lot more before Christmas or if an event inspires people to write songs. In the Seventies, things would get pressed on vinyl. That's dwindled to nothing. Now I get tapes, which is unfortunate for record collectors like me."

A music historian, Demento had privately accumulated more than 200,000 records dating from 1897. To represent the way he'd made a living, Rhino Records released *Dr. Demento 20th Anniversary Collection: The Greatest Novelty Records of All Time*, an anthology featuring the 36 most-requested tracks of classic dementia. Some names were familiar to pop fans—Steve Martin ("King Tut") and Frank Zappa ("Dancin' Fool"). But others were culled from the Doctor's vaults—among others, Nervous Norvus ("Transfusion"), Napoleon XIV ("They're Coming to Take Me Away, Ha-Haaa!") and Spike Jones (1942's "Der Fuehrer's Face").

In support of the double-CD set, the "dean of novelty records" hit the road. "Dement-O-Rama" was a mini-film festival featuring vintage short films, movie trailers, cartoons and classic music clips. Dr. Demento (he was born Barry Hansen), dressed in his trademark top hat and tux, served as the master of ceremonies.

"I've been a record man most of my life," he explained. "But now video versions exist of things that I play on my radio show, so the tour seems like a natural—some really great celluloid from campy old B-grade horror films and songs by people like Cab Calloway and Fats Waller. And, of course, 'Weird Al' Yankovic." ■

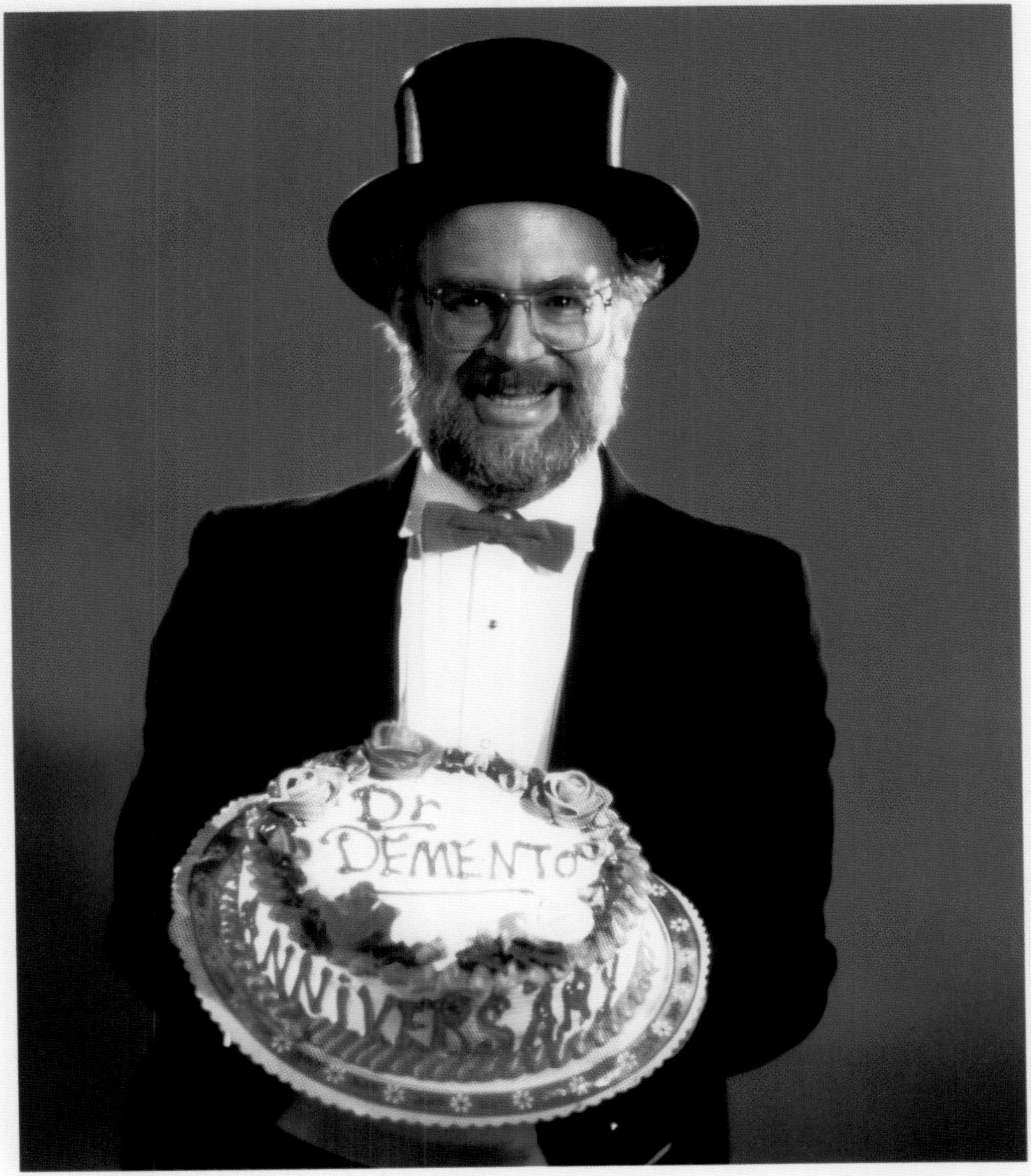

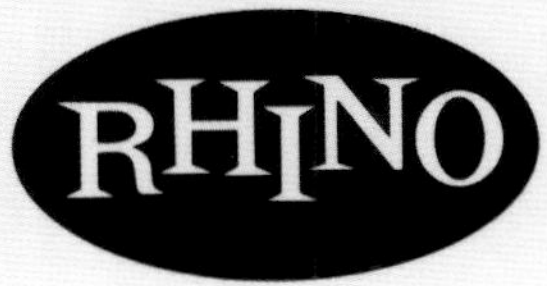

DR. DEMENTO

20TH ANNIVERSARY COLLECTION

RHINO RECORDS INC.
2225 COLORADO AVE.
SANTA MONICA, CA 90404
(213) 828-1980
FAX: (213) 453-5529

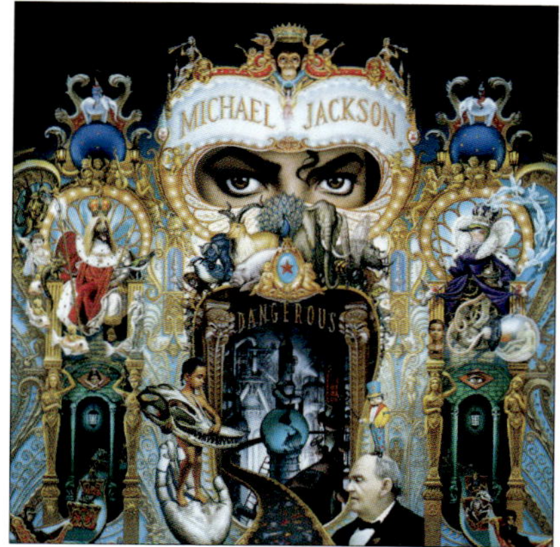

Based on record sales, **Michael Jackson**'s *Dangerous* won *Billboard*'s award for the top Worldwide Album, and "Black and White" snared Worldwide Single.

Billboard 200: *Dangerous* (No. 1)
Billboard Hot 100: "Black and White" (No. 1); "Remember the Time" (#3); "In the Closet" (#6); "Jam" (#26); "Who Is It" (#14); "Heal the World" (#27); "Will You Be There" (#7)

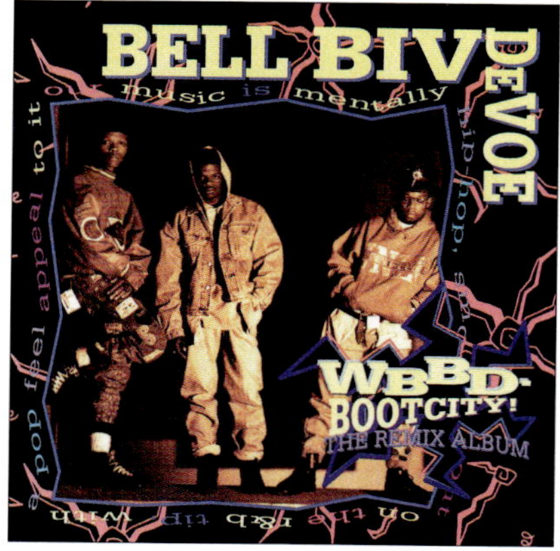

Featuring original members of New Edition, the new jack swing trio **Bell Biv Devoe** put out *WBBD - Bootcity!*, remixes from the group's debut album, *Poison*.

Billboard 200: *WBBD - Bootcity!* (#18)

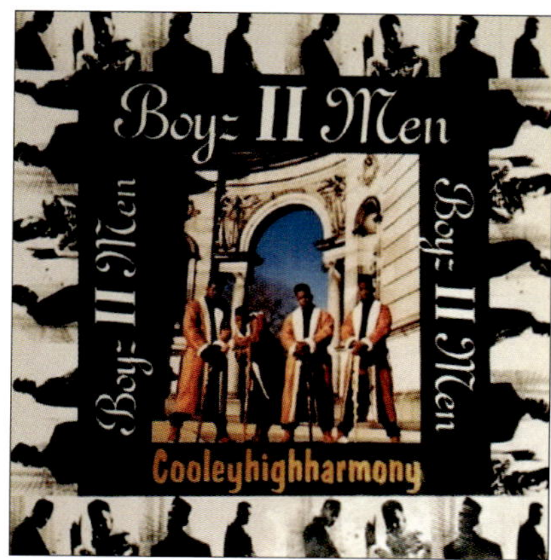

Boyz II Men's "hip-hop doo-wop" sound produced "Motownphilly" and "It's So Hard to Say Goodbye to Yesterday," both No. 1 R&B hits and Top 5 pop hits.

Billboard 200: *Cooleyhighharmony* (#3)
Billboard Hot 100: "Motownphilly" (#3); "It's So Hard to Say Goodbye to Yesterday" (#2); "Uhh Ahh" (#16); "Please Don't Go" (#49)

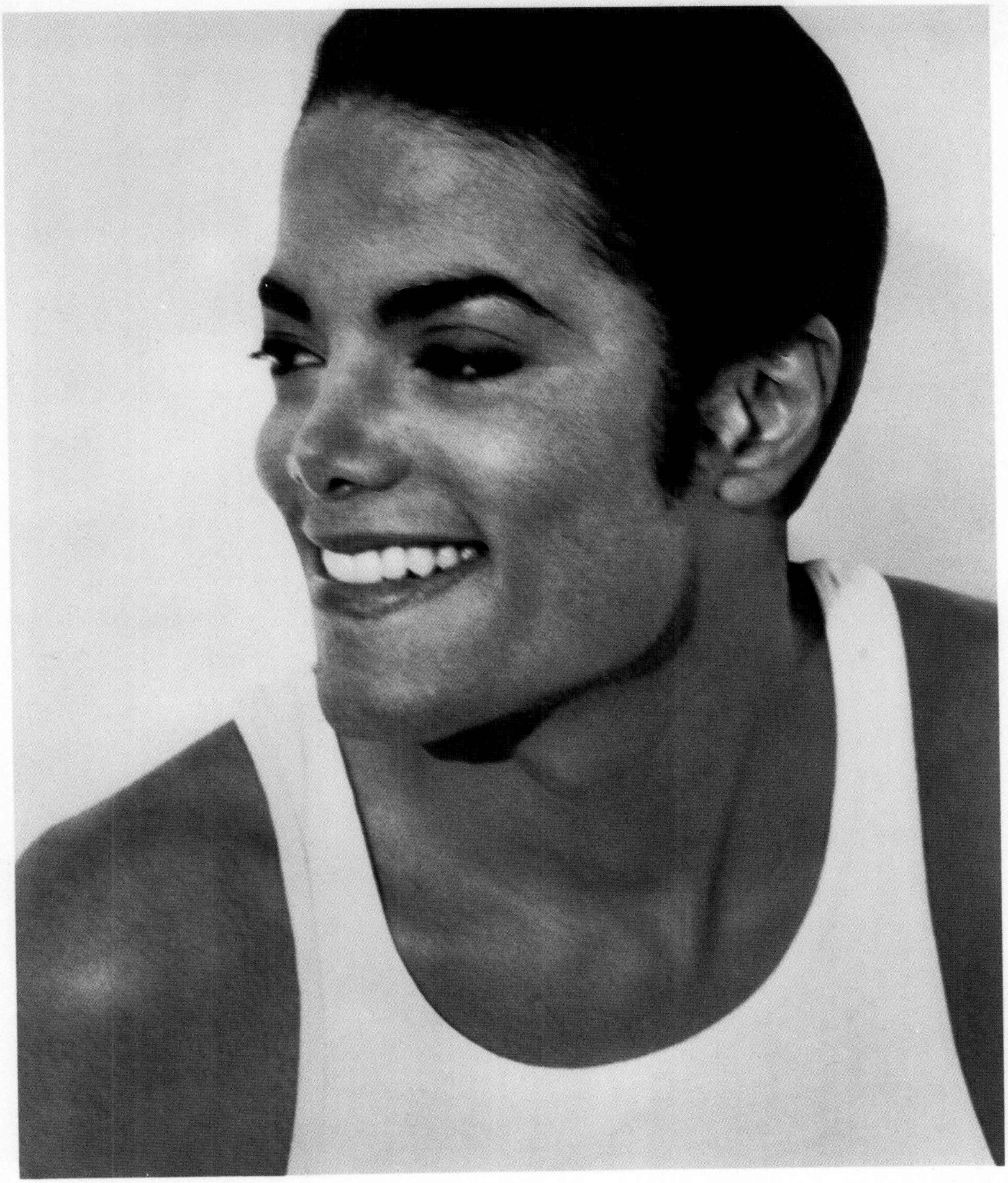

Photo Credit: Herb Ritts

MICHAEL JACKSON

9110

© 1991 Sony Music. Permission to reproduce this photography is limited to editorial uses in regular issues of newspapers and other regularly published periodicals and television news programming.

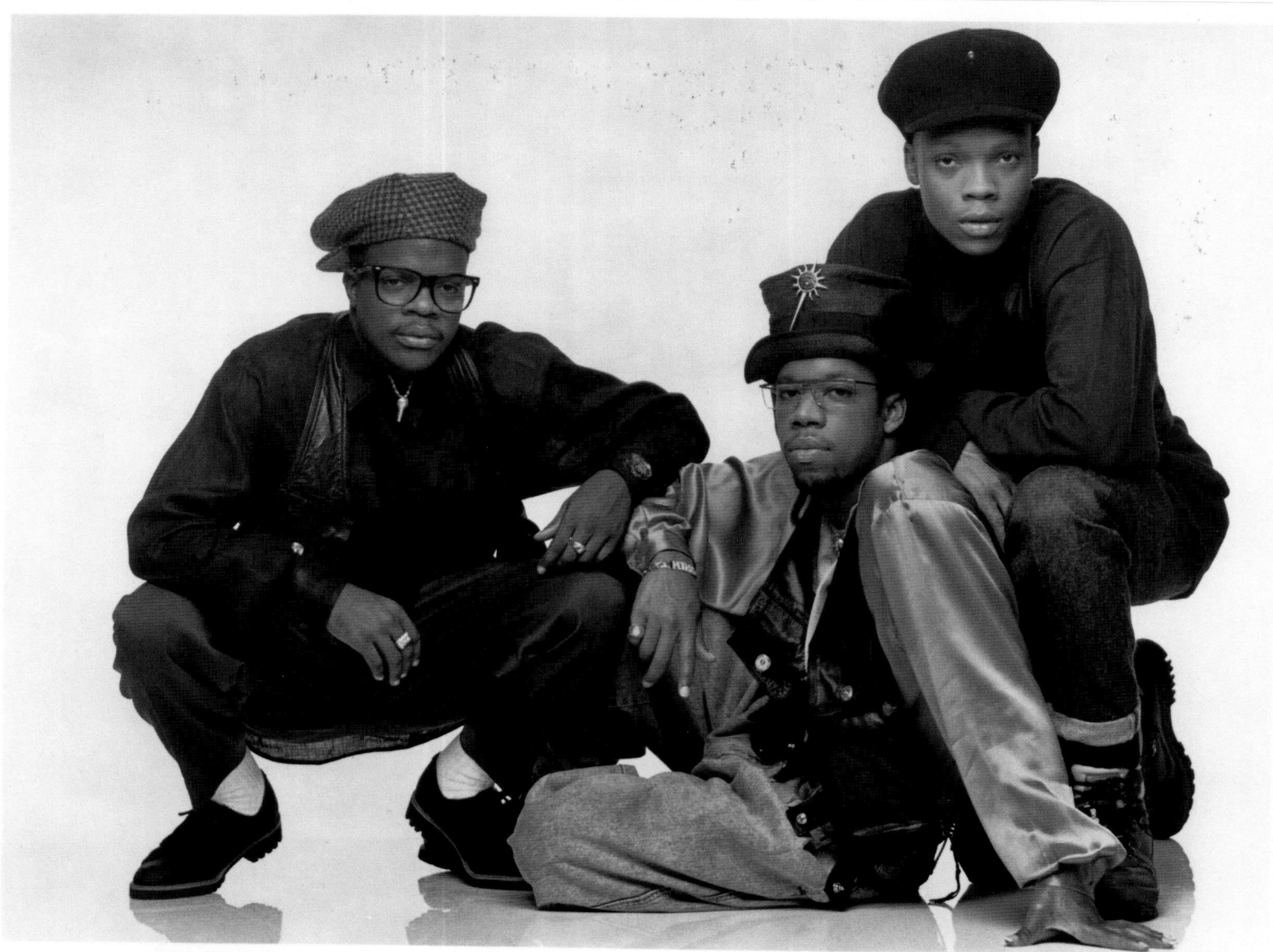

Photo Credit: David Roth

BELL BIV DEVOE

6/90

MCA RECORDS

©1990 MCA RECORDS, INC.

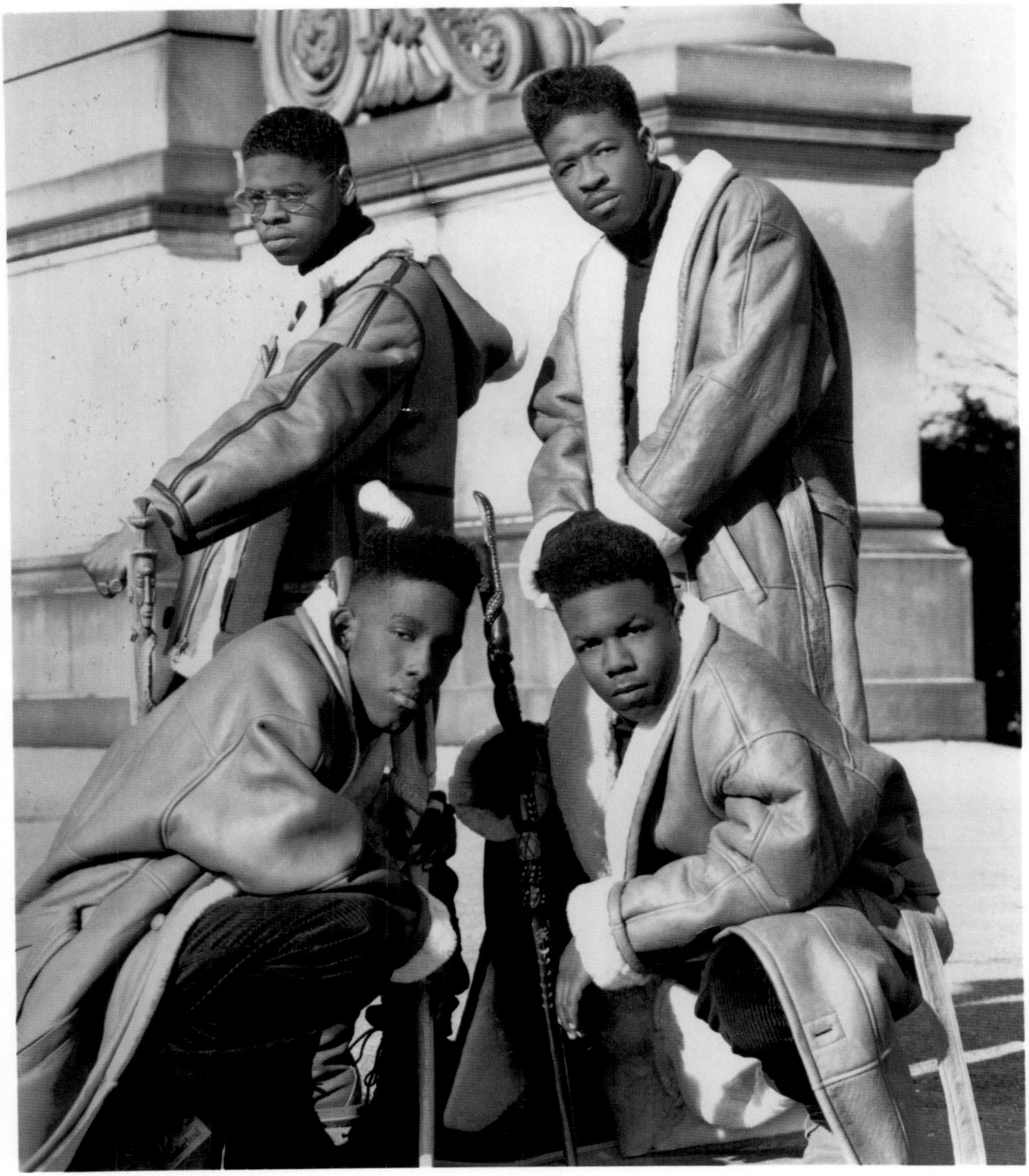

Boyz **II** Men

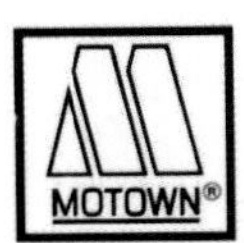

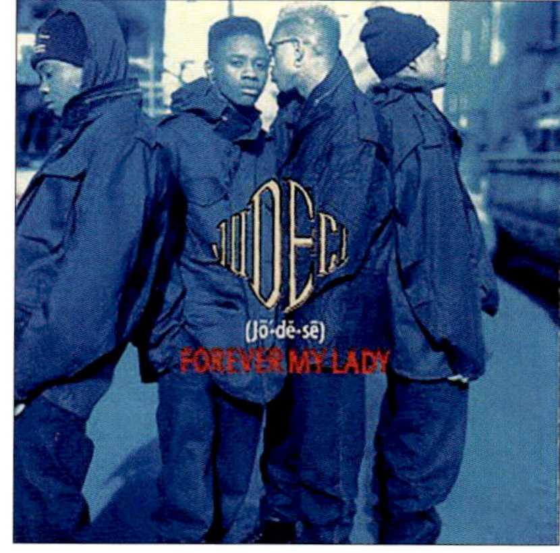

"Come and Talk to Me" and "Forever My Lady" brought **Jodeci** mainstream success, establishing the group's rowdy reputation as "the bad boys of R&B."

Billboard 200: *Forever My Lady* (#18)
Billboard Hot 100: "Forever My Lady" (#25); "Stay" (#41); "Come and Talk to Me" (#11); "I'm Still Waiting" (#85)

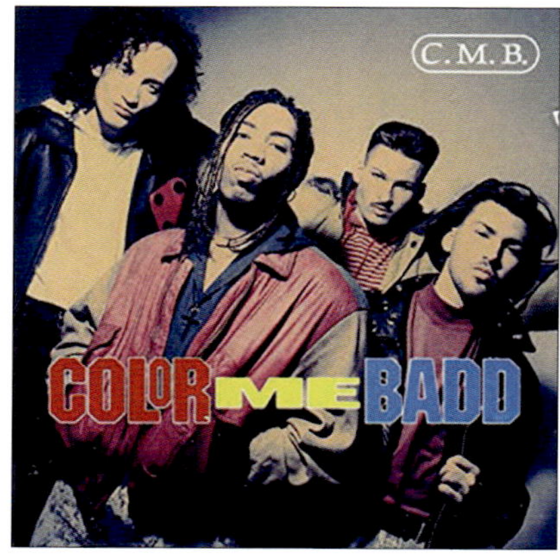

C.M.B., the debut album by R&B vocal quartet **Color Me Badd**, spawned five smash singles, led by "I Wanna Sex You Up," "I Adore Mi Amor" and "All 4 Love."

Billboard 200: *C.M.B.* (#3)
Billboard Hot 100: "I Wanna Sex You Up" (#2); "I Adore Mi Amor" (No. 1); "All 4 Love" (No. 1); "Thinkin' Back" (#16); "Slow Motion" (#18)

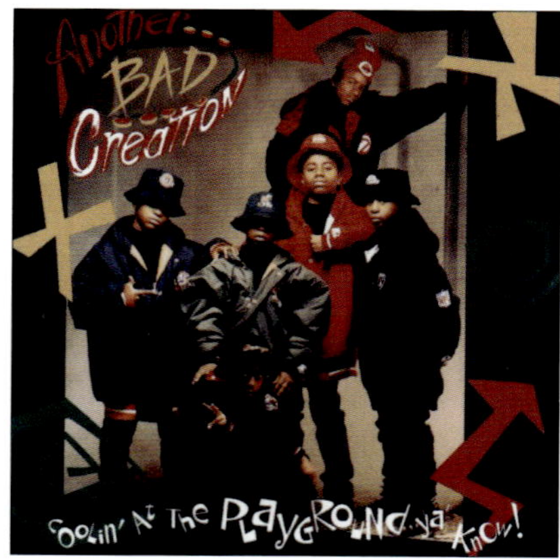

Discovered and managed by New Edition and Bell Biv DeVoe member Michael Bivins, **Another Bad Creation** bagged the pop-rap hits "Iesha" and "Playground."

Billboard 200: *Coolin' at the Playground Ya Know!* (#7)
Billboard Hot 100: "Iesha" (#9); "Playground" (#10)

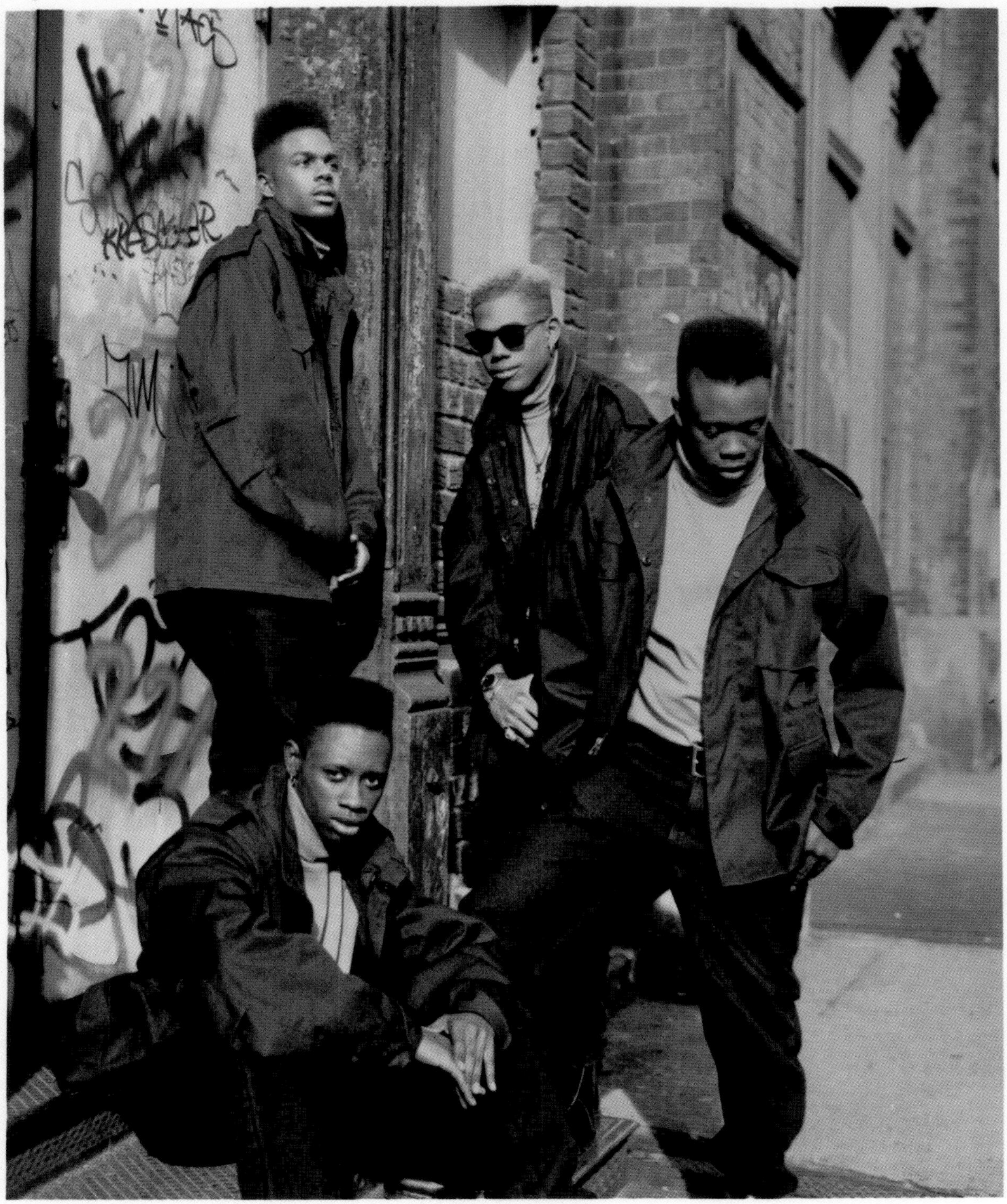

PHOTO CREDIT: ENIS SEFERSAH

DALVIN DEVANTE

K-CI JOJO

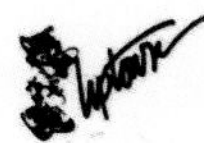

JODECI

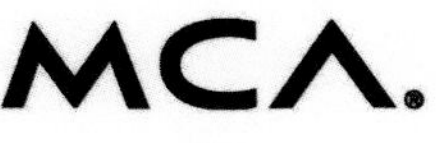

3/91

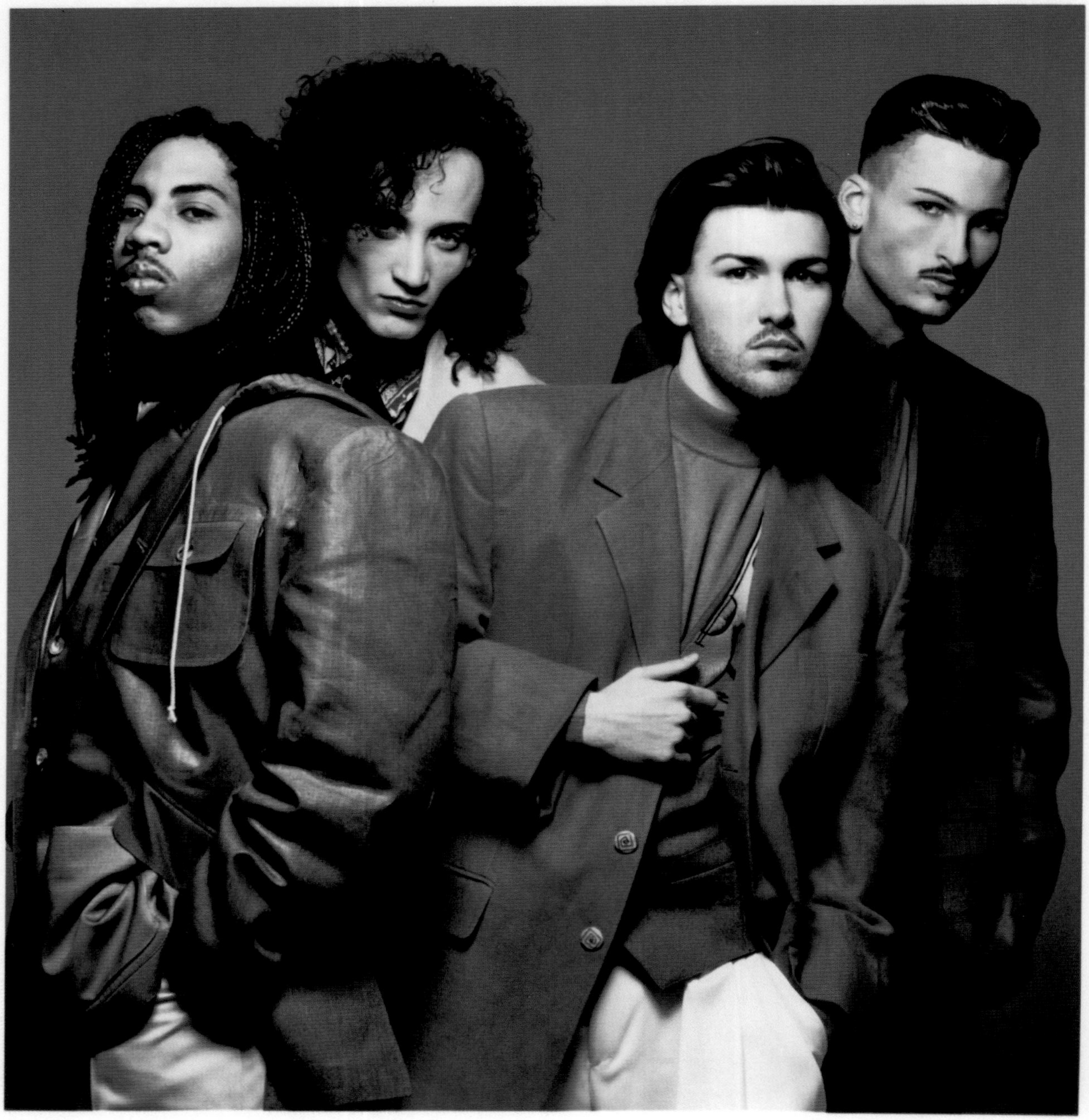

Photo Credit: Michael Lavine

Kevin Thornton Sam Watters Mark Calderon Bryan Abrams

Color Me Badd

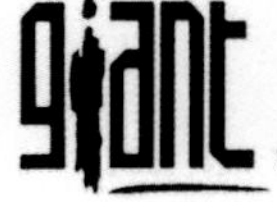

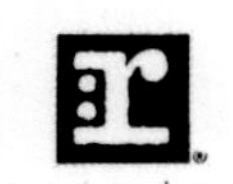

© 1991 Reprise Records/Permission to reproduce limited to editorial uses in newspapers and other regularly published periodicals and television news programming.

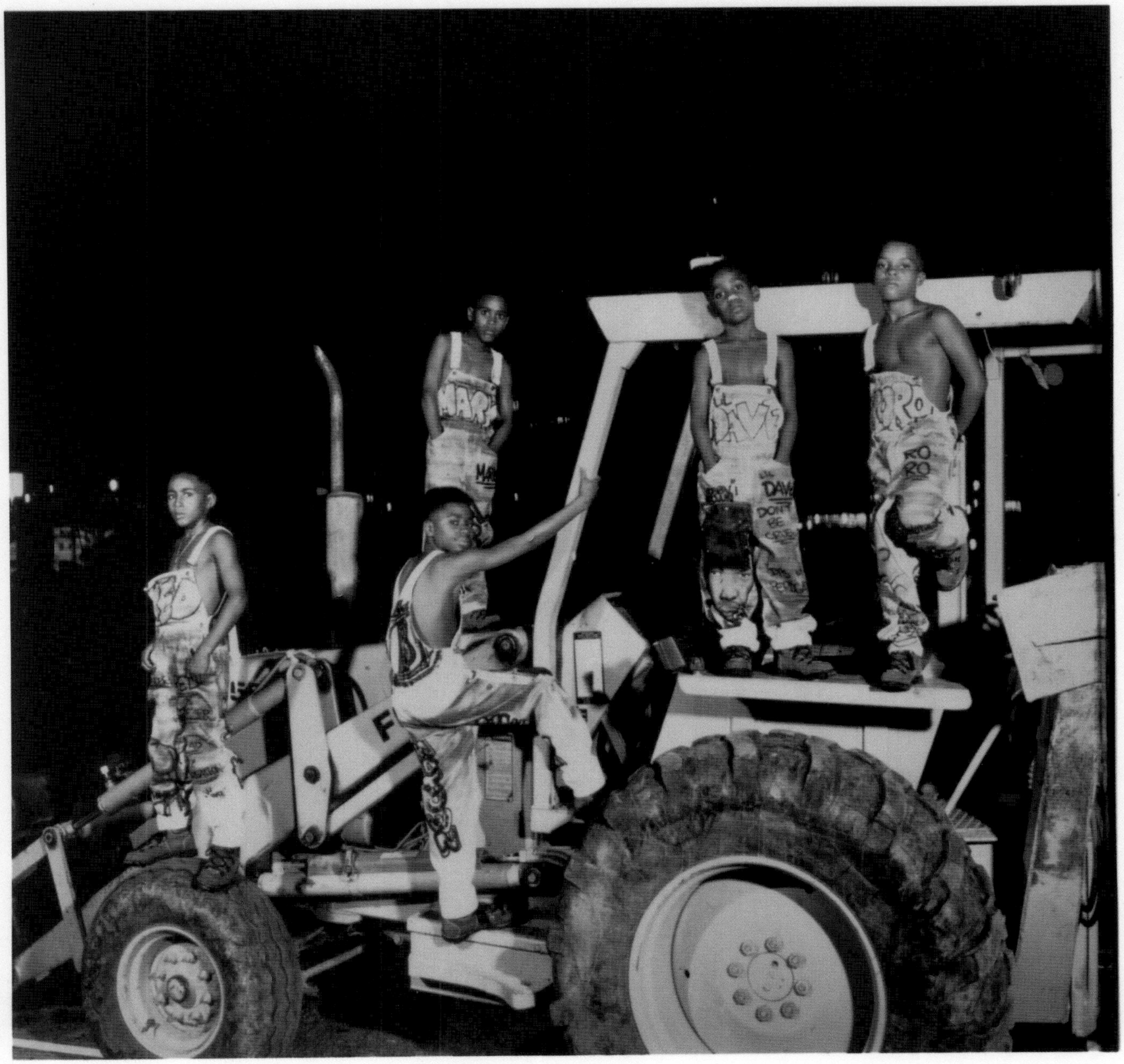

Mark

Red

Chris

Lil Dave

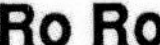

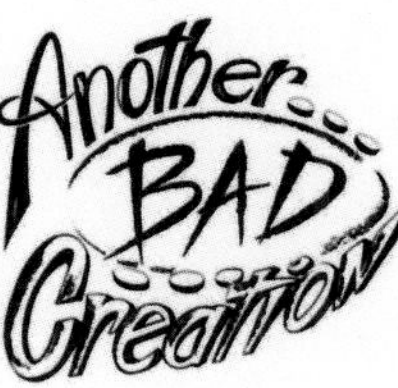

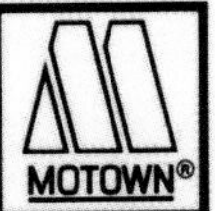

Record producers Robert Clivillés and David Cole employed rappers and singers to vocalize **C+C Music Factory**'s debut album, *Gonna Make You Sweat.*

Billboard 200: *Gonna Make You Sweat* (#2)
Billboard Hot 100: "Gonna Make You Sweat (Everybody Dance Now)" (No. 1); "Here We Go (Let's Rock & Roll)" (#3); "Things That Make You Go Hmmmm…" (#4); "Just a Touch of Love (Everyday)" (#50)

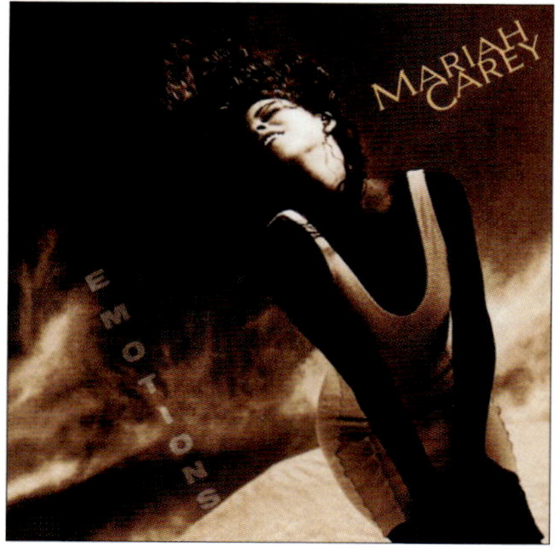

The title track from *Emotions*, **Mariah Carey**'s second album, peaked at No. 1, marking a record fifth consecutive single to top the *Billboard* Hot 100 chart.

Billboard 200: *Emotions* (#4)
Billboard Hot 100: "Emotions" (No. 1); "Can't Let Go" (#2); "Make It Happen" (#5)

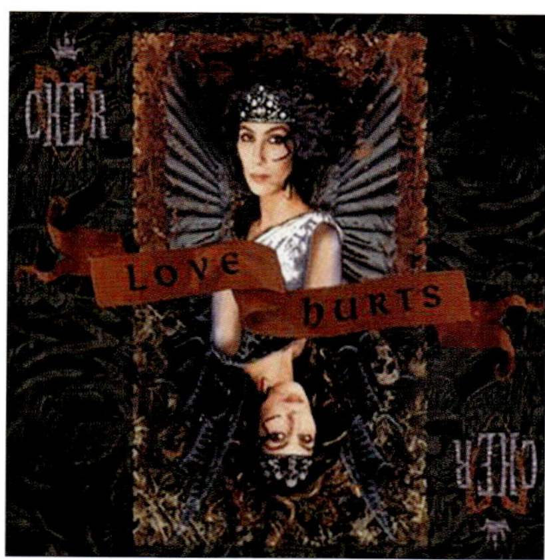

Love Hurts, **Cher**'s last release during her "metal babe" phase, became her first No. 1 album in the UK and yielded the hit, "Love and Understanding," in the US.

Billboard 200: *Love Hurts* (#48)
Billboard Hot 100: "Love and Understanding" (#17); "Save Up All Your Tears" (#37)

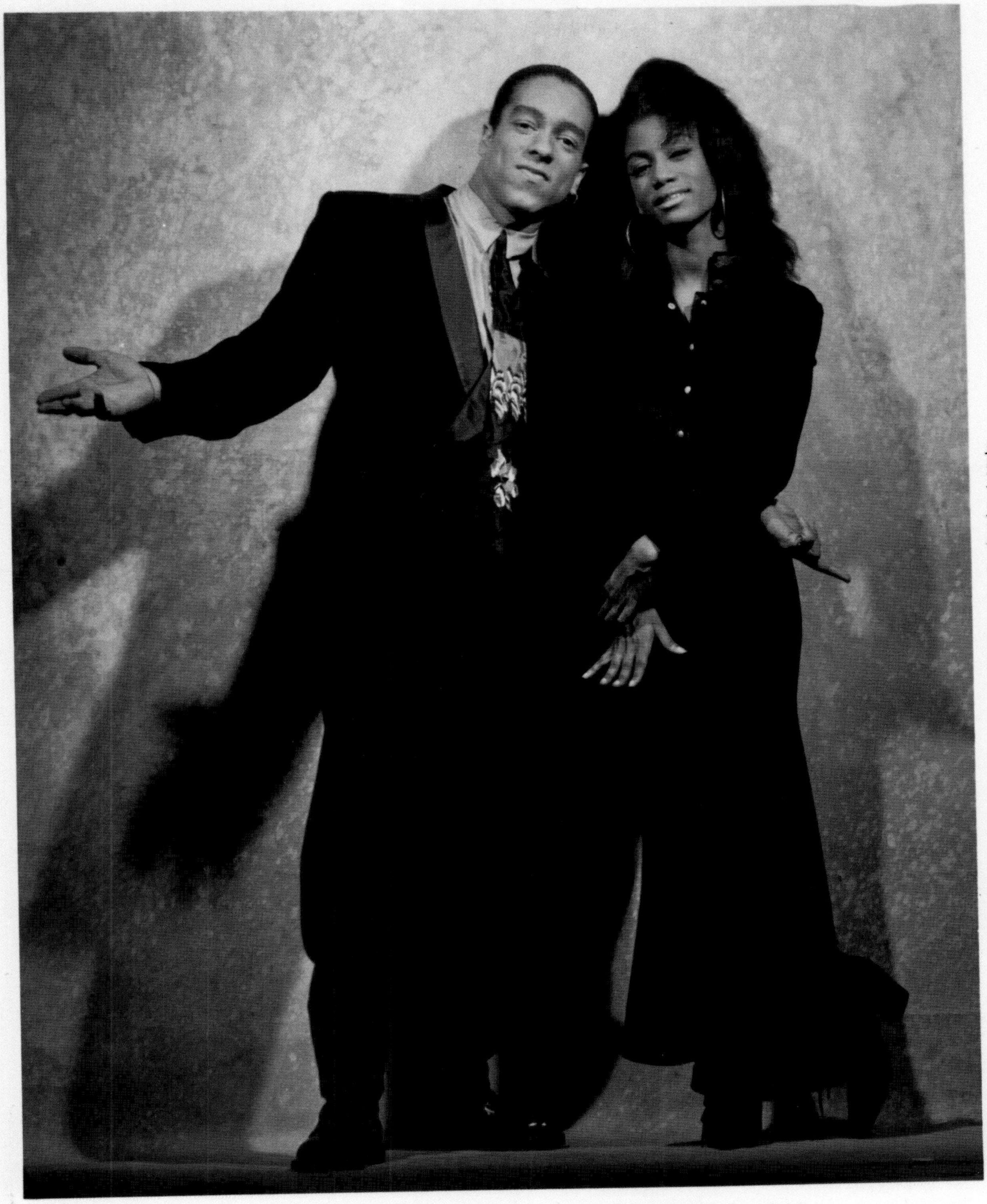

PHOTOGRAPH: FRANK OCKENFELS 3

© 1990 CBS Records Inc. Permission to reproduce this photography is limited to editorial uses in regular issues of newspapers and other regularly published periodicals and television news programming.

FREEDOM WILLIAMS (left) and ZELMA DAVIS (right).

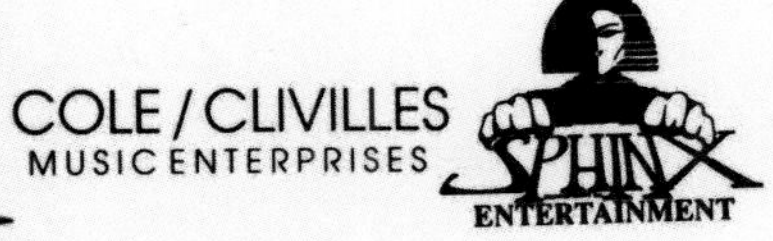

C+C music factory

FAMOUS
FAMOUS ARTISTS AGENCY, INC.

Columbia
9012

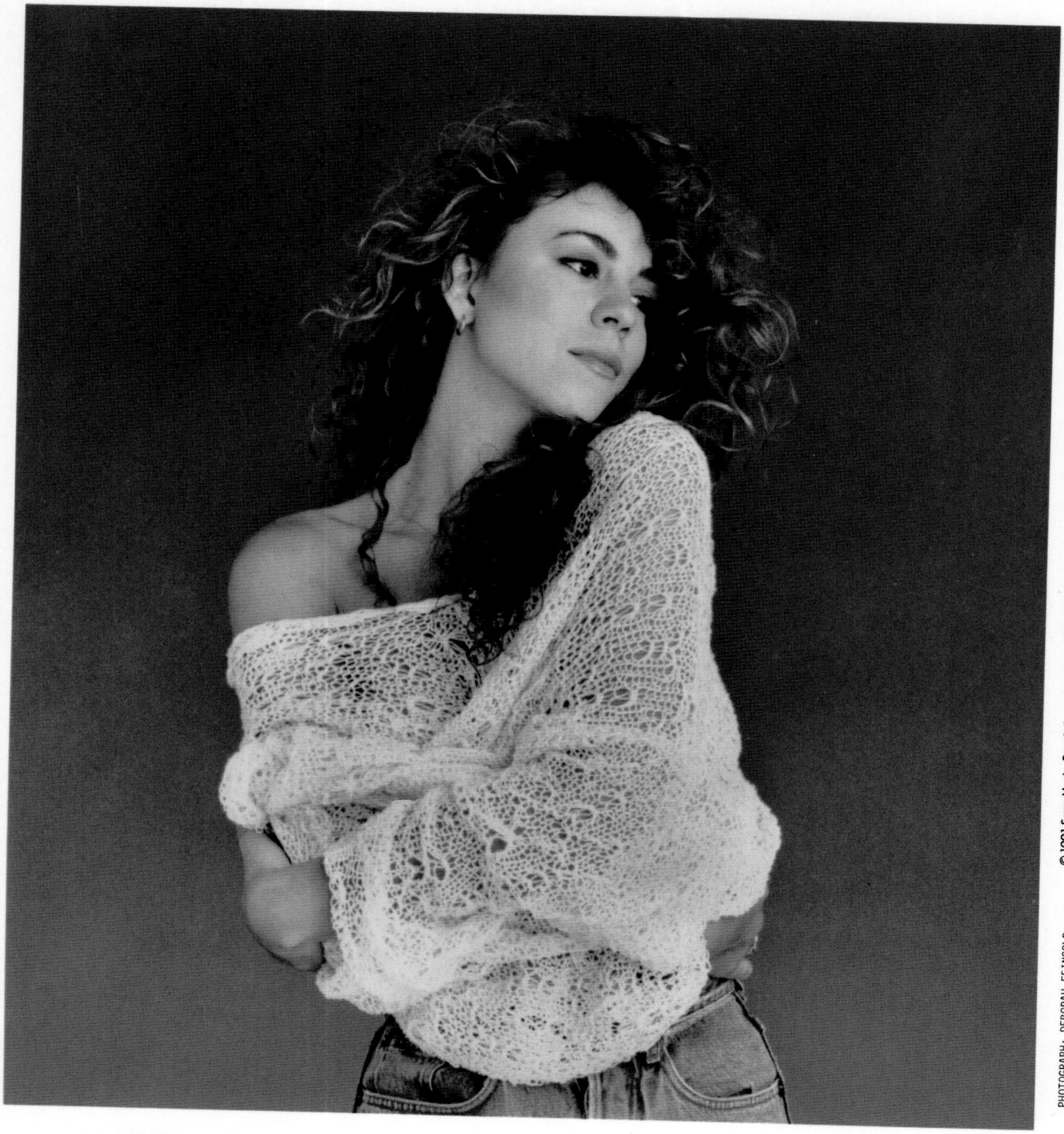

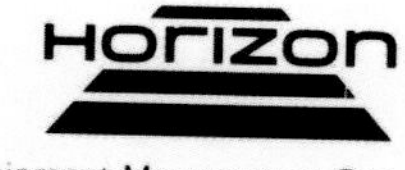

Entertainment Management Group, Inc.

MARIAH CAREY

Columbia
9108

PHOTOGRAPH: DEBORAH FEINGOLD

© 1991 Sony Music. Permission to reproduce this photography is limited to editorial uses in regular issues of newspapers and other regularly published periodicals and television news programming.

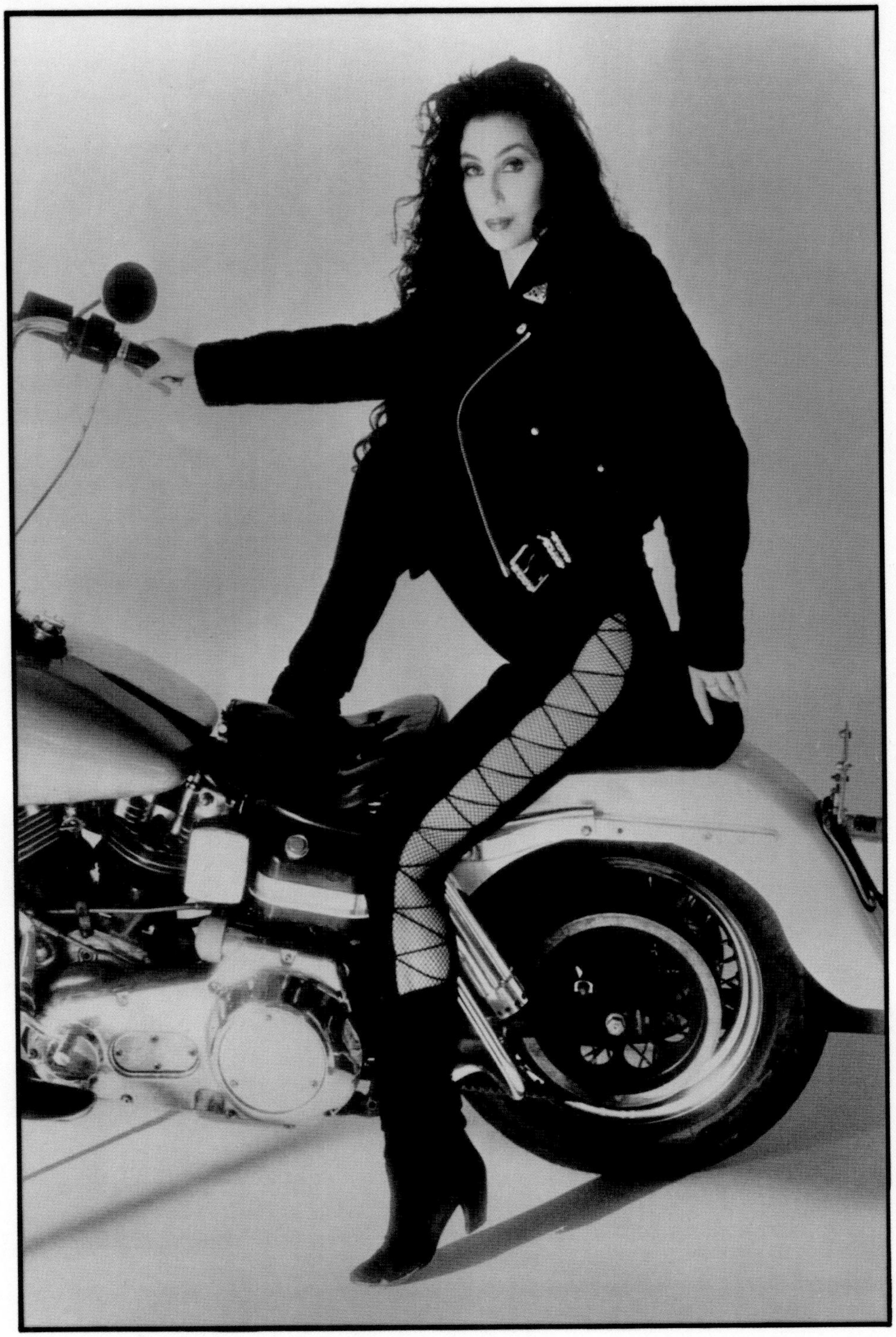

Photo Credit: Herb Ritts

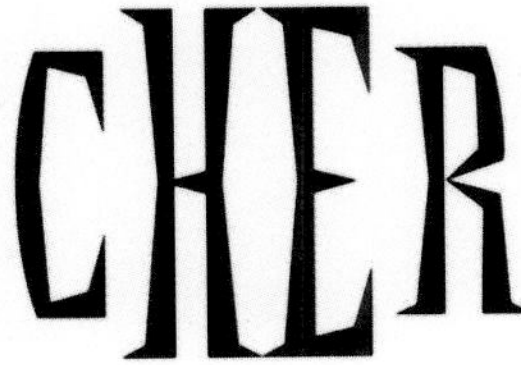

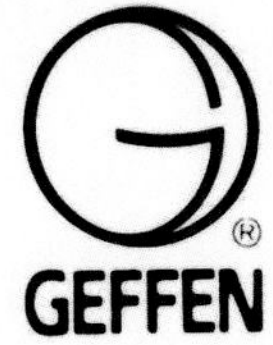

© 1991 The David Geffen Company/Permission to reproduce limited to editorial uses in newspapers and other regularly published periodicals and television news programming.

A Tribe Called Quest released its sophomore album, the jazz-inflected *The Low End Theory*, a benchmark for intelligent, artistic alternative hip-hop music.

Billboard 200: *The Low End Theory* (#45)
Billboard Hot 100: "Scenario" (#57)

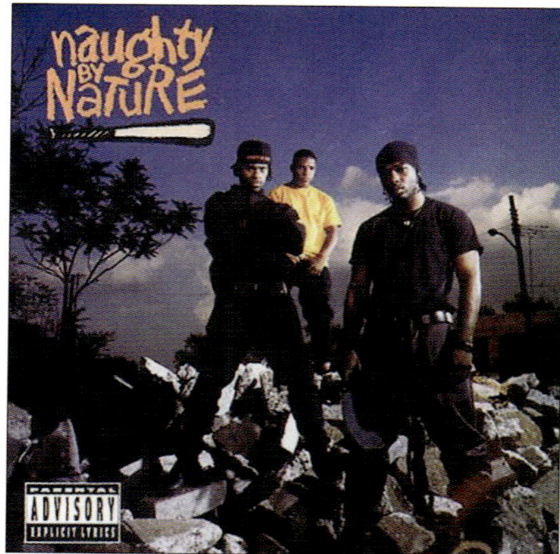

Naughty by Nature's "O.P.P.," which sampled the Jackson 5's 1970 hit "ABC," was one of the first rap songs to emerge as an inescapable pop smash.

Billboard 200: *Naughty by Nature* (#16)
Billboard Hot 100: "O.P.P." (#6); "Everything's Gonna Be Alright" (#53)

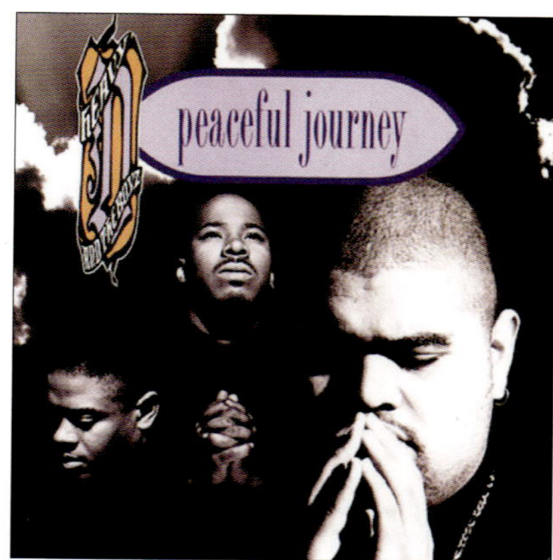

A modernized version of "Now That We Found Love," originally recorded by the O'Jays, provided a breakthrough single for the hip-hop trio **Heavy D. & the Boyz**.

W*Billboard* 200: *Peaceful Journey* (#21)
Billboard Hot 100: "Is It Good to You" (#32); "Now That We Found Love" (#11)

©1991 Zomba Recording Corp. Permission to reproduce this photography is limited to editorial uses in regular issues of newspapers and other regularly published periodicals and television news programming.

PHOTO CREDIT: JOE GRANT

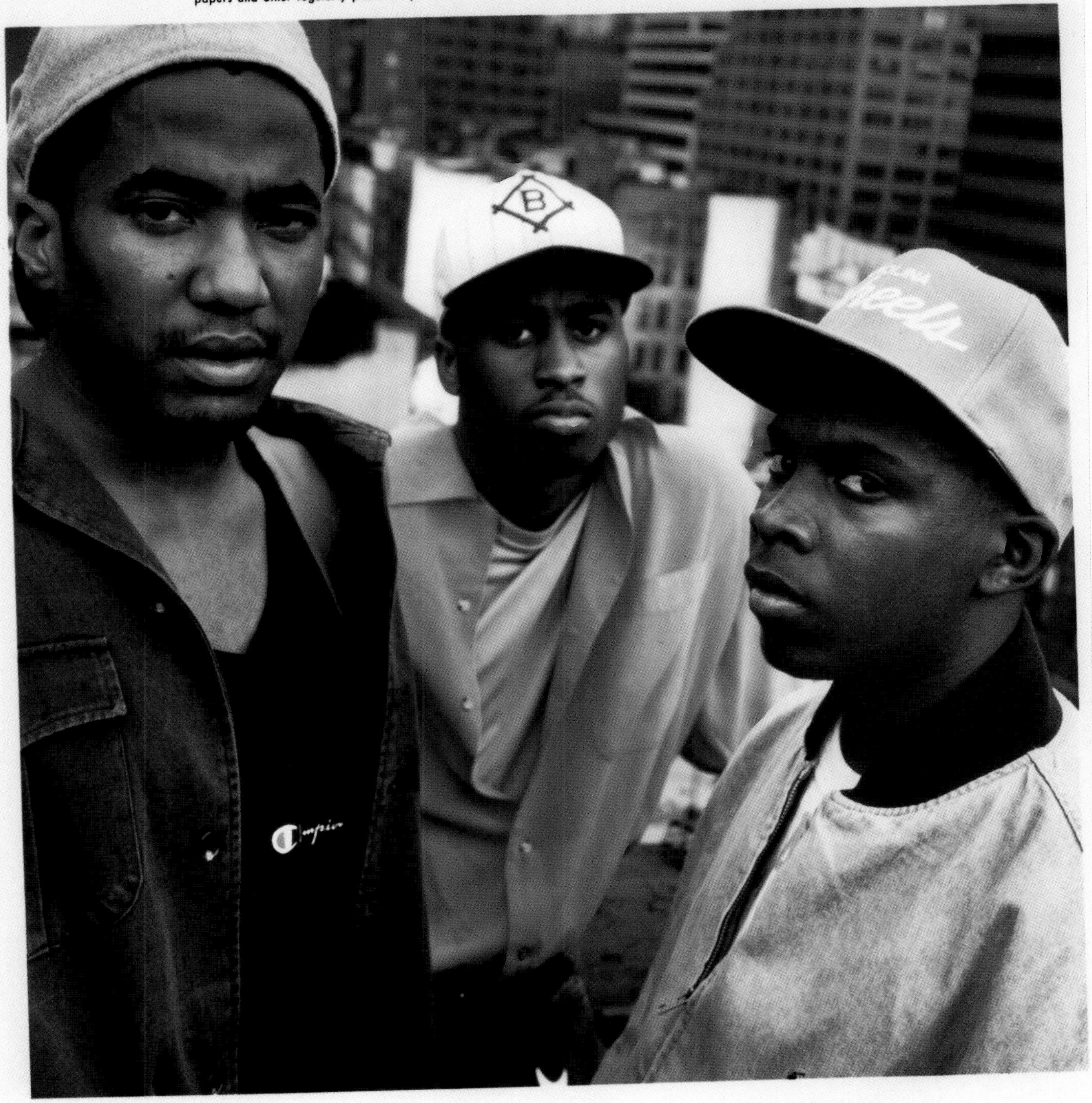

A TRIBE CALLED QUEST

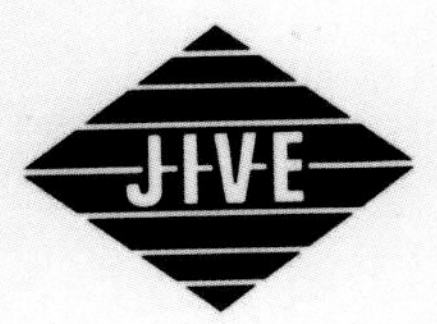

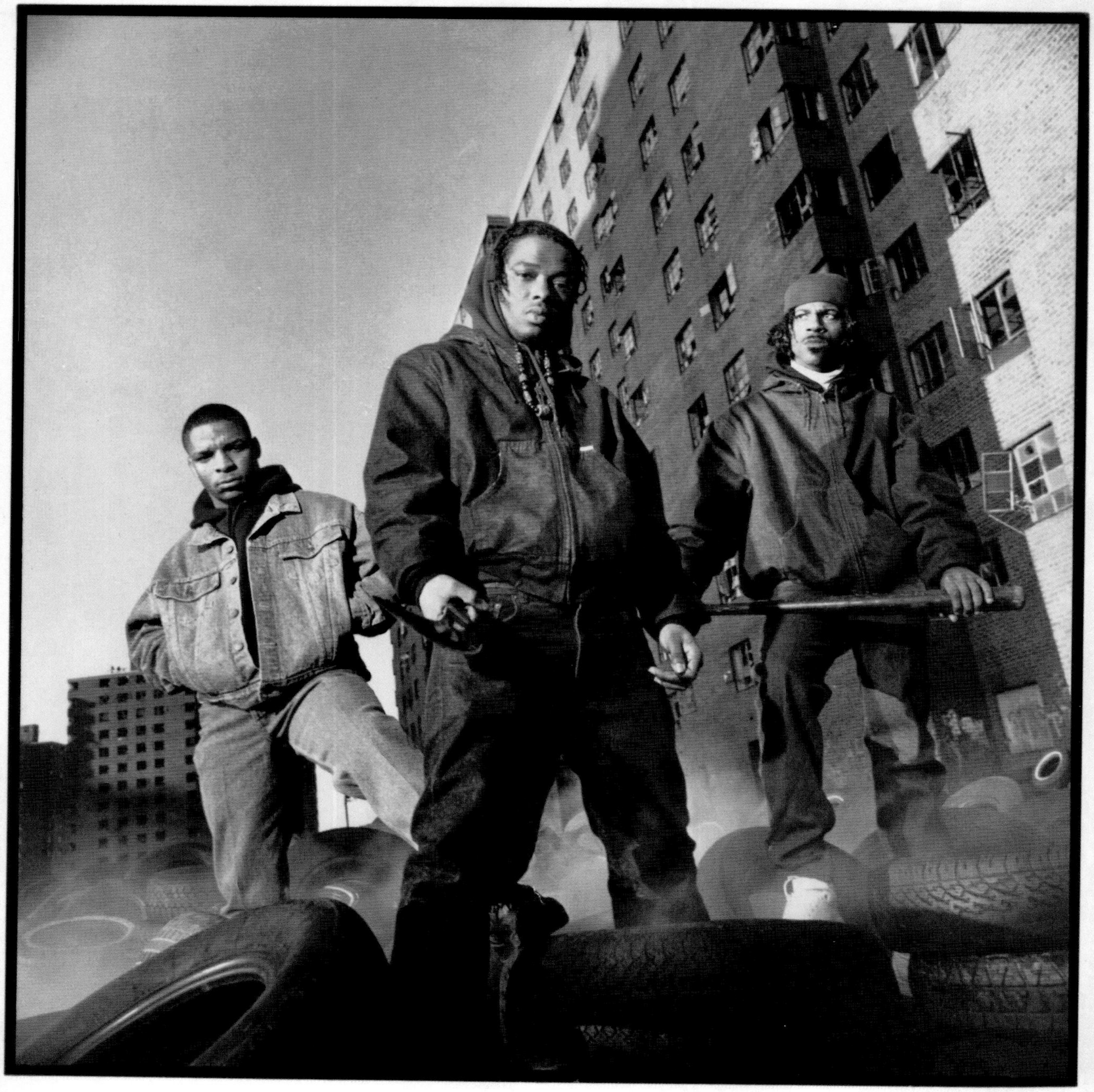

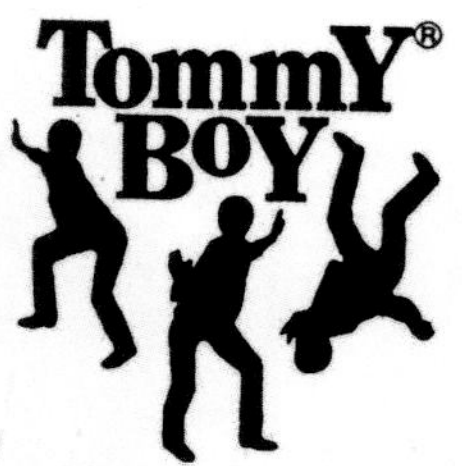
TommY®
BoY

naughty
BY
NaTuRE

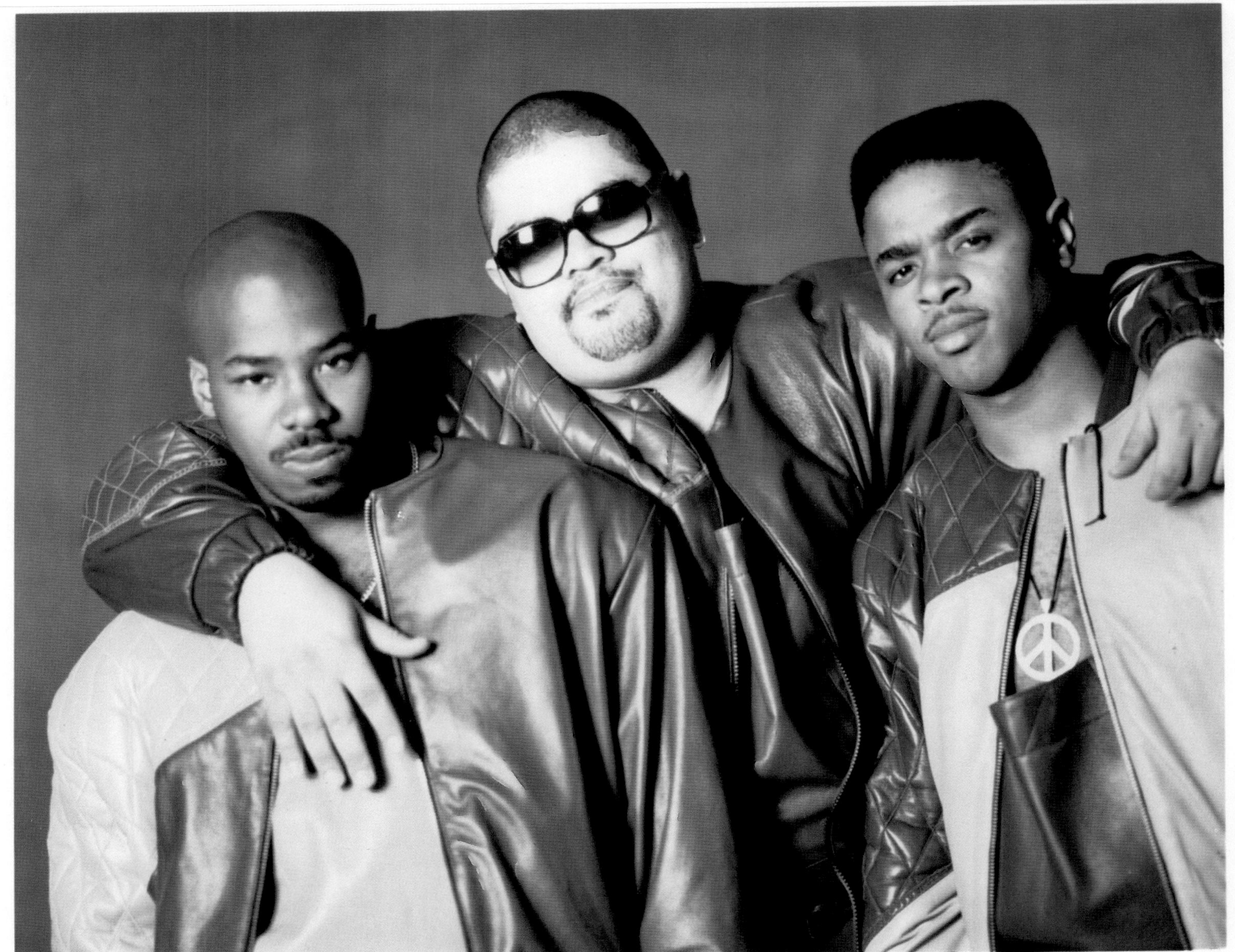

Photo: NICK BARETTA

Heavy D. & The BOYZ

MCA.

June 1991

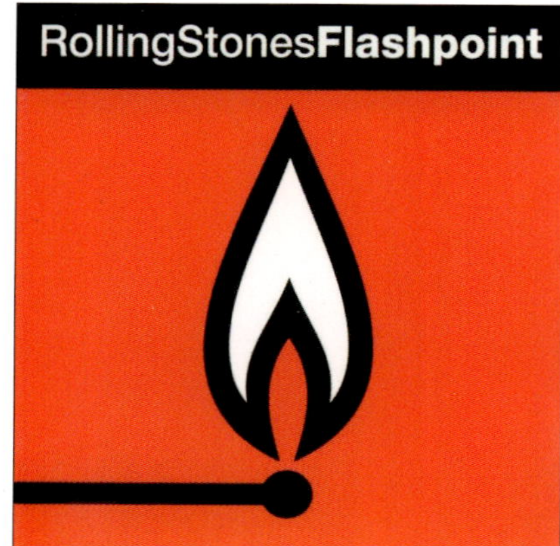

The Rolling Stones culled the live album *Flashpoint* from the North American "Steel Wheels" and European "Urban Jungle" legs of the band's world tour.

Billboard 200: *Flashpoint* (#16)
Billboard Hot 100: "Highwire" (#57)

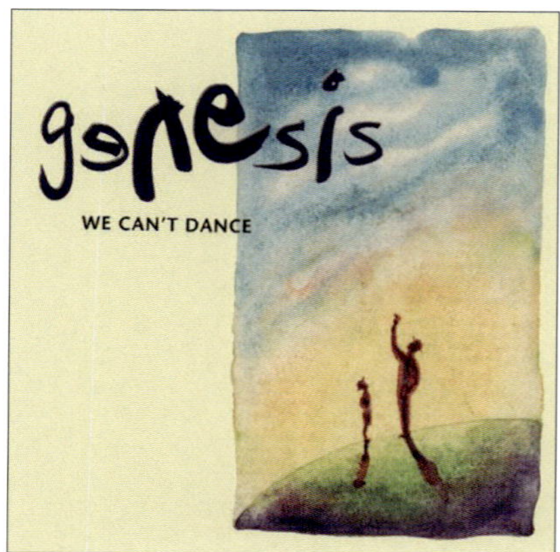

After each member had done solo work—and Phil Collins had become a superstar on his own—**Genesis** issued *We Can't Dance*, driven by five hit singles.

Billboard 200: *We Can't Dance* (#4)
Billboard Hot 100: "No Son of Mine" (#12);
"I Can't Dance" (#7); "Hold on My Heart" (#12);
"Jesus He Knows Me" (#23); "Never a Time" (#21)

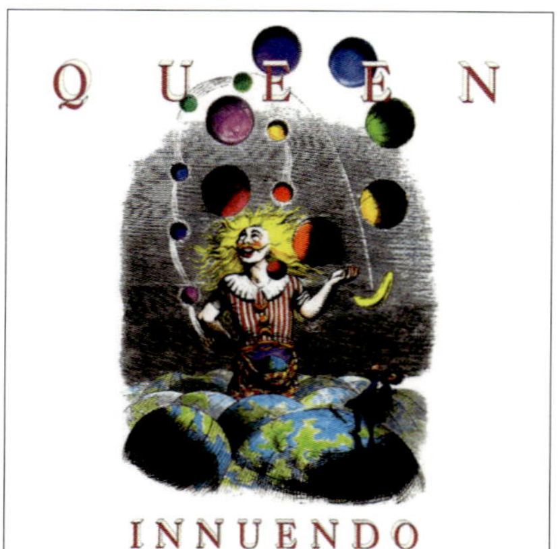

Innuendo by **Queen** was released in early 1991 to impressive European sales, nine months before singer Freddie Mercury died of complications from AIDS.

Billboard 200: *Innuendo* (#30)

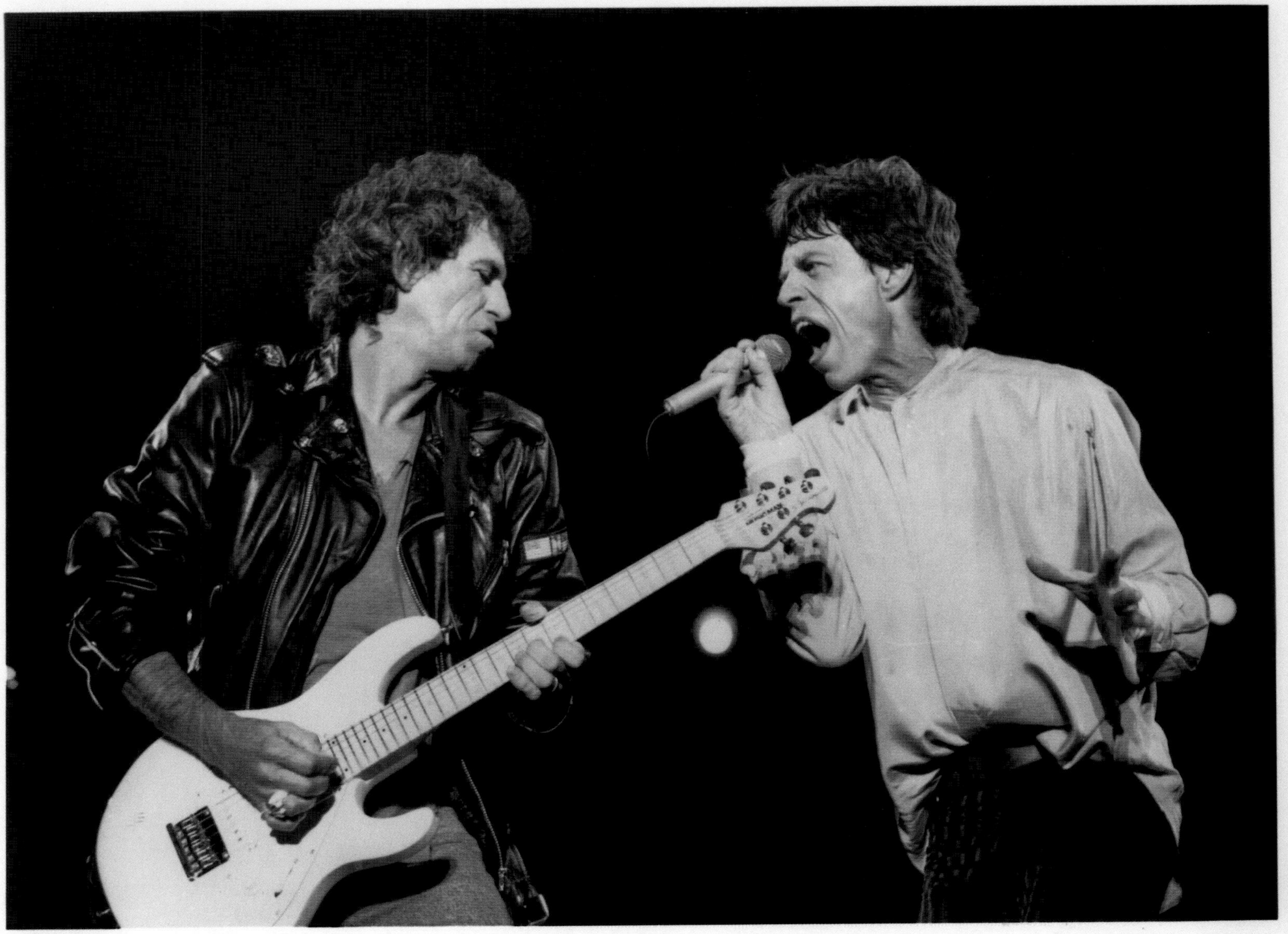

© 1991 Sony Music. Permission to reproduce this photography is limited to editorial uses in regular issues of newspapers and other regularly published periodicals and television news programming.

THE ROLLING STONES

PHOTOGRAPH: EUGENE ADEBARI

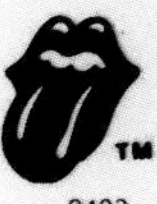

9103

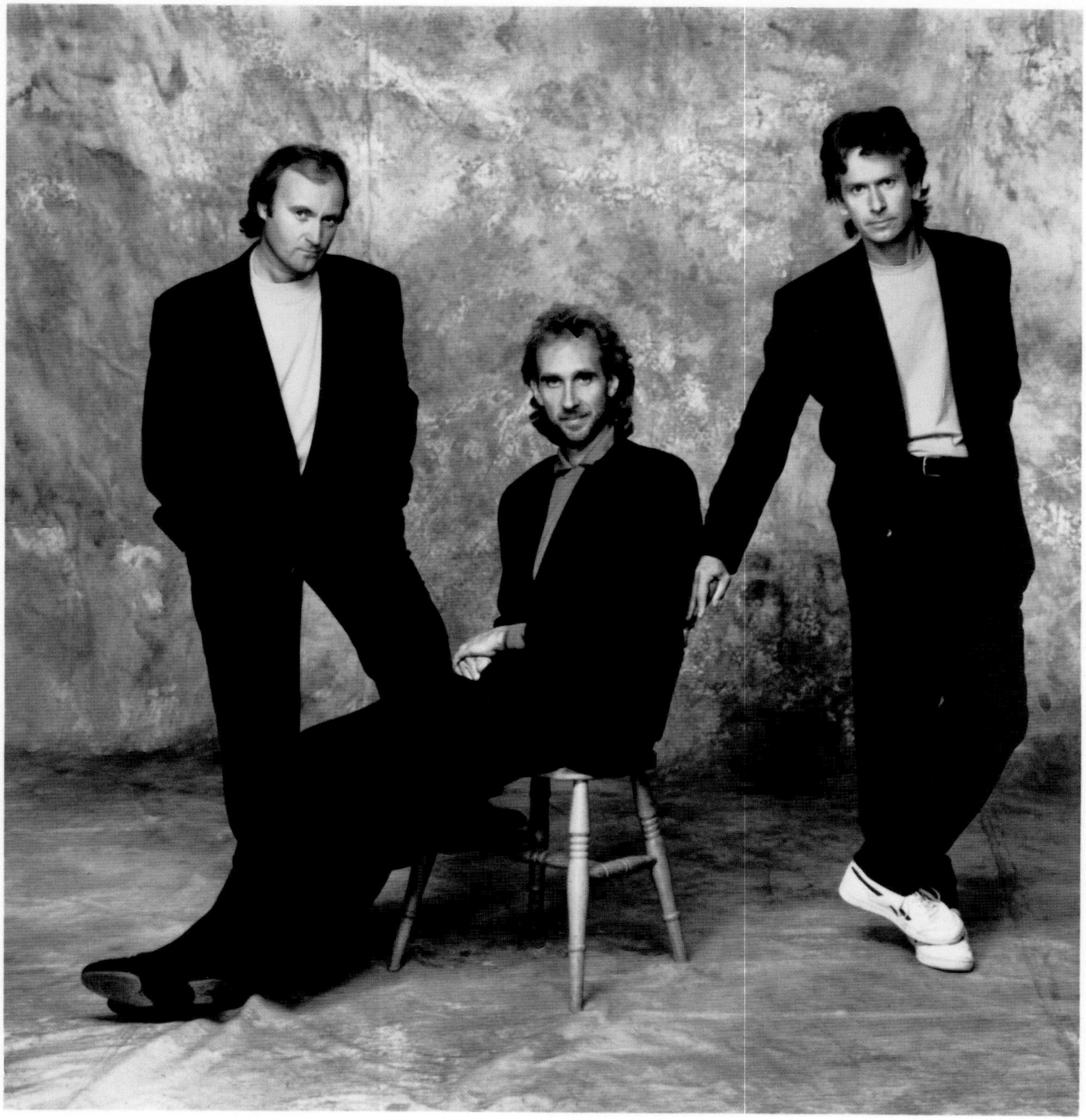

PHIL COLLINS MIKE RUTHERFORD TONY BANKS

Photo © CARL STUDNA

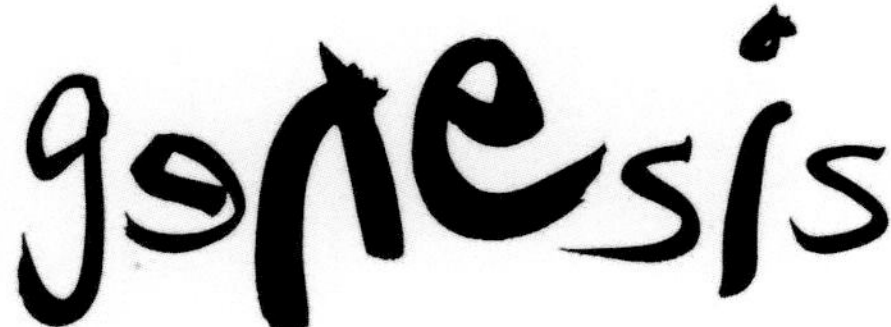

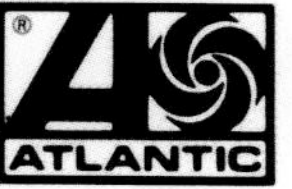

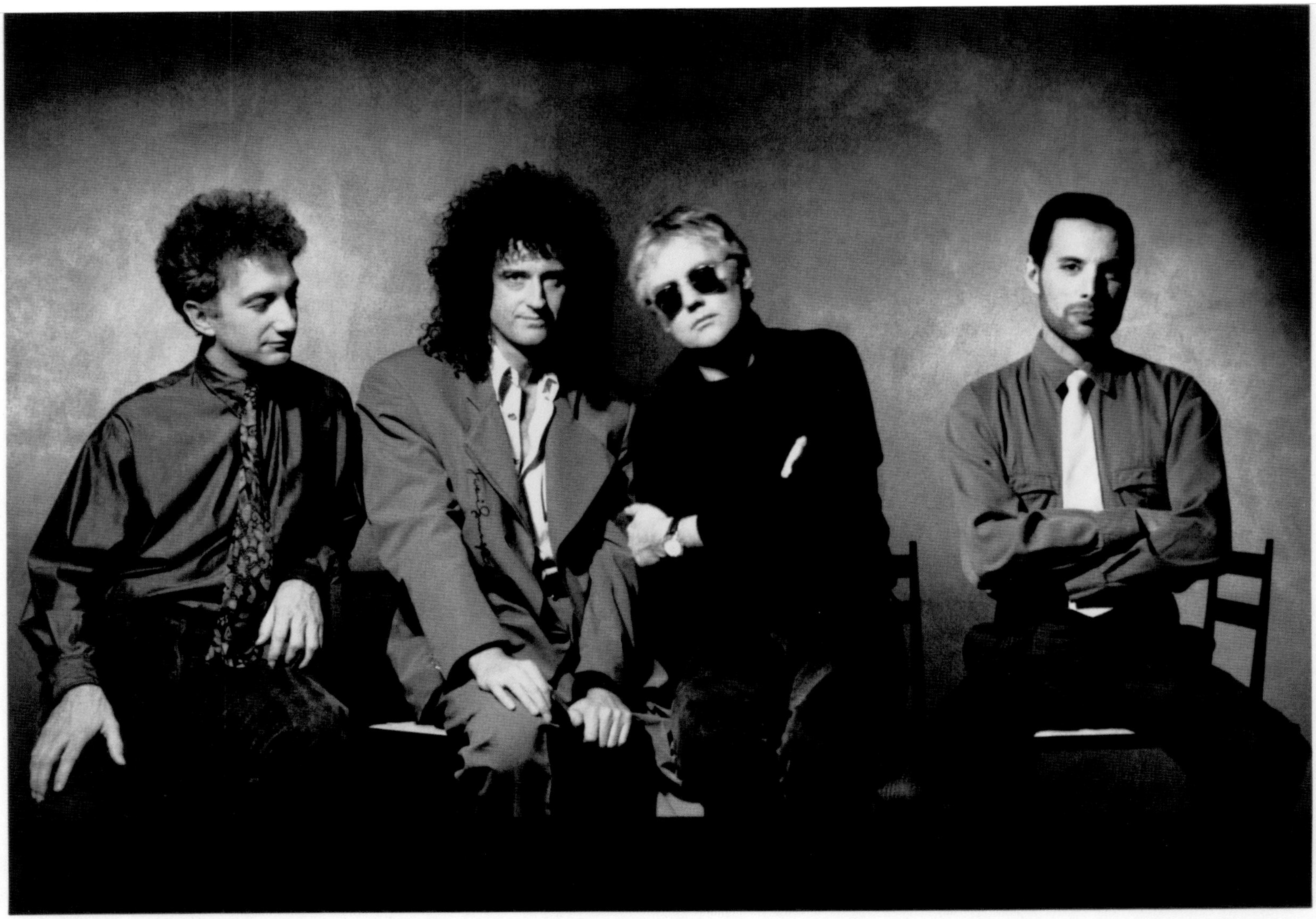

photo credit: Simon Fowler

John Deacon Brian May Roger Taylor Freddie Mercury

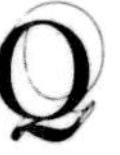

QUEEN

12/90

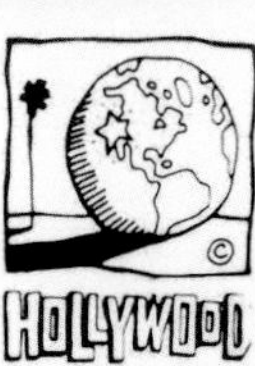

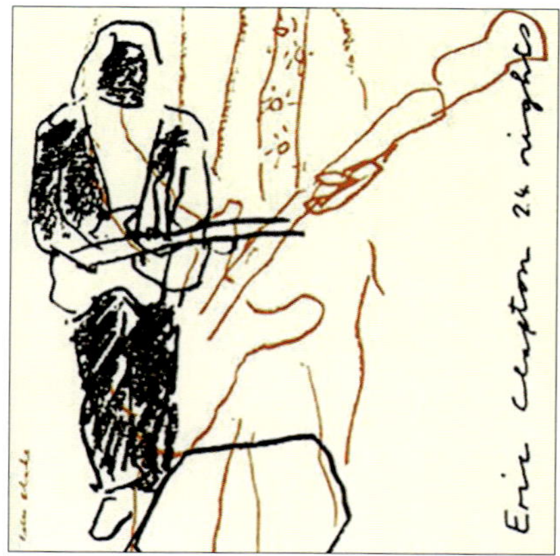

While he grieved the accidental death of his four-year-old son, **Eric Clapton** released *24 Nights*, culled from a series of concerts at London's Royal Albert Hall.

Billboard 200: *24 Nights* (#38)

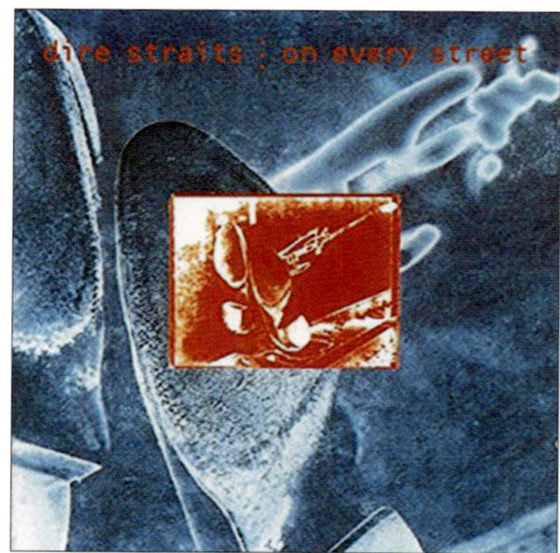

On Every Street, **Dire Straits**' final studio album, produced the singles "Calling Elvis," "The Bug" and "Heavy Fuel," a No.1 hit on the mainstream rock charts.

Billboard 200: *On Every Street* (#12)

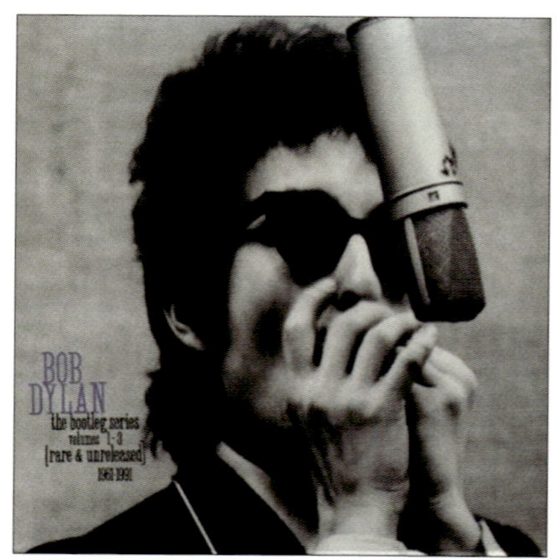

The Bootleg Series Volumes 1-3 (Rare & Unreleased) 1961-1991 marked the first previously unissued **Bob Dylan** material to be made officially available.

Billboard 200: *The Bootleg Series Volumes 1-3* (#49)

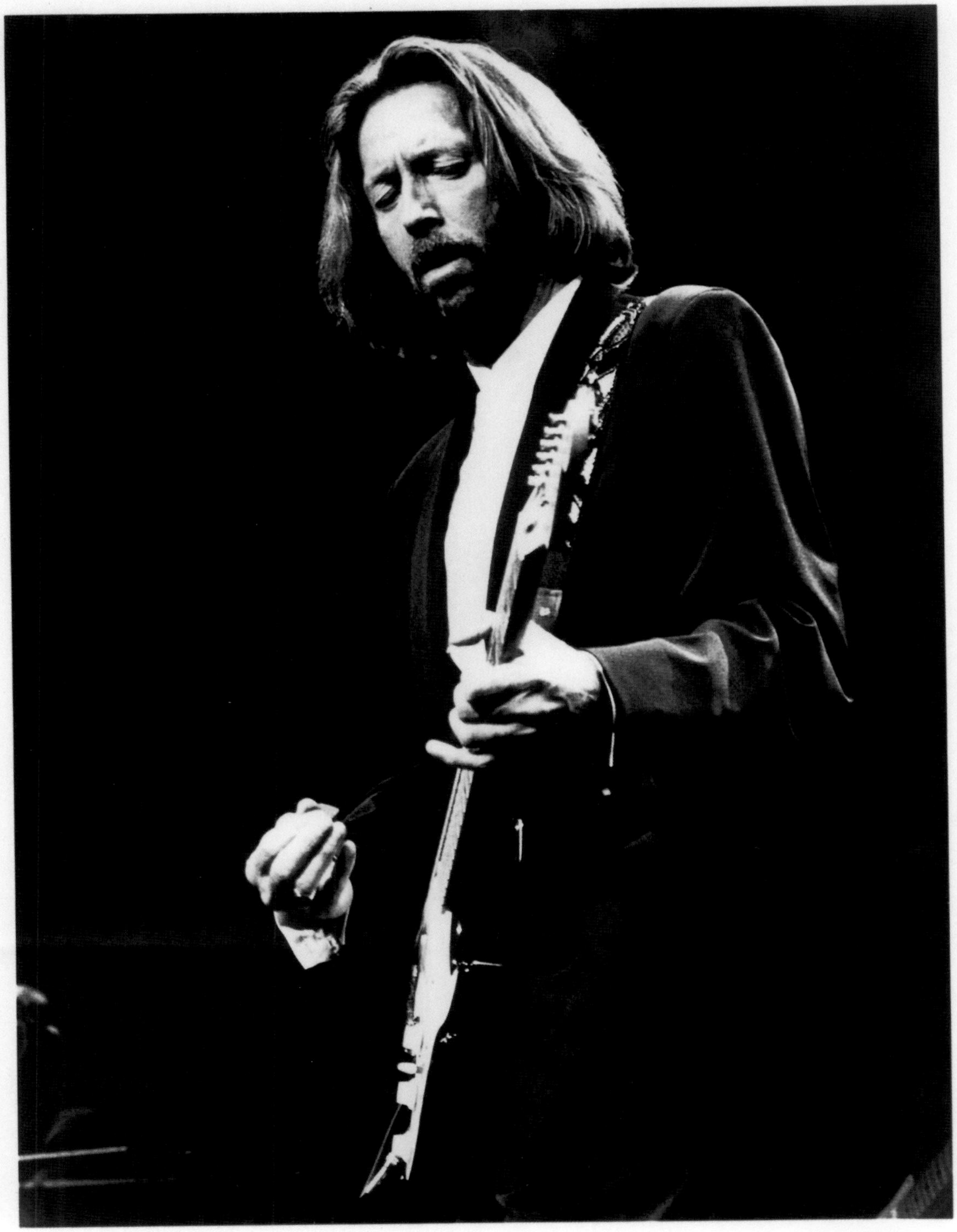

Photo Credit: Carl Studna

Eric Clapton

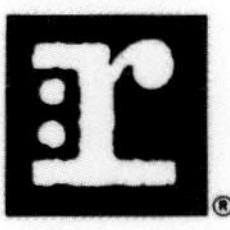

reprise

© 1991 Reprise Records/Permission to reproduce limited to editorial uses in newspapers and other regularly published periodicals and television news programming.

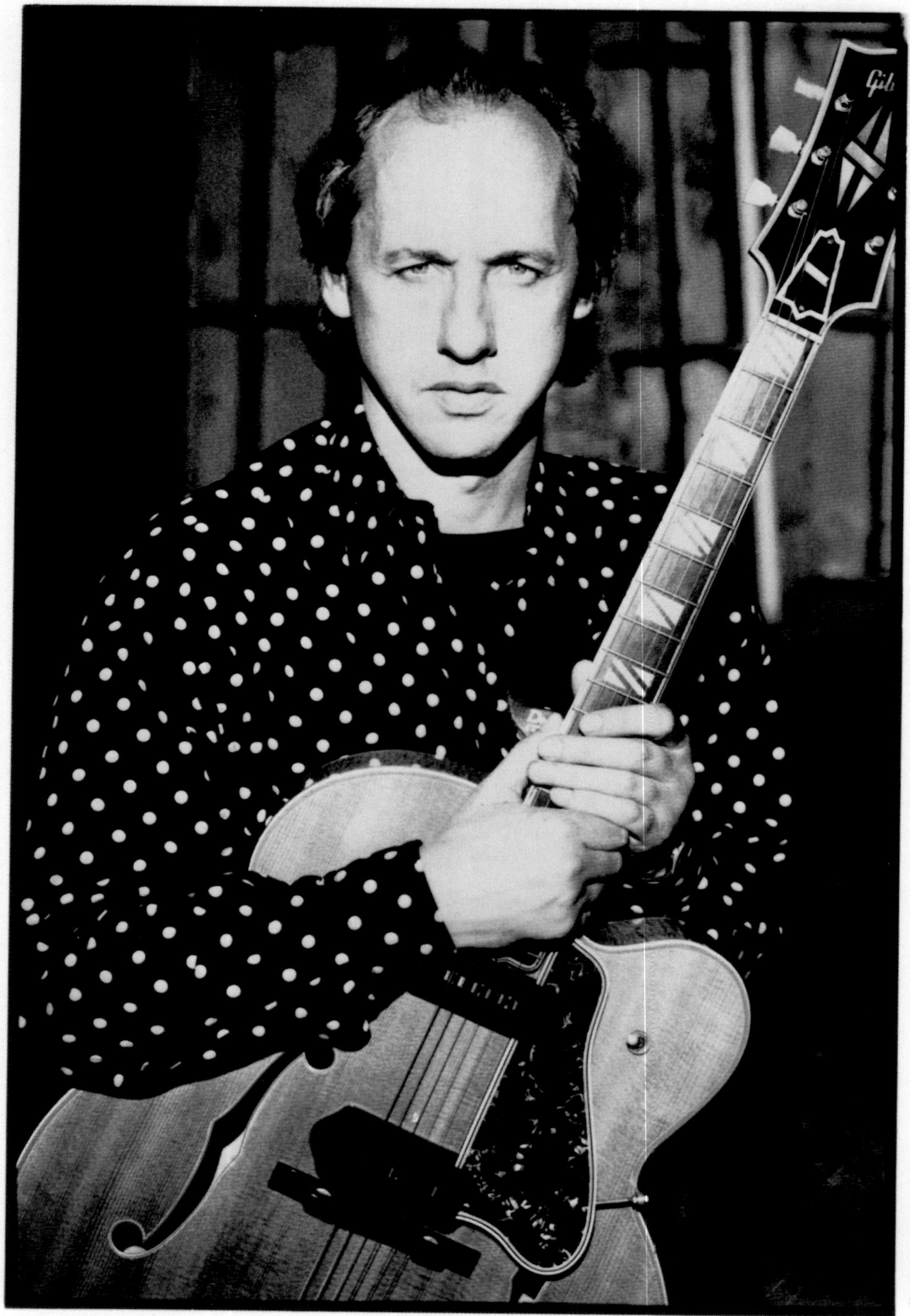

Photo Credit: Paul Cox

Mark Knopfler of

dire straits

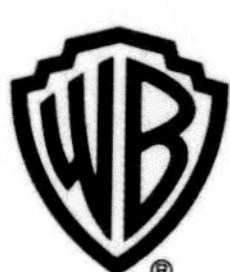

© 1991 Warner Bros. Records/Permission to reproduce limited to editorial uses in newspapers and other regularly published periodicals and television news programming.

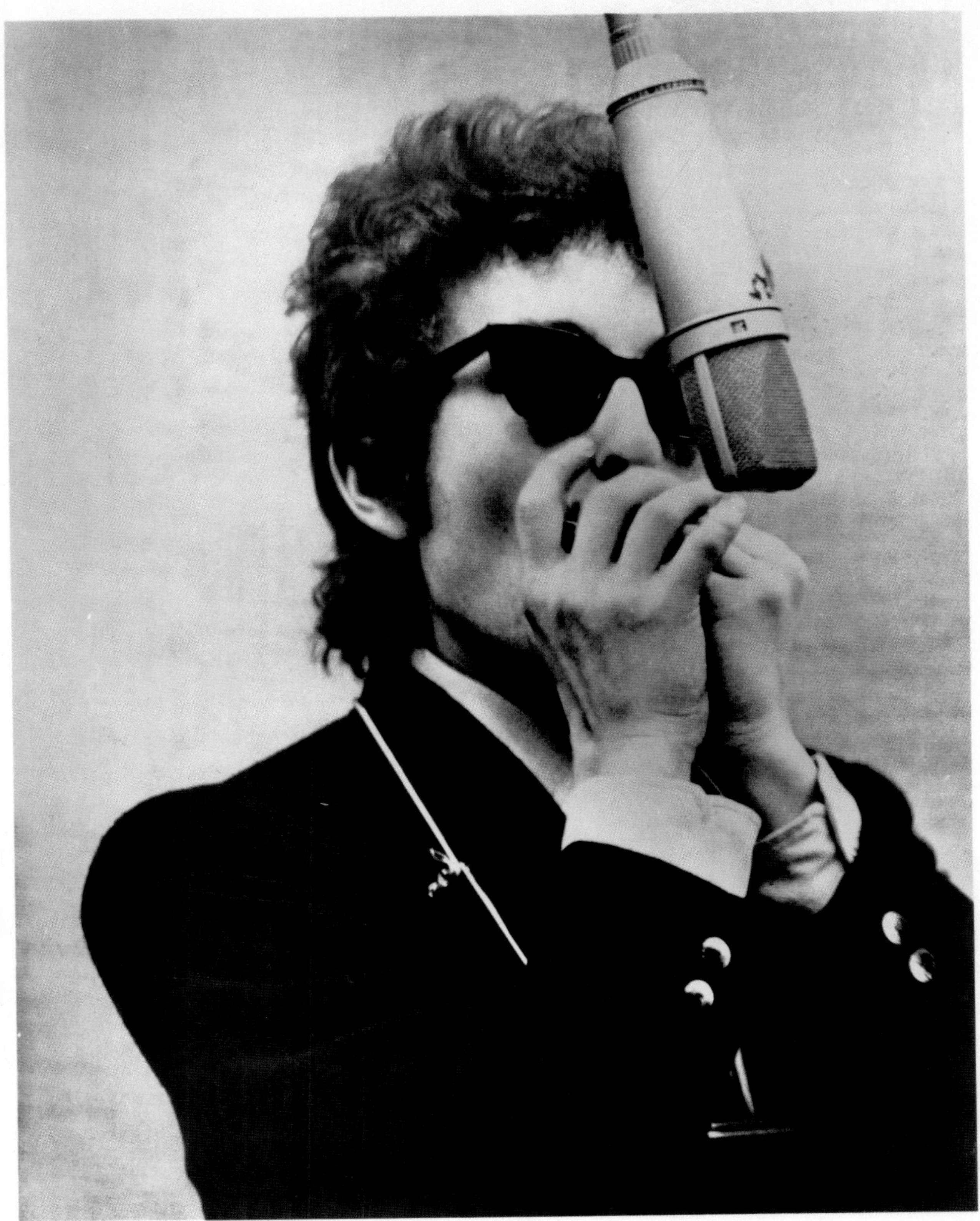

PHOTOGRAPH: DON HUNSTEIN

© 1991 Sony Music. Permission to reproduce this photography is limited to editorial uses in regular issues of newspapers and other regularly published periodicals and television news programming.

BOB DYLAN

Columbia

9103

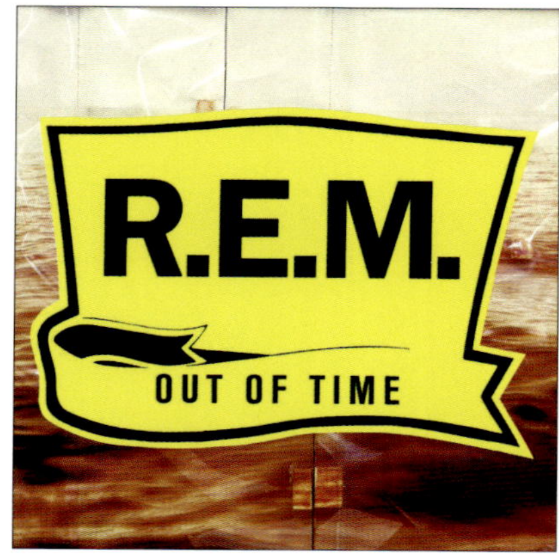

Boasting the hits "Losing My Religion" and "Shiny Happy People," *Out of Time* topped both the US and UK charts and catapulted **R.E.M.** to international fame.

Billboard 200: *Out of Time* (No. 1)
Billboard Hot 100: "Losing My Religion" (#4); "Shiny Happy People" (#10)

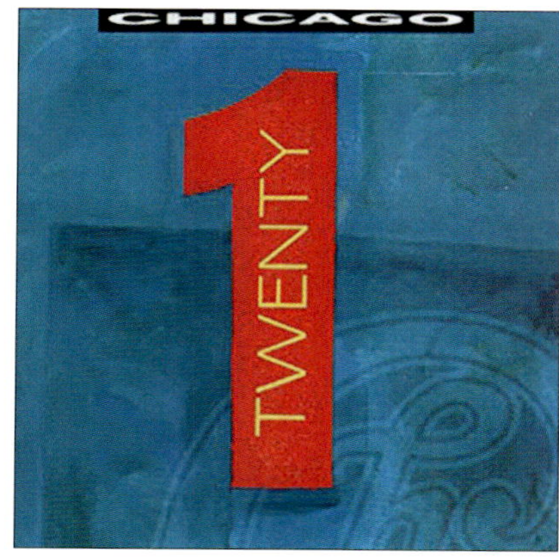

Having experienced significant lineup changes, **Chicago** put out its 21st album overall, and *Twenty 1* spun off a lone Top 40 hit, "Chasin' the Wind."

Billboard 200: *Twenty 1* (#66)
Billboard Hot 100: "Chasin' the Wind" (#39)

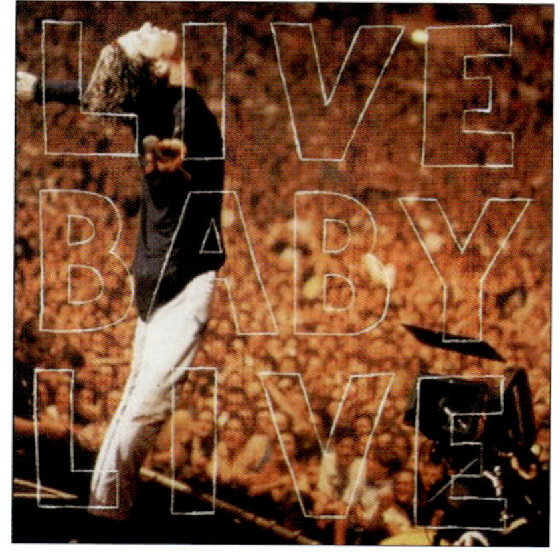

"Shining Star," a new studio track, was released ahead of *Live Baby Live*, **INXS**' first live album recorded during the Australian rock band's international tour.

Billboard 200: *Live Baby Live* (#72)

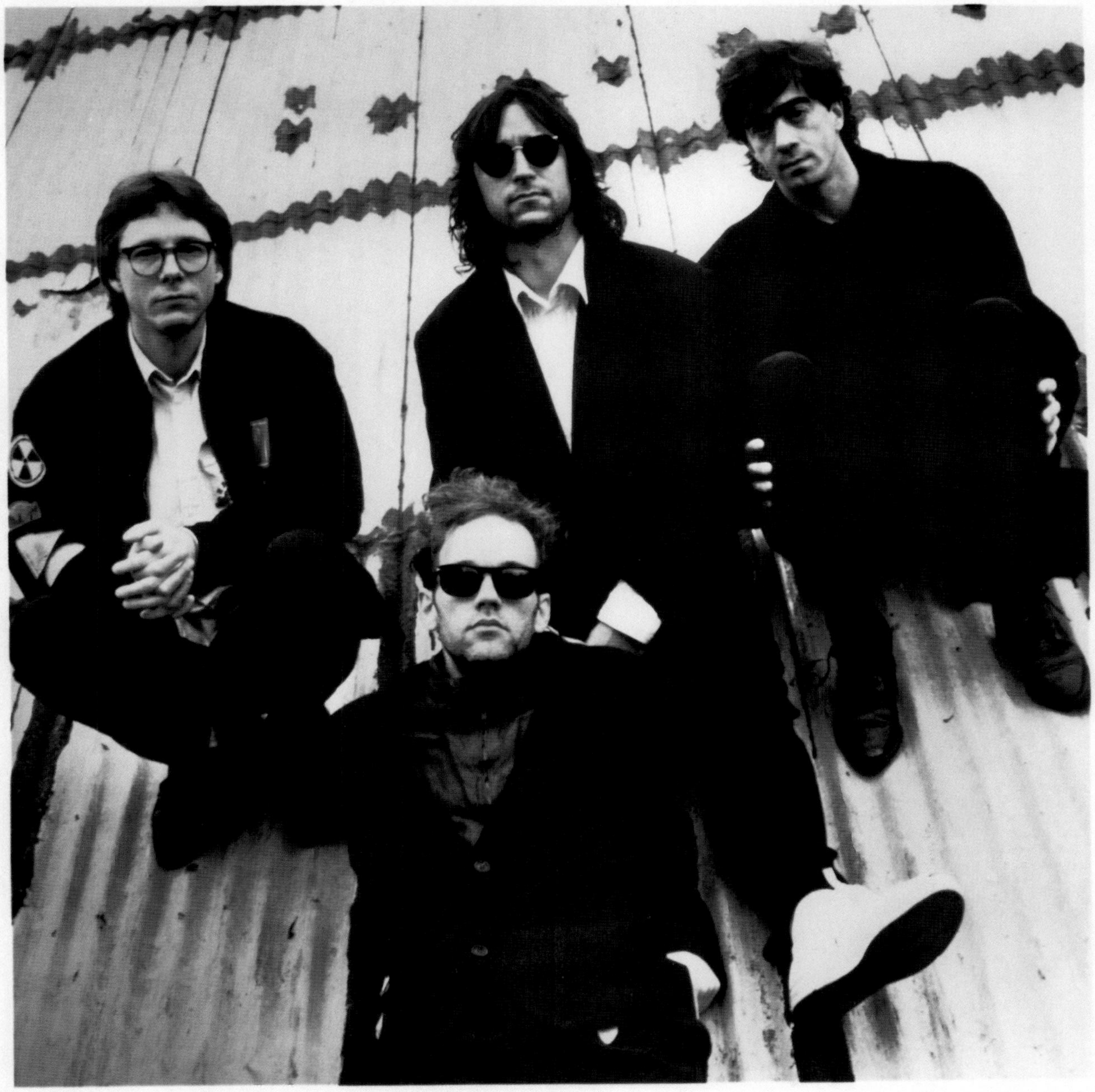

Photo Credit: Frank Ockenfels

R.E.M.

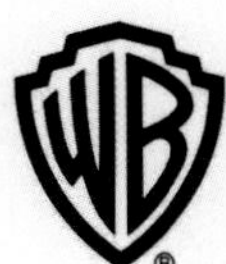

© 1991 Warner Bros. Records/Permission to reproduce limited to editorial uses in newspapers and other regularly published periodicals and television news programming.

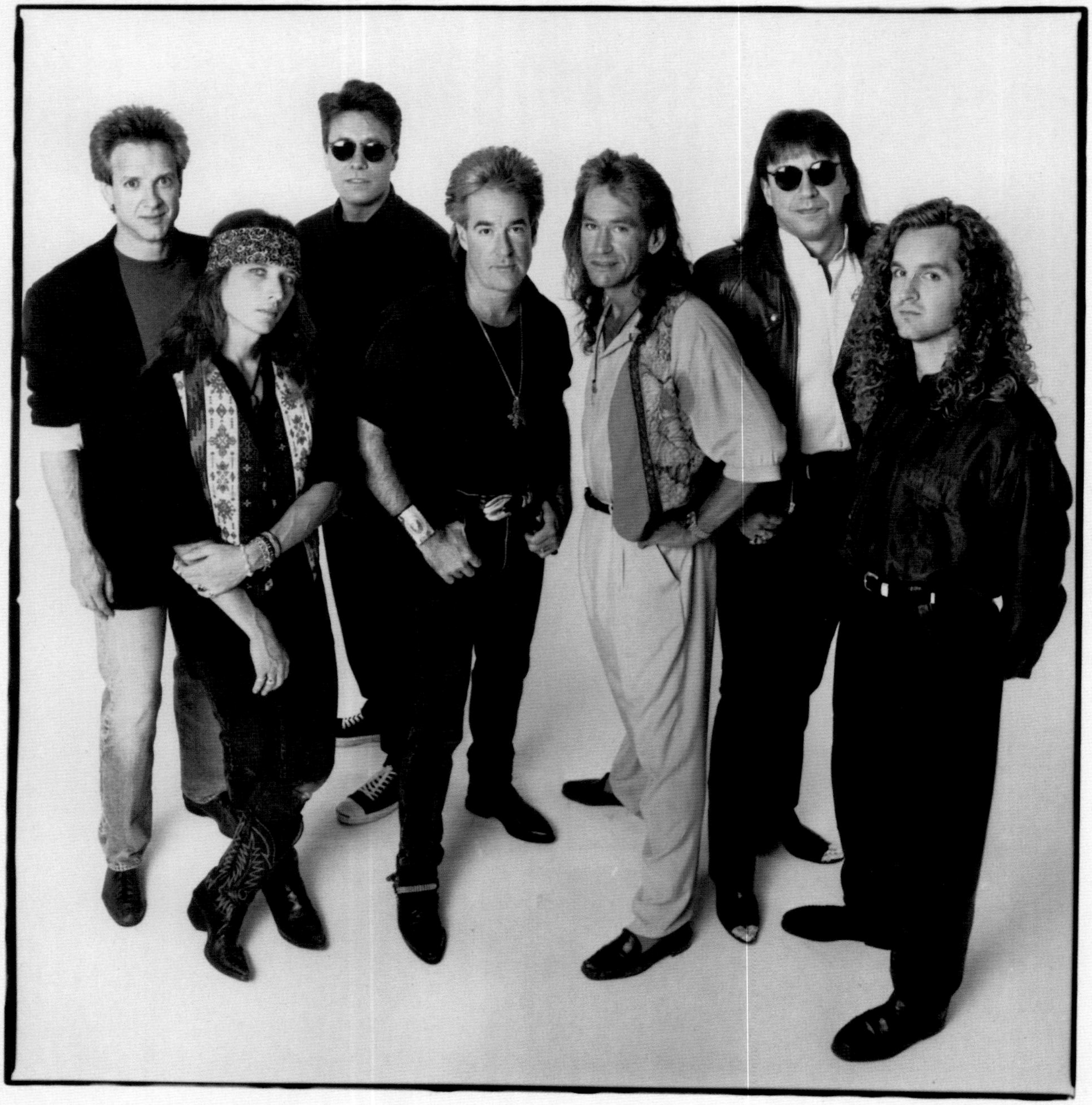

Photo Credit: Chris Cuffaro/Visages

Lee Loughnane Dawayne Bailey Robert Lamm James Pankow Bill Champlin Walt Parazaider Jason Scheff

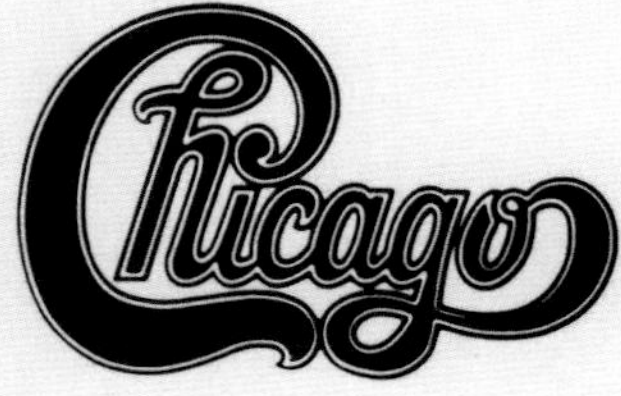

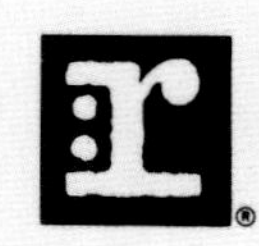

reprise

© 1990 Reprise Records/Permission to reproduce limited to editorial uses in newspapers and other regularly published periodicals and television news programming.

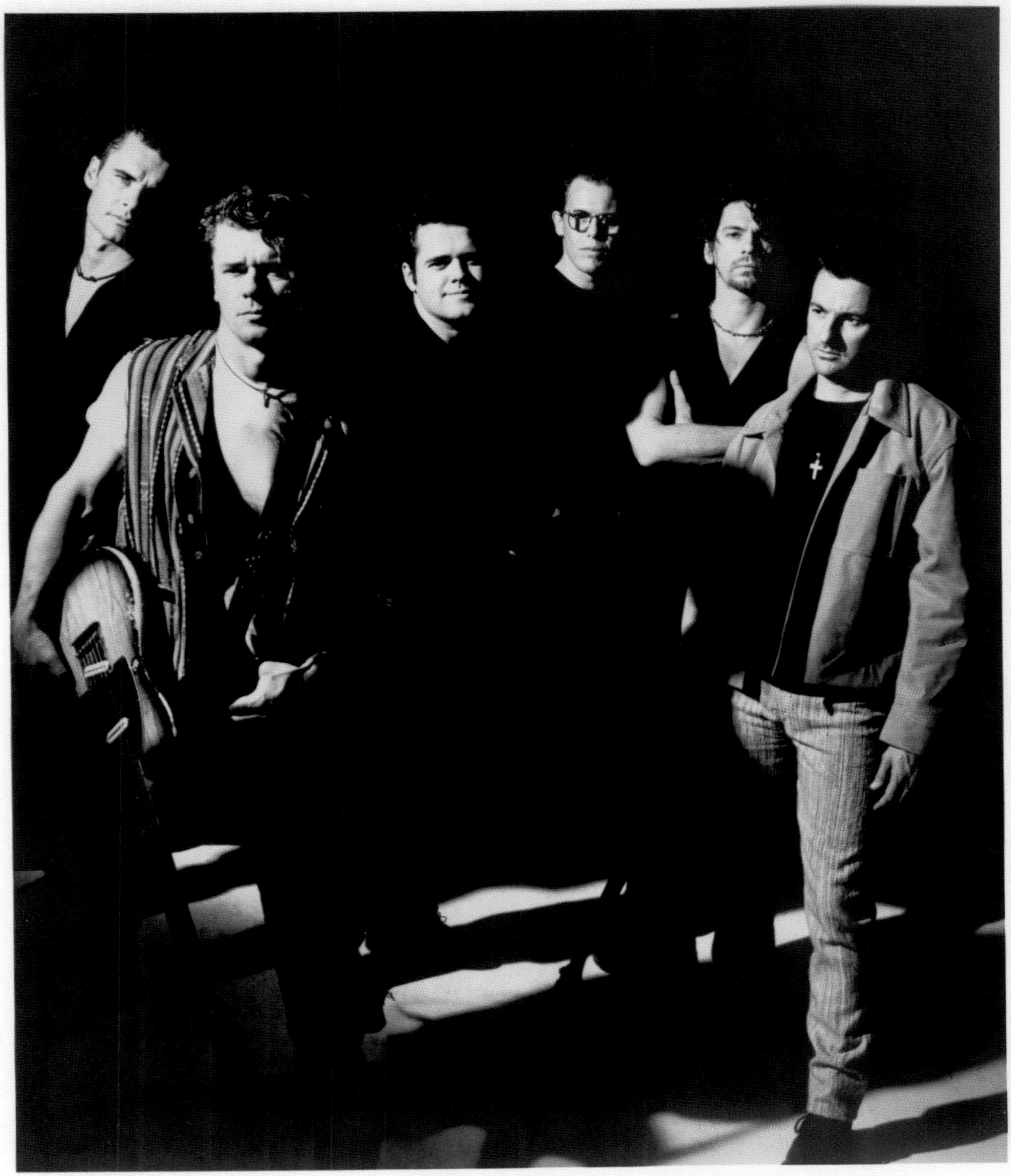

JON FARRISS TIM FARRISS ANDREW FARRISS KIRK PENGILLY MICHAEL HUTCHENCE GARRY GARY BEERS

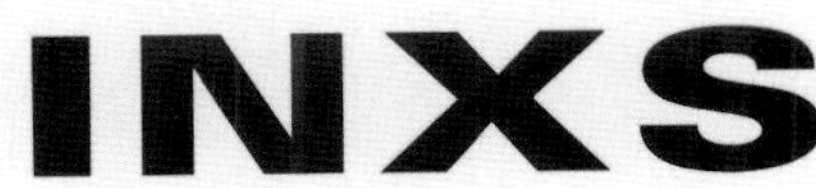

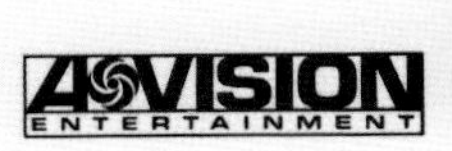

ATLANTIC

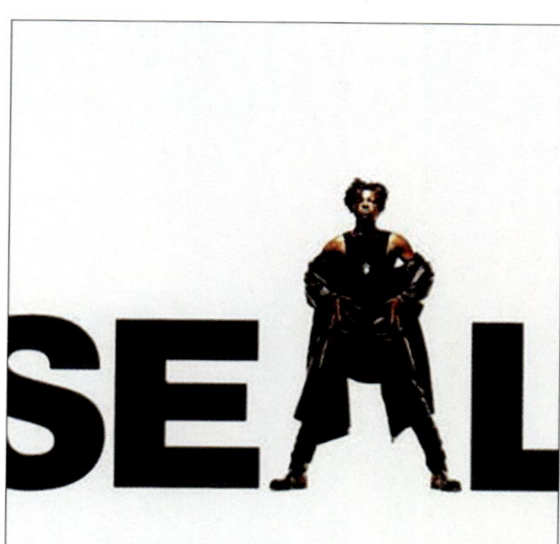

British singer-songwriter **Seal**, born Seal Henry Samuel, recorded his debut album with producer Trevor Horn, and "Crazy" became an international hit.

Billboard 200: *Seal* (#27)
Billboard Hot 100: "Crazy" (#7); "Killer" (#100)

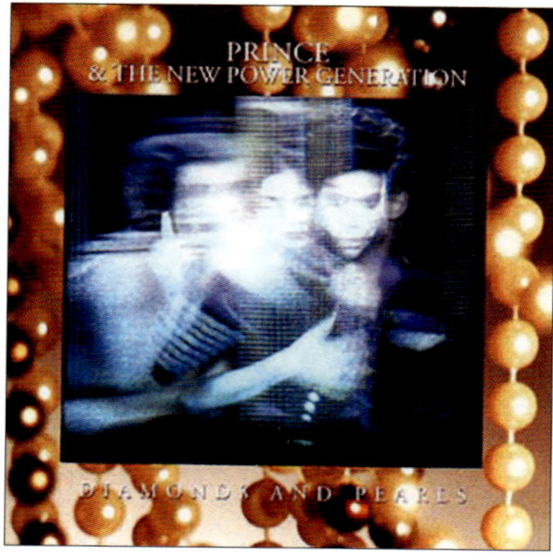

Prince assembled a versatile new backing band, the New Power Generation, which debuted on *Diamonds and Pearls*, generating the No. 1 single "Cream."

Billboard 200: *Diamonds and Pearls* (#3)
Billboard Hot 100: "Gett Off" (#21); "Cream" (No. 1); "Diamonds and Pearls" (#3); "Money Don't Matter 2 Night" (#23)

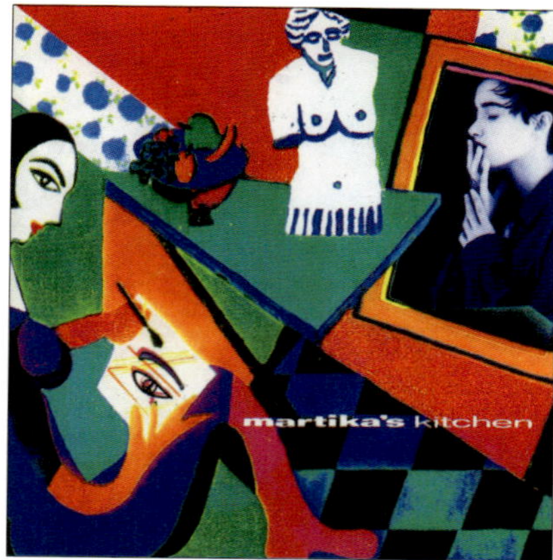

Pop singer **Martika** approached Prince to write and produce some new tracks, and "Love... Thy Will Be Done," which began as a prayer, became a Top 10 hit.

Billboard 200: *Martika's Kitchen* (#111)
Billboard Hot 100: "Love... Thy Will Be Done" (#10); "Martika's Kitchen" (#93)

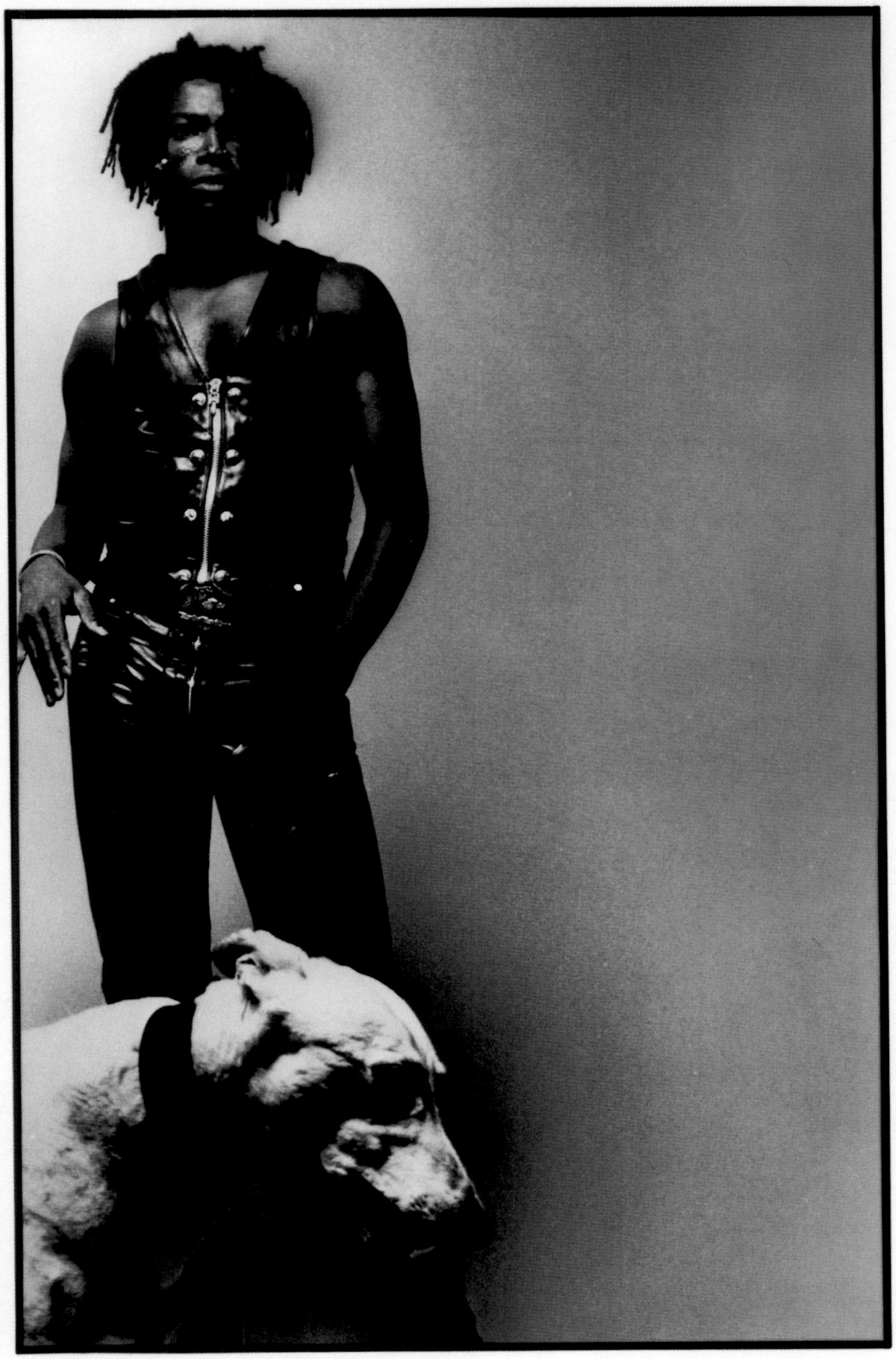

SEAL

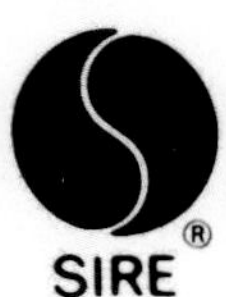

© 1991 Sire Records Company/Permission to reproduce limited to editorial uses in newspapers and other regularly published periodicals and television news programming

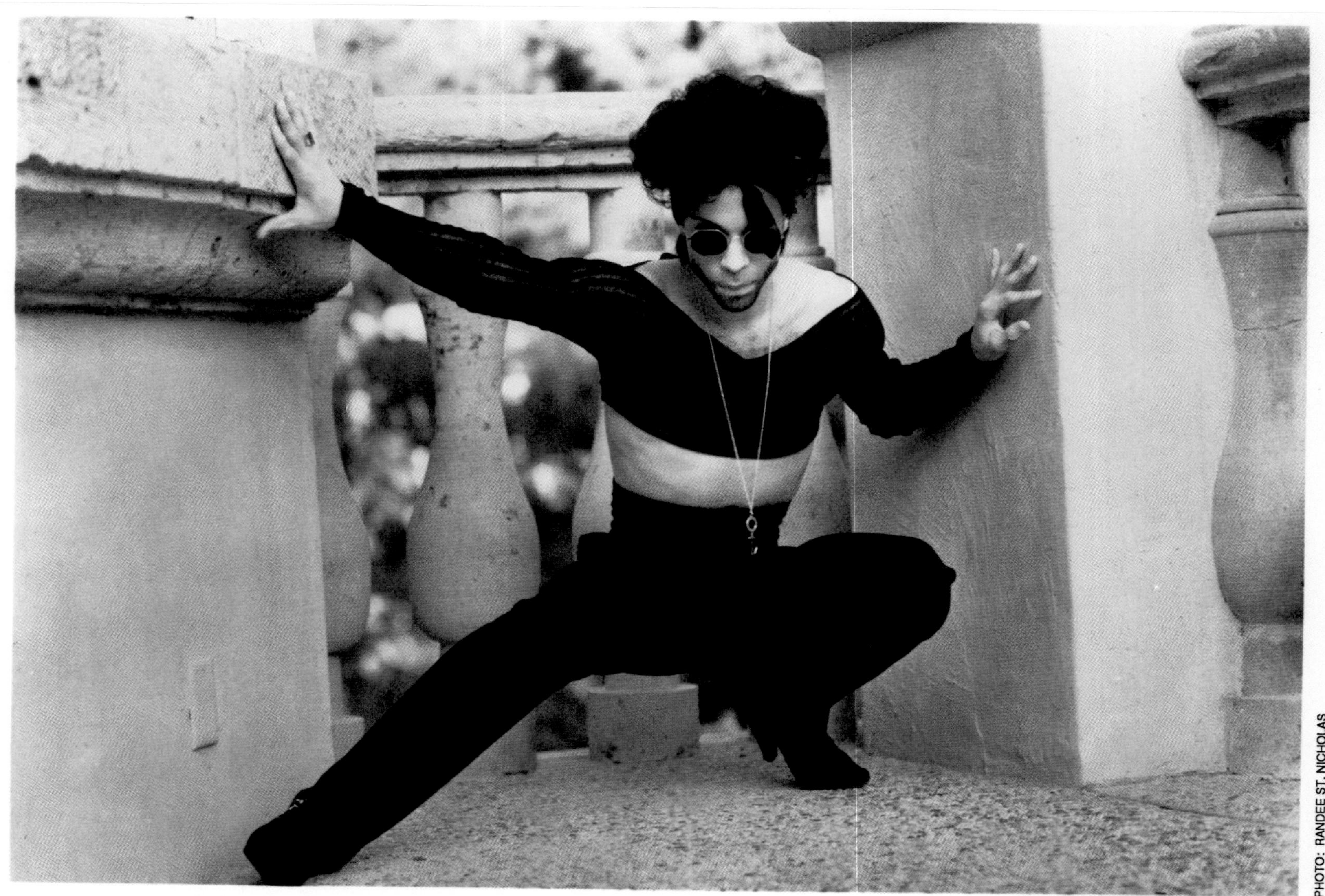

PHOTO: RANDEE ST. NICHOLAS

PRINCE

Paisley Park

© 1991 Paisley Park Records/Permission to reproduce limited to editorial uses in newspapers and other regularly published periodicals and television news programming.

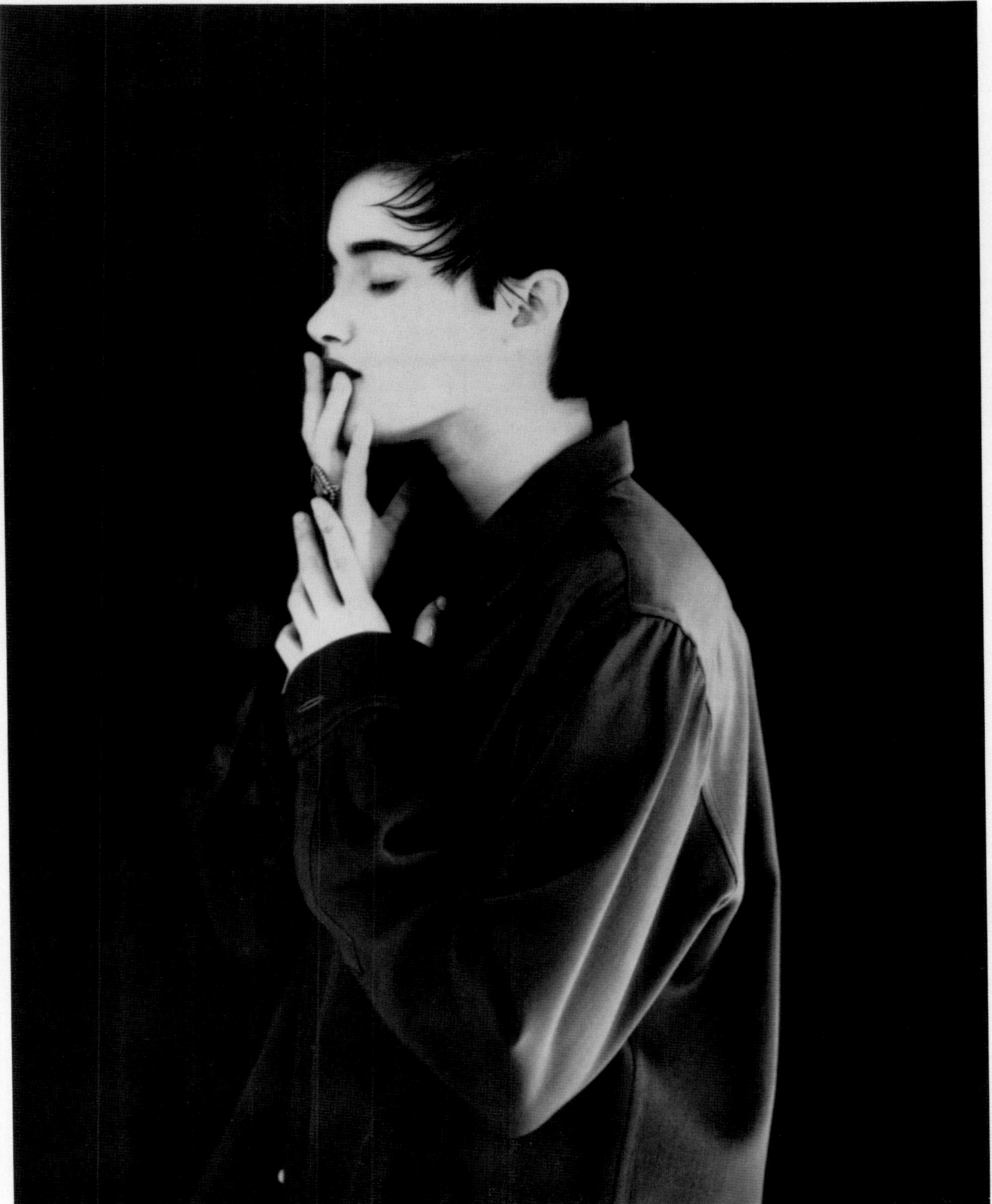

© 1991 Sony Music. Permission to reproduce this photography is limited to editorial uses in regular issues of newspapers and other regularly published periodicals and television news programming.

Photo Credit: David Jensen

MARTIKA

Columbia

9106

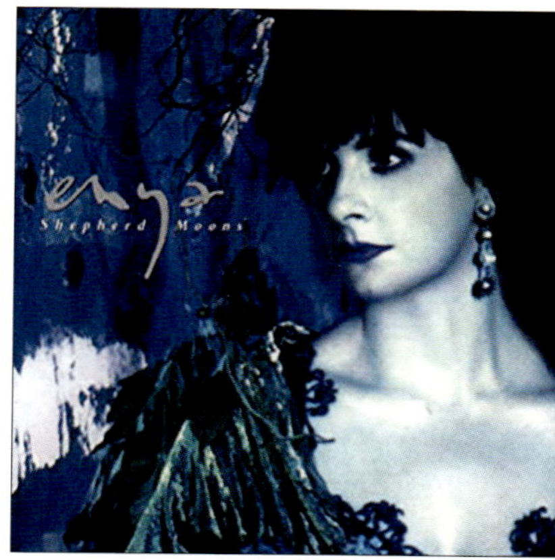

Featuring "Caribbean Blue," an elegant, rosy waltz, **Enya**'s *Shepherd Moons* would win the Irish musician her first Grammy Award, for Best New Age Album.

Billboard 200: *Shepherd Moons* (#17)
Billboard Hot 100: "Caribbean Blue" (#79)

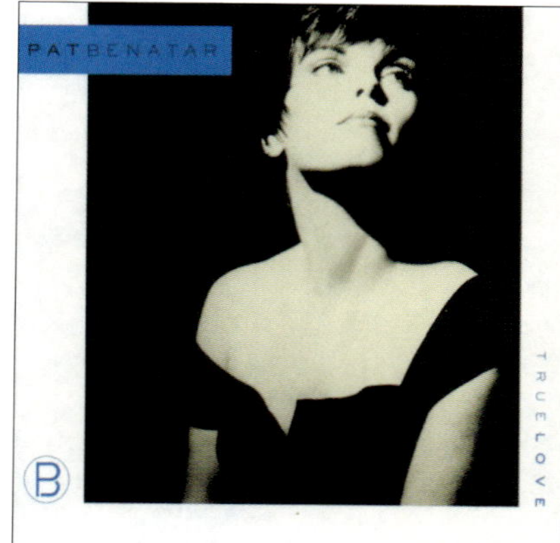

Mainstream rock singer **Pat Benatar** shifted musical gears, issuing *True Love*, a jump blues record featuring the Roomful of Blues horn section and drummer.

Billboard 200: *True Love* (#37)

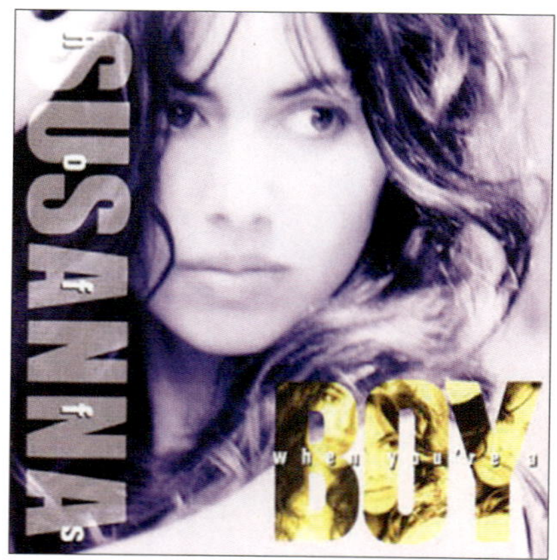

Susanna Hoffs, a co-founder of the Bangles, released *When You're a Boy*, and the debut solo album generated a Top 40 hit with "My Side of the Bed."

Billboard 200: *When You're a Boy* (#83)
Billboard Hot 100: "My Side of the Bed" (#30)

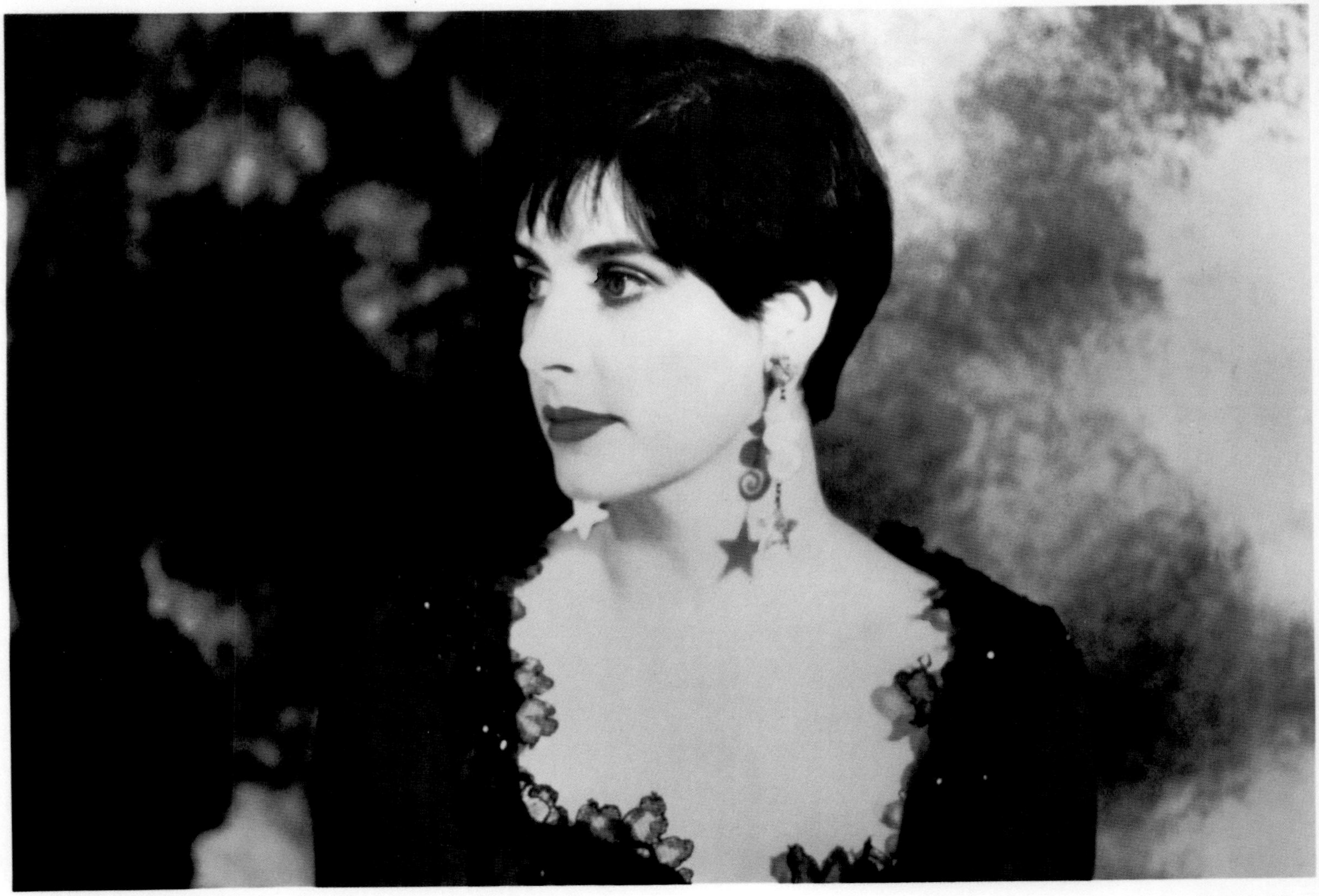

Photo Credit: Steve Rapport

ENYA

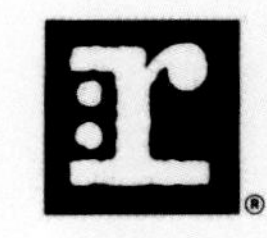

reprise

© 1991 Reprise Records/Permission to reproduce limited to editorial uses in newspapers and other regularly published periodicals and television news programming.

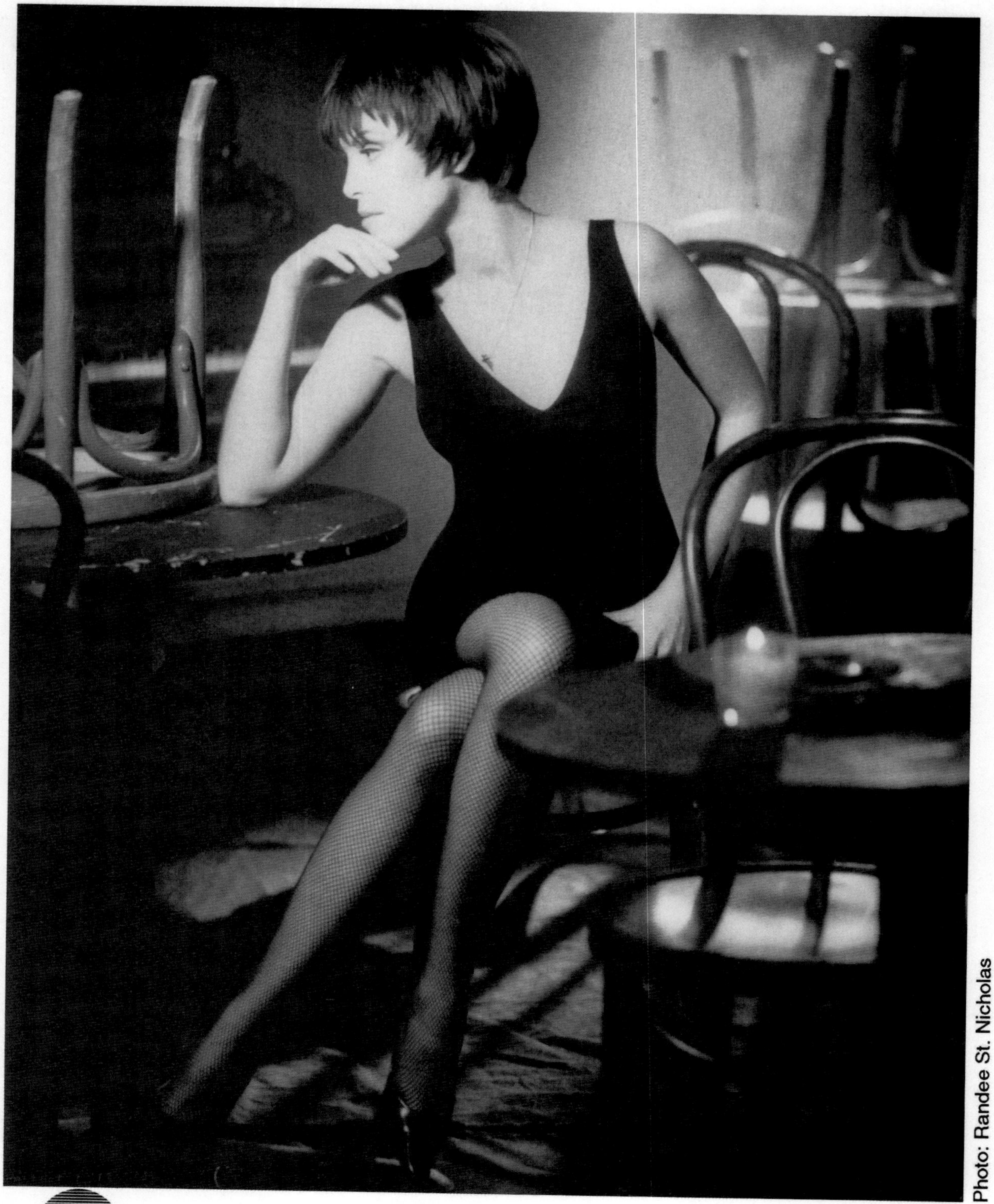

Photo: Randee St. Nicholas

Gold Mountain®

PAT BENATAR

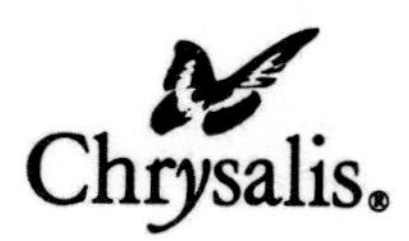

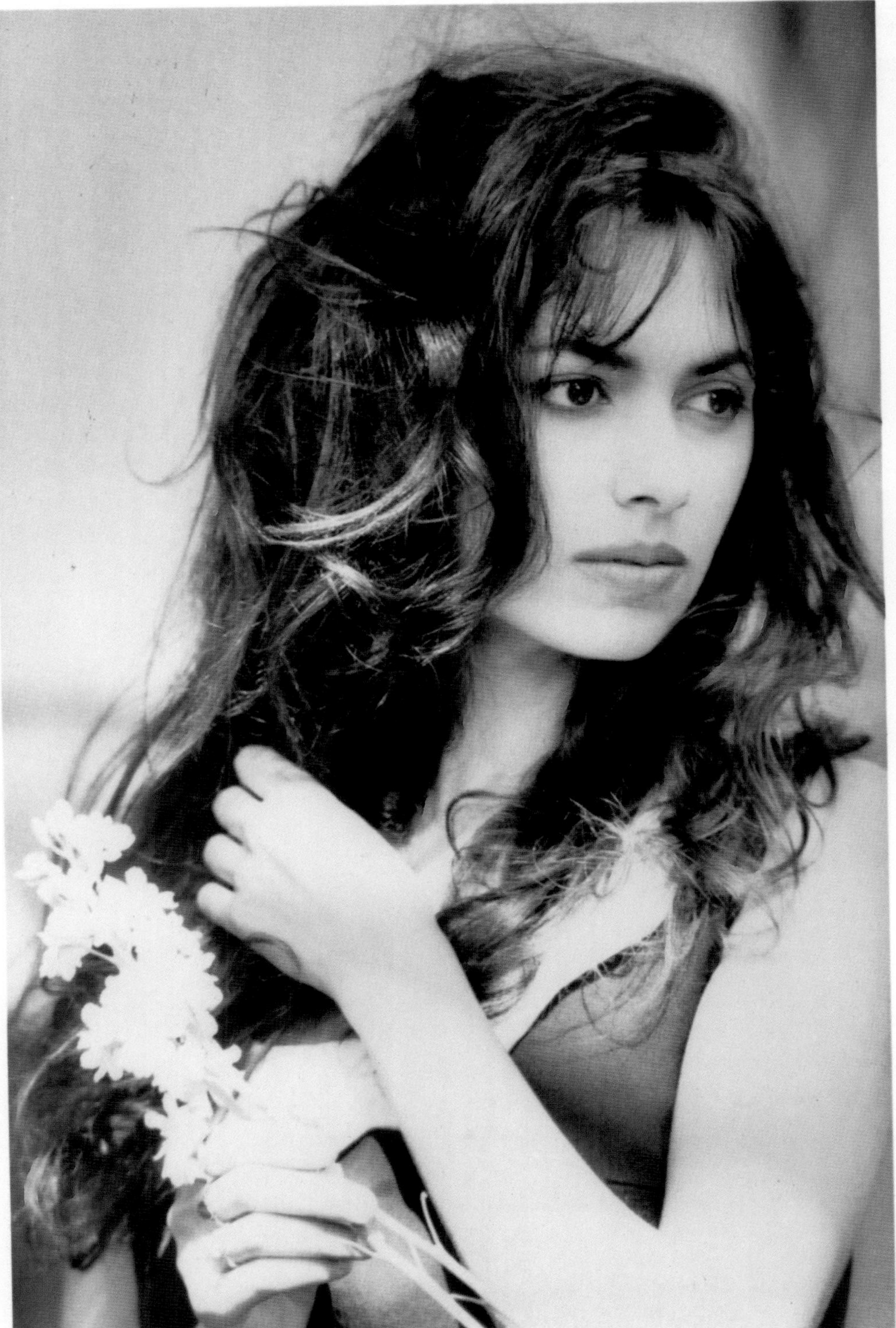

© 1990 CBS Records Inc. Permission to reproduce this photography is limited to editorial uses in regular issues of newspapers and other regularly published periodicals and television news programming.

Photo Credit: Randee St. Nicholas

STIEFEL PHILLIPS ENTERTAINMENT

SUSANNA HOFFS

Columbia

9012

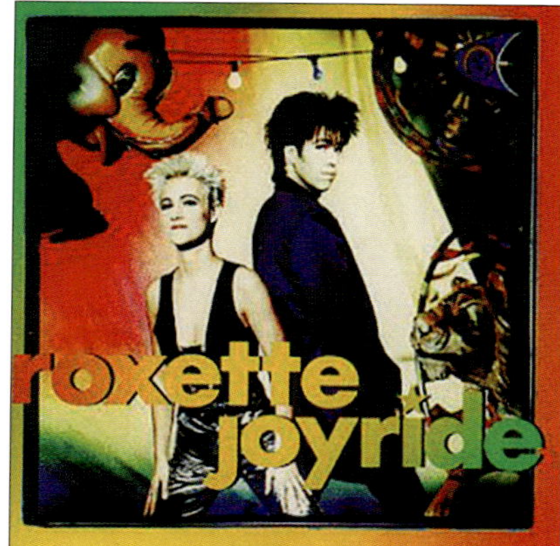

Roxette, the Swedish pop-rock duo of vocalist Marie Fredriksson and songwriter Per Gessle, delivered *Joyride* and dominated the charts around the world.

Billboard 200: *Joyride* (#12)
Billboard Hot 100: "Joyride" (No. 1); "Fading Like a Flower (Every Time You Leave)" (#2); "Spending My Time" (#32); "Church of Your Heart" (#36)

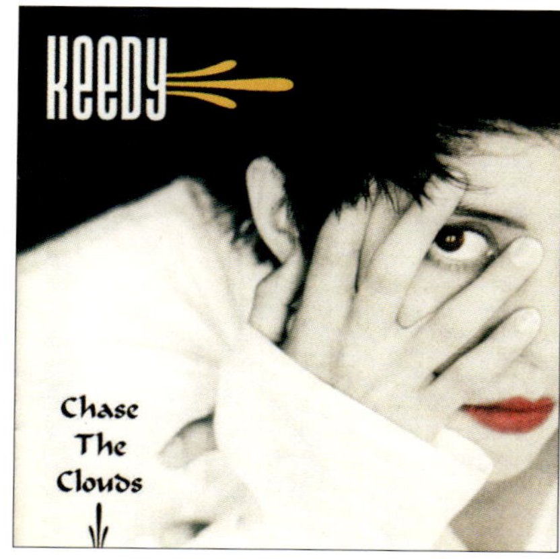

From her debut album, *Chase the Clouds*, promising pop singer **Keedy** shined on the rollicking "Save Some Love," her only Top 20 hit in a fleeting career.

Billboard Hot 100: "Save Some Love" (#15); "Wishing on the Same Star" (#86)

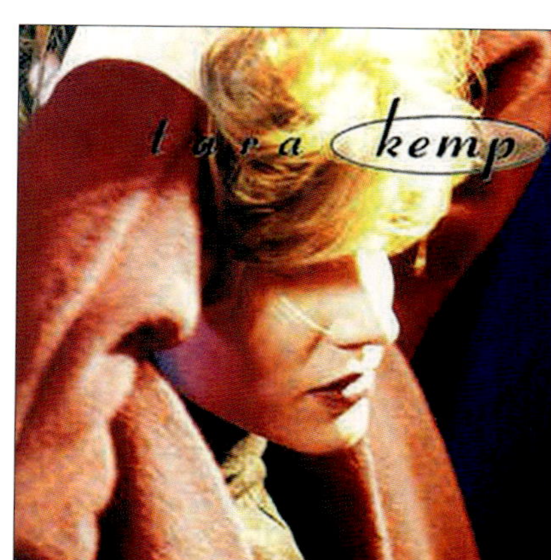

Bay Area singer **Tara Kemp**'s short-lived success consisted of two Top 10 singles, "Hold You Tight" and "Piece of My Heart," from her self-titled first album.

Billboard 200: *Tara Kemp* (#109)
Billboard Hot 100: "Hold You Tight" (#3); "Piece of My Heart" (#7); "Too Much" (#95)

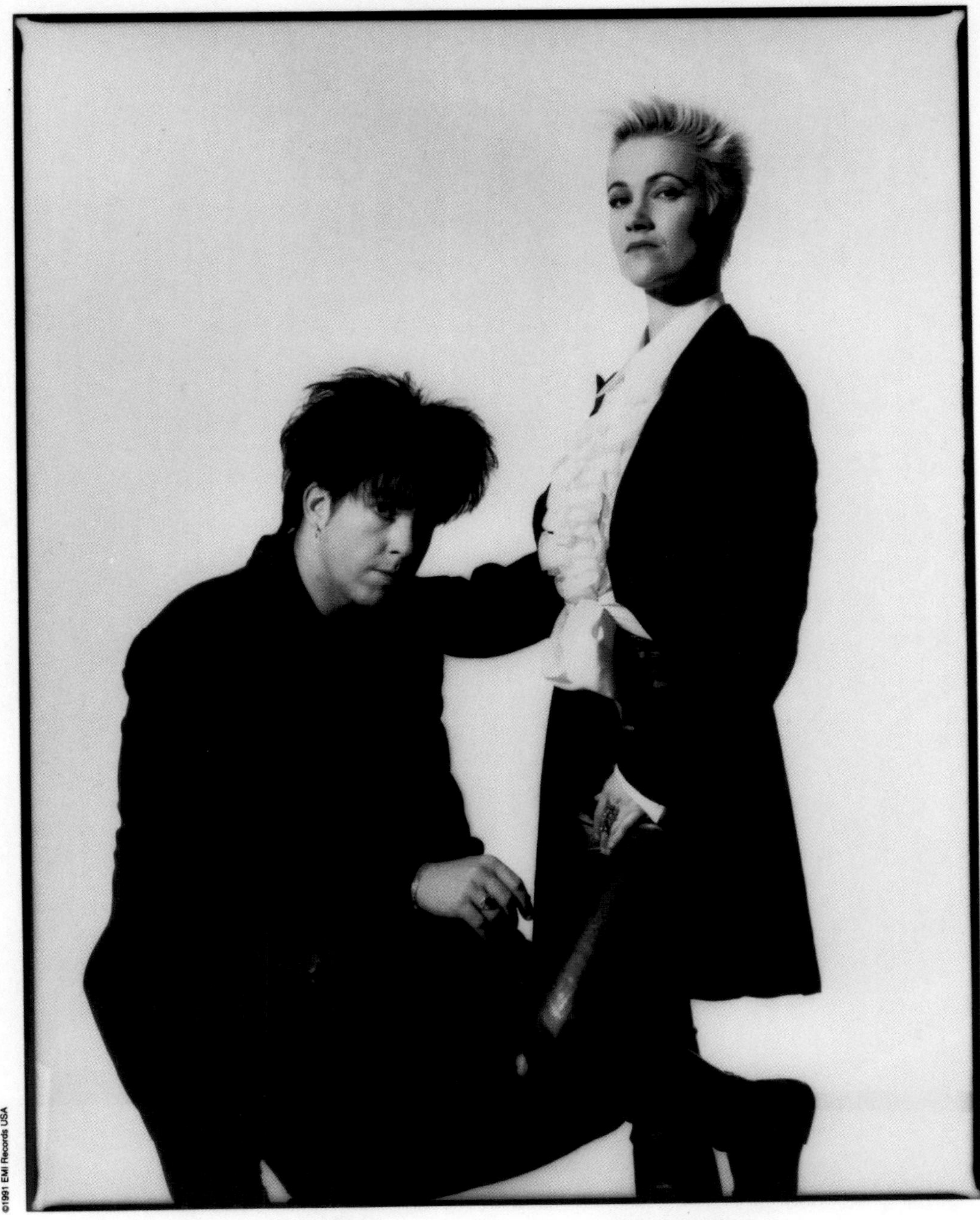

©1991 EMI Records USA

Photography: Timothy White

per gessle marie fredriksson

roxette

EMI

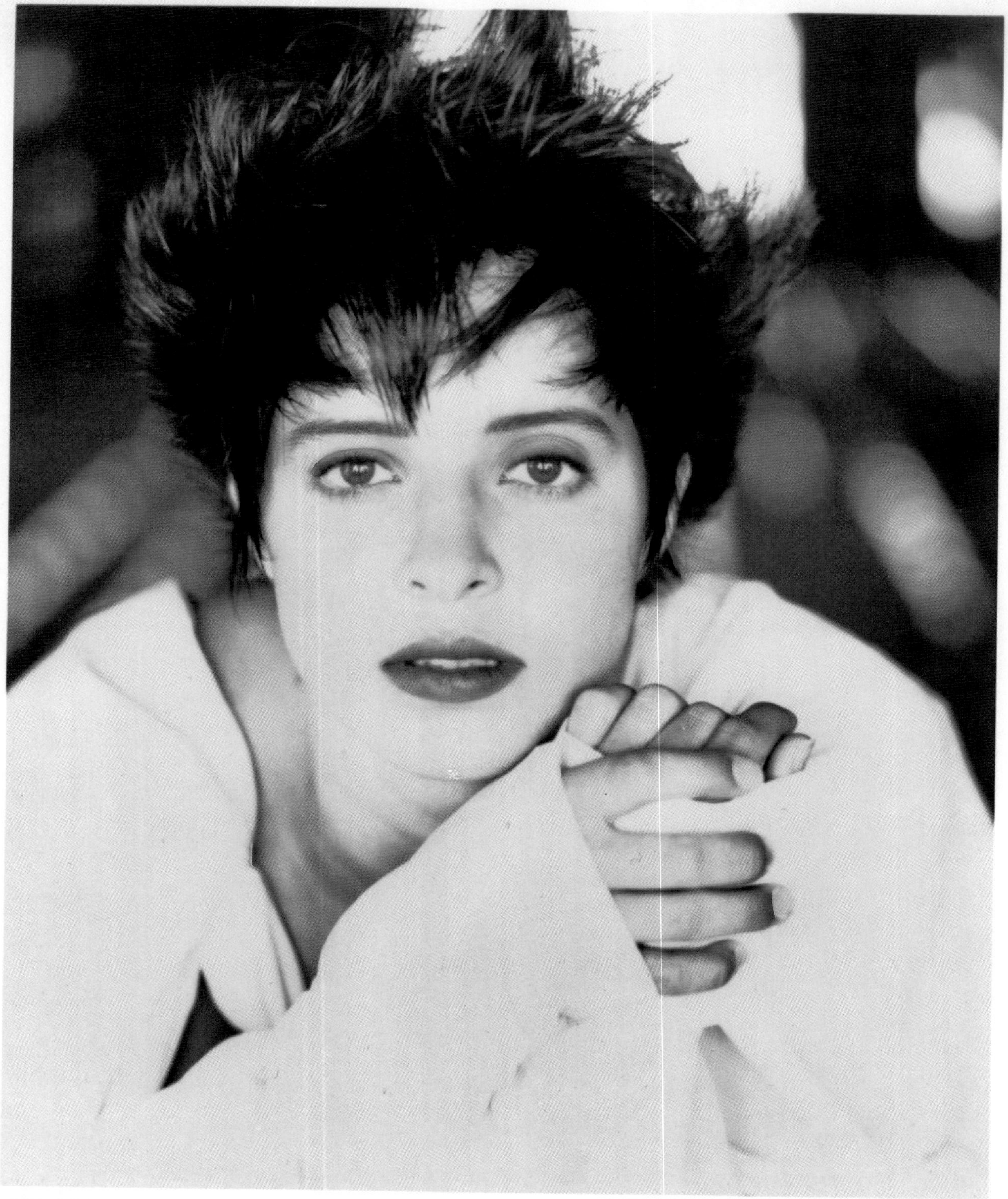

<u>Management</u>:

Rod Beaudoin

GERARD ENTERTAINMENT GROUP
4560 N. 60th Street
Milwaukee, WI 53218

tel: 414/463-6555

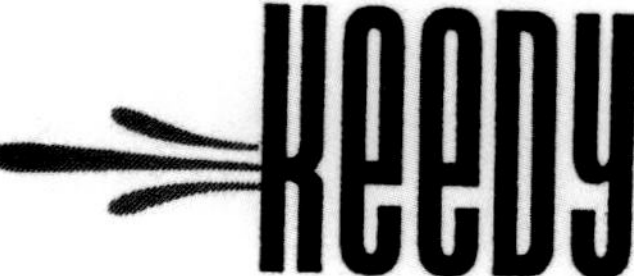

ARISTA™

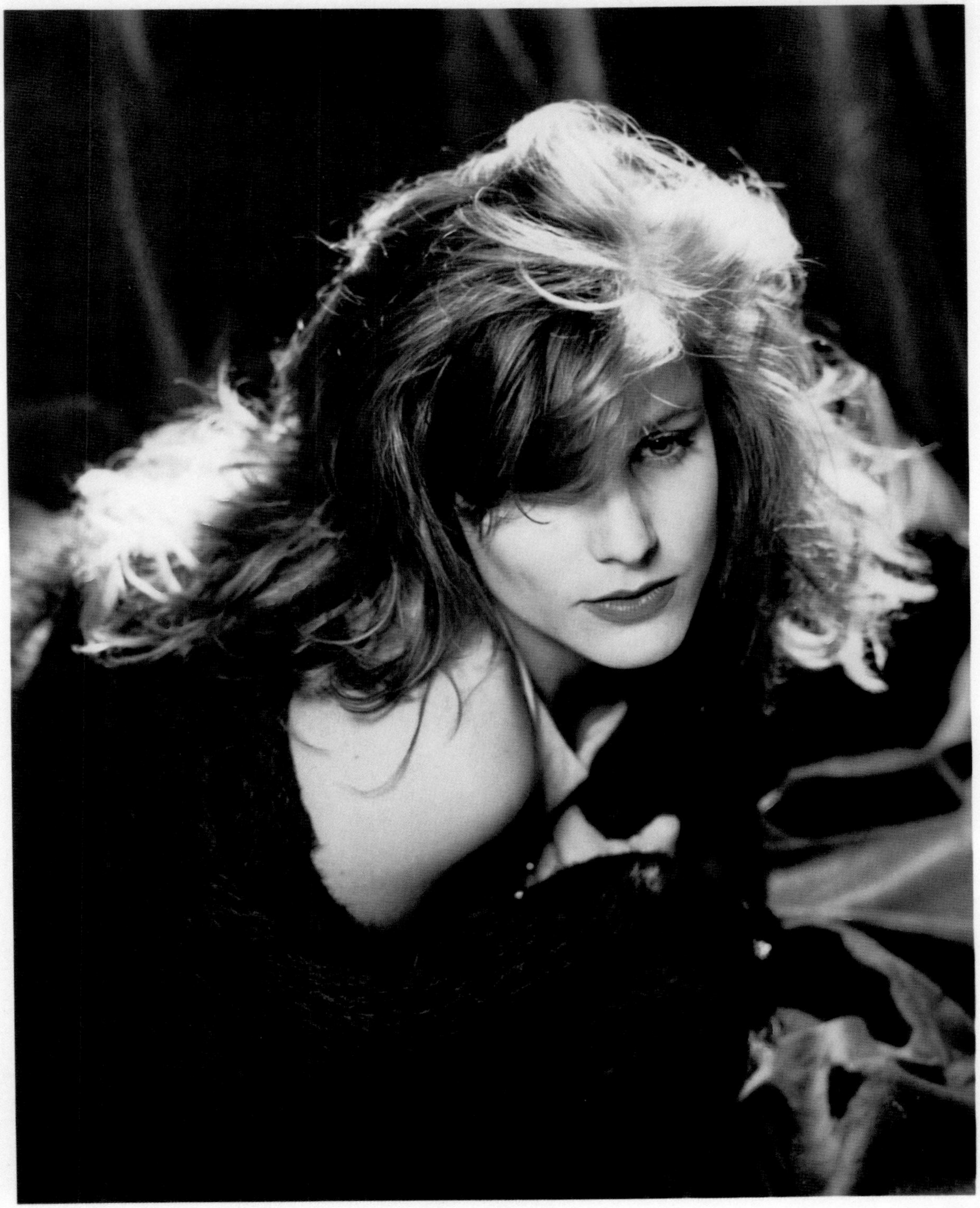

Photo Credit: Bernard Belair

tara kemp

© 1990 Warner Bros. Records/Permission to reproduce limited to editorial uses in newspapers and other regularly published periodicals and television news programming.

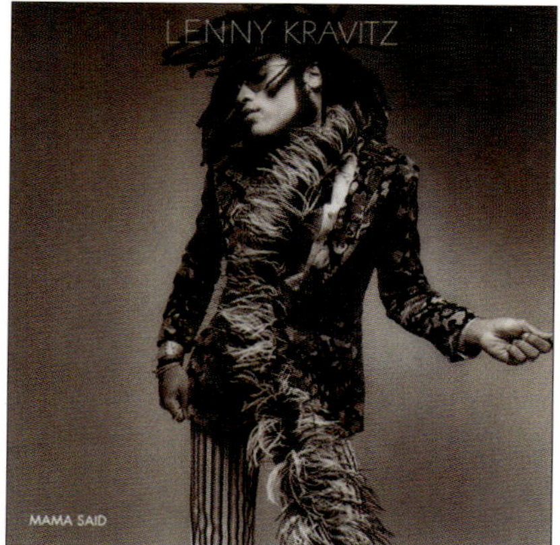

Mama Said, the first album by **Lenny Kravitz** to reach the Top 40, featured the soul ballad, "It Ain't Over 'til It's Over," the musician's most successful single.

Billboard 200: *Mama Said* (#39)
Billboard Hot 100: "It Ain't Over 'til It's Over" (#2); "Stand by My Woman" (#76)

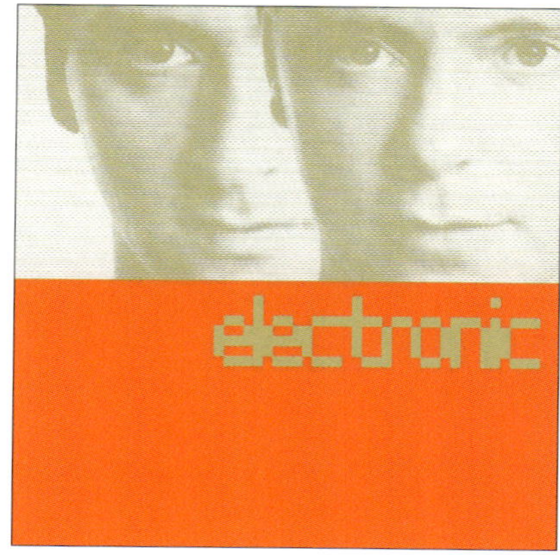

Electronic, a project formed by New Order's Bernard Sumner and ex-Smiths guitarist Johnny Marr, scored a No. 1 modern rock track with "Get the Message."

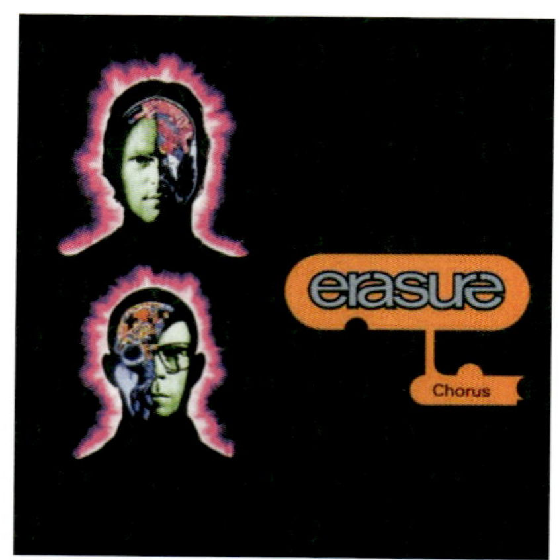

Chorus gave **Erasure**, the English synth-pop duo of singer-songwriter Andy Bell and keyboardist Vince Clarke, a charting US hit with the pristine title track.

Billboard 200: *Chorus* (#29)
Billboard Hot 100: "Chorus" (#83)

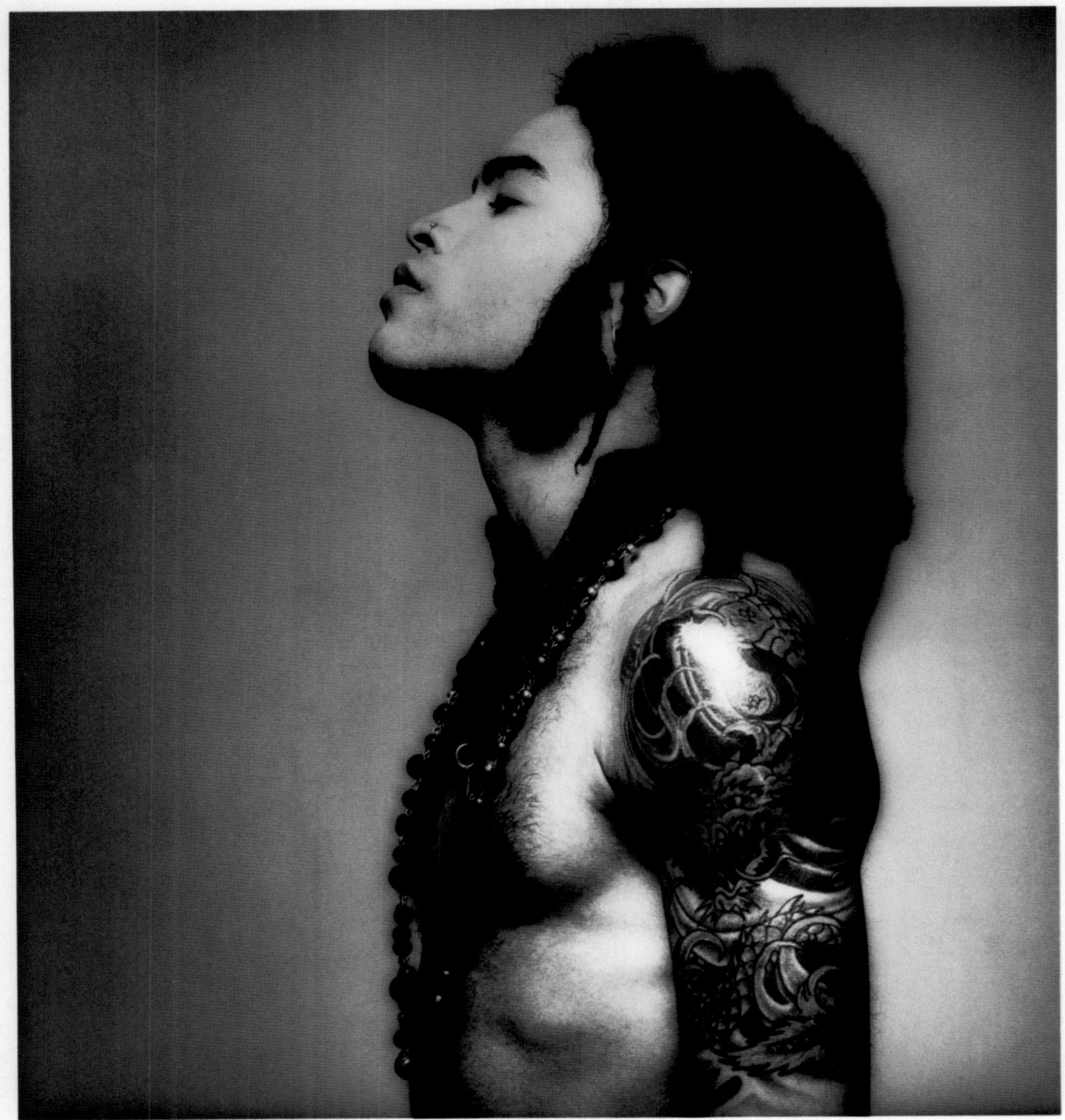

Photo Credit: James Calderaro 0291

LENNY KRAVITZ

Virgin

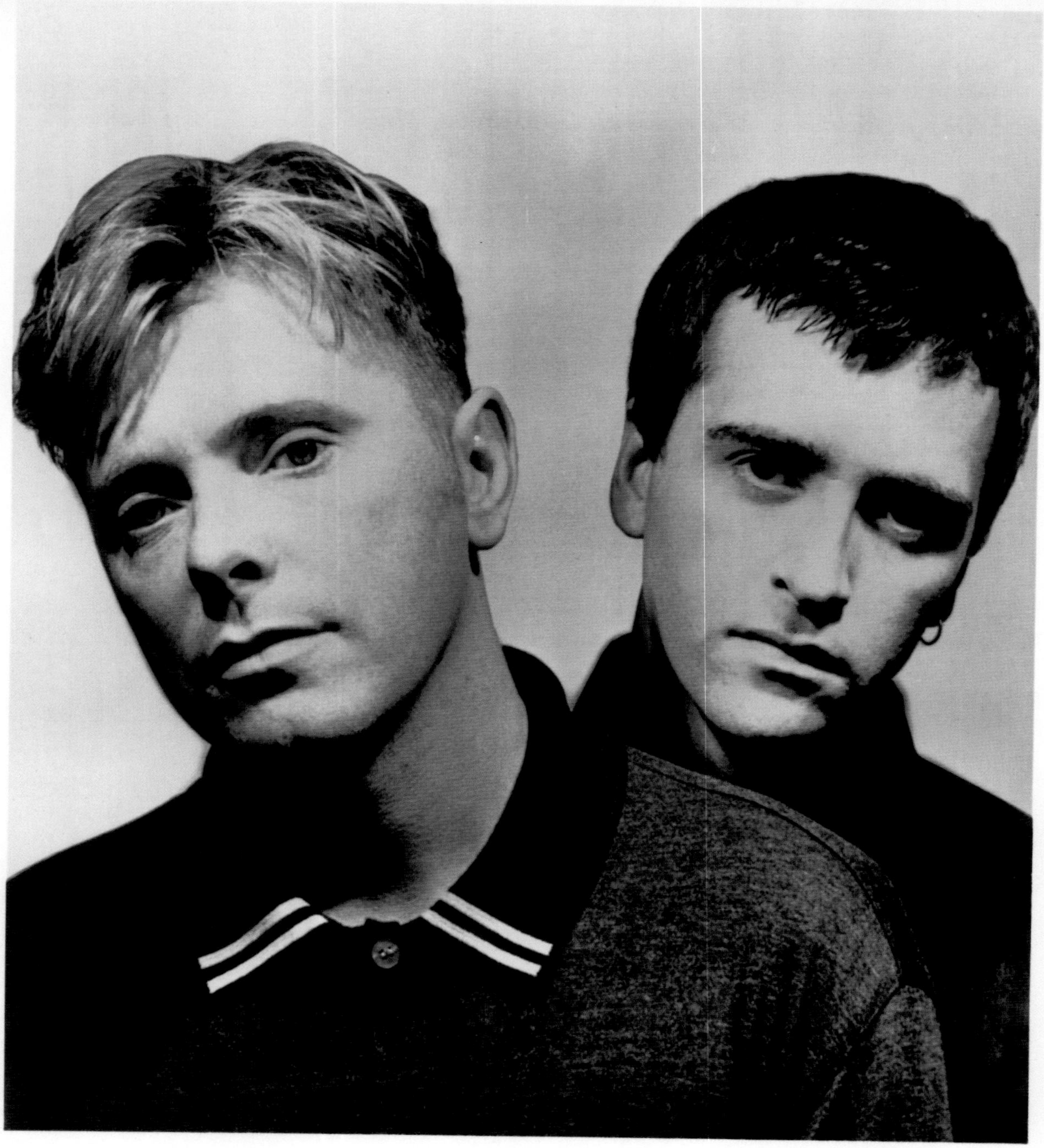

Photo Credit: Todd Fath

Bernard Sumner

Johnny Marr

Electronic

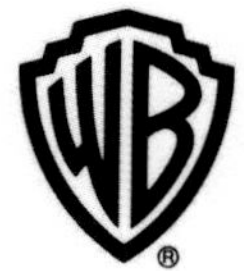

© 1991 Warner Bros. Records/Permission to reproduce limited to editorial uses in newspapers and other regularly published periodicals and television news programming.

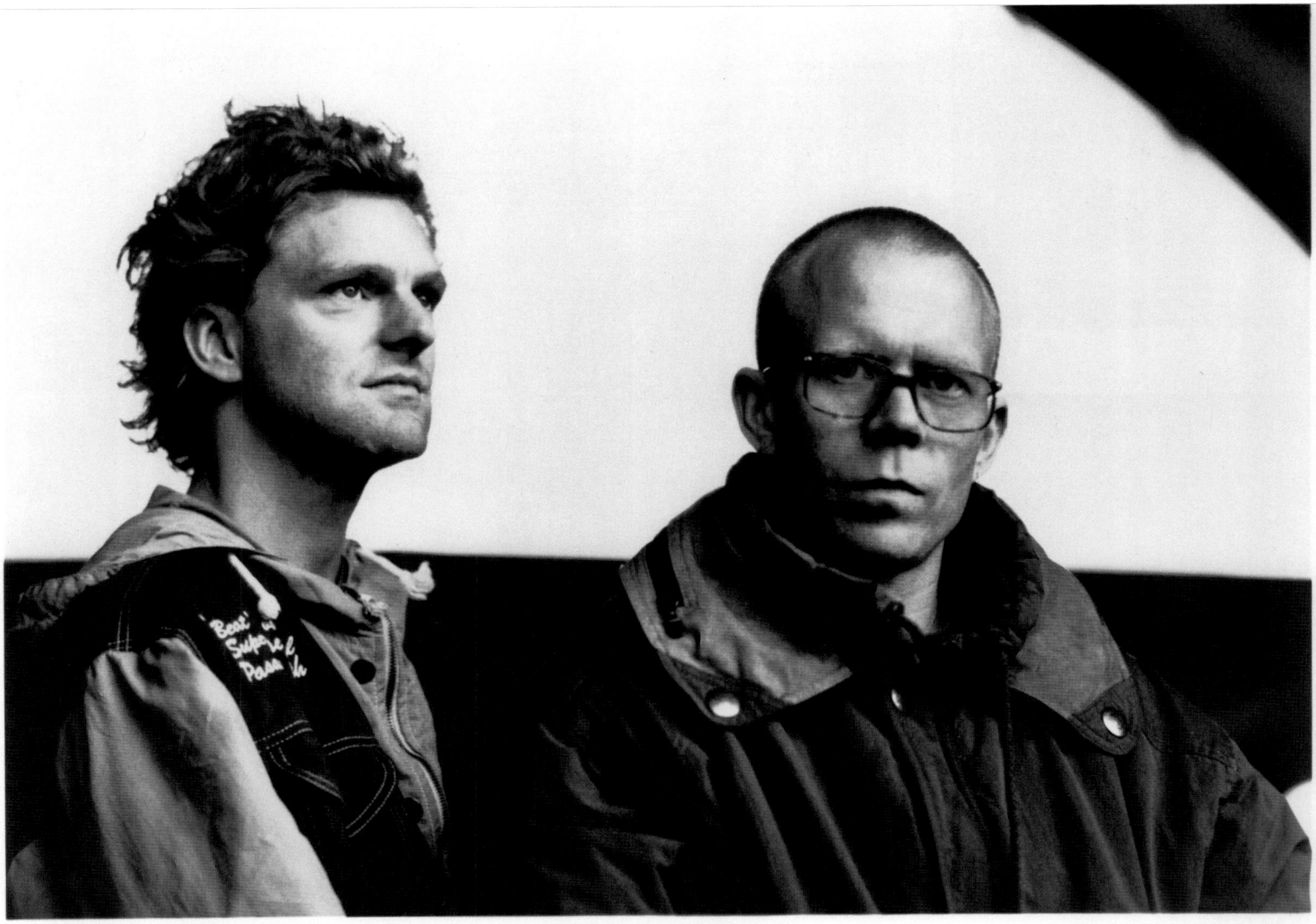

ERASURE

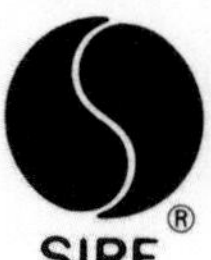

SIRE®

reprise®

© 1991 Reprise Records/Permission to reproduce limited to editorial uses in newspapers and other regularly published periodicals and television news programming.

Photo Credit: The Douglas Brothers

With "I've Been Thinking About You," **Londonbeat** scored a worldwide No. 1 hit, propelling the British dance-pop band to international prominence.

Billboard 200: *In the Blood* (#21)
Billboard Hot 100: "I've Been Thinking About You" (No. 1); "A Better Love" (#18)

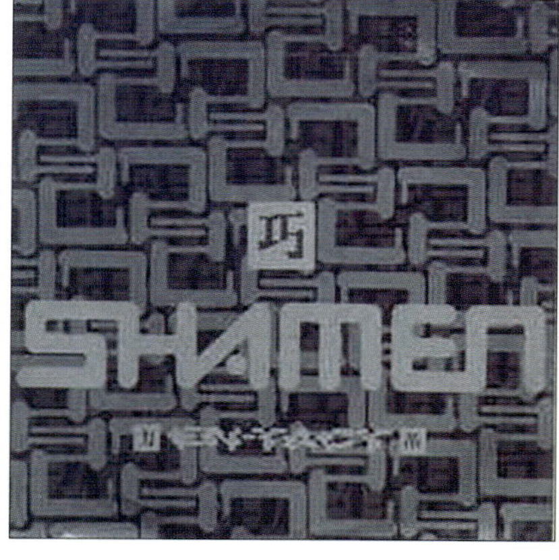

The Shamen's techno-pop anthem, "Move Any Mountain," was the Scottish electronic group's only Top 40 hit in the US, with a remix by the Beatmasters.

Billboard 200: *En-Tact* (#138)
Billboard Hot 100: "Move Any Mountain" (#38)

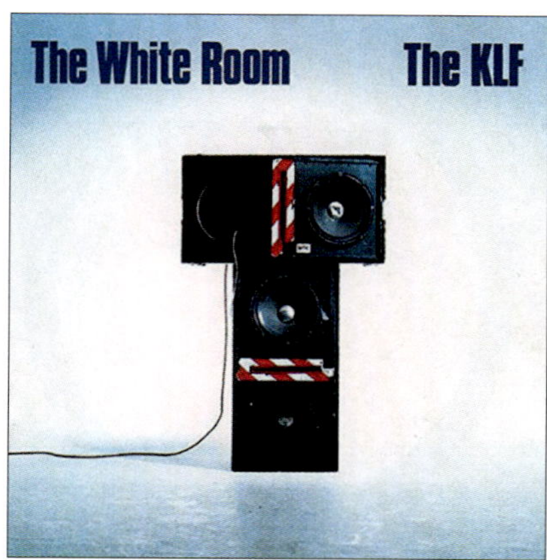

The KLF's version of "3 A.M. Eternal" and a "Justified & Ancient" cover with country queen Tammy Wynette were the British electronic group's last releases.

Billboard 200: *The White Room* (#39)
Billboard Hot 100: "3 A.M. Eternal" (#5); "What Time Is Love?" (#57); "Justified & Ancient" (#11)

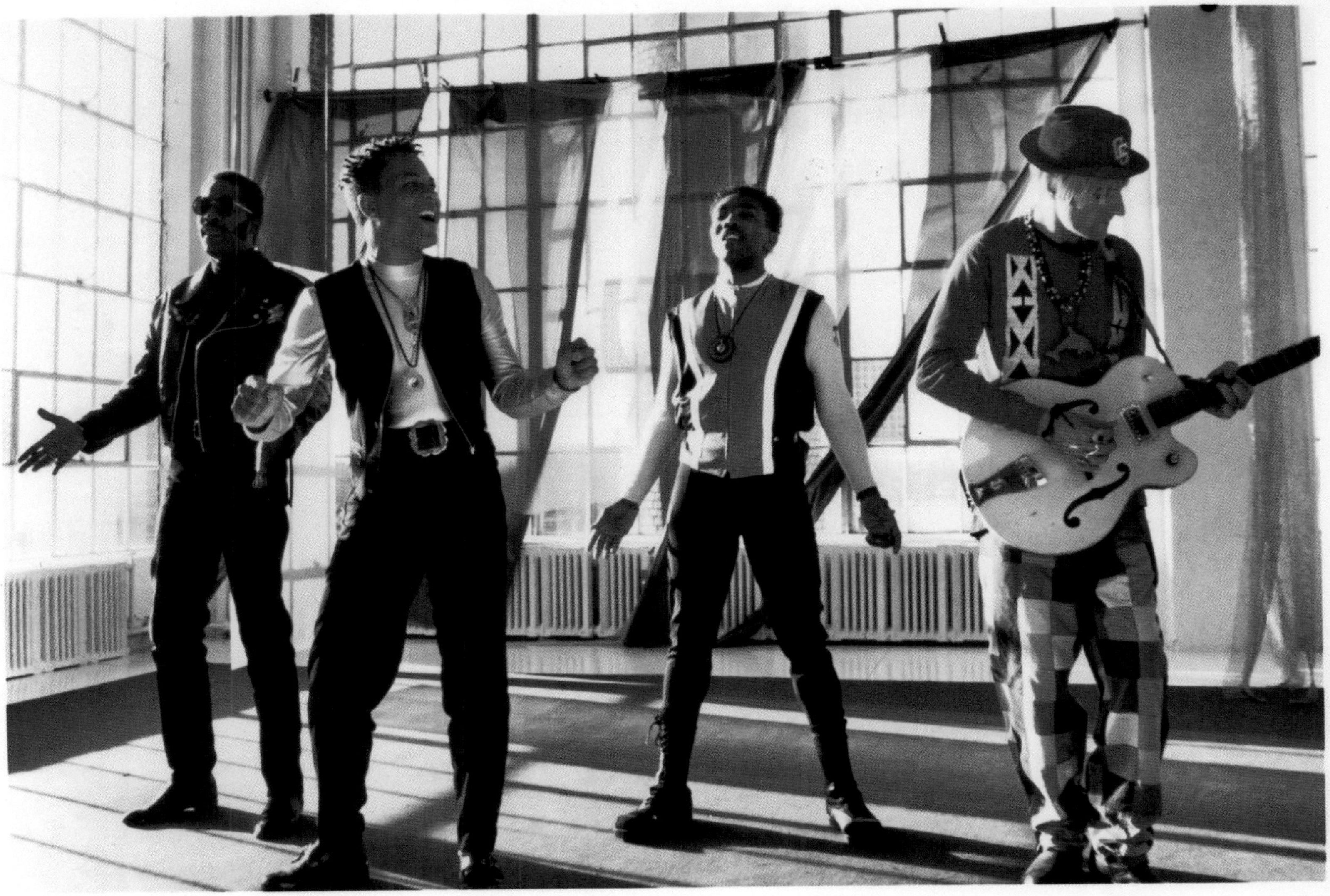

Photo credit: Daniel Root

1/91

LONDONBEAT

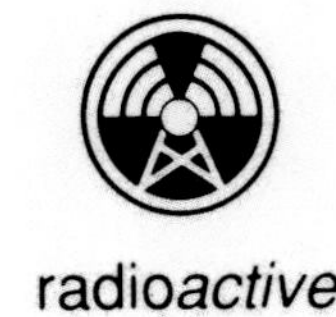

radio*active*

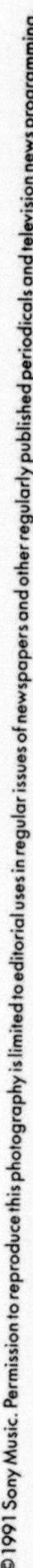
© 1991 Sony Music. Permission to reproduce this photography is limited to editorial uses in regular issues of newspapers and other regularly published periodicals and television news programming.

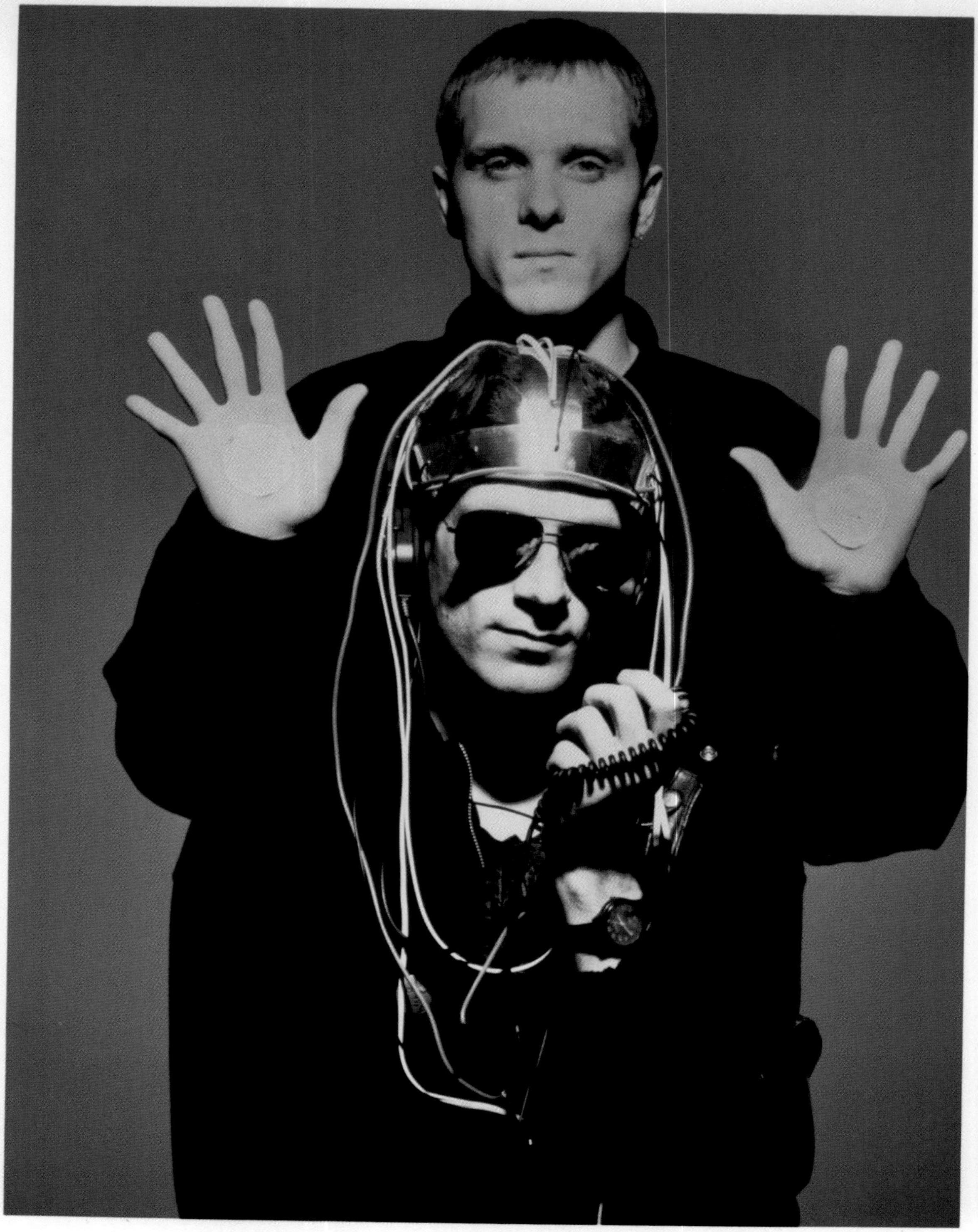

PHOTO CREDIT: STEVE DOWBLE

TOP: MR. C (RAPPER)   BOTTOM: COLIN SHAMEN (PRODUCER, VOCALIST)

THE SHAMEN

9110

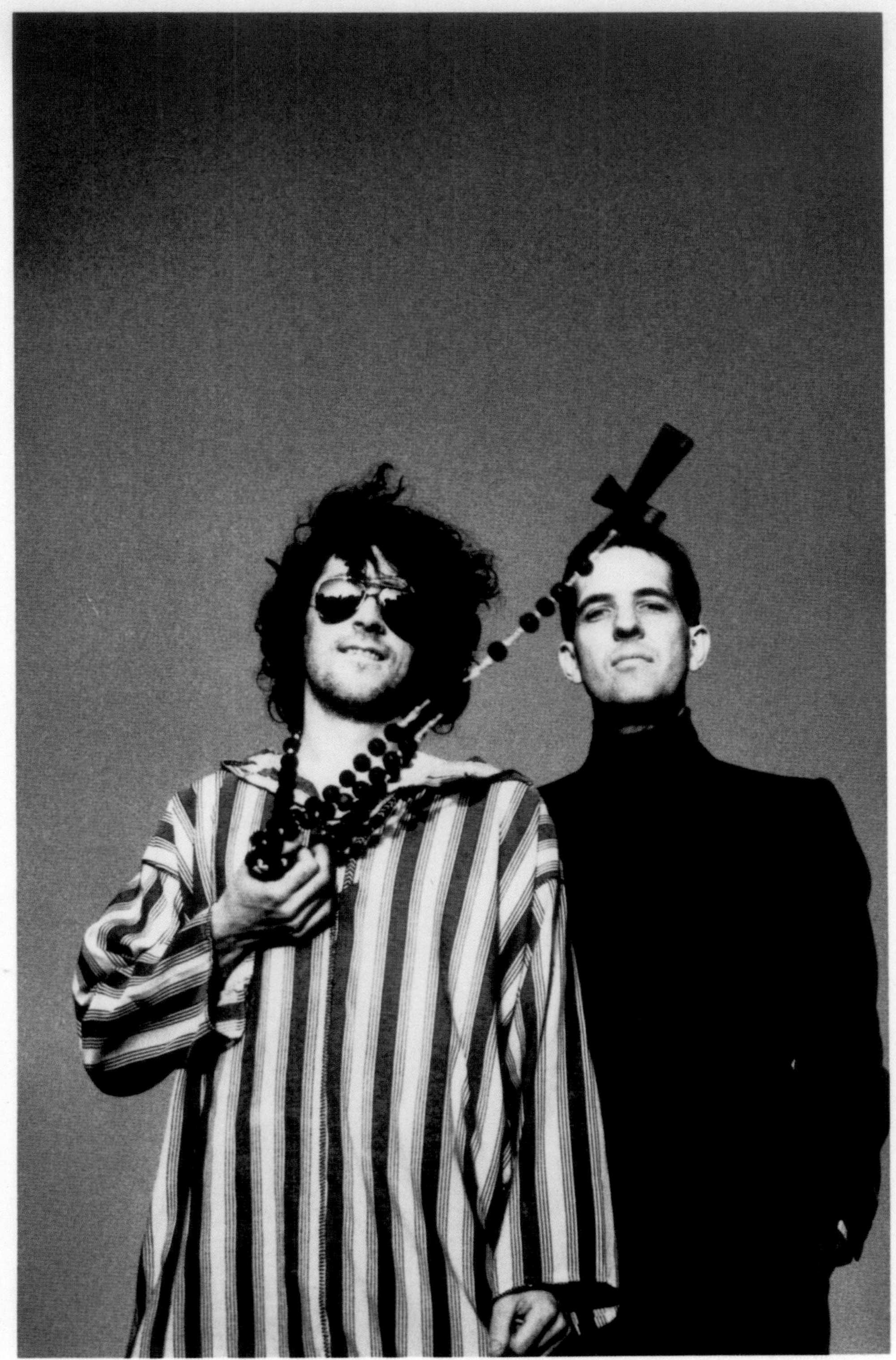

The KLF Jimmy Cauty Bill Drummond ARISTA™

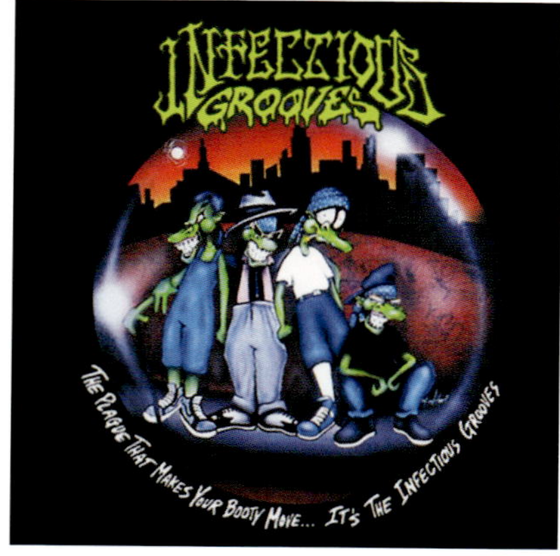

"Therapy" by **Infectious Grooves**, a funk-metal project led by Suicidal Tendencies frontman Mike Muir, featured Ozzy Osbourne screeching the chorus.

Billboard 200: *The Plague That Makes Your Booty Move... It's the Infectious Grooves* (#198)

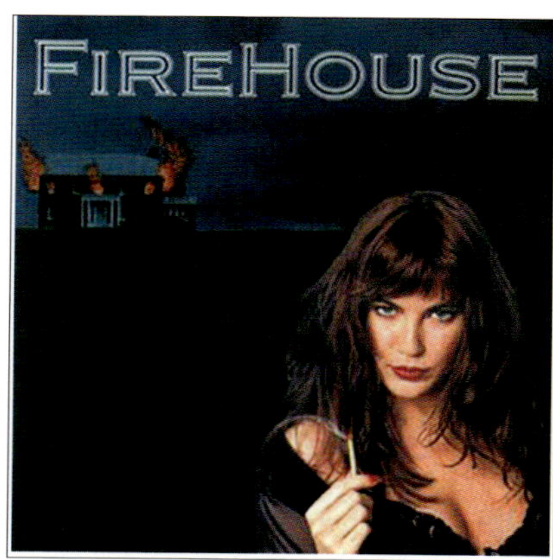

"Love of a Lifetime," the lone power ballad from **FireHouse**'s self-titled debut album, landed the pop-metal band a Top 10 hit and soaring sales.

Billboard 200: *FireHouse* (#21)
Billboard Hot 100: "Don't Treat Me Bad" (#19); "Love of a Lifetime" (#3); "All She Wrote" (#58)

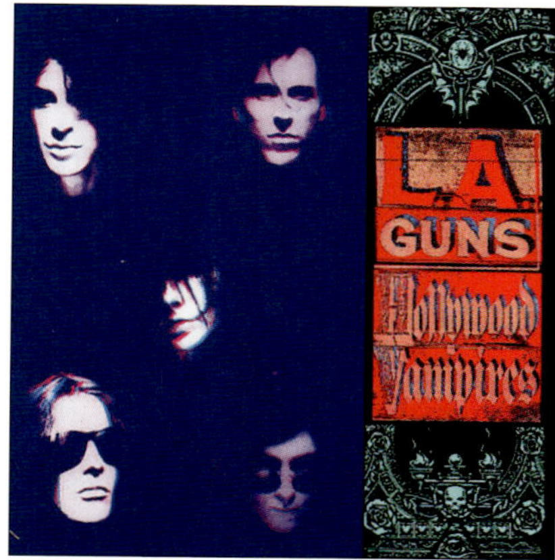

With the arrival of grunge, **L.A. Guns**' glam-metal style fell out of commercial favor soon after the release of *Hollywood Vampires*, the band's third album.

Billboard 200: *Hollywood Vampires* (#42)

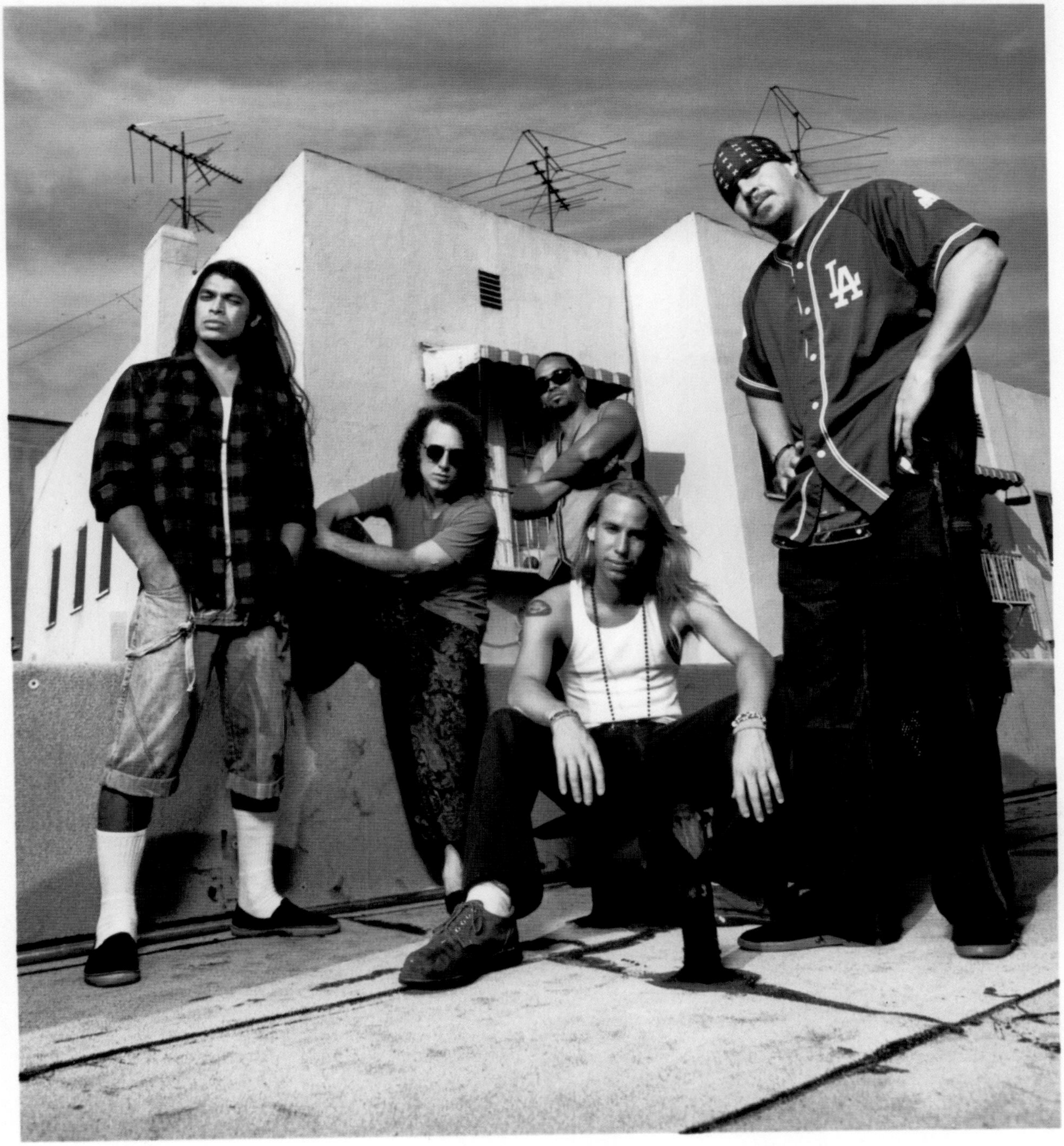

Photo Credit: Ross Hallin

L to R: Robert Trujillo, Stephen Perkins, Dean Pleasants (standing), Adam Siegel, Mike Muir

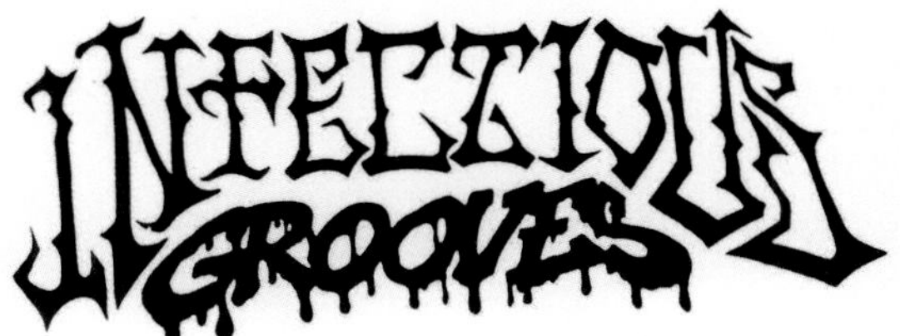

© 1991 Sony Music. Permission to reproduce this photography is limited to editorial uses in regular issues of newspapers and other regularly published periodicals and television news programming.

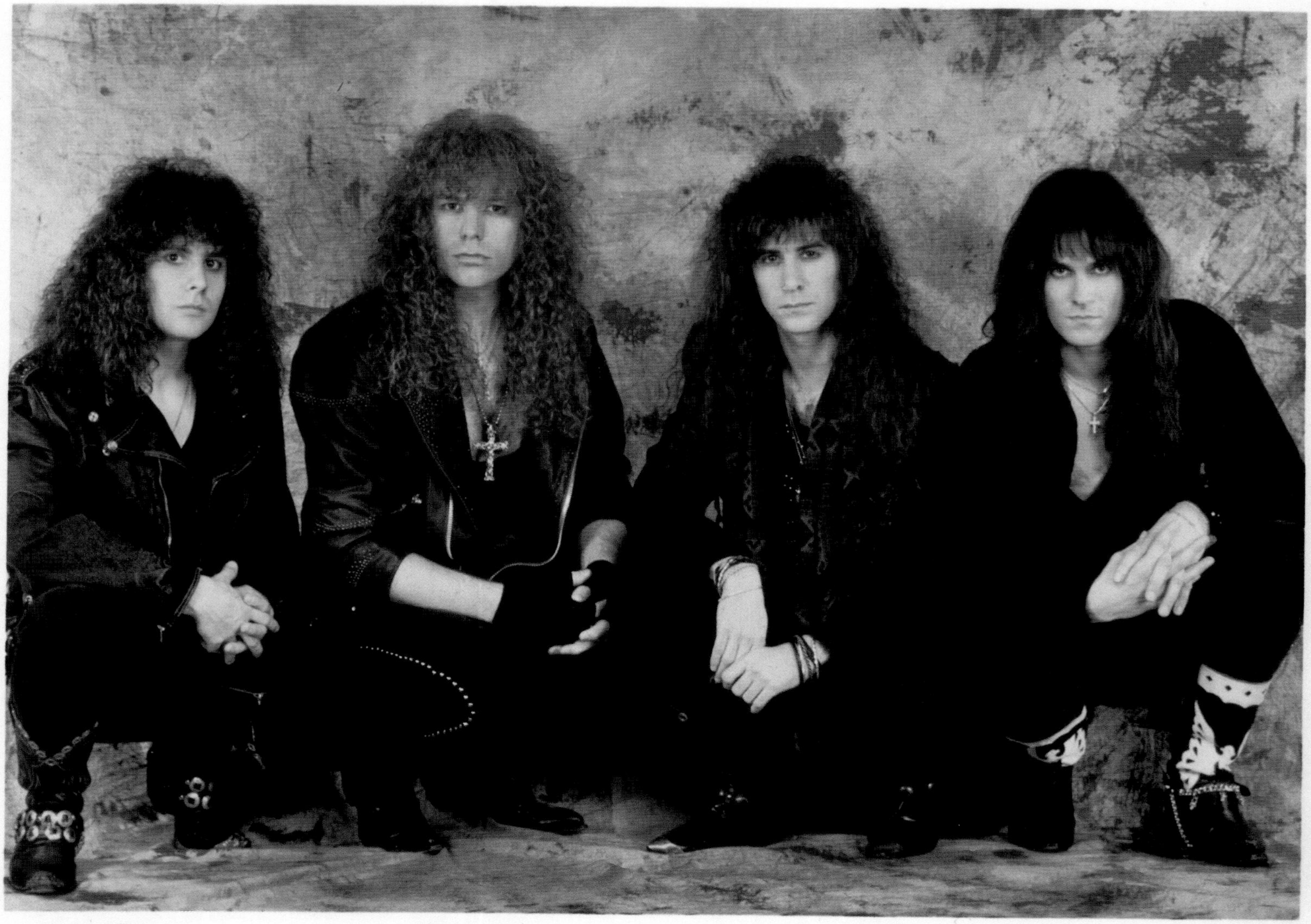

© 1991 Sony Music. Permission to reproduce this photography is limited to editorial uses in regular issues of newspapers and other regularly published periodicals and television news programming.

PHOTO CREDIT: TODD KAPLAN

MICHAEL FOSTER
(DRUMS)

PERRY RICHARDSON
(BASS GUITAR)

C.J. SNARE
(LEAD VOCALS)

BILL LEVERTY
(GUITARS)

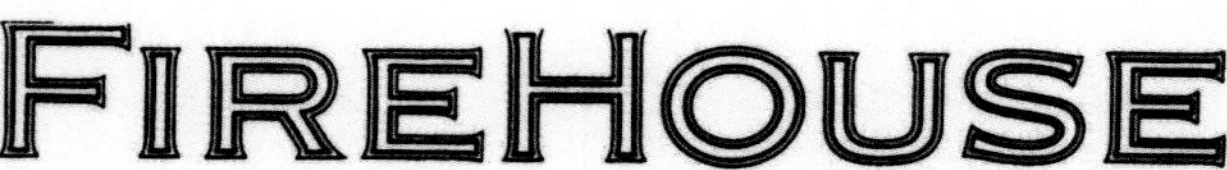

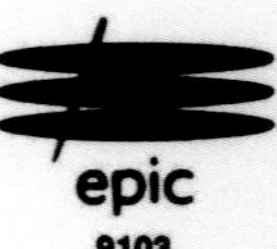

9103

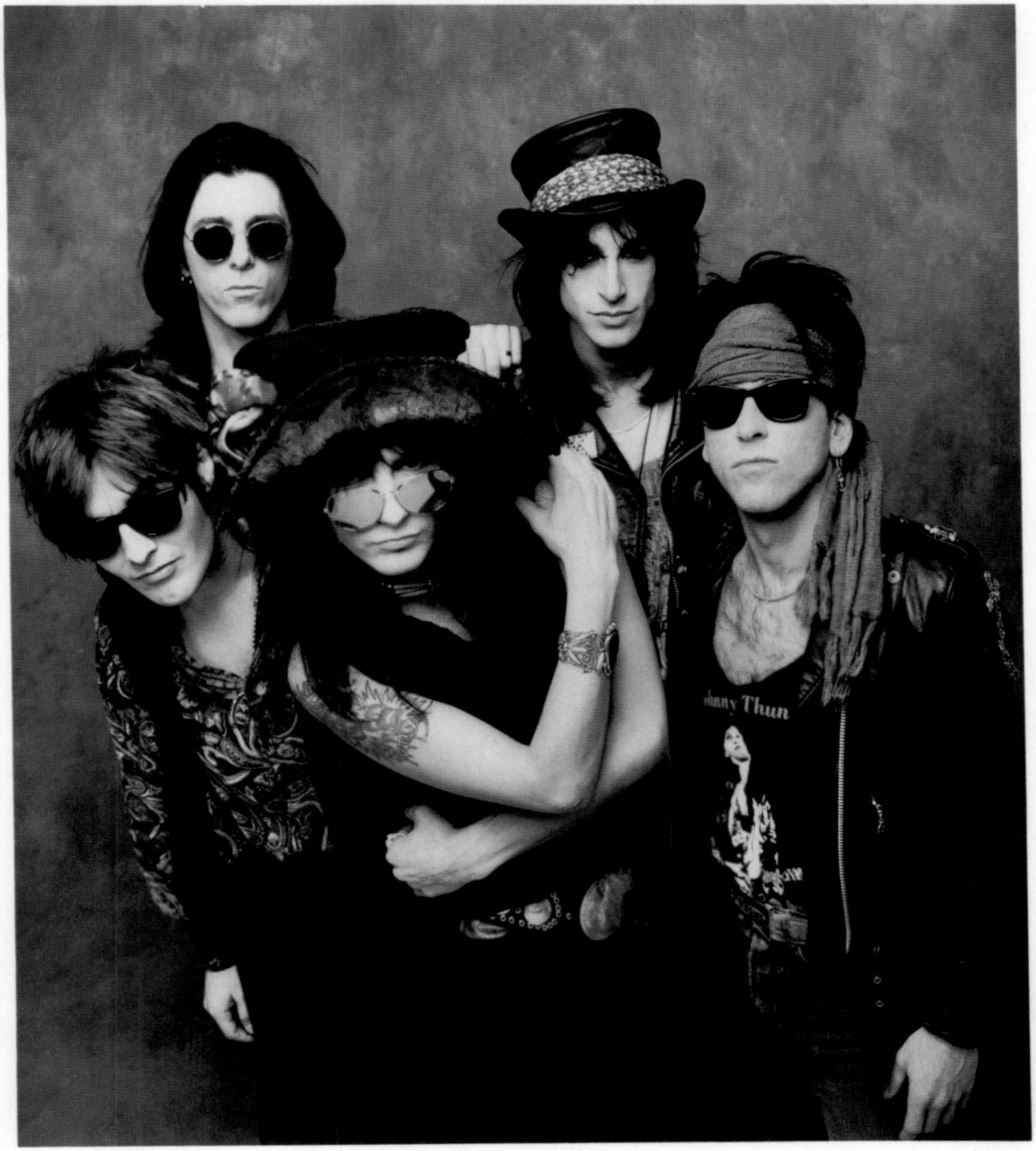

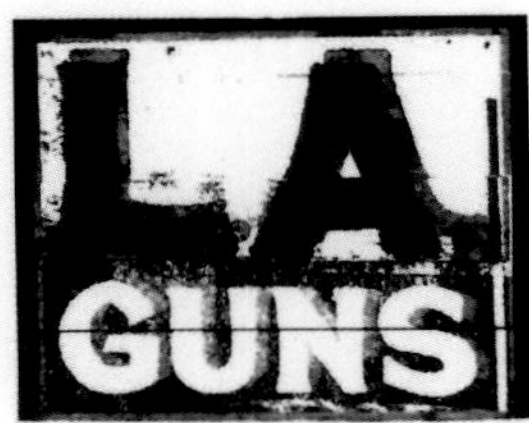
L.A.
GUNS

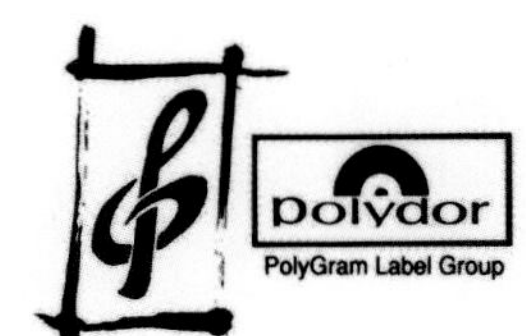
Polydor
PolyGram Label Group

"Pop Goes the Weasel," a dis of fellow Caucasian rapper Vanilla Ice for cultural theft, gave **3rd Bass** a No. 1 track on *Billboard*'s Top Rap Singles chart.

Billboard 200: *Derelicts of Dialect* (#19)
Billboard Hot 100: "Pop Goes the Weasel" (#29)

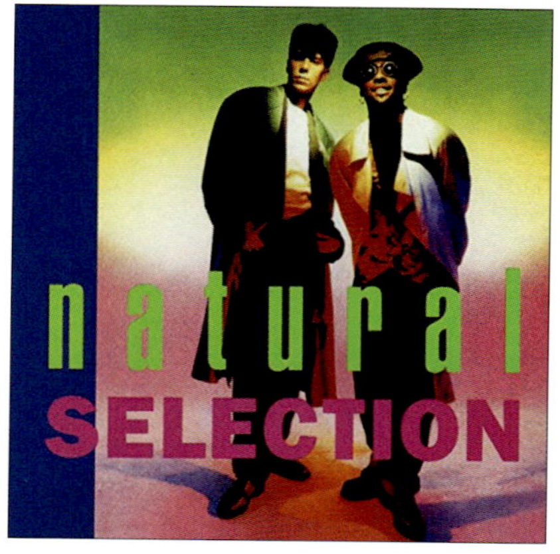

Natural Selection's "Do Anything" was given a national release after it caught on at a Minnesota radio station, and the song reached #2 on the pop charts.

Billboard Hot 100: "Do Anything" (#2); "Hearts Don't Think (They Feel)!" (#28)

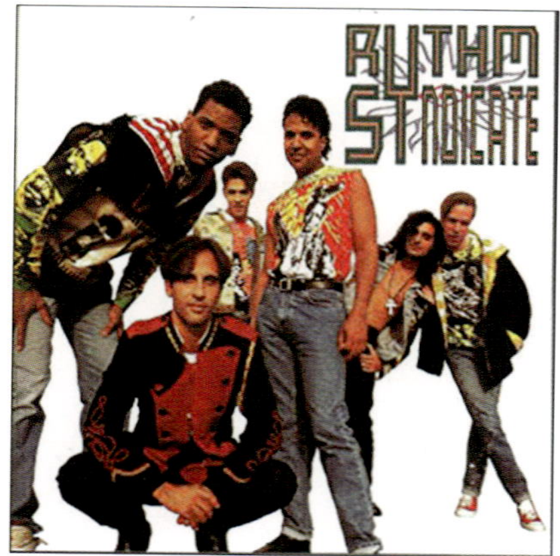

Rythm Syndicate, a six-piece multiracial dance-rock band from Connecticut, enjoyed two irresistible summer radio hits, "P.A.S.S.I.O.N." and "Hey Donna."

Billboard Hot 100: "P.A.S.S.I.O.N." (#2); "Hey Donna" (#13); "Blinded by Love" (#76)

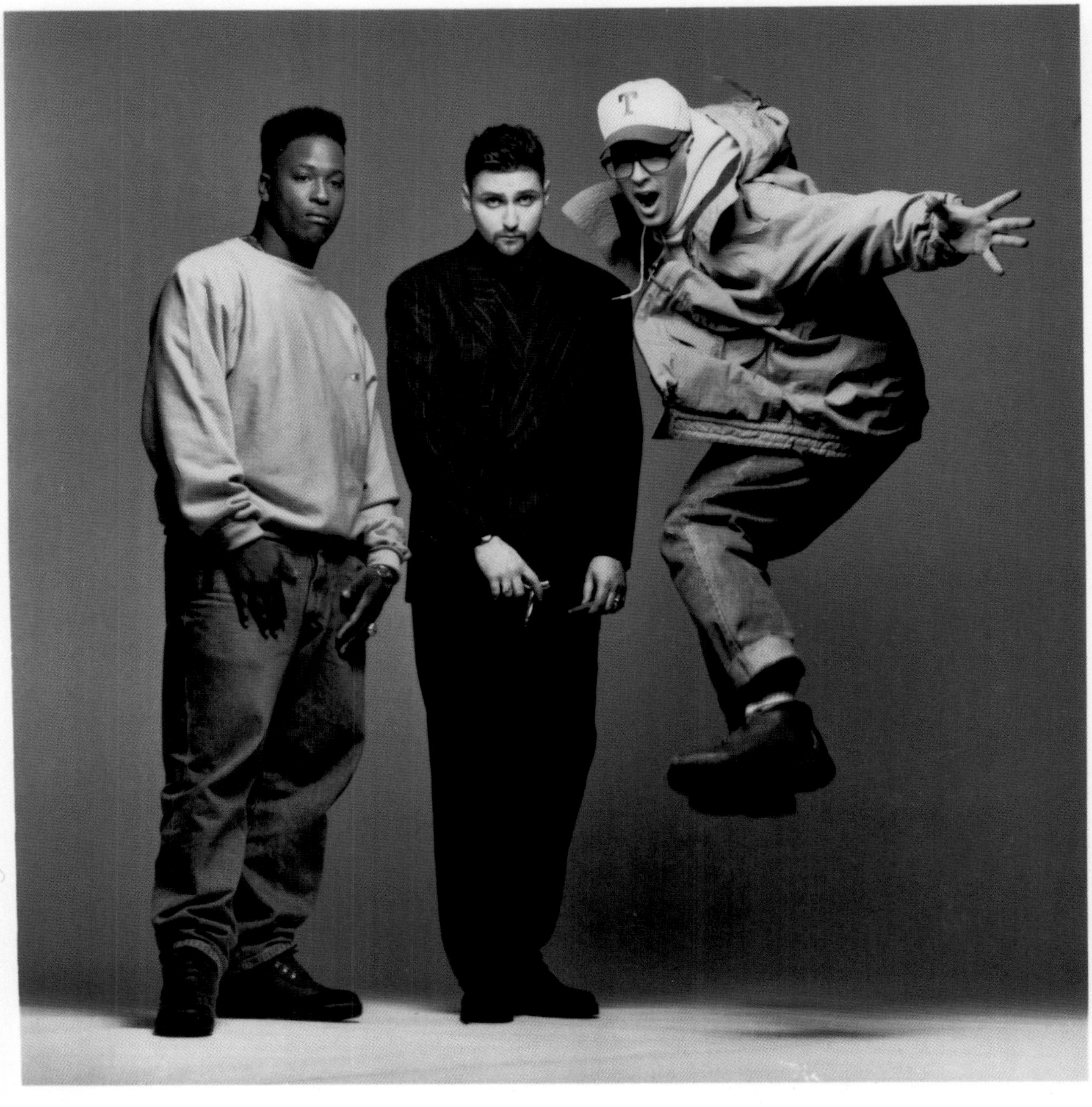

© 1991 Sony Music. Permission to reproduce this photography is limited to editorial uses in regular issues of newspapers and other regularly published periodicals and television news programming.

PHOTOGRAPH: MICHAEL LAVINE

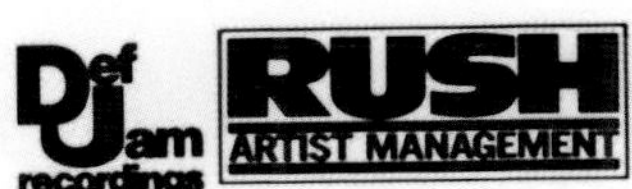

3RD BASS

Columbia
9104

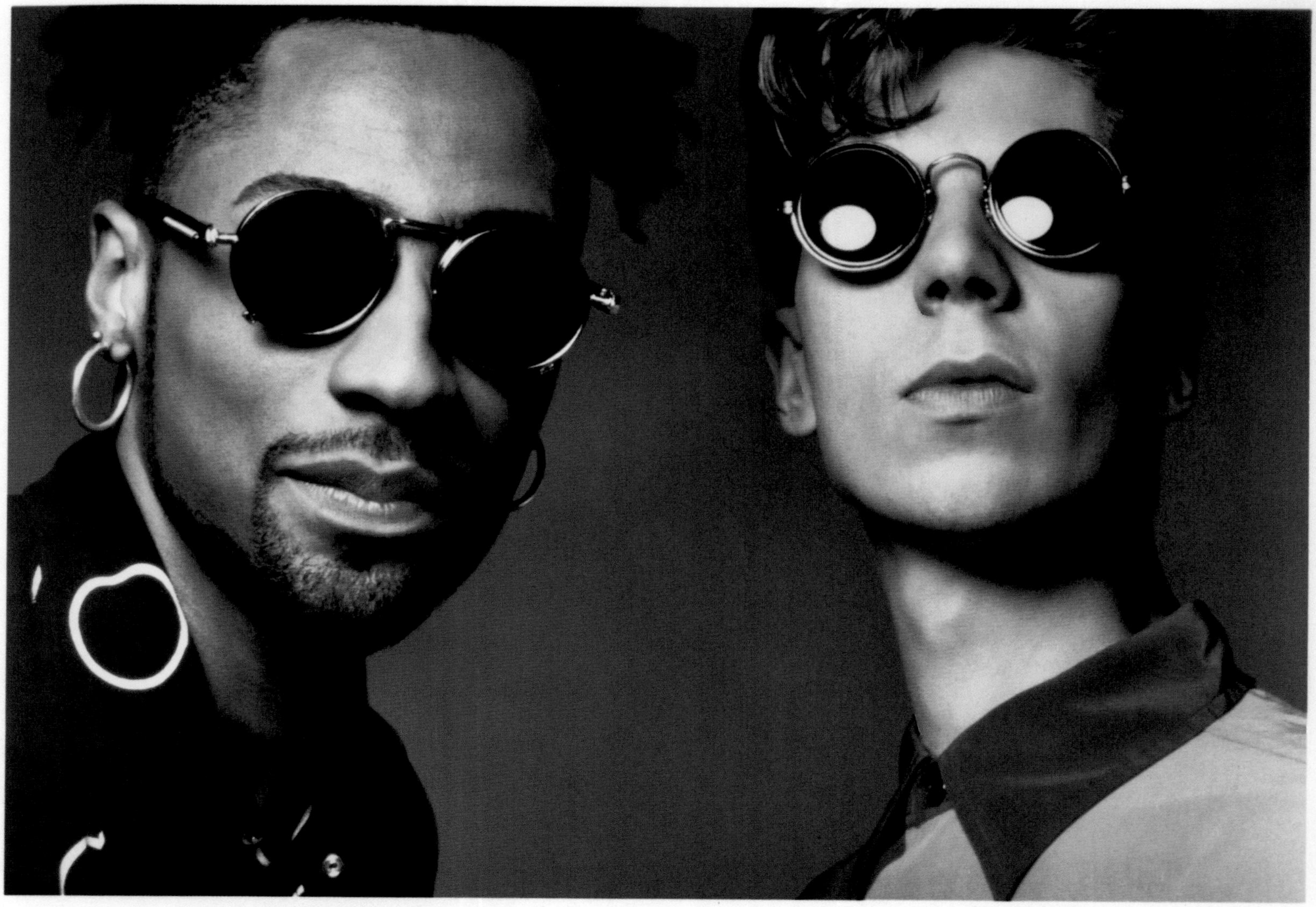

FREDERICK THOMAS

ELLIOT ERICKSON

Photo © MICHAEL LAVINE

natural
SELECTION

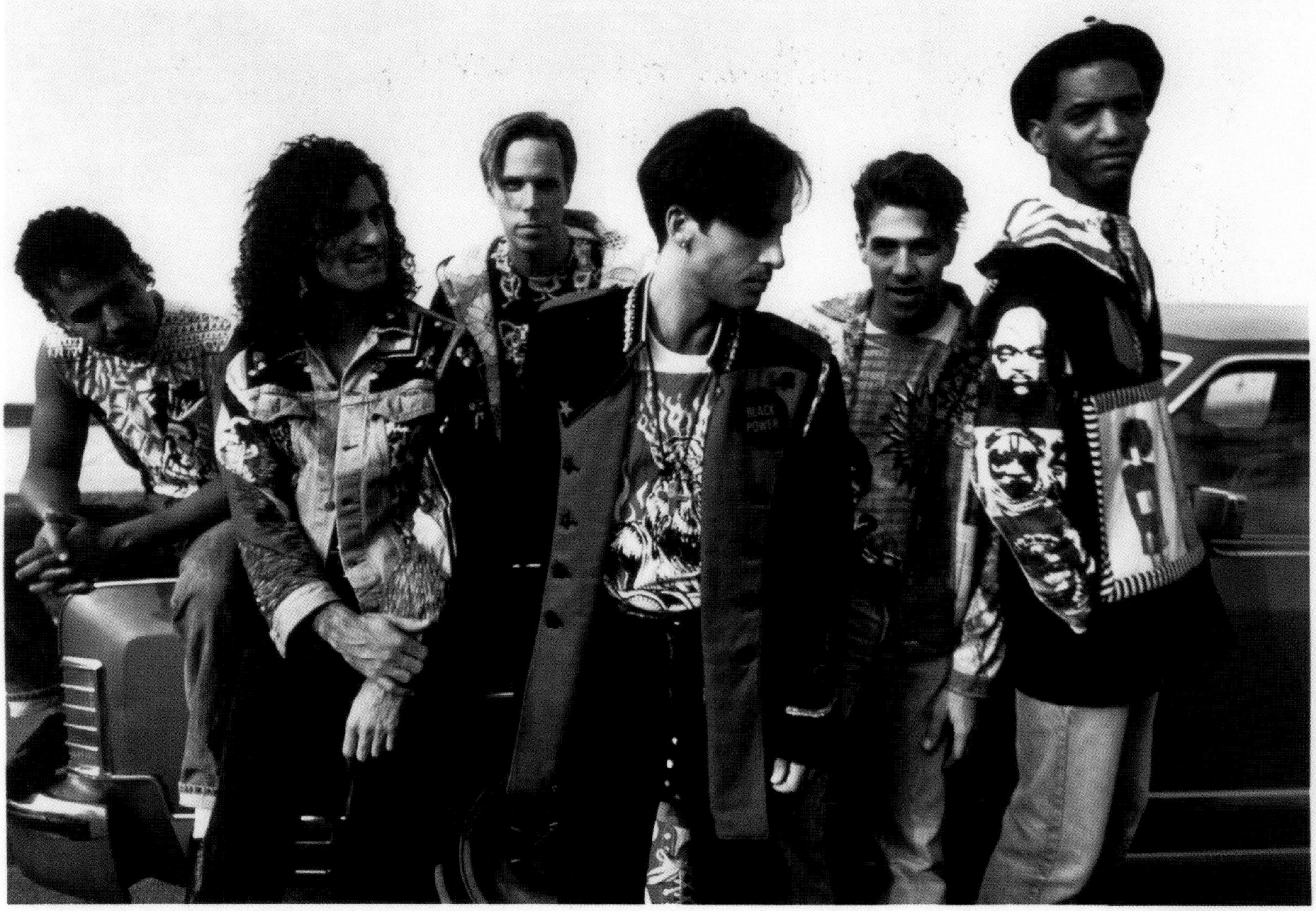

RYTHM SYNDICATE

Photo credit: Dewey Nicks

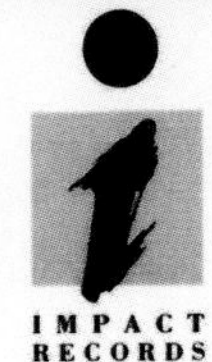

From *Rush Street*, his third consecutive multi-platinum album, "Keep Coming Back" and "Hazard" kept **Richard Marx** on top of the adult contemporary charts.

Billboard 200: *Rush Street* (#35)
Billboard Hot 100: "Keep Coming Back" (#12);
"Hazard" (#9); "Take This Heart" (#20);
"Chains Around My Heart" (#44)

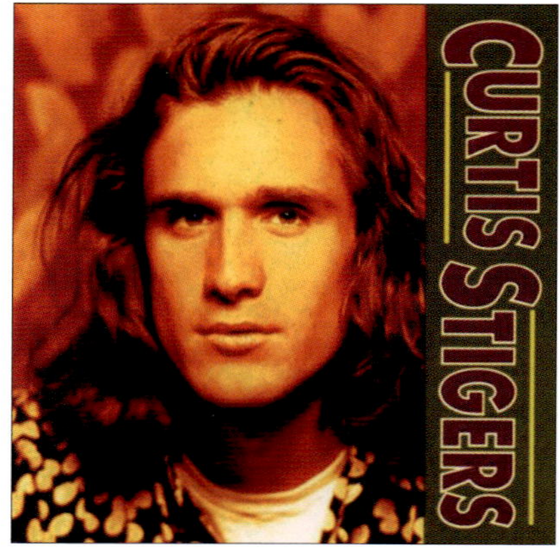

Jazz singer, songwriter and saxophonist **Curtis Stigers** achieved an international hit with the emotional "I Wonder Why," from his self-titled debut album.

Billboard 200: *Curtis Stigers* (#101)
Billboard Hot 100: "I Wonder Why" (#9); "You're All That Matters to Me" (#98); "Sleeping with the Lights On" (#96)

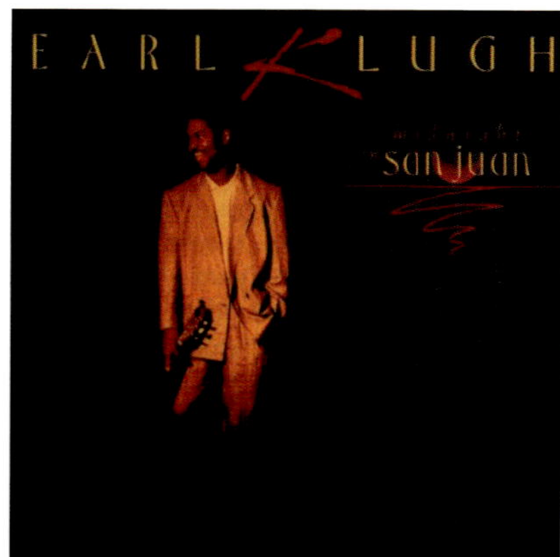

With an emphasis on Latin and Caribbean elements, acoustic guitarist **Earl Klugh**'s *Midnight in San Juan* hit No. 1 on the contemporary jazz album charts.

Billboard 200: *Midnight in San Juan* (#189)

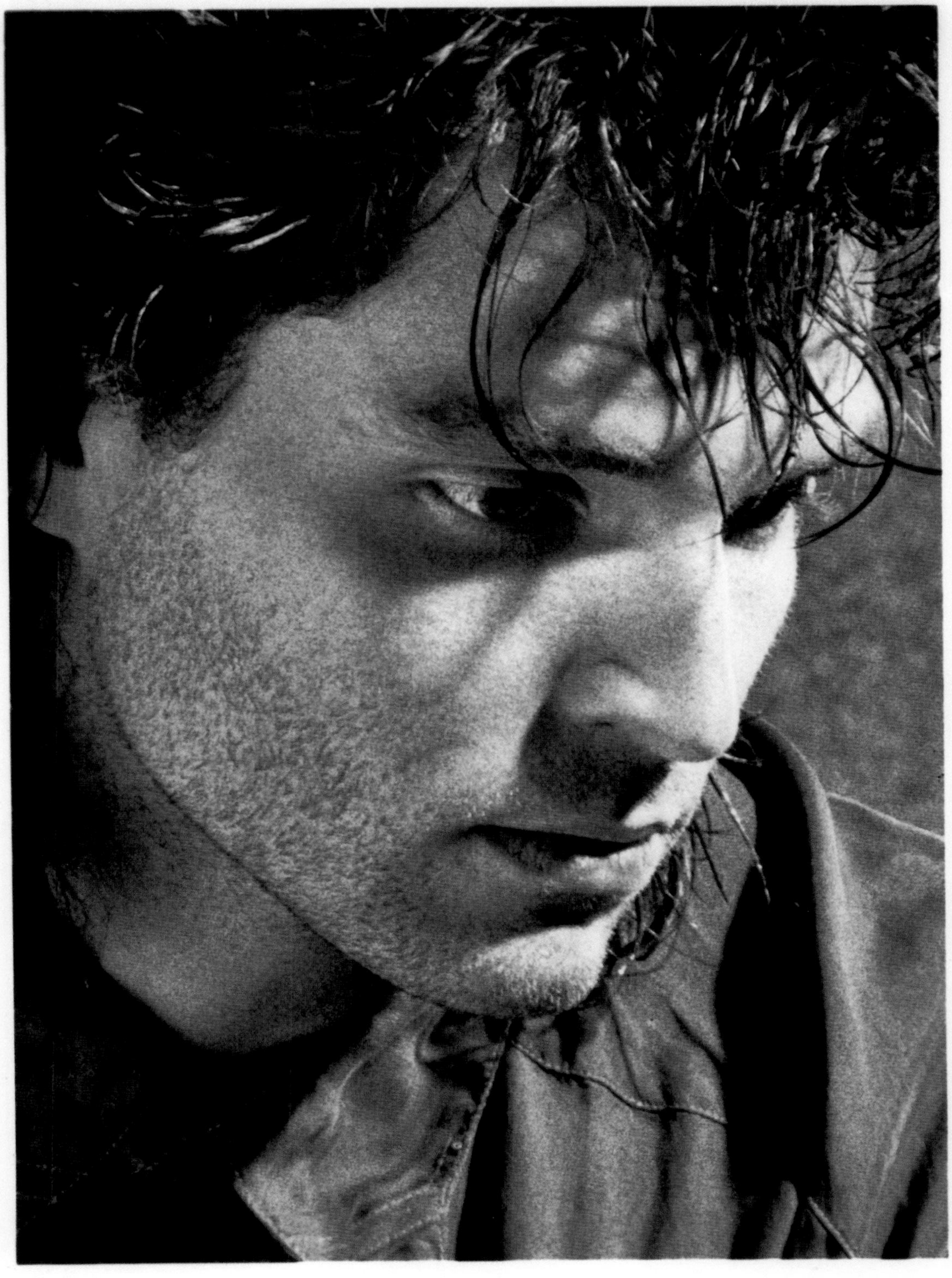

RICHARD MARX

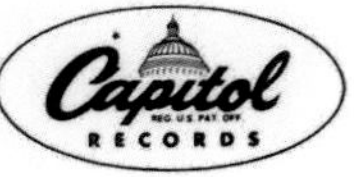

PHOTO: NELS ISRAELSON / 1991

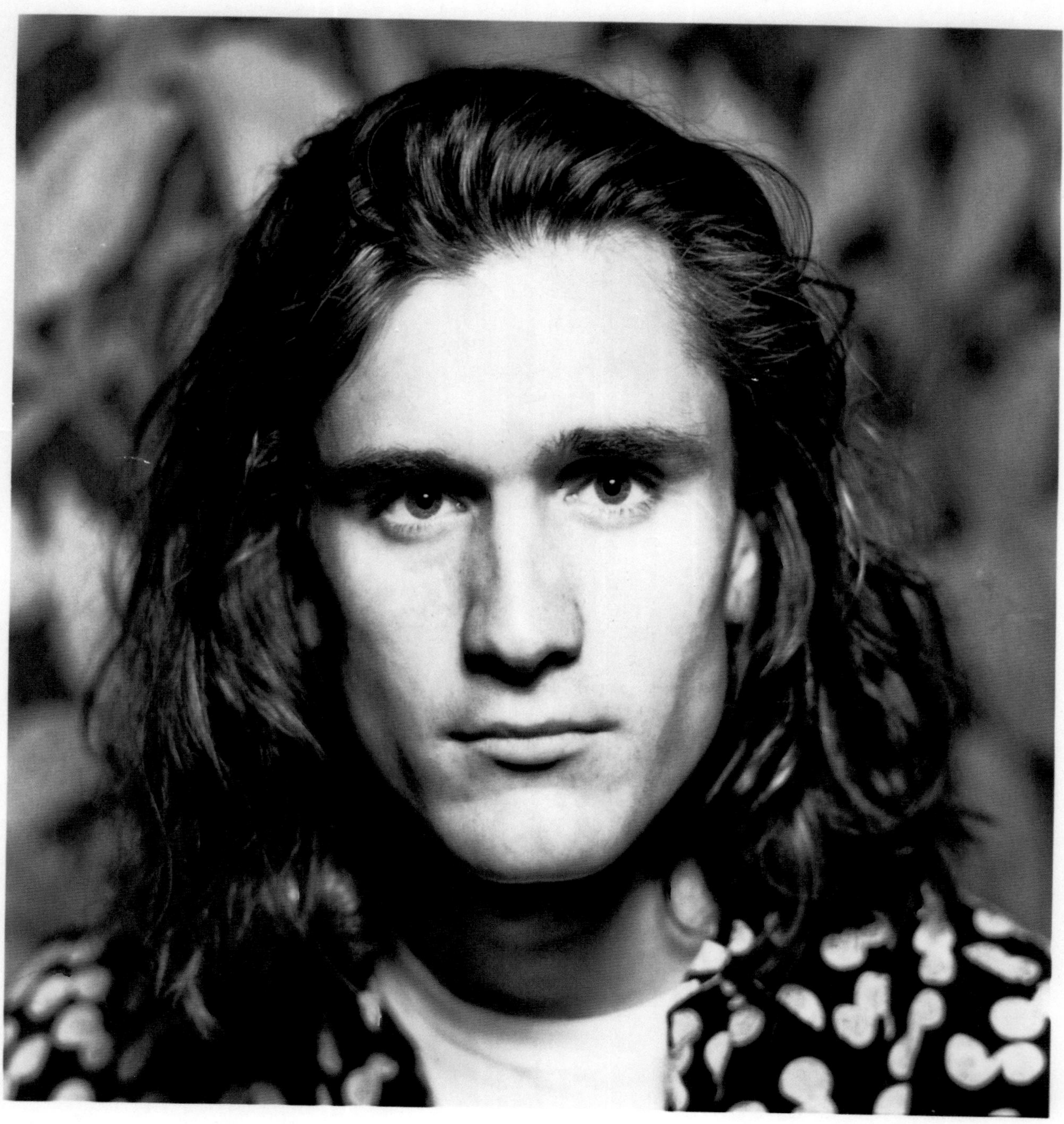

C. WINSTON SIMONE
MANAGEMENT
1780 BROADWAY
SUITE 1201
NEW YORK, NY 10019
212 974-5322
FAX 212 974-3988

CURTIS STIGERS

ARISTA™

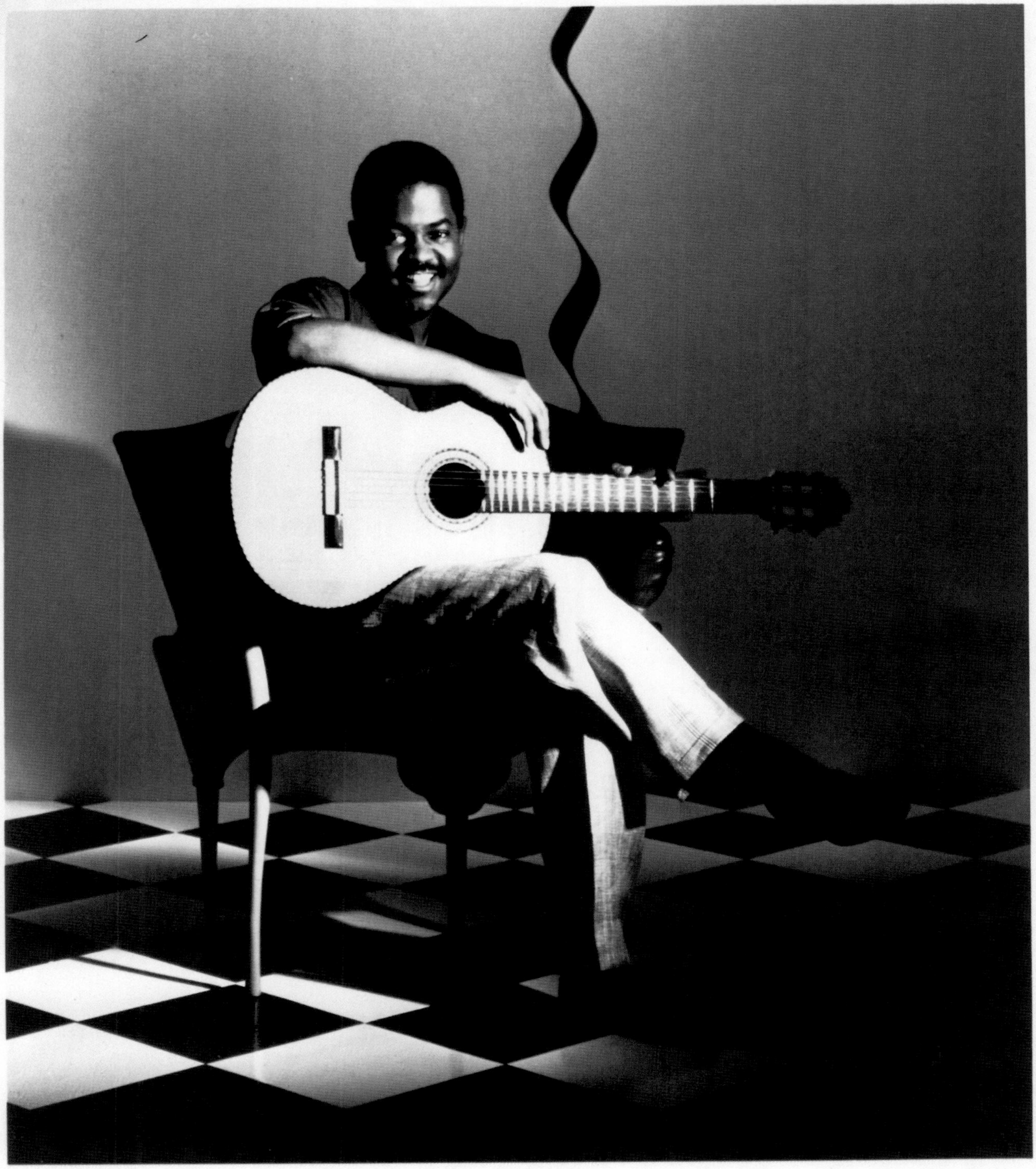

Photo Credit: Adriel Givens

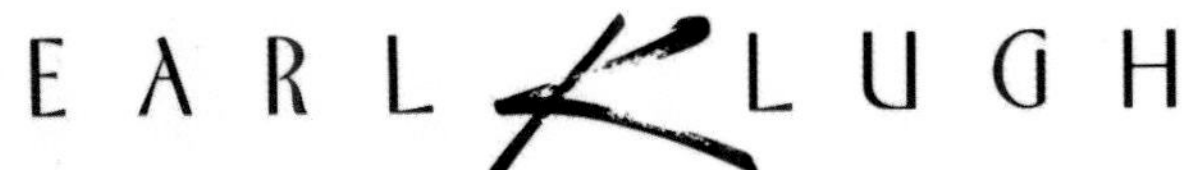

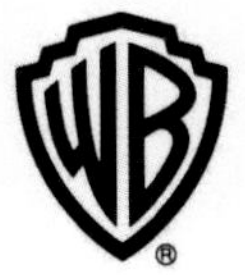

© 1991 Warner Bros. Records/Permission to reproduce limited to editorial uses in newspapers and other regularly published periodicals and television news programming.

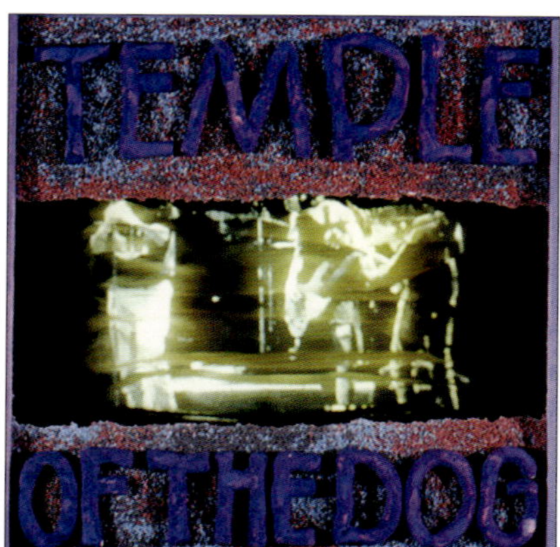

Soundgarden's Chris Cornell joined members of Pearl Jam to form a one-off tribute to the late Seattle musician Andrew Wood, **Temple of the Dog**.

Billboard 200: *Temple of the Dog* (#5)

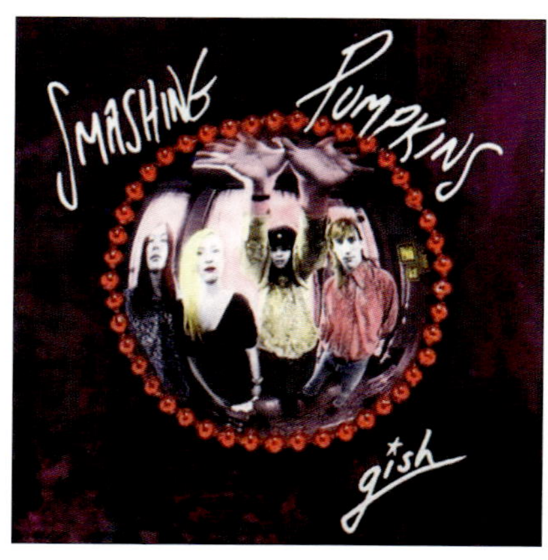

Smashing Pumpkins made a splash with *Gish*, their debut studio album, when the sweeping "Rhinoceros" received airplay on college and modern rock radio.

Billboard 200: *Gish* (#195)

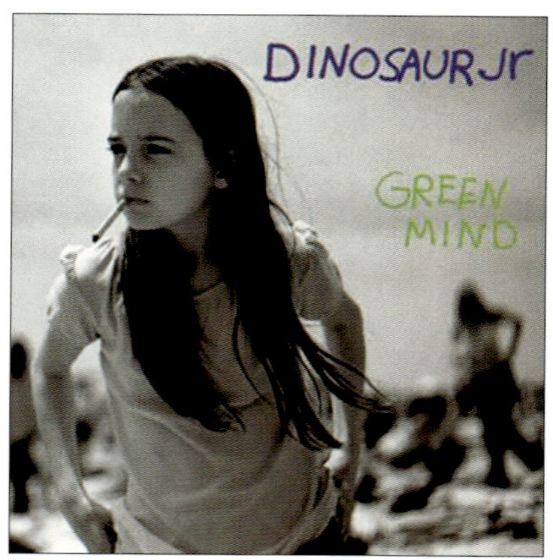

After bassist Lou Barlow's departure, **Dinosaur Jr** came out with *Green Mind*, its first major-label album, with frontman J Mascis playing most of the instruments.

Billboard 200: *Green Mind* (#168)

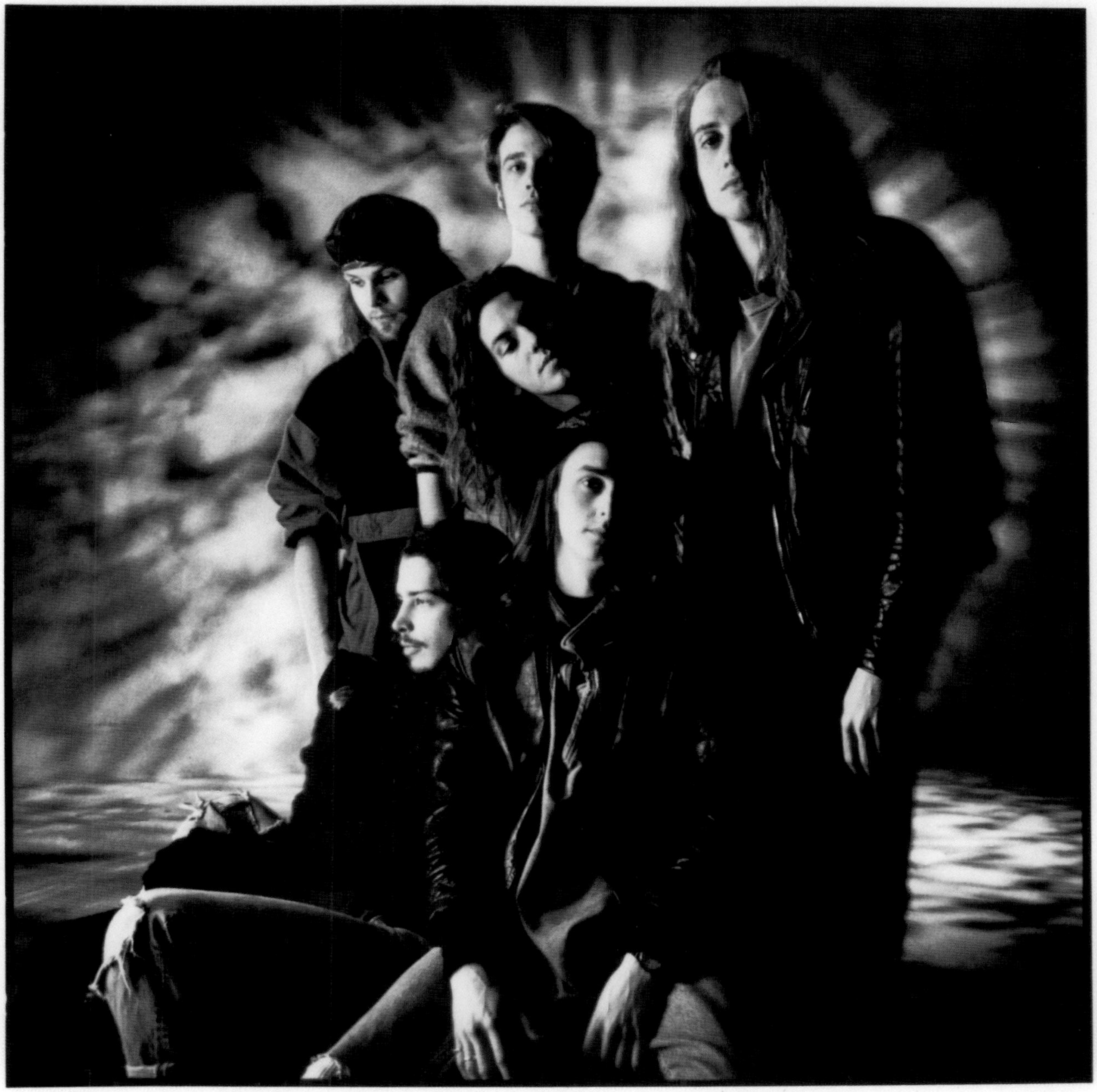

Photo Credit: Moskowitz

Jeff Ament Matt Cameron Stone Gossard
Eddie Vedder
Chris Cornell Mike McCready

TEMPLE OF THE DOG

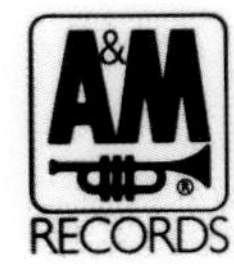

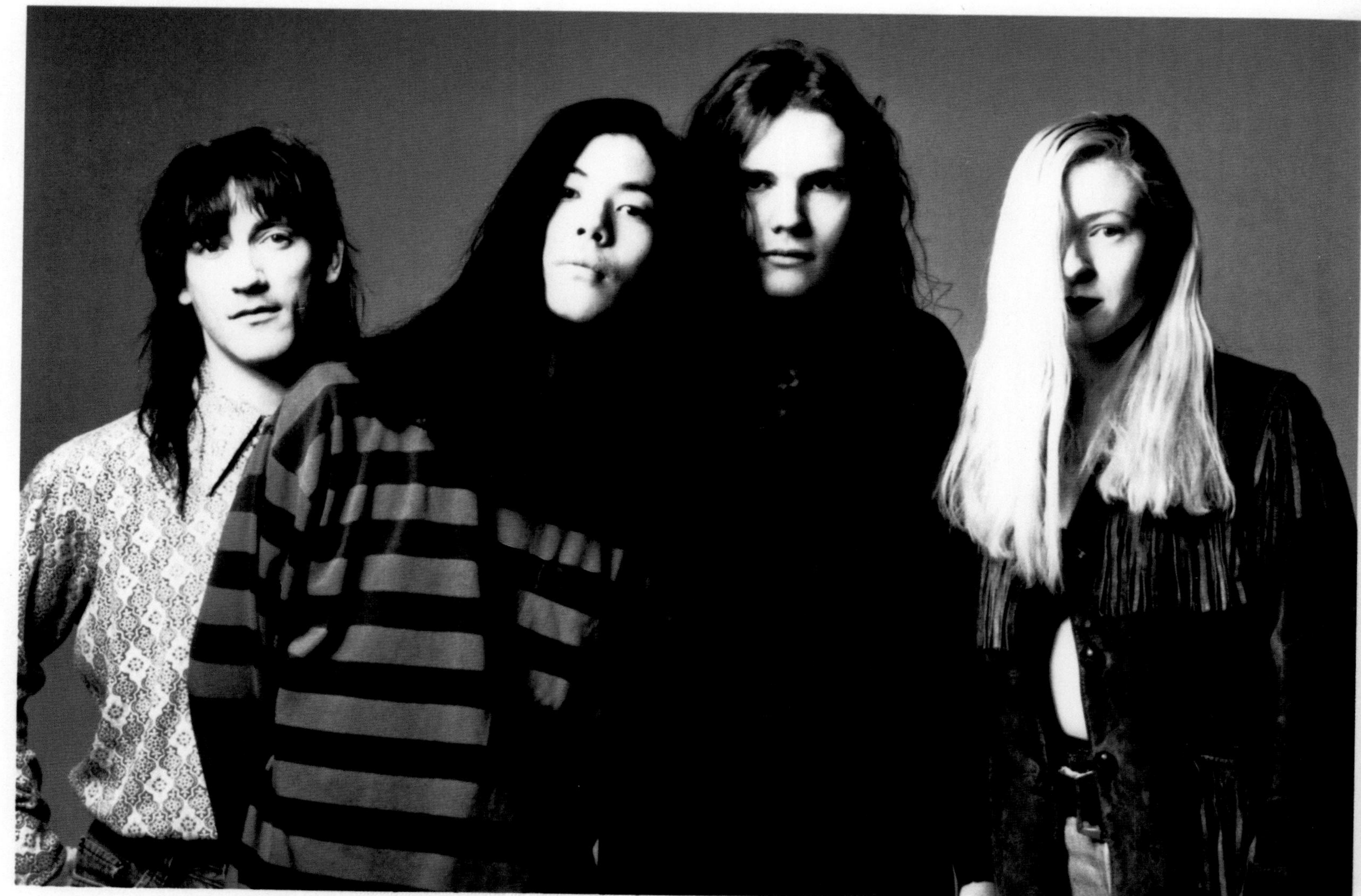

Photo Credit: Michael Lavine

SMASHING PUMPKINS

CAROLINE

CAROLINE RECORDS, INC., 114 WEST 26th STREET, NEW YORK, N.Y. 10001

(212) 989-2929

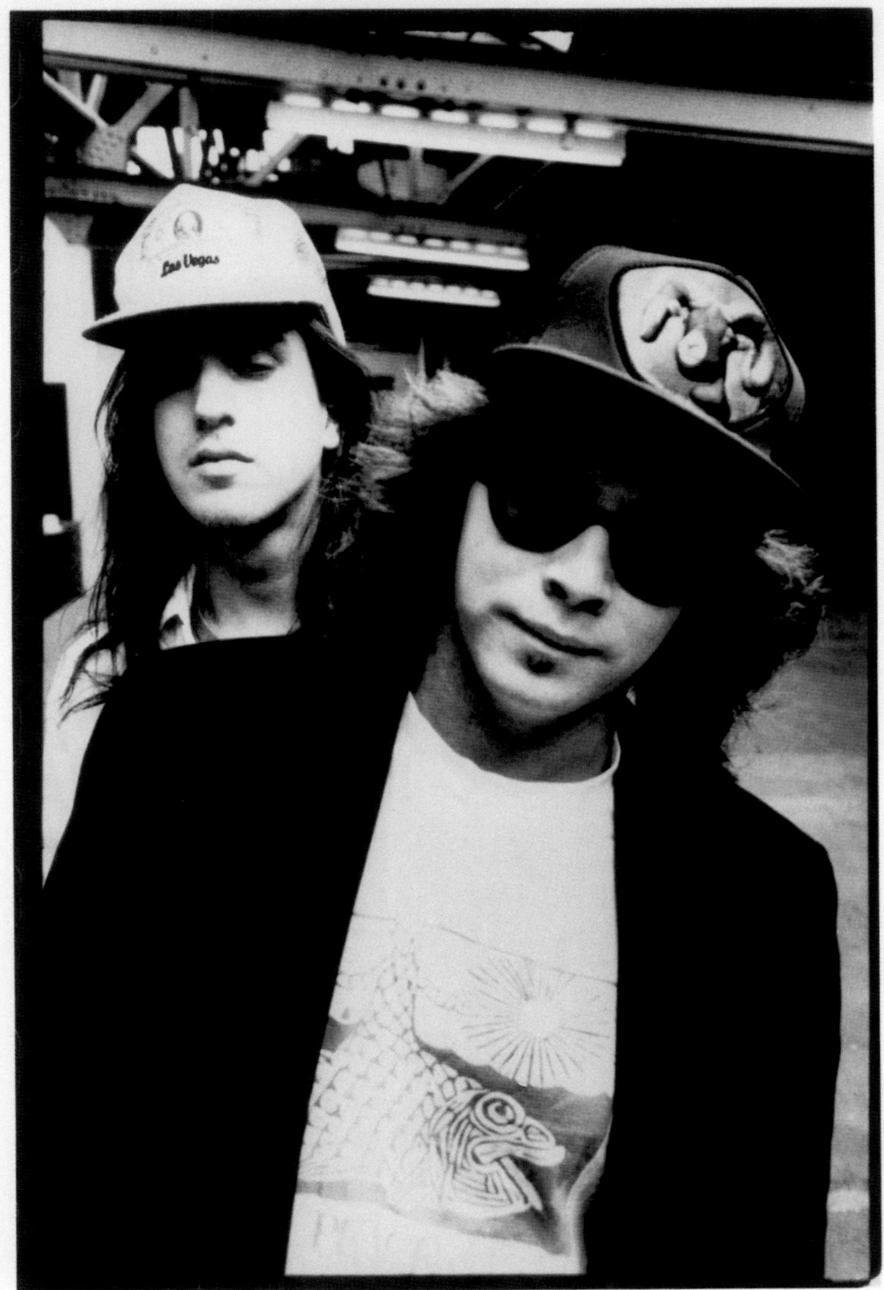

Photo Credit: Robert Goldstein

J Mascis Murph

DINOSAUR Jr

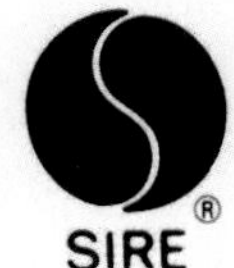

© 1991 Sire Records Company/Permission to reproduce limited to editorial uses in newspapers and other regularly published periodicals and television news programming.

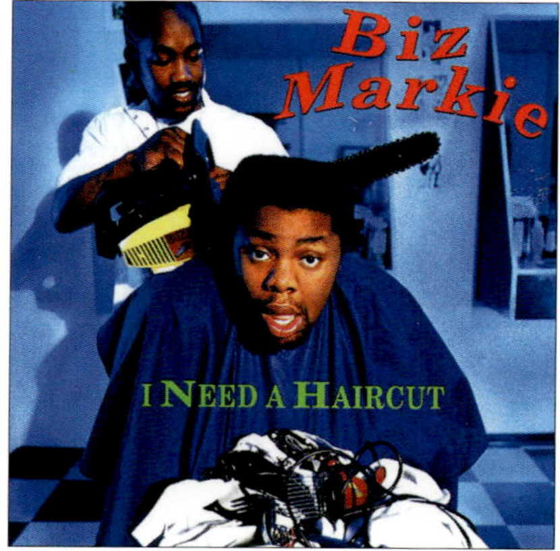

Biz Markie's track "Alone Again" incorporated an unauthorized sample from Gilbert O'Sullivan's 1972 hit "Alone Again (Naturally)," inspiring a major lawsuit.

Billboard 200: *I Need a Haircut* (#113)

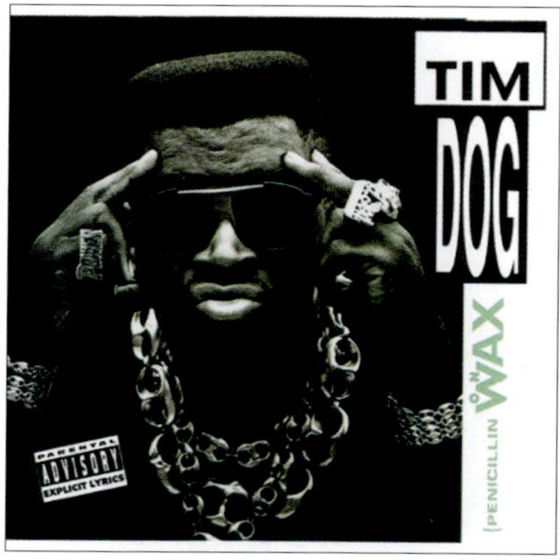

Resenting the promotion and ascendency of the West Coast hip-hop scene, Bronx rapper **Tim Dog** dropped the scathing underground hit "Fuck Compton."

Billboard 200: *Penicillin on Wax* (#155)

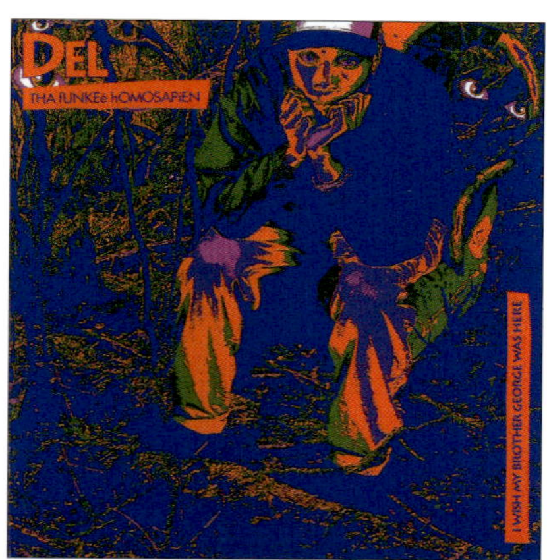

With an assist from his cousin Ice Cube, hip-hopper **Del Tha Funkee Homosapien** launched his first solo release, *I Wish My Brother George Was Here*.

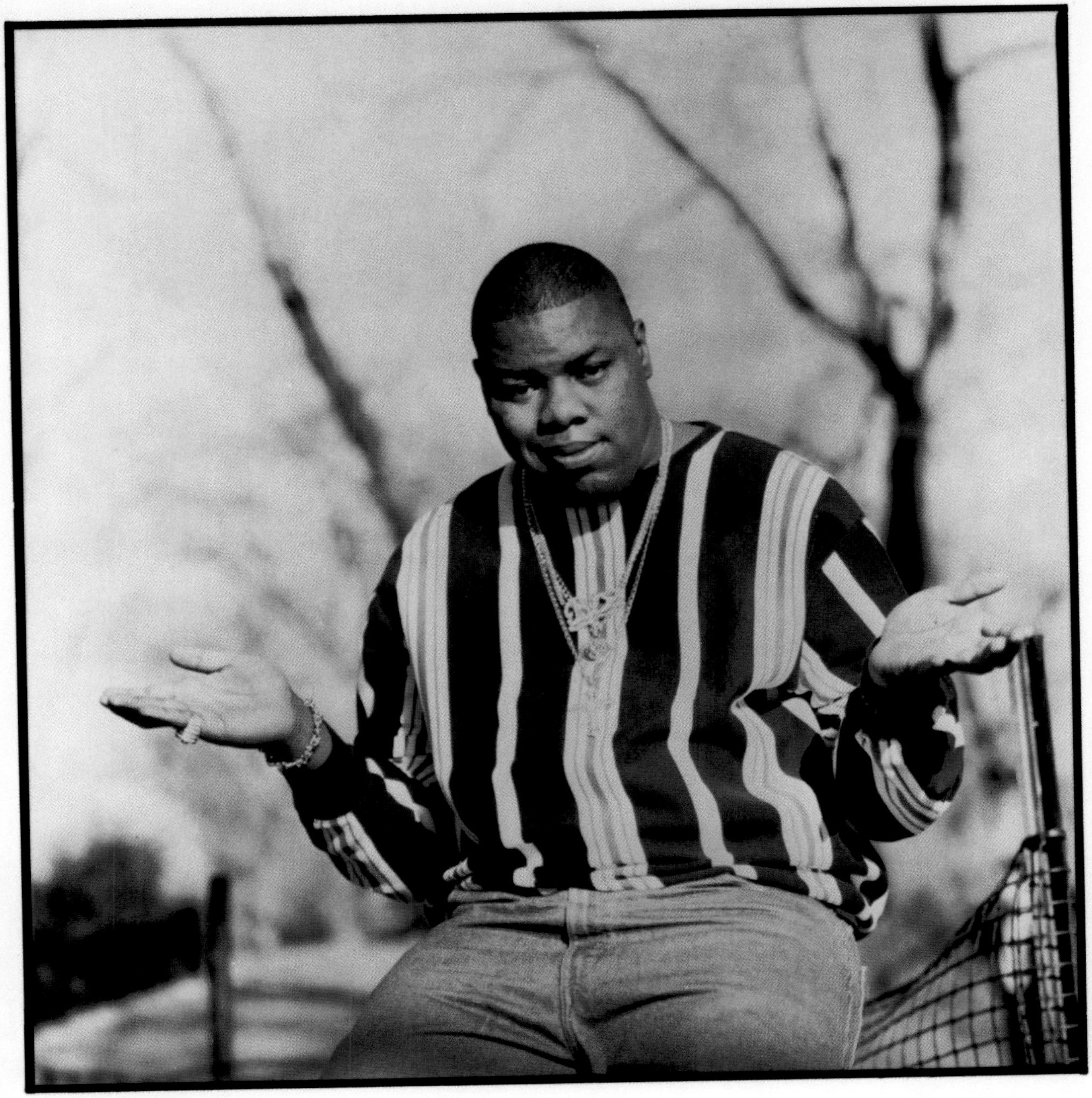

Photo Credit: George DuBose

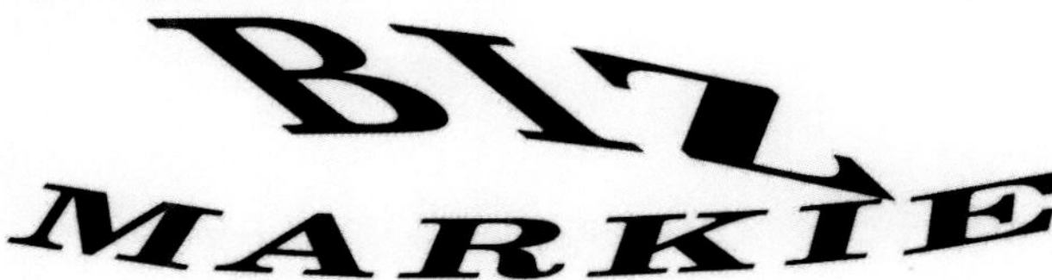

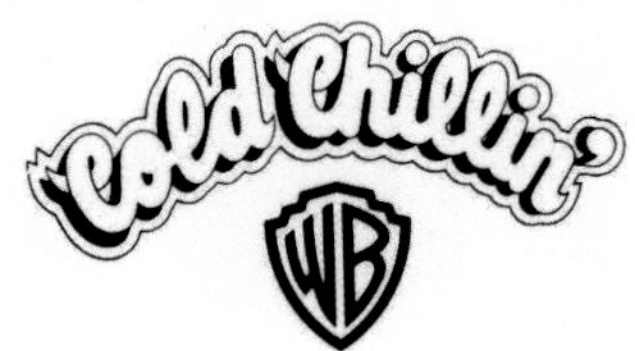

© 1991 Warner Bros. Records/Permission to reproduce limited to editorial uses in newspapers and other regularly published periodicals and television news programming.

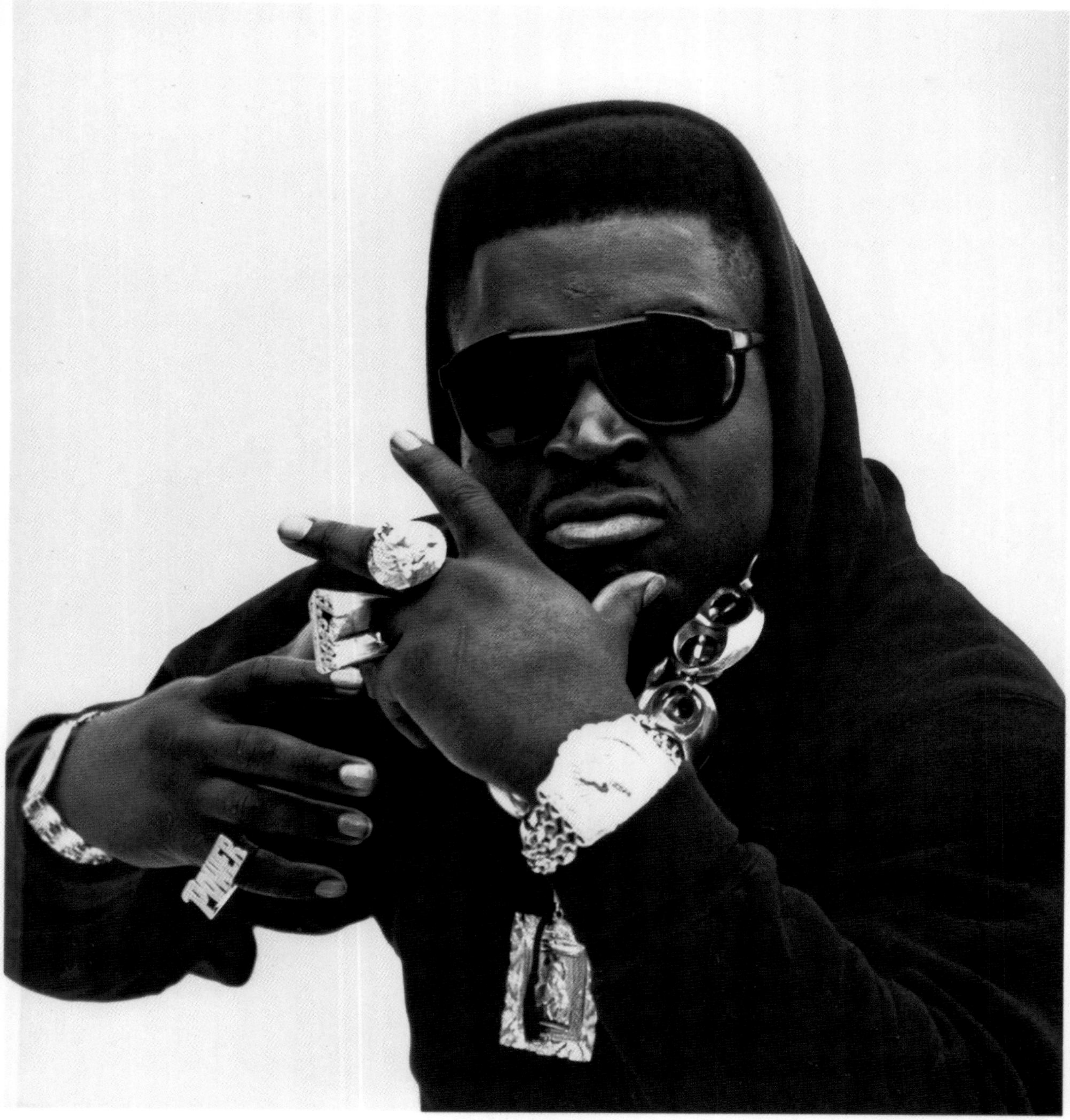

PHOTOGRAPH: JESSE FROHMAN

© 1991 Sony Music. Permission to reproduce this photography is limited to editorial uses in regular issues of newspapers and other regularly published periodicals and television news programming.

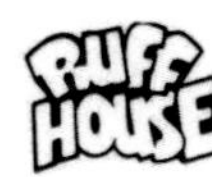

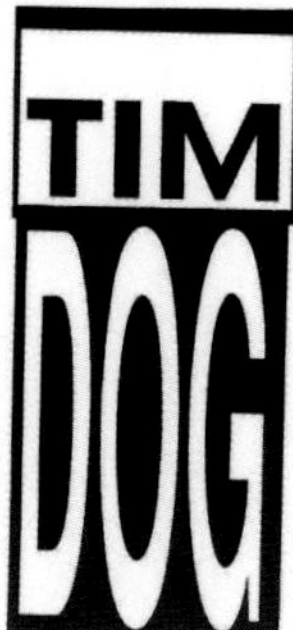

Columbia
9107

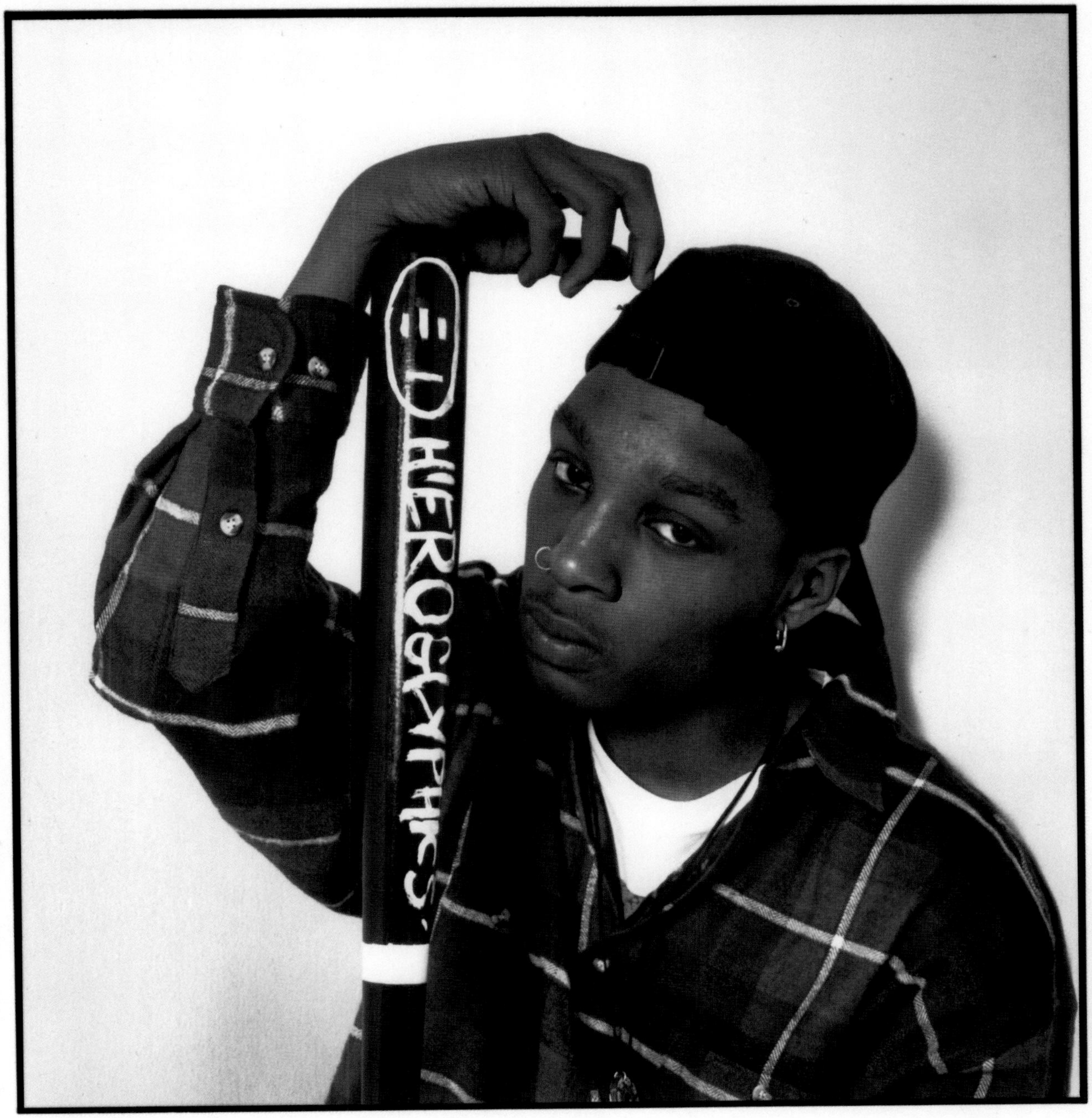

PHOTO CREDIT: JESSE FROHMAN

DEL THA fUNKEé hOMOSAPiEN

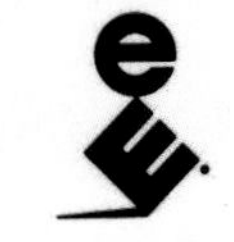

Elektra Entertainment

Luther Vandross' *Power of Love* yielded "Power of Love/Love Power," the singer's biggest pop hit and a Grammy winner in the Best R&B Song category.

Billboard 200: *Power of Love* (#7)
Billboard Hot 100: "Power of Love/Love Power" (#4); "Don't Want to Be a Fool" (#9); "The Rush" (#73)

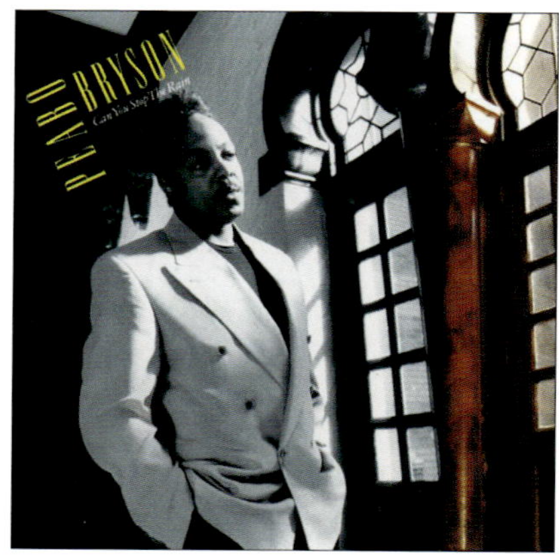

The title track of **Peabo Bryson**'s 15th album, *Can You Stop the Rain*, reached No. 1 on the R&B chart and earned the soul balladeer a gold record.

Billboard 200: *Can You Stop the Rain* (#88)
Billboard Hot 100: "Can You Stop the Rain" (#52)

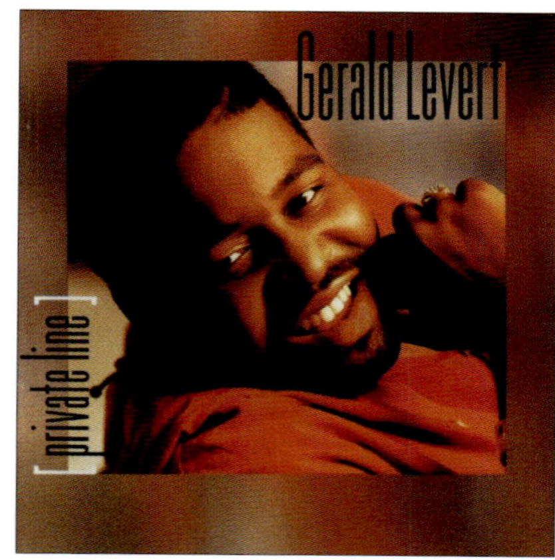

Following his tenure with the group LeVert, **Gerald Levert** went solo with the album *Private Line*, which topped the R&B charts and spawned four singles.

Billboard 200: *Private Line* (#48)
Billboard Hot 100: "Baby Hold On to Me" (#37)

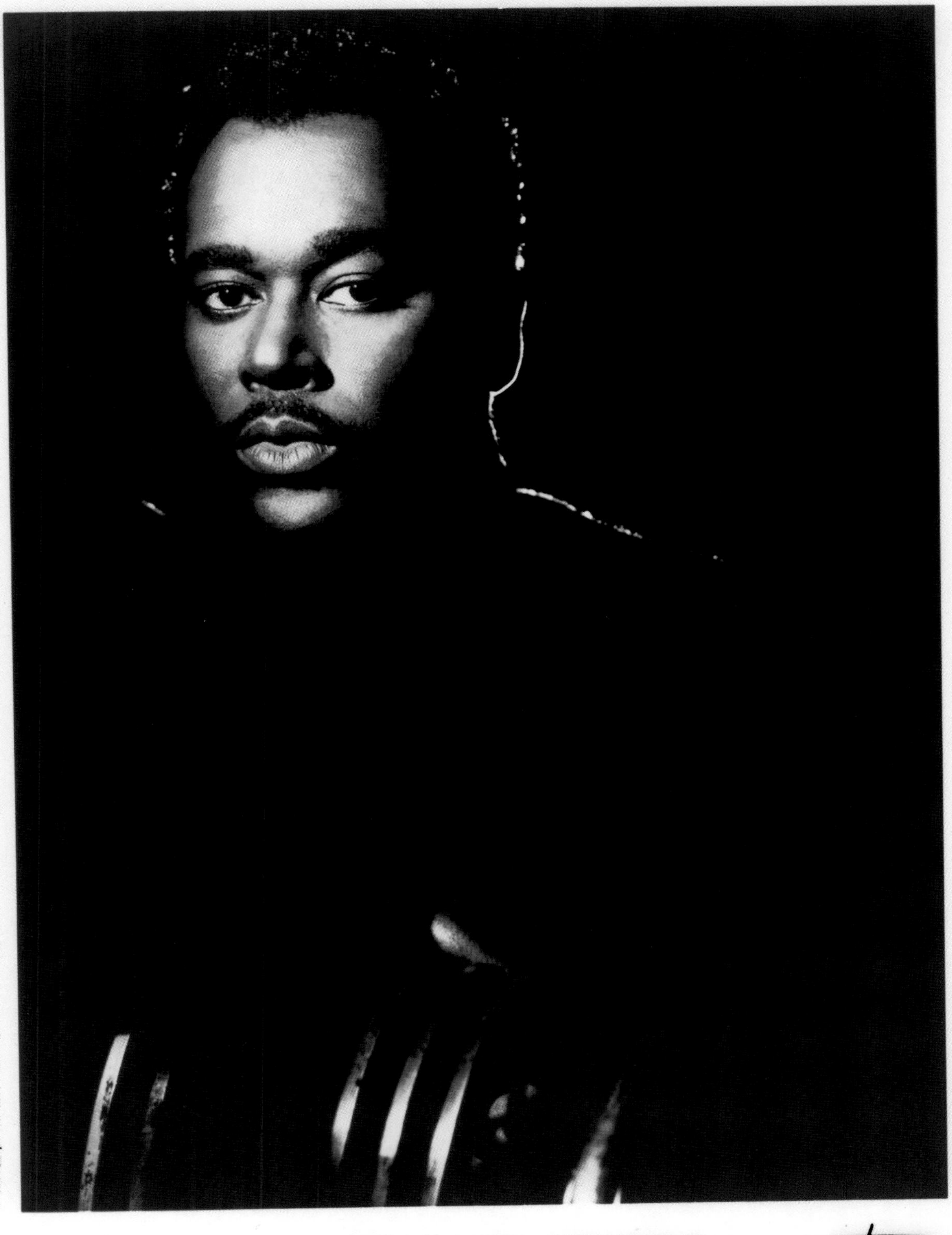

© 1991 Sony Music Permission to reproduce this photography is limited to editorial uses in regular issues of newspapers and other regularly published periodicals and television news programming

PHOTO: MATTHEW ROLSTON

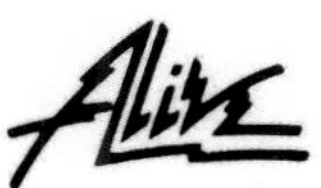

LUTHER VANDROSS

epic
9104

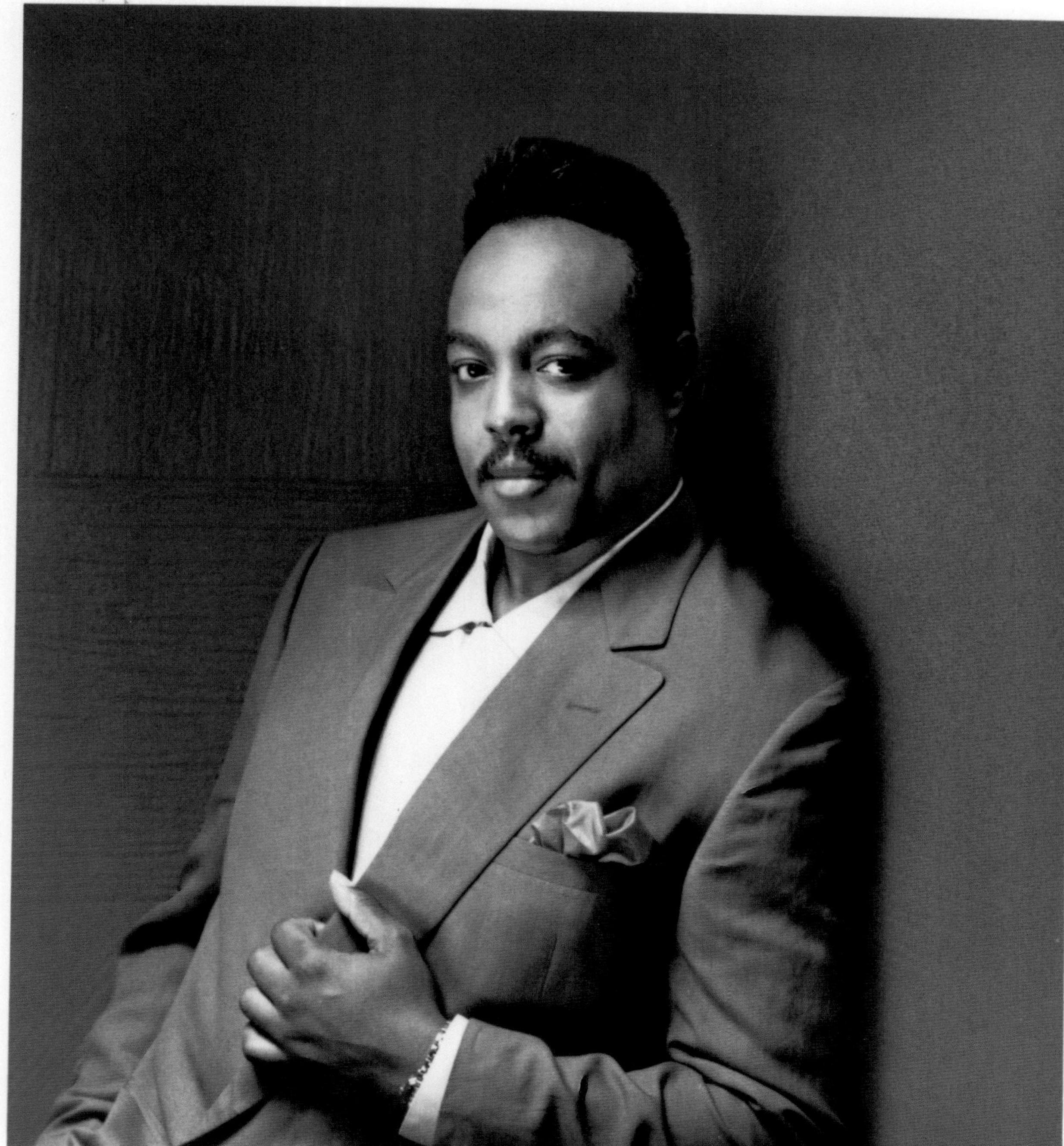

PHOTOGRAPH: E.J. CAMP

© 1991 Sony Music. Permission to reproduce this photography is limited to editorial uses in regular issues of newspapers and other regularly published periodicals and television news programming.

PEABO BRYSON

Columbia

9105

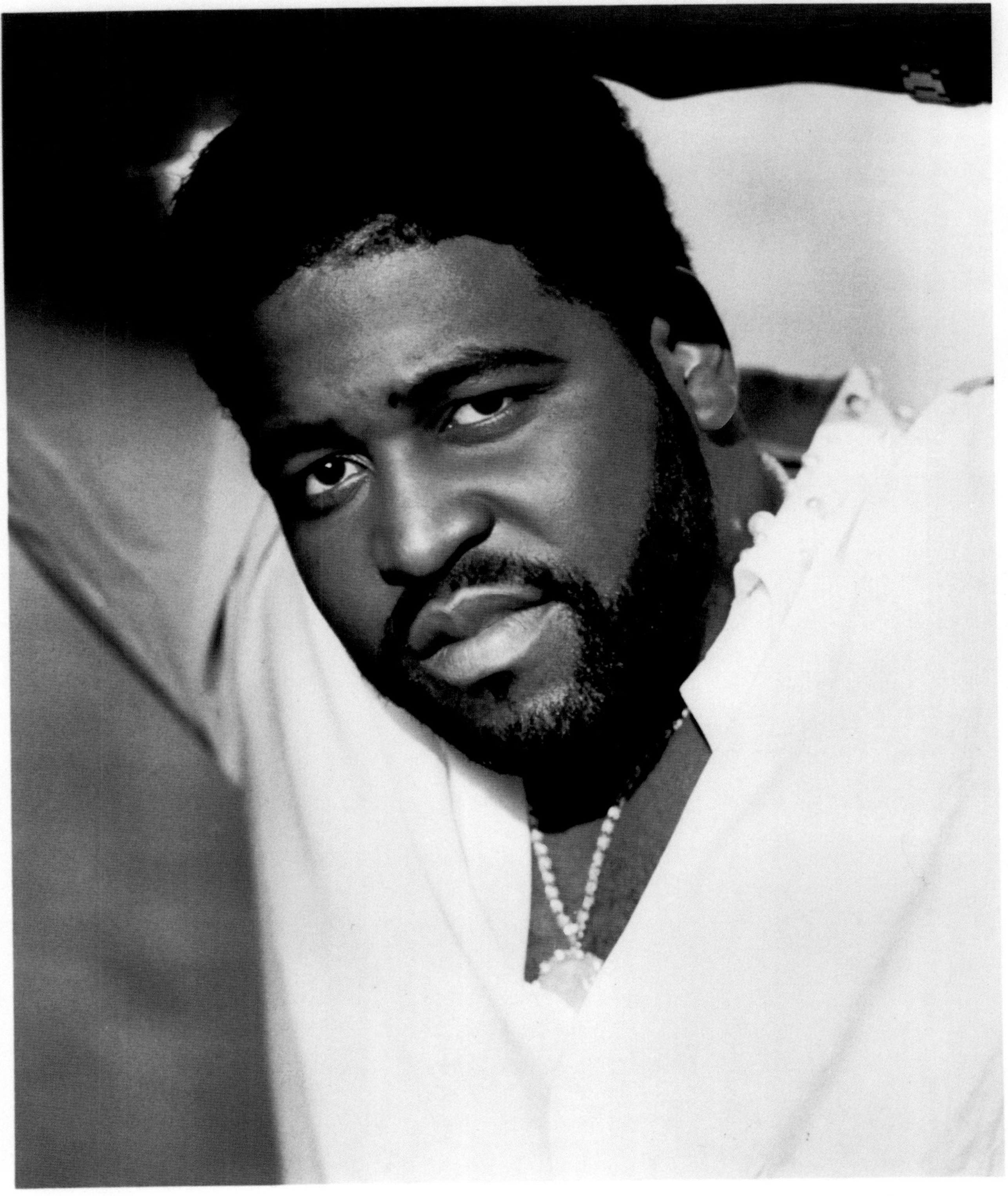

Photo © DAVID ROTH

Gerald Levert

ew

eastwest records america

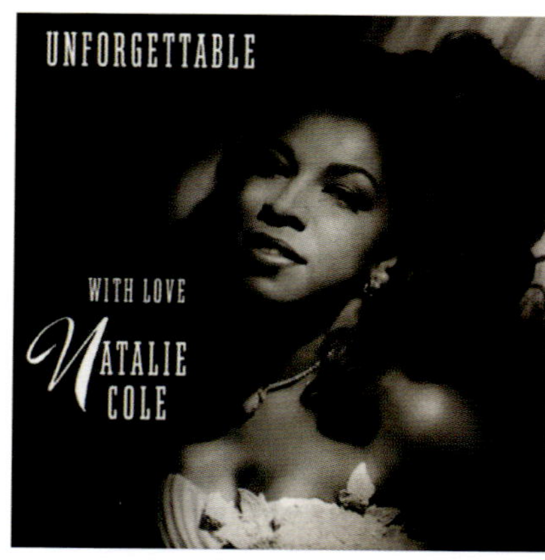

Natalie Cole paid tribute to her late father Nat King Cole on *Unforgettable...with Love*, a No. 1 album which won the Grammy Award for Album of the Year.

Billboard 200: *Unforgettable...with Love* (No. 1)
Billboard Hot 100: "Unforgettable" (#14)

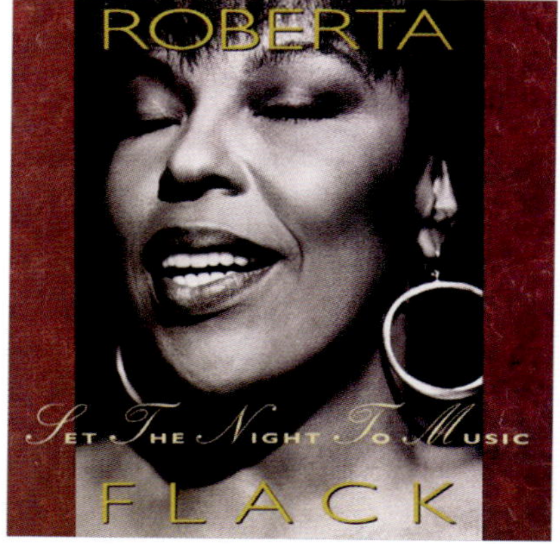

Singer **Roberta Flack** returned to the Top 10 on the pop charts with "Set the Night to Music," a hit collaboration with British reggae vocalist Maxi Priest.

Billboard 200: *Set the Night to Music* (#110)
Billboard Hot 100: "Set the Night to Music" (#6)

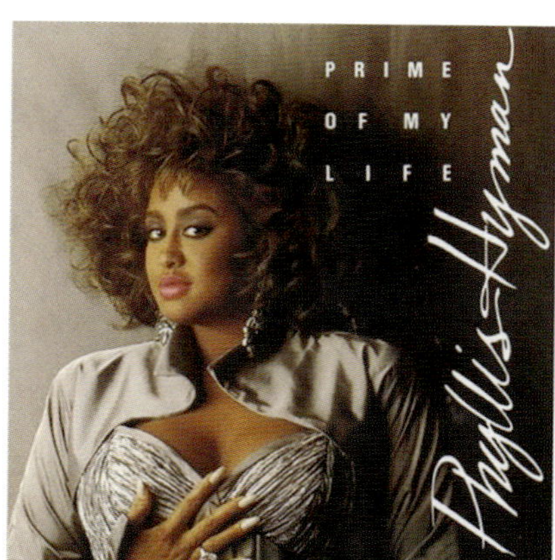

Featuring the sassy pop hit, "Don't Wanna Change the World," **Phyllis Hyman**'s *Prime of My Life* emerged as the best-selling album in the soul singer's career.

Billboard 200: *Prime of My Life* (#117)
Billboard Hot 100: "Don't Wanna Change the World" (#68)

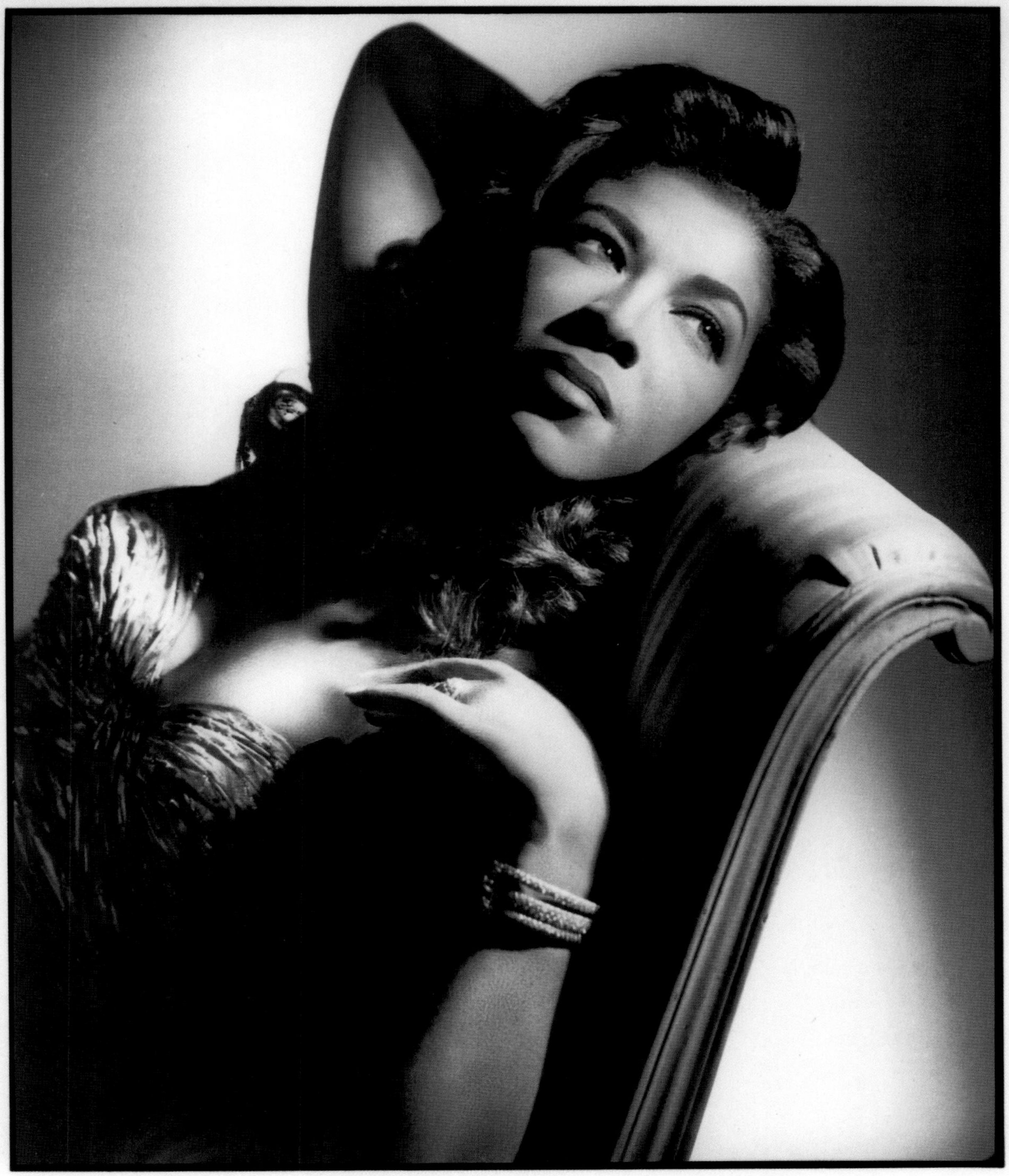

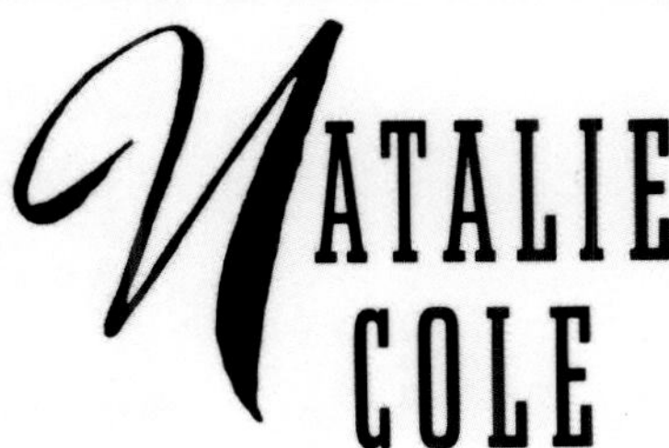

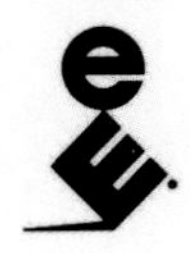

Elektra Entertainment

Dan Cleary Management

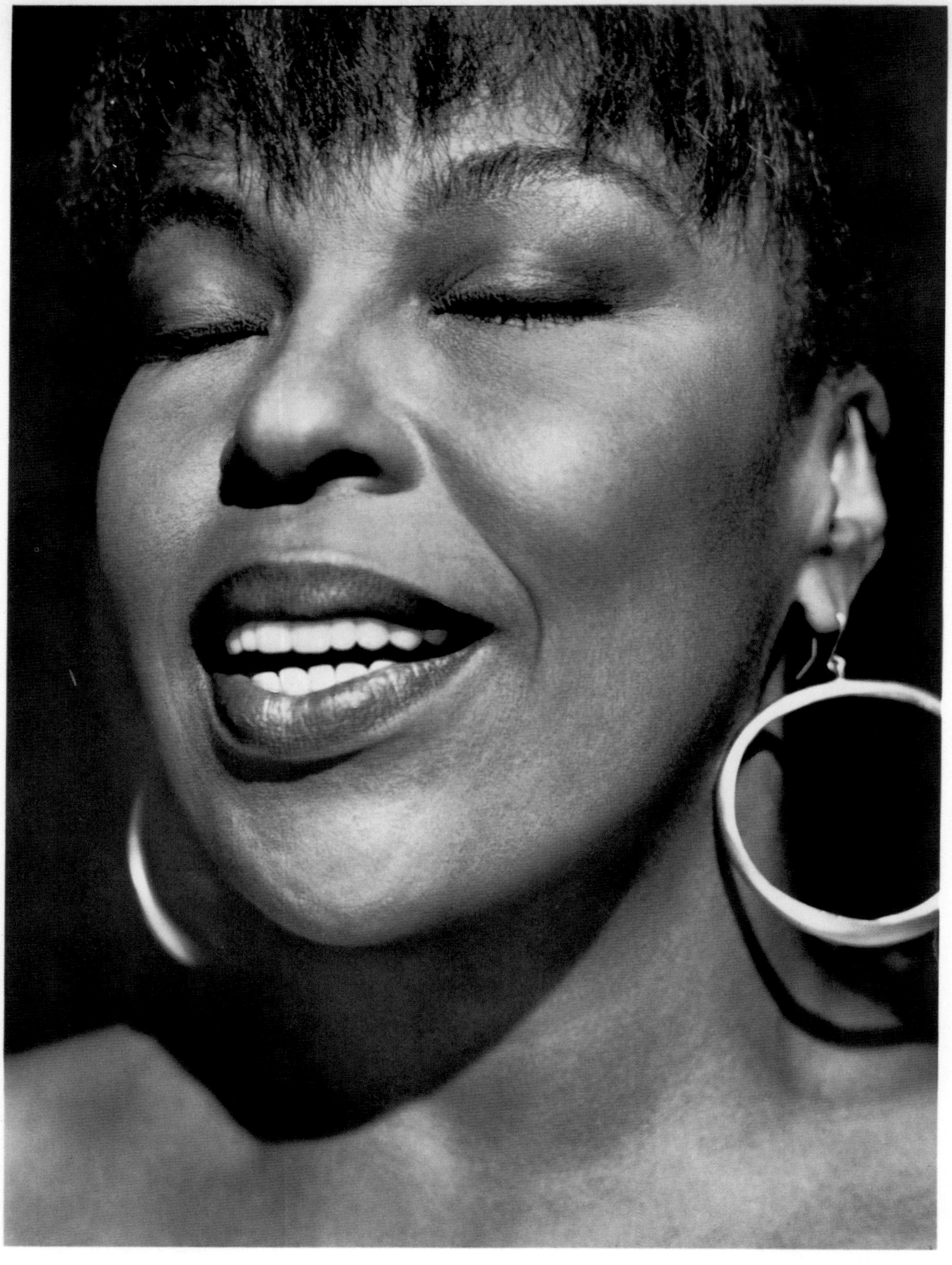

ROBERTA
FLACK

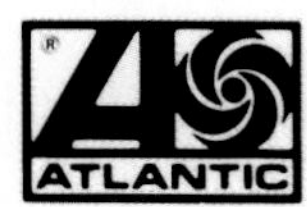

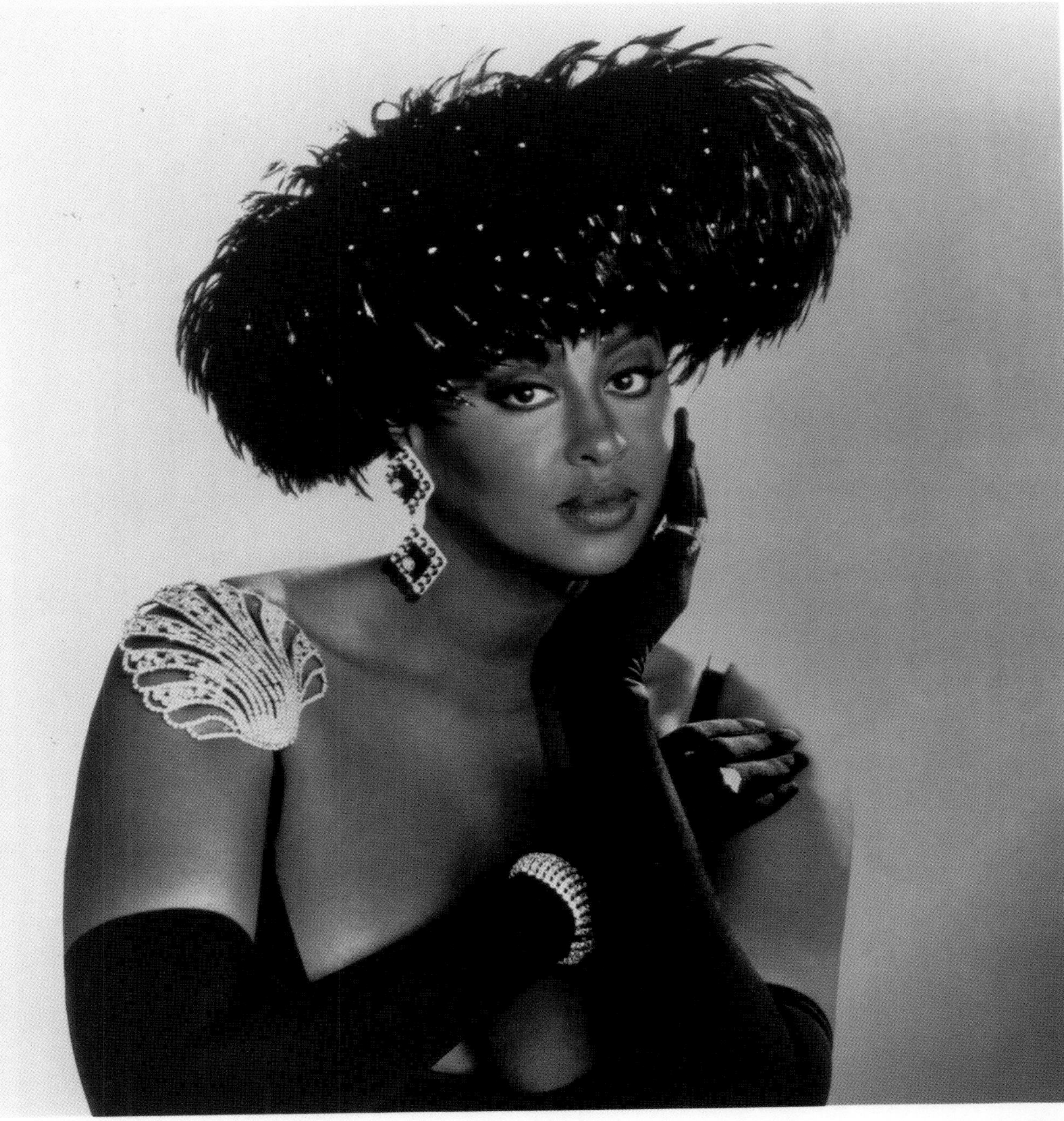

Photo: Phyllis Cuington

Phyllis Hyman

PR
PHILADELPHIA INTERNATIONAL RECORDS

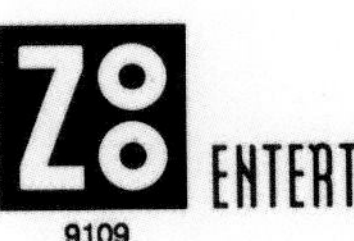

ENTERTAINMENT 6363 Sunset Boulevard, Hollywood, California 90028 TEL 213 468 4200 FAX 213 468 4207

9109

© 1991 Zoo Entertainment. Permission to reproduce this photography is limited to editorial uses in regular issues of newspapers and other regularly published periodicals and television news programming.

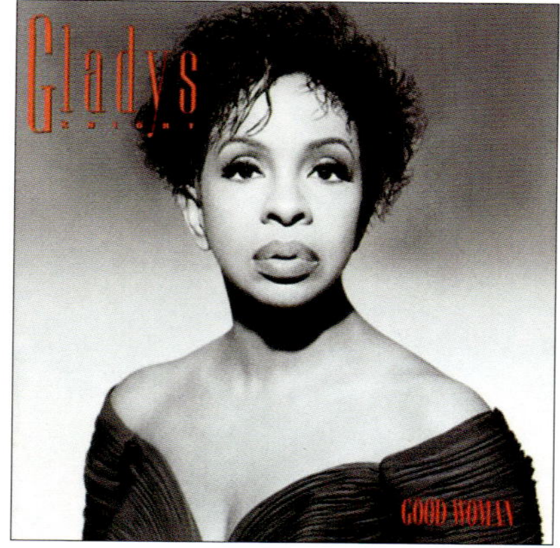

Known for the massive hits she recorded with the Pips, **Gladys Knight** released her most successful solo album, *Good Woman*, hitting No. 1 on the R&B chart.

Billboard 200: *Good Woman* (#45)

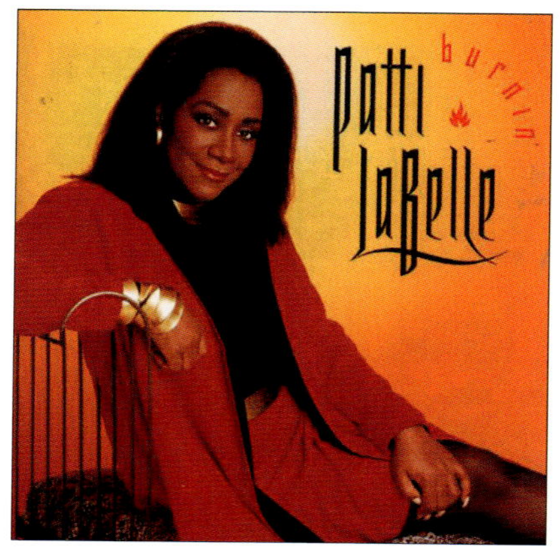

In a rare tie, **Patti LaBelle**'s *Burnin'* album shared a Grammy for Best Female R&B Vocal Performance with Lisa Fischer's single, "How Can I Ease the Pain."

Billboard 200: *Burnin'* (#71)

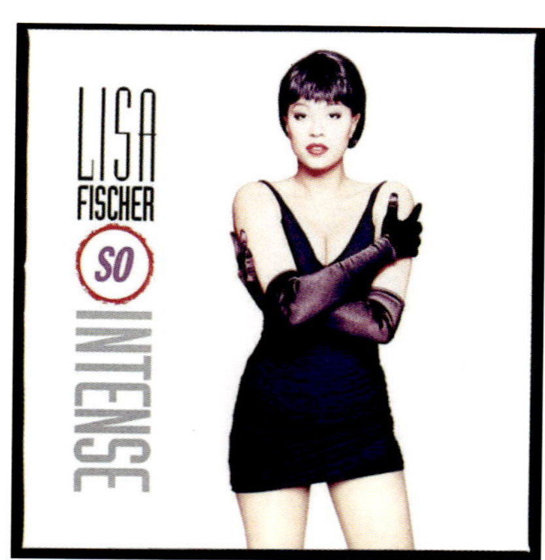

A longstanding background singer, **Lisa Fischer** rose to solo fame with her debut album, *So Intense*, writing the No. 1 R&B hit, "How Can I Ease the Pain."

Billboard 200: *So Intense* (#100)
Billboard Hot 100: "How Can I Ease the Pain" (#11);
"Save Me" (#74)

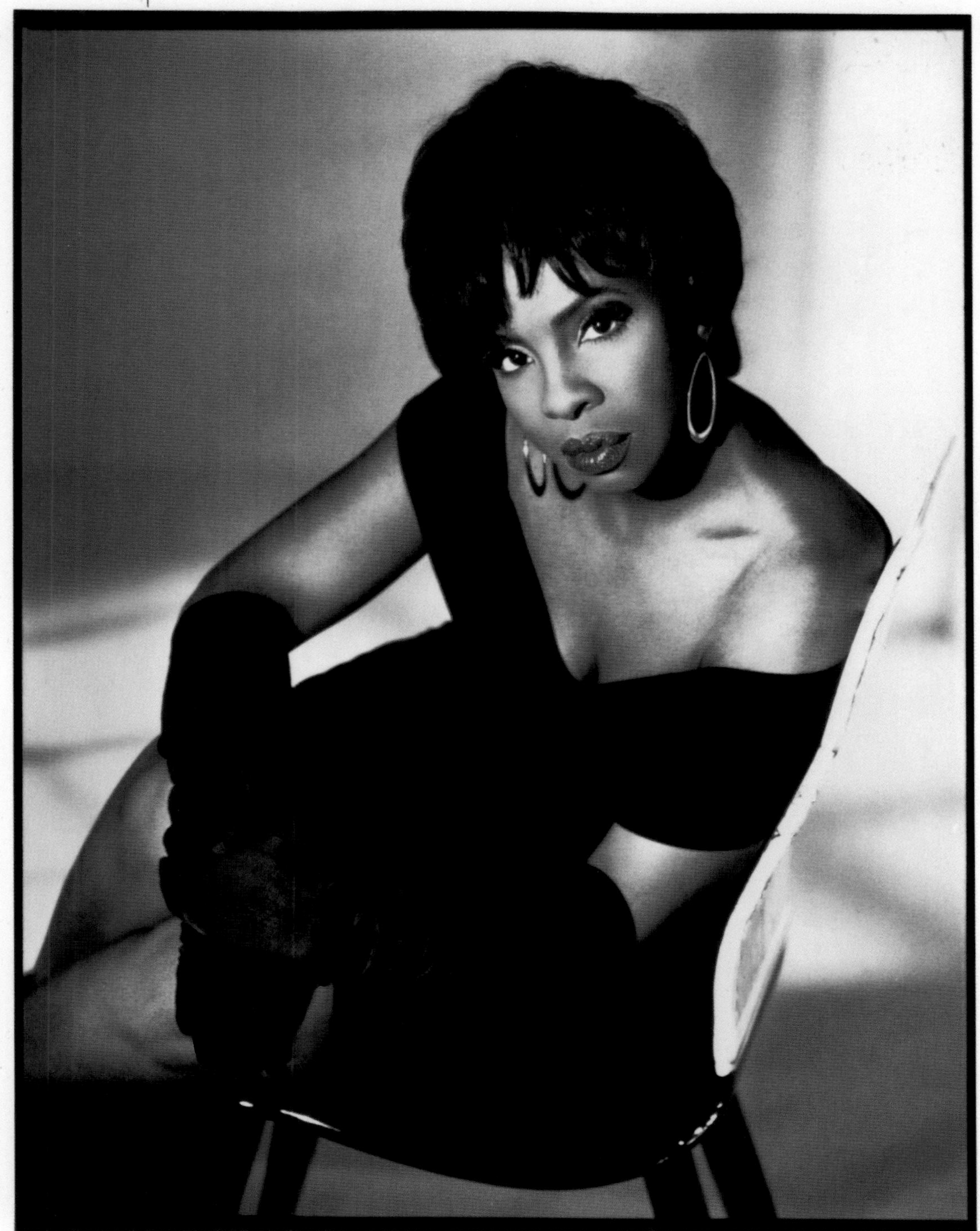

Photo Credit : Randee St. Nicholas

Gladys
KNIGHT

7/91

MCA

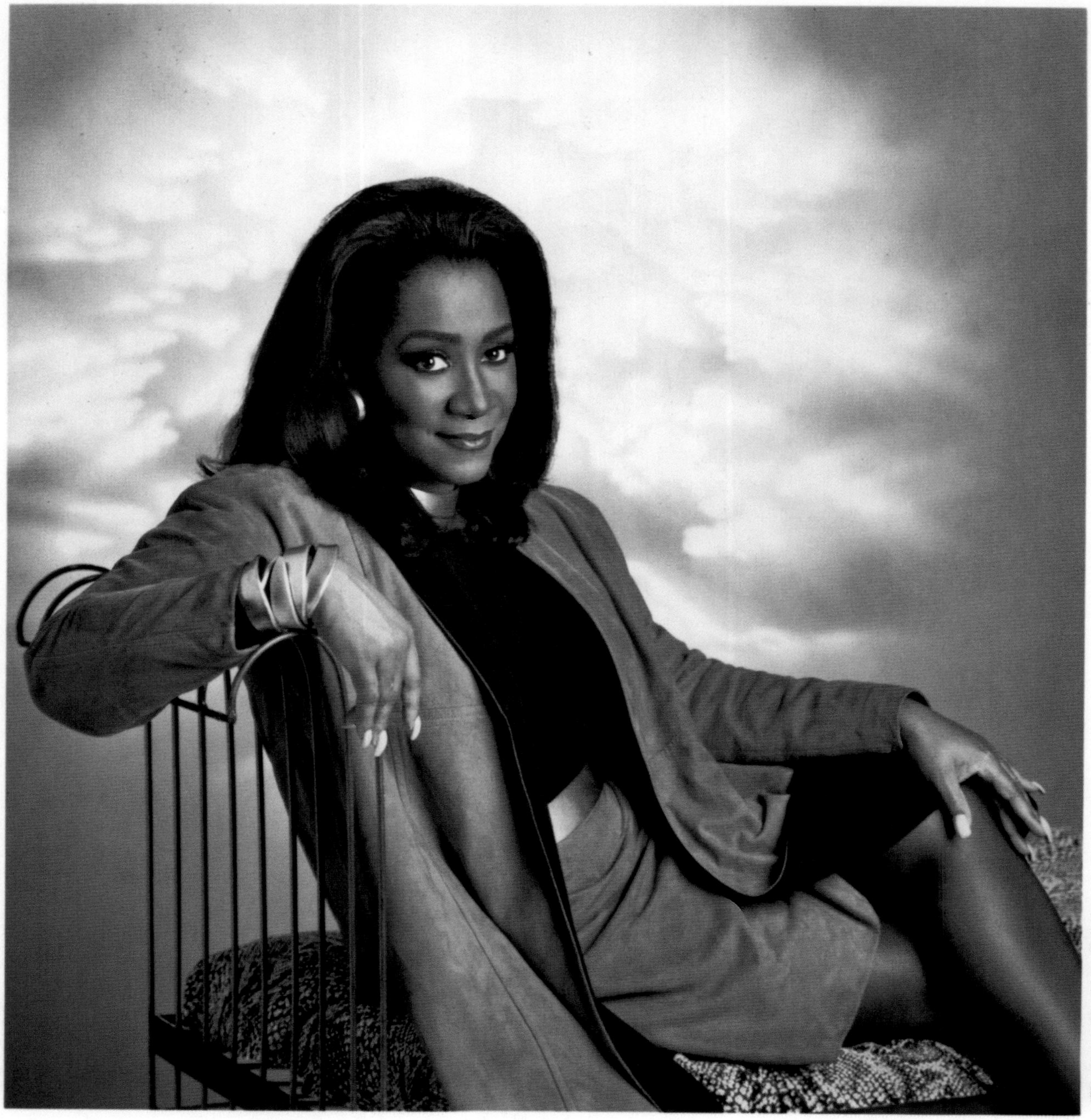

Photo credit: Marc Raboy

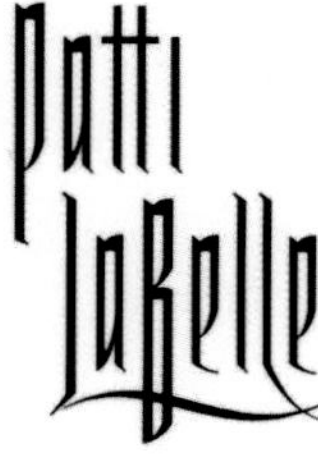

10/91

MCA

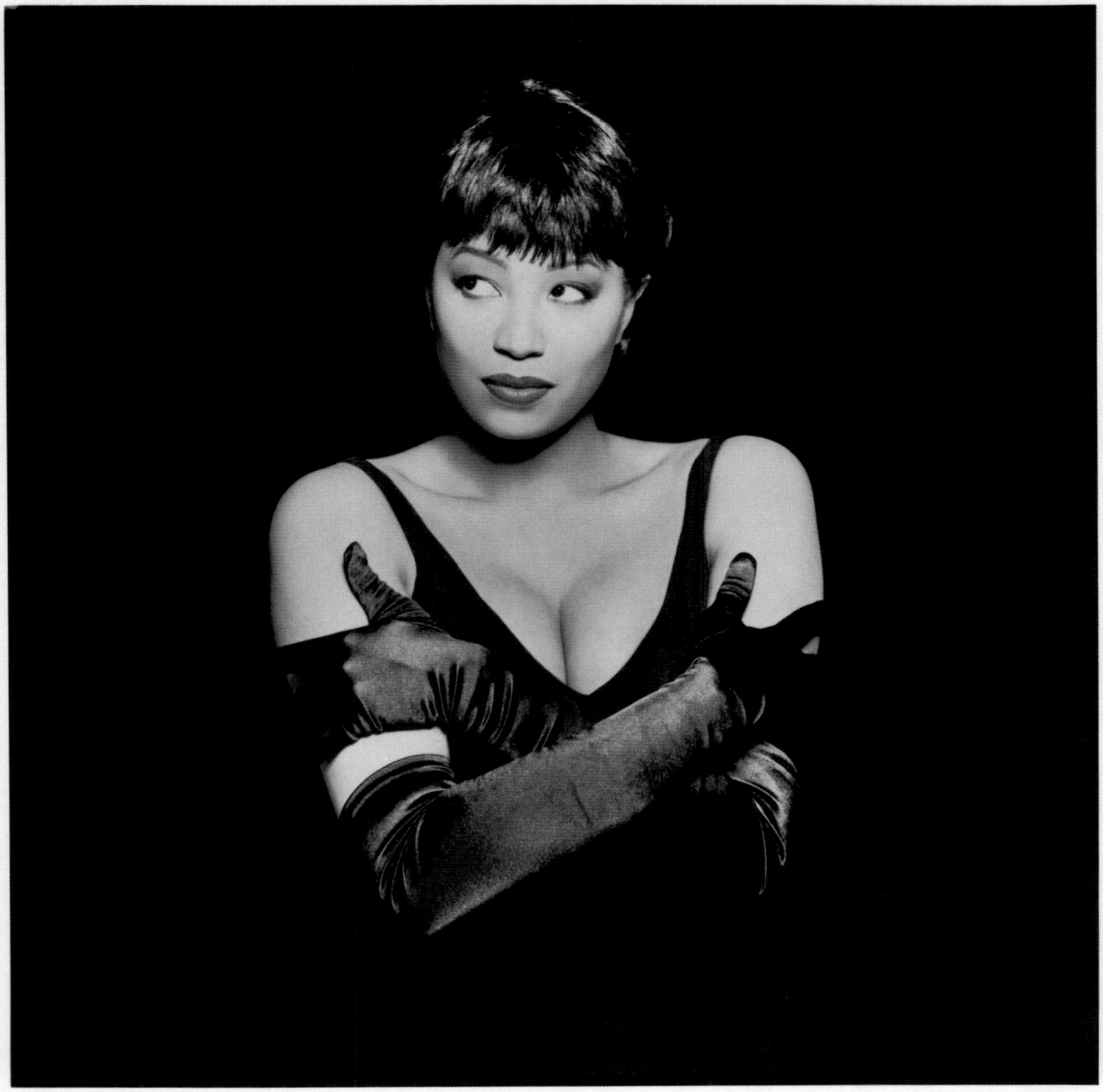

PHOTO CREDIT: WAYNE MASER

LISA
FISCHER

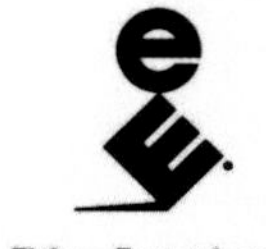

Elektra Entertainment

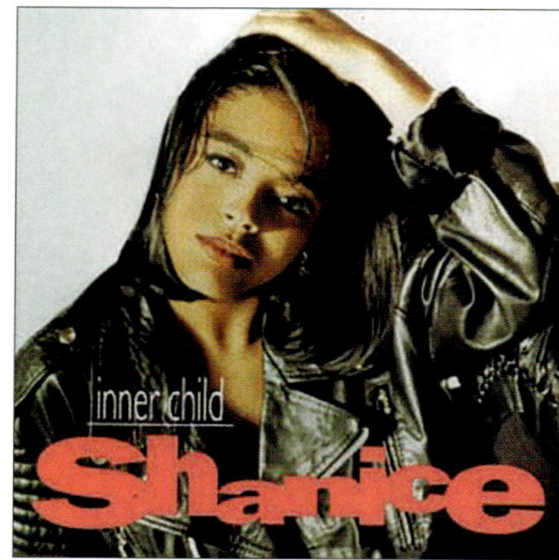

Teenager **Shanice** released *Inner Child*, her debut album, and an irresistible R&B single, "I Love Your Smile," proceeded to reach the Top 10 in 16 countries.

Billboard 200: *Inner Child* (#83)
Billboard Hot 100: "I Love Your Smile" (#2); "Silent Prayer" (#31)

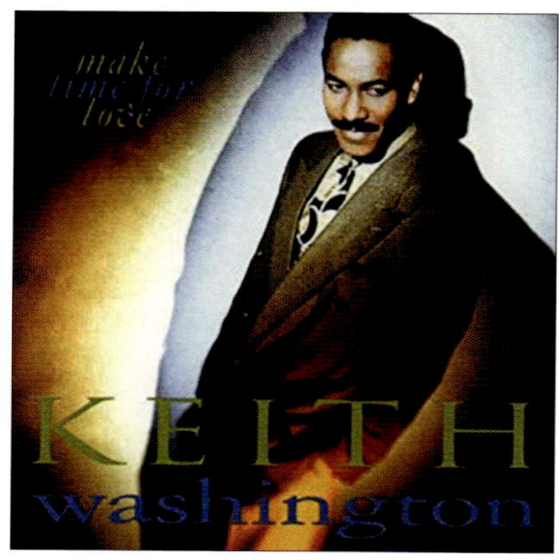

Romantic balladeer **Keith Washington** surfaced with the alluring "Kissing You," a No. 1 R&B smash from the Detroit native's debut album, *Make Time for Love*.

Billboard 200: *Make Time for Love* (#48)
Billboard Hot 100: "Kissing You" (#40)

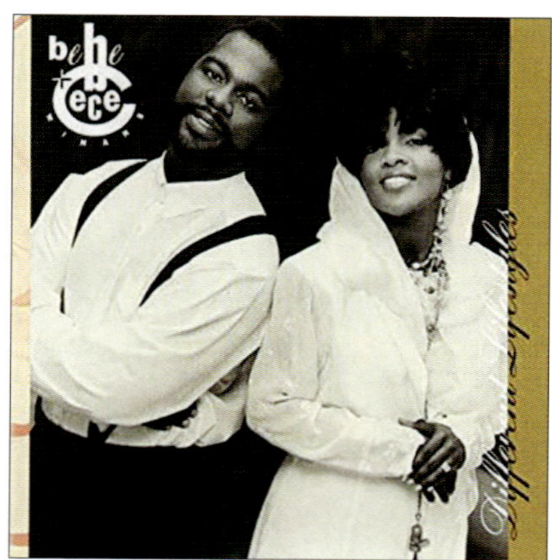

The brother-and-sister gospel duo of **BeBe & CeCe Winans** topped the R&B chart with "Addictive Love" and a cover of the Staples Singers' "I'll Take You There."

Billboard 200: *Different Lifestyles* (#74)

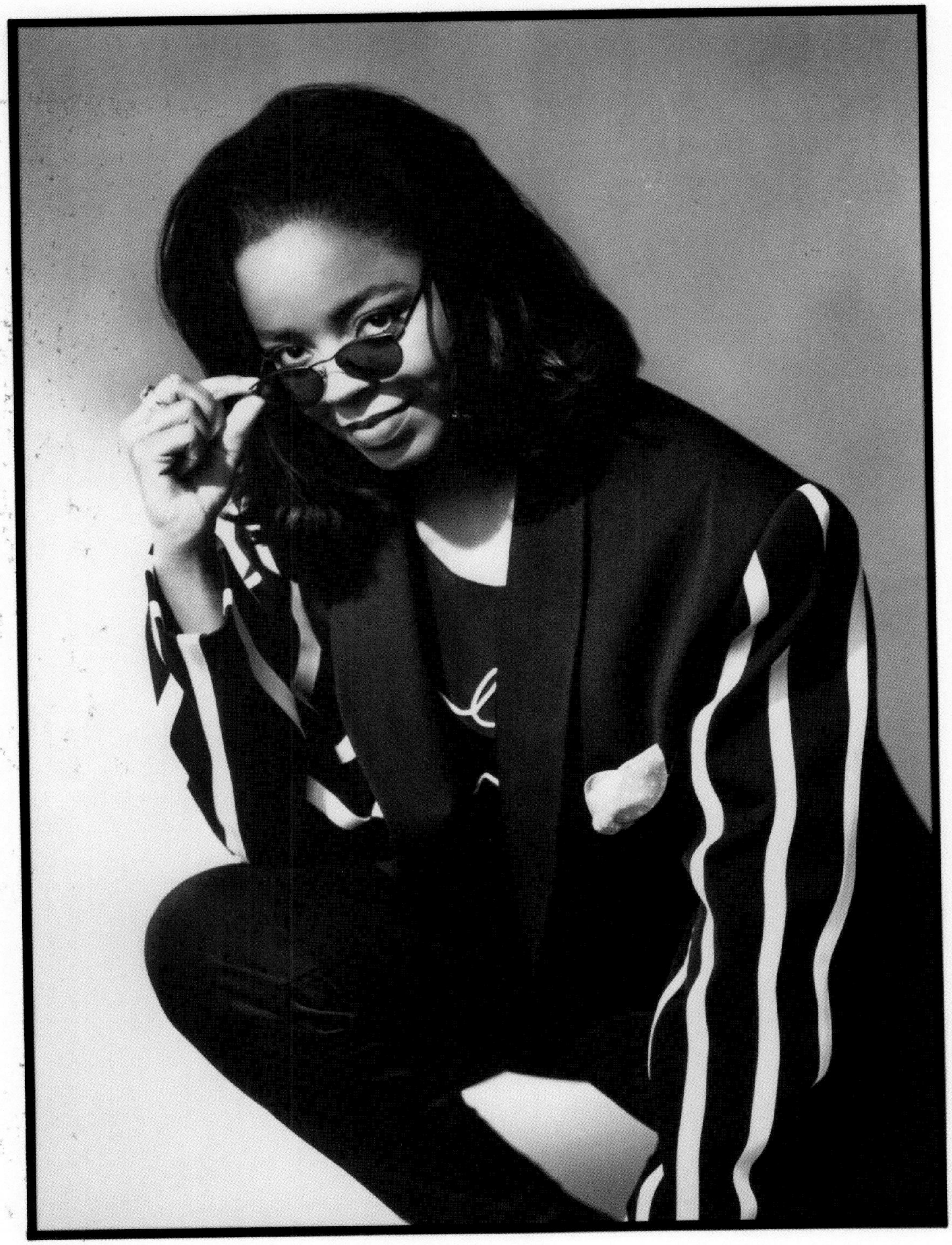

Shanice

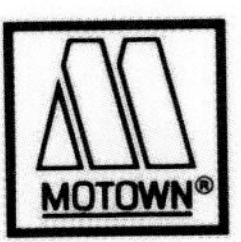

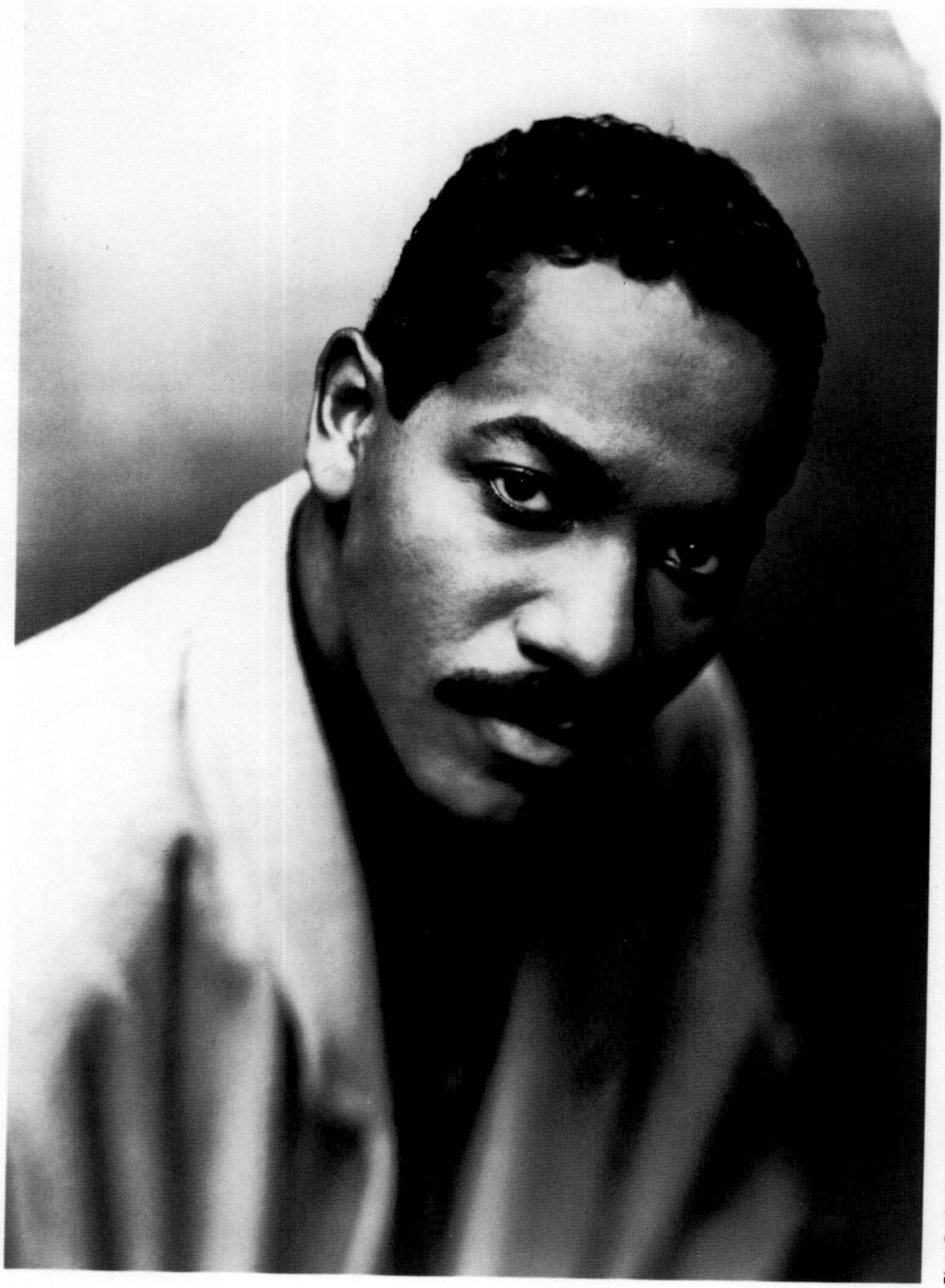

Photo Credit: Diego Uchitel

KEITH
washington

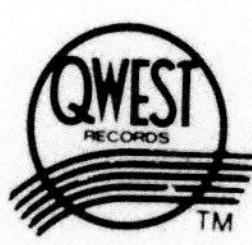

© 1991 Warner Bros Records Permission to reproduce limited to editorial uses in newspapers and other regularly published periodicals and television news programming

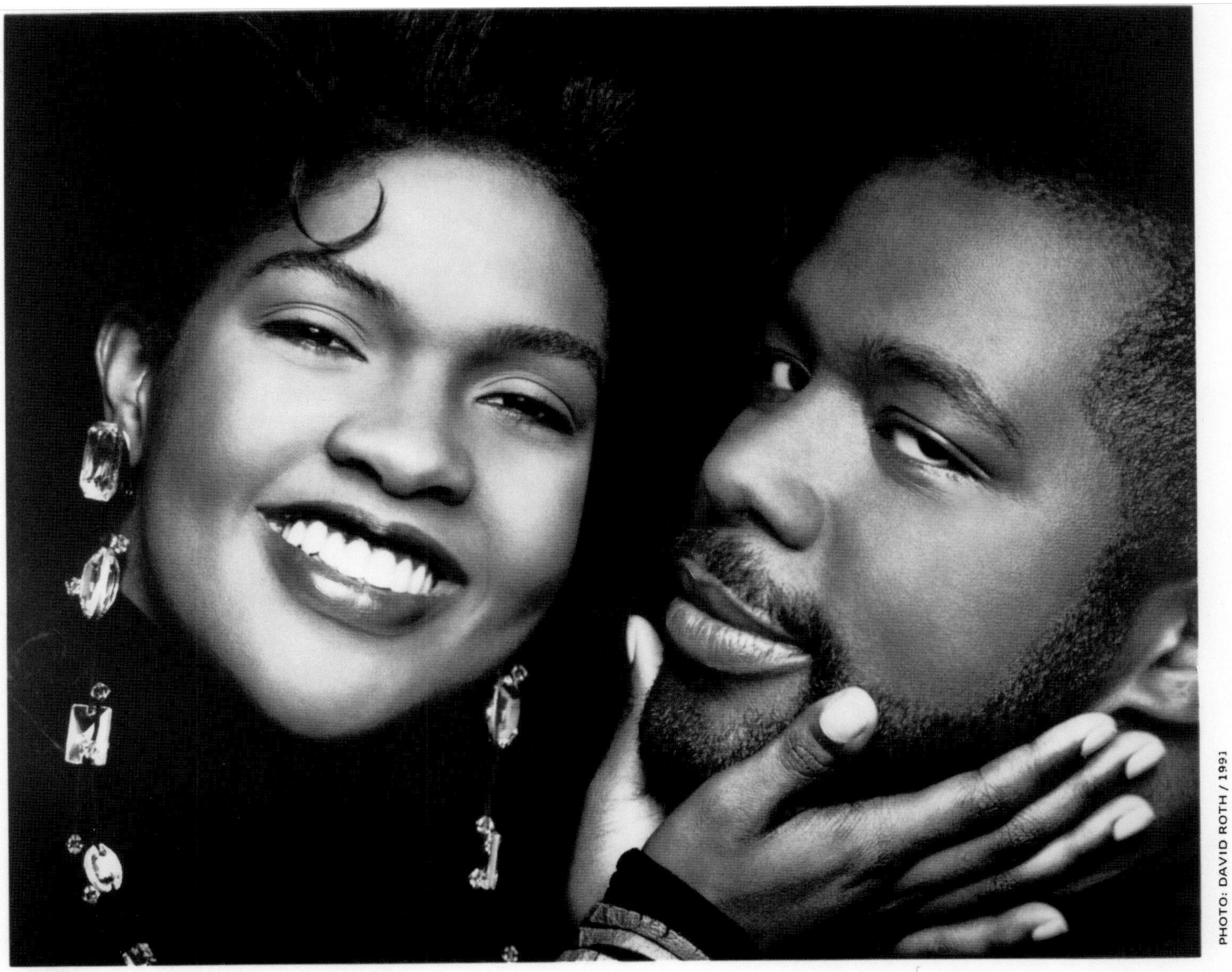

CeCe BeBe

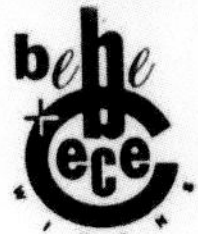

BEBE & CECE WINANS

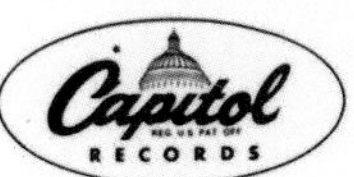

PHOTO: DAVID ROTH / 1991

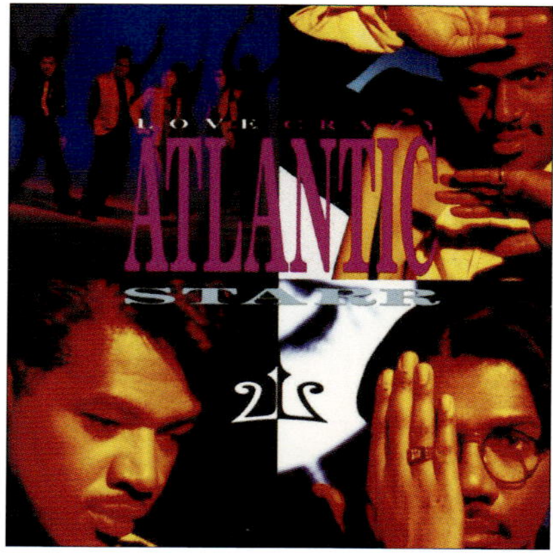

Atlantic Starr's *Love Crazy* featured "Masterpiece," a soft and easy ballad and one of the East Coast band's biggest R&B, pop and adult contemporary hits.

Billboard 200: *Love Crazy* (#134)
Billboard Hot 100: "Love Crazy" (#75); "Masterpiece" (#3)

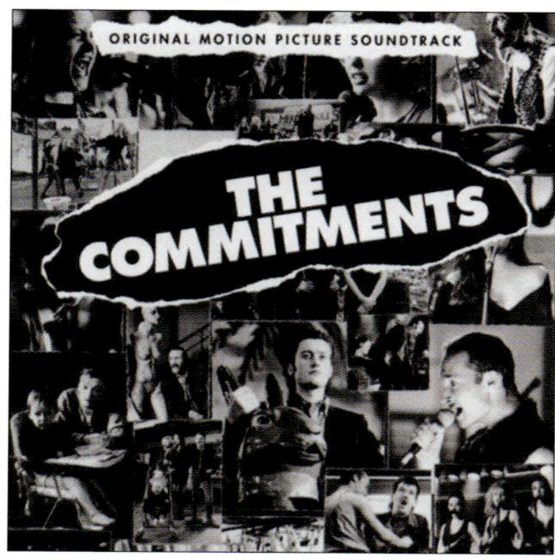

The soundtrack album to *The Commitments* featured cover versions of R&B and soul standards, most of which the titular group showcased in the hit film.

Billboard 200: *The Commitments (Original Motion Picture Soundtrack)* (#8)

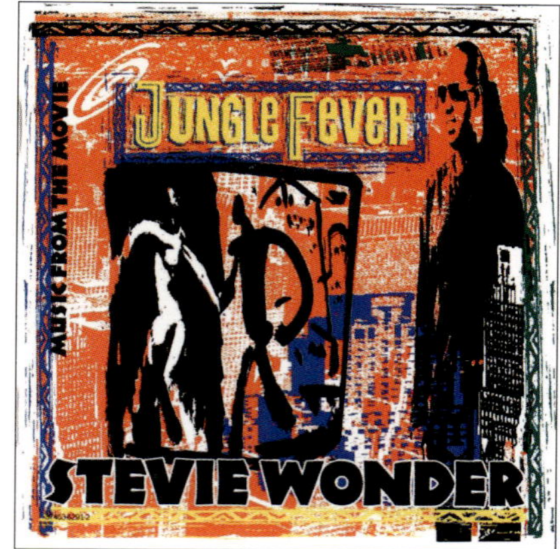

To compose the soundtrack to the film *Jungle Fever*, Stevie Wonder purportedly sat through a screening with director Spike Lee relating each scene to him.

Billboard 200: *Jungle Fever* (#24)
Billboard Hot 100: "Gotta Have You" (#92)

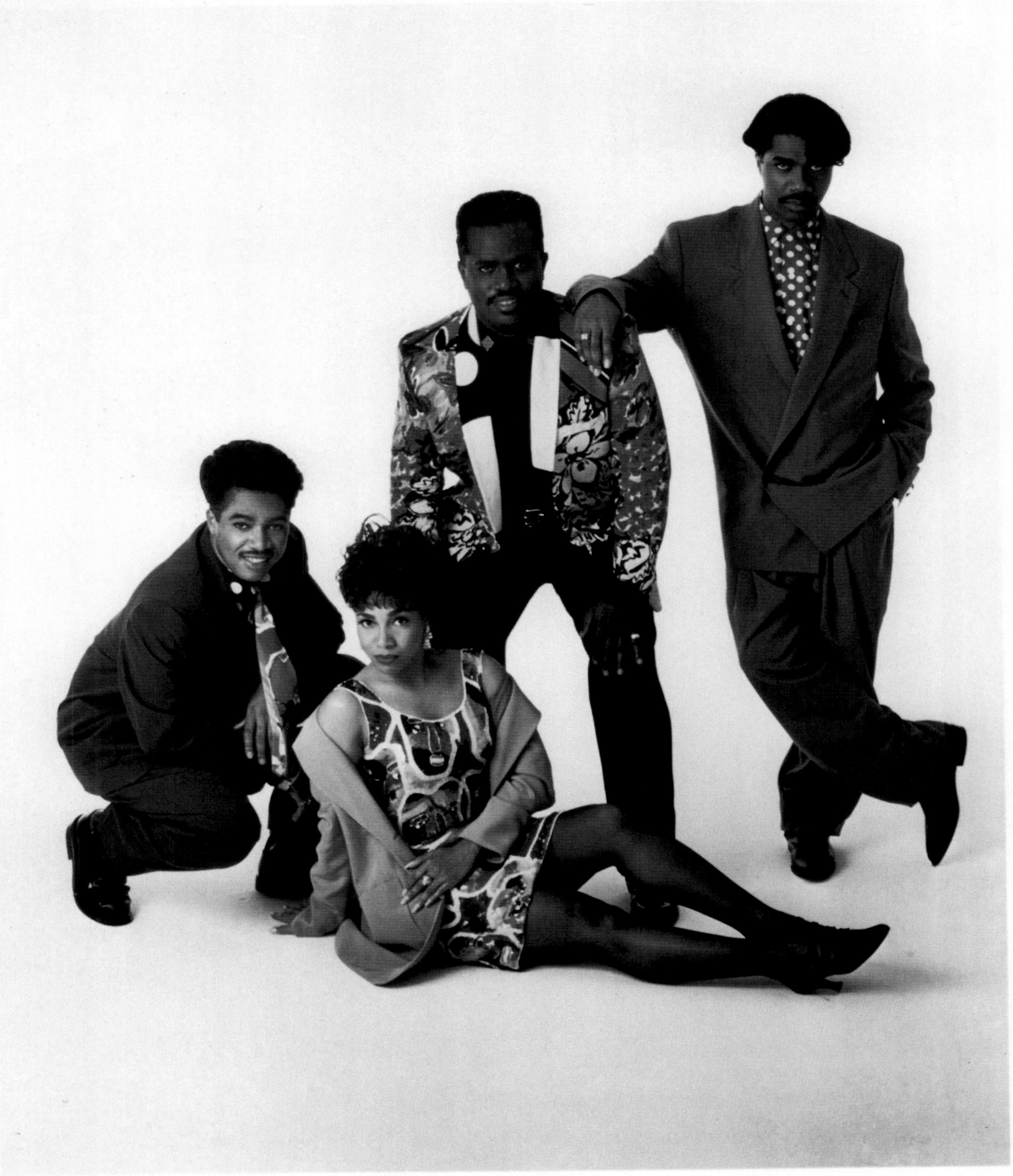

David Lewis Rachel Oliver Jonathan Lewis Wayne Lewis

Photo Credit: Scott Morgan

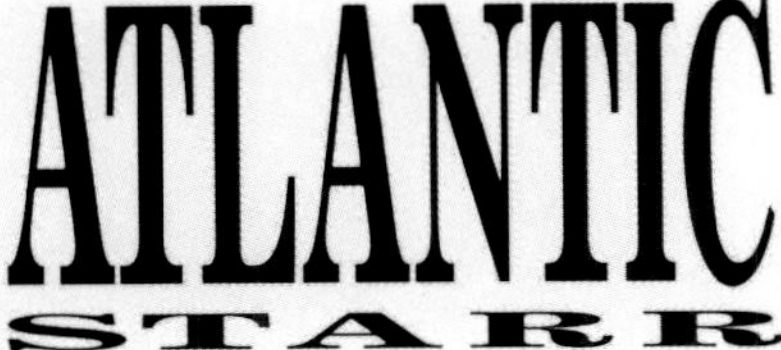

reprise

© 1991 Reprise Records/Permission to reproduce limited to editorial uses in newspapers and other regularly published periodicals and television news programming.

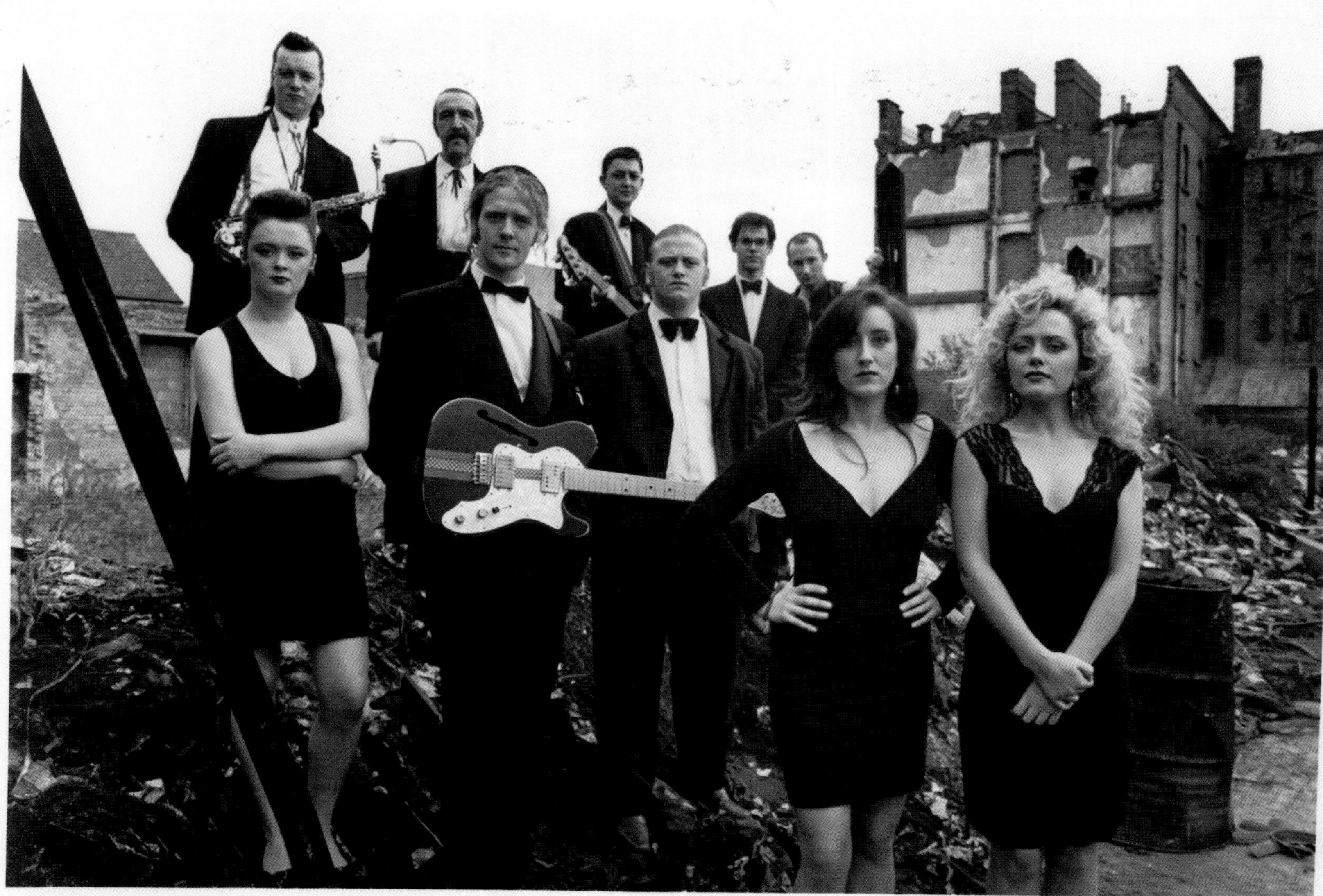

Copyright © 1991 Beacon Communications Corp.
All rights reserved.
Permission is hereby granted to newspapers and other periodicals to reproduce this photograph for publicity or advertising except for the endorsement of products. This must not be sold, leased or given away.
Printed in U.S.A

THE COMMITMENTS
A Twentieth Century Fox Release

TC-3 The Commitments. Back row, left to right: Dean (**FELIM GORMLEY**), Joey "The Lips" (**JOHNNY MURPHY**), Derek (**KENNETH McCLUSKEY**), Steven (**MICHAEL AHERNE**) and Mickah (**DAVE FINNEGAN**). Front row, left to right: Bernie (**BRONAGH GALLAGHER**), Outspan (**GLEN HANSARD**), Deco (**ANDREW STRONG**), Natalie (**MARIA DOYLE**) and Imelda (**ANGELINE BALL**) in Alan Parker's new film, "**THE COMMITMENTS**."

Photo credit: David Appleby

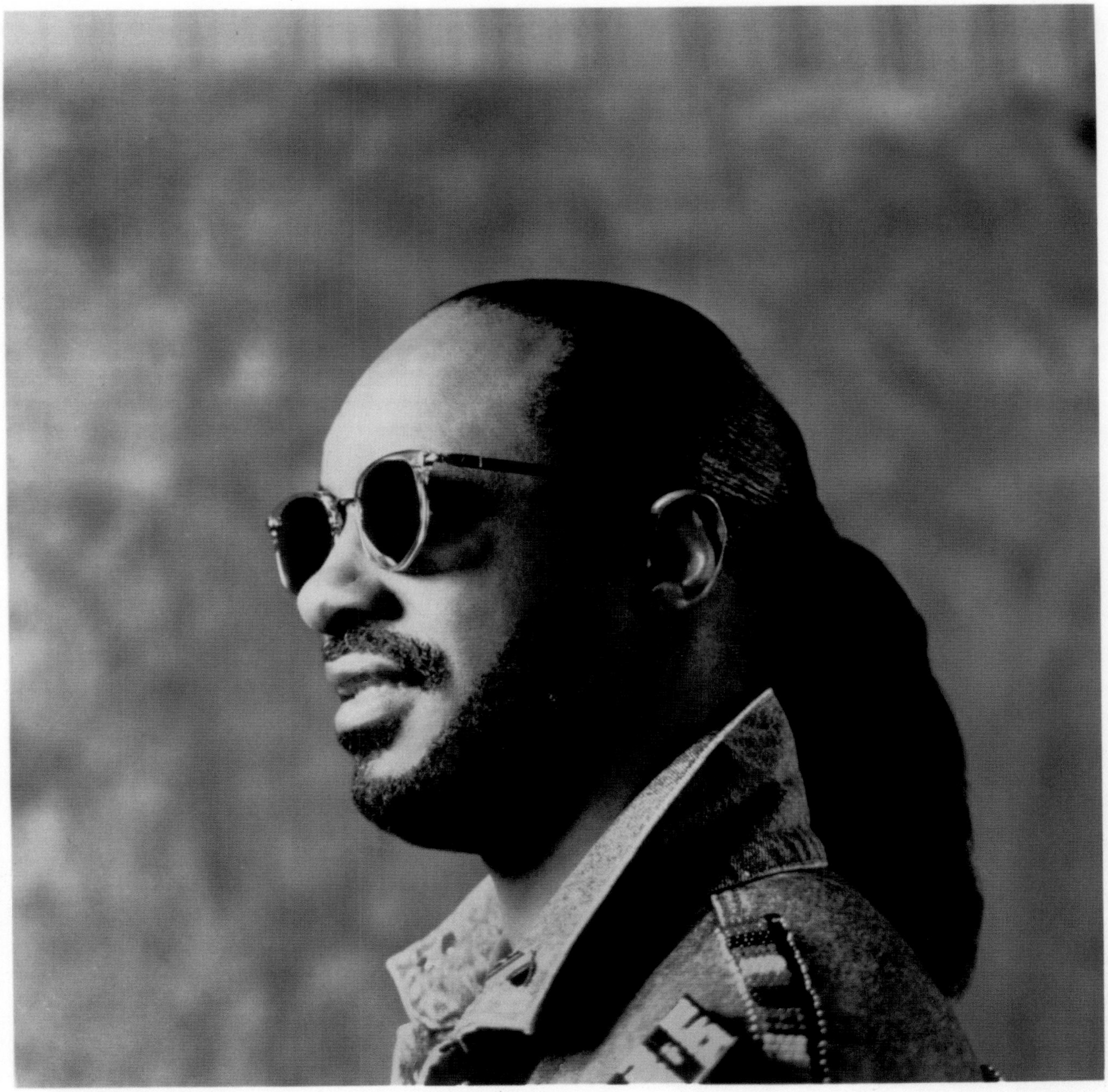

STEVIE WONDER

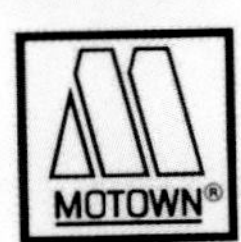

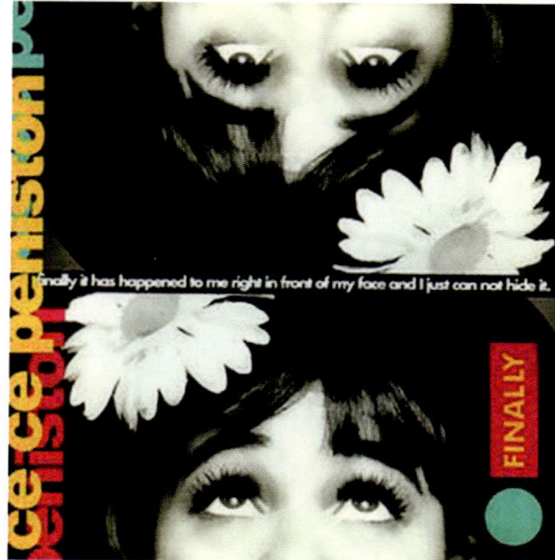

CeCe Peniston's "Finally" became an instant dance club anthem and the former Miss Black Arizona's biggest hit song, peaking at #5 on *Billboard*'s Hot 100.

Billboard 200: *Finally* (#70)
Billboard Hot 100: "Finally" (#5); "We Got a Love Thang" (#20); "Keep On Walkin'" (#15); "Inside That I Cried" (#94); "Crazy Love" (#97)

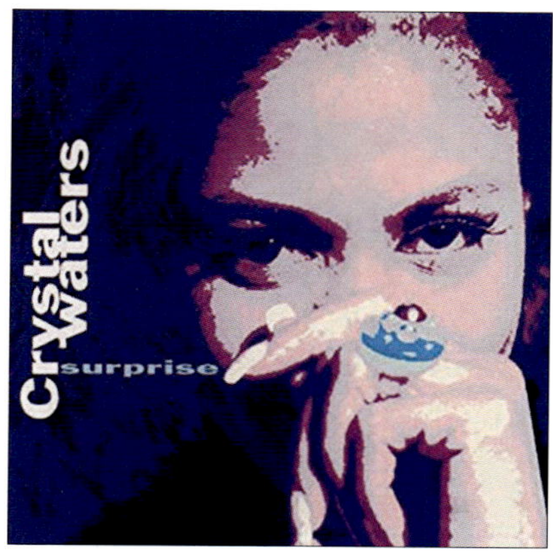

From her debut album, *Surprise*, singer-songwriter Crystal Waters had a No. 1 dance hit with the house-music treasure, "Gypsy Woman (She's Homeless)."

Billboard 200: *Surprise* (#197)
Billboard Hot 100: "Gypsy Woman (She's Homeless)" (#8)

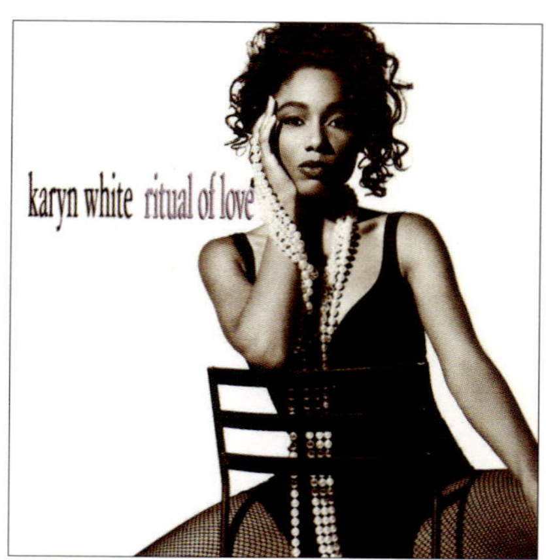

On the No. 1 hit single, "Romantic," R&B singer Karyn White worked with Jimmy Jam & Terry Lewis, the prolific production duo behind Janet Jackson's success.

Billboard 200: *Ritual of Love* (#53)
Billboard Hot 100: "Romantic" (No. 1); "The Way I Feel About You" (#12)

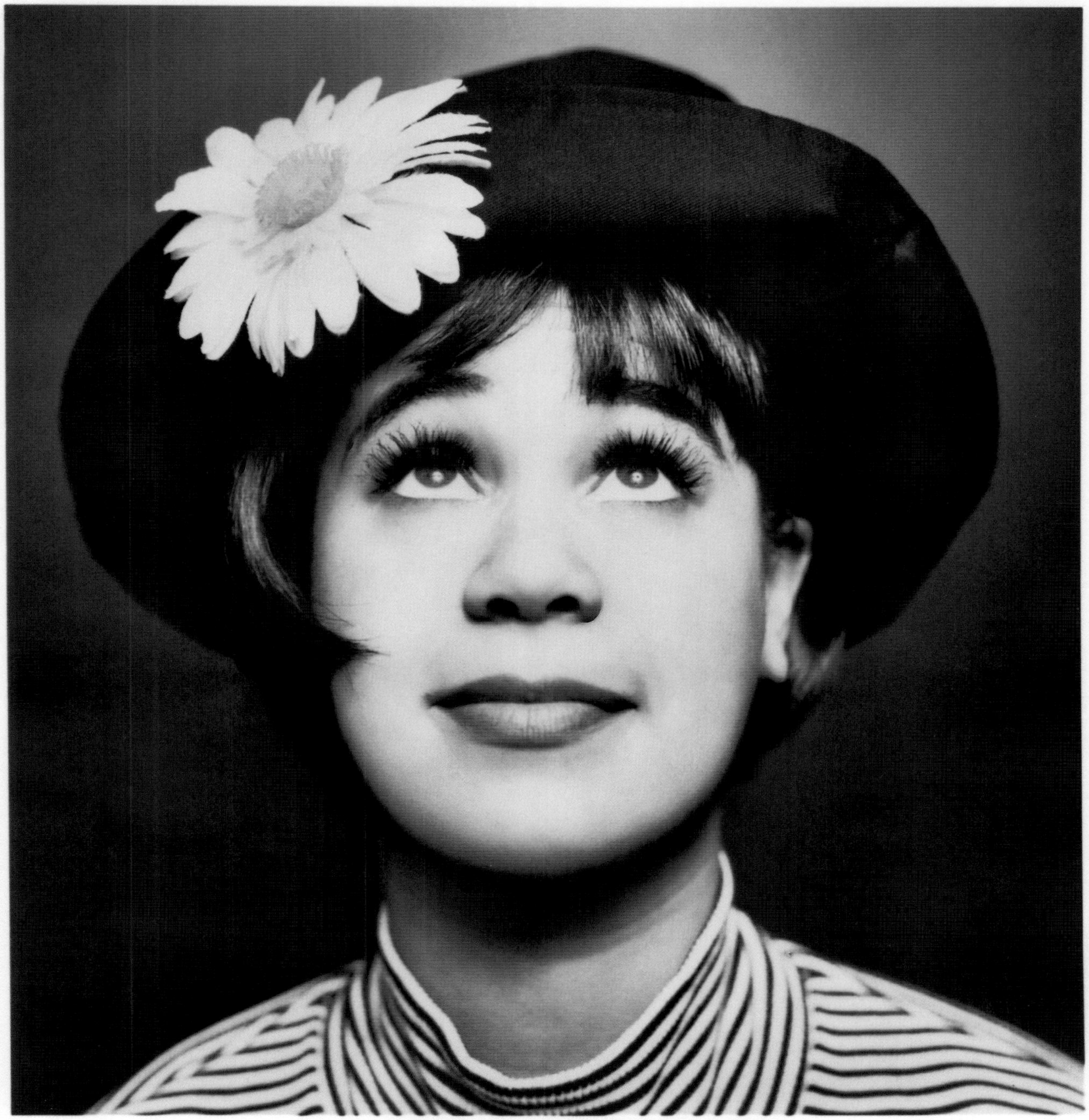

PHOTO: PEGGY SIROTA

CE CE PENISTON

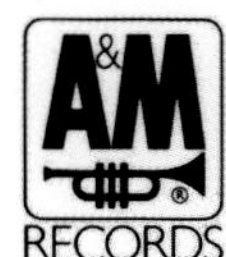

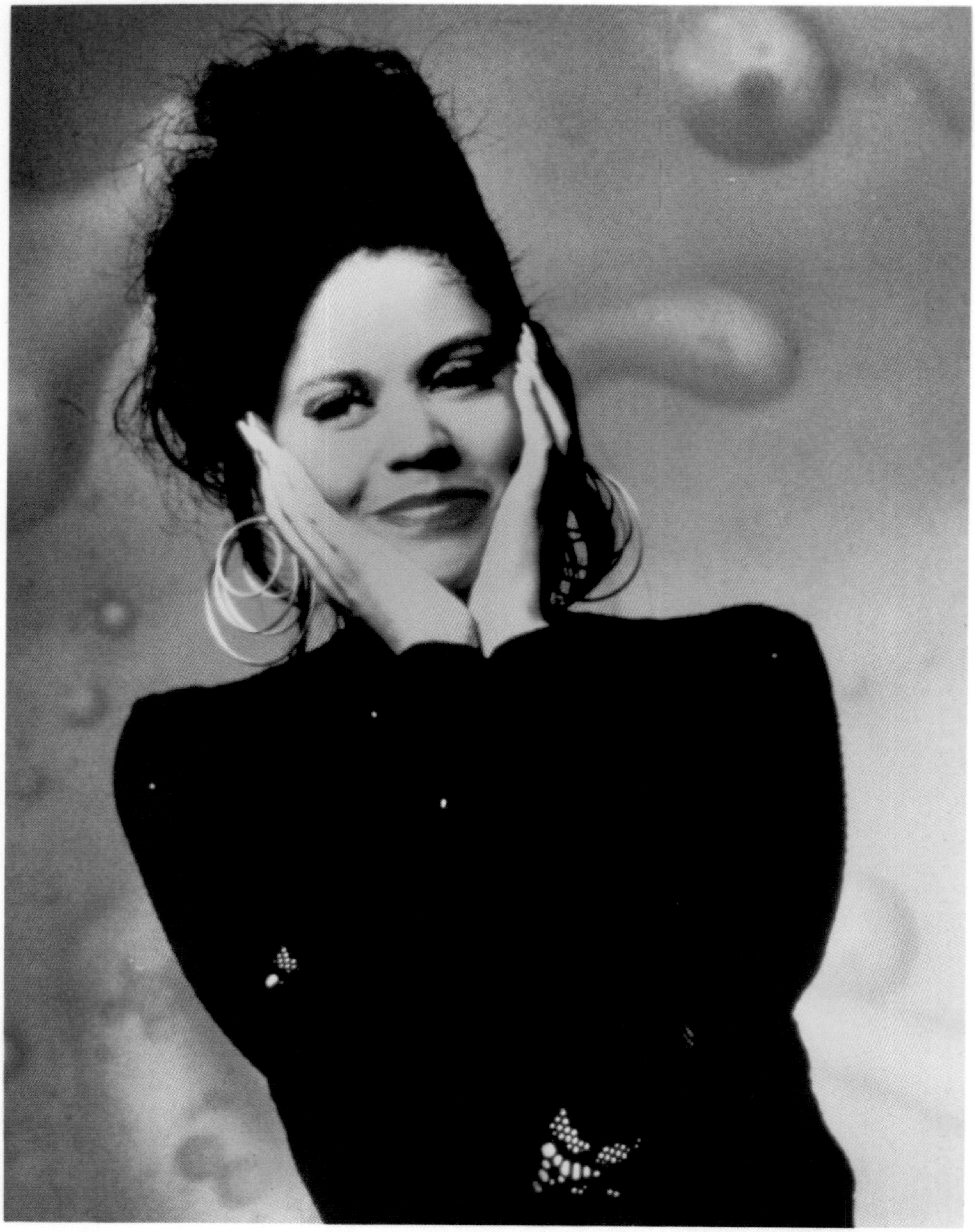

© PolyGram 1991

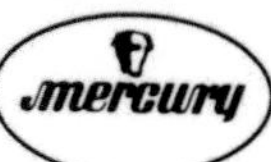

CRYSTAL WATERS

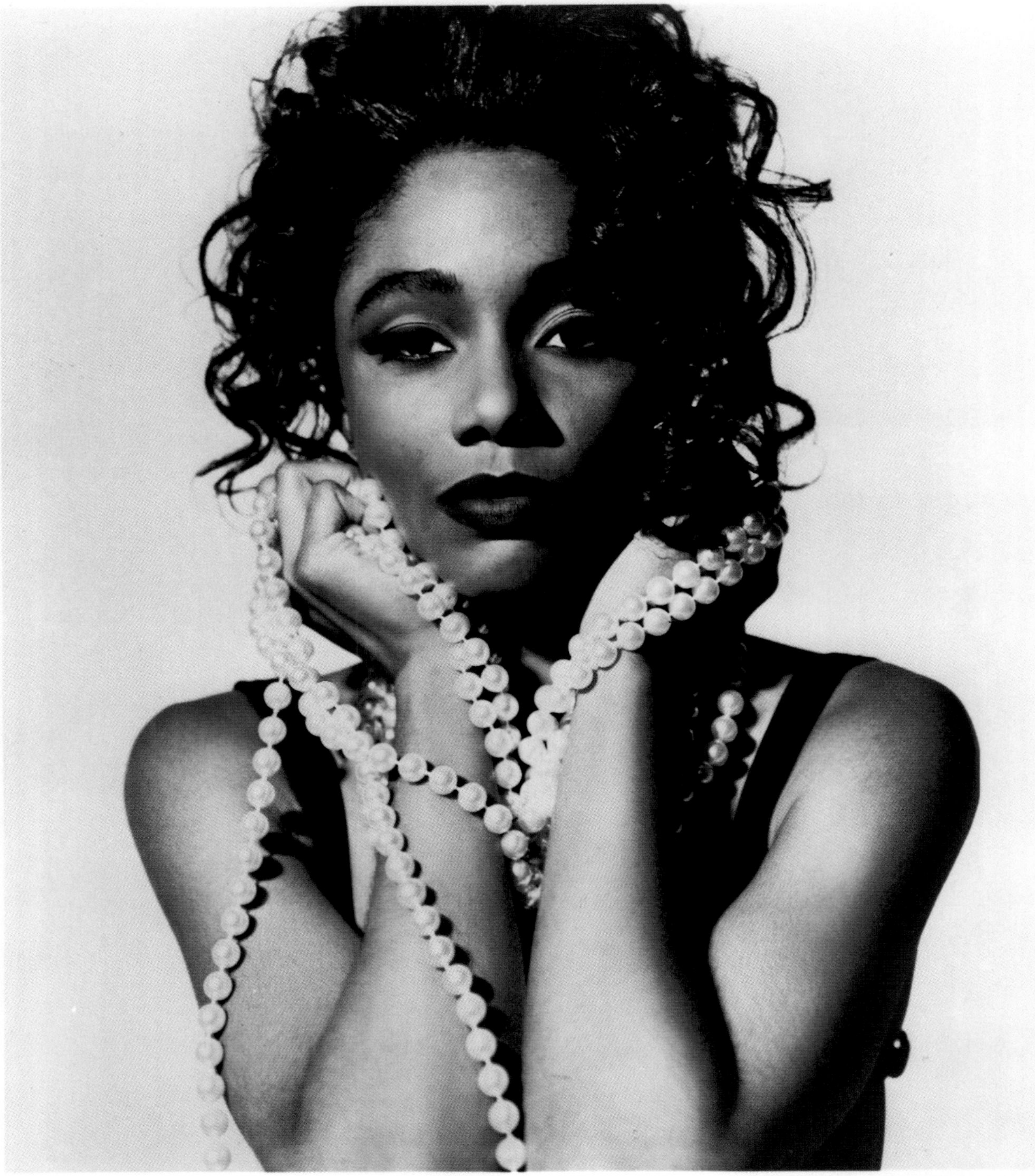

Karyn White

Photo Credit: Chris Cuffaro

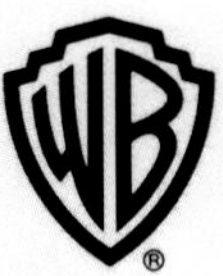

© 1991 Warner Bros. Records/Permission to reproduce limited to editorial uses in newspapers and other regularly published periodicals and television news programming.

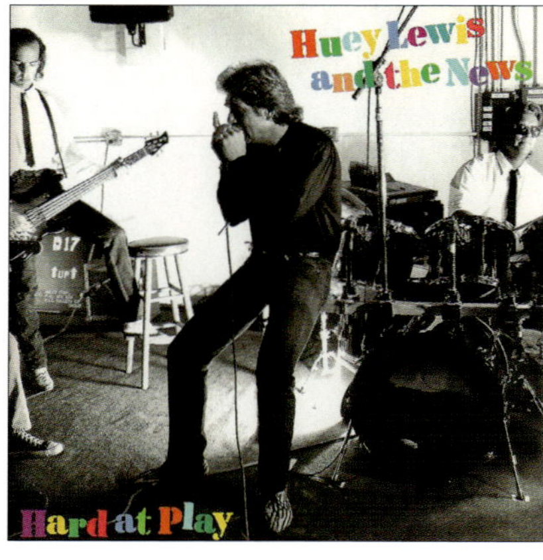

Huey Lewis & the News extended their commercial heyday with *Hard at Play*, which generated two hits, "Couple Days Off" and "It Hit Me Like a Hammer."

Billboard 200: *Hard at Play* (#27)
Billboard Hot 100: "Couple Days Off (#11); "It Hit Me Like a Hammer" (#21)

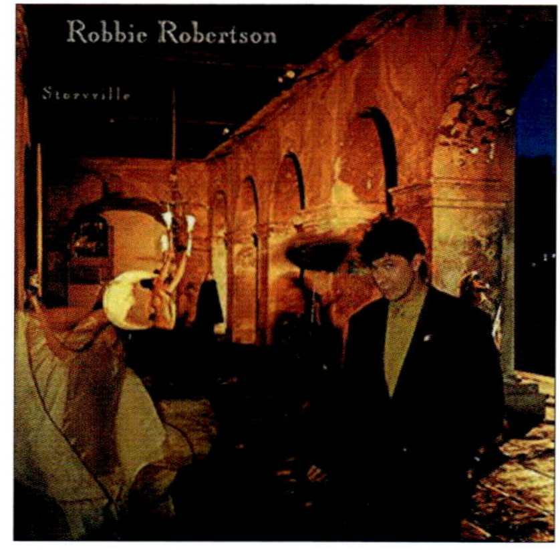

The Band's **Robbie Robertson** recorded his second solo album, *Storyville*, focusing on the sounds and imagery of the famed jazz district of New Orleans.

Billboard 200: *Storyville* (#69)

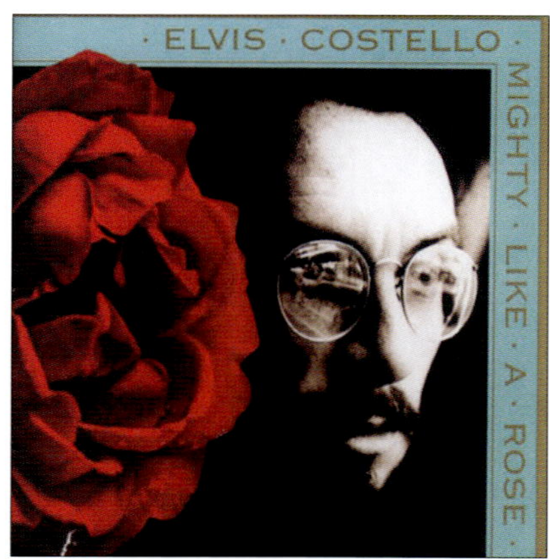

"The Other Side of Summer," a Beach Boys pastiche from **Elvis Costello**'s *Mighty Like a Rose*, reached No. 1 on *Billboard*'s Modern Rock Tracks chart.

Billboard 200: *Mighty Like a Rose* (#55)

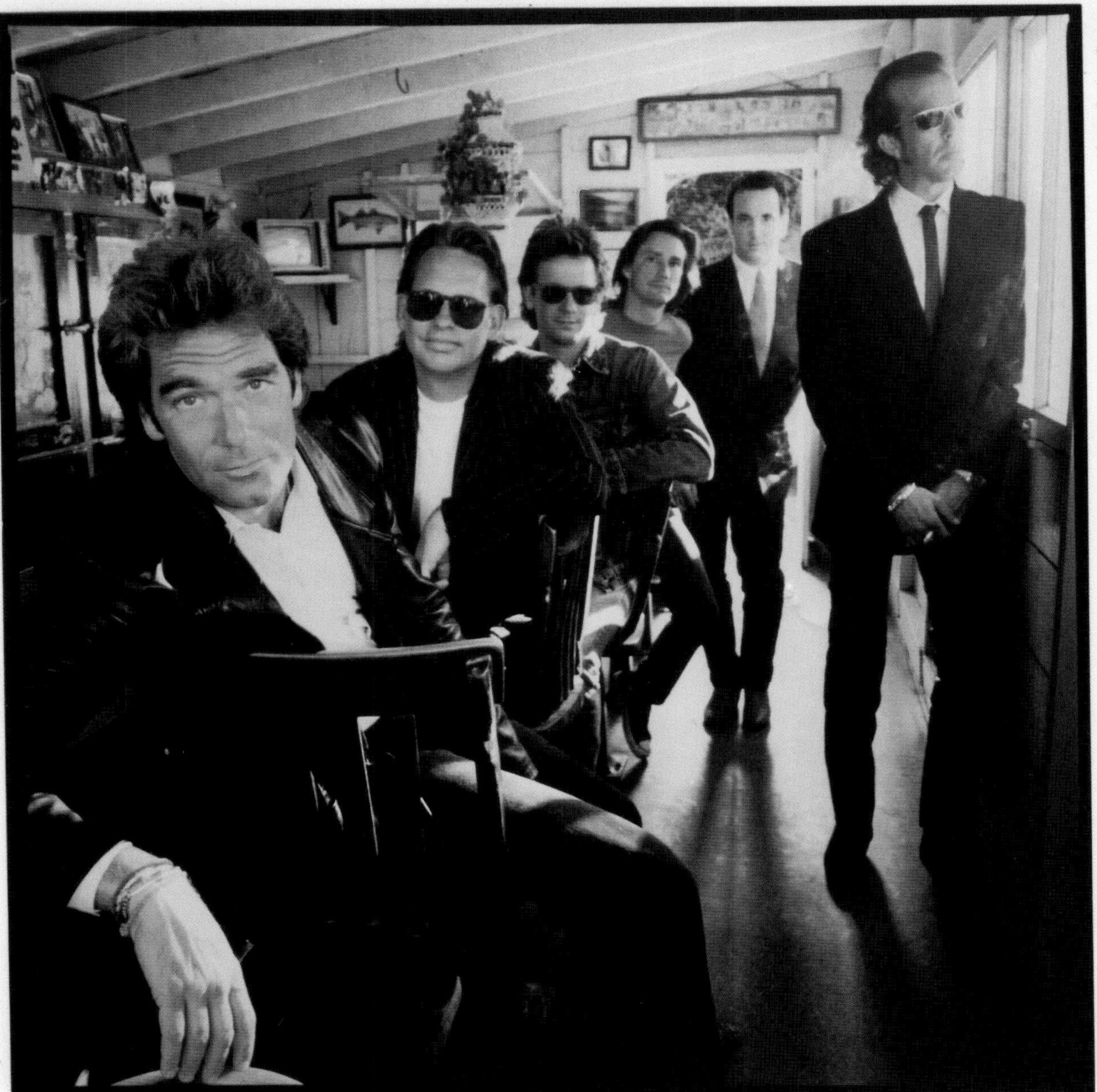

Photography: Aaron Rapoport

©1991 EMI Records USA

Huey Lewis and the News

FROM EMI

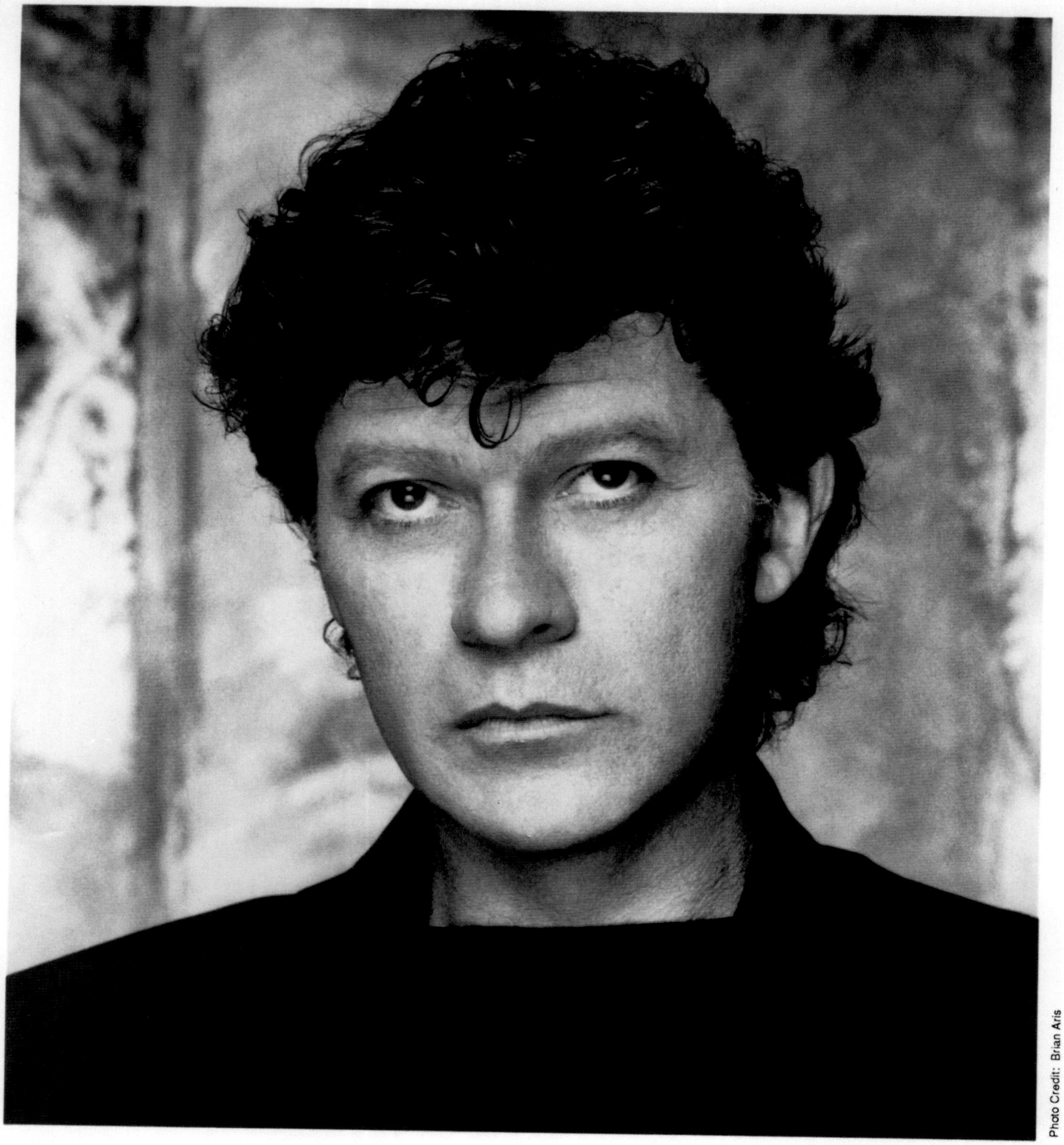

Photo Credit: Brian Aris

Robbie Robertson

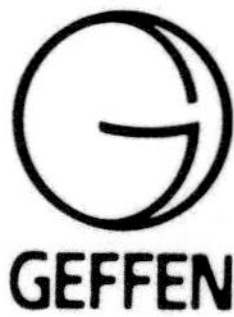

© 1991 The David Geffen Company. Permission to reproduce limited to editorial uses ir newspapers and other regularly published periodicals and television news programminq

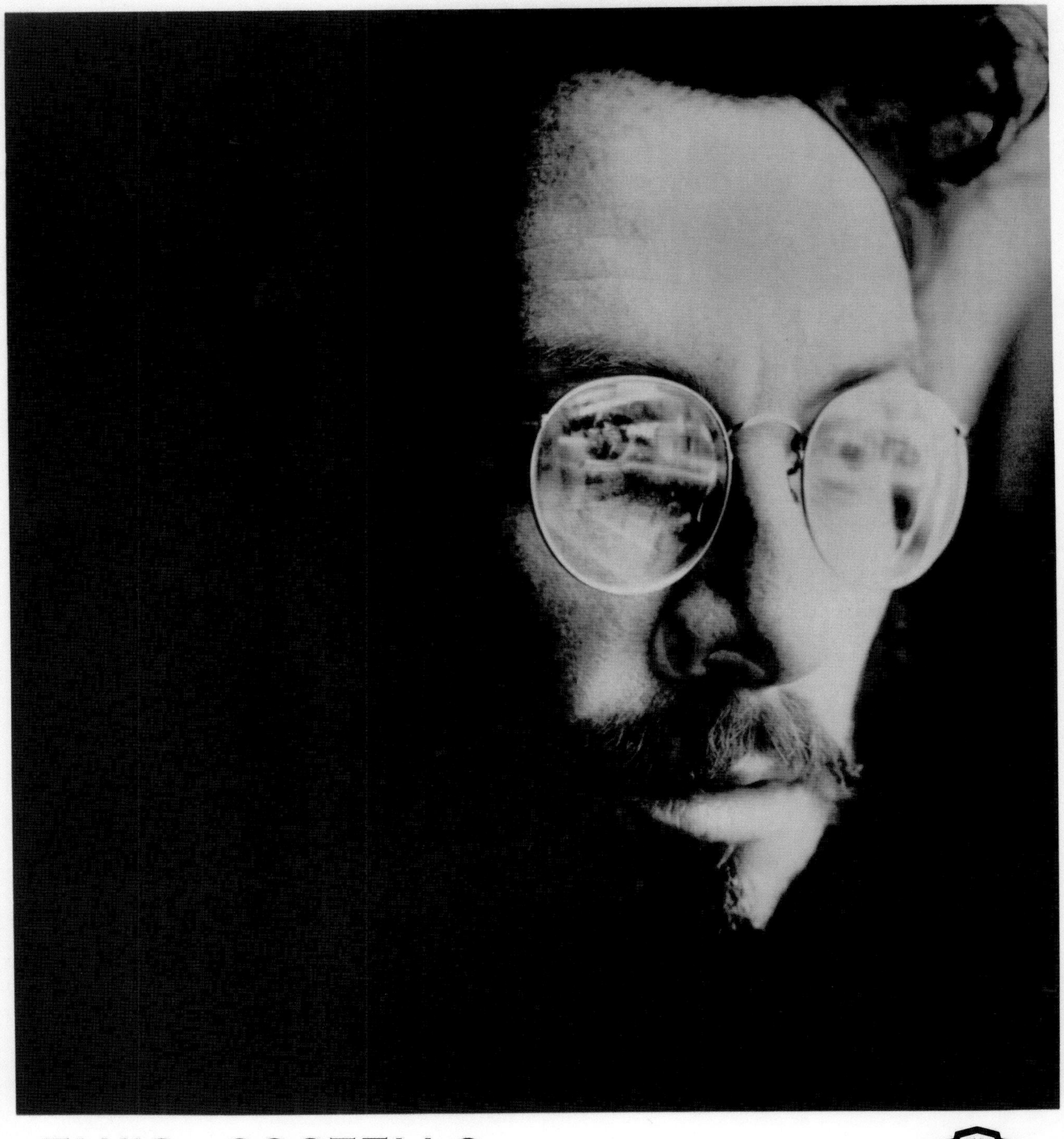

Photo Credit: Amelia Stein

· ELVIS · COSTELLO ·

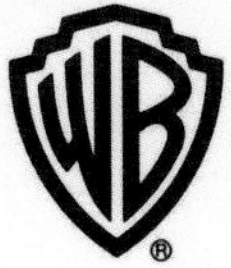

© 1991 Warner Bros. Records/Permission to reproduce limited to editorial uses in newspapers and other regularly published periodicals and television news programming.

Marketed after **Stevie Ray Vaughan**'s 1990 death, *The Sky Is Crying* compiled studio outtakes, such as an instrumental cover of Jimi Hendrix' "Little Wing."

Billboard 200: *The Sky Is Crying* (#10)

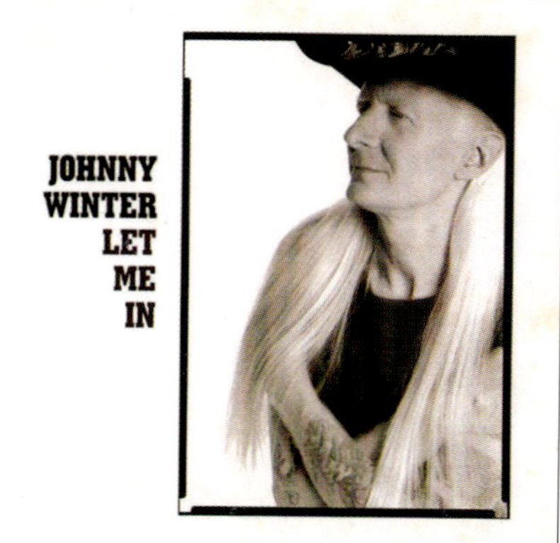

Texas guitar slinger **Johnny Winter** returned to straight-ahead blues material on the album *Let Me In*, an approach which garnered a Grammy nomination.

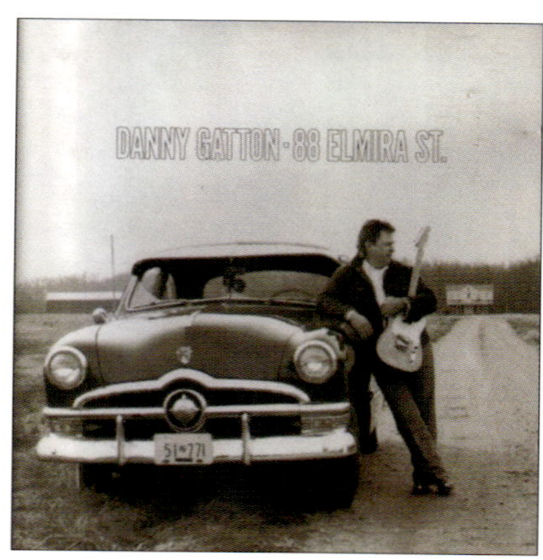

Nicknamed "the world's greatest unknown guitarist," **Danny Gatton** signed his first major-label deal and released the instrumental album *88 Elmira Street.*

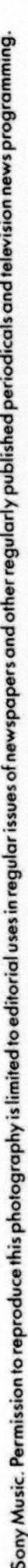
© 1991 Sony Music. Permission to reproduce this photography is limited to editorial uses in regular issues of newspapers and other regularly published periodicals and television news programming.

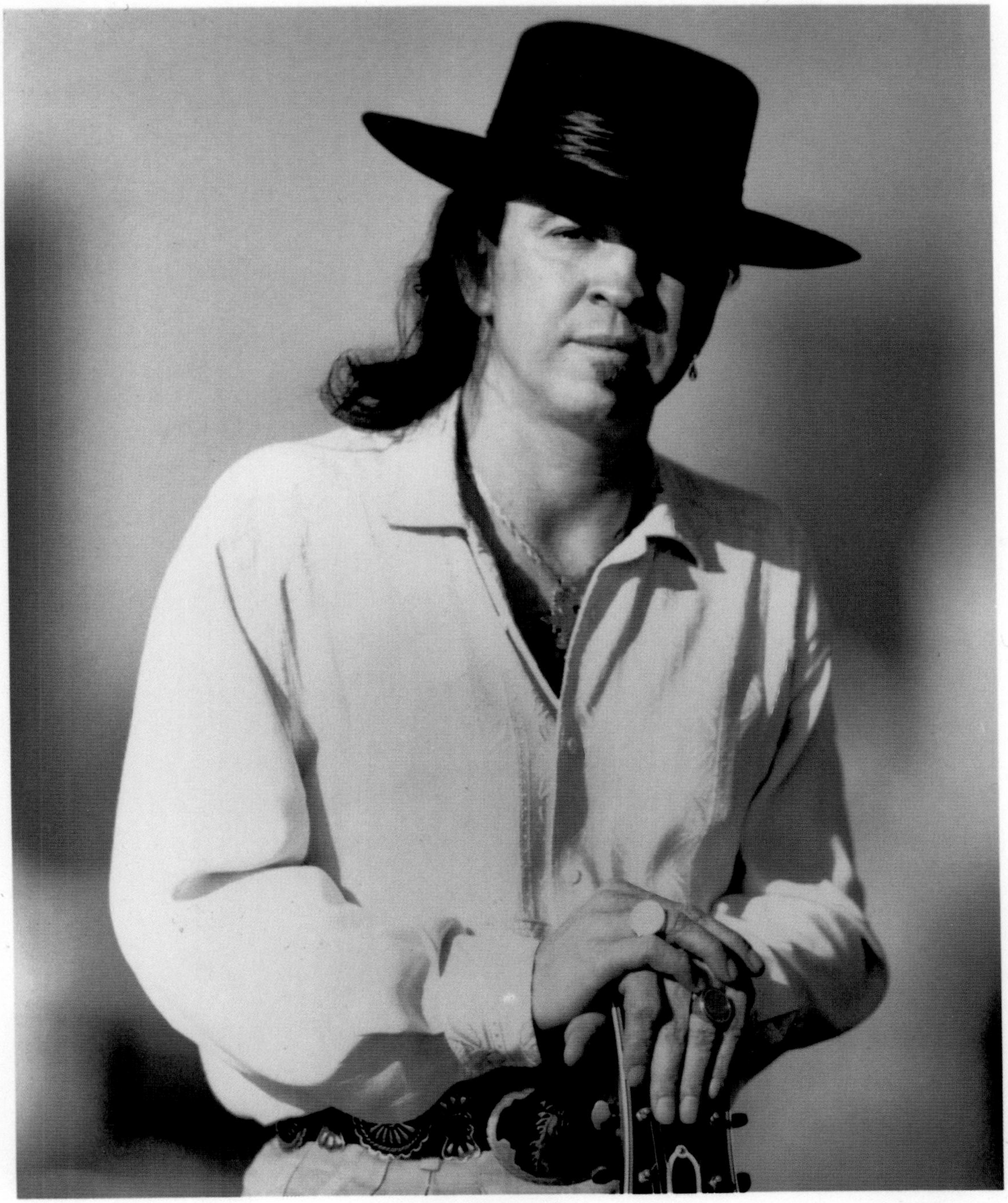

Stevie Ray Vaughan
and Double Trouble

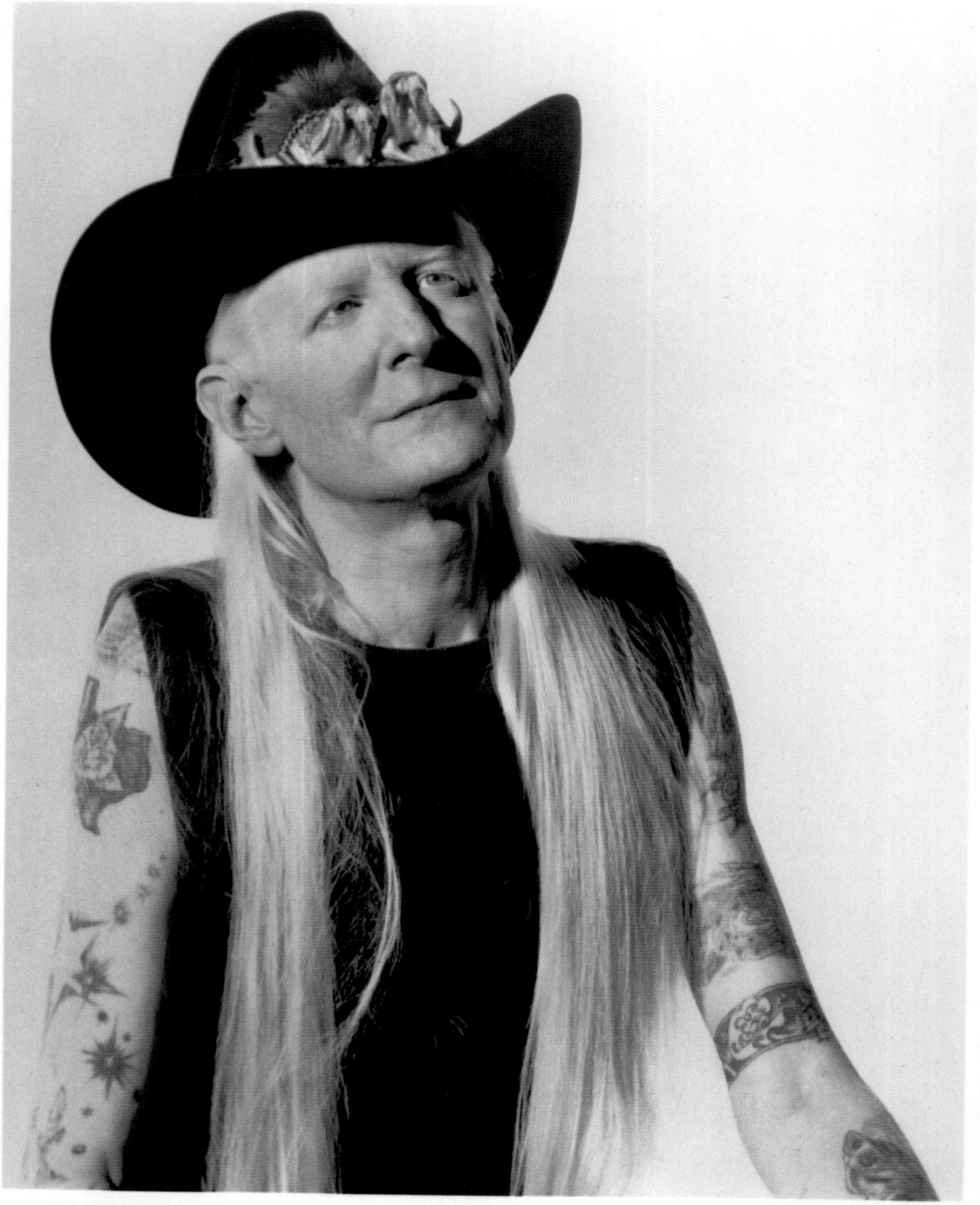

Photo Credit: Mark Weiss 8/91

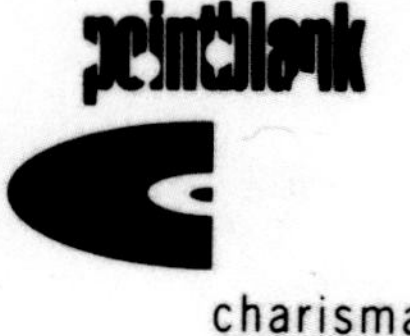

JOHNNY WINTER

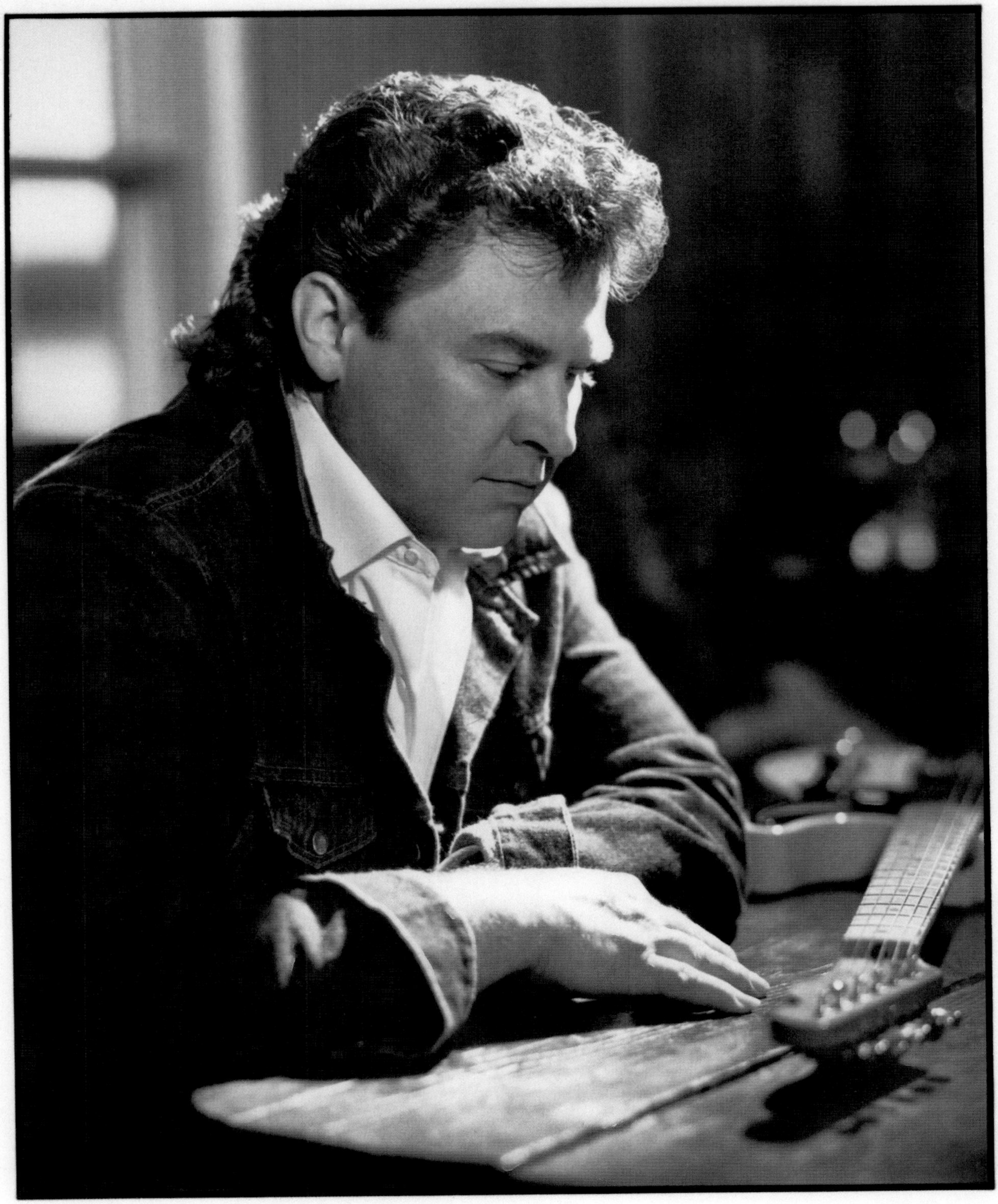

DANNY GATTON

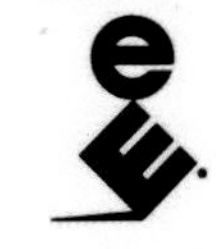

Elektra Entertainment

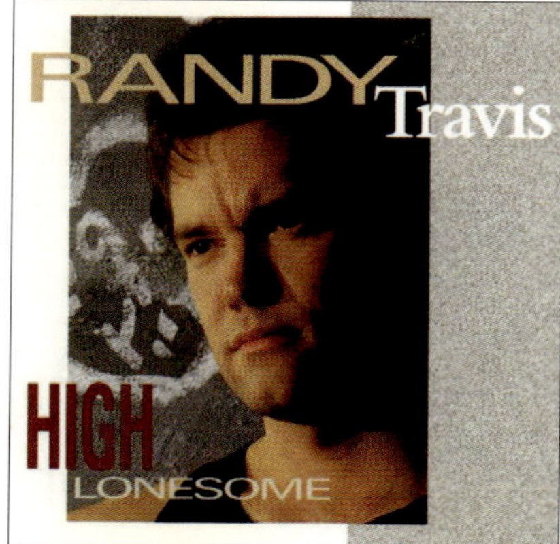

Randy Travis' *High Lonesome* contained a trio of country hits co-written on tour with fellow artist Alan Jackson, including the No. 1 track, "Forever Together."

Billboard 200: *High Lonesome* (#43)

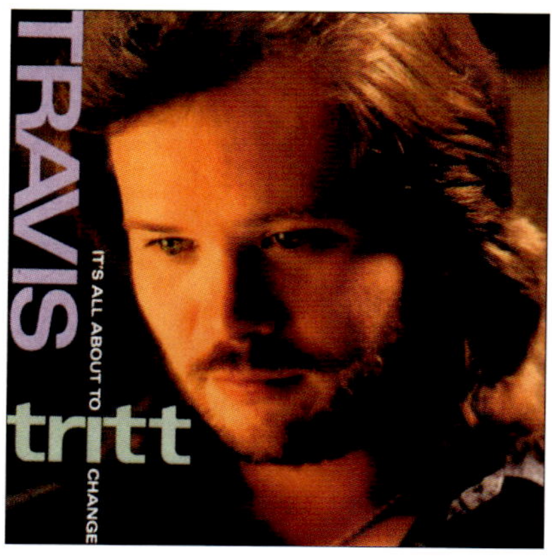

Four country singles from **Travis Tritt**'s *It's All About to Change* reached the Top 5, notably the Grammy-winning Marty Stuart duet, "The Whiskey Ain't Workin'."

Billboard 200: *It's All About to Change* (#22)

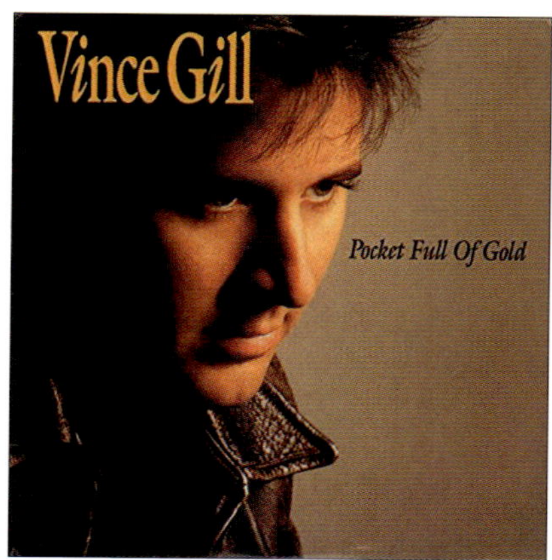

Country music star **Vince Gill**'s platinum *Pocket Full of Gold* placed four Top 10 songs on the charts, including the smash, "Take Your Memory with You."

Billboard 200: *Pocket Full of Gold* (#37)

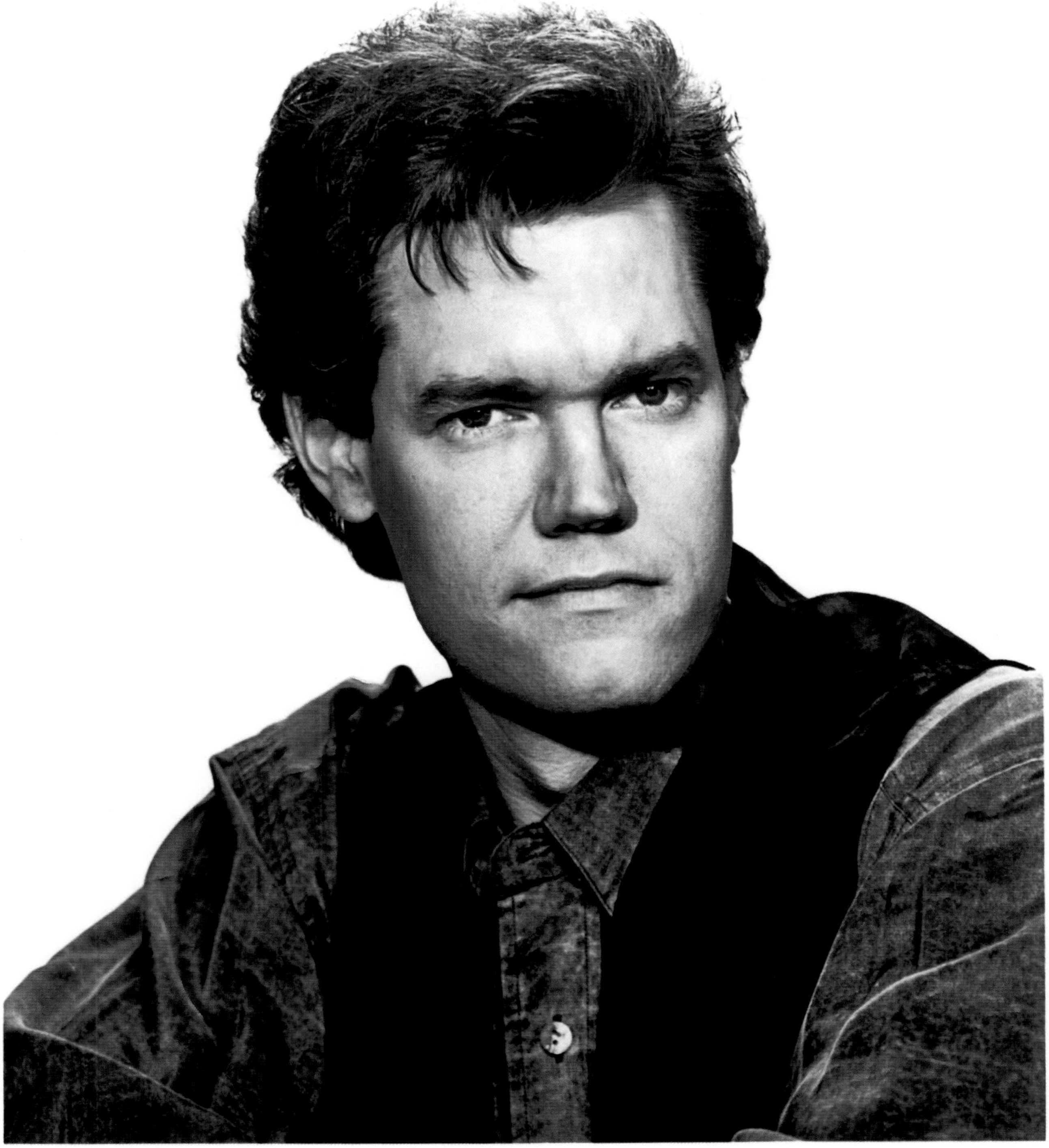

photo: Dennis Carney

RANDY TRAVIS

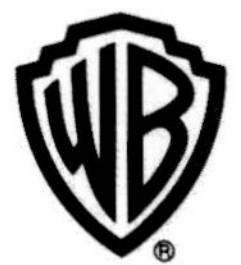

© 1991 Warner Bros. Records/Permission to reproduce limited to editorial uses in newspapers and other regularly published periodicals and television news programming.

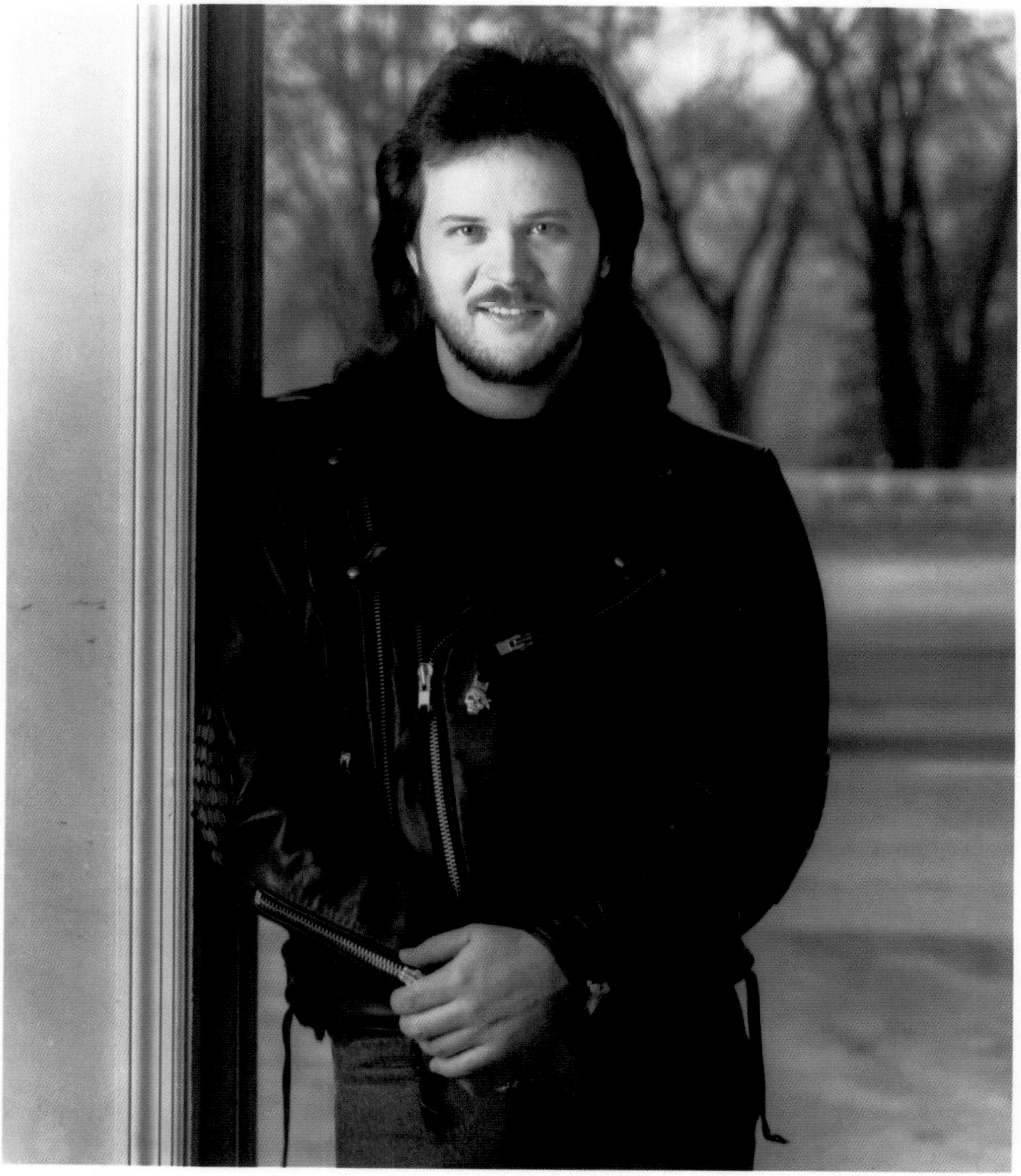

photo: Dean Dixon 5/91

TRAVIS TRITT

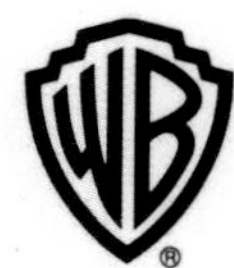

© 1991 Warner Bros. Records/Permission to reproduce limited to editorial uses in newspapers and other regularly published periodicals and television news programming.

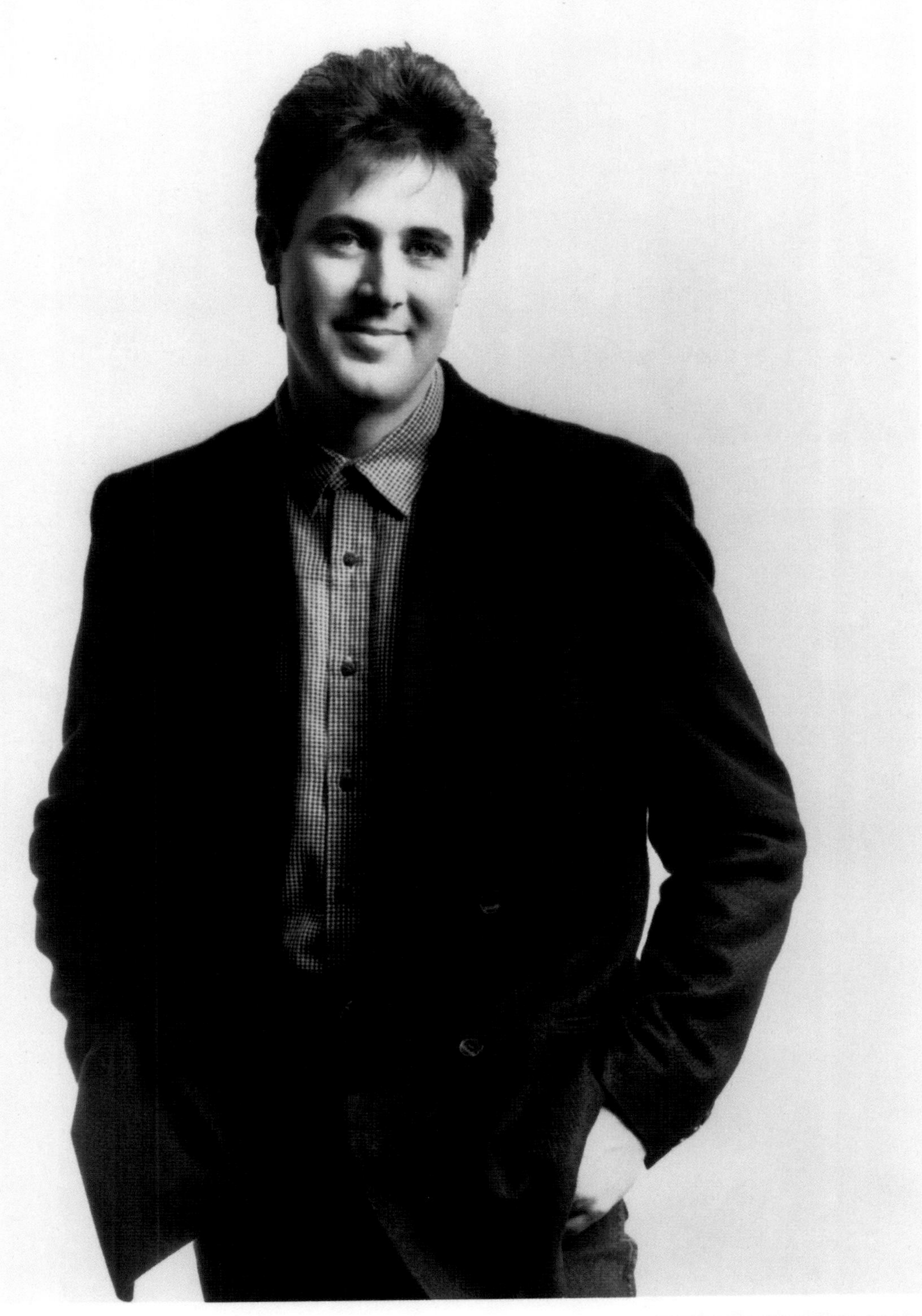

VINCE GILL

MCA RECORDS
NASHVILLE

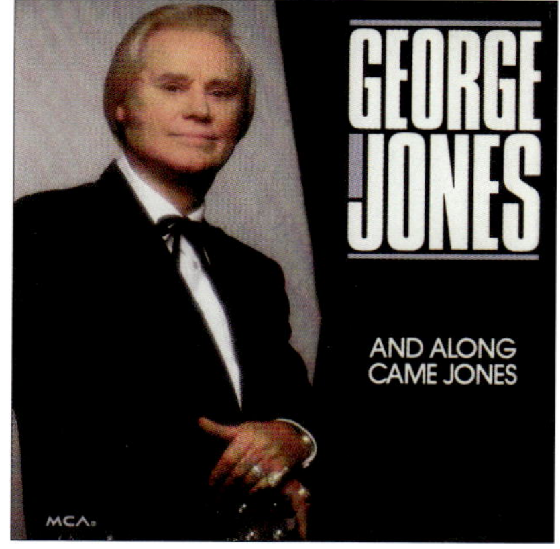

Losing favor on country radio to younger stars, **George Jones** ended his relationship with producer Billy Sherrill and quickly released *And Along Came Jones.*

Billboard 200: *And Along Came Jones* (#148)

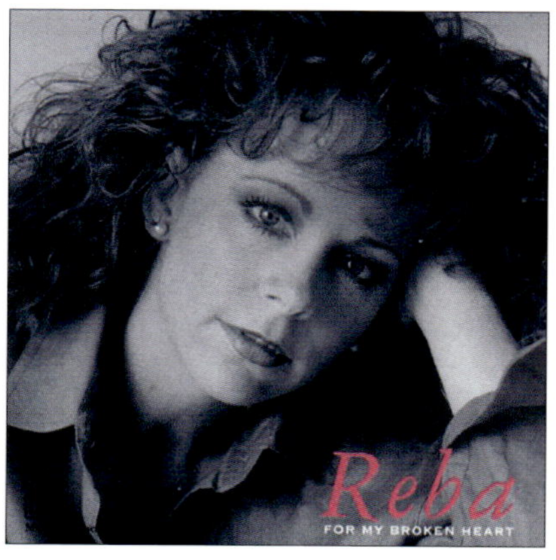

After a plane crash killed eight members of her touring entourage, country vocalist **Reba McEntire** dedicated her hit album *For My Broken Heart* to them.

Billboard 200: *For My Broken Heart* (#13)

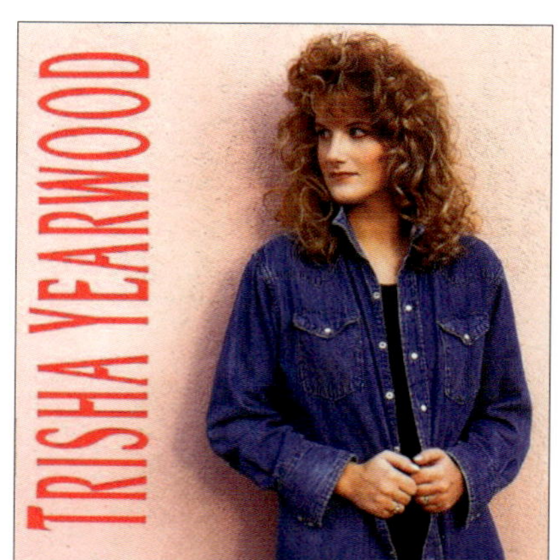

Trisha Yearwood rocketed to stardom with her debut single, "She's in Love with the Boy," which became the singer's first No. 1 hit on the country charts.

Billboard 200: *Trisha Yearwood* (#31)

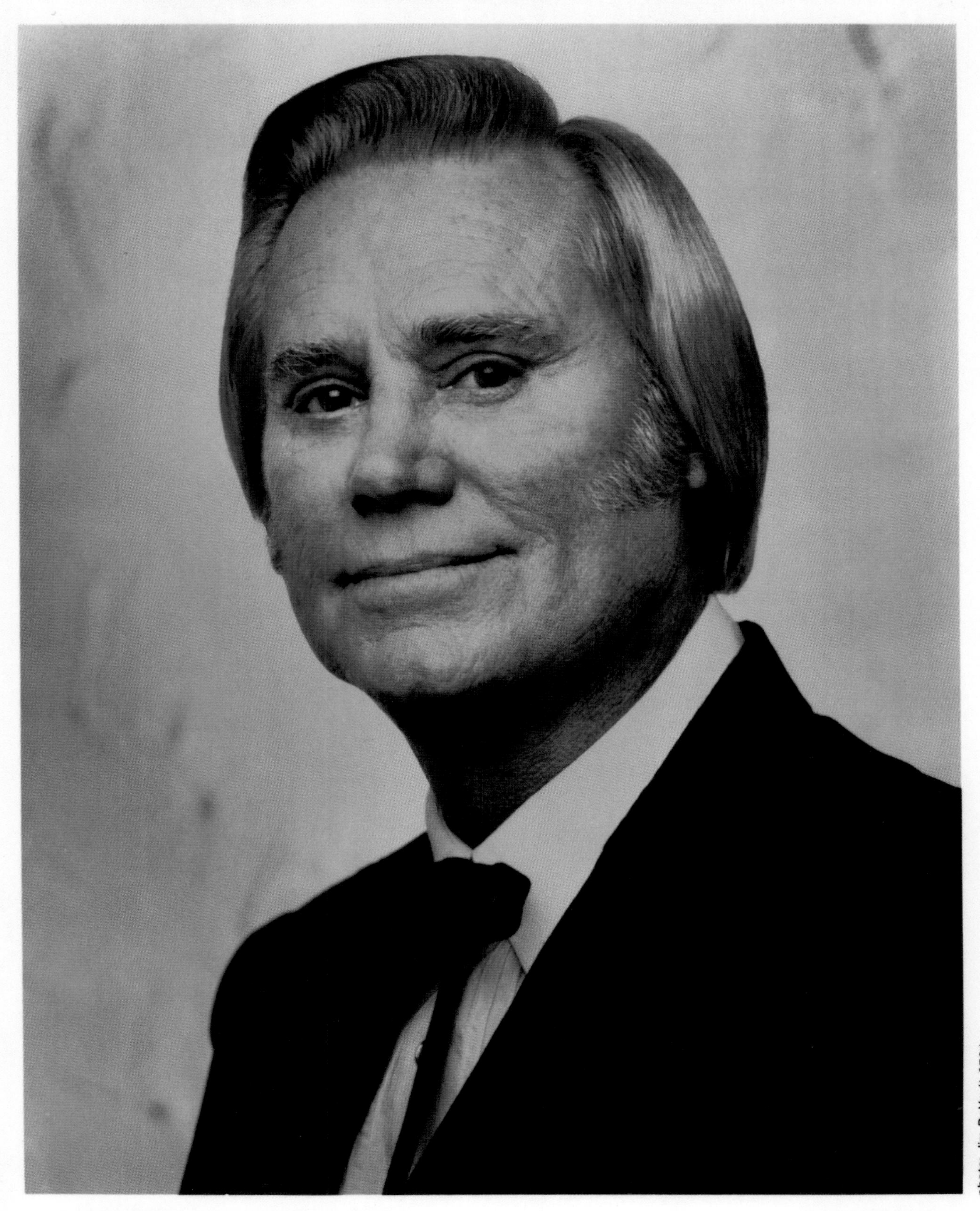

photo: Jim DeVault 0791

GEORGE JONES

MCA
NASHVILLE

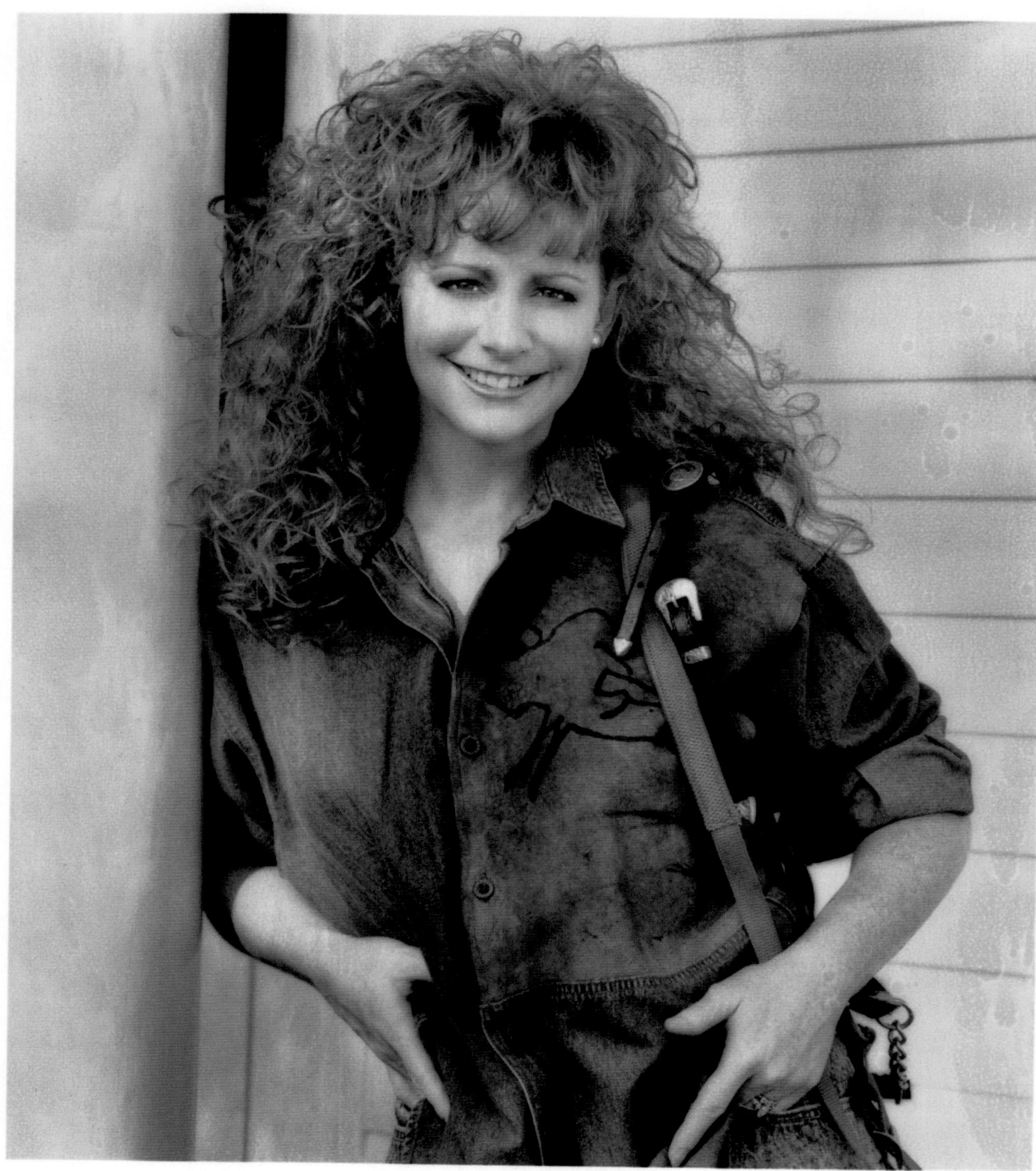

photo: McGuire 0991A

REBA McENTIRE

MCA
NASHVILLE

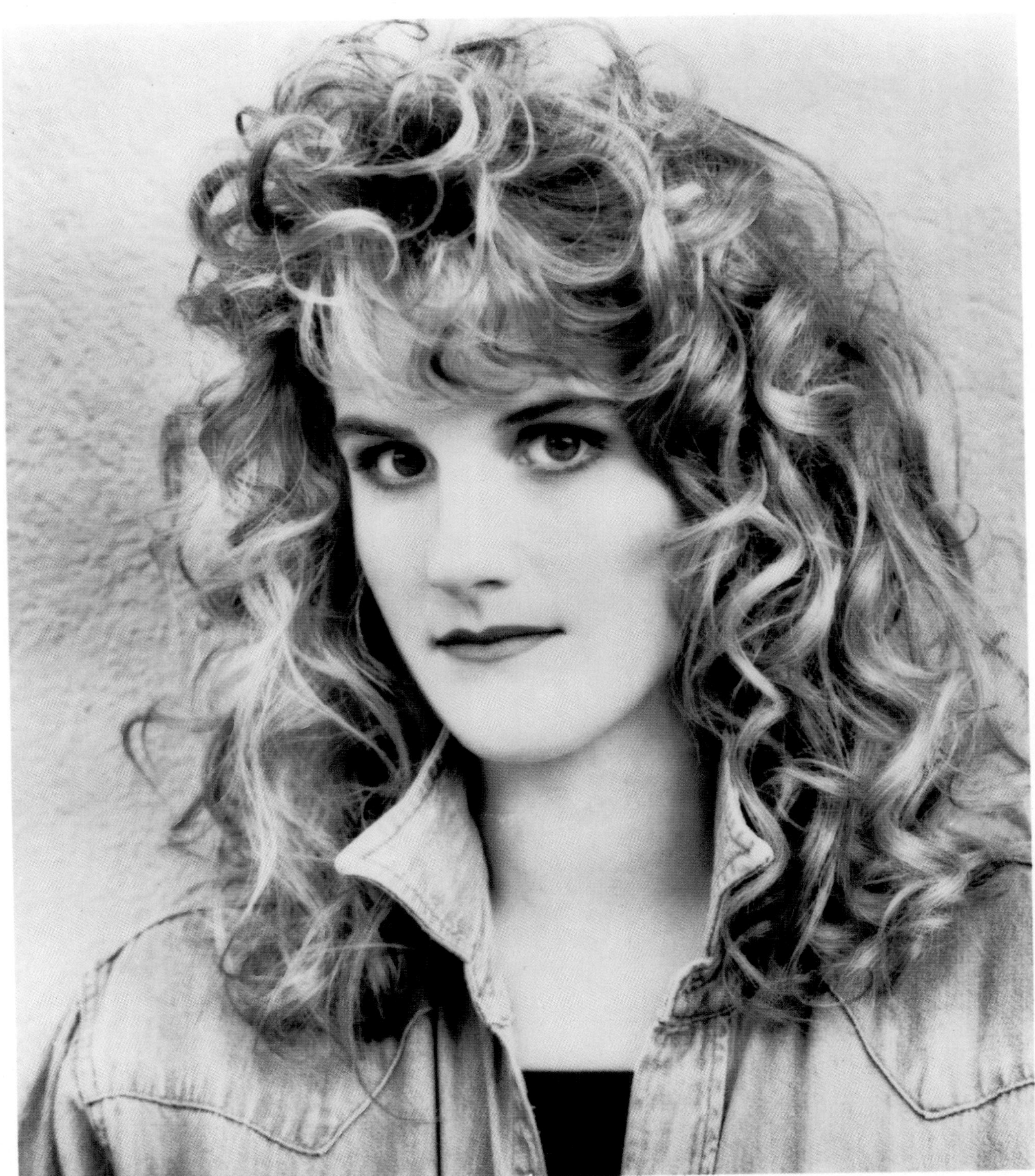

photo: McGuire 0491A

TRISHA YEARWOOD

MCA
NASHVILLE

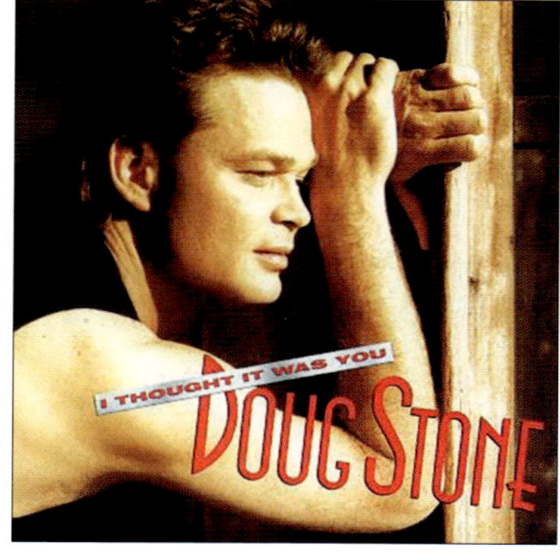

The platinum-selling *I Thought It Was You* yielded singer **Doug Stone**'s second No. 1 lament on the country music charts, "A Jukebox with a Country Song."

Billboard 200: *I Thought It Was You* (#74)

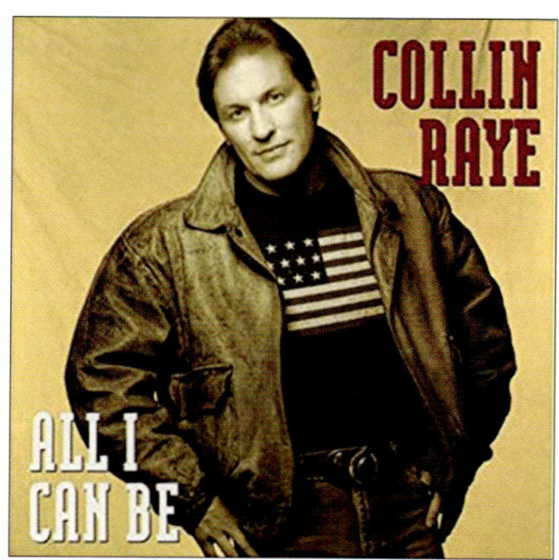

Collin Raye debuted with *All I Can Be*, and "Love, Me" shot to No. 1 on *Billboard*'s Hot Country Singles chart and became a popular song for funerals.

Billboard 200: *All I Can Be* (#54)

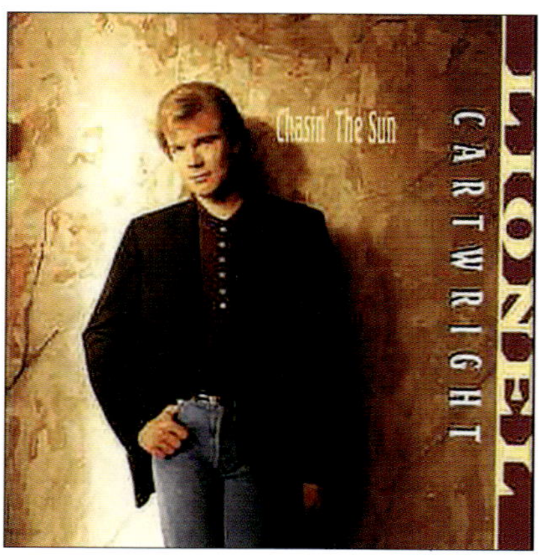

From *Chasin' the Sun*, his third album, singer-songwriter **Lionel Cartwright** chalked up his first chart-topping country hit with the single, "Leap of Faith."

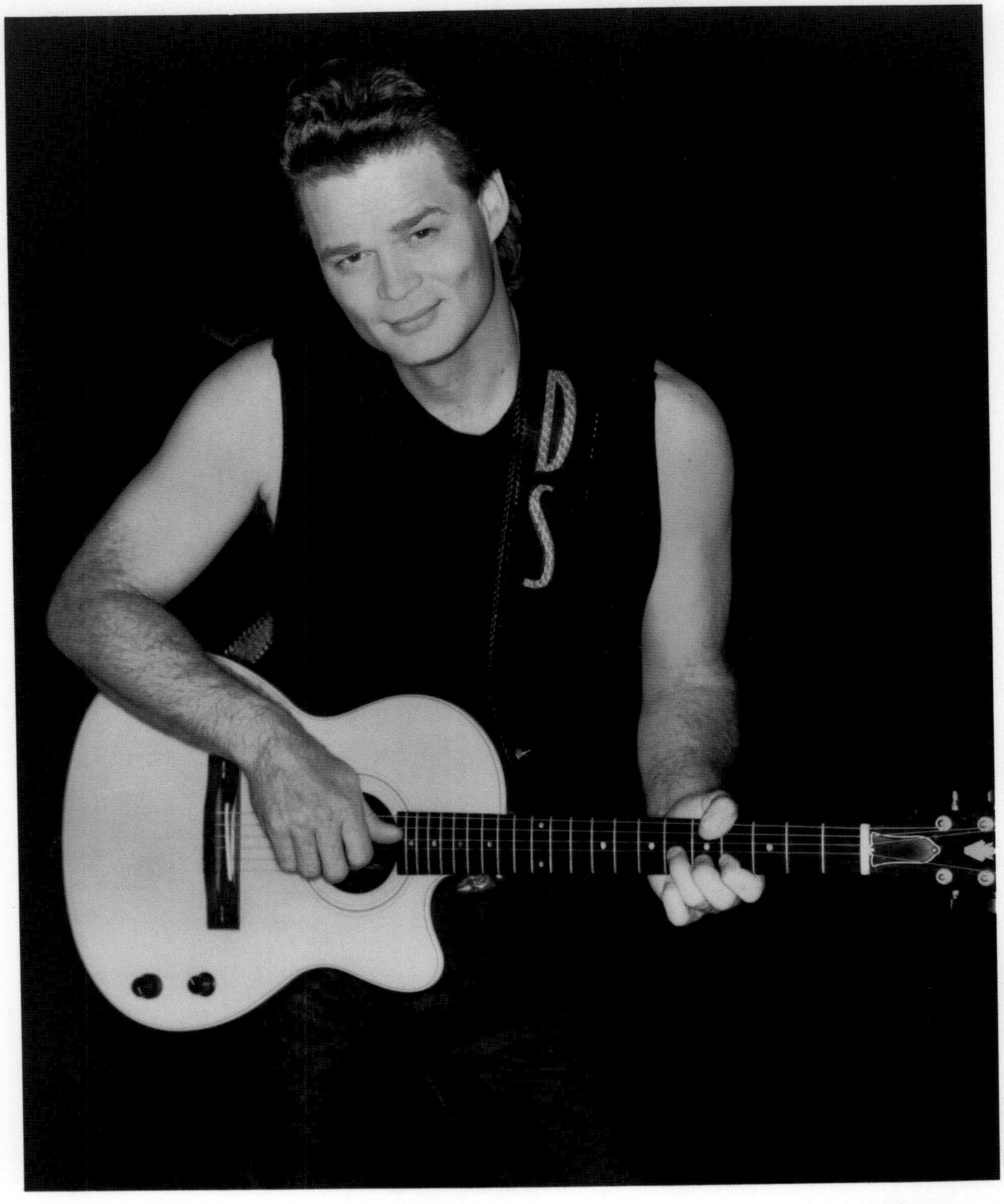

photo: Randee St.Nicholas

DOUG STONE

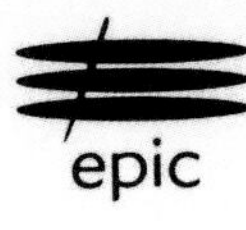

9106

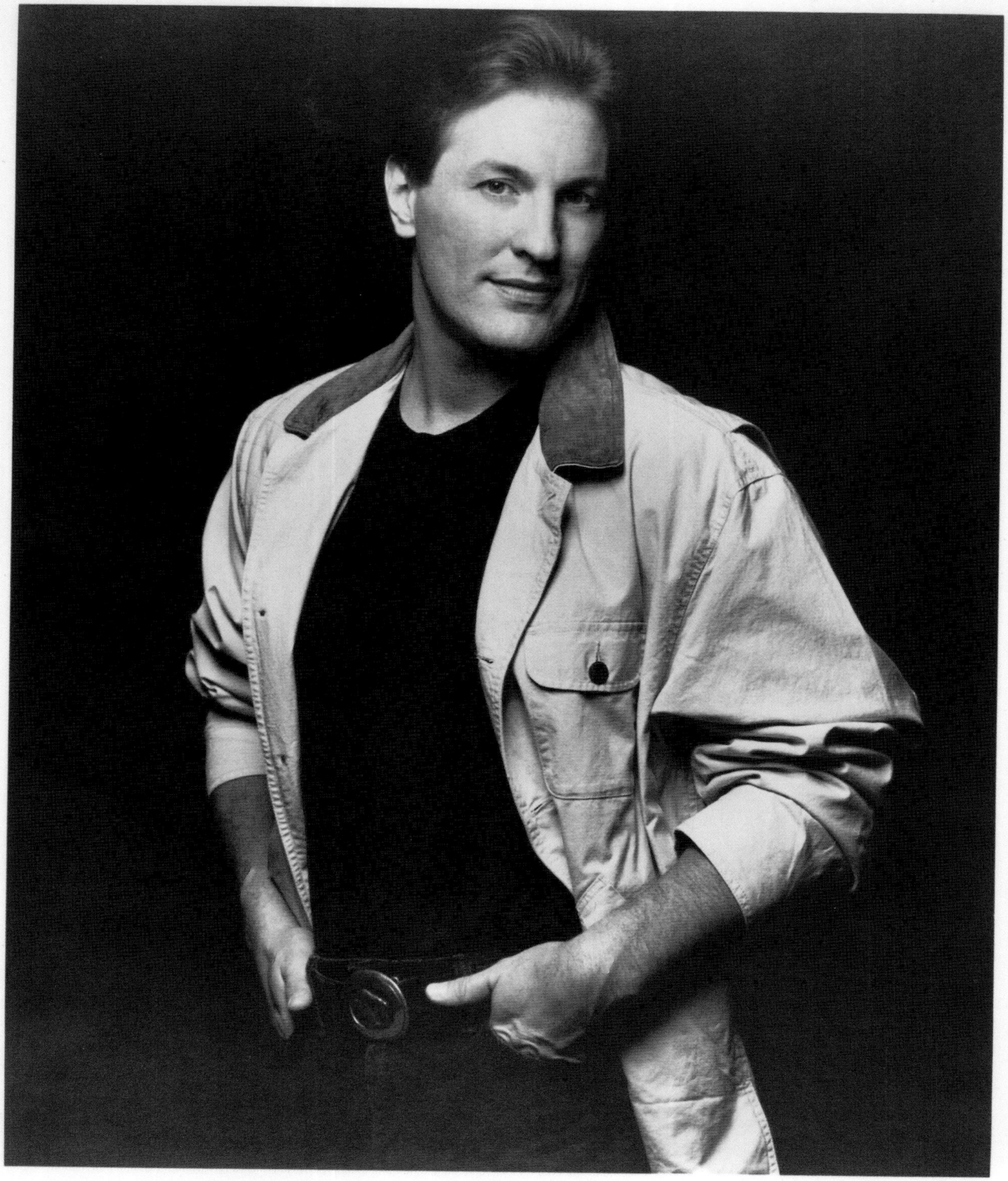

photo: Chris Carroll

COLLIN RAYE

9107

© 1991 Sony Music. Permission to reproduce this photography is limited to editorial uses in regular issues of newspapers and other regularly published periodicals and television news programming.

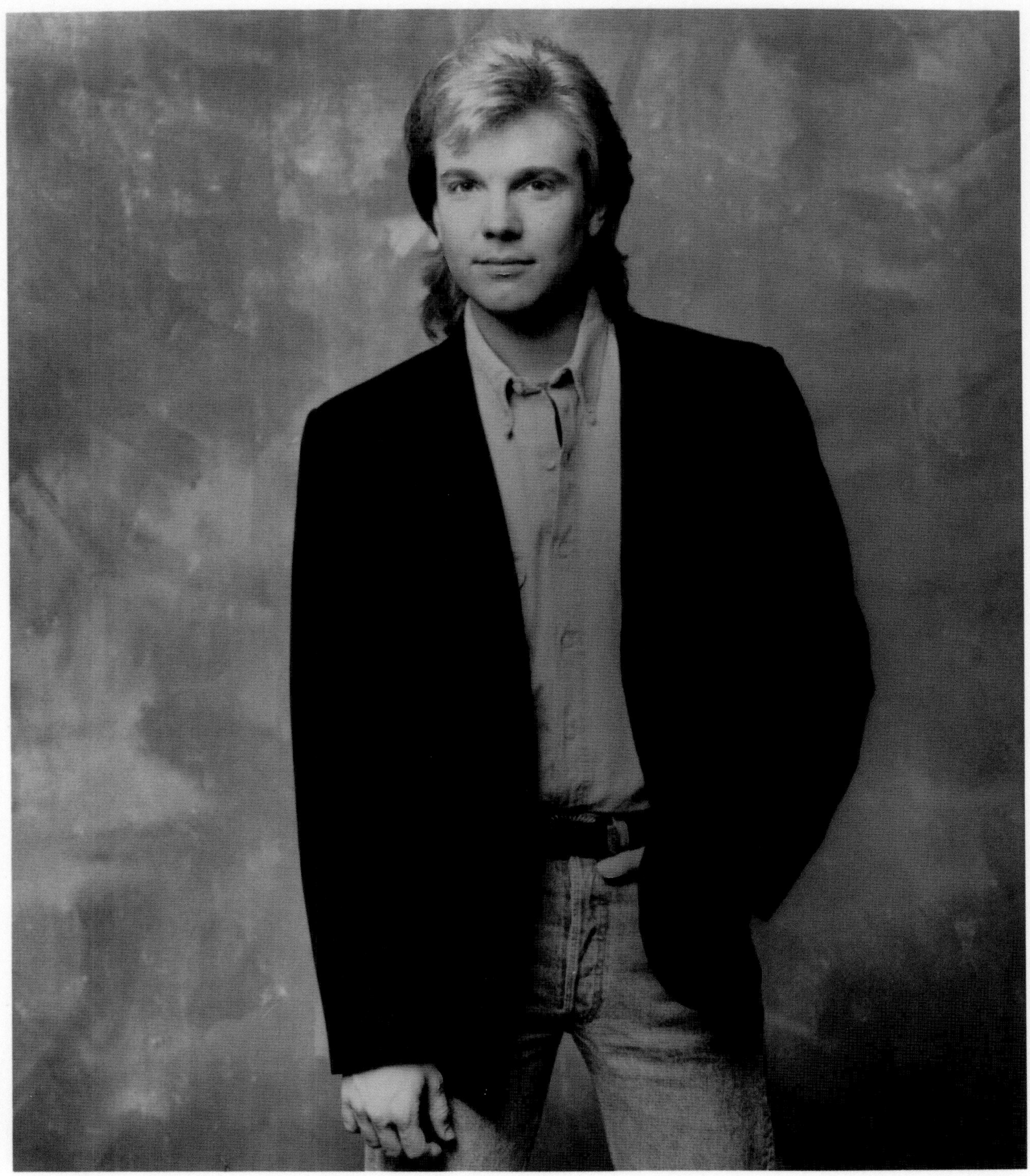

photo: McGuire 0691A

LIONEL CARTWRIGHT

MCA NASHVILLE

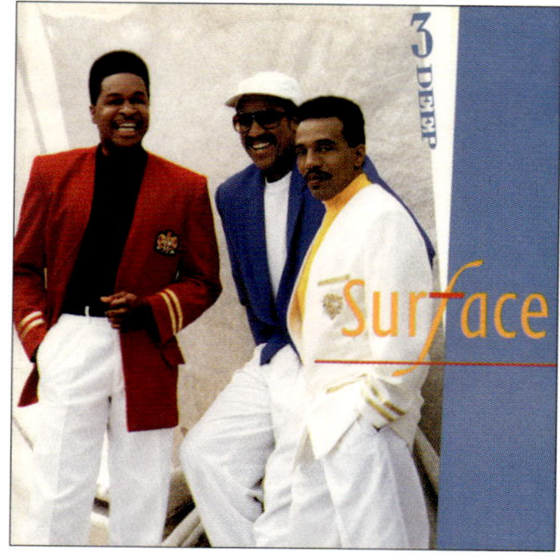

The soulful balladeers **Surface** scored a trifecta when the romantic splendor of "The First Time" hit No. 1 on the R&B, pop and adult contemporary charts.

Billboard 200: *3 Deep* (#65)
Billboard Hot 100: "The First Time" (No. 1);
"Never Gonna Let You Down" (#17)

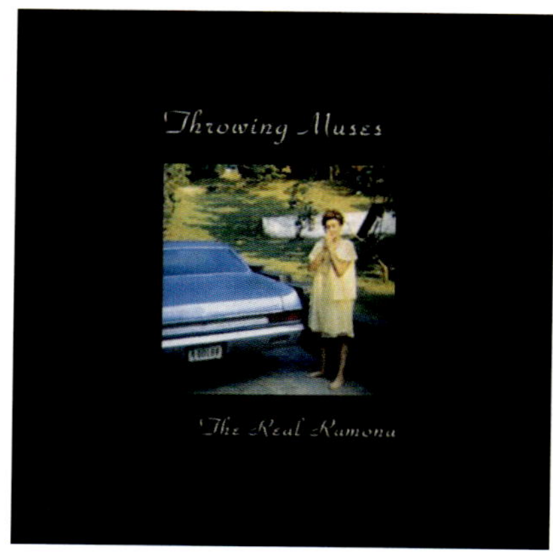

On *The Real Ramona*, acclaimed alternative-rock outfit **Throwing Muses** equalized Kristen Hersh's stark songwriting and Tanya Donelly's pop tendencies.

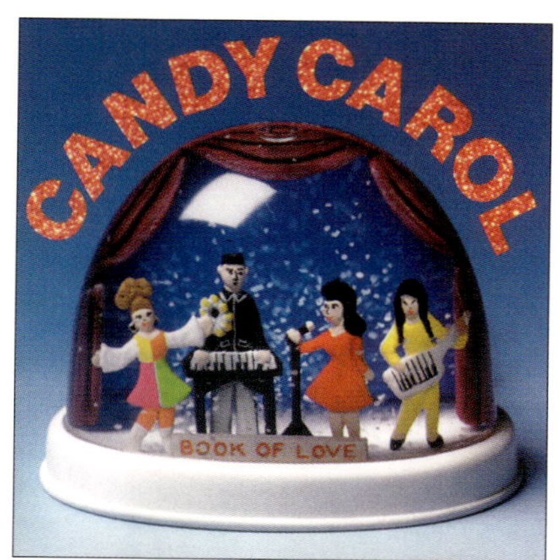

Book of Love moved in a sweeter direction with the synth-pop ditty "Alice Everyday," sustaining the New York art-school quintet's allure in the dance clubs.

Billboard 200: *Candy Carol* (#174)

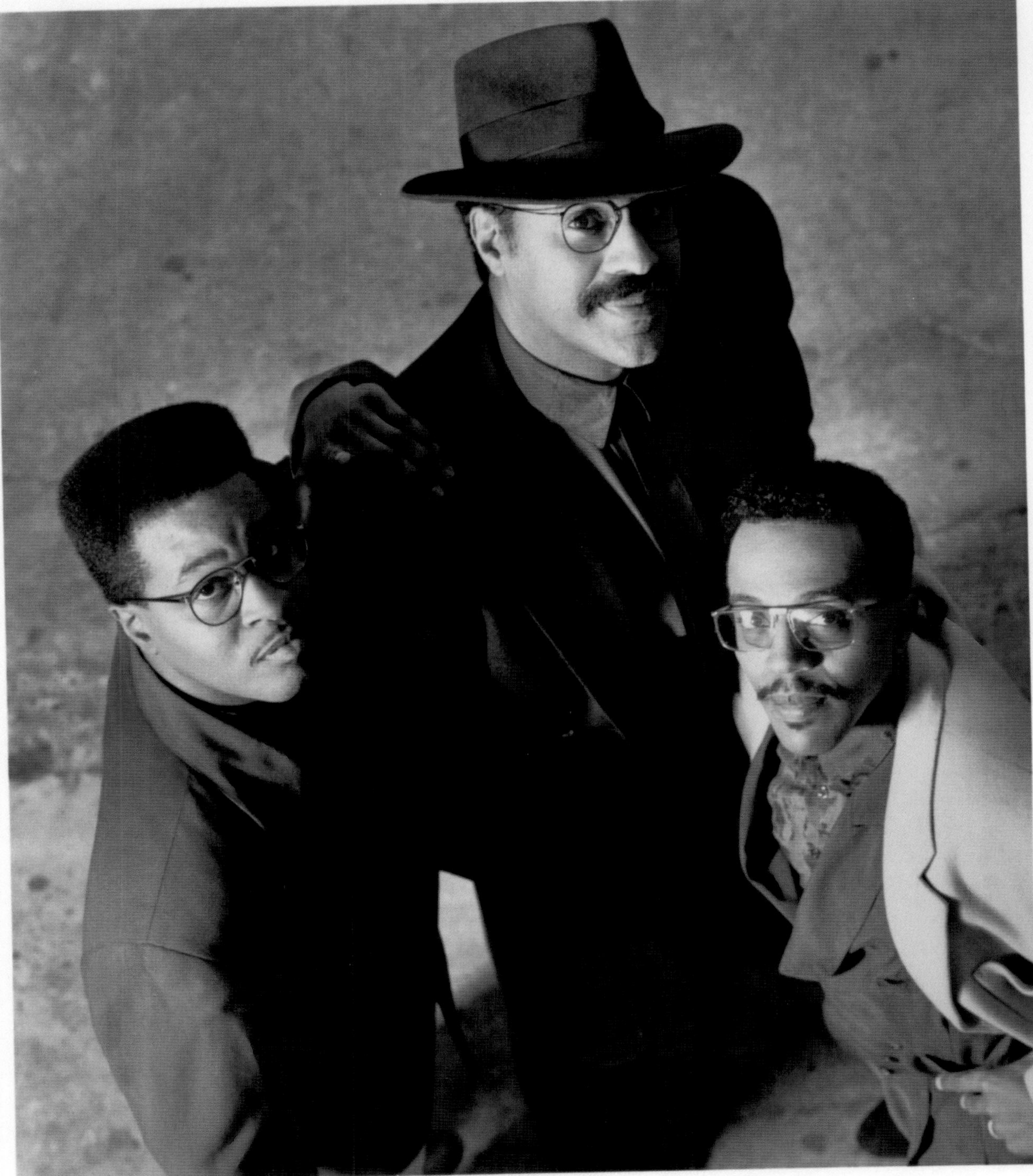

Photo Credit: Jeff Katz

© 1991 Sony Music. Permission to reproduce this photography is limited to editorial uses in regular issues of newspapers and other regularly published periodicals and television news programming.

Bernard Jackson David Townsend David "Pic" Conley

MANAGEMENT·
COLE CLASSIC MANAGEMENT·
4150 RIVERSIDE DR., SUITE 207
BURBANK, CA 91505

SURFACE

Columbia

9101

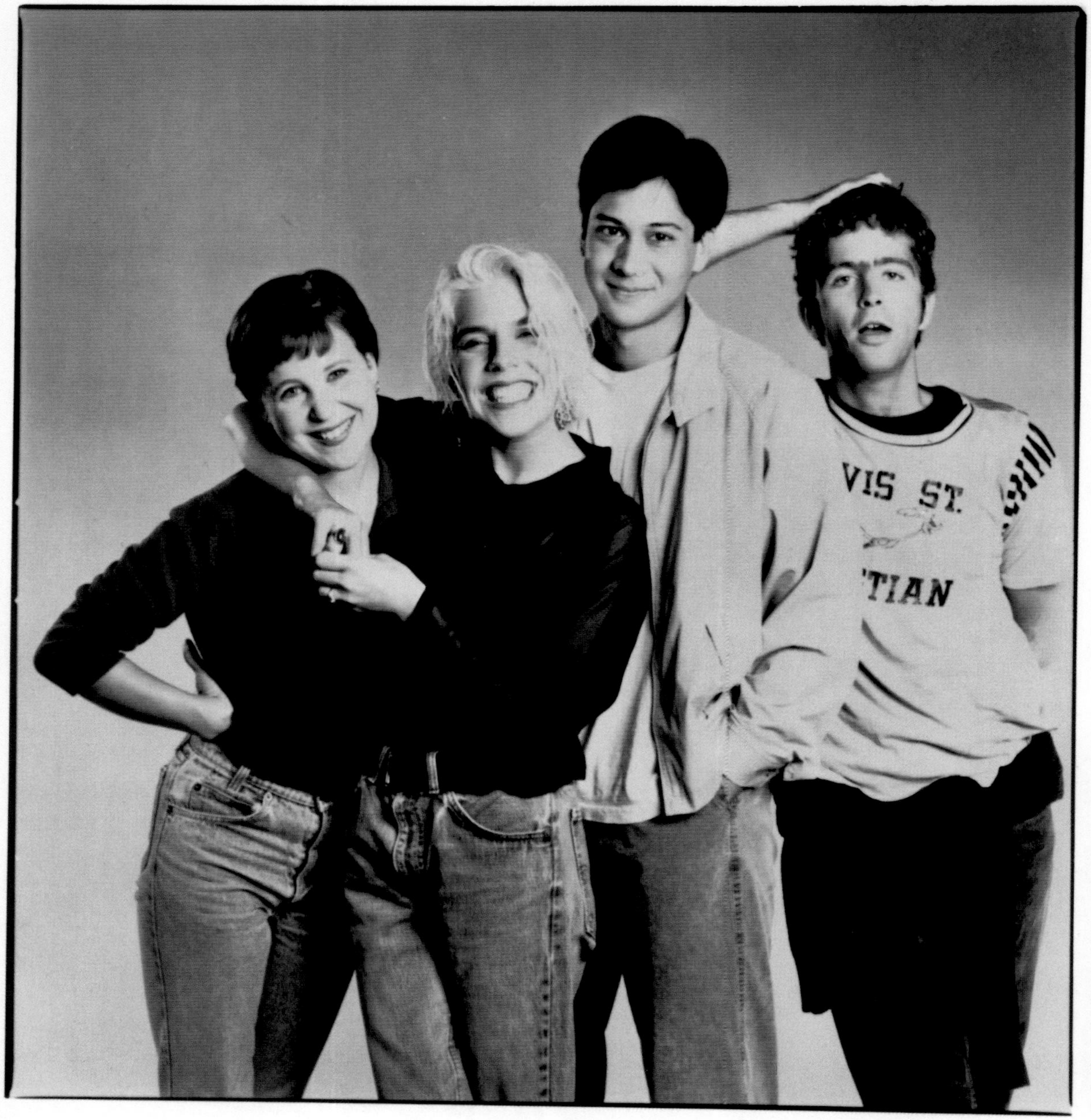

Photo Credit: Andrew Catlin

Kristin Hersh | Tanya Donelly | Fred Abong | David Narcizo

Throwing Muses

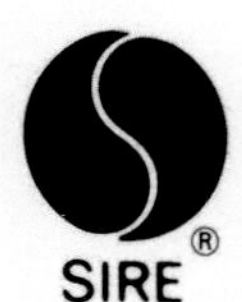

© 1991 Sire Records Company/Permission to reproduce limited to editorial uses in newspapers and other regularly published periodicals and television news programming.

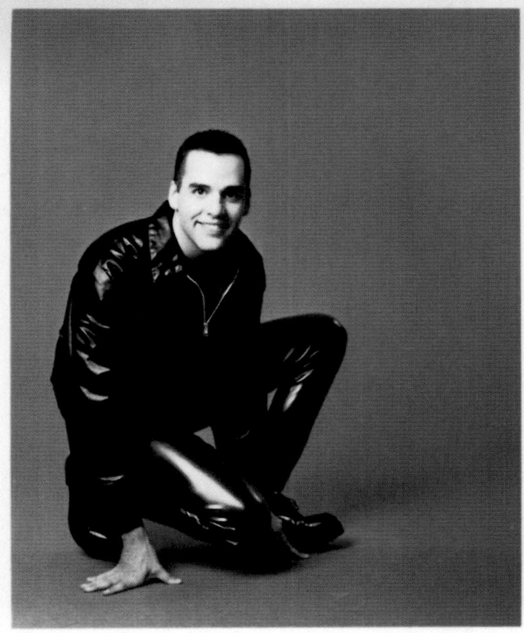

Ted Ottaviano

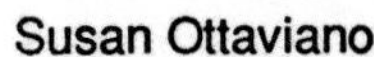

Susan Ottaviano

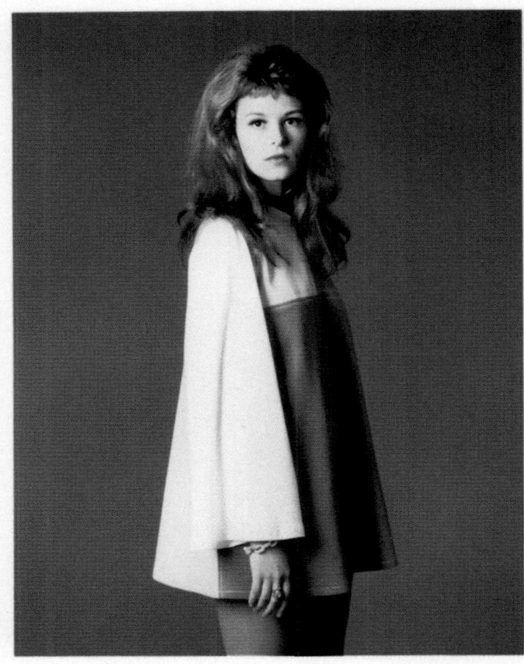

Lauren Roselli

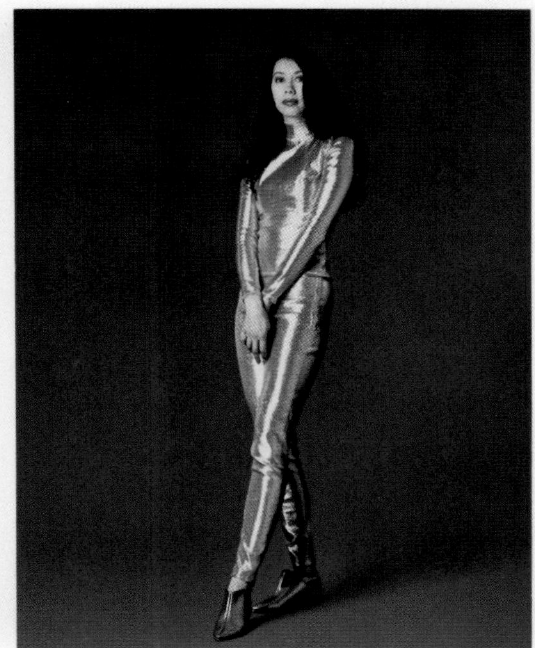

Jade Lee

Photo Credit: Janette Beckman

BOOK OF LOVE

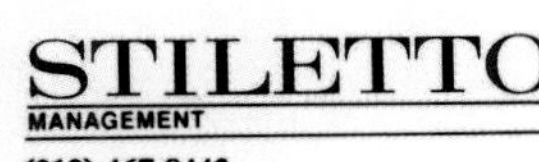

(213) 467-9442

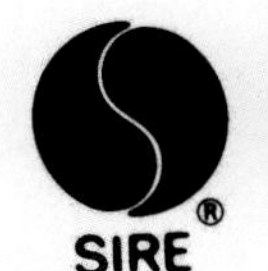

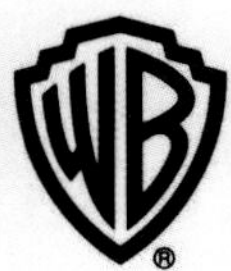

© 1991 Warner Bros. Records/Permission to reproduce limited to editorial uses in newspapers and other regularly published periodicals and television news programming.

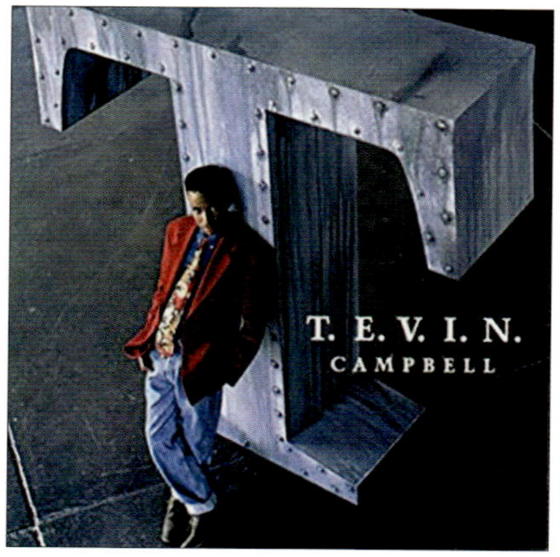

T.E.V.I.N., the debut album by 14-year-old crooner **Tevin Campbell**, spawned two No. 1 R&B hits, "Tell Me What You Want Me to Do" and "Alone with You."

Billboard 200: *T.E.V.I.N.* (#38)
Billboard Hot 100: "Round and Round" (#12); "Just Ask Me To" (#88); "Tell Me What You Want Me to Do" (#6); "Goodbye" (#85); "Strawberry Letter 23" (#53); "Alone with You" (#72)

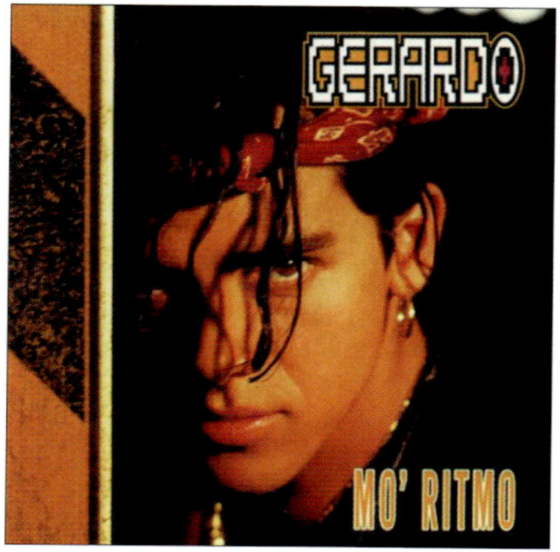

Toggling between both English and Spanish, **Gerardo**'s boisterous summer hit, "Rico Suave," appeared on the Ecuadorian native's debut album, *Mo' Ritmo*.

Billboard 200: *Mo' Ritmo* (#36)

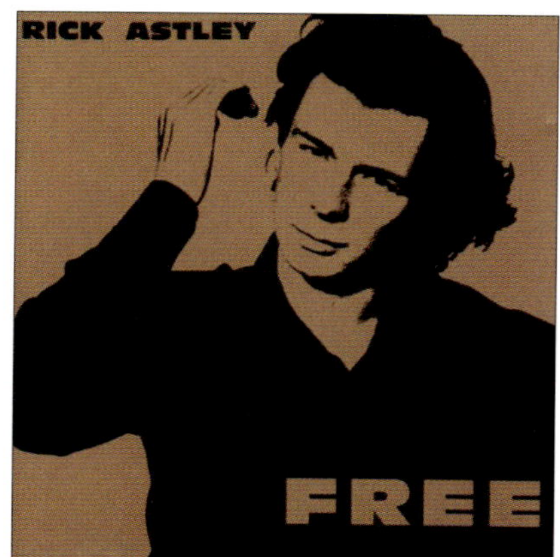

Abandoning connections with his dance-pop days, British singer **Rick Astley** swerved towards soul and got another hit single with the ballad, "Cry for Help."

Billboard 200: *Free* (#31)
Billboard Hot 100: "Cry for Help" (#7); "Move Right Out" (#81)

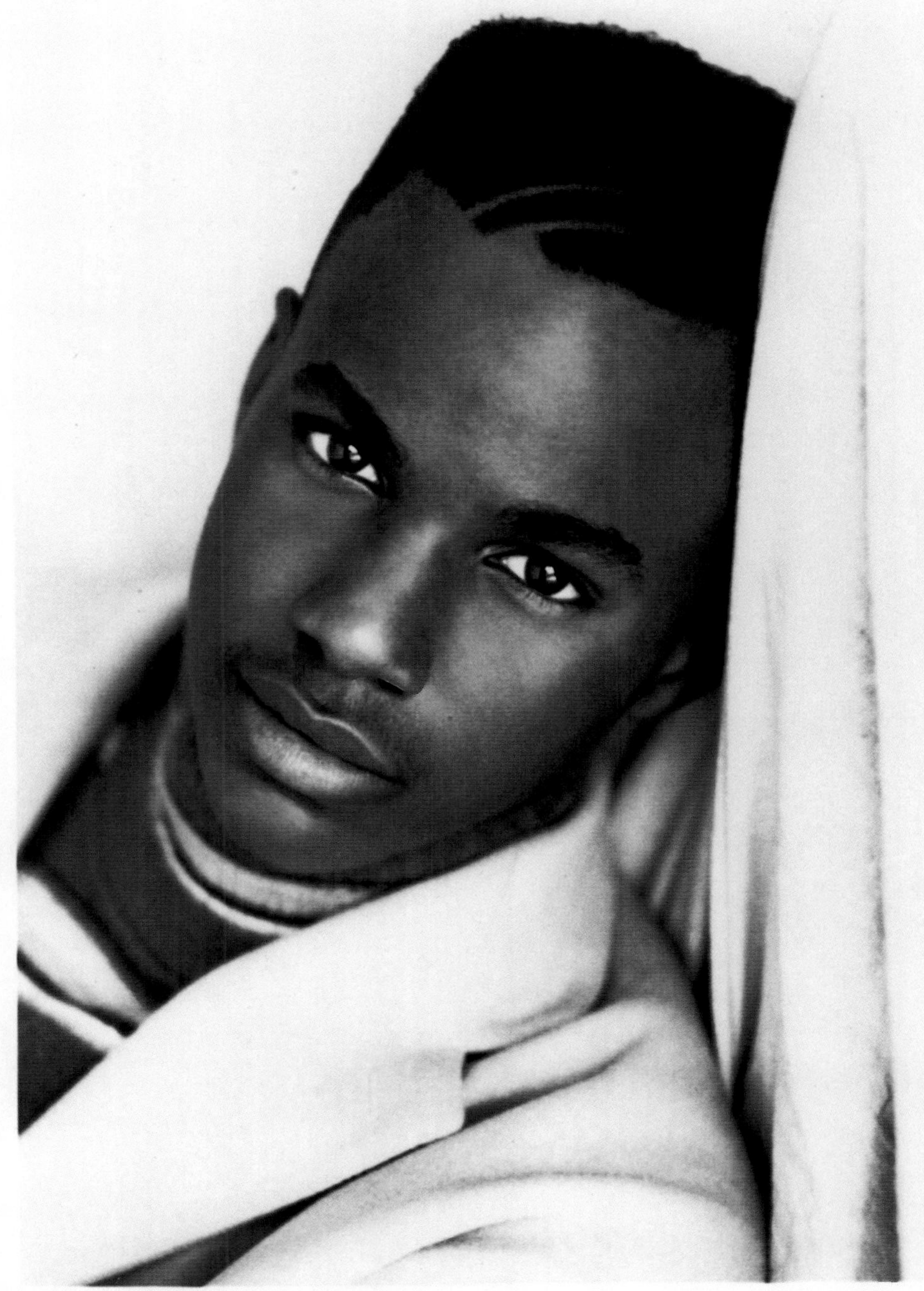

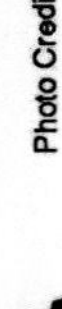

T. E. V. I. N.
CAMPBELL

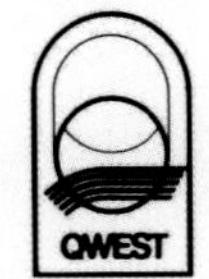

© 1991 Warner Bros. Records/Permission to reproduce limited to editorial uses in newspapers and other regularly published periodicals and television news programming.

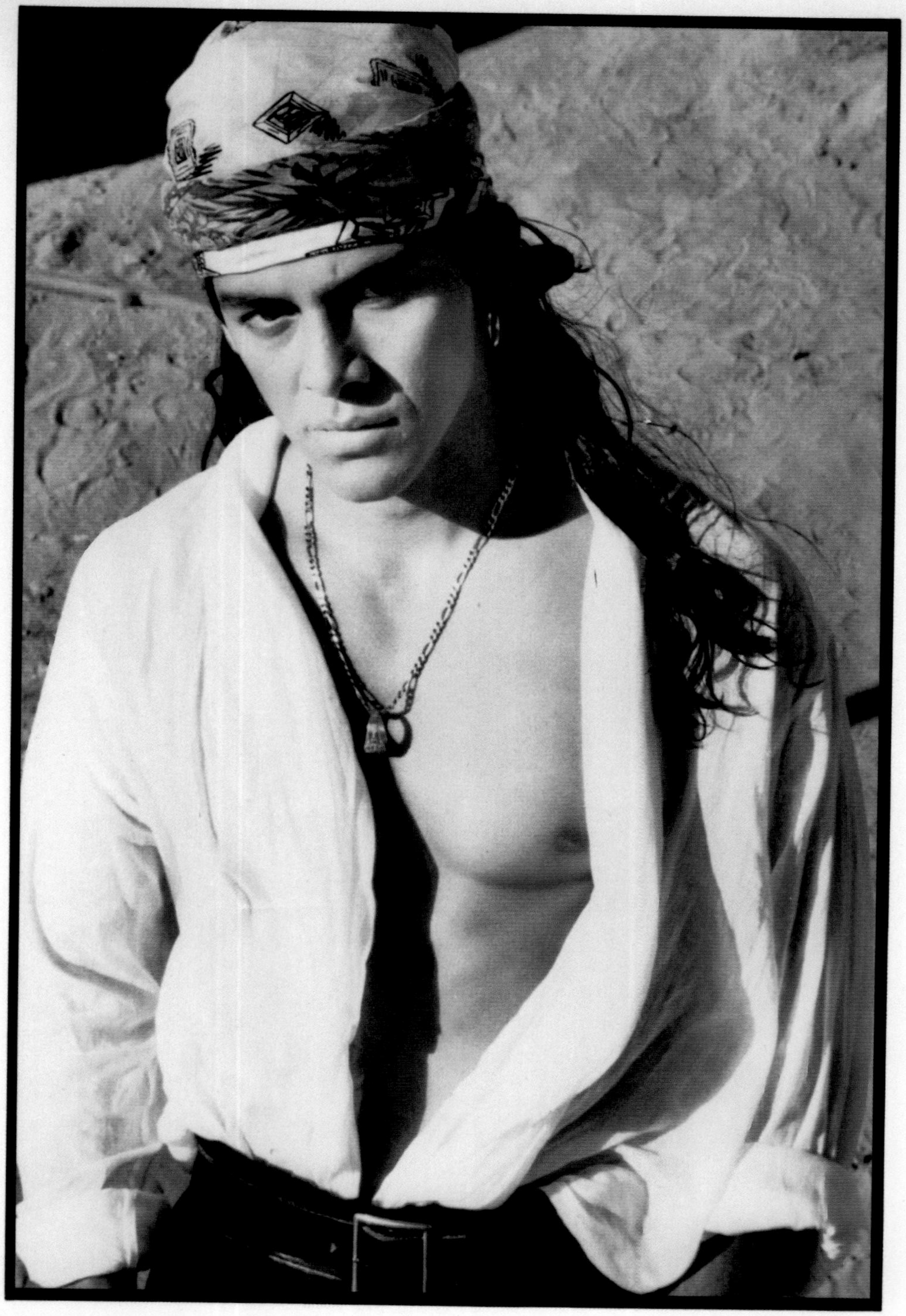

PHOTO CREDIT: RANDEE ST. NICHOLAS/1990

GERARDO

©1990 Interscope Records, Inc./ Permission to reproduce limited to editorial uses in newspapers and other regularly published periodicals and television news programming. All other rights are reserved.

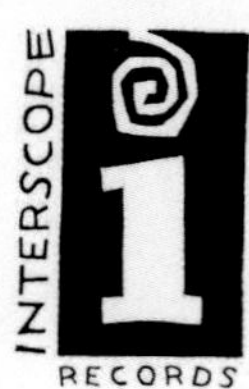

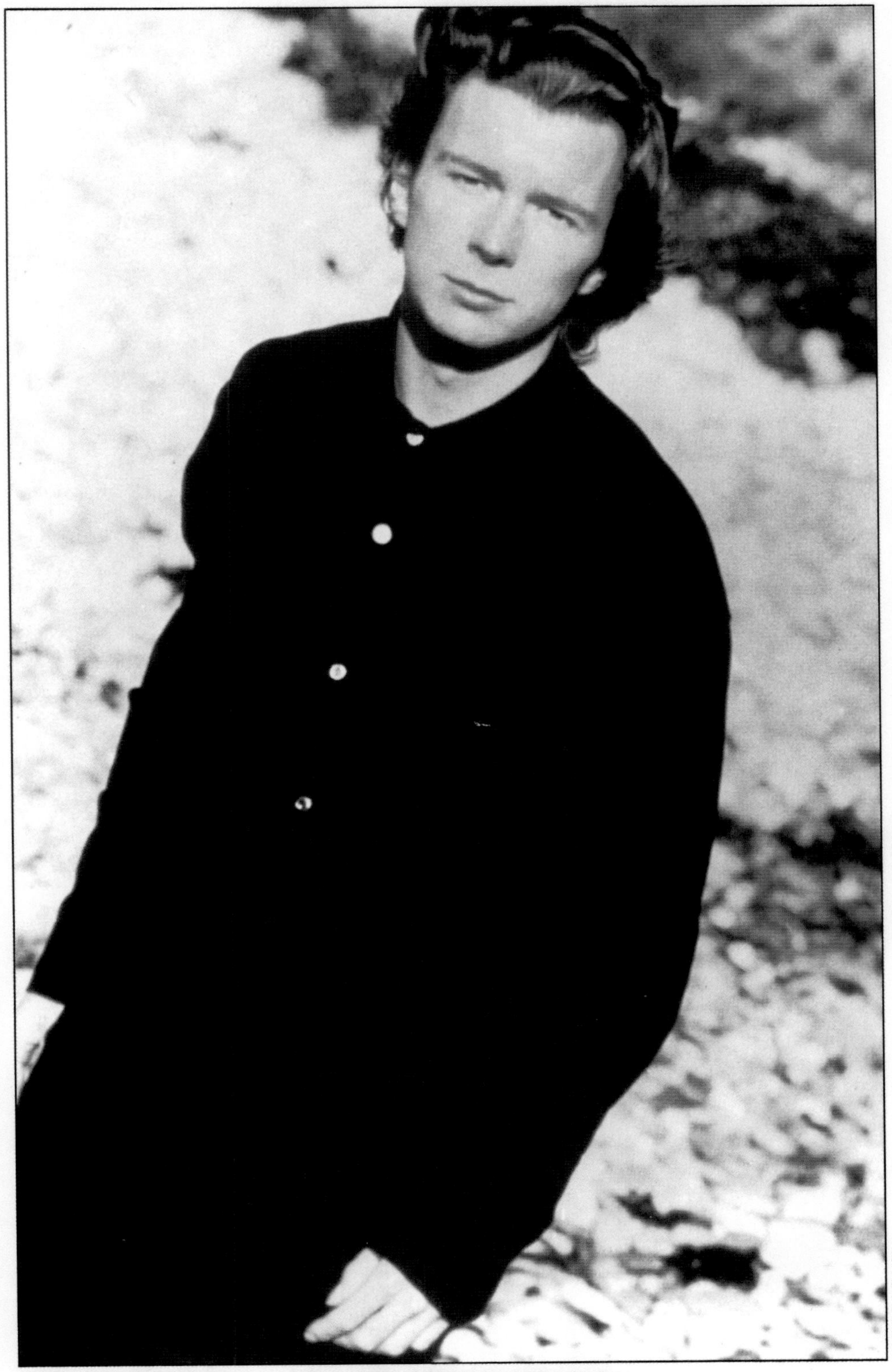

Photo Credit: Paul Cox

RICK ASTLEY

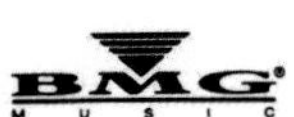

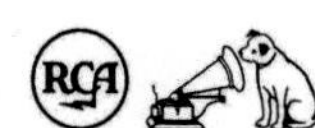

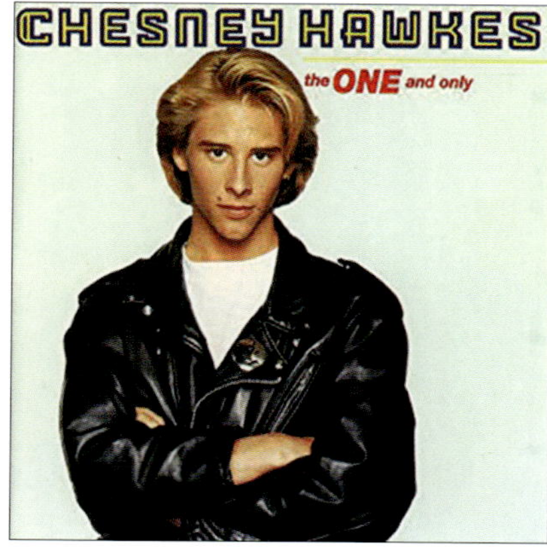

British teen singer **Chesney Hawkes** topped the UK charts and reached the Top 10 in the US with "The One and Only," his one and only successful single.

Billboard Hot 100: "The One and Only" (#10)

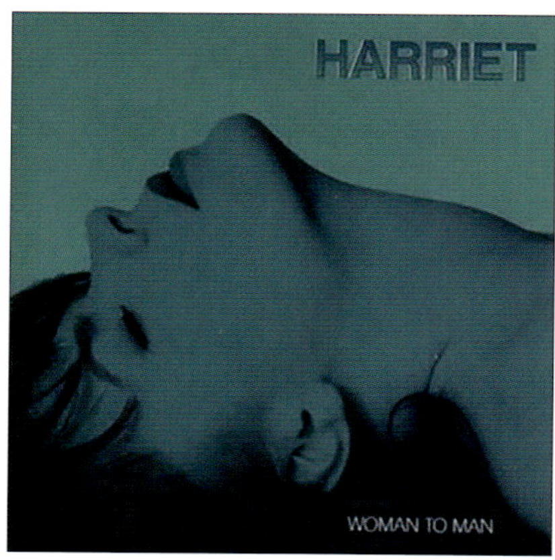

Attractive pop-soul singer **Harriet** squeaked into the dance singles charts and the Top 40 with "Temple of Love," her one hit from the album *Woman to Man.*

Billboard Hot 100: "Temple of Love" (#39)

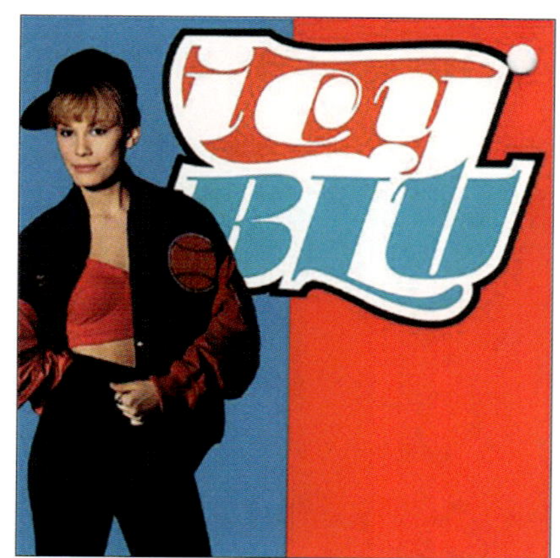

Nicknamed "the female Vanilla Ice," **Icy Blu** experienced a brief pop career with the trifling singles, "Pump It (Nice an' Hard)" and "I Wanna Be Your Girl."

Billboard Hot 100: "Pump It (Nice an' Hard)" (#78);
"I Wanna Be Your Girl" (#46)

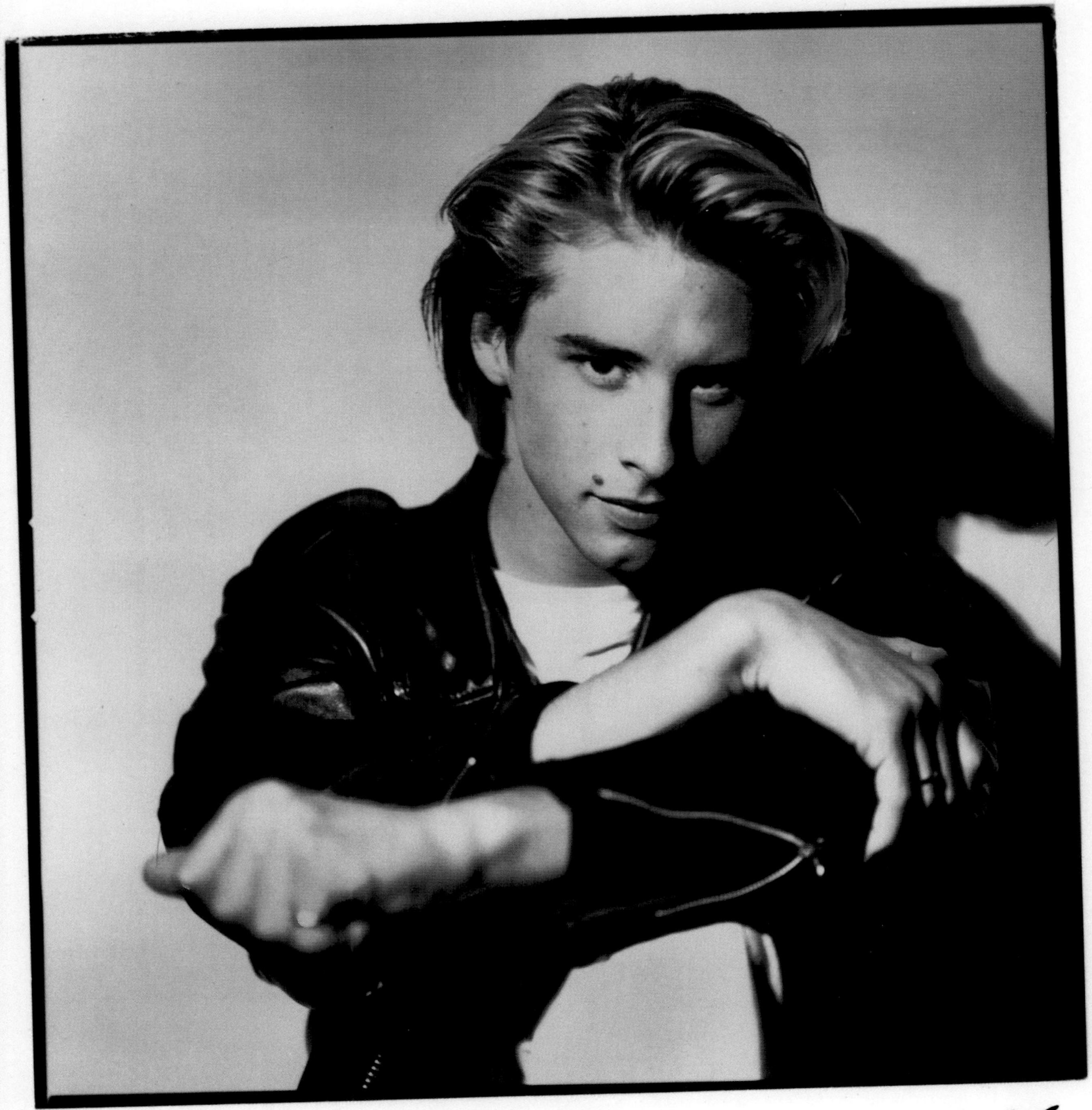

Chesney Hawkes

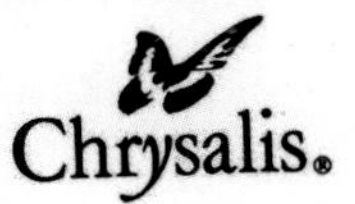

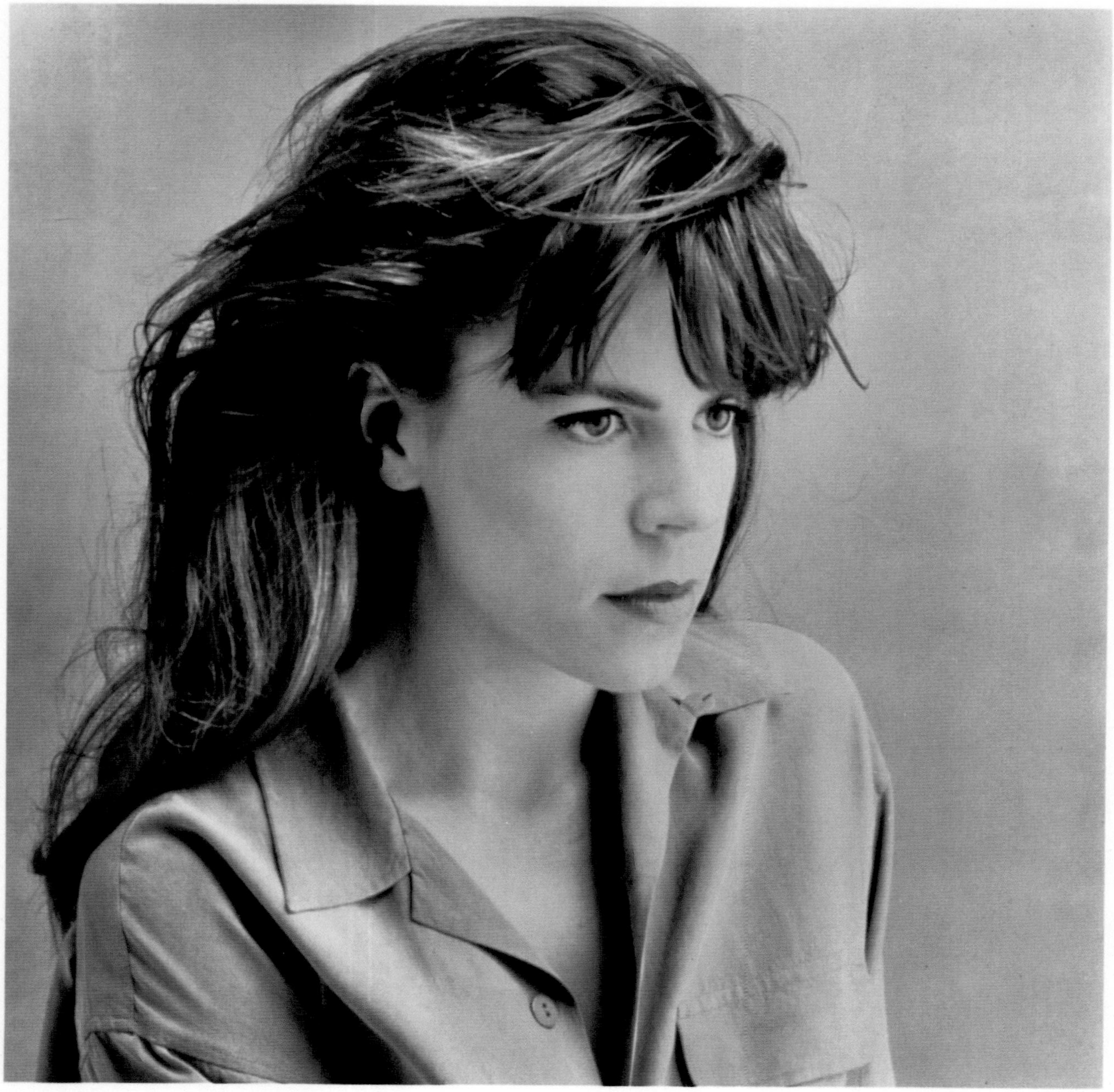

HARRIET

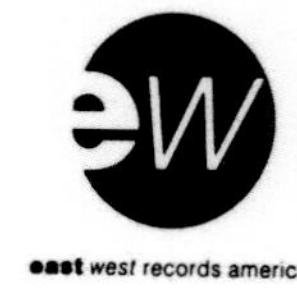

east west records america

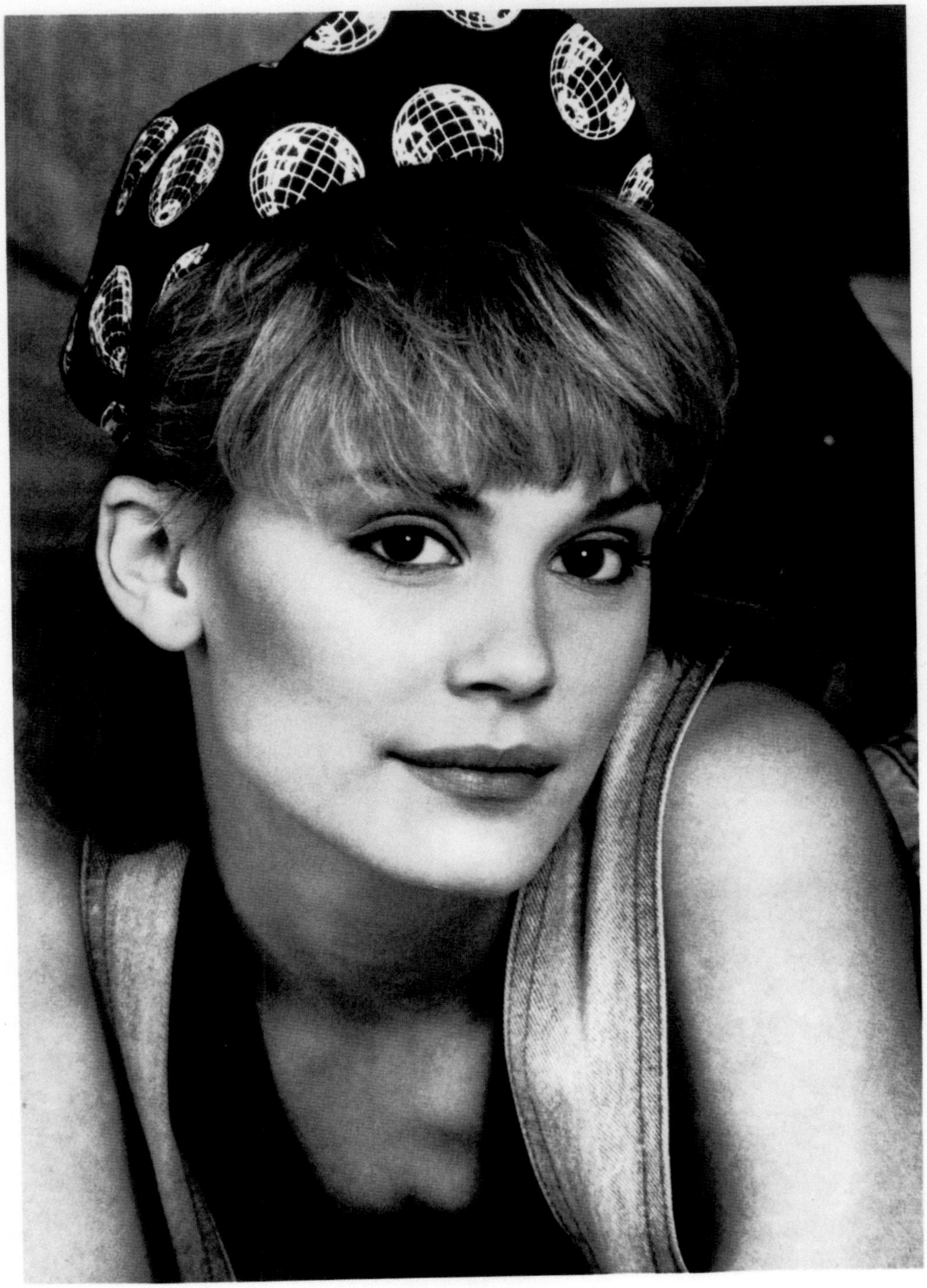

Photo Credit: Yvonne Taylor

Icy Blu

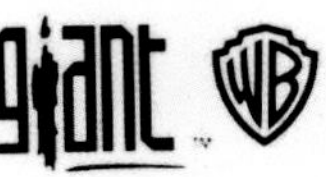

© 1991 Warner Bros. Records Permission to reproduce limited to editorial uses in newspapers and other regularly published periodicals and television news programming.

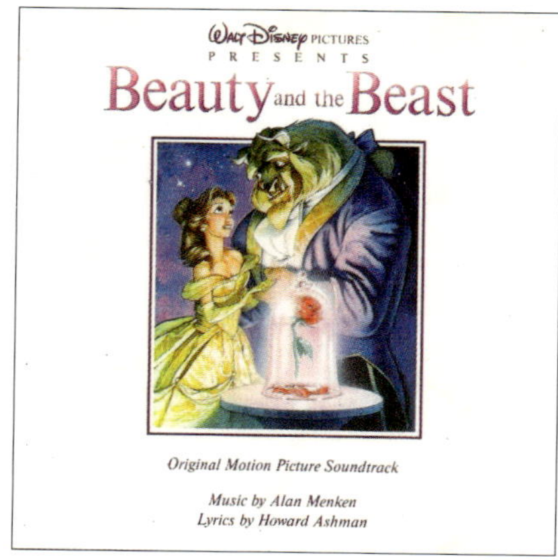

The official soundtrack album to the Disney animated film ***Beauty and the Beast*** showcased Celine Dion duetting with Peabo Bryson on the title track.

Billboard 200: *Beauty and the Beast* (#19)
Billboard Hot 100: "Beauty and the Beast" (#9)

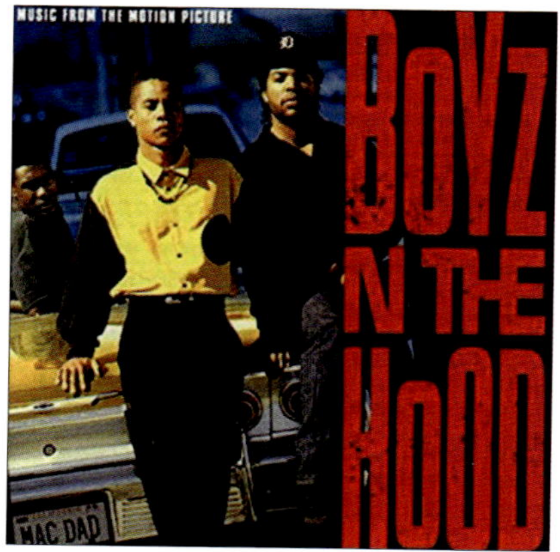

The soundtrack to the film ***Boyz N the Hood***, John Singleton's debut as a director, generated singer Tevin Campbell's Top 10 R&B hit, "Just Ask Me To."

Billboard 200: *Boyz N the Hood* (#12)
Billboard Hot 100: "Just Ask Me To" (#88)

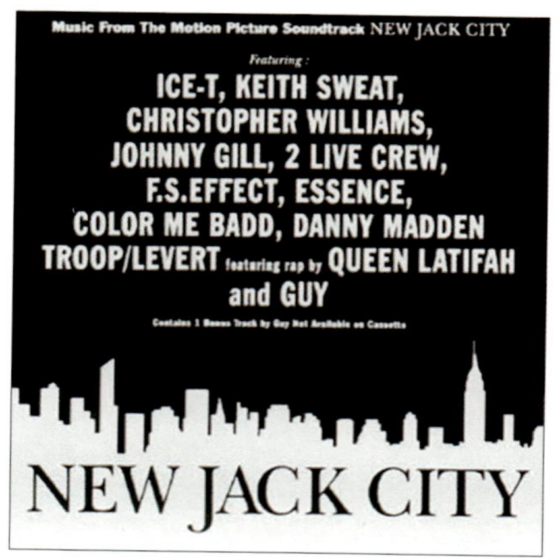

"I'm Dreamin'" by Christopher Williams, a No. 1 R&B single, and Ice-T's "New Jack Hustler (Nino's Theme)" appeared on the soundtrack for ***New Jack City***.

Billboard 200: *New Jack City* (#2)
Billboard Hot 100: "I'm Dreaming" (#89);
"New Jack Hustler" (#67)

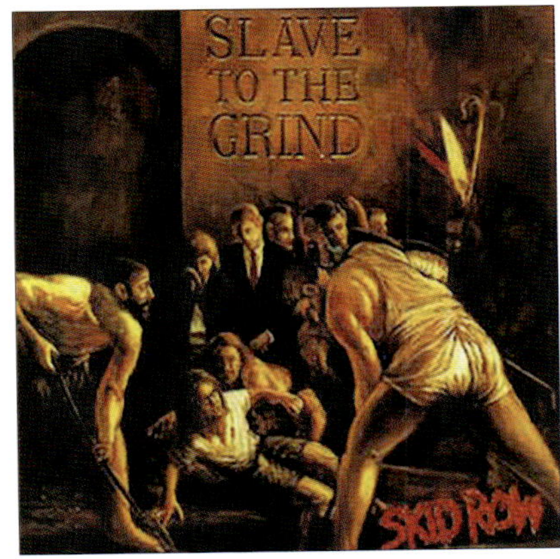

Skid Row retained its devoted fandom as *Slave to the Grind*, the mainstream metal band's second album, debuted atop the *Billboard* 200 and went platinum.

Billboard 200: *Slave to the Grind* (No. 1)
Billboard Hot 100: "Wasted Time" (#88)

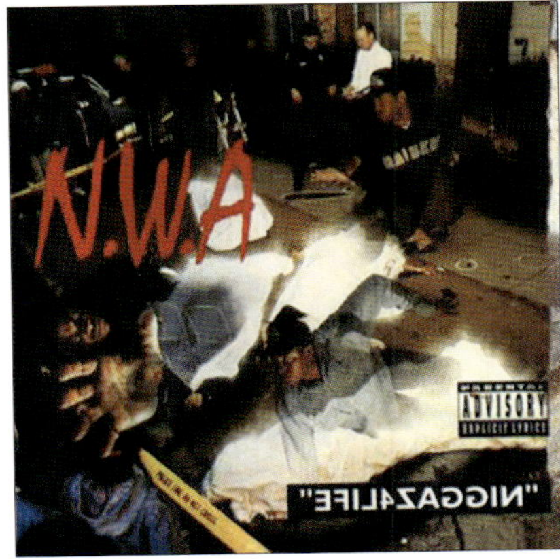

Owing to the music's explicit lyrics, *Niggaz4Life* by **N.W.A.** courted controversy as the first gangsta rap album to climb to No. 1 on the *Billboard* 200 chart.

Billboard 200: *Niggaz4Life* (No. 1)

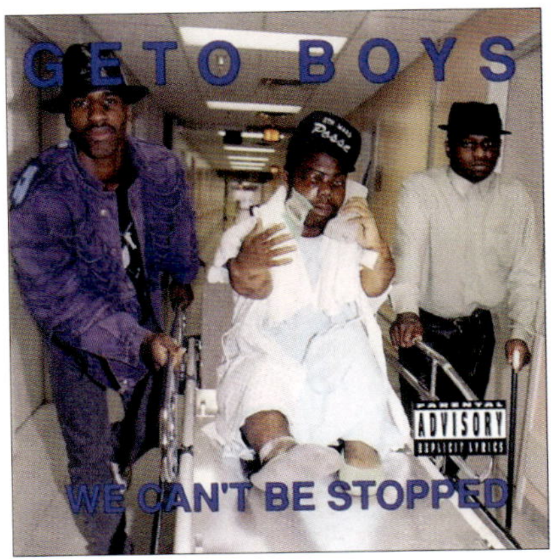

A rap outfit from Houston's Fifth Ward community, **Geto Boys** fueled a fracas with "Mind Playing Tricks on Me," a disconcerting vignette of inner-city life.

Billboard 200: *We Can't Be Stopped* (#24)
Billboard Hot 100: "Mind Playing Tricks on Me" (#23)

De La Soul's second album, *De La Soul Is Dead*, a series of distinct, uninterrupted skits, gave the rap group a minor hit in "Ring Ring Ring (Ha Ha Hey)."

Billboard 200: *De La Soul Is Dead* (#26)

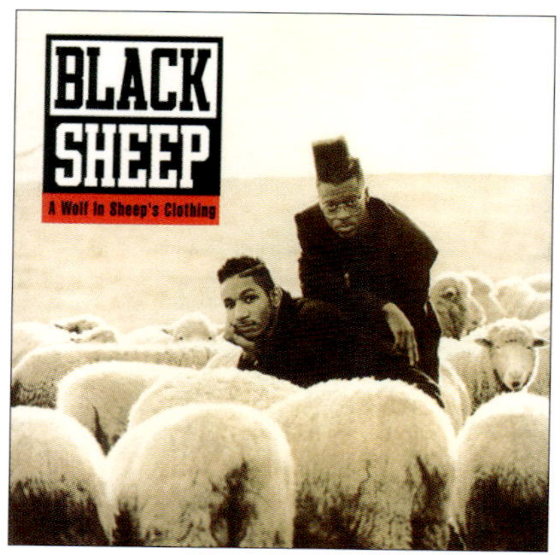

Having affiliated with the New York City-based collective Native Tongues, the hip-hop duo **Black Sheep** launched with the hit track, "Flavor of the Month."

Billboard 200: *A Wolf in Sheep's Clothing* (#30)
Billboard Hot 100: "The Choice Is Yours" (#57); "Strobelite Honey" (#80)

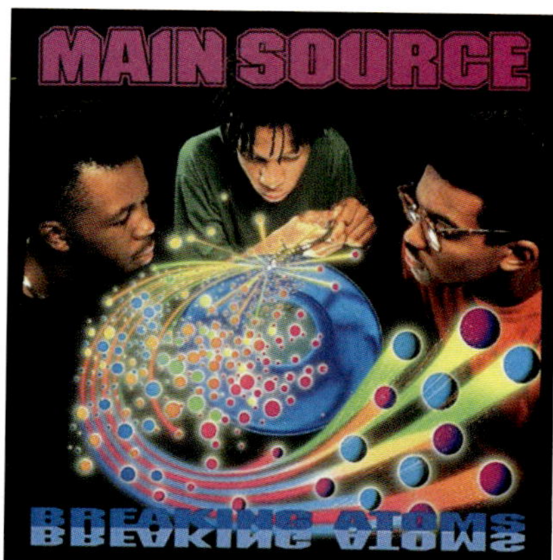

Breaking Atoms, the inaugural album by **Main Source**, earned critical reverence for its substantial and unconventional use of jazz and soul music samples.

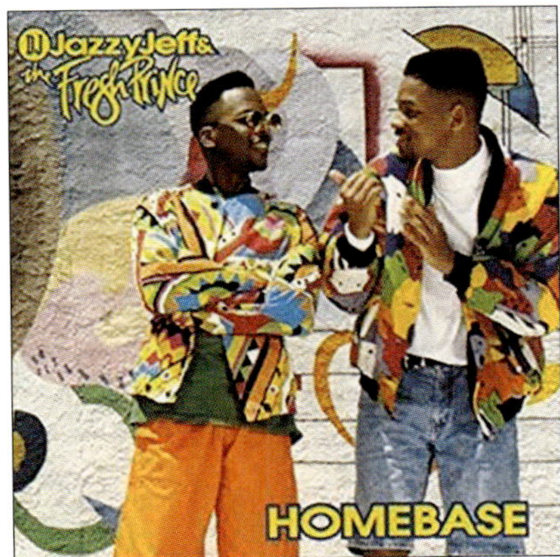

DJ Jazzy Jeff & the Fresh Prince—Jeff Townes and Will Smith—rejoined from Smith's TV sitcom *The Fresh Prince of Bel Air* to produce the pop hit, "Summertime."

Billboard 200: *Homebase* (#12)
Billboard Hot 100: "Summertime" (#4); "Ring My Bell" (#20)

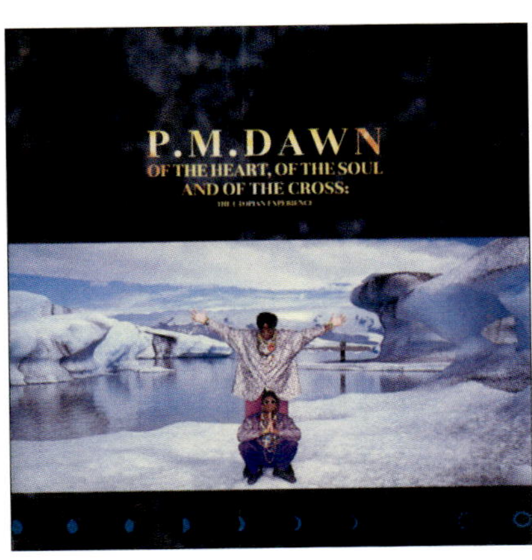

The international hit "Set Adrift on Memory Bliss" by hip-hop group **P.M. Dawn** was constructed around a sample of Spandau Ballet's new wave classic, "True."

Billboard 200: *Of the Heart, of the Soul and of the Cross: The Utopian Experience* (#48)
Billboard Hot 100: "Set Adrift on Memory Bliss" (No. 1); "Paper Doll" (#28)

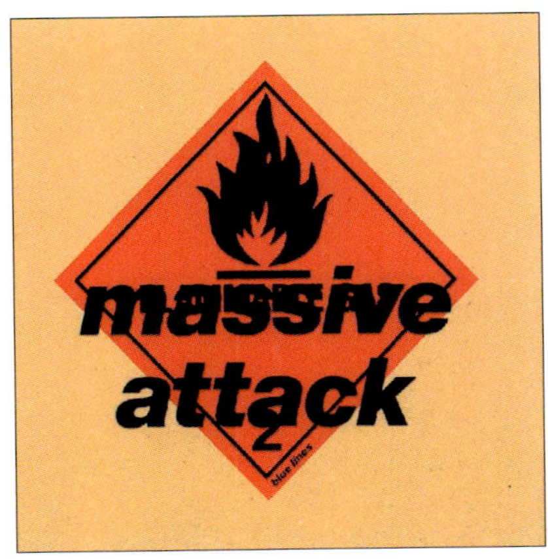

British electronic group **Massive Attack** released the hypnotic debut *Blue Lines*, forging a blueprint for what came to be known as the trip-hop genre.

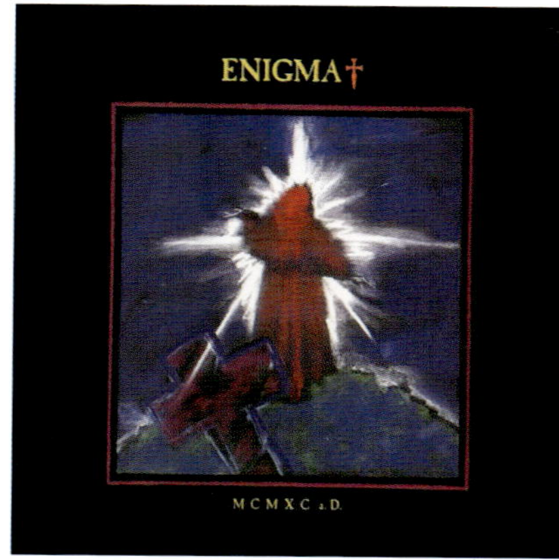

Established by Romanian composer and producer Michael Cretu, the musical project **Enigma** mixed Gregorian chants and dance beats on "Sadeness (Part 1)."

Billboard 200: *MCMXC a.D.* (#6)
Billboard Hot 100: "Sadeness Part 1" (#5)

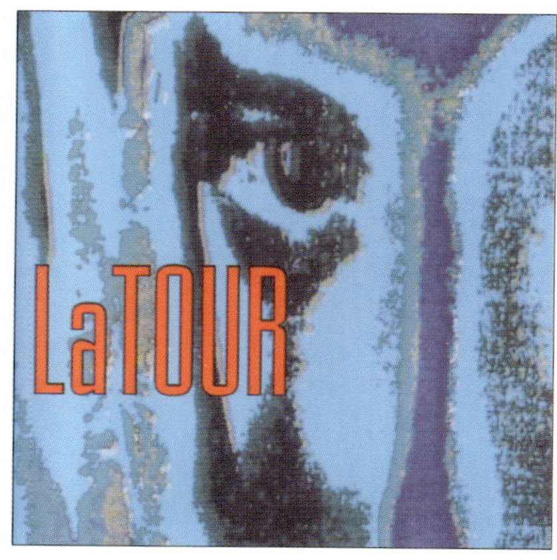

LaTour, the alias of Chicago house music producer William Latour, reached No. 1 on the dance charts with the novelty song, "People Are Still Having Sex."

Billboard Hot 100: "People Are Still Having Sex" (#35)

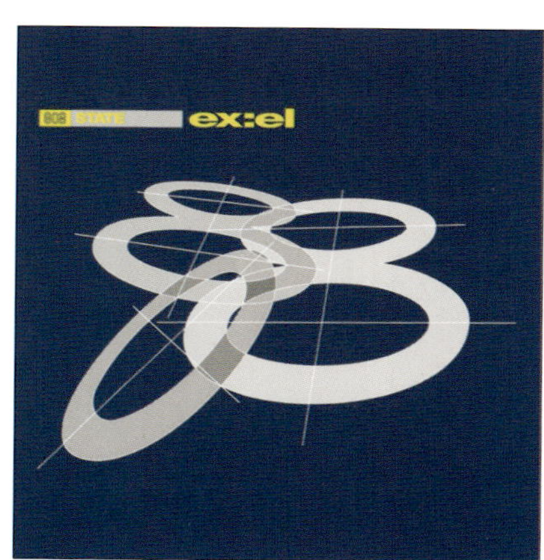

808 State, a UK techno group formed in Manchester, featured the guest vocals of Björk and New Order's Bernard Sumner on the influential album *Ex:el.*

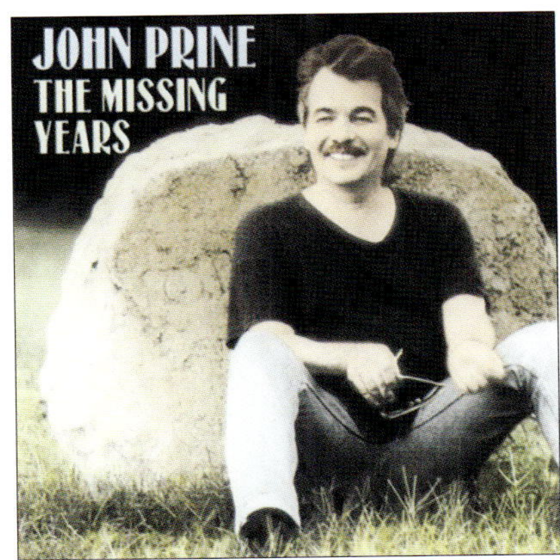

Produced by Howie Epstein of the Heartbreakers, **John Prine**'s 10th release, *The Missing Years*, took home the Grammy for Best Contemporary Folk Album.

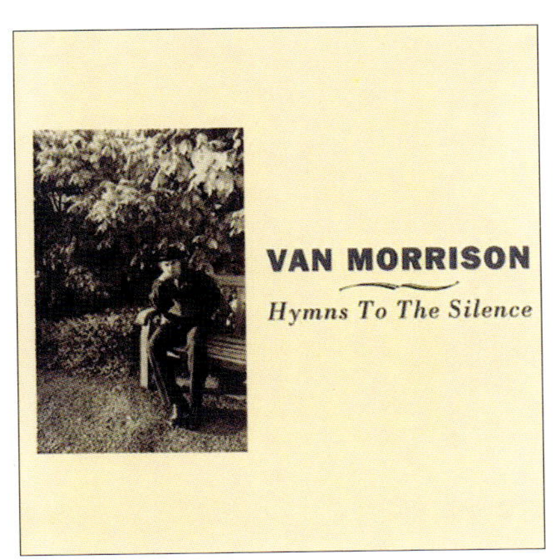

Hymns to the Silence, **Van Morrison**'s double album, notably put the melody for his 1971 classic "Tupelo Honey" to the song, "Why Must I Always Explain?"

Billboard 200: *Hymns to the Silence* (#99)

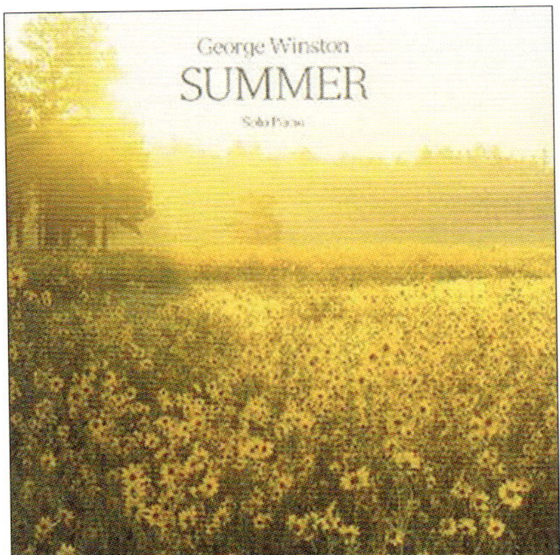

George Winston resurfaced with *Summer*, his fourth collection of impressionistic, seasonally themed piano musings for the new age label Windham Hill.

Billboard 200: *Summer* (#55)

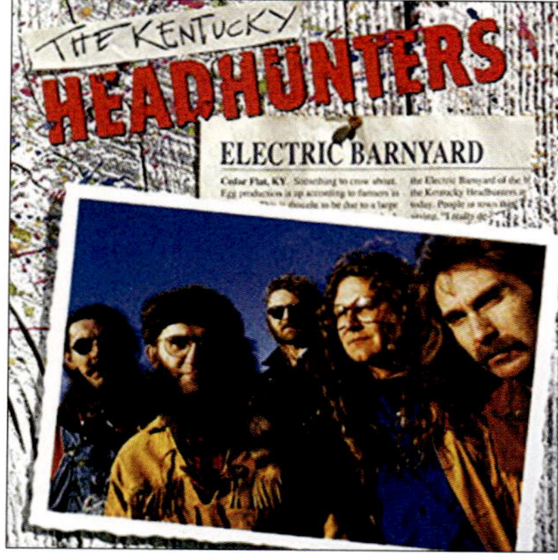

The Kentucky Headhunters released *Electric Barnyard*, a Southern rock and country combination and the final album to feature the band's original lineup.

Billboard 200: *Electric Barnyard* (#29)

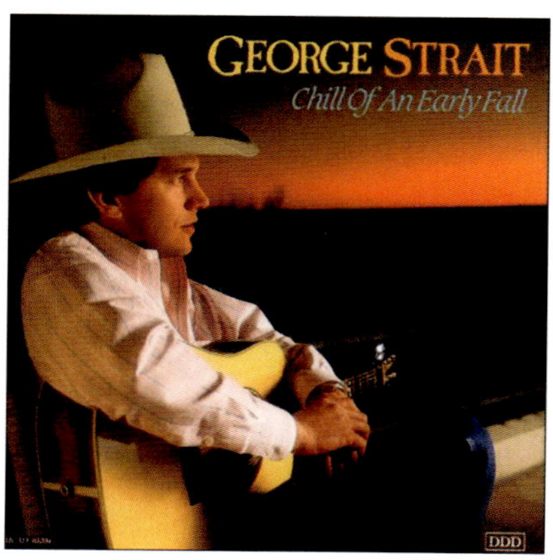

Despite a logjam of neotraditionalist country singers, George Strait broke through with the No. 1 tracks, "If I Know Me" and "You Know Me Better Than That."

Billboard 200: *Chill of an Early Fall* (#45)

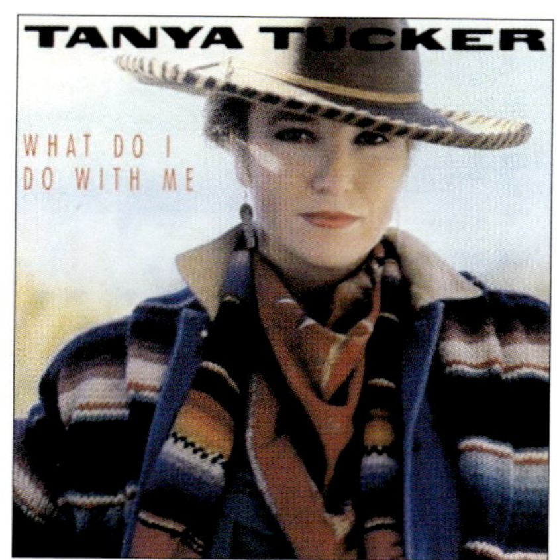

A child country sensation in the early Seventies, Tanya Tucker extended her success into adulthood with *What Do I Do with Me*, her first platinum album.

Billboard 200: *What Do I Do with Me* (#48)

With saxophonist Bob Mintzer unofficially joining the fusion unit, **Yellowjackets**' *Greenhouse* hit No. 1 on *Billboard*'s Top Contemporary Jazz Albums chart.

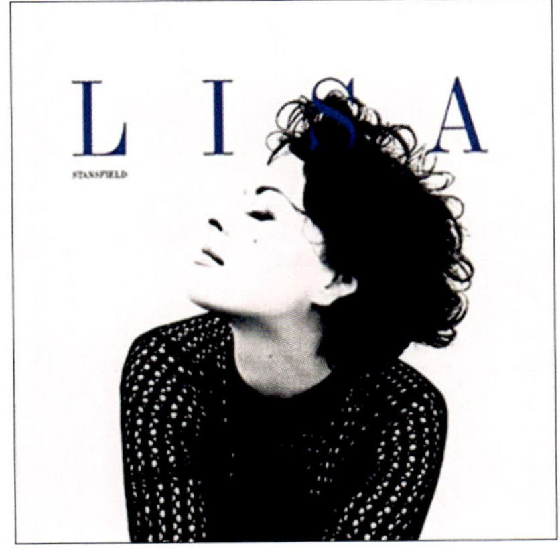

British R&B singer **Lisa Stansfield** released her second album, the soul-inspired *Real Love*, and the stylish "Change" became a smash in the dance clubs.

Billboard 200: *Real Love* (#43)
Billboard Hot 100: "Change" (#27); "All Woman" (#56)

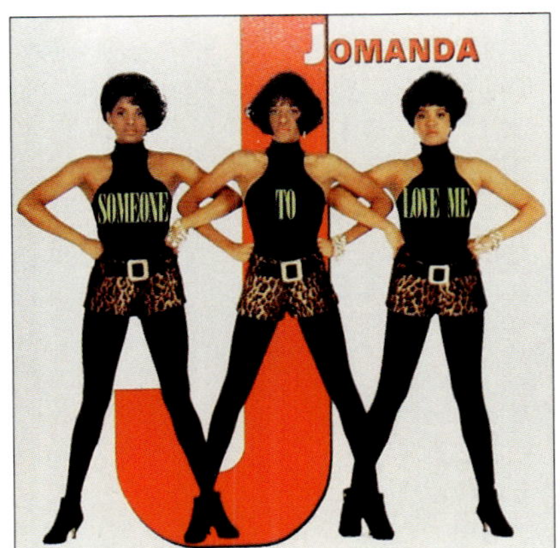

Formed in New Jersey, the female vocal trio **Jomanda** climbed to No. 1 on the dance charts with the progressive house jam, "Got a Love for You."

Billboard Hot 100: "Got a Love for You" (#40)

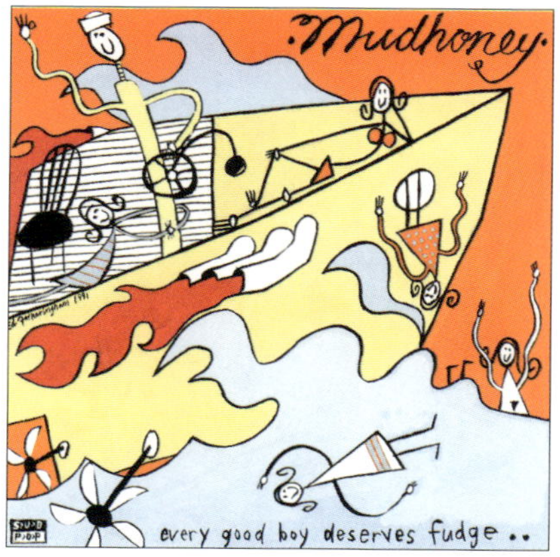

Every Good Boy Deserves Fudge, **Mudhoney**'s sophomore album for the independent label Sub Pop, had a mighty influence on the Seattle grunge movement.

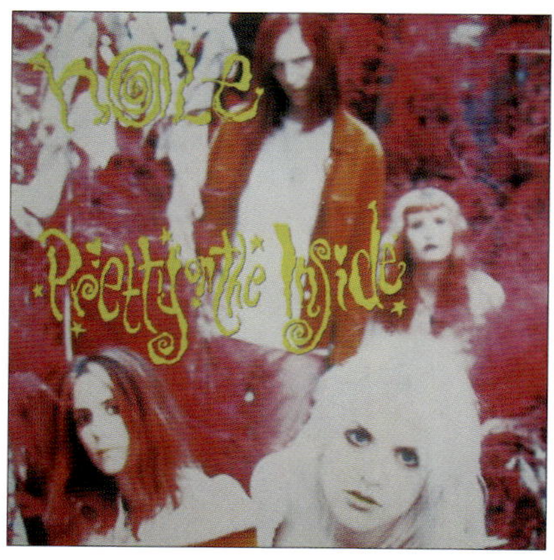

An alternative-rock band fronted by singer, songwriter and guitarist Courtney Love, **Hole** released its debut album, the noisy, caustic *Pretty on the Inside*.

Billboard 200: *Pretty on the Inside* (#73)

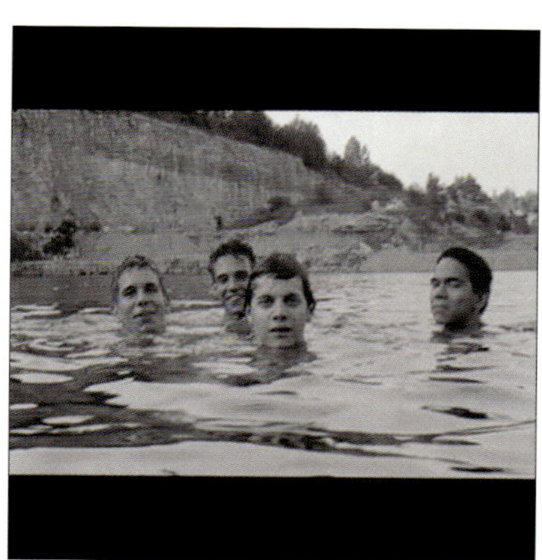

The underground rock community bequeathed accolades on Louisville, Kentucky's **Slint** for its second album, the creative and iconoclastic *Spiderland*.

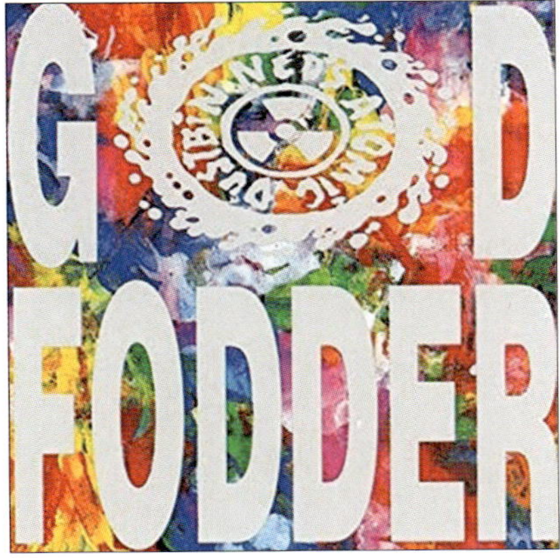

Popularized by the college radio hits, "Grey Cell Green" and "Kill Your Television," the English band **Ned's Atomic Dustbin** found a cult following in the US.

Billboard Hot 100: "Grey Cell Green" (#91)

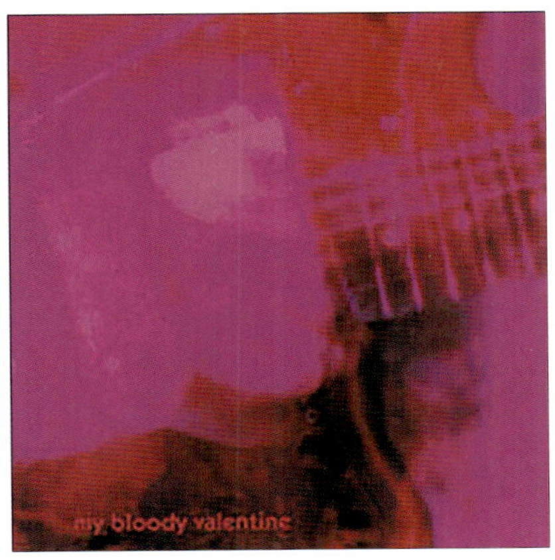

After extensive recording time, Kevin Shields' harsh guitars and ethereal vocals defined **My Bloody Valentine**'s *Loveless* as a coup of the shoegaze genre.

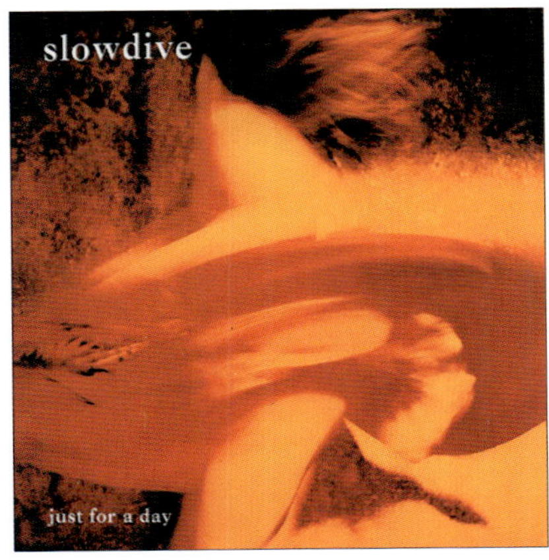

With the debut *Just for a Day*, **Slowdive** was tagged as a "dream-pop" band on the UK indie scene but acquired a significant following in America.

{ IN MEMORY OF **JOHN ALFRED RIZZI** }

ACKNOWLEDGMENTS

Many people were essential to the creation of this book. My first thanks go to my amazing publishing team—Jon Rizzi for bringing his special brand of editorial wit and intelligence, and Kate Glassner Brainerd for her design artistry and unflagging pursuit of excellence. Special appreciation goes to the Michael & Patricia Matthews Fund, whose facilitation was indispensable.

Chip Garofalo, Mark Zaremba, Jay Elowsky, Dave Zobl, Jennifer Soulé, Matt Rue, Sandra Jonas, Mark Lewis and Mike Dickson contributed expertise and resources. I am especially indebted to my dear friend Michael Jensen, as well as Sue Satriano, Janice Azrak, Bryn Bridenthal, Byron Hontas, Kathy Acquaviva, Shelly Selover, Sue Sawyer, Glen Brunman, Rick Ambrose, Bob Merlis, Bill Bentley, Heidi Ellen Robinson, Les Schwartz, Rick Gershon, Judi Kerr and Susan Blond—all of whom supported my efforts.

I specifically treasure the beneficence of Dave Rothstein, Greg Phifer, John Tope, Kevin Knee, Dick Merkle, Jeff Cook, Michael Brannen, Zak Phillips, Rich Garcia, Jason Minkler, Burt Baumgartner, Mitch Kampf, Don Zucker, Carl Walters, Charlie Reardon, Robin Wren, Jimmy Smith, Sharona White, John Ryland, Geina Horton, Michael Linehan, Mike Prince and Jeffrey Naumann, who all graciously furnished information and assistance.

I also salute Leland Rucker, Steve Knopper, David Menconi, Jon Iverson, Gil Asakawa, Mark Bliesener and Justin Mitchell, whose writings formed a vital index for the music-obsessed.

Finally, I would like to acknowledge with gratitude my beloved wife, Bridget, for her constant devotion and kindness. I cherish her—the love of my life.

EDITOR | **JON RIZZI**
ART DIRECTOR | **KATE GLASSNER BRAINERD**

Copyright ©2020 Colorado Music Experience
ALL RIGHTS RESERVED. No portion of this book may be reproduced, stored in retreival system, or transmitted in any form, by any means, mechanical, electronic, photocopying, recording or otherwise, without the written permission of the publisher.

ISBN 978-0-9915668-5-3 PRINTED IN CHINA | Asia Pacific Offset

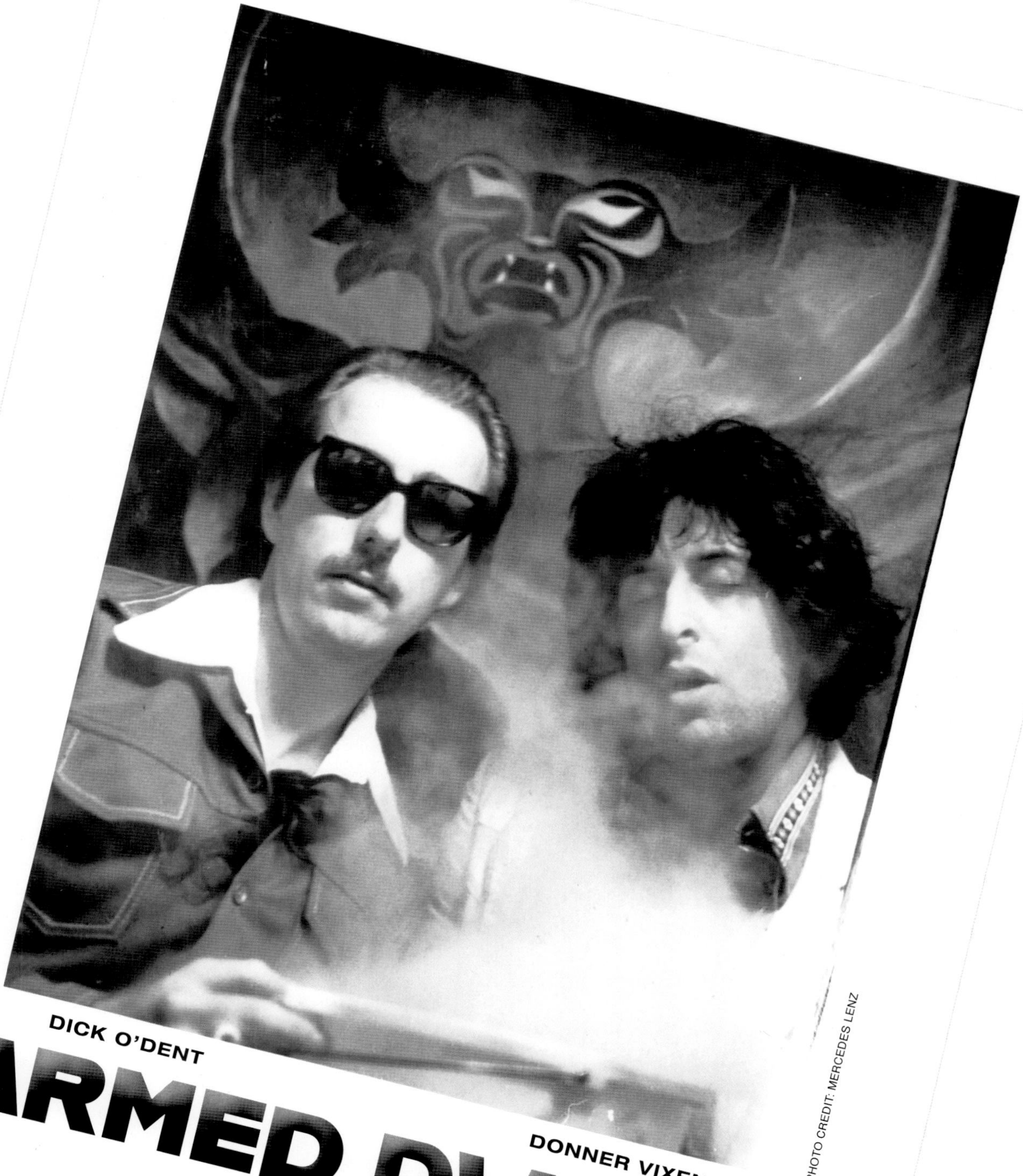

DICK O'DENT

ARMED DWARF

DONNER VIXEN

PHOTO CREDIT: MERCEDES LENZ

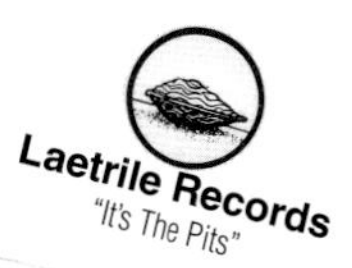

Next in the *ON RECORD* book series

Vol.4 1981

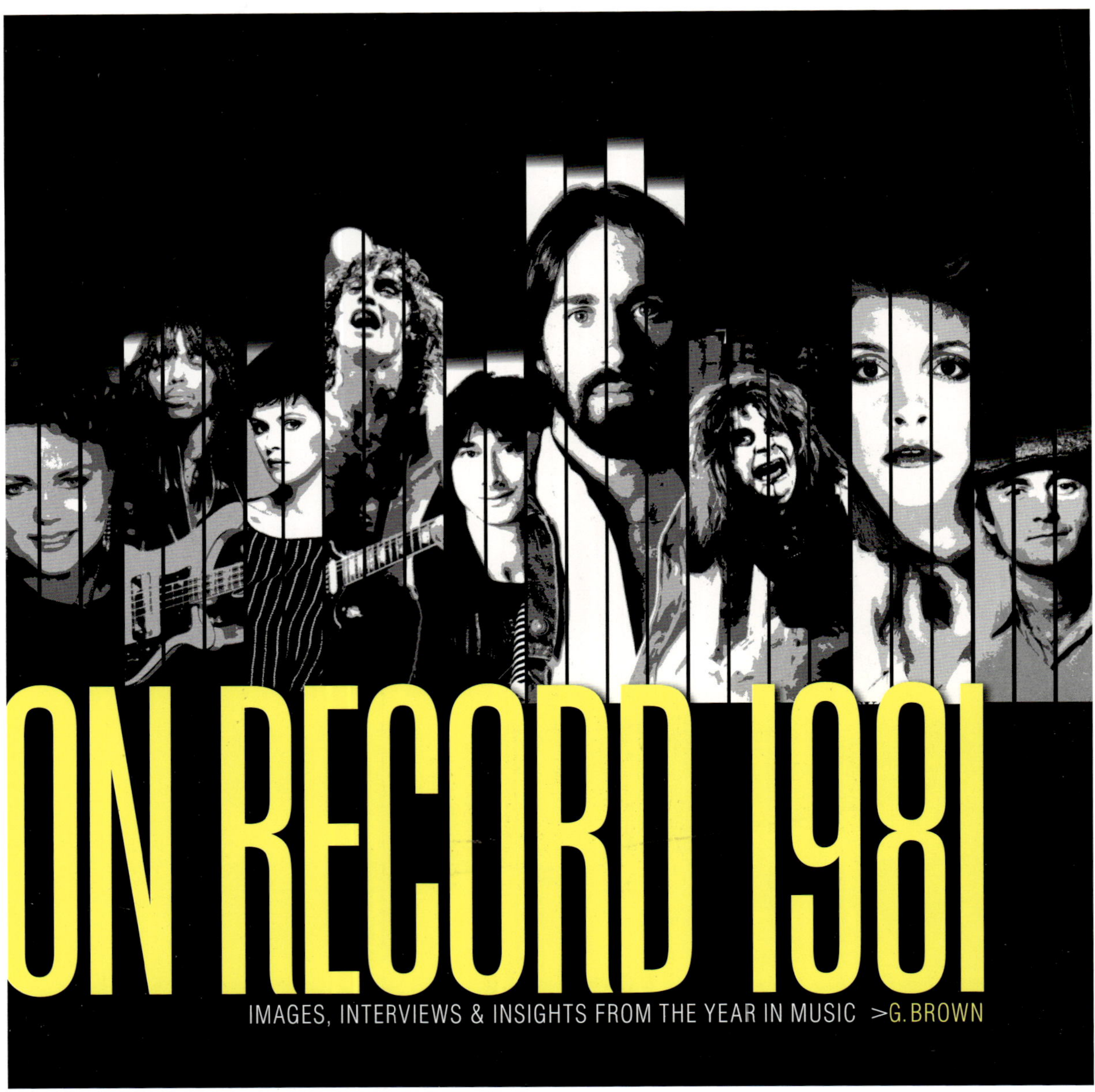